T0214526

Lecture Notes in Artificial Intelligence   11481

Subseries of Lecture Notes in Computer Science

More information about this series at http://www.springer.com/series/1244

Marcello Balduccini · Yuliya Lierler ·
Stefan Woltran (Eds.)

Logic Programming and Nonmonotonic Reasoning

15th International Conference, LPNMR 2019
Philadelphia, PA, USA, June 3–7, 2019
Proceedings

 Springer

Editors
Marcello Balduccini ⓘ
Saint Joseph's University
Philadelphia, PA, USA

Yuliya Lierler ⓘ
University of Nebraska at Omaha
Omaha, USA

Stefan Woltran ⓘ
TU Wien
Vienna, Austria

ISSN 0302-9743   ISSN 1611-3349 (electronic)
Lecture Notes in Artificial Intelligence
ISBN 978-3-030-20527-0   ISBN 978-3-030-20528-7 (eBook)
https://doi.org/10.1007/978-3-030-20528-7

LNCS Sublibrary: SL7 – Artificial Intelligence

This Springer imprint is published by the registered company Springer Nature Switzerland AG
The registered company address is: Gewerbestrasse 11, 6330 Cham, Switzerland

Preface

This volume contains the papers presented at the 15th International Conference on Logic Programming and Nonmonotonic Reasoning (LPNMR 2019) held June 3–7, 2019, at Saint Joseph's University in Philadelphia, USA. The conference was co-located with the Datalog 2.0 Workshop, the Workshop on Bidirectional Transformations, and the Workshop on Theory and Practice of Provenance at the Philadelphia Logic Week 2019.

LPNMR 2019 was the 15th in the series of international meetings on logic programming and non-monotonic reasoning. LPNMR is a forum for exchanging ideas on declarative logic programming, non-monotonic reasoning, and knowledge representation. The aim of the conference is to facilitate interactions between researchers and practitioners interested in the design and implementation of logic-based programming languages and database systems, and those working in knowledge representation and nonmonotonic reasoning. LPNMR strives to encompass theoretical and experimental studies that have led or will lead to advances in declarative programming and knowledge representation, as well as their use in practical applications. This year's edition of the conference attempted to raise submissions discussing the use of LPNMR techniques in emerging applications stemming from such areas as deep learning, robotics, cybersecurity, modeling cyberphysical systems, and human-aware AI. LPNMR 2019 thus brought together researchers from LPNMR core areas and application areas of the aforementioned kind in order to share research experiences, promote collaboration, and identify directions for joint future research.

LPNMR received 45 submissions in three categories: technical papers, system descriptions, and application descriptions. Of these, 22 submissions were accepted as regular papers and three as short papers, yielding an acceptance rate of 55%. Each reviewed paper was examined by at least three experts and discussed amongst them, the Program Committee (PC) members, and the program chairs. This volume contains versions of these articles that have been revised by their authors according to the comments provided in the reviews. Two of the papers were selected for Springer Best Paper Awards: "Pruning External Minimality Checking for ASP Using Semantic Dependencies" by Thomas Eiter and Tobias Kaminski (Best Student Paper Award), and "Splitting Epistemic Logic Programs" by Pedro Cabalar, Jorge Fandinno and Luis Fariñas del Cerro (Best Paper Award).

In addition to the oral presentations of the technical papers, the scientific program featured invited talks by:

- Esra Erdem, Sabanci University, Turkey
- Michael Gelfond, Texas Tech University, USA
- V. S. Subrahmanian, Dartmouth College, USA

The program also included sessions dedicated to the Answer Set Programming Challenge and the Doctoral Consortium of the conference. The conference proceedings contain abstracts for the invited talks and the Answer Set Programming Challenge. The main conference was preceded by several workshops offering an inspiring start to the event.

The LPNMR 2019 conference received generous support from several organizations. We gratefully acknowledge our sponsors, *Artificial Intelligence* journal, Association for Logic Programming (ALP), Haub School of Business at Saint Joseph's University, European Association for Artificial Intelligence (EurAI), National Science Foundation (NSF), and Potassco Solutions. We also would like to thank Springer for the longstanding, successful cooperation with the LPNMR series. The possibilities for fast-track journal publications in *Artificial Intelligence* and *Theory and Practice of Logic Programming*, as well as the best paper prize offered by Springer, brought additional value and motivation. The conference was managed with the help of EasyChair.

Many people played an important role in the success of LPNMR 2019 and deserve our acknowledgment: the PC members and additional reviewers for their timely expertise in carefully reviewing the submissions. The organizers of the Answer Set Programming Challenge, Carmine Dodaro, Christoph Redl, and Peter Schüller dedicated themselves to designing a sequel to the ASP Competition series in order to let LPNMR systems face novel and challenging real-world benchmarks. Fangkai Yang and Jörg Pührer organized an excellent Doctoral Consortium program, guiding young researchers to plan their research and careers. Mario Alviano's contribution was invaluable in coordinating the workshop program and Gregory Gelfond advertised the conference through a number of channels. We also wish to thank all authors who submitted papers and all the conference participants for fruitful discussions. Last but not least, special thanks go to the local organization team and, in particular, to Virginia Miori, Joseph DiAngelo, Lara Guerrini, Jeannine Shantz, Ruixin "Reese" Guo, Andrew Westveer, Elizabeth Angelucci, and Kelsey Neri, for their support and for being our hosts during the wonderful days at Saint Joseph's University.

June 2019

Marcello Balduccini
Yuliya Lierler
Stefan Woltran

Organization

Program Committee Chairs

Yuliya Lierler	University of Nebraska at Omaha, USA
Stefan Woltran	TU Wien, Austria

General Chair

Marcello Balduccini	Saint Joseph's University, USA

Workshops Chair

Mario Alviano	University of Calabria, Italy

Publicity Chair

Gregory Gelfond	University of Nebraska at Omaha, USA

Doctoral Consortium Chairs

Fangkai Yang	NVIDIA Corporation, USA
Jörg Pührer	TU Wien, Austria

Marketing Chairs

Elizabeth Angelucci	Saint Joseph's University, USA
Kelsey Neri	Saint Joseph's University, USA

Answer Set Programming Challenge 2019

Carmine Dodaro	University of Genoa, Italy
Christoph Redl	TU Wien, Austria
Peter Schüller	TU Wien, Austria

Program Committee

Chitta Baral	Arizona State University, USA
Bart Bogaerts	Vrije Universiteit Brussel (VUB), Belgium
Martin Brain	University of Oxford, UK
Gerhard Brewka	Leipzig University, Germany
Pedro Cabalar	Corunna University, Spain
Francesco Calimeri	University of Calabria, Italy

Daniele Theseider Dupré	Università del Piemonte Orientale, Italy
Matthias Thimm	Universität Koblenz-Landau, Germany
Hans Tompits	Vienna University of Technology, Austria
Mirek Truszczynski	University of Kentucky, USA
Agustin Valverde	Universidad de Malaga, Spain
Johannes P. Wallner	Vienna University of Technology, Austria
Kewen Wang	Griffith University, Australia
Yisong Wang	Guizhou University, China
Renata Wassermann	University of São Paulo, Brazil
Antonius Weinzierl	Vienna University of Technology, Austria
Jia-Huai You	University of Alberta, Canada
Yuanlin Zhang	Texas Tech University, USA
Yi Zhou	University of Technology Sydney, Australia

Additional Reviewers

Weronika T. Adrian	Johannes Oetsch
Carmine Dodaro	Francesco Pacenza
Francesco Fabiano	Javier Romero
Jorge Fandinno	Lukas Schweizer
Markus Hecher	Fabio Tardivo
Man Luo	Zhun Yang
Philipp Obermeier	Jessica Zangari

Sponsors and Collaborators

Artificial Intelligence Journal, Elsevier
Association for Logic Programming (ALP)
Haub School of Business, Saint Joseph's University
European Association for Artificial Intelligence (EurAI)
NSF - National Science Foundation
Potassco Solutions
Theory and Practice of Logic Programming, Cambridge University Press

Abstracts of Invited Contributions

Logic Programming and Non-monotonic Reasoning from 1991 to 2019: A Personal Perspective

Michael Gelfond

Texas Tech University, Lubbock, Texas, USA
Michael.Gelfond@ttu.edu

Abstract. The field of logic programming and nonmonotic reasoning was born in 1991, when a number of researchers working in "the theoretical ends" of logic programming and artificial intelligence gathered in Washington D.C. for the first LPNMR workshop, which was organized by Anil Nerode, Wiktor Marek, and V. S. Subrahmanian. I was privileged to attend this meeting; to closely observe the development of the field over the past 28 years; and to witness many remarkable achievements, which in 1991 I would not have believed to be possible. In this talk I plan to discuss some of these achievements and share a number of personal observations on the field's history, current state, and possible future directions. Among other things, I will comment on the development of powerful knowledge representation languages, the design and implementation of non-monotonic reasoning systems, and use of these languages and systems in formalizing various types of knowledge and reasoning tasks. The talk is not meant to be a survey of the field, rather it is my personal perspective limited to a small, but important, collection of topics I am most familiar with.

Integrating AI and Robotics
Using Answer Set Programming

Esra Erdem

Faculty of Engineering and Natural Sciences, Sabanci University,
Istanbul, Turkey
esraerdem@sabanciuniv.edu

Abstract. Successful deployment of robotic assistants in social environments necessitates these systems to be furnished with high-level cognitive abilities, such as planning and diagnostic reasoning, to be able to deal with high complexity and wide variability of their surroundings, and perform typical everyday tasks robustly and without sacrificing safety. In the presence of humans, robotic agents need further abilities, such as commonsense reasoning, explanation generation, and epistemic reasoning, to be able to collaborate, communicate and live with humans. We have been investigating the use of Answer Set Programming to endow robotic agents with such cognitive capabilities, considering various robotic domains, such as service robotics, medical robotics, and cognitive factories. In this talk, we will share our experiences of using Answer Set Programming in robotics applications, and discuss its strengths and weaknesses as a knowledge representation and reasoning paradigm to integrate Artificial Intelligence and Robotics.

Logic for Machine Learning Based Security

V. S. Subrahmanian

Dartmouth College, Hanover, New Hamsphire, USA
vs@dartmouth.edu

Abstract. The talk will cover 2 broad areas: (i) the role of logic in providing human-understandable explanations of forecasts produced by complex machine learning models, (ii) the use of logic based methods for reasoning about deception in cybersecurity. In the first part, I will describe BEEF, a framework that generates logic-based "balanced" explanations (which explain both why a forecast might be correct and why it might be incorrect). BEEF is capable of operating "on top" of any binary classifier. In the second part, I will describe logic-based methods to lead an attacker astray when he successfully penetrates a system by providing him fake results in response to scan requests. I will conclude with suggestions on how the LPNMR community may build upon these ideas.

The ASP Challenge 2019

Carmine Dodaro[1], Christoph Redl[2], and Peter Schüller[2]

[1] Department of Informatics, Robotics and Systems Engineering (DIBRIS),
University of Genova
dodaro@dibris.unige.it
[2] Institut für Logic and Computation, Technische Universität Wien
{redl,ps}@kr.tuwien.ac.at

The Answer Set Programming Challenge 2019 is run jointly among the Technische Universität Wien (Austria) and the University of Genoa (Italy), in Spring 2019. The event is the sequel to the ASP Competition series, which was held biannually since 2007. Unlike the previous ASP Competitions, the ASP Challenge 2019 focuses on challenging persons and teams rather than systems. To this end, five real problems from research and industry have been collected and are to be solved by researchers and students using arbitrary available systems, which do not necessarily have to be developed by the participants. Indeed, participants are encouraged to use any available system(s) and to combine ASP with other formalisms, as long as ASP or an extension thereof plays a crucial role. Submissions are expected to comprise the used systems and an encoding.

The challenge benefits the ASP community as challenging real-world research and industrial benchmarks become available, and it also benefits the problem providers as they get solutions to their problems.

Differently from previous editions, we host the challenge on the StarExec platform at https://www.starexec.org/ with two aims: (i) attracting expert and non-expert participants, and (ii) providing timely feedback to solutions and permitting participants to adjust solutions instead of collecting encodings and solvers, running the competition offline, and publishing the results afterwards.

We use the following problem domains:

- The *House Reconfiguration Problem* is an abstract version of (re-)configuration problems occurring in practice. The task is, given a legacy configuration, to find an (optimal) reconfiguration satisfying various constraints.
- The industrial *Insurance Referees Assignment Problem* is a scheduling problem from the insurance domain, where referees are to be assigned to insurance cases according to various hard and soft constraints.
- The *Automated Warehouse Scenario* is a planning problem where robots have to deliver products to picking stations to fulfill orders.
- In the *Fastfood Problem*, given a set of restaurants, the task is to select a number of them as depots such that the sum of distances from each restaurant to the closest depot is minimized.

– The problem of *Checking Policies for Reactive Agents* comes from the planning domain. An agent in a grid environment has to find a goal, where the environment and obstacles are only partially observable.

For details we refer to https://sites.google.com/view/aspcomp2019/.

Contents

Knowledge Representation and Reasoning

Systems

Applications

Train Scheduling with Hybrid ASP

Dirk Abels[2] , Julian Jordi[2], Max Ostrowski[1], Torsten Schaub[1,3,4,5(✉)] ,
Ambra Toletti[2] , and Philipp Wanko[1,3]

[1] Potassco Solutions, Potsdam, Germany
[2] SBB, Bern, Switzerland
[3] University of Potsdam, Potsdam, Germany
torsten@cs.uni-potsdam.de
[4] Simon Fraser University, Burnaby, Canada
[5] Griffith University, Brisbane, Australia

Abstract. We present an ASP-based solution to real-world train
scheduling problems, involving routing, scheduling, and optimization.
To this end, we pursue a hybrid approach that extends ASP withdif-
ference constraints to account for a fine-grained timing. More precisely,
we exemplarily show how the hybrid ASP system *clingo*[DL] can be
used to tackle demanding planning-and-scheduling problems. In particular, we investigate how to boost performance by combining distinct ASP
solving techniques, such as approximation, heuristic, and optimization
strategies.

1 Introduction

Densely-populated railway networks transport millions of people and carry millions of tons of freight daily; and this traffic is expected to increase even further.
Hence, for using a railway network to capacity, it is important to schedule trains
in a flexible and global way. This is however far from easy since the generation
of railway timetables is already known to be intractable for a single track [3].
While this is not so severe for sparse traffic, it becomes a true challenge when
dealing with dense networks. This is caused by increasing dependencies among
trains due to connections and shared resources.

We take up this challenge and show how to address real-world train scheduling with hybrid Answer Set Programming (ASP [10]). Our hybrid approach
allows us to specifically account for the different types of constraints induced by
routing, scheduling, and optimization. While we address paths and conflicts with
regular ASP, we use difference constraints (over integers) to capture fine timings.
Similarly, to boost (multi-objective) optimization, we study approximations of
delay functions of varying granularity. This is complemented by various domain-
specific heuristics aiming at improving feasibility checking as well as solution
quality. We implement our approach with the hybrid ASP system *clingo*[DL] [8],
an extension of *clingo* [7] with difference constraints. Our approach provides us

---

This work was partially funded by DFG grants SCHA 550/9 and 11.

M. Balduccini et al. (Eds.): LPNMR 2019, LNAI 11481, pp. 3–17, 2019.
https://doi.org/10.1007/978-3-030-20528-7_1

with an exemplary study of using a variety of techniques for solving demanding real-world planning-and-scheduling problems with hybrid ASP.

To begin with, we introduce in Sect. 3 a dedicated formalization of the train scheduling problem. This is indispensable to master the complexness of the problem. Moreover, it guides the development of our hybrid ASP encodings, presented in Sect. 4. We evaluate our approach along with various enhancements in Sect. 5 on increasingly difficult problem instances with up to 467 trains.

2 Background

We expect the reader to be familiar with the basic syntax, semantics, and terminology of logic programs under stable models semantics, and focus below on the introduction of non-standard concepts. The base syntax of our logic programs follows the one of *clingo* [5]; its semantics is detailed in [4].

clingo[DL] extends the input language of *clingo* by (theory) atoms representing *difference constraints*. That is, atoms of the form '`&diff{u-v}<= `d', where u, v are symbolic terms and d a numeral term, represent difference constraints such as '$u - v \leq d$', where u, v serve as integer variables and d stands for an integer.[1] For instance, assume that '`&diff{e(T)-b(T)}<= `D' stands for the condition that the difference between the end and the beginning of a task T must be less or equal than some duration D. This may get instantiated to '`&diff{e(7)-b(7)}<= 42`' to require that `e(7)` and `b(7)` take integer values such that '$e(7) - b(7) \leq 42$'. Note that u, v can be arbitrary terms; we exploit this below to use tuples like (T,V) as integer variables. Among the alternative semantic couplings between (theory) atoms and constraints offered by *clingo*[DL] (cf. [6,8]), we follow the *defined, non-strict* approach (i) tolerating theory atoms in rule heads and (ii) enforcing their corresponding constraints only if the atoms are derivable. Hence, if a theory atom is false, its associated constraint is ignored. This approach has the advantage that we only need to consider difference constraints occurring in the encoding and not their negations. Obviously, the overall benefit of using such constraints is that their variables are not subject to grounding.

For boosting performance, we take advantage of *clingo*'s heuristic directives of form '`#heuristic `$a:B$`. `$[w,m]$', where a is an atom and B is a body; w is a numeral term and m a heuristic modifier, indicating how the solver's heuristic treatment of a should be changed whenever B holds. We use modifiers `sign` and `false`. Whenever a is chosen by the solver, `sign` enforces that it becomes either true or false depending on whether w is positive or negative, respectively. Similarly, with `false`, a is always assigned false and additionally pushed on priority level w (where 0 is the default; cf. [5]).

3 Real-World Train Scheduling

The train scheduling problem can be divided into three distinct tasks: routing, conflict resolution and scheduling.

---

[1] Strictly speaking, we had to distinguish the integer from its representation.

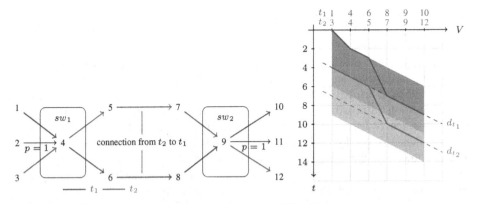

Fig. 1. Routing of two trains through a railway network. (Color figure online)

Fig. 2. Scheduling of two trains. (Color figure online)

First, each train is routed through a railway network. The directed graph in Fig. 1 shows an example of such a network. It consists of all edges regardless of coloring, and nodes numbered from 1 to 12 mark the entry (or exit) of different edges of the track. Furthermore, Fig. 1 depicts a valid routing of two trains, t_1 and t_2, through the network. Blue edges are traveled by t_1 and red edges by t_2. In this example, both trains have access to the whole network and may chose among possible start nodes 1, 2 and 3, and end nodes 10, 11 and 12, respectively.

Second, edges of the railway network are associated with resources, and whenever the paths of two trains lead through an edge associated with the same resource, there is a possible conflict and a decision has to be made which train accesses the edge first. The train going second has to wait until the first one leaves the edge plus a safety period. Each edge in the directed graph is associated with a resource representing the track, thus prohibiting two trains from entering it simultaneously. Furthermore, resources like railway switches may span several edges. Here, there are two switches, sw_1 and sw_2, represented by rectangles cutting the assigned edges. For instance, given the paths of t_1 and t_2, the two trains have resource conflicts on edges $(1, 4)$ and $(3, 4)$, and similarly, on $(9, 10)$ and $(8, 10)$, since the pairs of edges are assigned to sw_1 and sw_2, respectively.

Finally, for each train and each node visited by the trains, a time point has to be scheduled avoiding conflicts between trains and meeting all timing requirements, such as earliest arrival at nodes or connections between trains. For all trains and each node, an earliest point of arrival is defined, as well as, optionally, a latest point of arrival. Together, these two time points define the time span in which the train might be at a node in its path. Given the paths in Figs. 1, 2 shows the time spans and a valid schedule for t_1 and t_2. The horizontal axis indicates the nodes that the trains travel and the vertical axis the time. The light blue and light red areas show the possible arrival times for t_1 and t_2, respectively. The light violet area indicates that both trains may arrive in this time period. For instance, t_1 may arrive at node 4 between time points 2 and 7, and t_2 at node 5 between 6 and 11. The blue and red lines represent a feasible schedule for t_1 and t_2, respectively. In our example, every edge takes one time unit to pass, whenever conflicts are resolved, the second train may enter one time unit after the first has left, and connecting trains have to arrive one time unit before the train that ought to receive cargo or passengers leaves. The schedule in Fig. 2 always prioritizes t_1 in resource conflicts and schedules the points of arrival as soon as possible. Resource conflicts at switch sw_1 do not impact t_2's schedule since t_1 leaves these edges several time points before t_2 may arrive. Train t_1 has to wait for t_2 in between nodes 6 and 8 due to their connection, and is allowed to leave at the earliest at time point 7, one time point after t_2 has entered edge $(5, 7)$. The resource conflicts induced by switch sw_2 forces t_2 to wait until time point 10, one time unit after t_1 leaves sw_2.

After obtaining a valid routing and scheduling, the resulting solution is evaluated regarding delay and quality of the trains' paths. For that purpose, edges are assigned penalties. Edges with higher penalties represent, for instance, tracks that can take less workload. In our example, only edges $(2, 4)$ and $(9, 11)$ are penalized, viz. $p = 1$. Figure 2 shows the time points after which trains t_1 and t_2 are considered delayed via dashed lines d_{t_1} and d_{t_2}, respectively. Every time point below the dashed lines is penalized for the respective train. Since both trains avoid the penalized edges and manage to travel their routes without delay, the solution shown in Fig. 2 is optimal.

We formalize the train scheduling problem as a triple (N, T, C). N stands for the railway network (V, E, R, m, a, b), where (V, E) is a directed graph, R is a set of resources, $m : E \rightarrow \mathbb{N}$ assigns the minimum travel time of an edge, $a : R \rightarrow 2^E$ allocates resources in the railway network, and $b : R \rightarrow \mathbb{N}$ gives the time a resource is blocked after it was accessed by a train. Elements (S, L, e, l, w) of T are trains to be scheduled on network N, where (S, L) is an acyclic subgraph of (V, E), $e : S \rightarrow \mathbb{N}$ and $l : S \rightarrow \mathbb{N} \cup \{\infty\}$ give the earliest and latest time a train may arrive at a node, respectively, and $w : L \rightarrow \mathbb{N}$ is the time a train has to wait on an edge. Note that all functions are total unless specified otherwise and we use seconds as the time unit. Elements (t_1, e_1, t_2, e_2, c) of C are connections, denoting that $t_1 \in T$ on edge $e_1 \in E$ has a connection to $t_2 \in T$ on $e_2 \in E$ requiring t_2 not to leave e_2 before t_1 has arrived by at least c seconds at e_1.

In Fig. 1, the train scheduling problem is defined as: $V = \{1, \ldots, 12\}$, $E = \{(1, 4), (2, 4), \ldots, (9, 11), (9, 12)\}$, $R = \{sw_1, sw_2\} \cup \{r_e \mid e \in E\}$, $m(e) = 1$ and $a(r_e) = \{e\}$ for $e \in E$, $a(sw_1) = \{(1, 4), (2, 4), (3, 4), (4, 5), (4, 6)\}$, $a(sw_2) = \{(7, 9), (8, 9), (9, 10), (9, 11), (9, 12)\}$, $b(r) = 1$ for $r \in R$, $T = \{t_1, t_2\}$ with $t_1 = (S_1, L_1, e_1, l_1, w_1), t_2 = (S_2, L_2, e_2, l_2, w_2)$, where (V, E) equals $(S_1, L_1) = (S_2, L_2)$, e_1, l_1, e_2, l_2 are the upper and lower coordinates of the colored areas in Fig. 2, $w_1(e) = w_2(e) = 0$ for $e \in E$, and $C = \{(t_2, (5, 7), t_1, (6, 8), 1), (t_2, (6, 8), t_1, (5, 7), 1)\}$.

A solution (P, A) to a train scheduling problem (N, T, C) is a pair of (i) a function P assigning each train the path it takes through the network, and (ii) an assignment A of arrival times to each train at each node on their path.

A path p is a connected sequence of nodes. We write $v \in p$ and $e \in p$ to denote that node $v \in V$ and edge $e \in E$ are contained in path p, respectively. A path $P(t) = (v_1, \ldots, v_n)$ for $t = (S, L, e, l, w) \in T$ with $v_i \in S$ for $1 \leq i \leq n$ has to satisfy:

$$(v_j, v_{j+1}) \in L \text{ for } 1 \leq j \leq n-1 \tag{1}$$

$$in(v_1) = 0 \text{ and } out(v_n) = 0, \tag{2}$$

where in and out give the in- and out-degree of a node in graph (S, L), respectively. Intuitively, Condition (1) forces the path to be connected and feasible for the train in question and Condition (2) ensures that the path is between a possible start and end node.

An assignment A is a partial function $T \times V \to \mathbb{N}$, where $A(t, v)$ is undefined for $v \notin P(t)$. Given paths P, an assignment has to satisfy:

$$A(t, v_i) \geq e(v_i) \tag{3}$$

$$A(t, v_i) \leq l(v_i) \tag{4}$$

$$A(t, v_j) + m((v_j, v_{j+1})) + w((v_j, v_{j+1})) \leq A(t, v_{j+1}) \tag{5}$$

for all $t = (S, L, e, l, w) \in T, P(t) = (v_1, \ldots, v_n), 1 \leq i \leq n, 1 \leq j \leq n-1$,

$$\text{either } A(t_1, v') + b(r) \leq A(t_2, u) \text{ or } A(t_2, u') + b(r) \leq A(t_1, v) \tag{6}$$

for $r \in R, \{t_1, t_2\} \subseteq T, t_1 \neq t_2, (v, v') \in P(t_1), (u, u') \in P(t_2)$ with $\{(v, v'), (u, u')\} \subseteq a(r)$, and

$$A(t_1, v) + c \leq A(t_2, u') \tag{7}$$

for $(t_1, (v, v'), t_2, (u, u'), c) \in C$ with $(v, v') \in P(t_1)$ and $(u, u') \in P(t_2)$.

Intuitively, conditions (3), (4) and (5) ensure that a train arrives neither too early nor too late and that waiting and traveling times are accounted for. Furthermore, Condition (6) resolves conflicts between two trains that travel edges sharing a resource, so that either the second train can only enter after the first train has left for a specified time or vice versa. Finally, Condition (7) handles connections between two trains: a train with a connection can only leave if the other train has arrived for a specified time. Note that connections only apply if both trains travel the specified edges.

For our solution in Fig. 2, $P(t_1) = (1, 4, 6, 8, 9, 10)$, $P(t_2) = (3, 4, 5, 7, 9, 12)$, and $A(t_1, 1) = 0, \ldots, A(t_1, 8) = 7, \ldots, A(t_1, 10) = 9, A(t_2, 3) = 4, \ldots, A(t_2, 5) = 6, A(t_2, 7) = 10, \ldots, A(t_2, 12) = 12$.

To determine the quality of a solution, the aggregated delay of all trains as well as the quality of the paths through the network is taken into account. For that purpose, we consider two functions: the delay function d and route penalty function rp. Given train $t = (S, L, e, l, w) \in T$ and a node $s \in S$, $d(t, s) \in \mathbb{N}$ returns the time point after which the train t is considered late at node s. Note that $e(s) \leq d(t, s) \leq l(s)$. Given an edge $e \in E$, $rp(e) \in \mathbb{N}$ is the penalty a solution receives for each train traveling edge e. The quality of a solution (P, A) is determined via the following equation:

$$\sum_{((t,v),a)\in A} \max\{(a - d(t, v)), 0\}/60 + \sum_{e\in\{u|p\in P, u\in p, e\in E\}} rp(e) \qquad (8)$$

In our example, we get $rp((2, 4)) = 1, rp((9, 11)) = 1$ and $rp(v) = 0$ for $v \in V \setminus \{(2, 4), (10, 12)\}$, and, for instance, $d(t_1, 1) = 4, d(t_1, 10) = 9$ and $d(t_2, 3) = 7, d(t_2, 12) = 12$. As mentioned, our solution obtains the optimal quality value of 0.

4   An ASP-Based Solution to Real-World Train Scheduling

In this section, we present our hybrid solution to the train scheduling problem. We start by describing the factual representation of problem instances, continue with the problem encoding and finish by introducing several domain-specific heuristics aimed at improving solving performance and solution quality.

Fact Format. A train scheduling problem (N, T, C) with $N = (V, E, R, m, a, b)$ is represented by

$$\texttt{train}(t) \quad \texttt{edge}(t, v, v') \quad \texttt{m}((v, v'), m((v, v'))) \quad \texttt{w}(t, (v, v'), w((v, v')))$$

for every $t = (S, L, e, l, w) \in T$ and $(v, v') \in L$. For every $s \in S$, we add

$$\texttt{e}(t, s, e(s)) \quad \texttt{l}(t, s, l(s)), \quad \text{and} \quad \texttt{start}(t, s) \quad \text{or} \quad \texttt{end}(t, s)$$

if $in(s) = 0$ or $out(s) = 0$ in (S, L), respectively. We assign unique terms to each train for identifiability. For example, facts `train(t1)`, `edge(t1,1,4)`, `e(t1,1,0)`, `l(t1,1,6)`, `start(t1,1)`, `m((1,4),1)` and `w(t1,(1,4),0)` express that train `t1` may travel between nodes 1 and 4 taking at least 1 s, waiting on this edge for 0 s, and arrives between time points 0 and 6 at node 1, which is a possible start node. Furthermore, we add

$$\texttt{resource}(r, e) \quad \texttt{b}(r, b(r))$$

for $r \in R$ and $e \in a(r)$. Akin to trains, resources are assigned unique terms to distinguish them. For example, facts `resource(sw1,(1,4))`, `resource (sw1,(4,5))` and `b(sw1,1)` assign resource `sw1` to edges $(1, 4)$ and $(4, 5)$ and the resource is blocked for 1 s after a train has left it. Finally, we add

$$\texttt{connection}(t, (v, v'), t', (u, u'), c)$$

for all $(t, (v, v'), t', (u, u'), c) \in C$. The fact that `t1` may not leave $(6, 8)$ before `t2` spent at least 1 s in $(5, 7)$ is encoded by `connection(t2,(5,7), t1,(6,8),1)`.

Given delay and route penalty functions d and rp, we add

$$\texttt{potlate}(t, s, u, p) \quad \texttt{penalty}(m, rp(m))$$

for $t = (S, L, e, l, w) \in T, s \in S, m \in L$ with $\{u, p\} \subseteq \mathbb{N}, d(t, s) < u \leq l(t, s)$ to evaluate a solution. While we encode route penalty optimization exactly, delay optimization is approximated via a combination of difference constraints and standard ASP optimization schemes. Intuitively, a fact `potlate(t1,1,5,1)` denotes that a solution receives a penalty of 1 if train `t1` travels over node 1 and arrives there at time point 5 or later. In Sect. 4, we introduce several schemes to create such facts and approximate the objective function to different degrees. For brevity, we cannot present the full instance representing the example in Figs. 1 and 2 but make it available here[2].

Encoding. In the following, we describe the general problem encoding. We separate it into three parts handling path constraints, conflict resolution and scheduling.

Listing 1.1. Encoding of path constraints.

```
1   1 { visit(T,V)        : start(T,V)        } 1 :- train(T).
2   1 { route(T,(V,V')) : edge(T,V,V') } 1 :- visit(T,V), not end(T,V).
3   visit(T,V')         :- route(T,(V,V')).
```

The first part of the encoding in Listing 1.1 covers routing. First, exactly one valid start node is chosen for each train to be visited (Line 1). From a node that is visited by a train and is not an end node, an edge in the relevant sub-graph is chosen as the next route (Line 2). The new route in turn leads to a node being visited by the train (Line 3). This way, each train is recursively assigned a valid path. Since those paths begin at a start node, finish at an end node and are connected via edges valid for the respective trains, conditions (1) and (2) are ensured.

Listing 1.2. Encoding of conflict resolution.

```
4    shared(T,(V,V'),T',(U,U')) :- edge(T,V,V'), edge(T',U,U'), T!=T',
5                                   resource(R,(V,V')), resource(R,(U,U')), b(R,B),
6                                   e(T,V,E), l(T,V',L), e(T',U,E'),
7                                   E <= E', E' < L+B.
8    shared(T',E',T,E)     :- shared(T,E,T',E').
9    conflict(T,E,T',E')   :- shared(T,E,T',E'), T < T',
10                             route(T,E), route(T',E').
11   { seq(T,E,T',E') } :-   conflict(T,E,T',E').
12     seq(T',E',T,E)   :-   conflict(T,E,T',E'), not seq(T,E,T',E').
```

The next part of the encoding shown in Listing 1.2 detects and resolves resource conflicts. A resource conflict is possible, if two trains have an edge in their sub-graphs that is assigned the same resource (lines 4 and 5), and they travel through the edges around the same time (lines 6 and 7), more precisely, whenever the time intervals in which the trains may enter and leave the edges in question, extended by the time the resource is blocked, overlap. Now, if both trains are routed through those edges a conflict occurs (lines 9 and 10). We resolve the conflict by making a choice which train passes through their edge first (lines 11 and 12).

---

[2] github.com/potassco/train-scheduling-with-clingo-dl/blob/master/example.lp.

Listing 1.3. Encoding of scheduling.

```
13  &diff{ 0-(T,V) } <= -E   :- e(T,V,E), visit(T,V).
14  &diff{ (T,V)-0 } <= L    :- l(T,V,L), visit(T,V).
15  &diff{ (T,V)-(T,V') }  <= -D :- route(T,(V,V')), E = (V,V'),
16                                D=#sum{ M,m : m(E,M); W,w : w(T,E,W) }.
17  &diff{ (T,V')-(T',U) } <= -M :- seq(T,(V,V'),T',(U,U')),
18                                M = #max{ B : resource(R,(V,V')), b(R,B) }.
19  &diff{ (T,V)-(T',U') } <= -W :- connection(T,(V,V'),T',(U,U'),W),
20                                route(T,(V,V')), route(T',(U,U')).
```

Finally, Listing 1.3 displays the encoding of scheduling via difference constraints. We represent arrival times of train t at node v with an integer variable (t,v). In the following, we use ground terms to describe how the rules function while in the encoding variables are used. Lines 13 and 14 encode that every train arrives at a node in their path neither too early nor too late, respectively. Given the earliest arrival e and latest arrival l of a train t at node v in their path, difference constraint atoms &diff{0-(t,v)}<= $-e$ and &diff{(t,v)-0}<= l are derived. This ensures that $e \leq$ (t,v) $\leq l$ holds, therefore fulfilling conditions (3) and (4). The rule in lines 15 and 16 first calculates the sum d of minimal travel and waiting time for train t at edge (v,v') in their path, which is the minimal difference between arrival times at nodes v and v' for train t. Then, difference constraint atom &diff{(t,v)-(t,v')}<= $-d$ is derived, which in turn ensures (t,v) $+ d \leq$ (t,v') (Condition (5)). The rule in lines 17 and 18 utilizes conflict detection and resolution from Listing 1.2. Given the maximum blocked time b of resources shared on (v,v') and (u,u'), and the decision that t takes precedence over t', we derive difference constraint atom &diff{(t,v')-(t',u)}<= $-b$ expressing linear constraint (t,v') $+ b \leq$ (t',u) for two conflicting trains t and t' on edges (v,v') and (u,u'). Hence, t' may only enter edge (u,u') b seconds after t has left (v,v') (Condition (6)). Note that if several resources induce a conflict for two trains on the same edges, only one difference constraint with the maximum blocked time suffices since $x + k \leq y$ implies $x + k' \leq y$ for $k \geq k'$. Finally, Line 19 handles connections in a similar fashion. If train t on (v,v') has a connection to t' on (u,u') with connection time w, a difference constraint atom &diff{(t,v)-(t',u')}<= $-w$ is derived, ensuring linear constraint (t,v) $+ w \leq$ (t',u') to hold (Condition (7)). This condition is required if both trains are routed through the edges (Line 20).

Optimization. As mentioned above, we use instances of potlate/4 to indicate when a train is considered late at a node and how to penalize its delay. For this purpose, we choose sets $D_{t,v} \subseteq \mathbb{N}$ whose elements act as thresholds for arrival time of train t at node v. Given delay function d, $d(t,v) \leq u \leq l(v)$ for every $u \in D_{t,v}$, train $t = (S, L, e, l, w) \in T$ and $v \in S$. We create facts potlate$(t,v,u,u-u')|$ for $u,u' \in D_{t,v}$ with $u' < u$ such that there is no $u'' \in D_{t,v}$ with $u' < u'' < u$. We add potlate$(t,v,u,u-d(t,v))$ for $u = \min(D_{t,v})$. Intuitively, we choose the penalty of a potential delay as the difference to the previous potential delay, or, if there is no smaller threshold, the difference to the time point after which the train is considered delayed. This way, the sum of penalties amounts to a lower bound on the train's actual delay

in seconds. For example, for $D_{t,v} = \{6, 10, 14\}$ and $d(t, v) = 5$, we create facts
`potlate(t,v,6,1)`, `potlate(t,v,10,4)` and `potlate(t,v,14,4)`. Now,
if t arrives at v at 12, it is above thresholds 6 and 10 and should receive a penalty
of 5. This penalty is a lower bound on the actual delay of 7, and we know that
the value has to be between 5 and 9 since the next threshold adds a penalty of
4. This method approximates the exact objective function in (8) in two ways.
First, we do not divide by 60 and penalize in minutes since this would lead to
rounding problems. Second, our penalty only gives a lower bound to the actual
delay if thresholds are more than one second apart. While our method allows
us to be arbitrarily precise in theory, in practice, creating a threshold for each
possible second of delay leads to a explosion in size. We employ two schemes for
generating sets $D_{t,v}$ given $t = (S, L, e, l, w) \in T$, $v \in S$ and delay function d.

Binary. This approximation detects if a train is a second late and penalizes it
by one, therefore, only the occurrence of a delay is detected while its amount
disregarded. We set $D_{t,v} = Bin_{t,v} = \{d(t,v) + 1\}$.

Linear. This scheme for $D_{t,v}$ evenly distributing thresholds m seconds apart
across the time span in which a delay might occur. Here, if train t arrives at
or after $n * m + d(t, v)$ at v, we know that the real delay is between $n * m$ and
$(n + 1) * m$ for $n \in \mathbb{N} \setminus \{0\}$. We also add $Bin_{t,v}$ to detect solutions without delay.
We set $D_{t,v} = Bin_{t,v} \cup Lin_{t,v}^{m}$ with $Lin_{t,v}^{m} = \{y \in \mathbb{N} \mid y = x * m + d(t,v), x \in \mathbb{N} \setminus \{0\}, y \leq l(v)\}$.

Listing 1.4. Delay and routing penalty minimization.

```
1  { late(T,V,D,W) : visit(T,V) } :- potlate(T,V,D,W).
2  &diff{ 0-(T,V) } <= -D  :- late(T,V,D,W).
3  &diff{ (T,V)-0 } <=  N  :- not late(T,V,D,W), potlate(T,V,D,W),
4                             N=D-1, visit(T,V).
5  #minimize{ W,T,V,D : late(T,V,D,W) }.
6  #minimize{ P,T,E : penalty(E,P), route(T,E) }.
```

Given thresholds $D_{t,v}$ for all trains and nodes and the corresponding instances
of predicate `potlate/4`, Listing 1.4 shows the implementation of the delay
minimization. The basic idea is to use regular atoms to choose whether a
train is delayed on its path for every potential delay (Line 1), deriving difference constraint atoms expressing this information (lines 2–4), and ultimately
using the regular atoms in a standard minimize statement (Line 5). In detail,
for every `potlate(t,v,u,w)`, a `late(t,v,u,w)` can be chosen if t visits v. If `late(t,v,u,w)` is chosen to be true, a difference constraint atom
`&diff{0-(t,v)}<= −u` is derived expressing $(t,v) \geq u$ and, therefore, that t
is delayed at v at threshold u. Otherwise, `&diff{(t,v)-0}<= u − 1` becomes
true so that $(t,v) < u$ holds. The difference constraints ensure that if the truth
value of a `late` atom is decided, the schedule has to reflect this information.
The minimize statement then sums up and minimizes the penalties of the `late`
atoms that are true.

Finally, Line 6 in Listing 1.4 shows the straight forward encoding of the routing penalty minimization. The minimize statement merely collects the paths of
the trains, sums up their penalties, and minimizes this sum.

Domain-Specific Heuristics. We devise several domain-specific heuristics to, first, improve solving performance, and second, improve quality of solutions regarding delay and routing.

*Sequence Heuristic.*The heuristic in Listing 1.5 attempts to order conflicting trains by their possible arrival times at the edges where the conflict is located. In essence, we analyze how the time intervals of the trains are situated and prefer their sequence accordingly. Line 1 derives those intervals by collecting the earliest and latest time a train might be at an edge. Given two trains t and t' with intervals $[e, l]$ and $[e', l']$ at the conflicting edges, respectively, we calculate $s = e' - e - (l - l')$ to determine whether t should be scheduled before t'. If s is positive, the preferred sign of the sequence atom is also positive, thus preferring t to go before t', if it is negative, the opposite is expressed. In detail, $e' - e$ is positive if t' may arrive later than t thus making it more likely that t can go first without delaying t'. Similarly, if $l - l'$ is negative, t' may leave later, suggesting t to go first. If the results of both expressions have the same sign, one interval is contained in the other and if the difference is positive, the center of the interval of t is located earlier than the center of the interval of t'. For example, in Fig. 2, we see that t_1 and t_2 share a resource in $(1, 4)$ and $(3, 4)$ and the time intervals in which they potentially arrive at those edges are $[0, 7]$ and $[4, 10]$, respectively. Due to $4 - 0 - (7 - 10) = 7$, we prefer t_1 to be scheduled before t_2, which in the example clearly is the correct decision, since t_1 precedes t_2 without delaying t_2.

Listing 1.5. Heuristic that orders conflicting trains by their possible arrival times.

```
1    range(T,(V,V'),E,L) :- edge(T,V,V'),e(T,V,E), l(T,V',L).
2    #heuristic seq(T,E,T',E') : shared(T,E,T',E'),
3                                range(T,E,L,U),
4                                range(T',E',L',U'). [L'-L - (U-U'),sign]
```

Delay Heuristic. Listing 1.6 gives a heuristic aimed at avoiding delay at earlier nodes in the paths. For that purpose, we first assign each node in the sub-graph of a train a natural number signifying their relative position (lines 1–4). Start nodes receive position 0, and from there, the number increases the farther a node is apart from the start nodes, indicating that they are visited later in the possible paths of the train. The maximum position of the end nodes is also the longest possible path minus one (Line 5). For a potential delay, we then select the position p and the maximum position m and modify the delay atom with value $m - p$ and modifier `false`. This accomplishes two things. First, the earlier the node, the higher the value, thus delays for earlier nodes are decided first. Second, the preferred sign of all delays is false. Intuitively, we assume that early delays are to be avoided since they likely lead to delays at subsequent nodes. Considering again our example in Fig. 2, node 1 for t_1 receives position 0 and node 5 position 3, respectively, while the maximum position is 5. Therefore, we receive values 5 and 2 for nodes 1 and 5, respectively, avoiding the delay at node 1 first, while also preferring t_1 to be on time at both nodes.

Listing 1.6. Heuristic discouraging delays early on.

```
1   node(T,(V;V'))     :- edge(T,V,V').
2   node_pos(T,V,0)    :- start(T,V).
3   node_pos(T,V',M+1) :- node(T,V'), not start(T,V'),
4                         M = #max{ P : node_pos(T,V,P), edge(T,V,V')}.
5   last_node(T,M)     :- train(T), M = #max{ P : node_pos(T,V,P), end(T,V) }.
6   #heuristic late(T,V,U,W) : potlate(T,V,U,W),
7                              node_pos(T,V,P),
8                              last_node(T,Max). [Max-P,false]
```

Routing heuristic. Akin to the straight-forward routing penalty minimization, the heuristic in Listing 1.7 merely tries to avoid routes where there is a penalty. The higher the penalty, the more those routes are to be avoided. In our example (Fig. 1), this amounts to t_1 and t_2 equally shunning $(2, 4)$ and $(9, 11)$.

Listing 1.7. Heuristic for avoiding paths with penalties.

```
1   #heuristic route(T,E) : train(T), penalty(E,P). [P,false]
```

Note that all three domain-specific heuristics are static, i.e., they are active immediately at the start of solving.

5   Experiments

We evaluate our train scheduling solution using the hybrid solver *clingo*[DL] v1.0, which is build upon the API of *clingo* 5.3.[3] We use nine real-world instances published by Swiss Federal Railway (SBB) to test different configurations of *clingo*[DL] with optimization strategies and domain-specific heuristics (60 in total). For brevity, we omit slight grounding and propagation optimizations in the encoding presented in Sect. 4; the full encoding and instance set is at github.com/potassco/train-scheduling-with-clingo-dl. We validate solution feasibility and quality via an external program also provided by SBB.[4] All benchmarks ran on Linux with a Xeon E3-1260L quad-core 2.9 GHz processors and 32 GB RAM; each run limited to 3 hours and 32 GB RAM. In detail, we examine the following techniques:

Optimization Schemes. (BB) *Model-guided* optimization iteratively producing models of descending cost until the optimum is found by establishing unsatisfiability of finding a model with lower cost. (USC) *Core-guided* optimization relying on successively identifying and relaxing unsatisfiable cores until a model is obtained. (nT) Natural number n determines the number of threads with which the solver is run. Threads use the same search space but might learn different clauses that are exchanged. If either BB or USC is additionally specified, both threads use the respective optimization scheme.

All other parameters are using the default of *clingo*[DL]. In particular, the default for 2T configures thread 1 with BB and thread 2 with USC in the hope that the shared information improves overall performance and solution quality.

---

[3] We use the releases for both *clingo*[DL] and *clingo* that are available at github.com/potassco/clingoDL and github.com/potassco/clingo.

[4] www.crowdai.org/challenges/train-schedule-optimisation-challenge.

Objective Function Approximation. We only vary delay optimization and use the same minimize statement for route penalty (see Sect. 4). (BIN) Delay approximation only penalizing instances and not amount of delay. We set $D_{t,v} = Bin_{t,v}$ for each train t at node v. (LIN) Delay approximation creating thresholds evenly within time span of possible delay. We set $D_{t,v} = Bin_{t,v} \cup Lin_{t,v}^{180}$ for each train t at node v. For LIN, we chose the distance of thresholds, viz. 180, such that there are 5 thresholds with a maximum threshold of 15 min. We also examined an exponential distribution of thresholds where the distance doubles every time so that the precision is higher for lower delays, and significant delays receive a greater penalty. We omit the results since the approach does not improve quality and displays worse performance compared to LIN.

Domain-Specific Heuristics. For details, see Sect. 4. (NONE) Domain-specific heuristics are disabled. (SEQ) Sequence heuristic in Listing 1.5. (DELAY) Delay heuristic in Listing 1.6. (ROUTES) Routing heuristic in Listing 1.7. (ALL) All heuristics SEQ, DELAY and ROUTES are enabled.

Table 1. Aggregated wall time and quality.

OPT	HEU									
	NONE		SEQ		DELAY		ROUTES		ALL	
	T	QU	T	QU	T	QU	T	QU	T	QU
BIN-1T	4767	175	4136	165	2578	165	3215	175	**684**	165
BIN-2T	933	181	*575	184	937	173	909	175	**574**	**165**
BIN-2T-BB	5050	166	4723	175	2481	165	1916	177	**600**	165
BIN-2T-USC	*877	165	581	184	*881	165	*881	175	**574**	173
LIN-1T	–	–	23343	33	6380	33	–	–	**705**	33
LIN-2T	1118	33	694	33	1264	33	926	33	**611**	33
LIN-2T-BB	–	–	16495	33	4561	33	11667	33	**605**	33
LIN-2T-USC	4047	33	**2351**	33	–	–	–	–	–	–

Table 2. Instance details and best results.

INS	#T	#N	#E	ALL-BIN-2T			ALL-LIN-2T-BB		
				T	AQU	QU	T	AQU	QU
1	4	159	159	2	0	0	2	0	0
2	58	1839	1816	5	0	0	5	0	0
3	143	2117	2090	8	0	0	9	0	0
4	148	2371	2352	12	0	0	13	0	0
5	149	2376	2356	19	8	165	42	21	33
6	365	3128	3109	149	0	0	144	0	0
7	467	3128	3109	252	0	0	251	0	0
8	133	3228	3314	127	0	0	139	0	0
9	287	34488	34827	–	–	–	–	–	–

In our experiments, we used *clingo*[DL] to report one optimal solution for each configuration. Table 1 shows the sum of wall time in seconds in columns T, and the value of the exact objective function as reported by the external validation tool in columns QU, for all combinations of optimization strategy (rows of the table) and domain-specific heuristics (columns of the table) that were able to report one valid optimal solution for instances 1 through 8. Note that all values are rounded to integers. We omit results for instance 9 since grounding was not possible within 32 GB of memory. Combinations where some instances timed out are marked with −. This way, we are able to exclude inferior results while being able to accurately compare performance and solution quality of successful configurations. The best results in a row and in a column for wall time and quality are marked bold and with *, respectively, unless at least two configurations achieved the same result.

Regarding wall time, ALL clearly performs best and improves performance up to one order of magnitude compared to NONE. While each domain-specific heuristic has a positive impact, either reducing wall time or allowing all instances to be solved optimally, we observe that SEQ has the most benefit on its own, but the joint effect of the three heuristics is vital in achieving the best possible performance. Furthermore, optimization approximation BIN performs best, displaying no timeouts and best aggregate wall time by a slight margin. Since weights in the optimization statement for BIN are all one, USC is very effective for it. For LIN, on the other hand, running both BB and USC simultaneously proved to be successful, most likely due to a mixture of different weight values and the benefit of the shared clauses between threads. As expected, the simple approximation of the objective function BIN is easier to solve but provides solutions of less quality. Note that while all the solutions returned by *clingo*[DL] were optimal, the value of the exact objective function varies. If there are several optimal solutions, a different one might be reported depending on heuristics or thread-based interference, i.e., we cannot guarantee that the same optimal model is found for different configurations. Approximations LIN has overall more timeouts and worse wall time, but solution quality is higher.

Table 2 shows for all instances the number of trains(#T), nodes(#N) and edges(#E) along with wall time(T), approximated quality(AQU) and exact quality(QU) for the configuration with the best performance, viz. ALL-BIN-2T, and best quality-performance ratio, viz. ALL-LIN-2T-BB. We found optimal solutions to the approximated objective functions for instances with up to 467 trains, 3228 nodes and 3314 edges within 5 min. Except for instances 4 and 5, which were crafted specifically to contain obstructions inducing delay, we could provide solutions without any penalties regarding the exact objective function. For Instance 4, the delay is negligible and for Instances 5, we achieve a value close to the best possible solution according to SBB. We see that BIN is a good choice for instances that are expected to be solvable without delay, but for more difficult instances, like Instance 5, the approximation is too inaccurate. On the other hand, LIN achieves more accuracy with similar performance mostly thanks to the domain-specific heuristics that steer the solving process to promising regions of the search space.

Overall, we observe that all domain-specific heuristics, SEQ in particular, linear approximation of delay optimization, and several threads with multiple optimization strategies, allow us to successfully solve the train scheduling problem for a variety of real-world instances in acceptable time.

6   Discussion

At its core, train scheduling is similar to classical scheduling problems that were already tackled by ASP. Foremost, job shop scheduling [16] is also addressed by *clingo*[DL] and compared to other hybrid approaches in [8]; solutions based on SMT, CP and MILP are given in [1,2,9,11], respectively. In fact, job shop scheduling can be seen as a special case of our setting, in which train paths are known beforehand. Solutions to this restricted variant via MILP and CP are presented in [12,15]. The difference to our setting is twofold: first, resource conflicts are not known beforehand since we take routing and scheduling simultaneously into account. Second, our approach encompasses a global view of arbitrary precision, i.e., we model all routing and scheduling decisions across hundreds of trains and possible lines down to inner-station conflict resolution. Furthermore, using hybrid ASP with difference constraints gives us inherent advantages over pure ASP and MILP. First, we show in [6] that ASP is not able to solve most shop scheduling instances since grounding all the integer variables leads to an explosion in problem size. We avoid this bottleneck by encapsulating scheduling in difference constraints and, hence, avoid grounding integer variables. Second, while difference constraints are less expressive than linear constraints in MILP, they are sufficient for expressing the timing constraint needed for train scheduling and are solvable in polynomial time. Finally, routing and conflict resolution require Boolean variables and disjunctions for which ASP has effective means.

Since we produce timetables from scratch, our train scheduling problem can be characterized as tactical scheduling [17]. In the future, we aim at addressing re-scheduling [13,14], where existing timetables have to be adapted to sudden deviations. While our hybrid ASP encoding can be easily modified to accommodate such advanced reasoning tasks, we currently could not address them in real-time. The main challenge lies in reducing the size of the problem. We have shown that, if grounding is possible, we can effectively solve real-world train scheduling with *clingo*[DL]. The problem size can be reduced by first, compressing the graph and removing nodes that are redundant in terms of timing constraints that they pose to the schedule, and second, identifying groups of conflicts of trains that only require a single decision to be resolved in a preprocessing step.

References

1. Baptiste, P., Pape, C.L., Nuijten, W.: Constraint-Based Scheduling: Applying Constraint Programming to Scheduling Problems, vol. 39. Springer, New York (2012)
2. Bofill, M., Palahí, M., Suy, J., Villaret, M.: Solving constraint satisfaction problems with SAT modulo theories. Constraints **17**(3), 273–303 (2012)
3. Caprara, A., Fischetti, M., Toth, P.: Modeling and solving the train timetabling problem. Oper. Res. **50**, 851–861 (2002)
4. Gebser, M., Harrison, A., Kaminski, R., Lifschitz, V., Schaub, T.: Abstract gringo. Theory Pract. Log. Program. **15**(4–5), 449–463 (2015)
5. Gebser, M., et al.: Potassco User Guide, 2nd edn. (2015). http://potassco.org
6. Gebser, M., Kaminski, R., Kaufmann, B., Ostrowski, M., Schaub, T., Wanko, P.: Theory solving made easy with clingo 5. In: Technical Communications of the International Conference on Logic Programming (ICLP 2016), vol. 52, pp. 2:1–2:15. OASIcs (2016)
7. Gebser, M., Kaminski, R., Kaufmann, B., Schaub, T.: Multi-shot ASP solving with clingo. Theory Pract. Log. Program. **19**(1), 27–82 (2019)
8. Janhunen, T., Kaminski, R., Ostrowski, M., Schaub, T., Schellhorn, S., Wanko, P.: Clingo goes linear constraints over reals and integers. Theory Pract. Log. Program. **17**(5–6), 872–888 (2017)

9. Janhunen, T., Liu, G., Niemelä, I.: Tight integration of non-ground answer set programming and satisfiability modulo theories. In: Proceedings of the Workshop on Grounding and Transformation for Theories with Variables (GTTV 2011), pp. 1–13 (2011)
10. Lifschitz, V.: Answer set planning. In: Proceedings of the International Conference on Logic Programming (ICLP 1999), pp. 23–37. MIT Press (1999)
11. Liu, G., Janhunen, T., Niemelä, I.: Answer set programming via mixed integer programming. In: Proceedings of the International Conference on Principles of Knowledge Representation and Reasoning (KR 2012), pp. 32–42. AAAI Press (2012)
12. Oliveira, E., Smith, B.: A job-shop scheduling model for the single-track railway scheduling problem. University of Leeds, LU SCS RR (21) (2000)
13. Pellegrini, P., Douchet, G., Marlière, G., Rodriguez, J.: Real-time train routing and scheduling through mixed integer linear programming: heuristic approach. In: Proceedings of the International Conference on Industrial Engineering and System Management, pp. 1–5 (2013)
14. Pellegrini, P., Marlière, G., Pesenti, R., Rodriguez, J.: RECIFE-MILP: an effective MILP-based heuristic for the real-time railway traffic management problem. IEEE Trans. Intell. Transp. Syst. **16**(5), 2609–2619 (2015)
15. Rodriguez, J.: A constraint programming model for real-time train scheduling at junctions. Transp. Res.: Methodol. **41**(2), 231–245 (2007)
16. Taillard, E.: Benchmarks for basic scheduling problems. Eur. J. Oper. Res. **64**(2), 278–285 (1993)
17. Törnquist, J.: Computer-based decision support for railway traffic scheduling and dispatching: a review of models and algorithms. In: Proceedings of the Workshop on Algorithmic Methods and Models for Optimization of Railways, vol. 2. OASIcs (2006)

Telco Network Inventory Validation
with NoHR

Vedran Kasalica[1], Ioannis Gerochristos[2], José Júlio Alferes[2],
Ana Sofia Gomes[2], Matthias Knorr[2], and João Leite[2(✉)]

[1] Department of Information and Computing Sciences, Utrecht University,
3584 CC Utrecht, The Netherlands
[2] NOVA LINCS, Departamento de Informática, FCT-NOVA Lisboa,
2829-516 Caparica, Portugal
jleite@fct.unl.pt

Abstract. Network database inventory is a critical tool for the operations of any telecommunication company, by supporting network configuration and maintenance, as well as troubleshooting of network incidents.
Whereas an incorrect inventory can often lead to severe implications
and financial losses, the sheer size of a telecommunication network, the
number of equipment involved, and other operational constraints, often
lead to outdated inconsistent inventories, which are usually validated
and updated *by hand*, during change management processes – a time-
consuming task highly prone to human error. In this paper, we describe
a solution to automate the validation of network inventories within the
context of a multinational telecommunication company, with operations
in several different countries, using NoHR, a reasoner that allows the
user to query (hybrid) knowledge bases composed of ontologies and non-
monotonic rules, both of which are necessary to perform the kind of
reasoning required by this task. In addition, to address severe performance issues – essentially in terms of memory – resulting from NoHR
v3.0's need to pre-process the entire database into OWL assertions or rule
facts, in this paper, we also present v4.0 of NoHR, which extends NoHR
v3.0 with native support for Databases, solving not only the memory
consumption problems, but also improving the average reasoning times.

1   Introduction

Network database inventory is a critical tool for any telecommunication company, maintaining information on what network nodes exist and their characteristics (model, band, frequency, etc.); how nodes connect with each other,
their physical and logical paths; and general topology configuration. Network
inventory supports many different parts of a telecommunication organization.
In particular, it provides important inputs for planning and provisioning, but
it is absolutely critical to network operations, by supporting network configuration and maintenance, as well as troubleshooting of network incidents. However,
given the sheer size of a telecommunication network, and the number of equipment involved, network inventories are often outdated, providing a misleading

© Springer Nature Switzerland AG 2019
M. Balduccini et al. (Eds.): LPNMR 2019, LNAI 11481, pp. 18–31, 2019.
https://doi.org/10.1007/978-3-030-20528-7_2

image of the network configuration. On a network operation service, an incorrect inventory can lead, for instance, to a wrong assessment of the problem root-cause, evaluating an incident with the incorrect priority, or setting up an insufficient work-around to restore operations. In any case, an incorrect inventory can often lead to financial losses and implications.

Normally, on any telecommunication company, network inventories are stored in the back-end of some specialized enterprise system, supported by some relational database. While some tools and processes may exist to automate inventory validation and correctness, these are normally very limited and incomplete.

Most enterprise inventory solutions incorporate some constraints over the data being inserted and updated, e.g., that a Radio Base Station (RBS) cannot be inserted without a related Location, or that a Cell can only be created for a given parent RBS. However, these validations are very limited and rely on simple database constraints defined by the vendor. Additionally, since engineers interact with the inventory at a user interface level without the context of a transaction, they often may need to leave the database in an inconsistent state during a planned work. As such, these solutions cannot implement very strong constraints over what is being inserted, and one may, e.g., find a 3G RBS station (aka NodeB) with a defined connection to a 2G Radio Controller (aka BSC), although that simply cannot be the case.

Other more sophisticated solutions exist, which connect to the live network and then compare it with the network inventory. However, these can overload the live network with requests and impact network service, which requires that they be planned with care, managed as low priority requests, and validation can take several hours/days depending on the network size. Additionally, these solutions rely on having connectors to each of the different telco hardware vendors and technologies, which make the solution considerably expensive. In fact, all vendors have closed and proprietary protocols to connect to each of their network nodes, which may change (and be charged differently) depending on the technology or even the equipment's firmware version. Moreover, most telecommunication companies have at least three generations of equipment and have contracts with several different vendors. As a consequence, normally only some part of the network is scanned with these tools, due to prohibitive integration costs. Finally, these solutions do not perform any validation per se. They just update the inventory with the current image of that day, and cannot validate if network nodes are implemented according to the organization's best-practices and rules.

Due to all these reasons, often these network inventories are simply validated and updated *by hand*, during change management processes, which is a time-consuming task highly prone to human error.

In this paper, we describe an implemented solution to automate the validation of network inventories within the context of a multinational telecommunication company, with operations in several different countries, based on NoHR (Nova Hybrid Reasoner) [6,11,17]. NoHR v3.0 [17] is a reasoner theoretically founded on the formalism of Hybrid MKNF under the well-founded semantics [15], with support for paraconsistent reasoning [13], which allows the user to query (hybrid) knowledge bases composed of both ontologies and non-monotonic rules. Using a top-down reasoning approach, which means that only the part of the ontology and rules that is relevant for the query is actually evaluated, NoHR is implemented in a way that combines the capabilities of the DL reasoners ELK [14], HermiT [9], and Konclude [21] with the rule engine XSB Prolog,[1] to deliver very fast interactive response times.

Turning back to the network inventory validation problem, on closer inspection of the existing inventory data, we observe that even though operations in different countries rely on data managed with very different levels of maturity – from those with state-of-the-art enterprise inventory systems to those where most up-to-date data is stored in very basic excel spreadsheets – ultimately, all is accessible through a standard database connector such as ODBC. Also, although the enterprise systems implemented in each of the countries are very different, network inventories are, in their essence, all the same for any telecommunication company. Namely, a Mobile Network is normally split into three domains and networks: radio access network (RAN) which comprises the necessary equipment for the interaction with a Client User Equipment; the CORE network that comprises all the equipment and technology to provide Voice, Data and any other service; and the Transmission (Tx) Network that deals with transport between the nodes and between the RAN and CORE. As a result, such generic knowledge and concepts of a Mobile Network that are required to make sense and validate the network inventories are naturally modelled through an ontology. Additionally, over the years, the telecommunication company has maintained a body of knowledge gathered from experts, encoding their reasoning when validating the network inventory. This knowledge mostly encodes possible (and somewhat typical) problems usually found in inventories. For example, the experts know that, except from those using Long Term Evolution (LTE) technology, every active station must be connected to exactly one active controller, which means that any non-LTE active station, in the inventory, with no connection to one active controller, or with more than one active controller connected to it, must represent an error in the inventory. What this body of knowledge reveals is that the kind of reasoning carried out by these experts – for example, referring to defaults and exceptions – is the same kind of reasoning that requires and can be expressed as non-monotonic rules.

Whereas, in principle, NoHR v3.0 would be sufficient to deal with all the data and knowledge used in the validation of network inventories problem – besides directly using the ontology and encoding the experts' reasoning rules, we would extract the data from the databases, convert it to a format that is acceptable by the reasoner and then load it into the memory – this would be complicated, time-consuming, and, depending on the data size, sometimes not even feasible. Additionally, it would likely be far from optimal in the sense that the working memory would likely be loaded with huge amounts of facts from the database not required for the reasoning process. Finally, the static interaction with database management systems would mean that any change in the database

---

[1] http://xsb.sourceforge.net.

would yield an inconsistency with the working memory, which would require the data extraction process to restart. It turns out that this is not a limitation specific to the validation of network inventories problem: most of the data used in modern industry is stored in some type of database management system, and its use within NoHR would always result in a similar problem.

Addressing this issue, in this paper, we also describe v4.0 of NoHR, which extends NoHR v3.0 with native support for Databases. From a theoretical standpoint this support is encoded through the concept of *mappings* between predicates in the hybrid knowledge base (both in the rules and the ontology) and SQL query results from the corresponding database systems. In particular, the mappings allow to transparently and simultaneously integrate data stored in different databases, which is of crucial importance to deal with the validation of network inventories. From a practical perspective, the mappings are implemented using ODBC drivers, thus allowing the integration of NoHR with all major database management systems, together with a user interface.

The evaluation has shown that this implementation of NoHR v4.0 not only solves the problems of memory consumption and preprocessing in case of loading large amounts of data, but also managed to considerably improve the average reasoning time over this data when making use of query optimizations based on state-of-the-art database technology.

2   Background on NoHR

We start by providing some background information on the hybrid knowledge bases considered within NoHR.

2.1   Description Logics

Description logics (DLs)[2] are commonly decidable fragments of first-order logic, defined over disjoint countably infinite sets of *concept names* N_C, *role names* N_R, and *individual names* N_I, matching unary and binary predicates, and constants, respectively. *Complex concepts* (and *complex roles*) can be defined based on these sets and the logical constructors a concrete DL admits to be used. An *ontology* $\mathcal{O}$ is a finite set of *inclusion axioms* of the form $C \sqsubseteq D$ where C and D are both (complex) concepts (or roles) and *assertions* of the form $C(a)$ or $R(a, b)$ for concepts C, roles R, and individuals a, b. The semantics of such ontologies is defined in a standard way for first-order logic.

The DL $\mathcal{SROIQ}$ [10] underlying the W3C standard OWL 2 is very general and highly expressive, but reasoning with it is highly complex, which is why the profiles OWL 2 EL, OWL 2 QL and OWL 2 RL have been defined [18], for which reasoning is tractable. NoHR supports all three profiles, in fact, even a combination of the constructors provided by them [17].[3]

---

[2] We refer to [2] for a more general and thorough introduction to DLs.

[3] We refer to [6,11,17] and pointers therein for all constructors supported by NoHR.

For the use case, we require $\mathcal{EL}_\perp^+$, a large fragment of the DL underlying OWL 2 EL, which only allows conjunction of concepts, existential restriction of concepts, hierarchies of roles, and disjoint concepts, and, in addition, symmetric roles. Hence, we use a combination of constructors from different OWL 2 profiles.

2.2 Hybrid Knowledge Bases

The hybrid knowledge bases we consider here are MKNF knowledge bases (KBs), which build on the logic of minimal knowledge and negation as failure (MKNF) [16]. Among the two different semantics defined for these [15,19], we focus on the well-founded one [15], due to its lower computational complexity and amenability to top-down querying without computing the entire model. Again, we only point out important notions, and refer to [1,15] for the details.

A *rule* r is of the form $H \leftarrow A_1, \ldots, A_n, \textbf{not}\ B_1, \ldots, \textbf{not}\ B_m$ where the *head* of r, H, and all A_i with $1 \le i \le n$ and B_j with $1 \le j \le m$ in the *body* of r are atoms, possibly built from the unary and binary predicates occurring in the ontology.[4] A *program* $\mathcal{P}$ is a finite set of rules, $\mathcal{O}$ is an ontology, and an *MKNF knowledge base* $\mathcal{K}$ is a pair $(\mathcal{O}, \mathcal{P})$. A rule r is *safe* if all its variables occur in at least one A_i with $1 \le i \le n$, and $\mathcal{K}$ is *safe* if all its rules are safe.[5]

The semantics of MKNF knowledge bases $\mathcal{K}$ is given by a translation π into an MKNF formula $\pi(\mathcal{K})$, i.e., a formula over first-order logic extended with two modal operators $\textbf{K}$ and $\textbf{not}$. The well-founded MKNF model can be computed efficiently [15] in a bottom-up fashion, and queried based on $\textbf{SLG}(\mathcal{O})$, as defined in [1]. This procedure extends SLG resolution with tabling [4] with an *oracle* to $\mathcal{O}$ that handles ground queries to the DL-part of $\mathcal{K}$ by returning (possibly empty) sets of atoms that, together with $\mathcal{O}$ and information already proven true, allows us to derive the queried atom. We refer to [1] for the full account of $\textbf{SLG}(\mathcal{O})$.

3 Validating Telco Network Inventory Data

In this section, we illustrate how the knowledge relevant for the validation of telco network inventory data can be expressed in an MKNF knowledge base so that the reasoner NoHR can be applied to solve this problem. Following Sect. 1, we thus have to represent the ontology on network inventories, the expert knowledge on validating network inventories, and the data itself within an MKNF KB.

As outlined in the introduction, the ontology describes generic knowledge of the network inventory, common to the inventories in all countries of the multinational telco company. E.g., the knowledge that RAN, CORE, and Tx are all

---

[4] Conceptually, this allows to simultaneously view certain predicates under the closed world semantics in rules and under the open world semantics in the ontology, and admits the bidirectional flow of information between both the rules and the ontology.

[5] In general, the notion of DL-safety is used in this context which requires that these variables occur in atoms that do themselves not occur in the ontology, but due to the reasoning method employed in NoHR, we can relax that restriction.

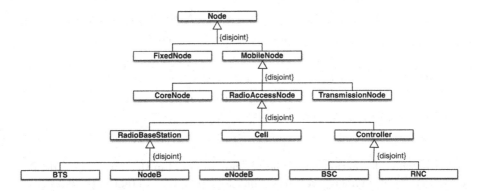

Fig. 1. Part of the inventories ontology

(disjoint) Mobile Nodes can be expressed as follows.

$$Core \sqsubseteq MobileNode \qquad RAN \sqsubseteq MobileNode \qquad Tx \sqsubseteq MobileNode$$
$$Core \sqsubseteq \neg RAN \qquad Core \sqsubseteq \neg Tx \qquad RAN \sqsubseteq \neg Tx$$

A further part of this hierarchical knowledge as shown in Fig. 1 can be represented similarly. Moreover, there are several axioms in the ontology encoding specific knowledge about the telecom network topology. For example:

- Every BTS station is always connected to a BSC controller:

$$BTS \sqsubseteq \exists isConnected.BSC \tag{1}$$

- If a Radio Base Station is directly connected to a core node, then it is a 4G station (aka eNodeB):

$$\exists isConnected.CoreNode \sqcap RBS \sqsubseteq eNodeB \tag{2}$$

Note that these axioms do not represent integrity constraints. Rather, they allow us to infer knowledge that is not explicitly present in the knowledge base, i.e., to compensate for some incompleteness in the inventory. This is especially important because not all inventories in the different countries have a detailed specification of all kinds of nodes, and sometimes leave the specification at higher levels in the taxonomy.

The expert knowledge about possible problems in the inventories can be encoded using non-monotonic rules. For example, the experts' knowledge that, except from those using Long Term Evolution (LTE) technology, every active station must be connected to exactly one active controller, means that any non-LTE active station in the inventory with no connection to one active controller, or more than one connection to an active controller, must represent an error in the inventory. Using rules, this can be encoded as follows.

$$badnLTEConn(X) \leftarrow RBS(X), \textbf{not } lteNode(X), active(X),$$
$$\textbf{not } controllerConnected(X)$$
$$lteNode(X) \leftarrow eNodeB(X)$$
$$controllerConnected(X) \leftarrow isConnected(X,Y), active(Y), Controller(Y),$$
$$\textbf{not } duplicateController(X,Y)$$
$$duplicateController(X,Y) \leftarrow isConnected(X,Z), active(Z), Z \neq Y,$$
$$Controller(Z), Controller(Y)$$

Note that the information on $active(X)$ can be found in the database, and that isConnected is a symmetric role in the ontology based on content in the database.

We emphasize that encoding this problem requires the usage of default negation, e.g., because we want to determine nodes that are not known to be connected, i.e., connections not present in the database, as well as ontological inference, since the inventory usually does not explicitly store information on controllers, but rather on more specific types of equipment that, according to the ontology, can be inferred to be controllers, and since LTE nodes can be inferred from the ontology given its connections (cf. axiom (2)). Further cases of such expert knowledge can also be encoded with rules and will be discussed in Sect. 5.

Finally, regarding the data,[6] it can be included in the reasoning process by transforming it into rule facts or ontology assertions. As mentioned, in principle, this readily allows the usage of NoHR v3.0 for validation of network inventory data. However, this transformation of the data would be complicated, time consuming, and, depending on the data size, sometimes not even feasible. Moreover, we would possibly load huge amounts of facts from the database not required for the reasoning process,[7] and any change in the database would require the data extraction process to restart. This is why we next present the new version of NoHR that overcomes these problems by providing native support for databases.

4   NoHR: Database Integration

In this section, we describe the new version of NoHR, NoHR v4.0, and discuss several features of its implementation, with a particular focus on the novel native support for databases including new functionalities and the associated benefits.

4.1   A Third Component for Hybrid KBs

In order to support the integration with external datasets, we have to extend MKNF KBs. Such an extension could be realized by the addition of a database component, effectively turning MKNF KBs into a triple comprising an ontology, a program (of non-monotonic rules), and a database to which we wish to connect. However, in the context of validating data of network inventory, in particular

---

[6] As the actual database schemas are confidential, we cannot disclose them here.

[7] E.g., there are around 200K of facts for one of the countries involved.

on a multi-national scale, it is clearly preferable to admit several databases to be integrated. Arguably, one could join several databases into one for the sake of the formalism, but this is not necessarily easy as it would require, e.g., to handle (partially) repeated columns with potentially contradictory data, and, from a practical point of view, we would like to simply consult data in tables of different databases, and MKNF KBs should be conceptually close to this idea.

To tackle the integration of several databases within an MKNF KB, we introduce the concepts of mappings and of a mapping knowledge base.[8]

Definition 1. *Let p be a predicate, db a database and q a query defined over db, where p and the tuples returned by q have the same arity. A triple $\langle p, db, q \rangle$ is called a* mapping *for p, where the result set from db for the query q is mapped to the predicate p. A set of mappings $\mathcal{M}$ is called a* mapping knowledge base.

Essentially, mappings are used to create predicates that are populated with the result set obtained from queries to external databases. Based on this we can extend MKNF KBs as follows.

Definition 2. *An MKNF knowledge base $\mathcal{K}$ is a triple $\mathcal{K} = (\mathcal{O}, \mathcal{P}, \mathcal{M})$, where $\mathcal{O}$ is an ontology, $\mathcal{P}$ is a finite set of rules, and $\mathcal{M}$ is a mapping knowledge base.*

For the semantics of such MKNF knowledge bases, we can extend the translation function to mappings and the mapping knowledge base by turning, for each triple $\langle p, db, q \rangle$ in $\mathcal{M}$, all tuples for p into rule facts. Based on this, it can be shown that all technical results for the well-founded MKNF semantics [15], as well as for top-down querying in $\mathbf{SLG}(\mathcal{O})$ [1] hold.

For reasons of space, we omit the details here, and proceed by showing how this extension is reflected in the architecture of NoHR.

4.2   Architecture of NoHR

NoHR is available as a plugin for Protégé[9], a well-known and widely used ontology editor, and we describe the system architecture of this plugin NoHR v4.0 as shown in Fig. 2. When compared with NoHR v3.0, the architecture has been extended with external databases, corresponding ODBC drivers and the integration of the mapping knowledge base (all labelled with a green background).

The input for the plugin consists of an OWL file, a rule file and a mappings file. All three components can be edited in Protégé, using the built-in interface for the ontology and the custom "NoHR Rules" and "NoHR Mappings" tabs, provided by the plugin, for the rule and mapping components. After the inputs (which can be empty) and the first query are provided, the ontology is translated into a set of rules, using one of the provided reasoners, ELK [14], HermiT [9] or Konclude [21], depending on the DL in which the ontology is written. This

---

[8] Similar concepts have been used before for adding database support to rule systems, such as DLV^{DB} [22], and in ontology based data access, such as in ontop [3].

[9] https://protege.stanford.edu/.

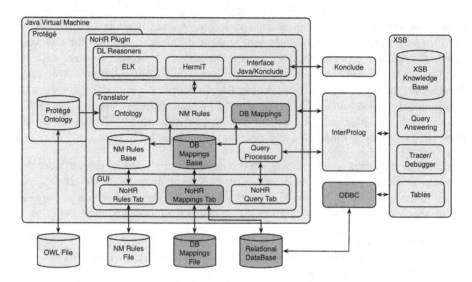

Fig. 2. System architecture of NoHR v4.0 with native database support

resulting set of rules is not equivalent to the ontology in general, but it yields exactly the same answers for ground queries (for more details cf. [6,11,17]). The resulting set is then combined with the rules and mappings provided by the input. This joined result serves as input to XSB Prolog via InterProlog[10], which is an open-source Java front-end, allowing the communication between Java and a Prolog engine, and the query is sent via the same interface to XSB to be executed. During the execution, mappings are providing facts from the external databases as they are requested in the reasoning process. This procedure is supported by the installed ODBC connections and handled within XSB, thus providing full control over the database access during querying and taking advantage of the built-in optimization to access only the relevant part of the database. Answers are returned to the query processor, which displays them to the user in a table (in the Query Tab). The user may pose further queries, and the system will simply send them directly to XSB, without any repeated preprocessing. If the knowledge base is edited, the system recompiles only the part that was changed.

4.3 Implementing Database Support

We now discuss several of the design decisions on implementing database support within NoHR 4.0 and the benefits we were able to leverage.

First, the connection to various databases is realized via the *XSB - ODBC Interface*, because it is part of the query engine XSB used in NoHR, it supports all major database management systems (DBMSs), and it provides an easy-to-use and well-known connection driver independently of the operating system.

---

[10] http://interprolog.com/java-bridge/.

Among the three levels of interaction with the database the *XSB - ODBC Interface* provides, *SQL level, relation level* and *view level*, we chose the SQL level, because, unlike the other two, it allows the usage of standard SQL syntax and provides the flexibility to map an arbitrary SQL query to the predicate, which also provides considerable performance gains compared to the other two.

To allow the user to create the necessary mappings, i.e., combinations of a predicate, an SQL query and a database connection, the "Mappings Tab" has been introduced to the Protégé plugin version of NoHR. It contains a parametrizable mapping form, which offers two different approaches to create mappings, namely mapping with the SQL Designer and Manual SQL mappings.

The *SQL Designer* allows the creation of mappings based on the user's specification of what columns from which tables of which database should be combined, where the underlying SQL queries are dynamically generated, based on the structure of the schema. As this interface has full control over the structure of the SQL query, several optimizations are applied, including improved handling of floating point number unification and of bounded variables. For example, the WHERE clause of the SQL query is dynamically adjusted to fetch only the relevant tuples, depending on the bounded variables in the predicate.

In order to generalize the DBMS integration, we also provide support for *Manual SQL mappings*, i.e., arbitrary SQL queries, to take advantage of the capabilities of the specific DBMS at hand. This allows, e.g., the usage of nested queries and benefiting from the associated performance gains when querying.

5 Evaluation

Previous tests of NoHR have shown that different ontologies can be pre-processed into rules in reasonably short amounts of time (around one minute for Snomed CT with over 300,000 concepts), loading of rules is only linearly dependent on the size of the rule file, and querying can often be done with interactive response times (cf. [5,6,11,12,17]). Here, we evaluate three measures in the use case of validating the network inventory that show that the native support of databases comes with considerable performance benefits for the reasoning process of NoHR.

We compare NoHR 4.0 with its predecessor in terms of preprocessing time and memory usage. To replicate the tests in the telco company, we generated sets of facts corresponding to database instances of increasing size, closely resembling the data used in the network inventory validation use case, and tested the impact of loading these files in NoHR. All tests were performed on an i5-2.4 GHz processor with 8 GB under win64. The results are shown in Fig. 3.

We first note that, since NoHR v4.0 does not require preloading of facts corresponding to the data stored in a database, the observed values for NoHR v4.0 can serve as a (constant) baseline in both cases. In terms of memory for NoHR v3.0, we observe a steady increase of used memory until the limit of the free available RAM is reached (around 20K of facts with many arguments). From there on, memory usage does not increase any further. Rather virtual memory is used increasing the size of the virtual address space beyond the available amount of RAM using paging and/or swapping to secondary storage. We can observe that this has a considerable impact on the loading time, e.g., loading 100K of facts takes around 38 min since swapping/secondary storage is in general considerably slower. In fact, we tried loading 200K (roughly the amount of data corresponding to one of the countries in which validation of network inventory is applied) and it failed to upload within the set time-out of one hour. We note that the given times only consider the loading, and do not even include the time necessary to transform the database content into rule facts in the right format. Again, for NoHR v4.0, the problem ceases to exist, as there is no need to load large amounts of facts corresponding to the database content into memory, which makes the NoHR v4.0 usable also for applications with larger amounts of data.

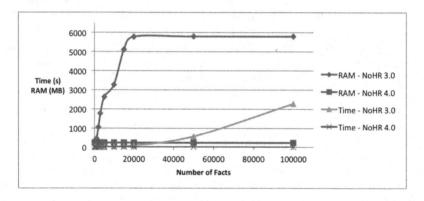

Fig. 3. Memory usage and time of data preloading for NoHR v3.0 and v4.0.

In order to evaluate the effect of using external databases on querying, we compare the time for answering several queries in the network inventory validation use case for NoHR v3.0 and NoHR v4.0. In fact, we consider two cases for NoHR v4.0: one with (simple) direct mappings from predicates to corresponding database columns, and one with advanced mappings using sophisticated queries to make use of optimizations in efficient state-of-the-art DBMS where possible. We use two sets of generated data instances of size 20K and 50K, resembling the actual data used, and five queries inspired by the real use case, namely: (1) find all active nodes that are located at a location that is marked as out of order; (2) find all nodes (equipments) manufactured by Ericsson before 1995 that are connected to Huawei equipment manufactured after 2010 (because they are incompatible); (3) find non-LTE active stations that are not connected to exactly one active controller (cf. Sect. 3); (4) find two locations that share the same coordinates and are both active; and (5) Find active nodes that are not connected to any other node. Among the two general purpose DL reasoners available in NoHR (given that the ontology does not fit one profile), we used HermiT, as it has been shown to be superior for all but the really large ontologies [17].

The results are shown in Fig. 4. As expected, NoHR v4.0 is slightly slower, on average, when querying, as the connection via ODBC adds an overhead to the query process. However, if we use advanced mappings, which allow to outsource certain joins over data from XSB to the DBMS, then NoHR v4.0 outperforms NoHR v3.0 by a considerable margin, in particular when advanced database joins reduce the amount of data that needs to be sent to XSB for reasoning.

Overall, we observe that NoHR v4.0 is competitive with NoHR v3.0 in terms of querying, and superior when part of the query can be processed by the DBMS directly, while eliminating the memory usage and preprocessing time problems.

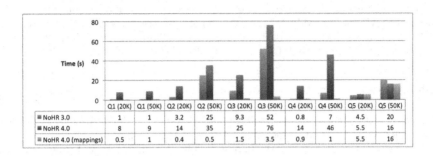

	Q1 (20K)	Q1 (50K)	Q2 (20K)	Q2 (50K)	Q3 (20K)	Q3 (50K)	Q4 (20K)	Q4 (50K)	Q5 (20K)	Q5 (50K)
■ NoHR 3.0	1	1	3.2	25	9.3	52	0.8	7	4.5	20
■ NoHR 4.0	8	9	14	35	25	76	14	46	5.5	16
■ NoHR 4.0 (mappings)	0.5	1	0.4	0.5	1.5	3.5	0.9	1	5.5	16

Fig. 4. Time of query answering in NoHR v3.0 and NoHR v4.0

6   Conclusions

We have presented an implemented solution to automate the validation of network inventories within the context of a multinational telecommunication company, with operations in several different countries, based on the reasoner NoHR. Since using NoHR v3.0 for this solution would require to load all the data into memory, which is problematic given the amount of data in the context of the multinational telco company, we also introduced NoHR v4.0, which extends NoHR v3.0 with native database support. We have described this database support in NoHR extending the underlying formalism by mappings and its integration in NoHR's architecture, and we have discussed important features such as the flexible XSB-ODBC interface, general support for SQL queries, and interfaces for the creation of optimized SQL queries. The evaluation confirms that using the new version is highly beneficial, in particular for use cases with large amounts of data, such as the validation of network inventories, because it avoids the overhead of transforming the database into facts in NoHR, reducing time and memory usage considerably, as well as during querying where we can make use of query optimizations that are based on state-of-the-art database technology.

In terms of future work, currently MySQL and Oracle DBMSs are fully supported, which sufficed for the validation use case. The XSB-OBDC interface is, however, flexible, and making the necessary adjustments so that all major DBMSs are supported is important, to admit the usage of NoHR in other use cases (with different DBMSs). Adapting ideas on dynamic hybrid KB's [20] and semi-automatic mapping creation [22] is also promising to further improve usability, and a comparison with the integration of databases with ontologies and rules in the HEX formalism [7], based on dl-programs [8], is of interest, even if arguably less general than hybrid MKNF [19]. A more ambitious objective is the integration of data on the Semantic Web, i.e., Linked Open Data. While, conceptually, the idea corresponds to database integration, the technical solution will certainly differ, due to different standards and formats employed. Given the wide-spread availability of Linked Open Data sets nowadays, such addition would provide a valuable extension to NoHR for knowledge integration.

Acknowledgments. We would like to acknowledge the helpful comments by the anonymous reviewers, the valuable contribution of N. Costa, V. Ivanov, and C. Lopes to the development of NoHR, and partial support by FCT projects RIVER (PTDC/CCI-COM/30952/2017) and NOVA LINCS (UID/CEC/04516/2013).

References

1. Alferes, J.J., Knorr, M., Swift, T.: Query-driven procedures for hybrid MKNF knowledge bases. ACM Trans. Comput. Log. **14**(2), 1–43 (2013)
2. Baader, F., Calvanese, D., McGuinness, D.L., Nardi, D., Patel-Schneider, P.F. (eds.): The Description Logic Handbook: Theory, Implementation, and Applications, 3rd edn. Cambridge University Press, Cambridge (2010)
3. Calvanese, D., et al.: Ontop: answering SPARQL queries over relational databases. Semant. Web **8**(3), 471–487 (2017)
4. Chen, W., Warren, D.S.: Tabled evaluation with delaying for general logic programs. J. ACM **43**(1), 20–74 (1996)
5. Costa, N., Knorr, M., Leite, J.: Querying LUBM with non-monotonic features in protege using NoHR. In: Proceedings of ISWC Demonstrations, CEUR Proceedings, vol. 1486 (2015)
6. Costa, N., Knorr, M., Leite, J.: Next step for NoHR: OWL 2 QL. In: Arenas, M., et al. (eds.) ISWC 2015. LNCS, vol. 9366, pp. 569–586. Springer, Cham (2015). https://doi.org/10.1007/978-3-319-25007-6_33
7. Eiter, T., Fink, M., Ianni, G., Krennwallner, T., Redl, C., Schüller, P.: A model building framework for answer set programming with external computations. TPLP **16**(4), 418–464 (2016)
8. Eiter, T., Ianni, G., Lukasiewicz, T., Schindlauer, R., Tompits, H.: Combining answer set programming with description logics for the semantic web. Artif. Intell. **172**(12–13), 1495–1539 (2008)
9. Glimm, B., Horrocks, I., Motik, B., Stoilos, G., Wang, Z.: Hermit: an OWL 2 reasoner. J. Autom. Reason. **53**(3), 245–269 (2014)
10. Horrocks, I., Kutz, O., Sattler, U.: The even more irresistible $\mathcal{SROIQ}$. In: Proceedings of KR. AAAI Press (2006)
11. Ivanov, V., Knorr, M., Leite, J.: A query tool for $\mathcal{EL}$ with non-monotonic rules. In: Alani, H., et al. (eds.) ISWC 2013. LNCS, vol. 8218, pp. 216–231. Springer, Heidelberg (2013). https://doi.org/10.1007/978-3-642-41335-3_14
12. Ivanov, V., Knorr, M., Leite, J.: Reasoning over ontologies and non-monotonic rules. In: Pereira, F., Machado, P., Costa, E., Cardoso, A. (eds.) EPIA 2015. LNCS (LNAI), vol. 9273, pp. 388–401. Springer, Cham (2015). https://doi.org/10.1007/978-3-319-23485-4_39
13. Kaminski, T., Knorr, M., Leite, J.: Efficient paraconsistent reasoning with ontologies and rules. In: Proceedings of IJCAI. AAAI Press (2015)

14. Kazakov, Y., Krötzsch, M., Simančík, F.: The incredible ELK: from polynomial procedures to efficient reasoning with $\mathcal{EL}$ ontologies. J. Autom. Reason. **53**, 1–61 (2013)
15. Knorr, M., Alferes, J.J., Hitzler, P.: Local closed world reasoning with description logics under the well-founded semantics. Artif. Intell. **175**(9–10), 1528–1554 (2011)
16. Lifschitz, V.: Nonmonotonic databases and epistemic queries. In: Mylopoulos, J., Reiter, R. (eds.) Proceedings of IJCAI. Morgan Kaufmann (1991)
17. Lopes, C., Knorr, M., Leite, J.: NoHR: integrating XSB prolog with the OWL 2 profiles and beyond. In: Balduccini, M., Janhunen, T. (eds.) LPNMR 2017. LNCS (LNAI), vol. 10377, pp. 236–249. Springer, Cham (2017). https://doi.org/10.1007/978-3-319-61660-5_22
18. Motik, B., Cuenca Grau, B., Horrocks, I., Wu, Z., Fokoue, A., Lutz, C. (eds.): OWL 2 Web Ontology Language: Profiles (Second Edition). W3C (2012)
19. Motik, B., Rosati, R.: Reconciling description logics and rules. J. ACM **57**(5), 93–154 (2010)
20. Slota, M., Leite, J., Swift, T.: On updates of hybrid knowledge bases composed of ontologies and rules. Artif. Intell. **229**, 33–104 (2015)
21. Steigmiller, A., Liebig, T., Glimm, B.: Konclude: system description. J. Web Semant. **27**, 78–85 (2014)
22. Terracina, G., Leone, N., Lio, V., Panetta, C.: Experimenting with recursive queries in database and logic programming systems. TPLP **8**(2), 129–165 (2008)

An ASP-Based Framework for the Manipulation of Articulated Objects Using Dual-Arm Robots

Riccardo Bertolucci[1], Alessio Capitanelli[2], Carmine Dodaro[2],
Nicola Leone[1], Marco Maratea[2(✉)], Fulvio Mastrogiovanni[2],
and Mauro Vallati[3]

[1] DeMaCS, University of Calabria, Rende, Italy
{bertolucci,leone}@mat.unical.it
[2] DIBRIS, University of Genova, Genova, Italy
{alessio.capitanelli,carmine.dodaro,
marco.maratea,fulvio.mastrogiovanni}@unige.it
[3] University of Huddersfield, Huddersfield, UK
m.vallati@hud.ac.uk

Abstract. The manipulation of articulated objects is of primary importance in robotics, and is one of the most complex robotics tasks. Traditionally, this problem has been tackled by developing ad-hoc approaches, that lack of flexibility and portability.

In this paper we present a framework based on Answer Set Programming (ASP) for the automated manipulation of articulated objects in a robot architecture. In particular, ASP is employed for representing the configuration of the articulated object, for checking the consistency of the knowledge base, as well as for generating the sequence of manipulation actions. The framework is validated both in simulation and on the Baxter dual-arm manipulator, showing the applicability of the ASP methodology in this complex application scenario.

1 Introduction

The manipulation of articulated objects plays an important role in real-world robot tasks, both in home and industrial environments [20,24]. Attention has been paid to the development of approaches and algorithms for generating the sequence of movements a robot has to perform in order to manipulate an articulated object. In the literature, the problem of determining the 2D configuration of articulated or flexible objects has received much attention in the past few years [7,8,27,31], whereas the problem of obtaining a target configuration via manipulation has been explored in motion planning [4,30,32]. A limitation of such manipulation strategies is that they are often crafted specifically for the problem at hand, with the relevant characteristics of the object and robot capabilities being either hard coded or assumed; thus, in these contexts generalisation property and scalability are somehow limited.

© Springer Nature Switzerland AG 2019
M. Balduccini et al. (Eds.): LPNMR 2019, LNAI 11481, pp. 32–44, 2019.
https://doi.org/10.1007/978-3-030-20528-7_3

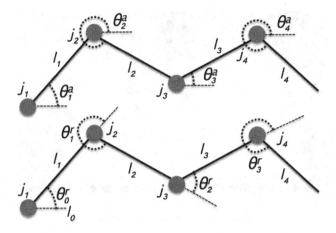

Fig. 1. Two possible representations: absolute (top) and relative (bottom).

In this paper we present a framework based on Answer Set Programming (ASP) [5,28] for the automated manipulation of articulated objects in a robot 2D workspace. ASP is a general, prominent knowledge representation and reasoning language with roots in logic programming and non-monotonic reasoning [17]. In particular, ASP is employed for performing all automated reasoning related tasks, i.e., both for planning actions that the robot has to execute, and for checking the consistency of the configurations of the articulated object as it changes over time. The validity of the framework is finally demonstrated both in simulation and on the Baxter dual-arm manipulator.

2 Problem Statement and the Reference Scenario

Our goal is to present (i) an efficient ASP-based planning and execution architecture for the manipulation of articulated objects in terms of perceptual features, their representation and the planning of manipulation actions, which maximises the likelihood of being successfully executed by robots, and (ii) given a specific object's goal configuration, determine a plan to attain it, in which each step involves one or more manipulation actions to be executed by a dual-arm robot. Our working assumptions are:

A_1 flexible objects can be appropriately modelled as articulated objects with a high number of links and joints, as it is customary [32];

A_2 an object's configuration is only affected by robot manipulation actions, or possibly by humans, and the effects of external forces such as gravity are not considered;

A_3 we do not consider possible issues related to grasping or dexterity during the manipulation task;

A_4 sensing is affected by noise, but the *symbol grounding problem*, i.e., the association between perceptual features and the corresponding symbols [19], is assumed to be solved.

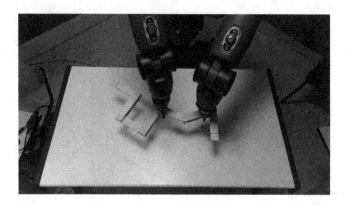

Fig. 2. The experimental scenario.

On the basis of assumption A_1, we focus on articulated objects only. We define an articulated object as a pair $\alpha = (\mathcal{L}, \mathcal{J})$, where $\mathcal{L}$ is the ordered set of its $|\mathcal{L}|$ links and $\mathcal{J}$ is the ordered set of its $|\mathcal{J}|$ joints. Each link $l \in \mathcal{L}$ is characterised by two parameters, namely a length λ_l and an orientation θ_l. We allow only for a limited number of possible orientations. This induces a set of allowed angle orientations A with size $|A|$. If α is represented using absolute angles (Fig. 1 on the top), then its configuration is a $|L|$-ple:

$$C_{\alpha,a} = \left(\theta_1^a, \ldots, \theta_{|L|}^a \right). \tag{1}$$

Otherwise, if relative angles are used (Fig. 1 on the bottom), then the configuration must be *augmented* with an initial *hidden* link l_0 in order to define a reference frame:

$$C_{\alpha,r} = \left(\theta_1^r, \theta_2^r, \ldots, \theta_{|L|}^r \right). \tag{2}$$

In fact, while in principle the relative approach could represent the configuration of an articulated object with one joint less compared to the absolute one, the resulting representation would not be unique, since the object maintains relative orientations among its parts even when rotated *as a whole*.

In order to comply with assumption A_2, we setup a scenario in which a Baxter robot manipulates an articulated object located on a horizontal table in front of it, assumed to be large enough to accommodate the object itself, see Fig. 2. Therefore, rotations occur only around an axis perpendicular to the table. We have crafted two wooden articulated objects of different size: the first has three 40 cm long links (which are connected by two joints), and the second is made up of seven 20 cm long links (connected by six joints). For both objects, links are 3 cm thick. The two objects can be easily manipulated by the Baxter's standard grippers, which complies with assumption A_3. The Baxter's *head* is equipped with a camera pointing downward to the table. QR tags are fixed to each object link l, which is aimed at meeting assumption A_4. Each QR code provides an overall link pose, which directly maps to an absolute link orientation

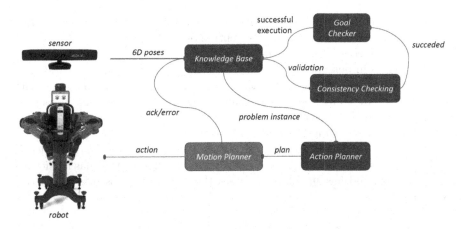

Fig. 3. The robot's architecture: in *green* the ASP-based modules, in *orange* the ROSPlan-based module. (Color figure online)

θ_l^a. Finally, if relative orientations are chosen, we compute them by performing an algebraic sum between the two absolute poses of two consequent links, e.g., $\theta_1^r = \theta_2^a - \theta_1^a$. After this general scenario introduction, in the next section we detail the architecture.

3   The Robot Architecture

The architecture of the Baxter from Rethink Robotics is shown in Fig. 3. It is noteworthy that, in principle, the architecture can be adapted to other robot platforms as well, either in simulation or in real-world conditions, as long as appropriate perception, low-level motion planning tools, and manipulation strategies are adopted.

In the current implementation, perception is managed using a camera sensor located on top of the robot's *head* and pointing downward, which provides 6D poses for each link, which update corresponding ASP-based representation structures in the *Knowledge Base* module. The *Consistency Checking* module performs a check for knowledge base validation. In case the check succeeds, the *Goal Checker* module is notified and relevant parts of the current ASP *Knowledge Base* are processed by the rules encoded in the *Goal Checker* module, aimed at detecting whether the (already computed) plan can be successfully executed, also in response to a possible human intervention. Whenever checks that influence the knowledge base status are performed, a problem instance may be generated, which depends on the target articulated object configuration and the current configuration maintained in the *Knowledge Base* module. The *Action Planner* module receives such problem instance and generates a plan in the form of a suitable sequence of actions to be performed. Once a plan is generated, its actions are processed sequentially to drive the overall behaviour of the robot *Motion Planner* module, which is responsible of the execution. For the use case described in this paper, each action involves one rotation operation on the target link. Rotations occur only around axes centred on the object's joints. Any action may be either successful or not, depending on a number of reasons related to noise and errors in perception, grasping, and manipulation in a real-world environment. If an action is successful, the *Motion Planner* module proceeds with the one that follows until the plan ends and the *Knowledge Base* module is notified about successful execution. Otherwise, an issue is raised and re-planning occurs, thereby reiterating the whole work-flow described above.

Note that all modules except *Motion Planner* (i.e., all *green* modules in Fig. 3) are based on ASP. The *Motion Planner* is the module that has to interact with the robot, and has therefore to follow the constraints posed by the actual machine.

4   ASP Modules

In this section we describe how ASP is used to implement the modules depicted in Fig. 3. In the following, we assume the reader is familiar with ASP and ASP-Core-2 input language specification [6].

4.1   Knowledge Base

The knowledge base consists of facts over atoms of the form `joint(J)`, `angle(A)`, `isLinked(J1,J2)`, `time(T)`, `hasAngle(J,A,T)`, and `goal(J,A)`, and the constants `granularity` and `timemax`. Atoms over the predicate `joint` represent the joints of the articulated object. Atoms over the predicate `angle` represent the possible angles reachable from the joints and they can range from 0 to 359. Actually, the atom `angle(0)` must be always part of the knowledge base and admissible angles are the ones that can be obtained by rotating a joint by the degrees specified by the constant `granularity`, e.g., if the granularity is 90°, then the admissible angles are 0, 90, 180, and 270. Atoms over the predicate `isLinked` represent links between joints J1 and J2. Atoms over the predicate `time` represent the possible time steps, and they range from 0, which represents the initial state, to `timemax`. Atoms over the predicate `hasAngle` represent the angle A of the joint J at time T. Actually, knowledge base only contains the initial state of each joint, i.e., its angle at time 0. Finally, atoms over the predicate `goal` represent the angle A that must be reached by the joint J at the time step specified by `timemax`. An example of the input is represented by the facts and constants reported in Fig. 4. Note that the constant `timemax` is not included in the example, its usage will be described in Sect. 4.3.

4.2   Consistency Checking Module

The module performs some consistency checking on the knowledge base by using the following ASP encoding:

```
joint(1..5).  angle(0).  angle(90).  angle(180).  angle(270).
isLinked(1,2).  isLinked(2,3).  isLinked(3,4).  isLinked(4,5).
hasAngle(1,90,0).  hasAngle(2,180,0).  hasAngle(3,180,0).
hasAngle(4,270,0).  hasAngle(5,270,0).  time(0..timemax).
goal(1,270).  goal(2,270).  goal(3,180).  goal(4,270).
goal(5,270).  #const granularity = 90.
```

Fig. 4. An example of an ASP knowledge base.

c_{1a} :- isLinked(J1,J2), not joint(J1).
c_{1b} :- isLinked(J1,J2), not joint(J2).
c_2 :- isLinked(J,J).
c_{3a} :- hasAngle(J,A,T), not joint(J).
c_{3b} :- hasAngle(J,A,T), not angle(A).
c_{3c} :- hasAngle(J,A,T), not time(T).
c_{4a} :- goal(J,A), not joint(J).
c_{4b} :- goal(J,A), not angle(A).
c_5 moreThanOneGoal(J) :- joint(J), #count{A:goal(J,A)}>1.
c_6 :- joint(J), moreThanOneGoal(J).
c_7 oneStartingAngle(J) :- joint(J), #count{A:hasAngle(J,A,0)}=1.
c_8 :- joint(J), not oneStartingAngle(J).
c_9 :- not time(0).
c_{10} :- not angle(0).
c_{11} possibleAngle(0).
c_{12} possibleAngle(X) :- possibleAngle(Y), X=Y+granularity, X<360.
c_{13} :- not angle(X), possibleAngle(X).
c_{14} :- angle(X), not possibleAngle(X).

In particular, rules c_{1a} and c_{1b} check whether atoms over the predicate isLinked represent the links between two joints, while c_2 checks whether there is no link between the same joint. Rules c_{3a}, c_{3b}, and c_{3c} check the correctness of the predicate hasAngle, whereas c_{4a} and c_{4b} check the correctness of the predicate goal. Rules c_5 and c_6 check whether at most one goal is specified for each joint, whereas rules c_7 and c_8 verify if each joint is in exactly one angle at time step 0. Rules c_9 and c_{10} simply check the existence of the first time step and angle 0, respectively. Finally, rules from c_{11} to c_{14} check whether atoms over the predicate angle represent the possible angles.

4.3 Action Planning Module

ASP is not a planning-specific language, but it can be also used to specify encoding for planning domains [26], like our target problem. We have defined several encodings variants, for what concerns either the manipulation modes and the strategy for computing plans. The encoding described in this section is embedded into a classical iterative deepening approach in the spirit of SAT-based planning [22], where `timemax` is initially set to 1 and then increased by 1 if a plan is not found, which guarantees to return the shortest possible plans for a sequential encoding, i.e., when the robot performs only one action for each step (see Sect. 6 for some details about the other strategies).

r_1 `joint(0).`
r_2 `hasAngle(0,0,0).`
r_3 `isLinked(0,1).`
r_4 `isLinked(J1,J2) :- isLinked(J2,J1).`
r_5 `{changeAngle(J1,J2,A,Ai,T) : joint(J1), joint(J2), J1>J2, angle(A),`
      `hasAngle(J1,Ai,T), A<>Ai, isLinked(J1,J2)} <= 1`
         `:- time(T), T < timemax, T > 0.`
r_6 `ok(J1,J2,A,Ai,T) :- changeAngle(J1,J2,A,Ai,T),`
      `F1=(A+granularity)\360, F2=(Ai\360), F1=F2, A < Ai.`
r_7 `ok(J1,J2,A,Ai,T) :- changeAngle(J1,J2,A,Ai,T),`
      `F1=(Ai+granularity)\360, F2=(A\360), F1=F2, A > Ai.`
r_8 `ok(J1,J2,A,0,T) :- changeAngle(J1,J2,A,0,T), A=360-granularity.`
r_9 `ok(J1,J2,0,A,T) :- changeAngle(J1,J2,0,A,T), A=360-granularity.`
r_{10} `:- changeAngle(J1,J2,A,Ai,T), not ok(J1,J2,A,Ai,T).`
r_{11} `affected(J1,An,Ac,T) :- changeAngle(J2,_,A,Ap,T), hasAngle(J1,Ac,T),`
      `J1>J2, angle(An), An=|(Ac + (A-Ap)) + 360|\360, time(T).`
r_{12} `hasAngle(J1,A,T+1) :- changeAngle(J1,_,A,_,T).`
r_{13} `hasAngle(J1,A,T+1) :- affected(J1,A,_,T).`
r_{14} `hasAngle(J1,A,T+1) :- hasAngle(J1,A,T), not changeAngle(J1,_,_,_,T),`
      `not affected(J1,_,_,T), T <= timemax.`
r_{15} `:- goal(J,A), not hasAngle(J,A,timemax).`

Fig. 5. Base encoding: it allows for forward manipulations only.

Figure 5 reports our base encoding. Note that it uses operations \ and $|\cdots|$, which are not defined in the ASP-Core-2 standard but supported by Clingo [15], and compute the remainder of the division and the absolute value, respectively.

Since we employ an absolute representation, r_1, r_2 and r_3 add to the knowledge base the `joint(0)`, its angle and link to joint 1. This joint will not be moved and it is used only to have a fixed reference between the robot and articulated object frames. Rule r_4 enforces that bidirectionality of linked joints, i.e., if `joint(1)` is linked to `joint(2)` then `joint(2)` is also linked to `joint(1)`. Rule r_5 selects an atom of the form `changeAngle(J1,J2,A,Ai,T)`, where `J1` is the joint to move, `J2` is the joint to keep steady, `A` is the desired angle, `Ai` is the current angle of `J1` and `T` is the current step. Rule r_{10} ensures the validity of the configuration represented by the atom `changeAngle(J1,J2,A,Ai,T)`, that is when each action has a desired angle `A` that can be reached in one step (rules r_6, r_7, r_8, and r_9). Rule r_{11} is used to identify which joints are affected from the atom selected in r_5. Rules r_{12} and r_{13} are used to update the joints angles for the next step, while r_{14} states that if neither r_{12} nor r_{13} have affected a joint then its angle remains unchanged. Finally, r_{15} states the the goal must be reached.

4.4   Goal Checker

During the execution of a plan an external agent may interact with the articulated object, e.g., a human may change the angle of some joints (see, e.g., [8]). In such a case, the system must react to the changes if they are not compatible with the plan executed by the robot. This is accomplished by asynchronously creating a new input configuration according to the current status of the object, so that the configuration is ready as soon as it is needed. The role of Goal Checker module is to check when there is no need to create a new configuration, that is when all goals have been reached. This is done by using rule r_{15} from the encoding in Fig. 5.

5   Validation of the Framework

A validation scenario where a robot has to manipulate a 5-link articulated object has been set up both in simulation and in real-world using the Baxter dual-arm manipulator. Objects composed by 5 links provide a very valuable ground for testing our approach, as they are not so long to make the manipulation difficult for the robot, and at the same time they are articulated enough to require to plan movements in order to reach a goal configuration. The use of Baxter is justified by its widespread adoption as a research platform and by the necessity to employ a robot with two arms in order to manipulate the object, i.e., the robot should be able to keep a link of an object with one arm while it rotates an adjacent one.

Simulations have some practical advantages in this scenario. Indeed, they allow to run a greater number of planning-execution cycles with minimal human supervision and shorter execution times. Moreover, they are less susceptible to uncertainty and low-level motion planning failures, which are outside of the scope of this work. Nevertheless, we also test with the real robot in order to provide a more robust proof-of-concept of the proposed architecture. A video showing the Baxter in operation, via the introduced framework, can be found at https:// tinyurl.com/yd6kqgjn.

In our setting, we employed (i) ALVAR, an AR tag tracking library, to detect the absolute pose of the object's links using a head-mounted camera; and (ii) MoveIt!, as the de facto standard for motion planning and execution in the robotic community. The system was implemented in the Robot Operating System (ROS, Indigo release) framework, while Gazebo 2 was used as simulation environment for the relevant part. The system has been tested on a machine with an Intel i7-4790 CPU and 16 GB of RAM. All the results of the evaluation are available at https://tinyurl.com/ydzyefux.

The evaluation procedure unfolds as follows. First, the object is set up in a random configuration coherent with the specified granularity and within an acceptable margin of error. The initial and goal configurations are then represented in terms of the ASP atoms reported in Sect. 4.1, and processed by the state-of-the-art ASP system Clingo [15] together with the encoding in Sect. 4.3 in order to generate a (valid) plan. Actions of the plan are then executed through

a_1 : `changeAngle(2,1,90,180,1)` a_2 : `changeAngle(1,0,180,90,2)`
a_3 : `changeAngle(3,2,90,180,3)` a_4 : `changeAngle(1,0,270,180,4)`

Fig. 6. The planning and execution process on the sample scenario: an excerpt of the answer set returned by Clingo ($a_1 \ldots a_4$ are compact references for the ground actions).

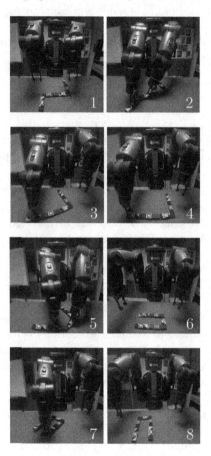

Fig. 7. The planning and execution process on the sample scenario: The robot actions and (intermediate) states induced by the computer plan.

the low-level motion planning layer, where an action consists of rotations around the object's joints perpendicular axes.

An example is shown in Figs. 4, 6 and 7: Fig. 4 reports the ASP representation of the scenario in which the number of joints composing the articulated object, their initial state and the goal to achieve are given, while Fig. 6 lists an excerpt of an answer set obtained by Clingo with the encoding in Sect. 4.3. Each atom of the form `changeAngle` in the answer set represents an action to perform on a joint with the meaning detailed in Sect. 4.1.

Eventually, Fig. 7 illustrates the execution process. In particular, starting from the initial configuration of the articulated object (Fig. 7(1)), Fig. 7(2), (4), (5) and (7) represent action's execution for a_1, a_2, a_3, and a_4, respectively (see Fig. 6), whereas Fig. 7(3), (4) and (6) represent intermediate configurations. Finally, Fig. 7(8) shows the final state that corresponds to the required goal configuration of the 5-link articulated object. It is important to note that Fig. 7(4) displays both a_3 execution and its resulting intermediate state since it was just a rotation of the whole object.

Other than the sample scenario, we have performed an experimental analysis on the Action Planning module by varying the number of joints (up to 14) and the granularity, and by randomly generating initial and final configurations, for a total of about 400 instances. On the successfully solved instances, Clingo took 1.5 s average processing time and could solve the problem in around 8 steps on average, with results as low 0.01 s/4 steps and never above 2.2 s/9 steps, which confirms the applicability of ASP reasoning in this context. All plans have been validated with the VAL tool [21]. Albeit the performance deteriorates when both the resolution and the links of the object are increased, they are encouraging considering current workspace dimensions and dexterity levels for bi-manual robots, which represent the true bottleneck in this scenario.

Remarkably, the proposed ASP approach is guaranteed to compute the shortest plan, due to the use of an iterative deepening procedure. This is pivotal, as it allows to minimise the actual execution time of the robot, which is the most consuming part.

6   Related Work

In Sect. 4.3 we have shown one of our encoding with one particular manipulation mode and search strategy but, as we already stated, we have designed a series of encodings (available at https://tinyurl.com/ycbp798j), including different manipulation modes, i.e., also backward (given our link ordering), and search strategies. As far as the strategies are concerned, we have designed encoding in which, imposing a reasonable `timemax` (i) by employing a strategy based on the algorithm *optsat* [9,18], where the heuristic of the solver is modified in order to prefer plans with increasing length, and (ii) by using a choice rule to select the timestep and we let the solver to find a plan, of course possibly loosing optimality (see also [10]).

In [7,8] a similar framework based on automated reasoning methodologies has been presented. Such framework employs PDDL language and automated planning engines for the planning module, and Description Logic (DL) solvers in the configuration module, where data are explicitly stored in an ontology, while we use a uniform language and approach (ASP-based) in the whole framework. Moreover, differently from most of our approaches, encodings and solvers employed in [7,8] are not currently able to return shortest plans, which is otherwise important, given that in this context executing the actions can be expensive. In [23], instead, a custom-designed multi-robot platform is presented, focused on

HRI in indoor service robot for understanding natural language requests. Planning is specified using the action language BC [25].

The ASP architecture used in this paper can be integrated with ROSo-Clingo [3], which is a system that combines the ASP solver Clingo (version 4) with the ROS middleware. In particular, it provides a high-level ASP-based interface to control the behaviour of a robot and to process the results of the execution of the actions. In our framework the interaction with ROS is handled by a custom script.

Moreover, it is worth pointing out that ASP has been employed in different domains, e.g., [1,2], including robotic, e.g., [3,12–14,29]. These consider logistic and ricochet robots domain, as well as cooperative robots, whose ultimate goal is not the validation and exploitation of the techniques on a real robot, as in our case. For a recent overview, the interested reader is referred to [11].

Focusing on planning encodings, recently the Plasp system [10] has been further extended with both SAT-inspired and genuine encodings. Some of them have helped to reduce the (still existing) gap with automated planning techniques. Our aim in the design of the encoding was to obtain a devoted and working solution for the problem at hand, rather than the fastest possible one. Nonetheless, results in [10] could be employed to further speed-up our Action Planning module.

7   Conclusions

In this paper we presented an ASP framework for the automated manipulation of articulated objects in a robot 2D workspace. We demonstrated the validity and usefulness of the proposed approach both in simulation and by running real-world experiments with a Baxter, which is widely adopted for research purposes. The experimental results of our validation also indicates that the proposed ASP-based approach, using Clingo as a solver, is capable of generating optimal results, with regards to the number of actions that the Baxter has to perform, in a very limited amount of time.

We see several avenues for future work. First, we are interested in validating the framework on different dual-arm robots, possibly manipulating different articulated objects: given the nature of the approach, we expect it to generalise with a reasonably limited effort. We also plan to integrate our approach with ROSoClingo, to simplify the interaction with robots. Then, we plan to extend our approach in order to cope with different types of robots (e.g., those with different number of arms/grippers), and to extend it to model and support the 3D manipulation of articulated objects. Finally, our instances could be an interesting benchmark domain for ASP Competitions (see, e.g., [16]).

References

1. Alviano, M., Dodaro, C., Maratea, M.: An advanced answer set programming encoding for nurse scheduling. In: Esposito, F., Basili, R., Ferilli, S., Lisi, F.A. (eds.) (AI*IA 2017). LNCS, vol. 10640, pp. 468–482. Springer, Heidelberg (2017). https://doi.org/10.1007/978-3-319-70169-1_35

2. Amendola, G., Dodaro, C., Leone, N., Ricca, F.: On the application of answer set programming to the conference paper assignment problem. In: Adorni, G., Cagnoni, S., Gori, M., Maratea, M. (eds.) AI*IA 2016. LNCS (LNAI), vol. 10037, pp. 164–178. Springer, Cham (2016). https://doi.org/10.1007/978-3-319-49130-1_13

3. Andres, B., Rajaratnam, D., Sabuncu, O., Schaub, T.: Integrating ASP into ROS for reasoning in robots. In: Calimeri, F., Ianni, G., Truszczynski, M. (eds.) LPNMR 2015. LNCS (LNAI), vol. 9345, pp. 69–82. Springer, Cham (2015). https://doi.org/10.1007/978-3-319-23264-5_7

4. Bodenhagen, L., et al.: An adaptable robot vision system performing manipulation actions with flexible objects. IEEE Trans. Autom. Sci. Eng. **11**(3), 749–765 (2014)

5. Brewka, G., Eiter, T., Truszczynski, M.: Answer set programming at a glance. Commun. ACM **54**(12), 92–103 (2011)

6. Calimeri, F., et al.: ASP-Core-2 Input Language Format (2013)

7. Capitanelli, A., Maratea, M., Mastrogiovanni, F., Vallati, M.: Automated planning techniques for robot manipulation tasks involving articulated objects. In: Esposito, F., Basili, R., Ferilli, S., Lisi, F. (eds.) AI*IA 2017. LNCS, pp. 483–497. Springer, Heidelberg (2017). https://doi.org/10.1007/978-3-319-70169-1_36

8. Capitanelli, A., Maratea, M., Mastrogiovanni, F., Vallati, M.: On the manipulation of articulated objects in human-robot cooperation scenarios. Robot. Auton. Syst. **109**, 139–155 (2018)

9. Di Rosa, E., Giunchiglia, E., Maratea, M.: Solving satisfiability problems with preferences. Constraints **15**(4), 485–515 (2010)

10. Dimopoulos, Y., Gebser, M., Lühne, P., Romero, J., Schaub, T.: *plasp* 3: towards effective ASP planning. In: Balduccini, M., Janhunen, T. (eds.) LPNMR 2017. LNCS (LNAI), vol. 10377, pp. 286–300. Springer, Cham (2017). https://doi.org/10.1007/978-3-319-61660-5_26

11. Erdem, E., Patoglu, V.: Applications of ASP in robotics. Künstliche Intelligenz **32**(2–3), 143–149 (2018)

12. Erdem, E., Patoglu, V., Saribatur, Z.G.: Integrating hybrid diagnostic reasoning in plan execution monitoring for cognitive factories with multiple robots. In: Proceedings of ICRA, pp. 2007–2013. IEEE (2015)

13. Erdem, E., Patoglu, V., Saribatur, Z.G., Schüller, P., Uras, T.: Finding optimal plans for multiple teams of robots through a mediator: a logic-based approach. Theory Pract. Log. Program. **13**(4–5), 831–846 (2013)

14. Gebser, M., et al.: Ricochet robots: a transverse ASP benchmark. In: Cabalar, P., Son, T.C. (eds.) LPNMR 2013. LNCS (LNAI), vol. 8148, pp. 348–360. Springer, Heidelberg (2013). https://doi.org/10.1007/978-3-642-40564-8_35

15. Gebser, M., Kaminski, R., Kaufmann, B., Ostrowski, M., Schaub, T., Wanko, P.: Theory solving made easy with clingo 5. In: Proceedings of the Technical Communications of the International Conference on Logic Programming (ICLP), pp. 2:1–2:15. Schloss Dagstuhl (2016)

16. Gebser, M., Maratea, M., Ricca, F.: The sixth answer set programming competition. J. Artif. Intell. Res. **60**, 41–95 (2017)

17. Gelfond, M., Lifschitz, V.: The stable model semantics for logic programming. In: Proceedings of the International Conference on Logic Programming (ICLP), pp. 1070–1080. MIT Press (1988)
18. Giunchiglia, E., Maratea, M.: Solving optimization problems with DLL. In: Brewka, G., Coradeschi, S., Perini, A., Traverso, P. (eds.) Proceedings of the 17th European Conference on Artificial Intelligence (ECAI 2006). Frontiers in Artificial Intelligence and Applications, vol. 141, pp. 377–381. IOS Press (2006)
19. Harnad, S.: The symbol grounding problem. Physica D **42**, 335–346 (1990)
20. Heyer, C.: Human-robot interaction and future industrial robotics applications. In: Proceedings of the IEEE/RSJ International Conference on Intelligent Robots and Systems (IROS), pp. 4749–4754. IEEE (2010)
21. Howey, R., Long, D., Fox, M.: VAL: automatic plan validation, continuous effects and mixed initiative planning using PDDL. In: Proceedings of the IEEE International Conference on Tools with Artificial Intelligence (ICTAI), pp. 294–301. IEEE Computer Society (2004)
22. Kautz, H.A., Selman, B.: Planning as satisfiability. In: Proceedings of the European Conference on Artificial Intelligence (ECAI), pp. 359–363 (1992)
23. Khandelwal, P., Zhang, S., Sinapov, J., Leonetti, M., Thomason, J., Yang, F., Gori, I., Svetlik, M., Khante, P., Lifschitz, V., Aggarwal, J.K., Mooney, R.J., Stone, P.: Bwibots: a platform for bridging the gap between AI and human-robot interaction research. Int. J. Robot. Res. **36**(5–7), 635–659 (2017)
24. Krüger, J., Lien, T.K., Verl, A.: Cooperation of human and machines in assembly lines. CIRP Ann. **58**(2), 628–646 (2009)
25. Lee, J., Lifschitz, V., Yang, F.: Action language BC: preliminary report. In: Rossi, F. (ed.) Proceedings of the 23rd International Joint Conference on Artificial Intelligence (IJCAI 2013), pp. 983–989. IJCAI/AAAI (2013)
26. Lifschitz, V.: Answer set programming and plan generation. Artif. Intell. J. **138**(1–2), 39–54 (2002)
27. Nair, A., et al.: Combining self-supervised learning and imitation for vision-based rope manipulation. In: Proceedings of the IEEE International Conference on Robotics and Automation (ICRA), pp. 2146–2153. IEEE (2017)
28. Niemelä, I.: Logic programs with stable model semantics as a constraint programming paradigm. AMAI **25**(3–4), 241–273 (1999)
29. Schäpers, B., Niemueller, T., Lakemeyer, G., Gebser, M., Schaub, T.: ASP-based time-bounded planning for logistics robots. In: Proceedings of the International Conference on Automated Planning and Scheduling (ICAPS), pp. 509–517. AAAI Press (2018)
30. Schulman, J., Ho, J., Lee, C., Abbeel, P.: Learning from demonstrations through the use of non-rigid registration. In: Inaba, M., Corke, P. (eds.) Robotics Research. STAR, vol. 114, pp. 339–354. Springer, Cham (2016). https://doi.org/10.1007/978-3-319-28872-7_20
31. Wakamatsu, H., Arai, E., Hirai, S.: Knotting/unknotting manipulation of deformable linear objects. Int. J. Robot. Res. **25**(4), 371–395 (2006)
32. Yamakawa, Y., Namiki, A., Ishikawa, M.: Dynamic high-speed knotting of a rope by a manipulator. IJARS **10**, 1–12 (2013)

C-ASP: Continuous ASP-Based Reasoning over RDF Streams

Thu-Le Pham[1]([⊠])(iD), Muhammad Intizar Ali[1](iD), and Alessandra Mileo[2]

[1] Insight Centre for Data Analytics, National University of Ireland, Galway,
IDA Bussiness Park, Lower Dangan, Galway, Ireland
{thule.pham,ali.intizar}@insight-centre.org
[2] Insight Centre for Data Analytics, Dublin City University,
Glasnevin, Dublin 9, Ireland
alessandra.mileo@insight-centre.org

Abstract. The ability to perform complex reasoning over data streams has recently become an important area of research in the Semantic Web community. Most of SPARQL-inspired engines have limitations in capturing sophisticated user requirements and dealing with complex reasoning tasks. To address these challenges, we propose and implement C-ASP, a reasoning system based on the Answer Set Programming (ASP) system Clingo and extended to handle continuous reasoning requests over RDF streams. We provide the syntax of the C-ASP language, as well as a set of examples in order to illustrate its expressive power. In addition, we present preliminary experimental results showing C-ASP performances.

Keywords: Stream reasoning · Answer Set Programming ·
Semantic Web · RDF

1 Introduction

In recent years, Semantic Web (SW) research has contributed to advancing the state-of-the-art in RDF Stream Processing (RSP) with several engines such as C-SPARQL [2] and CQELS [7], among others. Despite all these efforts, reasoning capabilities are still limited and cannot support complex reasoning such as the ability to handle defaults, preferences, recursion, and non-determinism. Some work in this direction leverages the expressive power of non-monotonic reasoning techniques to build a stream reasoning (SR) system, relying on both advances in RSP technologies for representing and processing data streams, and non-monotonic reasoning for performing complex rule-based inference. For instance, ASR [6] and StreamRule [8] rely on ASP by hard-coding a subprocess that performs repetitive calls to the ASP solver to infer new knowledge from data streams and a given rule set. Therefore, they do not provide a flexible way to seamlessly integrate the stream processing and reasoning functionalities.

This research is partially funded by Science Foundation Ireland (SFI) under grant No. SFI/12/RC/2289 and SFI/16/RC/3918.

© Springer Nature Switzerland AG 2019
M. Balduccini et al. (Eds.): LPNMR 2019, LNAI 11481, pp. 45–50, 2019.
https://doi.org/10.1007/978-3-030-20528-7_4

Recently, two new SR engines, namely Ticker [5] and Laser [3], have been implemented from a fragment of LARS [4]. LARS programs are encoded as ASP rules. However, Laser restricts its expressivity to positive and stratified programs and ASP encodings of Ticker's programs use mainly normal ASP rules. As a result, they do not fully exploit the expressive power of ASP, including the ability to handle disjunction, optimization, aggregations, and preferences. Moreover, they do not support the ability to query SW streams, which we believe is the key in ensuring the scalability of such systems when handling real IoT streams.

Aiming to (i) exploit full capabilities of ASP to perform reasoning over RDF streams, and (ii) seamlessly provide flexible ways of combining semantic stream processing and non-monotonic reasoning, this paper proposes C-ASP, an extension of ASP to support continuous reasoning over semantic streams. The C-ASP language allows users to specify their reasoning requests which include their sophisticated reasoning requirements, input streams, and how to access those streams. Such requests are registered with the C-ASP engine and continuously executed over RDF streams by the means of windows.

2   The C-ASP Processing Model

The processing model of C-ASP combines RSP and ASP-based reasoning in one single framework. Similarly to other RSP engines, C-ASP takes multiple RDF data streams as inputs and produces outputs as streams. It also supports the integration with background knowledge from static RDF knowledge bases. Users express their requirements and preferences in the form of *continuous reasoning requests* using the C-ASP language, an extension of the ASP language described in Sect. 3. A C-ASP reasoning request (RR) is registered with the C-ASP engine and evaluated continuously over the input streams and the knowledge bases.

Definition 1. *A C-ASP reasoning request RR is defined as $RR = (P, I, R, O)$ where P defines a set of constants indicating namespace prefixes; $I = I_{stream} \cup I_{kb}$, where I_{stream} identifies a set of RDF input streams and the windows to specify how to extract data elements from streams, and I_{kb} identifies a set of RDF static datasets; R identifies a set of ASP rules; and O identifies a selections of output data.*

When evaluating RR at time t, only a portion of the input stream is considered. The evaluation process can be broken down into 3 steps: windowing (from streams to relations) - select subsets of the most recent elements of the input streams; evaluating (from relations to relations) - perform reasoning on the finite and intermediate data portions; and streaming (from relations to streams) - convert the final solutions back into streams.

3   Implementation: The C-ASP Language

This section defines how a C-ASP reasoning request is expressed in an extension of the ASP language with RDF streaming features, and provides a set of examples.

3.1 C-ASP Reasoning Request

In Fig. 1, we provide the syntax to express each component in RR. First, to deal with RDF data format, we use a `PrefixClause` statement which captures each element in P. This `PrefixClause` is adopted from the syntax for prefixes used to abbreviate IRIs[1] in SW. The identification of input streams and static knowledge bases in I is expressed by means of `FromStreamClause` and `FromClause`, respectively. In `FromStreamClause`, each input stream is coupled with a window (represented by `Window`) to guide the C-ASP engine on how to extract related data from the stream. In `FromClause`, static knowledge bases are specified via their paths and the C-ASP engine integrates them with input streams before performing ASP-based reasoning over them.

```
PrefixClause → #prefix prefixName : ⟨IRI⟩;
FromStreamClause → #from stream streamIRI Window;
    Window → Time-basedWindow | Tuple-basedWindow
        Time-basedWindow → [time number TimeUnit step number TimeUnit]
            TimeUnit → d | h | m | s | ms
        Tuple-basedWindow → [count number step number]
FromClause → #from (knowledge base);
RuleClause → ASP rule;
OutputClause → #show predicateSymbol/number;
```

Fig. 1. C-ASP syntax

A rule in R follows the ASP-core2 language standard[2] and the C-ASP implementation relies on the Clingo solver. However, the extension of ASP rules to deal with RDF streams introduces predicate symbols, which are obtained from converting an RDF triple $\langle s, p, o \rangle$, in form of `prefixName_p`. The predicate symbol `prefixName_p` identifies that this predicate is from RDF input streams or RDF datasets while p (without `prefixName`) is an internal predicate defined and used within the ASP rules. In this way, an input RDF triple with a timestamp $(\langle s, p, o \rangle, t)$ is automatically converted into an ASP predicate of the form `prefixName_p`(s, o, t).

In addition, output statements identify output predicates the C-ASP engine needs to provide after reasoning. The syntax of an output statement in O is defined in `OutputClause`. The variable **number** in `OutputClause` identifies the number of arguments in `predicateSymbol`. If **number** $= 2$ then the C-ASP engine provides output as (timestamped) RDF streams by converting output atoms (i.e., `predicateSymbol(s,o)`) to triples (i.e., `<s,predicateSymbol,o>`) and assigning timepstamps to them (i.e., `(<s, predicateSymbol,o>, t)`). Otherwise, C-ASP outputs (timestamped) predicate-format streams.

---

[1] https://www.w3.org/TR/rdf11-concepts/#section-IRIs.

[2] https://www.mat.unical.it/aspcomp2013/files/ASP-CORE-2.03b.pdf.

3.2   Examples of a C-ASP Reasoning Request

In what follows we present some of the features of the C-ASP language defined above by providing examples of continuous reasoning requests.

RR1, illustrated in Listing 1, is a simple C-ASP reasoning request with aggregation[3]. The request is made by the travel company in order to know how many hotels have been booked during the last hour. It will notify the company every 30 min.

```
#from stream <http :// travel . org/booking> [time 1h step 30m];
bookedHotel (Hotel)  :-  tl_booked (User , Hotel , Time);
noH(N)  :-  N = #count {Hotel : bookedHotel (Hotel)};
#show noH/1;
```

Listing 1. RR1

Assume that the information of hotels and streets are stored in static RDF datasets, `hotelkb.rdf` and `streetkb.rdf` respectively. The company wants to know which 5-star hotels located on a main street have been booked in the last hour. The reasoning request *RR2* in Listing 2 shows the combination of static and streaming data.

```
#from stream <http :// travel . org/booking> [time 1h step 30m];
#from <hotelkb . rdf>;
#from <streetkb . rdf>;
bookedHotel (Hotel):- tl_booked (User , Hotel , Time);
fiveStar (Hotel):- bookedHotel (Hotel) ,  ht_star (Hotel , Star) ,
                Star = 5;
ex_fmHotel (Hotel , Street):- fiveStar (Hotel) ,
                        ht_located (Hotel , Street) ,
                        rdf_type (Street ," ct_MainStreet");
#show ex_fmHotel/2;
```

Listing 2. RR2

To illustrate an example of combining multiple input streams, we assume that the company also records information when a user cancels a booking. The reasoning request *RR3* (Listing 3) notifies the company on which below-3-star hotels located on a main street have been booked and then canceled during the last hour. This request also allows the company to decide how to deal with incomplete information about hotels' stars via the negation-as-failure rule `bcStar(Hotel):-bcHotel(Hotel), not hasStar(Hotel);`.

We now showcase an example of C-ASP that can capture more sophisticated requirements via optimization statements in ASP. Imagine that the company wants to know the most expensive and highest star hotels that have been booked during the last hour. They do not want to get notification of those hotels located

---

[3] Due to space limitation, we omit the `PrefixClause` of the following prefixes from the reasoning request: #prefix tl : ⟨http://travel.org/⟩; #prefix ht : ⟨http://hotel.org/⟩; #prefix ct : ⟨http://city.org/⟩; #prefix rdf : ⟨http://www.w3.org/1999/02/22-rdf-syntax-ns#⟩; #prefix ex : ⟨http://example.org/⟩;.

in a noisy area (we assume that a hotel located on a main street is noisy). Moreover, they are more interested in the most expensive hotels. *RR4* expresses such request as illustrated in Listing 4. This request takes advantage of the ability of ASP to handle expressive reasoning such as managing optimization statements.

```
#from stream <http://travel.org/booking> [time 1h step 30m];
#from stream <http://travel.org/canceling> [time 1h step 30m];
#from <hotelkb.rdf>;
#from <streetkb.rdf>;
bcHotel(Hotel):-tl_booked(User, Hotel, Time1),
                tl_canceled(User, Hotel, Time2), Time1<Time2;
bcStar(Hotel):-bcHotel(Hotel), ht_star(Hotel, Star), Star <= 3;
hasStar(Hotel):- ht_star(Hotel, Star);
bcStar(Hotel):-bcHotel(Hotel), not hasStar(Hotel);
ex_bcmHotel(Hotel, Street):-bcStar(Hotel),
                            ht_located(Hotel, Street),
                            rdf_type(Street,"ct_MainStreet");
#show ex_bcmHotel/2;
```

Listing 3. RR3

```
#from stream <http://travel.org/booking> [time 1h step 30m];
#from <hotelkb.rdf>;
#from <streetkb.rdf>;
1{bookedHotel(Hotel):tl_booked(User, Hotel, Time)}1;
noisyHotel(Hotel):-bookedHotel(Hotel),
                   ht_located(Hotel, Street),
                   rdf_type(Street,"ct_MainStreet");
:- noisyHotel(Hotel);
#maximize {Y@1 : ht_star(Hotel, Star), bookedHotel(Hotel)};
#maximize {Y@2 : ht_cost(Hotel, Cost), bookedHotel(Hotel)};
#show bookedHotel/1;
```

Listing 4. RR4

4 Evaluation

We compare the performance of C-ASP against one of the most mature RSP engines, C-SPARQL, with respect to latency and memory consumption, by using the well-known RSP benchmark CityBench [1]. The experiment was conducted on a machine with 24-core Intel(R) Xeon(R) 2.40 GHz and 96G RAM. First, we evaluate the performance of the two engines with a frequency $f = 1$ (i.e., replay streams at the original rate). We stream data for 10 min to C-SPARQL queries Q1C, Q2C, and Q10C as representative samples in terms of number of query patterns and presence of join operators (respectively, R1C, R2C, and R10C for C-ASP reasoning requests). Results indicate that the latency of C-ASP is minimal compared to C-SPARQL for all three queries. More specifically, C-ASP performs almost 3 times (or more) faster than C-SPARQL for queries

Q1C, Q2C and slightly faster for query Q10C. In addition, it is noticeable in those figures that the memory consumption of C-ASP is less than a half of the C-SPARQL memory consumption. We then increase the frequency of streams to $f = 2$ and re-run the experiment with the similar setting. We observe the similar results as in $f = 1$.

5   Conclusion and Future Work

This paper presents C-ASP, an ASP-based approach for performing complex reasoning over RDF streams. The C-ASP language, which leverages the full expressive power of ASP, allows users to express their requirements and preferences in the form of C-ASP reasoning requests. C-ASP enables the continuous reasoning capability in ASP by adding RDF streams to the input data types, windowing operators to capture the most relevant portions of data from streams, (stable model semantics) entailment at window-level, and streaming operators to stream out the results. The experimental evaluation shows that the C-ASP engine outperforms the state-of-the-art RSP engine C-SPARQL. Our future work includes optimization techniques to scale up the engine such as incremental evaluation as applied in [3,5] or parallel reasoning as applied in [9].

References

1. Ali, M.I., Gao, F., Mileo, A.: CityBench: a configurable benchmark to evaluate RSP engines using smart city datasets. In: Arenas, M., et al. (eds.) ISWC 2015. LNCS, vol. 9367, pp. 374–389. Springer, Cham (2015). https://doi.org/10.1007/978-3-319-25010-6_25
2. Barbieri, D.F., Braga, D., Ceri, S., Valle, E.D., Grossniklaus, M.: C-SPARQL: a continuous query language for RDF data streams. Int. J. Semant. Comput. **4**(01), 3–25 (2010)
3. Bazoobandi, H.R., Beck, H., Urbani, J.: Expressive stream reasoning with laser. In: d'Amato, C., et al. (eds.) ISWC 2017. LNCS, vol. 10587, pp. 87–103. Springer, Cham (2017). https://doi.org/10.1007/978-3-319-68288-4_6
4. Beck, H., Dao-Tran, M., Eiter, T.: LARS: a logic-based framework for analytic reasoning over streams. Artif. Intell. **261**, 16–70 (2018)
5. Beck, H., Eiter, T., Folie, C.: Ticker: a system for incremental ASP-based stream reasoning. Theory Pract. Log. Program. **17**(5–6), 744–763 (2017)
6. Do, T.M., Loke, S.W., Liu, F.: Answer set programming for stream reasoning. In: Butz, C., Lingras, P. (eds.) AI 2011. LNCS (LNAI), vol. 6657, pp. 104–109. Springer, Heidelberg (2011). https://doi.org/10.1007/978-3-642-21043-3_13
7. Le-Phuoc, D., Dao-Tran, M., Xavier Parreira, J., Hauswirth, M.: A native and adaptive approach for unified processing of linked streams and linked data. In: Aroyo, L., et al. (eds.) ISWC 2011. LNCS, vol. 7031, pp. 370–388. Springer, Heidelberg (2011). https://doi.org/10.1007/978-3-642-25073-6_24
8. Mileo, A., Abdelrahman, A., Policarpio, S., Hauswirth, M.: StreamRule: a nonmonotonic stream reasoning system for the semantic web. In: Faber, W., Lembo, D. (eds.) RR 2013. LNCS, vol. 7994, pp. 247–252. Springer, Heidelberg (2013). https://doi.org/10.1007/978-3-642-39666-3_23
9. Pham, T.-L., Ali, M.I., Mileo, A.: Enhancing the scalability of expressive stream reasoning via input-driven parallelization. Semantic Web, (Preprint), 1–17

Internet Routing and Non-monotonic Reasoning

Anduo Wang[✉] and Zhijia Chen

Temple University, Philadelphia, USA
{adw,zhijia.chen}@temple.edu

Abstract. Internet routing is the process of selecting paths across the Internet to connect the communicating hosts, it is unique in that path selection is *jointly* determined by a network of *independently* operated networks, known as domains or Autonomous Systems (ASes), that interconnect to form the Internet. In fact, the present routing infrastructure takes such an extreme position that it favors *local autonomy*—an AS can use arbitrary path preference to override the default shortest path policy, at the expense of potential *global oscillation*—a collection of AS preferences (policies) can fail to converge on a stable path, a path that is also the most preferred possible for every AS along the path. In this paper, we examine the route oscillation problem with non-monotonic reasoning. We observe that, in the absence of any AS specific policies, Internet routing degenerates into the monotonic computation of shortest path—a preferred (shorter) (super)path always extends another preferred (sub)path; But fully autonomous AS policies are *non-monotonic*—a path favored by one AS can be an extension of a less preferred path of a neighbor, to which an "upgrade" to a better path can cause this AS to downgrade to a less preferred path previously discarded. Based on this insight, we present an Answer Set Programming (ASP) formulation that allows for automatic oscillation detection. Our evaluation using the clingo ASP solver is promising: on realistic Internet topology and representative policies, clingo can detect anomalies within 35 s.

1 Introduction

The Internet is at once the world-wide information infrastructure that has revolutionized the computers and communications like nothing before. Behind its tremendous success as a means for information dissemination and a medium for collaboration and interaction between geographically distributed computers, is one common service—to provide end to end data paths that connect the communicating hosts. To select the much needed communication paths, the Internet relies on a process called routing.

© Springer Nature Switzerland AG 2019
M. Balduccini et al. (Eds.): LPNMR 2019, LNAI 11481, pp. 51–57, 2019.
https://doi.org/10.1007/978-3-030-20528-7_5

Routing on the global Internet is unique in that, the Internet is a network of *independently* operated networks—known as domains or Autonomous Systems (ASes) that are driven by their own economic concerns. This makes routing a process jointly determined by all the ASes along the path. In particular, border gateway protocol (BGP) [9] is currently the only interdomain (i.e. across ASes) routing protocol that stitches together the Internet, it allows the ASes to set arbitrary path preference—local policies—to override the path decision based on shortest path metric—by default, without any AS-specific policies, BGP behaves like the distributed execution of the Dijkstra algorithm on a (AS-level) graph and always selects the path with fewest AS hops.

This extreme position taken by BGP—favoring local autonomy, allowing an AS to influence path selection based solely on its own concerns without any global coordination—has an important consequence. The BGP protocol suffers a global anomaly called route oscillation [7]: BGP system is not guaranteed to converge on a unique best path. There exists some AS policies when the BGP system is unable to agree upon a global policy-compliant path, and keeps oscillating between several sub-optimal ones. Much efforts in the networking community [4–6] have been on using abstract combinatorial models and derived structures—e.g., state transition machines, circular dependency graphs—to understand and detect such routing oscillation.

In this position paper, instead of relying on specialized combinatorial structures or expert-guided reasoning, we use non-monotonic reasoning as a means to understand, explain, and automatically detect policies that can lead to routing oscillation.

We observe that, in the absence of any AS policies, Internet routing degenerates into the *monotonic* computation of shortest path: For a particular destination, any shortest path to that destination, denoted by P_x, selected by AS x, must also extend another shortest path that has been selected by some neighbor AS y that is one hop closer to the destination. This has been captured by the Bellman-Ford equation that lies at the heart of the Dijkstra algorithm—$P_x = sp_y\{x \text{ added to} P_y\}$, where sp is the aggregate function that returns the shortest path[1].

The Bellman-Ford equation implies that, path improvement to x's neighbor—y selects a better (thus shorter) path P'_y—can only benefit x, resulting in a P'_x no worse than before. Since the set of available paths are finite, all ASes will eventually converge on the path that is also their best possible choice. But independently set AS policies make path selection *non-monotonic*: The local policy of AS x may prefer a path (P_x) that extends a path (P_y) disliked by a neighbor y. As y learns and gets promoted to a better path—moving away from the less preferred P_y, it also unfortunately makes the much liked P_x unavailable at x, causing x to downgrade to a less preferred path.

---

[1] The original Bellman-Ford equation addresses computation of the cost of the shortest path. We presented a modified version for the shortest path—a list of nodes that constitute the path.

Based on this observation, we developed a systematic encoding of policy configurations in Answer Set Programming (ASP) [2,3] that allows for automated analysis. Our main result is that, the ASP solution to our policy formulation coincides with the paths selected by the policy-based routing system, thus providing a means to detect oscillation: The policies are guaranteed to converge on a single best path if the ASP solver gives a unique solution; The policies can lead to oscillation in some circumstances but converge in other cases if the ASP solver finds multiple solutions; The policies will result in permanent oscillation in any circumstances if the ASP solver cannot find any solution.

We also evaluated our ASP formulation using the clingo [1] solver, showing promising result: on realistic Internet topology with up to 10 k nodes and 51 k edges, clingo can correctly recognize routing oscillation problems for several representative policy configurations within 35 s; Our encoding also scales gracefully, the clingo searching time increases linearly with respect to the topology size (in terms of number of nodes under the same edge density).

2 Internet Routing and Non-monotonic Reasoning

In this section, we provide the necessary background on BGP and a detailed analysis of route oscillation with non-monotonic reasoning. We begin with a brief review of BGP using an abstract model called the stable path problem (SPP) formalism. SPP offers a simple semantics for AS policies while abstracting away all nonessential details, such as implementation specifics of BGP.

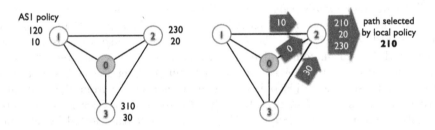

Fig. 1. (left) Example: the SPP model for AS policies. (right) Policy-based route selection.

An instance of SPP, $S = (G, P, R)$, as shown in Fig. 1 (left), is an AS graph G—0 is the pre-fixed destination of interests, together with the permitted paths P at each AS, and the path ranking (preference) functions R—a vertical list next to each AS, with the highest ranked path at the top going down to the lowest ranked path at the bottom. In Fig. 1 (left), each AS prefers the counter-clockwise path of length 2 over all other paths to 0. For example, AS1 prefers the longer path 120 over its direct path 10.

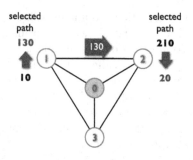

Fig. 2. Route selection with "disagreeing" AS policies is non-monotonic.

Given an SPP, BGP can be viewed as a distributed algorithm for finding the most preferred paths to 0: ASes exchange routing announcements with their neighbors. Each announcement is the current best path chosen by the sending AS, and it indicates that the sending AS is willing to carry traffic destined to 0 from the receiving AS. That is, traffic flow in the opposite direction, from announcement receivers to senders. When multiple announcements are received by an AS, one single best path is selected by the AS's local policy. In Fig. 1 (right), AS2, upon receiving three announcements from its neighbors, uses its local policy to filter out the path 210—which does not occur in the permitted path list, and picks the highest ranked path 210 as the selected one. It is also worth noting that, since an AS only selects one single best path, the announcement of a new (better) path implicitly retracts the previously exposed (older) path.

This path selection process was originally designed for using within an AS under one single administrative domain that often employs a single (global) ranking function—e.g., shortest path policy that always favors fewer hops. The global ranking ensures that all nodes will converge onto a stable path, a path that is not only globally optimal but also coincides with every node's local best.

But fully autonomous policies of BGP can lead to non-monotonic behavior. By fully autonomous we mean an AS is free to prefer a path that extends a path disliked by a neighbor. The ASes do not need to take a consistent view of the paths based on some universally agreed criteria. For example, in Fig. 1 (left), 210 is the most preferred path by AS2, but it extends the less preferred 10 from AS1. Note how this policy configuration diverges from the Bellman-Ford equation discussed in Sect. 1. Such "disagreeing" policies lead to route oscillation shown in Fig. 2: Suppose the current best path selected by AS1 and AS2 are 10 and 210, respectively. When AS1 learns a new path 30 from AS3, it will elevate 130 to be its best path and expose it to AS2, which also implicitly withdraws 10, resulting in the retraction of AS2's top choice 210. Now, AS2 needs to downgrade to the less preferred 10. In fact, all three ASes will keep exchanging route announcements and exhibit similar oscillation: their choices of best path bounce back and forth as the subpaths they depends on are announced and withdrawn by the corresponding neighbors.

3   An ASP Formulation for Automatic Oscillation Detection

An advantage of our non-monotonic reasoning approach is that it lends itself to an ASP formulation [2,3] that, readily recognizable by modern ASP solvers, allows for automatic analysis.

First, we present a straightforward ASP encoding of the AS policies defined in Sect. 2, thanks to ASP's native support for negation and constraints. Our formulation involves two predicates r and b: r(p) states that the path p is permitted at some AS, b(p) says that p is selected as the best path, and p is a tuple that contains the list of nodes along the path. To fully specify the policy-based route selection of an AS, we only need to describe how to generate the permitted and selected paths r,b.

A permitted path is either a direct path to the destination AS or an extension to paths received from a neighbor, which must also be that neighbor's current best path. Take AS2 in Fig. 1 (left) as an example, it can generate two permitted candidates, one direct path from itself to 0, and an indirect one extending the best path of AS1.

```
1  % direct path as known fact(s)
2  r((2,0)).
3  % an indirect path generated by route announcements from a neighbor
4  r((2,1,0)) :- b((1,0)).
```

The best paths are determined by the path ranking function, the encoding of which is also straightforward. For every p_i in a list of paths $p_1 \cdots, p_n$ ranked from the most preferred to the least preferred, we only need a rule of the form b(pi) :- r(pi), not r(p1-1), ..., not r(p1), meaning that, p_i can be promoted to be the best path only if it is available, while none of the more preferred paths are presented. Continuing with AS2, its ranking function is captured by the rules as follows.

```
1  % ranking function of the permitted paths at AS2
2  b((2,0)) :- r((2,0)), not r((2,1,0)).
3  b((2,1,0)) :- r((2,1,0)).
```

Finally, we need to ensure that only one best path is selected. To achieve this, we only need to make sure that, for any p_i from a list of permitted paths $p_1, \cdots, p_n$, the presence of p_i will prevent the derivation of $p_j, j \neq i$. In other words, for any $p_i, p_j (i \neq j)$, it follows that $b(p_i)$ and $b(p_j)$ cannot be simultaneously true. For the two paths—210,20—permitted at AS2, we have:

```
1  % only one permitted path can be selected as the best path
2  :- b((2,1,0)), b((2,0)).
```

The strength of this formulation is that, for a set of AS policies, the solution to this ASP encoding coincides with all the stable best paths that can be selected by the BGP system. For example, running the ASP program for Fig. 1 yields no solution. More importantly, this correspondence gives a method for detecting BGP oscillation, stated as follows:

Let L denote an ASP program that encodes a set of AS policies as described in this section, we can use the solution(s) to L to detect route oscillation as follows: (1) 0 solution implies permanent oscillation since the policies fail to give any stable path selection; (2) 1 solution indicates convergence since the policies will select a unique set of best paths under all circumstances—any ordering of route announcement exchanges; (3) multiple solutions mean-possible oscillation: depending on the ordering of route announcement exchange, the policies can converge onto different set of best paths, but it is also possible that the BGP system may oscillate on other circumstances.

4   Preliminary Evaluation

In this section, we evaluate our ASP formulation with the clingo solver [1, 3], on various network topologies and policy configurations. Our preliminary result is promising. Clingo can correctly recognize oscillation problem in all cases within 1 min. The solution time also scales well with the size of the network. All the experiments are performed on the macOS platform with 3.4 GHz Intel Core i5 processor and 16 GB 2400 MHz DDR4 RAM.

Setup. We use the popular GT-ITM tool [8] to generate various Internet-like topologies—2-level hierarchical graphs where the top level mimics a set of well connected network service providers, and the second layer represents smaller providers that access (and thus are customers of) the top providers. Compared to the actual Internet topology inferred from real-world network traffic, GT-ITM has the advantage of generating topologies of various sizes, allowing us to study the scalability of our ASP formulation. Specifically, we generate six topologies with 1000, 2000, 4000, 6000, 8000, 10000 nodes; 5092, 10304, 20766, 31595, 42880, 54954 edges; and a node-to-edge ratio of 0.196, 0.194, 0.192, 0.190, 0.187 and 0.182, respectively.

On every GT-ITM topology, we randomly pick a node as the destination of interest, and populate the rest of the nodes with all possible paths to that destination. The policy configurations we embed in the topology include three scenarios: In the "good" scenario, all paths are permitted and shortest path policy is used to rank the permitted paths. In the "disagree" scenario, we embed circular ranking (similar to Fig. 1 (left)) between two randomly picked neighbors and use shortest path for the rest of the nodes. In the last "bad" scenario, we embed the circular ranking of Fig. 1 (left). The bad configuration is known to exhibit permanent route oscillation while the disagree scenario only oscillates under certain ordering of route announcement exchanges.

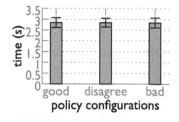

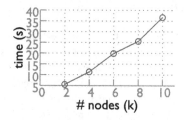

Fig. 3. Solution searching time for the good, disagree, and bad policies

Fig. 4. ASP scales gracefully: the searching time increases linearly

Correctness and Performance. Using the analysis method described in Sect. 3, clingo correctly recognizes the good, disagree, and bad policies on the graph with 1000 nodes and 5092 edges. The solution times for all three cases are depicted in Fig. 3: we plotted the average running time (the box height) and the standard deviation (the bar length) for 10 runs. The solution time on different cases are very close—2.843 s, 2.850 s and 2.846 s for good, disagree and bad case, respectively.

Scalability. Our formulation also scales gracefully. Figure 4 shows the searching time for the disagree case on various topology sizes: as the network size increases from 2000 nodes and 10304 edges to 10000 nodes and 54954 edges, clingo search time grows linearly from 6.578 s to 34.786 s. Each data point in the figure is averaged on 3 runs.

References

1. The clingo system. https://potassco.org/
2. Brewka, G., Eiter, T., Truszczyński, M.: Answer set programming at a glance. Commun. ACM **54**(12), 92–103 (2011)
3. Gebser, M., Kaufmann, B., Kaminski, R., Ostrowski, M., Schaub, T., Schneider, M.: Potassco: the Potsdam answer set solving collection. Ai Commun. **24**(2), 107–124 (2011)
4. Griffin, T.G., Shepherd, F.B., Wilfong, G.: The stable paths problem and interdomain routing. IEEE Trans. Netw. **10**, 232–243 (2002)
5. Griffin, T.G., Wilfong, G.: An analysis of BGP convergence properties. In: SIGCOMM (1999)
6. Griffin, T.G., Wilfong, G.: A safe path vector protocol. In: INFOCOM (2000)
7. McPherson, D., Gill, V., Walton, D., Retana, A.: Border Gateway Protocol (BGP) persistent route oscillation condition (2002)
8. Modeling Topology of Large Internetworks. http://www.cc.gatech.edu/projects/gtitm/
9. Rekhter, Y., Li, T., Hares, S.: A Border Gateway Protocol 4 (BGP-4) (2006)

Argumentation

Assessing Arguments with Schemes and Fallacies

Pierre Bisquert[1]([⊠]), Florence Dupin de Saint-Cyr[2]([iD]), and Philippe Besnard[2]

[1] INRA, Montpellier, France
pierre.bisquert@inra.fr
[2] IRIT - CNRS, Université Paul Sabatier, Toulouse, France
{florence.bannay,philippe.besnard}@irit.fr

Abstract. We present a logical framework allowing us to express assessment of facts (*is it proven?*) and arguments (*is it sound?*) together with a proof system to answer these questions. Our motivation is to clarify the notion of validity in the context of logic-based arguments along different aspects (such as the formulas used and the inference scheme). Originality lies in the possibility for the user to design their own argument schemes. We show that classical inference obtains when arguments are based on classical schemes (e.g. Hilbert axioms). We go beyond classical logic by distinguishing "proven" formulas from "uncontroversial" ones (whose negation is not proven). Hence a formal definition of a *fallacious argument*: it uses controversial formulas or schemes recognized as illicit. We express some rational arguments and fallacies in the form of schemes.

Keywords: Logic-based arguments · Fallacies · Soundness · Validity · Inference · Hilbert system

1 Introduction

Finding a good way to convince another individual (or oneself) is a crucial task that must have been done from the beginning of humanity and is still part of everyone's daily life. This may explain why this topic has been addressed by many researchers and is still a very hot topic which is studied from many different perspectives: philosophy, psychology, linguistics, logic, artificial intelligence, multi-agent communication, legal reasoning, etc.

There are at least two ways to interpret the word "argument" as expressed by Johnson and Blair [15]: (1) "An interaction, usually verbal and usually between two or more people, that is normally occasioned by a difference of opinion", we will call this option *Argumentation*, (2) "What someone makes or formulates (reasons or evidence) as grounds or support for an opinion (the basis for believing it)". We will call this second option *Assessing Arguments*. Hence the first sense is more related to dialogues where people *argue* by giving arguments and counter-arguments. In artificial intelligence, it concerns researchers working on action communication languages (see e.g. [2,10,25]), dialogues [3,30], and

© Springer Nature Switzerland AG 2019
M. Balduccini et al. (Eds.): LPNMR 2019, LNAI 11481, pp. 61–74, 2019.
https://doi.org/10.1007/978-3-030-20528-7_6

abstract argumentation [8] (where arguments are represented by vertices of a graph whose arcs are attacks between them). The second sense is the one we are going to use in this paper where, as expressed by [15], "The account for argument cogency is that of acceptability, relevance or sufficiency (or good grounds)". In this context, arguments are structures containing reasons and conclusions such that the reasons are intended to be seen as proofs of the conclusions. However, *Argumentation* and *Assessing Arguments* coincide when a proof is simulated by a dialogue between an agent PRO (in favor of a formula) and an agent CON (against it) [17]. Moreover, inquiry dialogues as defined by [30] show also the need to bring together "validity" and communication act since, in this type of dialogues, participants aim to jointly find a "proof" for a particular formula.

In contrast with the first view of *Argumentation* where the question of what is an argument is often not evoked at all, the definition of an argument is at the heart of the *Assessing Arguments* research field. A first definition could be found in the diagrams of [31]. Later, [27] decomposes structurally an argument in five sub-components (the Claim, the Data supporting this Claim, the Warrant providing a licence to infer the Claim from the Data, the Backing for this Warrant and the Rebuttal condition that encapsulates exceptions). A more recent work by [29] defines argument schemes on the basis of critical questions. Beyond this precise decomposition of an argument, there seems to be a consensus on the definition of a deductive structured argument with two parts (the premises and the claim) where the premises constitute a minimal proof of its claim. In that simpler context, assessing an argument amounts to check if it is *sound*, i.e. quoting Kelley [16]: "We evaluate [deductive] arguments by two basic standards: (1) Are the premises true? (2) How well do the premises support the conclusion?"

A major trend of research must be mentioned: the study of fallacy. Quoting Woods [32]: "in the broadest sense of the term, a fallacy is any error in reasoning. But the term is normally restricted to certain patterns of errors that occur with some frequency, usually because the reasoning involved has a certain surface plausibility. To the unwary, the premises of a fallacious argument seem relevant to the conclusion, even though they are not; or the argument seems to have more strength than it actually does. This is why fallacies are committed with some frequency". Understanding fallacious reasoning has two benefits: first, learn how to detect it in everyday life; second, progress in the understanding of what is a good argument by opposition to fallacies. This explains why fallacies have been broadly studied and seminal works [13] categorizing them in patterns is famous.

We propose a unified system for dealing with fallacies, since as far as we know, few authors [7,33,34] attempted to set a generic logical system that helps a user to assess an argument. Note that the introduction of meta-level predicates for assessing arguments has been explored but restricted to a dialectical argumentation framework [14,24]. Indeed, in this paper we propose a logical system that takes an argument and some knowledge as input then, either the argument is sound and the licit schemes that were implicitly used in the argument are listed to the user, or the argument is not sound and the system answers that some premises are missing and/or gives a list of the fallacious schemes that were used. It is important to note that the aim of our work is not to formalize argumentation schemes "à la Walton/Toulmin", but to provide a logic-based formalization of arguments considered as structured proofs. In this regard, the argumentation schemes of Walton/Toulmin are particular cases of "non standard" inference rules hence can be seen as licit schemes in our framework.

The paper is organized as follows: we define a formal language that enables us to give a formal definition of concepts related to argument assessment (validity, soundness, etc.) wrt. a set of argumentation schemes, and we show that this can mimic classical logic when the schemes amount to classical inference, exemplifying it with Hilbert axioms. We give a list of fallacious schemes (fallacies) and a definition of a fallacious argument wrt. a set of recorded (potentially fallacious) schemes. We show that a fallacious argument will be detected as "non robust".

2 Language

We use a language L split into two parts: $L = L_0 \cup L_1$, L_0 is the language for describing the world, L_1 is a metalanguage for describing inferences between arguments and formulas based on schemes and facts defined in the language. L_0 is based on a finite set of user-defined predicates P_0, a finite set of variables $\mathcal{X}_0$ and a finite set of constants $\mathcal{C}_0$. A term of L_0 is a variable of $\mathcal{X}_0$ or a constant of $\mathcal{C}_0$, a vector of terms is denoted $\mathbf{T}$. An atom has the form $p(\mathbf{T})$ where p is a n-ary predicate of P_0 and either $n = 0$ and $\mathbf{T}$ is empty; or for all $i \in [1...n]$, $\mathbf{T}[i]$ is a term. Let At_0 be the set of all atoms based on P_0, $\mathcal{X}_0$ and $\mathcal{C}_0$, they will represent factual information on the world. Let $\mathcal{X}_1$ be a set of variable symbols (starting with a capital letter) that can represent any member of At_0 (atoms of L_0), they will be used in L_1. Let I be an index set (serving as scheme identifiers).

Definition 1 (Syntax of L_0 and L_1)
$L_0 : \varphi, \psi :: p(\mathbf{T}); X; \varphi \to \psi; \neg\varphi$
$L_1 \qquad :: licit(\Psi, \varphi); proven(\varphi); sound(\Psi, \varphi); unctrv(\varphi); robust(\Psi, \varphi)$
where $\qquad p(\mathbf{T}) \in At_0 \quad$ *and* $\quad X \in \mathcal{X}_1 \quad$ *and* $\quad \Psi ::\{\}; \{\varphi\} \cup \Psi$

Let $K \subseteq L_0$ be a set of formulas representing a set of factual knowledge, and $S \subseteq I \times 2^{L_0} \times L_0$ be a list of triples of the form (id, Ψ, φ) where id is an identifier from I, Ψ is a set of formulas of L_0 (the premise) and φ is a formula of L_0 (the conclusion), that represent the recorded "schemes" defined on L_0. S needs not to represent axioms that capture classical logic. We will see both the cases where S allows to capture classical logic and where S captures other kinds of schemes.

Licit, proven, sound are L_1-counterparts to validity and soundness in classical logic. An *argument is licit* if obtained by a substitution upon a recorded scheme. Since using an argument can be viewed as applying an inference scheme, a formula is *proven* if it can be reached by a sequence of inference schemes from the knowledge base. An *argument is sound* if it is licit and its premises are proven.

Definition 2 (Semantics of licit, proven and sound)

- $K, S \models_L licit(\Psi, \varphi)$ *iff there exist* $(id, A, \alpha) \in S$ *and a substitution* $\sigma : \mathcal{X}_1 \to At_0$ *s.t.* $(\Psi, \varphi) = (\sigma(A), \sigma(\alpha))$.

- $K, S \models_L proven(\varphi)$ if $\varphi \in K$ or $\exists \Psi \in 2^{L_0}$ s.t. $K, S \models_L sound(\Psi, \varphi)$.
- $K, S \models_L sound(\Psi, \varphi)$ if $K, S \models_L licit(\Psi, \varphi)$ and $\forall \psi \in \Psi$, $K, S \models_L proven(\psi)$.
- The last two items are the only way to establish $proven(\varphi)$ and $sound(\Psi, \varphi)$ (structural minimality).

Example 1. Let K be a knowledge base expressing that it rains and that observing rain implies taking an umbrella $K = \{rain, rain \rightarrow take(umbrella)\}$. Let modus ponens be the only licit scheme, $S = \{(modusponens, \{X, X \rightarrow Y\}, Y)\}$.

The argument saying that "since it rains and due to the implication between rain and taking an umbrella, then the user should take an umbrella" is licit and sound, and allows us to prove that the user should take an umbrella. Formally, with $\Psi = \{rain, rain \rightarrow take(umbrella)\}$ and $\varphi = take(umbrella)$, it holds that $K, S \models_L licit(\Psi, \varphi)$ and $K, S \models_L sound(\Psi, \varphi)$ and $K, S \models_L proven(\varphi)$.

It is easier to visualize that a formula is proven by building a proof tree, according to Definition 3 and Proposition 1 (proof trees are used in some proofs).

Definition 3 (Proof tree, $\vdash_S$). Given a knowledge base K and a set of schemes S s.t. scheme $(id, \Psi, \varphi) \in S$, a graph $G = (V, E)$ where each vertex of V contains exactly one formula of L_0 is a proof tree for φ wrt. K and S iff

- either G is a tree of only one node v_0 containing φ which is a leaf: $G = (\{v_0\}, \emptyset)$ and $\varphi \in K$,
- or G is a directed tree of root v_0 containing φ and v_0 is a node with $k \leq \sup\{|\Psi| : (id, \Psi, \varphi) \in S\}$ children $v_1, \ldots, v_k$ s.t.
  - $\forall i \in [1, k]$, v_i contains a formula φ_i, v_i is the root of a proof tree of φ_i,
  - $(\{\varphi_1, \ldots, \varphi_k\}, \varphi)$ is s.t. there exist $(id, A, \alpha) \in S$ and a substitution $\sigma : \mathcal{X}_1 \rightarrow At_0$ s.t. $(\{\varphi_1, \ldots, \varphi_k\}, \varphi) = (\sigma(A), \sigma(\alpha))$.

Notation: $K \vdash_S \varphi$ iff there exists a finite proof tree for φ wrt K and S.

Proposition 1. $K, S \models_L proven(\varphi)$ iff $K \vdash_S \varphi$

In L_1 the expressions uncontroversial and robust are cautious counterparts of proven and sound as is standard [4,9]. A formula is uncontroversial if its negation is not proven and either it is a fact or the conclusion of a robust argument where a robust argument is a licit one whose premises are all uncontroversial.

Definition 4 (semantics of uncontroversial and robust)

- $K, S \models_L unctrv(\varphi)$ iff $K, S \not\models_L proven(\neg\varphi)$ and $(\varphi \in K$ or $\exists \Psi \in 2^L$ s.t. $K, S \models_L robust(\Psi, \varphi))$.
- $K, S \models_L robust(\Psi, \varphi)$ iff $K, S \models_L licit(\Psi, \varphi)$ and $\forall \psi \in \Psi$, $K, S \models_L unctrv(\psi)$.

Example 1 (continued): *Supplement K with color(umbrella, yellow) and $\neg rain$: $K' = \{rain \rightarrow take(umbrella), rain, \neg rain, color(umbrella, yellow)\}$. Then, $K, S \models_L proven(take(umbrella))$ and $K, S \not\models_L uncontroversial(take (umbrella))$. This is because the argument $(\{rain, rain \rightarrow take(umbrella)\}, take(umbrella))$ is no longer robust due to rain ceasing to be uncontroversial (now, both proven(rain) and proven($\neg rain$) hold).*

Even if K is inconsistent, it is possible to infer that some non absurd formula hold, since $K, S \models_L unctrv(color(umbrella, yellow))$ (there is no proof tree concluding $\neg color(umbrella, yellow)$ because the fact does not exist and no implication concludes this negation). Such an inference system is paraconsistent, although not very powerful: e.g. modus tollens is not a licit scheme in it.

The next property shows that uncontroversial is a particular case of proven.

Proposition 2. *If $K, S \models_L unctrv(\varphi)$ then $K, S \models_L proven(\varphi)$.*

Proof. If φ is uncontroversial then it is possible to build a particular proof tree for φ wrt. K and S (where each formula ψ of a node is such that $proven(\neg\psi)$ does not hold). Hence $K \vdash_S \varphi$.

3 Soundness and Completeness of this Framework

In this section we show that the framework is sound and complete when the set of schemes S is licit and complete wrt. classical logic. For any set of schemes $S = \bigcup_{i \in I_S} (i, \Psi_i, \varphi_i)$, we say that S is *cl-valid* (standing for valid wrt classical logic) iff $\forall i \in I_S, \Psi_i \models \varphi_i$. We say that S is *cl-complete* iff $\models \varphi$ implies $\vdash_S \varphi$.

Proposition 3 (cl-validity). *Let $S = \bigcup_{i \in I_S} (i, \Psi_i, \varphi_i)$ be a set of cl-valid schemes, $I_S \subseteq I$, $\forall\varphi \in L_0$, $\forall K \subseteq L_0$, if $K, S \models_L proven(\varphi)$ then $K \models \varphi$.*

Proof. Due to Proposition 1, $K, S \models_L proven(\varphi)$ implies $K \vdash_S \varphi$. Since S is cl-valid, this implies that $K \models \varphi$.

Proposition 4 (cl-completeness). *Let $S = \bigcup_{i \in I_S} (i, \Psi_i, \varphi_i)$ be a cl-complete set, $I_S \subseteq I$, $\forall\varphi \in L_0$, $\forall K \subseteq L_0$, if $K \models \varphi$ then $K, S \models_L proven(\varphi)$*

Proof. By mapping the classical proof tree of φ to a proof tree for $proven(\varphi)$ wrt. K and S (inverting the arcs) and using Proposition 1 we get $K, S \models_L proven(\varphi)$.

Next, as expected, we show that introducing the notions of *uncontroversial* and *robust* provides a nice way to circumvent the ex falso quodlibet[1].

Proposition 5 (Escaping ex falso quodlibet). *Let $S = \bigcup_{i \in I_S} (i, \Psi_i, \varphi_i)$ be a set of schemes, $I_S \subseteq I$. If S is both cl-valid and cl-complete then $\forall\varphi \in L_0$, $\forall K \subseteq L_0$, $K, S \models_L unctrv(\varphi)$ iff $K \not\models \bot$ and $K \models \varphi$*

---

[1] The *ex falso quodlibet* expresses that from inconsistency anything can be deduced.

Proof. ($\Rightarrow$) $K, S \models_L unctrv(\varphi)$ by Proposition 2, $K, S \models_L proven(\varphi)$, by Proposition 3, $K \models \varphi$. Now, $K, S \models_L unctrv(\varphi)$ implies $K, S \not\models_L proven(\neg\varphi)$, due to Proposition 4 $K \not\models \neg\varphi$, i.e., $K \not\models \bot$ (since $K \models \bot$ implies $\forall \psi, K \models \psi$).
($\Leftarrow$) Due to Proposition 4, $K \models \varphi$ implies $K, S \models_L proven(\varphi)$. Due to Proposition 1, $K \vdash_S \varphi$. Assume that there is a node v containing a formula ψ in this proof tree s.t. $K, S \models_L proven(\neg\psi)$ then due to Proposition 3 $K \models \neg\psi$, moreover v should be s.t. $K, S \models_L proven(\psi)$ (by Definition 1). Due to Proposition 3 this implies $K \models \psi$), i.e., $K \models \bot$. Hence if $K \models \varphi$ and $K \not\models \bot$ then there is a proof tree for φ in K, S s.t. for each node containing any formula ψ in this tree $K, S \not\models_L proven(\neg\psi)$ which is a particular proof tree translating that $K, S \models_L unctrv(\varphi)$.

4 Computing Licitness and Soundness of an Argument

A Prolog program has been implemented that assesses arguments. For the sake of efficiency, we define a predicate arg/2 with which the user declares all the arguments to be used in the proof. The implementation is an encoding of the above definitions via the predicates *proven, licit sound, uncontroversial, robust*. In Prolog, these predicates have a parameter which can be set to an unbound variable that will contain a list of schemes and facts to be used to prove a formula.

Example 1 (continued): *The knowledge base given above is implemented as*

```
|?- proven([take(umbrella)], Schemes).
Schemes = [[modusponens, fact(rain),
            fact(implies(rain, take(umbrella)))]]
```

This means that we are able to prove take(umbrella) *based on the facts* rain *and* rain → take(umbrella) *and the* modus ponens *scheme.*

4.1 Example of Implementation of an Hilbert System

We now show how our framework captures classical logic by encoding a Hilbert system, namely Mendelson's axiom system for *implies* and *not*. These axioms are all valid and *modus ponens* preserves validity. As to completeness, the case is similar hence the schemes corresponding to this Hilbert system allows us to capture classical entailment, as is stated by the next corollary.

Corollary 1 (Inference with Hilbert Schemes)

$Let\ S_H = \{(hilbertK, \varnothing, X \to (Y \to X)), \quad (modusponens, \{X, X \to Y\}, Y)$
$(hilbertS, \varnothing, (X \to (Y \to Z)) \to ((X \to Y) \to (X \to Z)))$
$(hilbertNot, \varnothing, (\neg Y \to \neg X) \to ((\neg Y \to X) \to Y))\}$
$\forall K \subseteq L_0,\ \forall \varphi \in L_0$, we have $K, S_H \models_L proven(\varphi)$ iff $K \models \varphi$

Proof. The Hilbert axiomatic system has been shown to be valid, *modus ponens* has been shown to preserve validity hence S_H is valid, using Proposition 3 we get the implication from left to right, Hilbert system with modus ponens has been show to be complete, using Proposition 4 we get the reverse implication.

It is then possible to check if $f \rightarrow f$ can be proven:

```
|?- proven([implies(f,f)], S).
S = [[modusponens,[modusponens,[hilbertK],[hilbertS]],[hilbertK]]]
```

This list gives the sequence of schemes that are used to prove $f \rightarrow f$: *hilbertK*, *hilbertS*, *modus ponens*, *hilbertK* and *modus ponens*.

5   Reasoning with Schemes and Fallacies

In this section, we show how our framework can be used to assess arguments using particular argument schemes or, possibly, fallacies.

5.1   Sound and Fallacious Use of the Expert Scheme

We start with an example in which it is possible to produce "expert arguments", i.e. arguments using an expert's opinion to support a conclusion. Such arguments can be fallacious or sound according to the credibility of the expert (called "Authority" in the fallacy 2a "Appeal to Authority", see next section). Let the facts $K_1 = \{expert(doctorWho, weather), topic(sunny, weather), said(doctorWho, sunny)\}$ and schemes $S_1 = \{\{(\ expertarg, \{expert\ (Agent, Topic), topic\ (Claim, Topic), said\ (Agent, Claim)\}, Claim\}\}$ form the knowledge base. It is possible to construct the argument: $a_1 = (\{expert\ (doctorWho, weather), topic\ (sunny, weather), said\ (doctorWho\ , sunny)\}, sunny)$ such that we have:

$$K_1, S_1 \models_L licit(a_1)\ \ K_1, S_1 \models_L robust(a_1)\ \ K_1, S_1 \models_L unctrv(sunny)$$

Indeed, the argument a_1 follows exactly the "expert argument" scheme provided in S_1 (a_1 is thus licit) and its premises belong to K (it is the case of no contradicting piece of information) so it is robust. Since the argument is robust, its conclusion *sunny* is uncontroversial. If K does not contain *expert(doctorWho, weather)* then argument a_1 is no longer sound (nor robust) but it remains licit wrt. S_1.

Let us now observe how the addition of new information may give another result regarding the robustness of a_1 with the following knowledge base:

$$K_2 = K_1 \cup \{nodiploma(doctorWho, weather),$$
$$nodiploma(Agent, Topic) \rightarrow \neg expert(Agent, Topic)\},$$
$$S_2 = S_1 \cup \{(modusponens, \{X, X \rightarrow Y\}, Y)\}.$$

With the argument $a_2 = (\{nodiploma\ (doctorWho, weather), nodiploma\ (Agent, Topic) \rightarrow \neg\ expert(Agent, Topic)\}, \neg\ expert(doctorWho, weather))$, we get:

$$K_2, S_2 \models_L licit(a_2)\ \ \ \ \ K_2, S_2 \models_L sound(a_2)$$
$$K_2, S_2 \not\models_L robust(a_2)\ \ \ K_2, S_2 \models_L proven(\neg expert(doctorWho, weather))$$

Because of a_2, the provability of one of the premises of a_1 has been challenged. I.e., we still have a proof for *expert(doctorWho,weather)*, but we also have a proof for its negation. And, thus, the conclusion of a_1 is not uncontroversial anymore:

$$K_2, S_2 \not\models_L unctrv(sunny) \qquad K_2, S_2 \models_L proven(sunny).$$

However, *sunny* is still proven since a_1 is still sound (its premises are still in the knowledge base). Our Prolog implementation provides the list of schemes used for assessing the argument or for proving the formula.

```
|?- proven([sunny], S).
S = [[expertarg]]

|?- proven([neg(expert(doctorWho, weather))], T).
T = [[modusponens]]
```

This provides the schemes used for proving respectively *sunny* (*expertarg*) and ¬*(expert(doctorWho,weather))*. Since we are able to list every scheme that is used then it is possible to detect those that are regarded fallacious, and to let the user know about it. We illustrate this on the following knowledge base:

$$K_3 = K_1 \cup \{young(doctorWho)\},$$

$$S_3 = S_1 \cup \{(tooyoung, \{young(Agent)\}), \neg expert(Agent, weather)\}.$$

This scheme expresses that a young person cannot be an expert about weather, which is fallacious (viewed as an instance of *Hasty Generalization* meaning that "young" implies "inexperienced" hence "not expert"). Yet, one can have argument

$$a_3 = (\{young(doctorWho)\}, \neg expert(doctorWho, weather)).$$

In this context, a_3 is licit regarding S_3 and it challenges a_1 in the same way as a_2. However, the possibility to detect this particular *tooyoung* fallacious scheme might allow to prompt the user to change its arguments or provide grounding for its (hitherto fallacious) scheme.

5.2 Encoding the Schemes of Some Usual Fallacies

In this section, we show how our framework is able to handle usual fallacies. Since Aristotle's *On Sophistical Refutations*, there have been a lot of work on fallacies, including [13], along time the list of fallacies is growing, and is exposed in books or even on web pages[2]. Here, we choose to use the classification given by [16] who studied fallacies with the same goal as many authors including Aristotle, i.e., first for helping people to identify and avoid them, second because "understanding why these patterns of arguments are fallacious will help us understand the nature of good reasoning". In this section, we propose to examine fallacies that Kelley

---

[2] See e.g. https://www.logicallyfallacious.com/tools/lp/Bo/LogicalFallacies.

discussed in [16], Chap. 5. For example we do not consider fallacies that refer to an opponent's argument like "strawman" (misrepresenting someone's argument to make it easier to attack). Quoting Kelley, "the varieties of bad reasoning are too numerous to catalog here" hence we restrict to Kelley's four categories:

1. Subjectivist fallacies: these are inferences that involve the violation of objectivity in one way or another.
   (a) Subjectivism: "I believe in p" or "I want p" **hence** p holds.
   (b) Appeal to majority: The majority believes p **hence** p is true.
   (c) Appeal to emotion: use (explicitly or implicitly) emotion instead of evidence to make accepted a belief.
   (d) Appeal to force (*Argumentum ad Baculum*): use a threat instead of evidence (which may be regarded as an appeal to the emotion "scared").
2. Fallacies involving credibility:
   (a) Appeal to Authority (*Argumentum ad Verecundiam*): agent A says p **hence** p is true. It is a fallacy when A has not been proven to be competent and objective, when the conditions of credibility are not satisfied.
   (b) *Ad Hominem*: using a negative trait of a speaker as evidence that his statement is false: A says p, A has some negative trait **hence** p is false.
3. Fallacies of Context: "jumping to conclusions."
   (a) False Alternative[3]: Either p or q, $\neg q$ **hence** p which is deductively valid but the soundness depends on whether the premises take into account all the relevant alternatives.
   (b) *Post Hoc*[4]: X occurred before Y **hence** X caused Y.
   (c) Hasty Generalization: drawing conclusions too quickly, on the basis of insufficient evidence (with not enough variety to be representative).
   (d) Accident or Hasty application: applying a generalization to a special case without regard to the circumstances that make the case an exception to the general rule.
   (e) Slippery Slope: Action X will lead to Y that will lead to Z, Z is very bad **hence** [5] X should be avoided.
   (f) Composition (and Division): inferring p is true of a part (the whole) must be true of the whole (a part) without considering whether the nature of p makes it rational.
4. Fallacies of Logical Structure
   (a) Begging the Question (Circular Argument): p **hence** p, usually p is formulated in two different ways[6].
   (b) Equivocation: a word used in premise and conclusion switches meaning.
   (c) Appeal to Ignorance: $\neg p$ has not been proven true **hence** p is true[7].

---

[3] Also called False Dichotomy when the premises posit just two alternatives.

[4] This is short for *post hoc ergo propter hoc*: "after this, therefore because of this.".

[5] There could be any number of items in the series of projected consequences.

[6] This fallacy occurs when the circle is enlarged to include more than one step: The conclusion p is supported by premise q, which in turn is supported by p (though there could be any number of intervening steps).

[7] One application is the legal principle that a person is innocent until proven guilty.

(d) Diversion: changing the issue in the middle of an argument. Another form of diversion is called the *Straw man* argument: distorts an opponent's position and then refutes it. An extreme form is the *Non sequitur* fallacy when the premises are completely unrelated to the conclusion.

Table 1 is a first attempt to encode the schemes that could be associated to these fallacies in our framework. *We regard all the items followed by a star as rational schemes.* However, a number of instances of these schemes are fallacious because they are used with unproven premises. As already said, this is the case for the *Authority* argument which is not fallacious by itself, it is fallacious when $expert(A, T)$ fails to be *unctrv*. It is also the case for *False Alternative*: the scheme is rational but the premise may not be true in the context, i.e., there may be other alternatives than Y when X does not hold ($\neg X \rightarrow Y$ is false).

Table 1. Proposal of fallacious schemes encoding.

Fallacy	Scheme
Subjectivism	$(f1a, \{likeable(X)\}, X)$
Majority	$(f1b, \{majoritarian(X)\}, X)$
Authority*	$(f2a, \{expert(A, T), topic(X, T), said(A, X)\}, X)$
Ad Hominem	$(f2b, \{said(A, X), \neg likeable(A)\}, \neg X)$
False alternative*	$(f3a, \{X \rightarrow \neg Y, \neg X \rightarrow Y, \neg X\}, Y)$
Post Hoc	$(f3b, \{before(X, Y)\}, cause(X, Y))$
Hasty generalization	$(f3c, \{hasProp(X, P), Y \rightarrow X\}, hasProp(Y, P))$
Accident	$(f3d, \{hasProp(X, P), X \rightarrow Y\}, hasProp(Y, P)$
Slippery slope	$(f3e, \{cause(X, Y), cause(Y, Z)\neg likeable(Z)\}, \neg do(X)\}$
Composition	$(f3f, \{hasProp(X, P), part(X, Y)\}, hasProp(Y, P))$
Begging the question*	$(f4a, \{X\}, X)$

The items for which no scheme is proposed in the table are those that either are based on natural language or semantic interpretations like *Emotion, Force, Equivocation* and *Non Sequitur*. *Appeal to Ignorance* is of another type since it is a meta-argument that speaks about provability; we could encode it with $(f4c, \{\neg holds(X)\}, \neg X)$, however this would require to have a more complex definition of the language L_0 that includes the predicate *holds*. This would lead to a more complex definition of the semantics of L.

Definition 5. *Given a knowledge base K and a set of (rational and sophistic) schemes $S = S_R \cup S_S$ and an argument $a \in 2^{L_0} \times L_0$:*

$$a \text{ is fallacious wrt. } K, S \text{ iff } K, S_R \not\models robust(a)$$

This definition allows us to emphasize the fallacious aspects of arguments in our model: $a = (\Psi, \varphi)$ is fallacious in the following cases:

1. $\exists \psi \in \Psi$, $K, S_R \not\models_L proven(\psi)$: it uses a premise that is not rationally proven,
2. $\forall \psi \in \Psi$, $K, S_R \models_L proven(\psi)$ and $\exists \psi' \in \Psi$ $K, S_R \models_L proven(\neg\psi')$: there is a controversial premise,
3. $K, S_R \not\models_L licit(a)$: it uses a sophistic scheme or an unrecorded scheme.

The last case allows us to characterize the *Non Sequitur* fallacy which seems appropriate here. This also enables us to cover cases like *Appeal to Emotion* and *Appeal to Force* where the use of a premise that refers to emotion or threat is not following any rational deductive scheme towards a conclusion. The occurrence of the third case may disappoint a user by pointing out that her argument is not licit because not based on a recorded scheme. However our program will inform her about all the licit schemes and uncontroversial premises that she has used.

Proposition 6. *Given a knowledge base K and a set of schemes $S = S_R \cup S_S$ s.t. $K \cup \{(\sigma(\Psi) \rightarrow \sigma(\varphi) \mid \sigma \in \mathcal{X}_1 \rightarrow At_0, (id, \Psi, \varphi) \in S_R\} \not\vdash \bot$, for any argument $a \in 2^{L_0} \times L_0$, a is fallacious wrt. K, S iff $K, S_R \not\models_L sound(a)$*

This last result shows that when the rational schemes do not allow to infer inconsistent formulas from the knowledge base then a fallacious argument is simply an unsound argument. Hence a "non fallacious" argument uses the rational schemes with proven premises (which cannot be controversial in this context). This goes beyond classical logic because schemes $((id, \Psi, \varphi))$ need not be cl-valid ($\Psi \models \varphi$) to be applied (i.e. to belong to S_R).

6   Discussion and Related Work

This framework, and its Prolog implementation, allows us to assess arguments with regard to a knowledge base and a set of argumentation schemes. A merit of our work is to clarify various forms of validity depending on the nature of the target. Namely, we have distinguished three targets: logical deduction, instantiated argument, generic argument scheme. Each of them can be associated with a different definition of validity, which leads us to propose different names for them: "valid/unvalid" applies to a deduction between logical formulas, "licit/illicit" and "sound/unsound" concern an instantiated argument, a "rational scheme" is opposed to a "sophism" in order to qualify an argument scheme. More precisely, an instantiated argument is said to be licit if it follows a recognized scheme. It is said to be sound (or robust) if it has proven (or uncontroversial) premises. Distinguishing between proven and uncontroversial formulas allows in turn to circumvent the ex falso quodlibet that derives anything. Our framework is flexible enough to represent Hilbert axioms, granting the possibility to express classical logic, but could also be used with "argument schemes" or even sophistic schemes. One benefit of the encoding in a formal logical language is the ability to express and decide about soundness of arguments in the logical language itself.

The idea to axiomatize invalid statements is not new: it is called rejection calculi, first introduced by Łukasiewicz [18] and has been developed for different logics like classical logic, intuitionistic logic, modal logics [11,22,26]. Some proposals were dedicated to the detection of one particular fallacy, like [19]'s dialogue game for detecting the fallacy of *petitio principii*. In contrast, our approach deals with multiple fallacies and is highly flexible since it may be used with any user-defined inference scheme. For instance, by allowing the user to define non-classical inference schemes, our system may allow the closed world assumption or defeasible reasoning. This unified formalism may also allow us to better circumscribe usual commonsense inferences done with e.g., causes and counterfactuals that should deserve specific schemes (as also claimed by [20]).

While this paper is about the assessment of arguments, there are interesting links with the other interpretation of the word "argument", that is the subject of dialectical argumentation. The latter focuses on the study of argument validity in the sense of winning the dispute: "can this argument defend itself against any other argument?". We take the viewpoint of logic through argumentation, trying to extract the intrinsic validity of an argument, i.e. its soundness, from the way it is built. Some approaches like ABA [21], ASPIC+ [23] and Carneades [12] are relating structured arguments to Dung like interaction argumentation, and base the assessment of argument on its relation to counter-arguments. The problem with such approaches is that they use argumentation semantics, where these semantics do not depend on the intrinsic content of arguments but is only based on the interactions, leading to counter-intuitive results as proven in [1]. An idea could be to detect fallacies based on the existence of attacks. Moreover, if no counter-argument has been stated against a given (fallacious) argument, this does not mean that the argument is a correct evidence for its conclusion.

Our work is but an opening for a number of new studies. Thus, it would be interesting to study what schemes can be added to cover more types of rational reasoning (and their possible flaws). Another perspective is to extend our definitions so as to allow for more complex arguments, e.g. directly referring to another argument (as a premise or counterargument) with the long term view to handle dialogues. Our aim is not to help users build convincing tricky fallacies, our aim is to help people build efficiently *sound* arguments and to allow them to fight fallacies: the closer a fallacy is from a sound argument the more the agent can be inclined to use it especially in case of low cognitive availability [6].

Our long term goal is to use our framework to offer a protocol governing the authorized moves in a dialogue. It would be worth incorporating it as a part of a "dialogue support system" that could ensure for instance the correct use of the speech act *Argue* (that commits the agent to be able to provide a sound proof of her claim from some premises). So, our proposal enables an automatic verification of compliance of this speech act with regard to a set of rational schemes. The dialog support system could make the user aware of her biased reasoning and prompt her to give "better" grounds for her argumentation. An idea could be to take into account the notion of critical questions [5,27,29] in order to assess arguments and following the work of Verheij [28] we could help a user to provide more accurate justifications for any unproven premises (via other arguments), or even to introduce new justified schemes in her base.

References

1. Amgoud, L., Besnard, P.: Logical limits of abstract argumentation frameworks. J. Appl. Non-class. Log. **23**(3), 229–267 (2013)
2. Amgoud, L., Maudet, N., Parsons, S.: An argumentation-based semantics for agent communication languages. In: 15th European Conference on Artificial Intelligence, vol. 2, pp. 38–42 (2002)
3. Bench-Capon, T., Dunne, P., Leng, P.: A dialogue game for dialectical interaction with expert systems. In: 12th Annual Conference Expert Systems & Applications, pp. 105–113 (1992)
4. Benferhat, S., Dubois, D., Prade, H.: Argumentative inference in uncertain and inconsistent knowledge bases. In: 9th Conference on Uncertainty in AI, pp. 411–419 (1993)
5. Besnard, P., et al.: Introducing structured argumentation. Argum. Comput. **5**(1), 1–4 (2014)
6. Bisquert, P., Croitoru, M., de Saint Cyr, F.D., Hecham, A.: Formalizing cognitive acceptance of arguments: durum wheat selection interdisciplinary study. Minds Mach. **27**(1), 233–252 (2017)
7. D'Agostino, M., Modgil, S.: Classical logic, argument and dialectic. Artif. Intell. J. **262**, 15–51 (2018)
8. Dung, P.M.: On the acceptability of arguments and its fundamental role in non-monotonic reasoning, logic programming and n-person games. Artif. Intell. J. **77**, 321–357 (1995)
9. Elvang-Gøransson, M., Krause, P., Fox, J.: Dialectic reasoning with inconsistent information. In: 9th Conference on Uncertainty in AI, pp. 114–121 (1993)
10. FIPA: ACL message structure specification. Foundation for Intelligent Physical Agents (2002). http://www.fipa.org/specs/fipa00061/SC00061G.html. Accessed 30 June 2004
11. Goranko, V.: Refutation systems in modal logic. Stud. Log. **53**(2), 299–324 (1994)
12. Gordon, T.F., Prakken, H., Walton, D.: The Carneades model of argument and burden of proof. Artif. Intell. J. **171**(10–15), 875–896 (2007)
13. Hamblin, C.L.: Fallacies. Methuen, London (1970)
14. Hunter, A.: Reasoning about the appropriateness of proponents for arguments. In: 23rd AAAI Conference on Artificial Intelligence, pp. 89–94 (2008)
15. Johnson, R.H., Blair, J.A.: Logical Self-defense. IDEA, New York (2006)
16. Kelley, D.: The Art of Reasoning: An Introduction to Logic and Critical Thinking. W.W. Norton & Company, New York (2013)
17. Lorenz, K., Lorenzen, P.: Dialogische Logik. WBG, Darmstadt (1978)
18. Lukasiewicz, J.: Aristotle's Syllogistic from the Standpoint of Modern Formal Logic, 2nd edn. Clarendon Press, Oxford (1957)
19. Mackenzie, J.D.: Question-begging in non-cumulative systems. J. Philos. Log. **8**(1), 117–133 (1979)
20. Mendelson, E.: Introduction to Mathematical Logic, 6th edn. CRC Press, Boca Raton (2015)
21. Modgil, S., Prakken, H.: A general account of argumentation with preferences. Artif. Intell. J. **195**, 361–397 (2013)
22. Oetsch, J., Tompits, H.: Gentzen-type refutation systems for three-valued logics with an application to disproving strong equivalence. In: Delgrande, J.P., Faber, W. (eds.) LPNMR 2011. LNCS (LNAI), vol. 6645, pp. 254–259. Springer, Heidelberg (2011). https://doi.org/10.1007/978-3-642-20895-9_28

23. Prakken, H.: An abstract framework for argumentation with structured arguments. Argum. Comput. **1**(2), 93–124 (2010)
24. Prakken, H., Wyner, A., Bench-Capon, T., Atkinson, K.: A formalization of argumentation schemes for legal case-based reasoning in ASPIC+. J. Log. Comput. **25**(5), 1141–1166 (2015)
25. Singh, M.P.: Agent communication languages: rethinking the principles. Computer **31**(12), 40–47 (1998)
26. Skura, T.: Refutation systems in propositional logic. In: Gabbay, D., Guenthner, F. (eds.) Handbook of Philosophical Logic, vol. 16, 2nd edn, pp. 115–157. Springer, Heidelberg (2011). https://doi.org/10.1007/978-94-007-0479-4_2
27. Toulmin, S.: The Uses of Argument. Cambridge University Press, Cambridge (1958)
28. Verheij, B.: Evaluating arguments based on Toulmin's scheme. Argumentation **19**(3), 347–371 (2005)
29. Walton, D., Gordon, T.F.: Critical questions in computational models of legal argument. In: Argumentation in Artificial Intelligence and Law Workshop, pp. 103–111. Wolf Legal Publishers (2005)
30. Walton, D., Krabbe, E.C.W.: Commitment in Dialogue: Basic Concepts of Interpersonal Reasoning. State University of New York Press, Albany (1995)
31. Wigmore, J.H.: The Principles of Judicial Proof, 2nd edn. Little, Brown (1931)
32. Woods, J.: Is the theoretical unity of the fallacies possible? Informal Log. **XVI**, 77–85 (1994)
33. Wooldridge, M., McBurney, P., Parsons, S.: On the meta-logic of arguments. In: Parsons, S., Maudet, N., Moraitis, P., Rahwan, I. (eds.) ArgMAS 2005. LNCS (LNAI), vol. 4049, pp. 560–567. Springer, Heidelberg (2006). https://doi.org/10.1007/11794578_3
34. Yuan, T., Manandhar, S., Kelly, T., Wells, S.: Automatically detecting fallacies in system safety arguments. In: Baldoni, M., et al. (eds.) IWEC/CMNA 2014-2015. LNCS (LNAI), vol. 9935, pp. 47–59. Springer, Cham (2016). https://doi.org/10.1007/978-3-319-46218-9_4

Simple Contrapositive Assumption-Based Frameworks

Jesse Heyninck[1]($\boxtimes$) and Ofer Arieli[2]

[1] Institute of Philosophy II, Ruhr University Bochum, Bochum, Germany
jesse.heyninck@rub.de
[2] School of Computer Science, The Academic College of Tel-Aviv, Tel Aviv, Israel
oarieli@mta.ac.il

Abstract. Assumption-based argumentation is one of the most prominent formalisms for logical (or structured) argumentation. It has been shown useful for representing defeasible reasoning and has tight links to logic programming. In this paper we study the Dung semantics for extended forms of assumption-based argumentation frameworks (ABFs), based on *any* contrapositive propositional logic, and whose defeasible rules are expressed by *arbitrary formulas* in that logic. In particular, new results on the well-founded semantics for such ABFs are reported, the redundancy of the closure condition is shown, and the use of disjunctive attacks is investigated. Finally, some useful properties of the generalized frameworks are considered.

1 Introduction

Assumption-based argumentation frameworks (ABFs), thoroughly described in [4], were introduced in the 1990s as a computational structure to capture and generalize several formalisms for defeasible reasoning, including logic programming [4,6]. Their definition was inspired by Dung's semantics for abstract argumentation and logic programming with its dialectical interpretation of the acceptability of negation-as-failure assumptions based on the notion of "no-evidence-to-the-contrary".

In this paper, which is a companion of [13], we study the Dung-style semantics [11] and the entailment relations induced from a large family of ABFs, called *simple contrapositive*, that are based on *any* contrapositive propositional logic, and whose defeasible rules are expressed by *arbitrary* formulas in that logic.[1] Among others, the following contributions and new findings concerning these frameworks are shown in this paper:

---

[1] While both this paper and [13] refer to Dung semantics for simple contrapositive ABFs, the topics that each paper addresses are different, thus the papers are complementary.

This work is supported by the Israel Science Foundation (grant number 817/15). The first author is also supported by the Sofja Kovalevskaja award of the Alexander von Humboldt-Foundation, funded by the German Ministry for Education and Research.

© Springer Nature Switzerland AG 2019
M. Balduccini et al. (Eds.): LPNMR 2019, LNAI 11481, pp. 75–88, 2019.
https://doi.org/10.1007/978-3-030-20528-7_7

(1) The well-founded semantics for ABFs is considered, and its strong relations to reasoning with maximally consistent subsets of the premises is shown. Moreover, we show that under a simple condition this semantics coincides with the grounded semantics for the same ABFs.

(2) We show that for simple contrapositive ABFs the closure requirement on the frameworks' extensions is in fact redundant. As a consequence, most of the concepts that are related to such ABFs are simplified, and their computation becomes easier. To the best of our knowledge, this is the first time that such a question has been asked and answered for assumption-based argumentation.

(3) We consider a generalization of the attack relation in ABFs, called *disjunctive attacks*. The use of these attacks avoids some problems of the grounded semantics under standard attacks. Concerning the other types semantics, we show that (as in the case of ordinary attacks), preferred and stable semantics are reducible to naive semantics, and that the correspondence to reasoning with maximally consistent subsets is preserved. This means that we define a formalism that preserves consistency and correspondence to maximal consistency-based reasoning even under disjunctive attacks, thus avoiding some of the long-standing problems that were reported by [7] for other logic-based argumentation formalisms using disjunctive attacks (called *undercut* in [7]).

(4) We show that the entailment relations induced from the ABFs with disjunctive attacks are preferential for skeptical reasoning and cumulative for credulous reasoning [14]. For these kinds of entailments the property of non-interference [5] is satisfied.

The remaining of this paper is organized as follows: in the next section we review some notions and relevant results from [13]. In Sect. 3 we provide some new results concerning the Dung-style semantics of simple contrapositive ABFs, and in Sect. 4 we consider some properties of the induced entailment relations. In Sect. 5 we discuss our results in light of related work and conclude.[2]

2   Preliminaries

In this section we define the notion of simple contrapositive ABFs, and recall the main results concerning their semantics (see [13]).

We denote by $\mathscr{L}$ an arbitrary propositional language. Atomic formulas in $\mathscr{L}$ are denoted by p, q, r, compound formulas are denoted by ψ, ϕ, σ, and sets of formulas in $\mathscr{L}$ are denoted by Γ, Δ. The powerset of $\mathscr{L}$ is denoted by $\wp(\mathscr{L})$.

Definition 1. A (propositional) *logic* for a language $\mathscr{L}$ is a pair $\mathfrak{L} = \langle \mathscr{L}, \vdash \rangle$, where $\vdash$ is a (Tarskian) consequence relation for $\mathscr{L}$, that is, a binary relation between sets of formulas and formulas in $\mathscr{L}$, which is reflexive (if $\psi \in \Gamma$ then $\Gamma \vdash \psi$), monotonic (if $\Gamma \vdash \psi$ and $\Gamma \subseteq \Gamma'$, then $\Gamma' \vdash \psi$), and transitive (if $\Gamma \vdash \psi$

---

[2] An extended abstract of this paper appears in the proceedings of AAMAS'2019.

and $\Gamma', \psi \vdash \phi$, then $\Gamma, \Gamma' \vdash \phi$). We also assume that $\vdash$ is *non-trivial* (there are Γ, ψ for which $\Gamma \nvdash \psi$), *structural* (i.e., closed under substitutions: for every substitution θ and every Γ, ψ, if $\Gamma \vdash \psi$ then $\{\theta(\gamma) \mid \gamma \in \Gamma\} \vdash \theta(\psi)$), and *finitary* (if $\Gamma \vdash \psi$ then there is a finite $\Gamma' \subseteq \Gamma$ such that $\Gamma' \vdash \psi$).

The $\vdash$-transitive closure of a set Γ of $\mathscr{L}$-formulas is $Cn_\vdash(\Gamma) = \{\psi \mid \Gamma \vdash \psi\}$. When the consequence relation is clear from the context we will sometimes just write $Cn(\Gamma)$.

We shall assume that the language $\mathscr{L}$ contains at least the following (primitive or defined) connectives: $\vdash$-*negation* $\neg$, satisfying: $p \nvdash \neg p$ and $\neg p \nvdash p$ (for every atomic p); $\vdash$-*conjunction* $\wedge$, satisfying: $\Gamma \vdash \psi \wedge \phi$ iff $\Gamma \vdash \psi$ and $\Gamma \vdash \phi$; $\vdash$-*disjunction* $\vee$, satisfying: $\Gamma, \phi \vee \psi \vdash \sigma$ iff $\Gamma, \phi \vdash \sigma$ and $\Gamma, \psi \vdash \sigma$; $\vdash$-*implication* $\supset$, satisfying: $\Gamma, \phi \vdash \psi$ iff $\Gamma \vdash \phi \supset \psi$; and $\vdash$-*falsity* constant F, satisfying: $\mathsf{F} \vdash \psi$ for every formula ψ.

For a finite set of formulas Γ we denote by $\bigwedge \Gamma$ (respectively, by $\bigvee \Gamma$), the conjunction (respectively, the disjunction) of the formulas in Γ. Also, we denote $\neg \Gamma = \{\neg \gamma \mid \gamma \in \Gamma\}$. We say that Γ is $\vdash$-*consistent*, if $\Gamma \nvdash \mathsf{F}$.

Definition 2. A logic $\mathfrak{L} = \langle \mathscr{L}, \vdash \rangle$ is *explosive*, if for $\mathscr{L}$-formula ψ, the set $\{\psi, \neg \psi\}$ is $\vdash$-inconsistent.[3] We say that $\mathfrak{L}$ is *contrapositive*, if for every Γ and ψ it holds that $\Gamma \vdash \neg \psi$ iff either $\psi = \mathsf{F}$, or for every $\phi \in \Gamma$ we have that $\Gamma \setminus \{\phi\}, \psi \vdash \neg \phi$.

Example 1. Classical logic, intuitionistic logic, and modal logics with standard modal semantics, are all specific cases of explosive and contrapositive logics.

Next, we generalize the definition in [4] of assumption-based frameworks.

Definition 3. An *assumption-based framework* is a tuple $\mathbf{ABF} = \langle \mathfrak{L}, \Gamma, Ab, \sim \rangle$, where:

- $\mathfrak{L} = \langle \mathscr{L}, \vdash \rangle$ is a propositional Tarskian logic
- Γ (the *strict assumptions*) and Ab (the *candidate or defeasible assumptions*) are distinct countable sets of $\mathscr{L}$-formulas, where the former is assumed to be $\vdash$-consistent and the latter is assumed to be nonempty.
- $\sim\colon Ab \rightarrow \wp(\mathscr{L})$ is a contrariness operator, assigning a finite set of $\mathscr{L}$-formulas to every defeasible assumption in Ab, such that for every $\psi \in Ab$ where $\psi \nvdash \mathsf{F}$ it holds that $\psi \nvdash \bigwedge \sim \psi$ and $\bigwedge \sim \psi \nvdash \psi$.

A *simple contrapositive* ABF is an assumption-based framework $\mathbf{ABF} = \langle \mathfrak{L}, \Gamma, Ab, \sim \rangle$, where $\mathfrak{L}$ is an explosive and contrapositive logic, and $\sim \psi = \{\neg \psi\}$.

Note 1. Unlike the setting of [4], an ABF may be based on *any* Tarskian logic $\mathfrak{L}$. Also, the strict as well as the candidate assumptions are formulas that may not be just atomic. Concerning the contrariness operator, note that it is not a connective of $\mathscr{L}$, as it is restricted only to the candidate assumptions.

---

[3] That is, $\psi, \neg \psi \vdash \mathsf{F}$. In explosive logics every formula follows from inconsistent assertions.

Note 2. Traditionally, ABFs make use of some set of domain dependent rules as known from e.g. logic programming (i.e., rules of the form $\phi_1, \ldots, \phi_n \rightarrow \phi$, as in logic programming). It is not difficult to see that our setting also applies to this subclass of ABFs by assuming that the implication $\supset$ is deductive (i.e., it is an $\vdash$-implication, see above) and treating such rules as strict premises $\bigwedge_{i=1}^{n} \phi_i \supset \phi$. Such a framework is a simple contrapositive ABF if the rules are closed under contraposition.

Defeasible assertions in an ABF may be attacked by counterarguments.

Definition 4. Let $\mathbf{ABF} = \langle \mathfrak{L}, \Gamma, Ab, \sim \rangle$ be an assumption-based framework, $\Delta, \Theta \subseteq Ab$, and $\psi \in Ab$. We say that Δ *attacks* ψ iff $\Gamma, \Delta \vdash \phi$ for some $\phi \in \sim\psi$. Accordingly, Δ attacks Θ if Δ attacks some $\psi \in \Theta$.

The last definition gives rise to the following adaptation to ABFs of the usual semantics for abstract argumentation frameworks [11].

Definition 5. [4] Let $\mathbf{ABF} = \langle \mathfrak{L}, \Gamma, Ab, \sim \rangle$ be an assumption-based framework, and let $\Delta \subseteq Ab$. Below, maximum and minimum are taken with respect to set inclusion. Then:

- Δ is *closed* if $\Delta = Ab \cap Cn_{\vdash}(\Gamma \cup \Delta)$.
- Δ is *conflict-free* iff there is no $\Delta' \subseteq \Delta$ that attacks some $\psi \in \Delta$.
- Δ is *naive* iff it is closed and maximally conflict-free.
- Δ *defends* a set $\Delta' \subseteq Ab$ iff for every closed set Θ that attacks Δ' there is $\Delta'' \subseteq \Delta$ that attacks Θ.
- Δ is *admissible* iff it is closed, conflict-free, and defends every $\Delta' \subseteq \Delta$.
- Δ is *complete* iff it is admissible and contains every $\Delta' \subseteq Ab$ that it defends.
- Δ is *grounded* iff it is minimally complete.
- Δ is *preferred* iff it is maximally admissible.
- Δ is *stable* iff it is closed, conflict-free, and attacks every $\psi \in Ab \setminus \Delta$.
- Δ is *well-founded* iff $\Delta = \bigcap \{ \Theta \subseteq Ab \mid \Theta$ is complete$\}$.

The set of naive (respectively, complete, preferred, stable, grounded, well-founded) extensions of $\mathbf{ABF}$ is denoted by $\mathsf{Naive}(\mathbf{ABF})$ (respectively, $\mathsf{Com}(\mathbf{ABF})$, $\mathsf{Prf}(\mathbf{ABF})$, $\mathsf{Stb}(\mathbf{ABF})$, $\mathsf{Grd}(\mathbf{ABF})$, $\mathsf{WF}(\mathbf{ABF})$). Clearly, the well-founded extension of an ABF is unique.

In [13] the Dung-style extensions considered above are characterized in terms of the maximal consistent subsets of the defeasible assumptions:

Definition 6. Let $\mathbf{ABF} = \langle \mathfrak{L}, \Gamma, Ab, \sim \rangle$. A set $\Delta \subseteq Ab$ is *maximally consistent* in $\mathbf{ABF}$, if (a) $\Gamma, \Delta \nvdash \mathsf{F}$ and (b) $\Gamma, \Delta' \vdash \mathsf{F}$ for every $\Delta \subsetneq \Delta' \subseteq Ab$. The set of the maximally consistent sets in $\mathbf{ABF}$ is denoted $\mathsf{MCS}(\mathbf{ABF})$.

Proposition 1. [13] *Let* $\mathbf{ABF} = \langle \mathfrak{L}, \Gamma, Ab, \sim \rangle$ *be a simple contrapositive ABF. Then:* $\mathsf{Naive}(\mathbf{ABF}) = \mathsf{Prf}(\mathbf{ABF}) = \mathsf{Stb}(\mathbf{ABF}) = \mathsf{MCS}(\mathbf{ABF})$. *If* $\mathsf{F} \in Ab$ *then also* $\mathsf{Grd}(\mathbf{ABF}) = \bigcap \mathsf{MCS}(\mathbf{ABF})$.

Apart of the correspondence to reasoning with maximal consistency, Proposition 1 also shows that in simple contrapositive ABFs preferred and stable semantics collapse to naive semantics. This is not surprising, as similar results for specific argumentation frameworks are reported in [1] and [3]. Yet, as shown in [3], when more expressive languages, and/or attack relations, and/or entailment relations are involved, this phenomenon ceases to hold. This is also the case with ABFs, even when the definition of the contrariness operator is kept. Here is a simple example:

Example 2. Let $\mathbf{ABF} = \langle \mathfrak{L}, \{p \supset \neg q\}, \{p, q\}, \sim \rangle$ be an ABF where $\mathfrak{L}$ is a logic with a negation $\neg$, and implication $\supset$, and where $\sim A = \{\neg A\}$ for any $A \in \mathscr{L}$. Suppose further that Modus Ponens holds in $\mathfrak{L}$, but contraposition does not. Then $\{q\}$ is naive but not preferred, since q doesn't defend itself from the attack from $\{p\}$.

3 Some Generalizations

In this section we give a series of new results concerning Dung's semantics for simple contrapositive ABFs and some of is useful enhancements.

3.1 The Well-Founded Extension

First, we consider the well-founded semantics for ABFs (recall Definition 5). This semantics has not been considered in [13], and it is useful when there is no unique minimal complete extension.

The existence of a well-founded extension for any simple contrapositive ABF follows from the following claim:[4]

Proposition 2. *Any simple contrapositive ABF has a complete extension.*

Proof. Follows from Proposition 1 and the fact that every stable extension is complete. To see the latter, suppose for a contradiction that Δ is stable, yet some $A \in Ab \setminus \Delta$ is defended by Δ. Since Δ is stable $\Gamma, \Delta \vdash \neg A$. Since Δ defends A, Δ attacks itself, a contradiction to Δ being conflict-free. $\square$

The next example shows that, as in the case of the grounded semantics, the well-founded extension of an assumption-based framework $\mathbf{ABF}$ does not always coincide with $\bigcap \mathsf{MCS}(\mathbf{ABF})$.

Example 3. Let $\mathfrak{L}$ be classical logic (CL), $\Gamma = \emptyset$, and $Ab = \{p, \neg p, s\}$. A corresponding attack diagram is shown in Fig. 1. In this case, we have that $\mathsf{Com}(\mathbf{ABF}) = \{\emptyset, \{p, s\}, \{\neg p, s\}\}$, thus $\mathsf{WF}(\mathbf{ABF}) = \emptyset$. However, $\bigcap \mathsf{MCS}(\mathbf{ABF}) = \{s\}$.

Again (see Proposition 1), the situation in Example 3 can be avoided by requiring that $\mathsf{F} \in Ab$ (Intuitively, this means that any inconsistent set of arguments is attacked by the emptyset, thus any admissible set is defended from it).

---

[4] In the sequel, some proofs will be sketched or omitted altogether due to space restrictions.

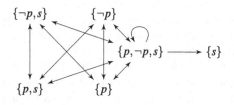

Fig. 1. An attack diagram for Example 3

Proposition 3. *Let* **ABF** $= \langle \mathscr{L}, \Gamma, Ab, \sim \rangle$ *be a simple contrapositive ABF. If* $\mathsf{F} \in Ab$ *then* $\mathsf{WF}(\mathbf{ABF}) = \bigcap \mathsf{MCS}(\mathbf{ABF})$.

Proof. In [13] it is shown that in case that $\mathsf{F} \in Ab$, there exists a unique grounded extension for any ABF. From this it follows that $\bigcup \mathsf{Grd}(\mathbf{ABF}) \subseteq \Delta$ for any $\Delta \in \mathsf{Com}(\mathbf{ABF})$. This implies that $\bigcap \mathsf{Com}(\mathbf{ABF}) = \bigcup \mathsf{Grd}(\mathbf{ABF})$, that is: $\mathsf{WF}(\mathbf{ABF}) = \mathsf{Grd}(\mathbf{ABF})$. □

By Propositions 1 and 3 we thus have:

Corollary 1. *Let* **ABF** $= \langle \mathscr{L}, \Gamma, Ab, \sim \rangle$ *be a simple contrapositive ABF. If* $\mathsf{F} \in Ab$ *then* $\mathsf{WF}(\mathbf{ABF}) = \mathsf{Grd}(\mathbf{ABF})$.

3.2 Lifting the Closure Requirement

According to Definition 5, extensions of an ABF are required to be closed. This is a standard requirement for ABFs (see, e.g., [4,9,18]), In this section we show that the closure condition is not necessary for simple contrapositive ABFs.

Definition 7. *Let* **ABF** $= \langle \mathfrak{L}, \Gamma, Ab, \sim \rangle$ *be an assumption-based framework, a subset* $\Delta \subseteq Ab$ *is* weakly admissible *(in* **ABF***) iff it is conflict-free, and defends every* $\Delta' \subseteq \Delta$. *We say that* Δ *is* weakly complete *(in* **ABF***) iff it is weakly admissible and contains every* $\Delta' \subseteq Ab$ *that it defends.*

Weakly admissibility (weak completeness) is thus admissibility (completeness) without the closure requirement.

Below, we fix a simple contrapositive argumentation framework **ABF** $= \langle \mathfrak{L}, \Gamma, Ab, \sim \rangle$. We show that closure is redundant in the definition of stable, naive and preferred semantics:

Proposition 4. *A set* $\Delta \subseteq Ab$ *is:*

- *stable iff it is conflict-free and attacks every* $\psi \in Ab \setminus \Delta$.
- *naive iff it is maximally conflict-free.*
- *preferred iff it is maximally weakly admissible.*

Concerning the grounded semantics, we note that when $\mathsf{F} \notin Ab$ the closure condition is not superfluous. For instance, when $\Gamma = \{s, s \supset q\}$ and $Ab = \{p, \neg p, q\}$, and classical logic is the base logic, the emptyset is minimally complete in Ab.[5] Yet, the emptyset is not closed, since $\Gamma \vdash q$.

When $\mathsf{F} \in Ab$, the following proposition shows that the grounded extension *is* closed.

Proposition 5. *If* $\mathsf{F} \in Ab$, *a set* $\Delta \subseteq Ab$ *is grounded iff it is minimally weakly complete.*

3.3   Using Disjunctive Attacks

The next generalization that we consider is concerned with the attack relation. Below, we allow disjunctive attacks rather than pointed attacks (Definition 4).

Definition 8. Let $\mathbf{ABF} = \langle \mathfrak{L}, \Gamma, Ab, \sim \rangle$ be a simple contrapositive ABF. We say that a set $\Delta \subseteq Ab$ *attacks* a set $\Theta \subseteq Ab$ if there is a finite subset $\Theta' \subseteq \Theta$ such that $\Gamma, \Delta \vdash \bigvee \neg \Theta'$.

Note 3. When the ABF is not simple (that is, when the contrariness operator is defined by sets of formulas), disjunctive attacks may be defined as follows: We let $\sim \theta' = \{\sim \nu \mid \nu \in \theta'\}$ and say that a set $\Delta \subseteq Ab$ attacks a set $\Theta \subseteq Ab$ if there is a finite subset $\Theta' \subseteq \Theta$ such that $\Gamma, \Delta \vdash \bigvee_{\theta' \in \Theta'} \bigvee_{\sigma' \in \Sigma' \subseteq \sim \theta'} \sigma'$.

Example 4. Let $\mathfrak{L} = \mathsf{CL}$, $\Gamma = \emptyset$, and $Ab = \{p, \neg p, s\}$. A corresponding attack diagram is shown in Fig. 2, where the strict lines represent standard attacks (Definition 4), and the dashed lines represent attacks that are applicable only according to the disjunctive version of attacks (Definition 8).

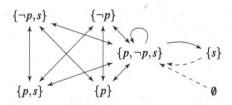

Fig. 2. An attack diagram for Example 4.

Note that the 'contaminating' set $\{p, \neg p, s\}$ attacks the set $\{s\}$. However, when disjunctive attacks are allowed the attacking set $\{p, \neg p, s\}$ is counter-attacked by the emptyset (since $\emptyset \vdash \neg p \vee \neg \neg p$), thus $\{s\}$ is defended by $\emptyset$ (which is not the case when only 'standard' attacks are allowed, cf. Example 3).

---

[5] In particular, the emptyset does not defend q from the attack $p, \neg p \vdash \neg q$.

In what follows we again fix some simple contrapositive ABF, this time with disjunctive attacks as in Definition 8. We further assume that the base logic $\mathfrak{L}$ respects the following de Morgan rules:

$$\text{de Morgan I: } \bigvee \neg \Delta \vdash \neg \bigwedge \Delta, \quad \text{de Morgan II: } \neg \bigwedge \Delta \vdash \bigvee \neg \Delta. \quad (1)$$

One clear benefit of using disjunctive attacks in this setting is that the inconsistency problems of argumentation-based extensions, first discussed in [7], are avoided. In that paper it was shown that in the framework of *deductive argumentation*, the use of preferred semantics in combination with disjunctive attacks might give rise to admissible (and thus preferred) extensions that contain arguments with mutually inconsistent conclusions. As shown next, the formalism of simple contrapositive ABFs provides a solution to this long-standing problem of finding a way to do consistent deductive argumentation using disjunctive attacks.

Proposition 6. *Let $\mathfrak{L}$ be a logic in which de Morgan's rules in (1) are satisfied, and let $\mathbf{ABF} = \langle \mathfrak{L}, \Gamma, Ab, \sim \rangle$ be a simple contrapositive ABF with disjunctive attacks. If $\Delta \subseteq Ab$ is conflict-free then there are no $\phi_1, \ldots, \phi_n \in \Delta$ such that $\Gamma, \Delta \vdash \neg \bigwedge_{i=1}^{n} \phi_i$.*

Proof. Suppose for a contradiction that $\Delta \subseteq Ab$ is conflict-free yet there are some $\phi_1, \ldots, \phi_n \in \Delta$ s.t. $\Gamma, \Delta \vdash \neg \bigwedge_{i=1}^{n} \phi_i$. By de Morgan II, $\Gamma, \Delta \vdash \bigvee \neg \{\phi_1, \ldots, \phi_n\}$. But then Δ attacks itself, a contradiction to the assumption that it is conflict-free. $\square$

Another benefit of using disjunctive attacks is that the notion of defense in Definition 5 can be independent of closed sets (see also Sect. 3.1). Indeed, the following definition is the same as Definition 5, but without any reference to closed sets.

Definition 9. *We say that Δ purely defends $\Delta' \subseteq Ab$ iff for every Θ that attacks Δ' there is some $\Delta'' \subseteq \Delta$ that attacks Θ.*

Proposition 7. *When disjunctive attacks are used, the notions of defense and pure defense coincide.*

Note 4. To see that the condition of having disjunctive attacks is indeed necessary for Proposition 7, consider again Example 4. As indicated in that example, when only standard attacks are used, $\{s\}$ cannot be purely defended from the attacking set $\{p, \neg p\}$. On the other hand, $\{s\}$ *is* defended according to Definition 5, simply because any attacker of $\{s\}$ not containing F is not closed (e.g., $\{p, \neg p\}$ is not closed since $\{p, \neg p\} \vdash F$).[6]

The main results of this section is that, again, in this case: (a) preferred and stable semantics are reducible to naive semantics, (b) the correspondence to

---

[6] This is exactly the reason why the restriction to closed sets is imposed when standard attacks are used, while for disjunctive attacks this is not necessary.

reasoning with maximally consistent subsets is preserved, and (c) the grounded extension is well-behaved for disjunctive attacks, even without requiring that $F \in Ab$.

To show these results we first indicate that when switching to the more generalized (disjunctive) attacks, the closure requirement in the definitions of naive, preferred, and stable extensions (Definition 5) remains redundant. Namely:

Proposition 8. *For a set $\Delta \subseteq Ab$, we have:*

1. Δ *is stable iff it is conflict-free in* **ABF** *and attacks every $\psi \in Ab \setminus \Delta$.*
2. Δ *is naive iff it is maximally conflict-free in* **ABF***.*
3. Δ *is preferred iff it is maximally weakly admissible in* **ABF***.*

Now we can show that also when disjunctive attacks are incorporated in simple contrapositive ABFs, preferred and stable semantics collapse to naive semantics and are related to maximally consistent subsets.

Theorem 1. *Let $\mathfrak{L}$ be a logic in which de Morgan's rules in (1) hold, and let* **ABF** $= \langle \mathfrak{L}, \Gamma, Ab, \sim \rangle$ *be a simple contrapositive ABF with disjunctive attacks. Then:*
$$\mathsf{Naive}(\mathbf{ABF}) = \mathsf{Prf}(\mathbf{ABF}) = \mathsf{Stb}(\mathbf{ABF}) = \mathsf{MCS}(\mathbf{ABF}).$$

Proof (outline). We show the following fragment of the theorem:

Proposition 9. Δ *is naive in* **ABF** *iff it is in* $\mathsf{MCS}(\mathbf{ABF})$*.*

Proof. [$\Rightarrow$]: Let Δ be a naive set in Ab. Suppose for a contradiction that $\Gamma, \Delta \vdash F$. By explosion, this means that $\Gamma, \Delta \vdash \bigvee \neg \Delta'$ for any $\Delta' \subseteq \Delta$, contradicting the conflict-freeness of Δ. Thus Δ is consistent. To see that Δ is maximally consistent in **ABF**, note that since Δ is maximally conflict-free, for every proper superset Δ' of Δ there is some $\Theta \subseteq \Delta'$ such that $\Gamma, \Delta' \vdash \bigvee \neg \Theta$. By de Morgan I and transitivity, then, $\Gamma, \Delta' \vdash \neg \bigwedge \Theta$. On the other hand, $\Theta \subseteq \Delta'$, and so $\Gamma, \Delta' \vdash \bigwedge \Theta$. This implies that $\Gamma, \Delta' \vdash F$. Thus, Δ is maximally consistent in **ABF**.
[$\Leftarrow$]: Let $\Delta \in \mathsf{MCS}(\mathbf{ABF})$ and suppose for a contradiction that $\Gamma, \Delta \vdash \bigvee \neg \Delta'$ for some $\Delta' \subseteq \Delta$. Again, by de Morgan I and transitivity we get on one hand that $\Gamma, \Delta \vdash \neg \bigwedge \Delta'$, and since $\Delta' \subseteq \Delta$, by reflexivity we get on the other hand that $\Gamma, \Delta \vdash \bigwedge \Delta'$, which together contradict the assumption that $\Gamma, \Delta \nvdash F$. Thus Δ is conflict-free. To see that Δ is maximally conflict-free, suppose for a contradiction that $\Delta \cup \{\phi\}$ is conflict-free for some $\phi \in Ab \setminus \Delta$. Since Δ is maximally consistent, $\Gamma, \Delta, \phi \vdash F$, thus by explosion $\Gamma, \Delta, \phi \vdash \neg \delta$ for every $\delta \in \Delta \cup \{\phi\}$, contradicting the assumption that $\Delta \cup \{\phi\}$ is conflict-free. $\square$

We now turn to the use of disjunctive attacks with the grounded semantics. The next example helps to appreciate the role of the former in such cases.

Example 5. Recall Examples 3 and 4 (together with, respectively, Figs. 1 and 2), in which $\mathfrak{L} = \mathsf{CL}$, $\Gamma = \emptyset$, and $Ab = \{p, \neg p, s\}$. As indicated in these examples, when only standard attacks are allowed, the grounded semantics is the emptyset, while when disjunctive attacks are allowed the grounded semantics is the set $\{s\}$ (which is defended by the emptyset). As s should not be contaminated by the inconsistency about p and $\neg p$, having $\{s\}$ as the grounded extension makes much more sense in this case, and – what is more – it holds that $\mathsf{Grd}(\mathbf{ABF}) = \{\{s\}\} = \{\bigcap \mathsf{MCS}(\mathbf{ABF})\}$ (cf. Theorem 2 below).

In what follows we shall show that the grounded extension is well-behaved for disjunctive attacks, even without requiring that $\mathsf{F} \in Ab$ (cf. Proposition 1). For this, we first consider an algorithm for constructing grounded extensions. As the following example shows, the standard iterative process that starts with non-attacked arguments and propagates through defended arguments (used for simple contrapositive ABF with standard attacks in [13]) needs to be slightly revised when disjunctive attacks are incorporated.

Example 6. Suppose that $\mathfrak{L}$ is a logic which does not satisfy the rule of resolution, and let $Ab = \{p, s, t\}$ and $\Gamma = \{p \supset (\neg s \vee \neg t)\}$. Since resolution is not available, formulas like $p \supset \neg s$ and $p \supset \neg t$ are not derivable from $\Gamma \cup \{t\}$ and $\Gamma \cup \{s\}$ respectively, and therefore neither t nor s is attacked. A process that gathers all the non-attacked defeasible assumptions will then include all the elements in $\{p, t, s\}$ in the result, although the set $\{s, t\}$ is attacked by p.

We therefore slightly generalize the construction of the grounded extension in [13]:

Definition 10. Let $\mathbf{ABF} = \langle \mathfrak{L}, \Gamma, Ab, \sim \rangle$ be an assumption-based framework. A set $\Delta \subseteq Ab$ is a *maximally unattacked set* of $\mathbf{ABF}$ iff it is not attacked by any $\Theta \subseteq Ab$ and any proper superset of Δ is attacked by some $\Theta \subseteq Ab$. We say that $\Delta \subseteq Ab$ is a *maximally defended set* of Δ' if Δ' defends Δ but Δ' does not defend any proper superset of Δ.

Definition 11. Let $\mathbf{ABF} = \langle \mathfrak{L}, \Gamma, Ab, \sim \rangle$ be an ABF. We denote:

$\mathscr{G}_0(\mathbf{ABF}) = \bigcap \{\Delta \subseteq Ab \mid \Delta \text{ is a maximally unattacked set of } \mathbf{ABF}\}$,
$\mathscr{G}_{i+1}(\mathbf{ABF}) = \mathscr{G}_i(\mathbf{ABF}) \cup \bigcap \{\Delta \subseteq Ab \mid \Delta \text{ is a maximally defended set of } \mathscr{G}_i(\mathbf{ABF})\}$,
$\mathscr{G}(\mathbf{ABF}) = \bigcup_{i \geqslant 0} \mathscr{G}_i(\mathbf{ABF})$.

When $\mathbf{ABF}$ is clear from the context we will often drop the reference to it and just write $\mathscr{G}_0$, $\mathscr{G}_i$ and $\mathscr{G}$.

Example 7 (Example 6 continued). In Example 6 we have that $\mathscr{G}_0 = \{p, s\} \cap \{p, t\} = \{p\}$. Since $\{p\}$ defends no other set of assumptions, $\mathscr{G} = \{p\}$.

We now state the adequacy of this definition and the relation of the grounded extension to maximally consistent subsets:

Theorem 2. *Let $\mathfrak{L}$ be a logic in which de Morgan's rules in (1) are satisfied, and let $\mathbf{ABF} = \langle \mathfrak{L}, \Gamma, Ab, \sim \rangle$ be a simple contrapositive assumption-based framework with disjunctive attacks. Then $\mathsf{Grd}(\mathbf{ABF}) = \{\mathscr{G}\} = \bigcap \mathsf{MCS}(\mathbf{ABF})$.*

4   Properties of the Induced Entailments

The results in the previous sections imply some properties of the entailment relations that are induced from ABFs by Dung's semantics. In this section we show a few of them.

Definition 12. For $\mathbf{ABF} = \langle \mathfrak{L}, \Gamma, Ab, \sim \rangle$, Sem $\in$ {Naive, Grd, Prf, Stb} and $\lambda \in$ {$\cup, \cap$}, we denote: $\mathbf{ABF} \mid\!\sim^{\lambda}_{\mathsf{Sem}} \psi$ iff $\psi \in \lambda_{\Delta \in \mathsf{Sem}(\mathbf{ABF})}(Cn_{\vdash}(\Gamma \cup \Delta))$.

Note 5. Unlike standard entailment relations, which are relations between sets of formulas and formulas, the entailments in Definition 12 are relations between ABFs and formulas. This will not cause any confusion in what follows.

In the following, when it holds that $\mathbf{ABF} \mid\!\sim \psi$ for some $\mathbf{ABF} = \langle \mathfrak{L}, \Gamma, Ab, \sim \rangle$, we shall sometimes just write $\Gamma, Ab \mid\!\sim \psi$.[7] Also, in this section we continue to assume that de Morgan's rules in (1) are satisfied in the base logic $\mathfrak{L}$.

4.1   Cumulativity, Preferentiality and Rationality

Theorems 1 and 2 are useful for showing cumulativity and preferentiality in the sense of Kraus, Lehmann and Magidor [14]:

Definition 13. A relation $\mid\!\sim$ between ABFs and formulas (like those in Definition 12) is called *cumulative*, if the following conditions are satisfied:

- *Cautious Reflexivity* (CR): For every $\vdash$-consistent ψ it holds that $\psi \mid\!\sim \psi$
- *Cautious Monotonicity* (CM): If $\Gamma, Ab \mid\!\sim \phi$ and $\Gamma, Ab \mid\!\sim \psi$ then $\Gamma, Ab, \phi \mid\!\sim \psi$
- *Cautious Cut* (CC): If $\Gamma, Ab \mid\!\sim \phi$ and $\Gamma, Ab, \phi \mid\!\sim \psi$ then $\Gamma, Ab \mid\!\sim \psi$
- *Right Weakening* (RW): If $\phi \vdash \psi$ and $\Gamma, Ab \mid\!\sim \phi$ then $\Gamma, Ab \mid\!\sim \psi$
- *Left Logical Equivalence* (LLE): If $\phi \vdash \psi$ and $\psi \vdash \phi$ then $\Gamma, Ab, \phi \mid\!\sim \rho$ iff $\Gamma, Ab, \psi \mid\!\sim \rho$

A cumulative relation is called *preferential*, if it satisfies the following condition:

- *Distribution* (OR): If $\Gamma, Ab, \phi \mid\!\sim \rho$ and $\Gamma, Ab, \psi \mid\!\sim \rho$ then $\Gamma, Ab, \phi \vee \psi \mid\!\sim \rho$.

Theorem 3. *Let $\mathfrak{L}$ be a logic in which de Morgan's rules in (1) hold, and let* $\mathbf{ABF} = \langle \mathscr{L}, \Gamma, Ab, \sim \rangle$ *be a simple contrapositive ABF with disjunctive attacks. Then $\mid\!\sim^{\cap}_{\mathsf{Sem}}$ is preferential for* Sem $\in$ {Naive, Grd, Prf, Stb}, *and $\mid\!\sim^{\cup}_{\mathsf{Sem}}$ is cumulative for* Sem $\in$ {Naive, Prf, Stb}.[8,9]

---

[7] Note that this writing is somewhat ambiguous, since, e.g. when Γ, Ab, ψ are the premises, ψ may be either a strict or a defeasible assumption. This will not cause problems in what follows.

[8] We refer to [13] for an example that shows that $\mid\!\sim^{\cup}_{\mathsf{Sem}}$ is not preferential even for ABFs with standard (non-disjunctive) attacks.

[9] Note that by Theorem 2, $\mid\!\sim^{\cup}_{\mathsf{Grd}} = \mid\!\sim^{\cap}_{\mathsf{Grd}}$, and so $\mid\!\sim^{\cup}_{\mathsf{Grd}}$ is not only cumulative, but also preferential.

Proof (outline). The proof is based on Theorems 1 and 2. Here we show, as an example, the property LLE for $\mathsf{Sem} \in \{\mathsf{Naive}, \mathsf{Prf}, \mathsf{Stb}\}$: Suppose that $\Gamma, Ab \hspace{1pt}\vdash^{\cap}_{\mathsf{Sem}} \psi$. By Theorem 1 we have that $\Gamma, \Delta \vdash \psi$ for every $\Delta \in \mathsf{MCS}(\mathbf{ABF})$. Thus, by cut with $\psi \vdash \phi$, it holds that $\Gamma, \Delta \vdash \phi$ for every $\Delta \in \mathsf{MCS}(\mathbf{ABF})$. By Theorem 1 again, $\Gamma, Ab \hspace{1pt}\vdash^{\cap}_{\mathsf{sem}} \phi$. The converse is dual.   □

We now consider the following more controversial rule from [14], called *Rational Monotonicity* (RM):

$$\text{If } \Gamma, Ab \hspace{1pt}\vdash \phi \text{ and } \Gamma, Ab \hspace{1pt}\not\vdash \neg\psi, \text{ then } \Gamma, Ab, \psi \hspace{1pt}\vdash \phi.$$

The next example shows that RM does not hold for skeptical entailments.

Example 8. [17] Let $\mathbf{ABF} = \langle \mathsf{CL}, \emptyset, Ab, \sim \rangle$ be an assumption-based framework in which $Ab = \{r, p \wedge q \wedge \neg r, (p \wedge r) \supset \neg q, \neg p \wedge q\}$. By the first item of Proposition 1 we may consider $\mathsf{MCS}(\mathbf{ABF}) = \{\{r, (p \wedge r) \supset \neg q, \neg p \wedge q\}, \{p \wedge q \wedge \neg r, (p \wedge r) \supset \neg q\}\}$. Note that none of the two members of $\mathsf{MCS}(\mathbf{ABF})$ implies $\neg p$, while both of them imply q.

Now, let $\mathbf{ABF}' = \langle \mathsf{CL}, \emptyset, Ab \cup \{p\}, \sim \rangle$. We get: $\mathsf{MCS}(\mathbf{ABF}') = \{\{r, (p \wedge r) \supset \neg q, \neg p \wedge q\}, \{p \wedge q \wedge \neg r, (p \wedge r) \supset \neg q, p\}, \{r, p, (p \wedge r) \supset \neg q\}\}$. Since $\{r, p, (p \wedge r) \supset \neg q\} \not\vdash_{\mathsf{CL}} q$, we have $\emptyset, Ab, p \hspace{1pt}\not\vdash^{\cap}_{\mathsf{Sem}} q$ (for every $\mathsf{Sem} \in \{\mathsf{Naive}, \mathsf{Prf}, \mathsf{Stb}\}$). Thus, rational monotonicity does not hold for $\hspace{1pt}\vdash^{\cap}_{\mathsf{Sem}}$.

For the credulous entailments, however, RM does hold:

Proposition 10. *Let $\mathfrak{L}$ be a logic in which de Morgan's rules in (1) hold, and let $\mathbf{ABF} = \langle \mathfrak{L}, \Gamma, Ab, \sim \rangle$ be a simple contrapositive ABF with disjunctive attacks. Then $\hspace{1pt}\vdash^{\cup}_{\mathsf{Sem}}$ satisfies RM for $\mathsf{Sem} \in \{\mathsf{Naive}, \mathsf{Prf}, \mathsf{Stb}\}$.*

4.2 Non-interference

Another property that is carried on to contrapositive ABFs with disjunctive attacks is non-interference [5]. Below, for $\mathbf{ABF}_i = \langle \mathfrak{L}, \Gamma_i, Ab_i, \sim_i \rangle$ $(i = 1, 2)$, we let:
$$\mathbf{ABF}_1 \cup \mathbf{ABF}_2 = \langle \mathfrak{L}, \Gamma_1 \cup \Gamma_2, Ab_1 \cup Ab_2, \sim_1 \cup \sim_2 \rangle.$$

Definition 14. *An entailment $\hspace{1pt}\vdash$ satisfies non-interference, if for every two frameworks $\mathbf{ABF}_1 = \langle \mathfrak{L}, \Gamma_1, Ab_1, \sim_1 \rangle$ and $\mathbf{ABF}_2 = \langle \mathfrak{L}, \Gamma_2, Ab_2, \sim_2 \rangle$ such that no atomic formula appears both in $\Gamma_1 \cup Ab_1$ and in $\Gamma_2 \cup Ab_2$, and where $\Gamma_1 \cup \Gamma_2$ is consistent, it holds that $\mathbf{ABF}_1 \hspace{1pt}\vdash \psi$ iff $\mathbf{ABF}_1 \cup \mathbf{ABF}_2 \hspace{1pt}\vdash \psi$ for every $\mathscr{L}$-formula ψ that mentions only atomic formulas in $\Gamma_1 \cup Ab_1$.*

Proposition 11. *For $\mathsf{Sem} \in \{\mathsf{Naive}, \mathsf{Grd}, \mathsf{Prf}, \mathsf{Stb}\}$, both $\hspace{1pt}\vdash^{\cup}_{\mathsf{Sem}}$ and $\hspace{1pt}\vdash^{\cap}_{\mathsf{Sem}}$ satisfy non-interference with respect to simple contrapositive ABFs with disjunctive attacks.*

Proof. By Theorems 1 and 2, and since $\mathbf{ABF}_1, \mathbf{ABF}_2$ do not have common atomic formulas, $\mathsf{MCS}(\mathbf{ABF}_1 \cup \mathbf{ABF}_2) = \{\Delta_1 \cup \Delta_2 \mid \Delta_1 \in \mathsf{MCS}(\mathbf{ABF}_1), \Delta_2 \in \mathsf{MCS}(\mathbf{ABF}_2)\}$.   □

5   Summary and Conclusion

Assumption-based argumentation is an outstanding method in the context of logical argumentation, which has obvious links to logic programming (see, e.g., [4,6]). In this paper we have considered the main Dung semantics for an extended family of assumption-based argumentation frameworks, based on any contrapositive propositional logic, where the defeasible assumptions are expressed by arbitrary formulas in the language, and attacks may be disjunctive. To the best of our knowledge, apart of the companion paper [13], the semantics of such ABFs have not been studied before.[10] Among the new insights provided in this paper are the following issues:

1. We delineated a class of problems in the application of the well-founded semantics and specified conditions under which these problems can be avoided. Similar problems have been discussed in [8], to which we suggest simple solutions.
2. The relation between well-founded semantics and grounded semantics in simple contapositive ABFs is clarified.
3. For simple contrapositive ABFs the argumentation semantics may be simplified (in comparison to those of [4]) by lifting the closure requirement.[11]
4. Attacks between arguments are extended to disjunctive variations. This assures some desirable properties of the grounded semantics that cannot be guaranteed for standard attacks (see [13]). This extension also provides a solution to the consistency problem of deductive argumentation with disjunctive attacks [7].
5. Relations to other general patterns of non-monotonic reasoning are investigated. In particular:
   - connections to the KLM theory [14] (including rational systems [15]) are studied, and
   - relations to reasoning with maximal consistency [16] that were investigated so far for other forms of logical argumentation (see, e.g., [2,3,7,19]), are now shown also for assumption-based frameworks. Note, also, that while all of the other approaches give rise to an infinite number of arguments even for a finite set Ab of defeasible assumptions, our approach avoids this problem by considering sets of assumptions as nodes in the argumentation graph, whose size is bounded by the size of the power-set of Ab.

---

[10] We note that works such as [12] use similar terminology when referring to attacks among arguments, but the nature of the attacks (disjunctive formulas vs. conjunctive formulas), as well as the context of those works (other structured frameworks), are different.

[11] The fact that a redundant closure condition reduces the computational complexity has been exploited in [10], for the analysis of flat ABFs (i.e., for ABFs in which no assumptions are derivable from other assumptions), in which case the closure assumption is indeed redundant. Our results now establish that for a wide class of non-flat ABFs, the closure condition can be safely dropped.

Future work includes, among others, the incorporation of more expressive languages, involving preferences among arguments, and the introduction of other kinds of contrariness operators.

References

1. Amgoud, L., Besnard, P.: A formal characterization of the outcomes of rule-based argumentation systems. In: Liu, W., Subrahmanian, V.S., Wijsen, J. (eds.) SUM 2013. LNCS (LNAI), vol. 8078, pp. 78–91. Springer, Heidelberg (2013). https://doi.org/10.1007/978-3-642-40381-1_7
2. Amgoud, L., Besnard, P.: Logical limits of abstract argumentation frameworks. J. Appl. Non-class. Log. **23**(3), 229–267 (2013)
3. Arieli, O., Borg, A., Straßer, C.: Reasoning with maximal consistency by argumentative approaches. J. Log. Comput. **28**(7), 1523–1563 (2018)
4. Bondarenko, A., Dung, P.M., Kowalski, R., Toni, F.: An abstract, argumentation-theoretic approach to default reasoning. Artif. Intell. **93**(1), 63–101 (1997)
5. Caminada, M., Carnielli, W., Dunne, P.: Semi-stable semantics. J. Log. Comput. **22**(5), 1207–1254 (2011)
6. Caminada, M., Schulz, C.: On the equivalence between assumption-based argumentation and logic programming. J. Artif. Intell. Res. **60**, 779–825 (2017)
7. Cayrol, C.: On the relation between argumentation and non-monotonic coherence-based entailment. In: Proceedings of the IJCAI 1995, pp. 1443–1448 (1995)
8. Čyras, K., Fan, X., Schulz, C., Toni, F.: Assumption-based argumentation: disputes, explanations, preferences. In: Handbook of Formal Argumentation, pp. 2407–2456 (2018)
9. Čyras, K., Toni, F.: Non-monotonic inference properties for assumption-based argumentation. In: Black, E., Modgil, S., Oren, N. (eds.) TAFA 2015. LNCS (LNAI), vol. 9524, pp. 92–111. Springer, Cham (2015). https://doi.org/10.1007/978-3-319-28460-6_6
10. Dimopoulos, Y., Nebel, B., Toni, F.: On the computational complexity of assumption-based argumentation for default reasoning. Artif. Intell. **141**(1/2), 57–78 (2002)
11. Dung, P.M.: On the acceptability of arguments and its fundamental role in non-monotonic reasoning, logic programming and n-person games. Artif. Intell. **77**, 321–358 (1995)
12. Gabbay, D.M., Gabbay, M.: Theory of disjunctive attacks, part I. Log. J. IGPL **24**(2), 186–218 (2016)
13. Heyninck, J., Arieli, O.: On the semantics of simple contrapositive assumption-based argumentation frameworks. In: Proceedings of the COMMA 2018. Frontiers in Artificial Intelligence and Applications, vol. 305, pp. 9–20. IOS Press (2018)
14. Kraus, S., Lehmann, D., Magidor, M.: Nonmonotonic reasoning, preferential models and cumulative logics. Artif. Intell. **44**(1), 167–207 (1990)
15. Lehmann, D.J., Magidor, M.: What does a conditional knowledge base entail? Artif. Intell. **55**(1), 1–60 (1992)
16. Rescher, N., Manor, R.: On inference from inconsistent premises. Theory Decis. **1**(2), 179–217 (1970)
17. Straßer, C.: Tutorial on nonmonotonic logics. In: Nat@Logic Workshop (2015)
18. Toni, F.: Assumption-based argumentation for epistemic and practical reasoning. Comput. Model. Law Lang. Dialogues Games Ontol. **4884**, 185–202 (2008)
19. Vesic, S.: Identifying the class of maxi-consistent operators in argumentation. J. Artif. Intell. Res. **47**, 71–93 (2013)

Argumentation-Based Explanations for Answer Sets Using ADF

Lena Rolf[1] (iD), Gabriele Kern-Isberner[1] (iD), and Gerhard Brewka[2]([⊠]) (iD)

[1] TU Dortmund, Dortmund, Germany
[2] Leipzig University, Leipzig, Germany
brewka@informatik.uni-leipzig.de

Abstract. This paper presents so-called *asl-explanation graphs* for answer set programming based on a translation of extended logic programs to abstract dialectical frameworks (ADF). The graphs show how a literal can be derived from the program, and they evaluate in an argumentative way why necessary assumptions about literals not contained in an answer set hold. With the set of all asl-explanation graphs for a literal and an answer set, it is possible to explain and justify thoroughly why the literal is or is not contained in that answer set. Additionally, we provide a criterion to improve the clarity of explanations by pruning nodes without loss of information and selecting most significant asl-explanation graphs.

Keywords: Answer set programming ·
Abstract dialectical frameworks · Argumentation · Explanation

1 Introduction

Explainable AI is a highly relevant topic of current research, see e.g. the DARPA XAI initiative (www.darpa.mil/program/explainable-artificial-intelligence). In this paper we focus on explanations in answer set programming (ASP). ASP has been applied to various problems of academic research and industry (cf. [4]). An example for the use in industry is the generation of teams of employees for the seaport of Gioia Tauro [7]. The utilization of ASP for decision support is examined for a lot of additional fields, e.g. physician-advisory systems [3] or logistics [13], in which ASP-based systems support users that are not familiar with logic programming. Because logic programs are nonmonotonic, it is difficult to retrace the results of a solver, i.e. even ASP-knowledgeable persons can sometimes hardly reconstruct why a literal is contained in an answer set. To improve a user's acceptance of suggestions by ASP-based decision support systems, it is helpful to explain why the suggested decision is chosen and alternative solutions, possibly expected by the user, are not.

This research has been supported by DFG (Research Unit 1513 and BR 1817/7-2).

M. Balduccini et al. (Eds.): LPNMR 2019, LNAI 11481, pp. 89–102, 2019.
https://doi.org/10.1007/978-3-030-20528-7_8

To provide helpful explanations, in this paper we focus on answering the question why a literal is or is not in a given answer set with abstract dialectical frameworks (ADFs), a generalization of Dung argumentation frameworks that allows for flexible modelling (cf. [1]). We develop a translation from extended logic programs with constraints to ADFs and show that there is a 1-to-1 relation between answer sets and stable models of the ADF. The transformation is used to construct argumentative *answer set literal-explanation (asl-explanation) graphs* based on the characterization of stable models by Sylwia Polberg in [10]. Every asl-explanation graph for a literal in an answer set contains a possible derivation of the literal based on the program and an explanation for why this derivation is not restrained. Moreover, for a literal not present in an answer set, asl-explanation graphs reveal why its derivation is inhibited. The set of all asl-explanation graphs can thus be used to explain why a literal is (not) contained in the given answer set. Additionally, we propose a criterion based on specificity to reduce the size and number of explanations. The main contributions of this paper which is based on [12] are:

- Translation from extended logic programs with constraints to ADF
- Definition of asl-explanation graphs based on positive dependency evaluations [10]
- Construction of asl-explanations from asl-explanation graphs

The rest of the paper is organized as follows: Sects. 2 and 3 contain background information on ASP and ADFs and an overview over related work. The translation from logic programs to ADFs and the relation between answer sets and stable models are described in Sect. 4. Based on that, the construction of asl-explanations and the reducing criterion are described in Sect. 5. Section 6 concludes and points out future work.

2   Preliminaries on ASP and ADF

Answer Set Programming. A *literal* L is an atom A or a strictly-negated atom $\neg A$ where A is an atomic formula of propositional logic. An *extended logic program* P is a set of rules of the form $H \leftarrow B_1, \ldots, B_n, not\, B_{n+1}, \ldots, not\, B_{n+m}$. with $m, n \geq 0$ where $H, \ldots, B_1, \ldots, B_{n+m}$ are literals and $B_{n+1}, \ldots, B_{n+m}$ *Negation-as-Failure (NAF)* literals. $Lit(P)$ denotes the set of all literals in P. For a rule r, the set $\{H\}$ is denoted by $head(r)$, the sets $\{B_1, \ldots, B_n\}$ resp. $\{B_{n+1}, \ldots, B_{n+m}\}$ are denoted with $body^+(r)$ resp. $body^-(r)$. Rules with $n + m = 0$ are called *facts* and denoted with H for short, rules with $head(r) = \emptyset$ are called *constraints*. For the remainder of this paper, *id* is a bijective mapping that maps a rule of P to an identifier. If not stated otherwise, the function maps every rule $r \in P$ to an identifier of $\{r_1, \ldots, r_{|P|}\}$ according to its appearance in P. As defined in [6], the *reduct* of P w.r.t. $S \subseteq Lit(P)$ is obtained from P by (1) deleting every rule $H \leftarrow B_1, \ldots, B_n, not\, B_{n+1}, \ldots, not\, B_{n+m}. \in P$ with $\{B_{n+1}, \ldots, B_{n+m}\} \cap S \neq \emptyset$ and (2) deleting all NAF literals in the remaining rules. A set $S \subseteq Lit(P)$ is an *answer set* of P iff S is the smallest subset of $Lit(P)$ that does not contain any complementary literals $A, \neg A$ so that $\{B_1, \ldots, B_n\} \subseteq S \Rightarrow \{H\} \cap S \neq \emptyset$ holds for every rule $H \leftarrow B_1, \ldots, B_n. \in P^S$

Abstract Dialectical Frameworks. According to [2], an *Abstract Dialectical Framework (ADF)* is a tuple $D = (S, L, C)$ with a set of statements S, a set of links $L \subseteq S \times S$ and a set of acceptance conditions C for statements of S. In this paper, an acceptance condition for a statement $s \in S$ is given as a propositional formula ϕ_s on the parents of s, i.e. the statements with direct link to s. For the rest of the paper, $\phi_s(S')$ for a set $S' \subseteq S$ denotes the formula that can be obtained from ϕ_s by replacing every occurrence of a statement s' with $\top$ (tautology) if $s' \in S'$ and with $\bot$ (contradiction) otherwise. As L is implicitly contained in C, it is not always specified explicitly in the following. $M \subseteq S$ is a *model* of D if $\phi_m(M) \equiv \top \Leftrightarrow m \in M$ holds. M is the *grounded model* of D if it is the least fixpoint of $\Gamma_D(A, R) = (acc(A, R), reb(A, R))$ for $A, R \subseteq S$ with

$$acc(A, R) = \{r \in S \mid \forall S', A \subseteq S' \subseteq (S \setminus R) : \phi_r(S') \equiv \top\}, \quad (1)$$
$$reb(A, R) = \{r \in S \mid \forall S', A \subseteq S' \subseteq (S \setminus R) : \phi_r(S') \equiv \bot\}. \quad (2)$$

M is a *stable model* of D if M is a model of D and the grounded model of the *reduct* D^M of D w.r.t. M with $D^M = (M, L \cap (M \times M), C^M)$ and $C^M = \{\phi_s[p/\bot : p \notin M] \mid s \in M\}$ where every occurrence of a statement $p \notin M$ in each formula ϕ_s is replaced by $\bot$.

3   Related Work

The approach described in this paper is related to the debugging of ASP programs (e.g. [8,9]) although these approaches reconstruct the computation of answer sets and aim at locating the source of unexpected behavior by a developer. Other related approaches in examining the characteristics of a logic program and understanding its results are based on graph representation of the programs. The approach in [11] also uses graphs to compute *offline-justifications* that illustrate how a literal depends on literals of the answer set for logic programs without strict negation. The Argument-Based Answer Set Justification in [14] and the different justifications in [15] use argumentation to explain why a literal is (not) in an answer set. Both papers use a translation from ASP to an ASPIC+ resp. assumption-based argumentation framework and construct justifications based on the arguments of a stable extension and relations between arguments. In [15], different labels indicate whether literals are facts or NAF-literals and if they are contained in the underlying stable extension. The approaches in [11,14,15] have something in common with the approach presented in this paper as they show different relations between literals, but there are important differences: The graphs constructed in [11] mainly show recursively how a literal can be derived from the rules of a program and which literals must not be in the answer set. The papers [14] and [15] use argumentation frameworks different from ADF for the translations and provide a different relation between answer sets and stable extensions. All three papers do not consider strict negation and constraints explicitly. Similar to the asl-explanation graphs in this paper, the justifications in [14] and [15] do not consider every literal in a derivation, but they do not give any criteria to compare justifications, or to reduce their size reasonably to improve clarity. The criterion presented in this paper is related to the notion of specificity used in *Defeasible Logic Programming* that is based on the sets of facts and defeasible rules in an argument (cf. [5]) while the specificity defined in this paper takes facts and default negated literals into account.

4   Translations and Relations Between ASP and ADFs

In this section, a translation from a logic program to a corresponding ADF is presented and it is shown that answer sets of the program correspond exactly to the stable models of the ADF. To be able to distinguish strict negation for literals in programs from negation in propositional formulas as used in ADFs, a mapping $^+$ is used that maps a literal to a corresponding statement s.t. an atom is mapped to itself and a strictly-negated atom $\neg A$ to $\overline{A}$ resp. a set of literals $\mathbf{L}$ to $\{L^+ \mid L \in \mathbf{L}\}$.

The statement set of an ADF corresponding to a logic program P contains the identifier of all rules of P, a statement for each literal in $Lit(P)$ and a statement $cmp(A)$ for every pair of complementary literals $A, \neg A \in Lit(P)$. Statements of the form $cmp(A)$ serve the purpose that no model of the ADF contains statements for complementary literals.

Definition 1 (Translation for extended logic programs). *Let P be an extended logic program and $Lit_C(P)$ resp. $Lit_R(P)$ sets of all identifiers of constraints resp. rules with non-empty rule-head. Then $ADF(P) = (S, C)$ is the ADF corresponding to P with:*

$$S = \{L^+ \mid L \in Lit(P)\} \cup \{cmp(A) \mid A, \neg A \in Lit(P)\} \cup Lit_C(P) \cup Lit_R(P)$$

$$C = \{\phi_{id(r)} = B_1^+ \wedge \cdots \wedge B_n^+ \wedge \neg B_{n+1}^+ \wedge \cdots \wedge \neg B_{n+m}^+ \mid$$
$$r = H \leftarrow B_1, \ldots, B_n, not\, B_{n+1}, \ldots, not\, B_{n+m}. \in P\}$$
$$\cup \{\phi_{id(c)} = \neg id(c) \wedge B_1^+ \wedge \ldots \wedge B_n^+ \wedge \neg B_{n+1}^+ \wedge \ldots \wedge \neg B_{n+m}^+ \mid$$
$$c = \leftarrow B_1, \ldots, B_n, not\, B_{n+1}, \ldots, not\, B_{n+m}. \in P\}$$
$$\cup \{\phi_{H^+} = \bigvee\nolimits_{\{H\}=head(r), r \in P} id(r) \mid H \in Lit(P)\}$$
$$\cup \{\phi_{cmp(A)} = \neg cmp(A) \wedge A \wedge \overline{A} \mid A, \neg A \in Lit(P)\}$$

We illustrate the construction of $ADF(P)$ in the following example.

Example 1. Let P be the logic program containing exactly the following rules associated with their rule identifiers:

$r_1 :\ bike \leftarrow not\, hurt, not\, \neg bike.$ $r_2 :\ \neg bike \leftarrow far, exhausting.$

$r_3 :\ \neg bike \leftarrow far, not\, \neg steep, not\, ebike.$ $r_4 :\ \neg bike \leftarrow heat, badWeather.$

$r_5 :\ car \leftarrow not\, bike, not\, \neg car.$ $r_6 :\ \neg car \leftarrow broke, not\, children.$

$r_7 :\ exhausting \leftarrow not\, \neg steep.$ $r_8 :\ badWeather \leftarrow winter.$

$r_9 :\ badWeather \leftarrow rainy, not\, warm.$ $r_{10} :\ hurried \leftarrow not\, holidays.$

$r_{11} :\ winter \leftarrow not\, \neg winter.$ $r_{12} :\ \neg winter \leftarrow not\, winter.$

$r_{13} :\ \leftarrow heat, winter.$

$r_{14} :\ warm.\ r_{15} :\ far.\ r_{16} :\ ebike.\ r_{17} :\ \neg steep.\ r_{18} :\ heat.\ r_{19} :\ broke.\ r_{20} :\ rainy.$

The ADF corresponding to P is given below by the set of acceptance conditions of all statements.

$$\phi_{r_1} = \neg hurt \wedge \neg\overline{bike} \qquad \phi_{r_2} = far \wedge exhausting \quad \phi_{r_3} = far \wedge \neg\overline{steep} \wedge \neg ebike$$
$$\phi_{r_4} = heat \wedge badWeather \qquad \phi_{r_5} = \neg bike \wedge \neg\overline{car} \qquad \phi_{r_6} = broke \wedge \neg children$$
$$\phi_{r_7} = \neg\overline{steep} \qquad\qquad\qquad \phi_{r_8} = winter \qquad\qquad \phi_{r_9} = rainy \wedge \neg warm$$
$$\phi_{r_{10}} = \neg holidays \qquad\qquad \phi_{r_{11}} = \neg winter \qquad\qquad \phi_{r_{12}} = \neg\overline{winter}$$
$$\phi_{r_{13}} = \neg r_{13} \wedge heat \wedge winter \quad \phi_{r_{14}} = \cdots = \phi_{r_{20}} = \top$$

$$\phi_{badWeather} = r_8 \vee r_9 \quad \phi_{bike} = r_1 \qquad \phi_{\overline{bike}} = r_2 \vee r_3 \vee r_4 \quad \phi_{broke} = r_{19}$$
$$\phi_{car} = r_5 \qquad\qquad \phi_{\overline{car}} = r_6 \qquad \phi_{children} = \bot \qquad\quad \phi_{ebike} = r_{16}$$
$$\phi_{exhausting} = r_7 \qquad \phi_{far} = r_{15} \qquad \phi_{heat} = r_{18} \qquad\quad \phi_{holidays} = \bot$$
$$\phi_{hurried} = r_{10} \qquad\quad \phi_{hurt} = \bot \qquad \phi_{\overline{steep}} = r_{17} \qquad\quad \phi_{rainy} = r_{20}$$
$$\phi_{warm} = r_{14} \qquad\quad \phi_{winter} = r_{11} \quad \phi_{\overline{winter}} = r_{12}$$

$$\phi_{cmp(bike)} = \neg cmp(bike) \wedge bike \wedge \overline{bike} \quad \phi_{cmp(car)} = \neg cmp(car) \wedge car \wedge \overline{car}$$
$$\phi_{cmp(winter)} = \neg cmp(winter) \wedge winter \wedge \overline{winter}$$

Obviously, for an acceptance condition $\phi_{id(r)}$ for a statement $id(r) \in Lit_R(P)$ and every set $M \subseteq Lit(P)$ it must hold that: $\phi_{id(r)}(M^+) \equiv \top \Leftrightarrow body^+(r) \subseteq M$ and $body^-(r) \cap M = \emptyset$. The acceptance condition for r_3 in Example 1, e.g., is satisfied by every set $S' \subseteq S$ with $far \in S'$ and $\{steep, ebike\} \cap S' = \emptyset$. For a constraint c, the cyclic dependency caused by the membership of $\neg id(c)$ in the acceptance condition effects that $id(c) \in S' \Rightarrow \phi_{id(c)}(S') \equiv \bot$ for every statement set $S' \subseteq S$ thus no model M of the ADF can satisfy $body^+(c) \subseteq M$ and $body^-(c) \cap M = \emptyset$. Because of the constraint $c =\leftarrow heat, winter.$ of P in Example 1, the corresponding ADF contains a statement r_{13} with $\phi_{r_{13}} = \neg r_{13} \wedge heat \wedge winter$. For a set $S' \subseteq S$ with $\{heat, winter\} \subseteq S'$, $\phi_{r_{13}}(S') \equiv \top$ holds iff $r_{13} \notin S'$ and $\phi_{r_{13}}(S') \equiv \bot$ holds iff $r_{13} \in S'$. Similarly, no model can contain two statements $A, \overline{A}$ for complementary literals $A, \neg A$.

$ADF(P)$ has been constructed in such a way that membership of a literal in an answer set corresponds to membership of the corresponding statement in a stable model and that answer sets have a 1-to-1 relation to stable models.

Theorem 1. *Let P be an extended logic program, $ADF(P) = (S, C)$ the ADF corresponding to P and $\overline{S} \subseteq S$ the set of statements corresponding to strictly negated literals of $Lit(P)$.*

1. *M is an answer set of P iff $M' = M^+ \cup \{id(r) \in Lit_R(P) \mid body^+(r) \subseteq M, body^-(r) \cap M = \emptyset\}$ is a stable model of $ADF(P)$.*
2. *M' is a stable model of $ADF(P)$ iff $M = \{A \in Lit(P) \mid A \in M' \setminus \overline{S}\} \cup \{\neg A \in Lit(P) \mid \overline{A} \in M' \cap \overline{S}\}$ is an answer set of P.*

Proof sketch. (1) If M is an answer set of P, M' is a model of $ADF(P)$ by construction of the acceptance conditions. It can be shown by induction over the steps of the Γ-operator that M' is the grounded model of $ADF(P)^{M'}$. If M' is a stable model of $ADF(P)$, M' does not contain statements corresponding to complementary literals $A, \neg A \in Lit(P)$ because of the cyclic dependency in $\phi_{cmp(A)}$. It can be shown that M satisfies every rule of P^M and that, if

M were not minimal, the Γ-operator for $ADF(P)^{M'}$ would have accepted a statement $s \in S \setminus M'$. (2) Every stable model of $ADF(P)$ is a subset of $\{l^+ \mid l \in Lit(P)\} \cup \{id(r) \in Lit_R\}$, because statements of the form $cmp(A)$ or $id(c)$ for a constraint c cannot be contained in a model of $ADF(P)$ by construction. The relation thus follows from (1).

Example 2. Program P of Example 1 has one answer set $M = \{warm, far, heat, ebike, broke, rainy, \neg steep, \neg winter, bike, \neg car, hurried\}$ thus the corresponding ADF has the corresponding stable model $M' = \{warm, far, heat, ebike, broke, rainy, \overline{steep}, \overline{winter}, bike, \overline{car}, hurried, r_1, r_6, r_{10}, r_{12}, r_{14}, \ldots, r_{20}\}$. M' contains statements for literals in M and the identifiers of those rules whose bodies are satisfied by M.

5   Construction of Explanations

The construction of asl-explanations is based on the translation presented in Sect. 4 and the characterization of stable models of ADFs in [10]. Useful definitions from [10] are recalled in the following.

Definition 2 (pdf, cf. [10]). *Let $D = (S, C)$ be an ADF, $E \subseteq S$ and $\mathcal{N}$ a fixed symbol. A positive dependency function (pdf) on E is a function pd that maps every $s \in E$ to a tuple (A_s, R_s) so that (1) $A_s \subseteq E, R_s \subseteq S$, (2) $\phi_s(S') \equiv \top$ for all S' with $A_s \subseteq S' \subseteq S \setminus R_s$, and (3) pd(s) is minimal[1] among all tuples (A, R) satisfying (1) and (2); or to the symbol $\mathcal{N}$ if no tuple (A_s, R_s) exists.*

Definition 3 (pde, [10]). *Let $D = (S, C)$ be an ADF, $E \subseteq S$ and pd a pdf on S. An (acyclic) positive dependency evaluation (pde) on E for a statement $e \in E$ is a tuple $((a_0, \ldots, a_n), B)$ with $a_n = e$ and (1) $(a_0, \ldots, a_n)$ is a sequence of distinct elements of E with $\forall a_i \in \{a_0, \ldots, a_n\} : pd(a_i) \neq \mathcal{N}$, (2) $A_i \subseteq \{a_0, \ldots, a_{i-1}\}$ for every $i \in \{1, \ldots, n\}$ with $pd(a_i) = (A_i, R_i)$, $A_0 = \emptyset$ for $pd(a_0) = (A_0, R_0)$, (3) $B = \bigcup_{i=0}^{n} R_i$ with (A_i, R_i) as defined in (2). $(a_0, \ldots, a_n)$ is called* sequence *and B* blocking set *of $((a_0, \ldots, a_n), B)$.*

In this paper, only acyclic pdes are used so a pde is assumed to be acyclic if not stated otherwise. A pde for a statement s can be interpreted as a part of an evaluation of the ADF in which s is accepted whenever every statement of B is rebutted, or in which operator Γ_D inserts the statements of the sequence, including s, in set (1) and the statements of B in set (2) during the recursion.

Definition 4 (Blocking, [10]). *Let $D = (S, C)$ be an ADF, $E \subseteq S$ and $((a_0, \ldots, a_n), B)$ a pde on E for a statement $e \in E$. A set $X \subseteq S$* blocks $((a_0, \ldots, a_n), B)$ *iff $\exists b \in B : b \in X$ or $\exists s \in \{a_0, \ldots, a_n\} : s \notin X$.*

Theorem 2 (cf. [10, Theorem 6.12]). *Let $D = (S, C)$ be an ADF and $E \subseteq S$ a model of D. Then E is a stable model of D iff there exists a pde on E for every $e \in E$ that is not blocked by E.*

---

[1] I.e., there is no other such tuple (A'_s, R'_s) with $A'_s \subseteq A_s$ and $R'_s \subseteq R_s$.

Proposition 1. *Let $D = (S, C)$ be an ADF, $\big((a_0, \ldots, a_n), B\big)$ a pde on S and $M \subseteq S$ a model of D. Then $\{a_0, \ldots, a_n\} \subseteq M$ if $M \cap B = \emptyset$.*

Proof. Let $M \cap B = \emptyset$, and assume $\{a_0, \ldots, a_n\} \not\subseteq M$. Then there is a statement $a_i \in \{a_0, \ldots, a_n\}$ with $a_i \notin M$ and $\{a_0, \ldots, a_{i-1}\} \subseteq M$. Then $\phi_{a_i}(S') \equiv \top$ holds for every $\{a_0, \ldots, a_{i-1}\} \subseteq S' \subseteq S \setminus B$ by Definition 3. Since $B \cap M = \emptyset$, $\phi_{a_i}(M) \equiv \top$ and that causes a contradiction because M is a model of D.

The characterization of stable models by Theorem 2 can be used to evaluate recursively why a pde is (not) blocked by a set of statements. Because of the relation between a logic program and the corresponding ADF in Theorem 1, the set of evaluations for all pdes for a given statement w.r.t. a stable model provides an explanation for why a literal is (not) in the corresponding answer set. Thus Proposition 1 yields the following helpful corollary.

Corollary 1. *Let P be a logic program, $ADF(P)$ its corresponding ADF, M an answer set of P and M' its corresponding stable model of $ADF(P)$. A literal $l \in Lit(P)$ is in M iff there is a pde for the corresponding statement l^+ on S with blocking set B and $M' \cap B = \emptyset$.*

A *justification tree* represents an evaluation for a statement w.r.t. a stable model by recursively checking the pdes of the statements in the blocking set.

Definition 5 (justification tree). *Let $D = (S, C)$ be an ADF, $M' \subseteq S$ a stable model of D, $s \in S$ a statement and $\mathcal{P}$ the set of pdes on S. A justification tree for s based on $\mathcal{P}$ w.r.t. M' is a marked tree $T = (V, E)$ such that the following conditions hold:*

- *The root node $v \in V$ is marked with*
  - *$label(v) = \big((a_0, \ldots, s), B, +\big)$ with $\big((a_0, \ldots, s), B\big) \in \mathcal{P}$ if $M' \cap B = \emptyset$ or*
  - *$label(v) = \big((a_0, \ldots, s), B, -\big)$ with $\big((a_0, \ldots, s), B\big) \in \mathcal{P}$ if $M' \cap B \neq \emptyset$.*
- *Every node $v \in V$ with $label(v) = \big((a_0, \ldots, a_n), B, +\big)$ has a child node $v' \in V$ with $label(v') = \big((a'_0, \ldots, a'_n), B', -\big)$ for every pde $\big((a'_0, \ldots, a'_n), B'\big) \in \mathcal{P}$ with $a'_n \in B$. v is a leaf iff no such child exists.*
- *Every node $v \in V$ with $label(v) = \big((a_0, \ldots, a_n), B, -\big)$ has exactly one child node $v' \in V$ for an $a'_n \in M' \cap B$ with $label(v') = \big((a'_0, \ldots, a'_n), B', +\big)$ for $\big((a'_0, \ldots, a'_n), B'\big) \in \mathcal{P}$ with $B' \cap M' = \emptyset$.*

T is positive resp. negative if the root node is marked with $+$ resp. $-$. A node $v \in V$ with $label(v) = \big((a_0, \ldots, s), B, l\big)$ is positive if $l = +$ and negative if $l = -$.

For a positive node, i.e., a pde that is not blocked by the stable model, all pdes for possibly blocking statements are evaluated to show that and why every of them is blocked by the stable model. For a negative node, i.e. a pde that is blocked by the stable model, one unblocked pde for one statement of the blocking set is evaluated. Thus there can be different justification trees for the same pde in the root node that represent different "strategies" how to block the not contained statements. Note that, by definition, every subtree of a justification tree is a justification tree.

Lemma 1. *Let $D = (S, C)$ be an ADF, $s \in S$, $\mathcal{P}$ the set of all pdes on S and M' a stable model of D.*

1. *There is a positive justification tree for s based on $\mathcal{P}$ w.r.t. M' iff $s \in M'$.*
2. *There is a negative justification tree for s based on $\mathcal{P}$ w.r.t. M' with root node v and $label(v) = \big((a_0, \ldots, s), B, -\big)$ for every pde $\big((a_0, \ldots, s), B\big) \in \mathcal{P}$ if $s \notin M'$.*

Lemma 1 states that there is a positive justification tree for a statement s iff it is contained in the stable model M' and that there are otherwise negative justification trees that show why every pde for s is blocked by M'. Although justification trees can be used to explain why a literal is (not) in an answer set in principle, they are unsuitable for practical use. The main reason for this is the large number of different pdes for one and the same statement: Definition 3 does not claim minimality of the sequence so that, for an ADF corresponding to a logic program, the set of rule identifiers in a pde need not be minimal w.r.t. set inclusion. Thus, a corresponding derivation may contain superfluous rules.

Definition 6. *Let P be a logic program, $ADF(P) = (S, C)$ its corresponding ADF and pde $= \big((a_0, \ldots, a_n), B\big)$ a pde on a set $S' \subseteq S$ for $s \in S$. pde is*

- *sequence-minimal iff there is no pde for $a_n = s$ with a sequence $(a'_0, \ldots, a'_m = a_n)$ and $\{a'_0, \ldots, a'_m\} \subset \{a_0, \ldots, a_n\}$.*
- *consistent iff (1) there is no $A \in Lit(P)$ with $A, \overline{A} \in \{a_0, \ldots, a_n\}$, and (2) there is no constraint r with $body^-(r) = \emptyset$ s.t. $body^+(r) \subseteq \{a_0, \ldots, a_n\}$.*

If pdes are interpreted as possible derivations of literals, inconsistent pdes are derivations that contain complementary literals or a set of literals that ensures that a constraint body is satisfied, i.e. they require sets of literals that cannot belong to the same answer set. Because of the construction of the acceptance conditions, an inconsistent pde can be blocked by every model of the ADF thus the evaluation of inconsistent pdes does not provide relevant information. For sake of clarity, a pde for a statement s is transformed into its *set representation* that is a tuple consisting of s, the sets of facts resp. rule identifiers in the sequence and the literals in its blocking set. Other literals which are derived by non-factual rules are omitted.

Definition 7 (set representation of a pde). *Let P be a logic program and $ADF(P) = (S, C)$ the corresponding ADF. The* set representation *of a pde $\big((a_0, \ldots, a_n), B\big)$ on S with $\{a_0, \ldots, a_n\} = Seq$ is*

$$\langle a_n, Seq \cap \{x^+ \mid x. \in P\}, B, Seq \cap \{id(r) \mid r \in P\}\rangle$$

Example 3. $p_1 = \big((r_{18}, heat, r_{11}, winter, r_8, badWeather, r_4, \overline{bike}), \{\overline{winter}\}\big)$ is a pde for the statement $\overline{bike}$ corresponding to literal $\neg bike$ of program P in Example 1. Because P contains constraint $r = \leftarrow heat, winter.$ with $body^-(r) = \emptyset$ and $\{winter, heat\} = body^+(r)$, p_1 is inconsistent. The set representation of p_1 is $\langle \overline{bike}, \{heat\}, \{\overline{winter}\}, \{r_{18}, r_{11}, r_8, r_4\}\rangle$. $\big((r_{18}, heat, r_{11}, winter, r_8, r_{20}, rainy, r_9, badWeather, r_4, \overline{bike}), \{\overline{winter}, warm\}\big)$ is not sequence-minimal. The derivation uses r_8 and r_9 with the rule head $badWeather$ so one rule is superfluous.

Definition 8 (asl-explanation graph). *Let P be a logic program, $ADF(P) = (S, C)$ the corresponding ADF, M' a stable model of $ADF(P)$, $l \in Lit(P)$, $\mathcal{P}$ the set of all consistent, sequence-minimal pdes on S and $T = (V, E)$ a positive resp. negative justification tree for l^+ based on $\mathcal{P}$ w.r.t. M' and root node w. Let f be a function that maps a node v with $label(v) = ((a_0, \dots, a_n), B, m)$ to a tuple $(\langle a_n, F, B, R \rangle, m)$ where $\langle a_n, F, B, R \rangle$ is the set representation of $((a_0, \dots, a_n), B)$. A graph $G = (V', E')$ with $V' = \{f(v) \mid v \in V\}$ and $E' = \{(f(v), f(v')) \mid (v, v') \in E\}$ is a positive resp. negative asl-explanation graph for l w.r.t. M'.*

Analogously to justification trees, a node with $m = -$ is called *negative*, and *positive* for $m = +$. For a positive resp. negative node, the outgoing edges are called *attack edges* resp. *defense edges*. $f(w) \in V'$ is called *goal node* of G where w is the root of T. Every positive node of $V' \setminus \{f(w)\}$ is called *defender in G*.

In asl-explanation graphs, only consistent, sequence-minimal pdes are considered by construction. The use of the set representation reduces the number of nodes, because two pdes with equal blocking sets and sequences that contain exactly the same statements, in a possibly different order, are combined to one node, and provide the most important information in the context of ASP. If the sets contain many statements, the visualization of the pde becomes confusing. In that case, for an implementation and use in practice, the number of showed statements can be limited and the full visualization can be restricted. Despite of these modifications, the existence of asl-explanation graphs is guaranteed in a way that is analogous to the existence of justification trees in Lemma 1.

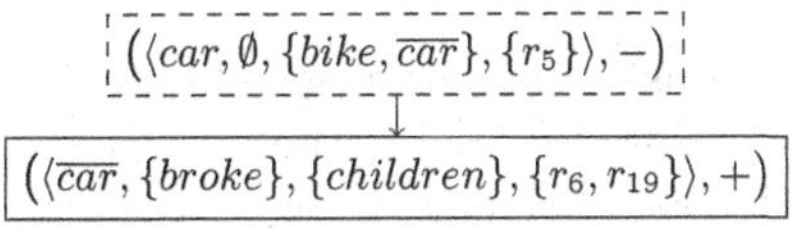

Fig. 1. asl-explanation graph G_1 for *car* (see Example 4), the goal node is surrounded by a dashed line, solid arrows represent defense edges

Example 4. Consider program P and $ADF(P)$ in Example 1 and the stable model M' of $ADF(P)$ (Example 2). Figures 1, 2 and 3 show all asl-explanation graphs G_1, G_2, G_3 for *car* w.r.t. M'. G_2 and G_3 differ only in the additional defending node for the pde for *ebike* that is only contained in G_2.

Definition 9 (asl-explanation). *Let P be a logic program, $ADF(P)$ the corresponding ADF, M an answer set of P, M' its corresponding stable model of $ADF(P)$ and $l \in Lit(P)$.*

- *If $l \in M$, every positive asl-explanation graph for l w.r.t. M' is a positive asl-explanation for l w.r.t. M.*
- *If $l \notin M$, the set of all asl-explanation graphs for l w.r.t. M' is the negative asl-explanation for l w.r.t. M.*

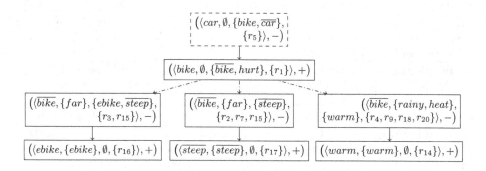

Fig. 2. asl-explanation graph G_2 for *car* (see Example 4), dash-dotted arrows represent attack edges

Example 5. The set of the asl-explanation graphs depicted in Figs. 1, 2 and 3 is a negative asl-explanation for *car* w.r.t. the answer set M in Example 2. For *bike*, there are two positive asl-explanations w.r.t. M that can be obtained from G_2 resp. G_3 in Figs. 2 and 3 by deleting the node $(\langle car, \emptyset, \{bike, \overline{car}\}, \{r_5\}\rangle, -)$ and the corresponding edge and setting $(\langle bike, \emptyset, \{\overline{bike}, hurt\}, \{r_1\}\rangle, +)$ as goal node.

An asl-explanation for a literal with respect to an answer set provides an explanation for why a literal is (not) in the given answer set. A positive asl-explanation for a literal l w.r.t. an answer set M is a positive asl-explanation graph and shows how l can be derived from facts and rules in the goal node and why required NAF-literals can be satisfied with respect to the answer set. A negative asl-explanation for a literal l w.r.t. an answer set M contains an asl-explanation graph with a corresponding goal node for every pde for l. A negative asl-explanation thus provides an explanation for why every possible derivation of l based on P is blocked by M resp. why there is at least one NAF-Literal that is necessary for the derivation but is not satisfied with respect to M. The negative asl-explanation is empty iff there is no pde for l on a set of statements.

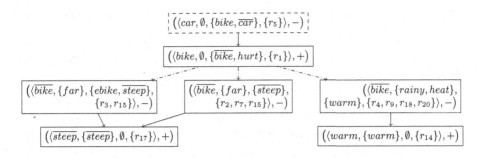

Fig. 3. asl-explanation graph G_3 for car (see Example 4)

Example 5 shows that different positive asl-explanations and the set of asl-explanation graphs in negative asl-explanations can contain similar relations between pdes that don't provide additional information. G_1 of Fig. 1 shows how the derivation in the goal node can be inhibited by $\overline{car}$ resp. $\neg car$. G_2 and G_3 in Figs. 2 and 3 show an alternative "defense-strategy" via $bike$. The comparison of G_2 and G_3 shows: The set of defending nodes in G_3 is a proper subset of the set of defending nodes in G_2, G_3 is thus a more compact way to defend the positive node with $bike$. Both graphs contain nodes $n_1 = (\langle \overline{bike}, \{far\}, \{ebike, \overline{steep}\}, \{r_3, r_{15}\}\rangle, -)$ and $n_2 = (\langle \overline{bike}, \{far\}, \{\overline{steep}\}, \{r_2, r_7, r_{15}\}\rangle, -)$ to evaluate why the corresponding pdes are blocked by the stable model. Intuitively, the evaluation of n_1 seems to be unnecessary because every explanation for why the pde corresponding to n_2 can be blocked is also an explanation for the pde corresponding to n_1. To improve the benefit of asl-explanations in practice w.r.t. these observations, a criterion to compare pdes is defined.

Definition 10 (specificity). *Let $ADF(P) = (S, C)$ be the ADF corresponding to a logic program P, $p = ((a_0, \ldots, a_n, s), B)$ with set representation $\langle s, F, B, R \rangle$ and $p' = ((a'_0, \ldots, a'_m, s), B')$ with set representation $\langle s, F', B', R \rangle$ two pdes for s on S. p is more specific than p' ($p \succ p'$) if (1) $F' \subseteq F$ and $B' \subset B$ or (2) $F' \subset F$ and $B' \subseteq B$ hold.*

Because specificity depends on statements for facts and the blocking set only, pdes with the same set-representation behave identically w.r.t. specificity. Specificity is used in Definition 11 to reduce the size of asl-explanation graphs by the restriction to least resp. most specific pdes for negative resp. positive nodes.

Definition 11 (reduced asl-explanation graph). *Let P be a logic program, $ADF(P)$ its corresponding ADF, M' a stable model of $ADF(P)$, $G = (V, E)$ an asl-explanation graph for $l \in Lit(P)$ w.r.t. M' and the goal node t. Let $G' = (V', E')$ be a subgraph of G with $t \in V'$ such that the following conditions hold:*

1. *For every positive node $(\langle s, F, B, R \rangle, +) \in V'$ and pde p corresponding to $\langle s, F, B, R \rangle$ there is no pde p' that is not blocked by M' s.t. $p' \succ p$.*

2. *For every negative node* $(\langle s, F, B, R \rangle, -) \in V'$ *and pde* p *corresponding to* $\langle s, F, B, R \rangle$ *there is no pde* p' *s.t.* $p \succ p'$.

The subgraph of G' *that contains goal node* t, *all nodes reachable from* t *and associated edges is a* reduced asl-explanation graph for l w.r.t. M'.

Based on reduced asl-explanation graphs, it is possible to build *reduced asl-explanations* that can be defined analogously to Definition 9 but based on the set of reduced asl-explanation graphs only.

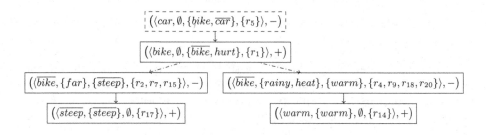

Fig. 4. reduced asl-explanation graph G'_2 for *car* (see Example 6)

Example 6. For program P in Example 1, there are two reduced asl-explanation graphs for *car* w.r.t. the stable model M' (see Example 2). The asl-explanation graph in Fig. 1 is reduced because it does not contain two nodes for the same literal, the second graph is depicted in Fig. 4. The reduced asl-explanation for *car* w.r.t. M thus consists of G_1 and G'_2.

A reduced asl-explanation graph contains no nodes with pdes that are comparable with respect to specificity (disregarding the goal node). Negative nodes in reduced asl-explanation graphs correspond to least specific pdes whose blocking set is minimal w.r.t. set inclusion. According to the definition of specificity and asl-explanation graphs, every node that can be linked to a node corresponding to a least specific pde via a defense edge can also be linked to a node for a more specific pde. The defenders in a reduced asl-explanation graph are thus particularly meaningful as the evaluation of the blocking set of the least specific pde explains why more specific pdes are blocked. Positive nodes in reduced asl-explanation graphs correspond to most specific pdes that are not blocked by the stable model. The set of evaluated outgoing attack edges for a most specific pde is a superset of the evaluated attack edges for nodes with a less specific pde. The evaluation of less specific pdes thus provides no additional information and the size of an asl-explanation graph can be reduced.

Specificity of pdes may also be used as a criterion to filter the set of positive resp. negative asl-explanation graphs w.r.t. their information content by comparing the pdes corresponding to the goal nodes and selecting only the graphs with the most resp. least specific ones. Another criterion to compare asl-explanation graphs for the same literal and answer set could be the sets of defending nodes. An asl-explanation graph with a set of defending nodes that is minimal w.r.t. set inclusion represents a very compact defending strategy. Further details on these two filtering strategies can be found in [12].

Due to the specificity criterion, the number of considered pdes and asl-explanation graphs can be reduced. Thus, for larger programs, the size and number of asl-explanation graphs for a literal do not necessarily increase.

6   Conclusion and Future Work

In this paper we presented asl-explanation graphs as a possibility to compose argumentative explanations for why a literal is or is not contained in a given answer set. A prototypical implementation allows one to compute (reduced) asl-explanations and the visualization of asl-explanation graphs, depending on user input, and is to provide explanations for logistics applications of ASP [13]. In [12], an extension of the translation shown in Sect. 4 is presented that is able to deal with disjunctive rules and cardinality rules, and provides the base for an adapted definition of asl-explanations. Furthermore, it is shown how the translation, particularly the statements for complementary literals and constraints, and (stable) model semantics of ADFs can be used to explain why a given literal set is not an answer set of the program. Directions for future work can be the development of further mechanisms to improve clarity, e.g. for non-ground input programs, or the consideration of other parts of the input language for solvers as conditional literals or optimization statements.

References

1. Brewka, G., Ellmauthaler, S., Strass, H., Wallner, J.P., Woltran, S.: Abstract dialectical frameworks. An overview. IFCoLog J. Log. Their Appl. **4**(8), 2263–2317 (2017)
2. Brewka, G., Strass, H., Ellmauthaler, S., Wallner, J.P., Woltran, S.: Abstract dialectical frameworks revisited. Proc. IJCAI **2013**, 803–809 (2013)
3. Chen, Z.: Automating disease management using answer set programming programming. In: Technical Communications of the 32nd International Conference on Logic Programming, ICLP 2016 TCs, pp. 22:1–22:10. OASICS (2016)
4. Erdem, E., Gelfond, M., Leone, N.: Applications of answer set programming. AI Mag. **37**(3), 53 (2016)
5. García, A.J., Simari, G.R.: Defeasible logic programming: an argumentative approach. Theory Pract. Log. Program. **4**(2), 95–138 (2004)
6. Gelfond, M., Lifschitz, V.: Classical negation in logic programs and disjunctive databases. New Gener. Comput. **9**(3), 365–385 (1991)
7. Grasso, G., Iiritano, S., Leone, N., Lio, V., Ricca, F., Scalise, F.: An ASP-based system for team-building in the Gioia-Tauro seaport. In: Carro, M., Peña, R. (eds.) PADL 2010. LNCS, vol. 5937, pp. 40–42. Springer, Heidelberg (2010). https://doi.org/10.1007/978-3-642-11503-5_5

8. Oetsch, J., Pührer, J., Tompits, H.: Catching the ouroboros: on debugging non-ground answer-set programs. Theory Pract. Log. Program. **10**(4–6), 513–529 (2010)

9. Oetsch, J., Pührer, J., Tompits, H.: Stepping through an answer-set program. In: Delgrande, J.P., Faber, W. (eds.) LPNMR 2011. LNCS (LNAI), vol. 6645, pp. 134–147. Springer, Heidelberg (2011). https://doi.org/10.1007/978-3-642-20895-9_13

10. Polberg, S.: Extension-based semantics of abstract dialectical frameworks. CoRR abs/1405.0406 (2014)

11. Pontelli, E., Son, T.C., El-Khatib, O.: Justifications for logic programs under answer set semantics. Theory Pract. Log. Program. **9**(1), 1–56 (2009)

12. Rolf, L.: Argumentation für Erklärung und Debugging von clingo-ASP-Lösungen (Argumentation for explaining and debugging of Clingo-ASP-solutions), TU Dortmund (2018)

13. Schieweck, S., Kern-Isberner, G., ten Hompel, M.: Various approaches to the application of answer set programming in order-picking systems with intelligent vehicles. In: Proceedings of the 9th International Joint Conference on Computational Intelligence, vol. 1, pp. 25–34 (2017)

14. Schulz, C., Sergot, M., Toni, F.: Argumentation-based answer set justification. In: Working Notes of the 11th International Symposium on Logical Formalizations of Commonsense Reasoning (2013)

15. Schulz, C., Toni, F.: Justifying answer sets using argumentation. Theory Pract. Log. Program. **16**(01), 59–110 (2016)

Foundations and Complexity

Treewidth and Counting Projected Answer Sets

Johannes K. Fichte[1] and Markus Hecher[2(✉)]

[1] TU Dresden, Dresden, Germany
johannes.fichte@tu-dresden.de
[2] TU Wien, Vienna, Austria
hecher@dbai.tuwien.ac.at

Abstract. In this paper, we introduce novel algorithms to solve *projected answer set counting (#PAs)*. #PAs asks to count the number of answer sets with respect to a given set of *projection atoms*, where multiple answer sets that are identical when restricted to the projection atoms count as only one projected answer set. Our algorithms exploit small treewidth of the primal graph of the input instance by dynamic programming (DP).

We establish a new algorithm for head-cycle-free (HCF) programs and lift very recent results from projected model counting to #PAs when the input is restricted to HCF programs. Further, we show how established DP algorithms for tight, normal, and disjunctive answer set programs can be extended to solve #PAs. Our algorithms run in polynomial time while requiring double exponential time in the treewidth for tight, normal, and HCF programs, and triple exponential time for disjunctive programs.

Finally, we take the exponential time hypothesis (ETH) into account and establish lower bounds of bounded treewidth algorithms for #PAs. Under ETH, one cannot significantly improve our obtained worst-case runtimes.

1 Introduction

Answer Set Programming (ASP) [6] is an active research area of artificial intelligence. It provides a logic-based declarative modeling language and problem solving framework for hard computational problems. In ASP, questions are encoded into rules and constraints that form a disjunctive (logic) program over atoms. Solutions to the program are so-called answer sets. Lately, two computational problems of ASP have received increasing attention, namely, #As [12] and #PAs [1]. The problem #As asks to *output the number of answer sets* of a given disjunctive program. When considering computational complexity #As can be classified as #·coNP-complete [12], which is even harder than counting the models of a Boolean formula. A natural abstraction of #As is to consider projected counting where we ask to count the answer sets of a disjunctive

This work extends an abstract [11] explaining only concepts, and a preliminary workshop paper, and has been supported by Austrian Science Fund (FWF): Y698 and DFG: HO 1294/11-1. Hecher is also affiliated with University of Potsdam, Germany.

M. Balduccini et al. (Eds.): LPNMR 2019, LNAI 11481, pp. 105–119, 2019.
https://doi.org/10.1007/978-3-030-20528-7_9

program with respect to a given set of *projection atoms* (#PAs). Particularly, multiple answer sets that are identical when reduced to the projection atoms are considered as only one solution. Intuitively, #PAs is needed to count answer sets without counting functionally independent auxiliary atoms. Under standard assumptions the problem #PAs is complete for the class $\#{\cdot}\Sigma_2 P$. However, if we take all atoms as projected, then #PAs is again #·coNP-complete and if there are no projection atoms then it is simply Σ_2^p-complete. But some fragments of ASP have lower complexity. A prominent example is the class of *head-cycle-free (HCF)* programs [2], which requires the absence of cycles in a certain graph representation of the program. Deciding whether a HCF program has an answer set is NP-complete.

A way to solve computationally hard problems is to employ parameterized algorithmics [7], which exploits certain structural restrictions in a given input instance. Because structural properties of an input instance often allow for algorithms that solve problems in polynomial time in the size of the input and exponential time in a measure of the structure, whereas under standard assumptions an efficient algorithm is not possible if we consider only the size of the input. In this paper, we consider the treewidth of a graph representation associated with the given input program as structural restriction, namely the *treewidth of the primal graph* [18]. Generally speaking, treewidth measures the closeness of a graph to a tree, based on the observation that problems on trees are often easier to solve than on arbitrary graphs.

Our results are as follows: We establish the classical complexity of #PAs and a novel algorithm that solves ASP problems by exploiting treewidth when the input program is restricted to HCF programs in runtime single exponential in the treewidth. We introduce a framework for counting projected answer sets by exploiting treewidth. Therefore, we lift recent results from projected model counting in the domain of Boolean formulas to counting projected answer sets. We establish algorithms that are (i) double exponential in the treewidth if the input is restricted to tight, normal or HCF programs and (ii) triple exponential in the treewidth if we allow disjunctive programs. Using the exponential time hypothesis (ETH), we establish that #PAs *cannot* be solved in time better than double exponential in the treewidth for tight, normal, and HCF programs, and not better than triple exponential for disjunctive programs, respectively.

Related Work. Gebser, Kaufmann and Schaub [14] considered projected enumeration for ASP. Aziz [1] introduced techniques to modify modern solvers to count projected answer sets. Fichte et al. [12] presented algorithms to solve #As for the full standard syntax of modern ASP solvers. Recently, Fichte et al. [13] gave DP algorithms for projected #SAT including lower bounds, c.f., Table 1.

2   Preliminaries

Basics and Combinatorics. For given sequence $\mathbf{s}$ and integer $i > 0$, $\mathbf{s}_{(i)}$ refers to the i-th element of $\mathbf{s}$ and $<_{\mathbf{s}} := \{(\mathbf{s}_{(i)}, \mathbf{s}_{(j)}) \mid 1 \leq i < j \leq |\mathbf{s}|\}$ denotes its *induced ordering.* Given finite sets X_1, X_2, ..., X_n, the generalized *inclusion-exclusion principle* states that $\left|\cup_{j=1}^n X_j\right| = \Sigma_{I \subseteq \{1,...,n\}, I \neq \emptyset}(-1)^{|I|-1} \left|\cap_{i \in I} X_i\right|$.

Computational Complexity. For parameterized complexity we refer to [7] and for counting complexity classes to [8]. Let Σ and Σ' be finite alphabets, $I \in \Sigma^*$ be an *instance* and $\|I\|$ denote its *size*. A *witness function* $\mathcal{W}: \Sigma^* \to 2^{\Sigma'^*}$ maps an instance $I \in \Sigma^*$ to its *witnesses*. A *parameterized counting problem* $L: \Sigma^* \times \mathbb{N} \to \mathbb{N}_0$ is a function that maps a given instance $I \in \Sigma^*$ and an integer $k \in \mathbb{N}$ to the cardinality of its witnesses $|\mathcal{W}(I)|$. Let $\mathcal{C}$ be a decision complexity class, e.g., P. Then, $\# \cdot \mathcal{C}$ denotes the class of all counting problems whose witness function $\mathcal{W}$ satisfies (i) there is a function $f : \mathbb{N}_0 \to \mathbb{N}_0$ such that for every instance $I \in \Sigma^*$ and every $W \in \mathcal{W}(I)$ we have $|W| \leq f(\|I\|)$ and f is computable in time $\mathcal{O}(\|I\|^c)$ for some constant c and (ii) for every instance $I \in \Sigma^*$ decision problem $\mathcal{W}(I)$ is in $\mathcal{C}$.

Answer Set Programming (ASP). We follow standard definitions of propositional disjunctive ASP. For comprehensive foundations, we refer to introductory literature [6]. Let ℓ, m, n be non-negative integers such that $\ell \leq m \leq n$, a_1, ..., a_n be distinct atoms. We refer by *literal* to an atom or the negation thereof. A *program* Π is a finite set of *rules* of the form $a_1 \vee \cdots \vee a_\ell \leftarrow a_{\ell+1}, \ldots, a_m, \neg a_{m+1}, \ldots, \neg a_n$. For a rule r, we let $H_r := \{a_1, \ldots, a_\ell\}$, $B_r^+ := \{a_{\ell+1}, \ldots, a_m\}$, and $B_r^- := \{a_{m+1}, \ldots, a_n\}$. We denote the sets of *atoms* occurring in a rule r or in a program Π by $\text{at}(r) := H_r \cup B_r^+ \cup B_r^-$ and $\text{at}(\Pi) := \cup_{r \in \Pi} \text{at}(r)$. Let Π be a program. A program Π' is a *sub-program* of Π if $\Pi' \subseteq \Pi$. Π is *normal* if $|H_r| \leq 1$ for every $r \in \Pi$. The *positive dependency digraph* D_Π of Π is the directed graph defined on the set of atoms from $\cup_{r \in \Pi} H_r \cup B_r^+$, where for every rule $r \in \Pi$ two atoms $a \in B_r^+$ and $b \in H_r$ are joined by an edge (a, b). A *head-cycle* of D_Π is an $\{a, b\}$-cycle[1] for two distinct atoms a, $b \in H_r$ for some rule $r \in \Pi$. Program Π is *tight* (*head-cycle-free* [2]) if D_Π contains no cycle (head-cycle).

An *interpretation* I is a set of atoms. I *satisfies* a rule r if $(H_r \cup B_r^-) \cap I \neq \emptyset$ or $B_r^+ \setminus I \neq \emptyset$. I is a *model* of Π if it satisfies all rules of Π, in symbols $I \models \Pi$. The *Gelfond-Lifschitz (GL) reduct* of Π under I is the program Π^I obtained from Π by first removing all rules r with $B_r^- \cap I \neq \emptyset$ and then removing all $\neg z$ where $z \in B_r^-$ from the remaining rules r [15]. I is an *answer set* of a program Π if I is a minimal model of Π^I. Deciding whether a disjunctive program has an answer set is Σ_2^P-complete [9]. The problem is called *consistency* (As) of an ASP program. If the input is restricted to normal programs, the complexity drops to NP-complete [3]. A head-cycle-free program Π can be translated into a normal program in polynomial time [2]. The following well-known characterization of answer sets is often invoked when considering normal programs [19]. Given a model I of a normal program Π and an ordering σ of atoms over I. An atom $a \in I$ is *proven* if there is a rule $r \in \Pi$ with $a \in H_r$ where (i) $B_r^+ \subseteq I$, (ii) $b <_\sigma a$ for every $b \in B_r^+$, and (iii) $I \cap B_r^- = \emptyset$ and $I \cap (H_r \setminus \{a\}) = \emptyset$. Then, I is an

---

[1] Let $G = (V, E)$ be a digraph and $W \subseteq V$. Then, a cycle in G is a W-cycle if it contains all vertices from W.

answer set of Π if (i) I is a model of Π, and (ii) every atom $a \in I$ is proven. This characterization vacuously extends to head-cycle-free programs by applying the results of Ben-Eliyahu and Dechter [2]. Given a program Π, we assume in the following that every atom $a \in \text{at}(\Pi)$ occurs in some head of a rule of Π.

Example 1. Consider $\Pi := \{\overbrace{a \vee b \leftarrow}^{r_1}; \overbrace{c \vee e \leftarrow}^{r_2}; \overbrace{d \vee e \leftarrow b}^{r_3}; \overbrace{b \leftarrow e, \neg d}^{r_4}; \overbrace{d \leftarrow \neg b}^{r_5}\}$. It is easy to see that Π is a head-cycle-free program. The set $A = \{b, c, d\}$ is an answer set of Π. Consider the ordering $\sigma = \langle b, c, d \rangle$, from which we can prove atom b by rule r_1, atom c by rule r_2, and atom d by rule r_3. Further answer sets are $B = \{a, c, d\}$, $C = \{b, e\}$, and $D = \{a, d, e\}$. ∎

Counting Projected Answer Sets. An instance is a pair (Π, P), where Π is a program and $P \subseteq \text{at}(\Pi)$ is a set of *projection atoms*. The *projected answer sets count* of Π with respect to P is the number of subsets $I \subseteq P$ such that $I \cup J$ is an answer set of Π for some set $J \subseteq \text{at}(\Pi) \setminus P$. The *counting projected answer sets problem (#PAs)* asks to output the projected answer sets count of Π, i.e., $|\{I \cap P \mid I \in S\}|$ where S is the set of all answer sets of Π. Note that #As is #PAs, where $P = \text{at}(\Pi)$, and that deciding As equals #PAs, where $P = \emptyset$.

Example 2. Consider program Π from Example 1 and its four answer sets $\{a, c, d\}$, $\{b, c, d\}$, $\{b, e\}$, and $\{a, d, e\}$, as well as the set $P := \{d, e\}$ of projection atoms. When we project the answer sets to P, we only have the three answer sets $\{d\}$, $\{e\}$, and $\{d, e\}$, i.e., the projected answer sets count of (Π, P) is 3. ∎

Theorem 1 ($\star^2$). *The problem #PAs is #$\cdot \Sigma_2 P$-complete for disjunctive programs and #$\cdot$NP-complete for head-cycle-free, normal or tight programs.*

Tree Decompositions (TDs). We follow standard terminology on graphs and digraphs. For a tree $T = (N, A, n)$ with root n and a node $t \in N$, we let children(t, T) be the sequence of all nodes t' in arbitrarily but fixed order, which have an edge $(t, t') \in A$. Let $G = (V, E)$ be a graph. A *tree decomposition (TD)* of graph G is a pair $\mathcal{T} = (T, \chi)$, where $T = (N, A, n)$ is a rooted tree, $n \in N$ the root, and χ a mapping that assigns to each node $t \in N$ a set $\chi(t) \subseteq V$, called a *bag*, such that the following conditions hold: (i) $V = \bigcup_{t \in N} \chi(t)$ and $E \subseteq \bigcup_{t \in N} \{\{u, v\} \mid u, v \in \chi(t)\}$; and (ii) for each r, s, t, such that s lies on the path from r to t, we have $\chi(r) \cap \chi(t) \subseteq \chi(s)$. Then, width$(\mathcal{T}) := \max_{t \in N} |\chi(t)| - 1$. The *treewidth* $tw(G)$ of G is the minimum width$(\mathcal{T})$ over all TDs $\mathcal{T}$ of G. For arbitrary but fixed $w \geq 1$, it is feasible in linear time to decide if a graph has treewidth at most w and, if so, to compute a TD of width w [4]. For simplifications *we always use so-called nice TDs*, which can be computed in linear time without increasing the width [5] and are defined as follows. For a node $t \in N$, we say that type(t) is *leaf* if children$(t, T) = \langle \rangle$; *join* if children$(t, T) = \langle t', t'' \rangle$ where $\chi(t) = \chi(t') = \chi(t'') \neq \emptyset$; *int* ("introduce") if children$(t, T) = \langle t' \rangle$, $\chi(t') \subseteq \chi(t)$

---

[2] Proofs marked with "$\star$" are in extended version at: https://tinyurl.com/y6gkrblc.

and $|\chi(t)| = |\chi(t')| + 1$; *rem* ("removal") if children$(t, T) = \langle t' \rangle$, $\chi(t') \supseteq \chi(t)$ and $|\chi(t')| = |\chi(t)| + 1$. If for every node $t \in N$, type$(t) \in \{leaf, join, int, rem\}$, and $\chi(t') = \emptyset$ for root and leaf t', the TD is *nice*.

Example 3. Figure 1 illustrates a graph G_1 and a tree decomposition of G_1 of width 2. By a property of tree decompositions [5], the treewidth of G_1 is 2. ■

3   Dynamic Programming on TDs

In order to use TDs for ASP solving, we need a dedicated graph representation of ASP programs [12]. The *primal graph* G_Π of program Π has the atoms of Π as vertices and an edge $\{a, b\}$ if there exists a rule $r \in \Pi$ and $a, b \in$ at(r).

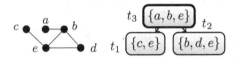

Fig. 1. Graph G_1 and a tree decomposition of G_1.

Example 4. Recall program Π from Example 1 and observe that graph G_1 in Fig. 1 is the primal graph G_Π of Π. ■

Let $\mathcal{T} = (T, \chi)$ be a TD of primal graph G_Π of a program Π. Further, let $T = (N, \cdot, n)$ and $t \in N$. The *bag-program* is defined as $\Pi_t := \{r \mid r \in \Pi, \text{at}(r) \subseteq \chi(t)\}$, the *program below t* as $\Pi_{\leq t} := \{r \mid r \in \Pi_{t'}, t' \in \text{post-order}(T, t)\}$, and the *program strictly below t* as $\Pi_{<t} := \Pi_{\leq t} \setminus \Pi_t$. It holds that $\Pi_{\leq n} = \Pi_{<n} = \Pi$ [12]. Analogously, we define the *atoms below t* by at$_{\leq t} := \cup_{t' \in \text{post-order}(T,t)} \chi(t')$, and the *atoms strictly below t* by at$_{<t} :=$ at$_{\leq t} \setminus \chi(t)$.

Algorithms that decide consistency or solve #As [12] proceed by *dynamic programming (DP)* along the TD (in post-order) where at each node of the tree information is gathered [5] in a table by a (local) *table algorithm* A. More generally, a *table* is a set of rows, where a *row* $\mathbf{u}$ is a sequence of fixed length. Similar as for sequences when addressing the i-th element, for a set U of rows (table) we let $U_{(i)} := \{\mathbf{u}_{(i)} \mid \mathbf{u} \in U\}$. The actual length, content, and meaning of the rows depend on the algorithm A. Since we later traverse the TD repeatedly running different algorithms, we explicitly state A-*row* if rows of this *type* are syntactically used for algorithm A and similar A-*table* for tables. In order to access tables computed at certain nodes after a traversal as well as to provide better readability, we attribute TDs with an additional mapping to store tables. Formally, a *tabled tree decomposition (TTD)* of graph G is a triple $\mathcal{T} = (T, \chi, \tau)$, where (T, χ) is a TD of G and τ maps nodes t of T to tables. If not specified otherwise, we assume that $\tau(t) = \{\}$ for every node t of T. When a TTD has been computed using algorithm A after traversing the TD, we call the decomposition the A-TTD of the given instance. DP for ASP performs the following steps:

Listing 1. Algorithm $DP_{\mathbb{A}}((\Pi, P), \mathcal{T})$: Dynamic programming on TTD $\mathcal{T}$, c.f., [12].

In: Problem instance (Π, P), TTD $\mathcal{T} = (T, \chi, \iota)$ of G_Π such that n is the root
of T, children$(t, T) = \langle t_1, \ldots, t_\ell \rangle$. **Out:** $\mathbb{A}$-TTD (T, χ, o), $\mathbb{A}$-table mapping o.
1 $o \leftarrow$ empty mapping
2 **for** iterate t *in* post-order *(T,n)* **do**
3    $\llcorner o(t) \leftarrow \mathbb{A}(t, \chi(t), \iota(t), (\Pi_t, P), \langle o(t_1), \ldots, o(t_\ell) \rangle)$
4 **return** (T, χ, o)

---

1. Given program Π, compute a tree decomposition of the primal graph P_Π.
2. Run algorithm $DP_{\mathbb{A}}$ (see Listing 1). It takes a TTD $\mathcal{T} = (T, \chi, \iota)$ with $T = (N, \cdot, n)$ and traverses T in post-order[3]. At each node $t \in N$ it computes a new $\mathbb{A}$-table $o(t)$ by executing the algorithm $\mathbb{A}$. Algorithm $\mathbb{A}$ has a "local view" on the computation and can access only t, the atoms in the bag $\chi(t)$, the bag-program Π_t, and $\mathbb{A}$-table $o(t')$ for any child t' of t.[4] Finally, $DP_{\mathbb{A}}$ returns an $\mathbb{A}$-TTD (T, χ, o).
3. Print the result by interpreting table $o(n)$ for root n of T.

Then, the actual computation of algorithm $\mathbb{A}$ is a somewhat technical case distinction of the types type(t) we see when considering node t. Algorithms for counting answer sets of disjunctive programs and its extensions [12] have already been established. Implementations of these algorithms can be useful also for solving [12], but the running time is clearly double exponential time in the treewidth in the worst case. We, however, establish an algorithm ($\mathbb{PHC}$) that is restricted to head-cycle-free programs. The runtime of our algorithm is factorial in the treewidth and therefore faster than previous algorithms. Our constructions are inspired by ideas used in previous DP algorithms. In the following, we first present the table algorithm for deciding whether a head-cycle-free program has an answer set (A_S). In the end, this algorithm outputs a new TTD, which we later reuse to solve the actual counting problem. Note that the TD itself remains the same, but for readability, we keep computed tables and nodes aligned.

Consistency of Head-Cycle-Free Programs. We can use algorithm $DP_{\mathbb{PHC}}$ to decide the consistency problem A_S for head-cycle-free programs and simply specify our new table algorithm ($\mathbb{PHC}$) that "transforms" tables from one node to another. As graph representation we use the primal graph. The idea is to implicitly apply along the TD the characterization of answer sets by Lin and Zhao [19] extended to head-cycle-free programs [2]. To this end, we store in table $o(t)$ at each node t rows of the form $\langle I, \mathcal{P}, \sigma \rangle$. The first position consists of an interpretation I restricted to the bag $\chi(t)$. For a sequence $\mathbf{u}$, we write $\mathcal{I}(\mathbf{u}) := \mathbf{u}_{(1)}$ to address the *interpretation part*. The second position consists of a set $\mathcal{P} \subseteq I$ that represents atoms in I for which we know that they have already been proven. The third position σ is a sequence of the atoms in I such that there is a

---

[3] Post-order(T, n) provides the sequence of nodes for tree T rooted at n.
[4] Note that in Listing 1, $\mathbb{A}$ takes in addition as input set P and table ι_t, used later. Later, P represents the projection atoms and ι_t is a table at t from an earlier traversal.

Listing 2. Table algorithm $\mathbb{PHC}(t, \chi_t, \cdot, (\Pi_t, \cdot), \langle \tau_1, \ldots \rangle)$.

In: Node t, bag χ_t, bag-program Π_t, $\langle \tau_1, \ldots \rangle$ is the sequence of $\mathbb{PHC}$-tables of children of t. **Out:** $\mathbb{PHC}$-table τ_t.

1 **if** type$(t) = leaf$ **then** $\tau_t := \{\langle \emptyset, \emptyset, \langle \rangle \rangle\}$
2 **else if** type$(t) = int$ and $a \in \chi_t$ *is the introduced atom* **then**
3 $\quad \Big| \tau_t := \{\langle J, \mathcal{P} \cup \text{proven}(J, \sigma', \Pi_t), \sigma' \rangle$
$\qquad\qquad\qquad | \langle I, \mathcal{P}, \sigma \rangle \in \tau_1, J \in \{I, I_a^+\}, J \models \Pi_t, \sigma' \in \text{ords}(\sigma, \{a\} \cap J)\}$
4 **else if** type$(t) = rem$ and $a \notin \chi_t$ *is the removed atom* **then**
5 $\quad \Big| \tau_t := \{\langle I_a^-, \mathcal{P}_a^-, \sigma_a^\sim \rangle \mid \langle I, \mathcal{P}, \sigma \rangle \in \tau_1, a \in \mathcal{P} \cup (\{a\} \setminus I)\}$
6 **else if** type$(t) = join$ **then**
7 $\quad \Big| \tau_t := \{\langle I, \mathcal{P}_1 \cup \mathcal{P}_2, \sigma \rangle \mid \langle I, \mathcal{P}_1, \sigma \rangle \in \tau_1, \langle I, \mathcal{P}_2, \sigma \rangle \in \tau_2\}$
8 **return** τ_t

$\sigma_{\sigma_i}^\sim := \langle \sigma_1, \ldots, \sigma_{i-1}, \sigma_{i+1}, \ldots, \sigma_k \rangle$ where $\sigma = \langle \sigma_1, \ldots, \sigma_k \rangle$, $S_e^+ := S \cup \{e\}$, $S_e^- := S \setminus \{e\}$.

super-sequence σ' of σ, which induces an ordering $<_{\sigma'}$. Our table algorithm $\mathbb{PHC}$ stores interpretation parts always restricted to bag $\chi(t)$ and ensures that an interpretation can be extended to a model of sub-program $\Pi_{\leq t}$. More precisely, it guarantees that interpretation I can be extended to a model $I' \supseteq I$ of $\Pi_{\leq t}$ and that the atoms in $I' \setminus I$ (and the atoms in $\mathcal{P} \subseteq I$) have already been *proven*, using some induced ordering $<_{\sigma'}$ where σ is a sub-sequence of σ'. In the end, an interpretation $\mathcal{I}(\mathbf{u})$ of a row $\mathbf{u}$ of the table $o(n)$ at the root n proves that there is a superset $I' \supseteq \mathcal{I}(\mathbf{u})$ that is an answer set of $\Pi = \Pi_{\leq n}$.

Listing 2 presents the algorithm $\mathbb{PHC}$. Intuitively, whenever an atom a is introduced (*int*), we decide whether we include a in the interpretation, determine bag atoms that can be proven in consequence of this decision, and update the sequence σ accordingly. To this end, we define for a given interpretation I and a sequence σ the set $\text{proven}(I, \sigma, \Pi_t) := \bigcup_{r \in \Pi_t, a \in H_r} \{a \mid B_r^+ \subseteq I, I \cap B_r^- = \emptyset, I \cap (H_r \setminus \{a\}) = \emptyset, B_r^+ <_\sigma a\}$ where $B_r^+ <_\sigma a$ holds if $b <_\sigma a$ is true for every $b \in B_r^+$. Moreover, given a sequence $\sigma = \langle \sigma_1, \ldots, \sigma_k \rangle$ and a set A of atoms, we compute the potential sequences involving A. Therefore, we let $\text{ords}(\sigma, A) := \{\sigma \mid A = \emptyset\} \cup \bigcup_{a \in A} \{\langle a, \sigma_1, \ldots, \sigma_k \rangle, \ldots, \langle \sigma_1, \ldots, \sigma_k, a \rangle\}$. When removing (*rem*) an atom a, we only keep those rows where a has been proven (contained in $\mathcal{P}$) and then restrict remaining rows to the bag (not containing a). In case the node is of type *join*, we combine two rows in two different child tables, intuitively, we are enforced to agree on interpretations I and sequences σ. However, concerning individual proofs $\mathcal{P}$, it suffices that an atom is proven in *one* of the rows.

Example 5. Recall program Π from Example 1. Figure 2 depicts a TD $\mathcal{T} = (T, \chi)$ of the primal graph G_1 of Π. Further, the figure illustrates a snippet of tables of the TTD (T, χ, τ), which we obtain when running DP$_{\mathbb{PHC}}$ on program Π and TD $\mathcal{T}$ according to Listing 2. In the following, we briefly discuss some selected rows of those tables. Note that for simplicity and space reasons, we write τ_j instead of $\tau(t_j)$ and identify rows by their node and identifier i in the figure. For example, the row $\mathbf{u}_{13.3} = \langle I_{13.3}, \mathcal{P}_{13.3}, \sigma_{13.3} \rangle \in \tau_{13}$ refers to the third row of table τ_{13} for node t_{13}. Node t_1 is of type *leaf*. Table τ_1 has only one row, which consists of the empty interpretation, empty set of proven atoms, and the empty sequence (Line 1). Node t_2 is of type *int* and introduces atom a. Executing Line 3 results in $\tau_2 = \{\langle\emptyset, \emptyset, \langle\rangle\rangle, \langle\{a\}, \emptyset, \langle a\rangle\rangle\}$. Node t_3 is of type *int* and introduces b. Then, bag-program at node t_3 is $\Pi_{t_3} = \{a \vee b \leftarrow\}$. By construction (Line 3) we ensure that interpretation $I_{3.i}$ is a model of Π_{t_3} for every row $\langle I_{3.i}, \mathcal{P}_{3.i}, \sigma_{3.i}\rangle$ in τ_3. Node t_4 is of type *rem*. Here, we restrict the rows such that they contain only atoms occurring in bag $\chi(t_4) = \{b\}$. To this end, Line 5 takes only rows $\mathbf{u}_{3.i}$ of table τ_3 where atoms in $I_{3.i}$ are also proven, i.e., contained in $\mathcal{P}_{3.i}$. In particular, every row in table τ_4 originates from at least one row in τ_3 that either proves $a \in \mathcal{P}_{3.i}$ or where $a \notin I_{3.i}$. Basic conditions of a TD ensure that once an atom is removed, it will not occur in any bag at an ancestor node. Hence, we also encountered all rules where atom a occurs. Nodes t_5, t_6, t_7, and t_8 are symmetric to nodes t_1, t_2, t_3, and t_4. Nodes t_9 and t_{10} again introduce atoms. Observe that $\mathcal{P}_{10.4} = \{e\}$ since $\sigma_{10.4}$ does not allow to prove b using atom e. However, $\mathcal{P}_{10.5} = \{b, e\}$ as the sequence $\sigma_{10.5}$ allows to prove b. In particular, in row $\mathbf{u}_{10.5}$ atom e is used to derive b. As a result, atom b can be proven, whereas ordering $\sigma_{10.4} = \langle b, e\rangle$ does not serve in proving b. We proceed similar for nodes t_{11} and t_{12}. At node t_{13} we join tables τ_4 and τ_{12} according to Line 7. Finally, $\tau_{14} \neq \emptyset$, i.e., Π has an answer set; joining interpretations I of yellow marked rows of Fig. 2 leads to $\{b, e\}$.   ∎

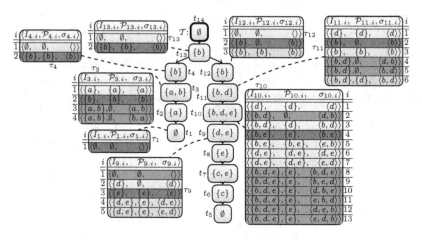

Fig. 2. Selected tables of τ obtained by $\mathsf{DP_{PHC}}$ on TD $\mathcal{T}$.

Next, we provide a notion to reconstruct answer sets from a computed TTD, which allows for computing for a given row its predecessor rows in the corresponding child tables, c.f., [13]. Let Π be a program, $\mathcal{T} = (T, \chi, \tau)$ be an A-TTD of G_Π, and t be a node of T where $\mathrm{children}(t, T) = \langle t_1, \ldots, t_\ell\rangle$. Given a sequence $\mathbf{s} = \langle s_1, \ldots, s_\ell\rangle$, we let $\langle\!\langle \mathbf{s}\rangle\!\rangle := \langle\{s_1\}, \ldots, \{s_\ell\}\rangle$. For a given A-row $\mathbf{u}$, we define the originating A-rows of $\mathbf{u}$ in node t by A-origins$(t, \mathbf{u}) := \{\mathbf{s} \mid \mathbf{s} \in \tau(t_1) \times \cdots \times \tau(t_\ell), \mathbf{u} \in \mathbb{A}(t, \chi(t), \cdot, (\Pi_t, \cdot), \langle\!\langle \mathbf{s}\rangle\!\rangle)\}$. We extend this to an A-table ρ by A-origins$(t, \rho) := \bigcup_{\mathbf{u} \in \rho}$ A-origins$(t, \mathbf{u})$.

Example 6. Consider program Π and $\mathbb{PHC}$-TTD (T, χ, τ) from Example 5. We focus on $\mathbf{u_{1.1}} = \langle \emptyset, \emptyset, \langle \rangle \rangle$ of table τ_1 of leaf t_1. The row $\mathbf{u_{1.1}}$ has no preceding row, since $\mathrm{type}(t_1) = \mathit{leaf}$. Hence, we have $\mathbb{PHC}\text{-origins}(t_1, \mathbf{u_{1.1}}) = \{\langle \rangle\}$. The origins of row $\mathbf{u_{11.1}}$ of table τ_{11} are given by $\mathbb{PHC}\text{-origins}(t_{11}, \mathbf{u_{11.1}})$, which correspond to the preceding rows in table τ_{10} that lead to row $\mathbf{u_{11.1}}$ of table τ_{11} when running algorithm $\mathbb{PHC}$, i.e., $\mathbb{PHC}\text{-origins}(t_{11}, \mathbf{u_{11.1}}) = \{\langle \mathbf{u_{10.1}}\rangle, \langle \mathbf{u_{10.6}}\rangle, \langle \mathbf{u_{10.7}}\rangle\}$. Origins of row $\mathbf{u_{12.2}}$ are given by $\mathbb{PHC}\text{-origins}(t_{12}, \mathbf{u_{12.2}}) = \{\langle \mathbf{u_{11.2}}\rangle, \langle \mathbf{u_{11.6}}\rangle\}$. Note that $\mathbf{u_{11.4}}$ and $\mathbf{u_{11.5}}$ are not among those origins, since d is not proven. Observe that $\mathbb{PHC}\text{-origins}(t_j, \mathbf{u}) = \emptyset$ for any row $\mathbf{u} \notin \tau_j$. For node t_{13} of type join and row $\mathbf{u_{13.2}}$, $\mathbb{PHC}\text{-origins}(t_{13}, \mathbf{u_{13.2}}) = \{\langle \mathbf{u_{4.2}}, \mathbf{u_{12.2}}\rangle, \langle \mathbf{u_{4.2}}, \mathbf{u_{12.3}}\rangle\}$. ∎

Next, we provide statements on correctness and a runtime analysis.

Theorem 2 ($\star$). *Given a head-cycle-free program Π and a TTD $T = (T, \chi, \cdot)$ of G_Π where $T = (N, \cdot, n)$ with root n. Then, $\mathrm{DP}_{\mathbb{PHC}}((\Pi, \cdot), T)$ returns the $\mathbb{PHC}$-TTD (T, χ, τ) such that Π has an answer set if and only if $\langle \emptyset, \emptyset, \langle \rangle \rangle \in \tau(n)$.*

Theorem 3 ($\star$). *Given a head-cycle-free program Π and a TD $T = (T, \chi)$ of G_Π of width k with g nodes. Algorithm $\mathrm{DP}_{\mathbb{PHC}}$ runs in time $\mathcal{O}(3^k \cdot k! \cdot g) = \mathcal{O}(2^{k \cdot \log(k)} \cdot g)$.*

A natural question is whether we can significantly improve this algorithm for fixed k. To this end, we take the *exponential time hypothesis (ETH)* into account [17], which states that there is some real $s > 0$ such that we cannot decide satisfiability of a given 3-CNF formula F in time $2^{s \cdot |F|} \cdot \|F\|^{\mathcal{O}(1)}$.

Proposition 1 ($\star$). *Unless ETH fails, consistency of head-cycle-free, normal or tight program Π cannot be decided in time $2^{o(k)} \cdot \|\Pi\|^{o(k)}$ where $k = tw(G_\Pi)$.*

In the construction above, we store an arbitrary but fixed ordering σ on the involved atoms. We believe that we cannot avoid these orderings in general, since we have to compensate arbitrarily "bad" orderings induced by the decomposition. Hence, we claim that As for head-cycle-free programs is slightly superexponential, rendering our algorithm asymptotically worst-case optimal. Lokshtanov, Marx and Saurabh confirm such an expectation [20] whenever orderings are required.

Conjecture 1. Unless ETH fails, consistency of a head-cycle-free program Π cannot be decided in time $2^{o(k \cdot \log(k))} \cdot \|\Pi\|^{o(k)}$ where $k = tw(G_\Pi)$.

4   Dynamic Programming for #PAs

In this section, we present our DP algorithm[5] $\mathrm{PCNT}_{\mathbb{A}}$, which allows for solving the projected answer set counting problem (#PAs). $\mathrm{PCNT}_{\mathbb{A}}$ is based on an approach of projected counting for Boolean formulas [13] where TDs are traversed multiple times. We show that ideas from that approach can be fruitfully extended to

---

[5] Later we use (among others) $\mathrm{PCNT}_{\mathbb{PHC}}$ where $\mathbb{A} = \mathbb{PHC}$.

Listing 3. Table algorithm $\mathbb{PROJ}(t, \cdot, \nu_t, (\cdot, P), \langle \pi_1, \ldots \rangle)$ for projected counting.

In: Node t, purged table mapping ν_t, projection atoms P, sequence $\langle \pi_1, \ldots \rangle$ of
$\mathbb{PROJ}$-tables of children of t. **Out:** $\mathbb{PROJ}$-table π_t of pairs $\langle \rho, c \rangle$, $\rho \subseteq \nu_t$, $c \in \mathbb{N}$.

1 $\pi_t \leftarrow \{ \langle \rho, \text{ipasc}(t, \rho, \langle \pi_1, \ldots \rangle) \rangle \mid \rho \in \text{sub-buckets}_P(\nu_t) \}$ **return** π_t

---

answer set programming. First, we construct the primal graph G_Π of the input program Π and compute a TD of Π. Then, we traverse the TD a first time by running $\text{DP}_\mathbb{A}$ (Step 2a), which outputs a TTD $\mathcal{T}_{\text{cons}} = (T, \chi, \tau)$, where $T = (N, \cdot, n)$. Afterwards, we traverse $\mathcal{T}_{\text{cons}}$ in pre-order and remove all rows from the tables that cannot be extended to an answer set (*"Purge non-solutions"*). In other words, we keep only rows $\mathbf{u}$ of table $\tau(t)$ at node t, if $\mathbf{u}$ is involved in those rows that are used to construct an answer set of Π, and let the resulting TTD[6] be $\mathcal{T}_{\text{purged}} = (T, \chi, \nu)$. We refer to ν as *purged table mapping*. In Step 2b ($\text{DP}_{\mathbb{PROJ}}$), we traverse $\mathcal{T}_{\text{purged}}$ to count interpretations with respect to the projection atoms and obtain $\mathcal{T}_{\text{proj}} = (T, \chi, \pi)$. From the table $\pi(n)$ at the root n of T, we can then read the projected answer sets count of the input instance. In the following, we only describe the table algorithm $\mathbb{PROJ}$, since the traversal in $\text{DP}_{\mathbb{PROJ}}$ is the same as before. For $\mathbb{PROJ}$, a row at a node t is a pair $\langle \rho, c \rangle \in \pi(t)$, where $\rho \subseteq \nu(t)$ is an $\mathbb{A}$-table and c is a non-negative integer. In fact, integer c stores the number of intersecting solutions (ipasc). However, we aim for the projected answer sets count (pasc), whose computation requires to extend previous definitions [13].

In the remainder, we assume (Π, P) to be an instance of #PAs, (T, χ, τ) to be an $\mathbb{A}$-TTD of G_Π and the mappings τ, ν, and π as used above. Further, let t be a node of T with children$(t, T) = \langle t_1, \ldots, t_\ell \rangle$ and let $\rho \subseteq \nu(t)$. The relation $=_P \subseteq \rho \times \rho$ considers equivalent rows with respect to the projection of its interpretations by $=_P := \{ (\mathbf{u}, \mathbf{v}) \mid \mathbf{u}, \mathbf{v} \in \rho, \mathcal{I}(\mathbf{u}) \cap P = \mathcal{I}(\mathbf{v}) \cap P \}$. Let buckets$_P(\rho)$ be equivalence classes induced by $=_P$ on ρ, i.e., buckets$_P(\rho) := (\rho/=_P) = \{ [\mathbf{u}]_P \mid \mathbf{u} \in \rho \}$, where $[\mathbf{u}]_P = \{ \mathbf{v} \mid \mathbf{v} =_P \mathbf{u}, \mathbf{v} \in \rho \}$. Further, sub-buckets$_P(\rho) := \cup_{S \mid \emptyset \neq S \subseteq \text{buckets}_P(\rho)} \{ S \}$.

Example 7. Consider program Π, set P, TTD (T, χ, τ), and table τ_{10} from Example 2 and Fig. 2. Rows $\mathbf{u}_{10.2}$ and $\mathbf{u}_{10.8}, \ldots, \mathbf{u}_{10.13}$ are removed (highlighted gray) during purging, since they are not involved in any answer set, resulting in ν_{10}. Then, $\mathbf{u}_{10.4} =_P \mathbf{u}_{10.5}$ and $\mathbf{u}_{10.6} =_P \mathbf{u}_{10.7}$. The set $\nu_{10}/=_P$ of equivalence classes of ν_{10} is buckets$_P(\nu_{10}) = \{ \{\mathbf{u}_{10.1}\}, \{\mathbf{u}_{10.3}\}, \{\mathbf{u}_{10.4}, \mathbf{u}_{10.5}\}, \{\mathbf{u}_{10.6}, \mathbf{u}_{10.7}\} \}$.

Later, we require to construct already computed projected counts for tables of children of a given node t. Therefore, we define the *stored* ipasc of a table $\rho \subseteq \nu(t)$ in table $\pi(t)$ by s-ipasc$(\pi(t), \rho) := \Sigma_{\langle \rho, c \rangle \in \pi(t)} c$. We extend this to a sequence $s = \langle \pi(t_1), \ldots, \pi(t_\ell) \rangle$ of tables of length ℓ and a set $O = \{ \langle \rho_1, \ldots, \rho_\ell \rangle, \langle \rho_1', \ldots, \rho_\ell' \rangle, \ldots \}$ of sequences of ℓ tables by s-ipasc$(s, O) = \Pi_{i \in \{1, \ldots, \ell\}}$ s-ipasc$(s_{(i)}, O_{(i)})$. So we select the i-th position of the sequence together with sets of the i-th positions.

Intuitively, when we are at a node t in algorithm $\text{DP}_{\mathbb{PROJ}}$ we have already computed $\pi(t')$ of $\mathcal{T}_{\text{proj}}$ for every node t' below t. Then, we compute the

---

[6] Table $\nu(t)$ contains rows obtained by recursively following origins of $\tau(n)$ for root n.

projected answer sets count of $\rho \subseteq \nu(t)$. Therefore, we apply the inclusion-exclusion principle to the stored projected answer sets count of origins. We define $\text{pasc}(t, \rho, \langle \pi(t_1), \ldots \rangle) := \Sigma_{\emptyset \subsetneq O \subseteq \mathbb{A}\text{-origins}(t,\rho)} \ (-1)^{(|O|-1)} \cdot \text{s-ipasc}(\langle \pi(t_1), \ldots \rangle, O)$. Intuitively, pasc determines the $\mathbb{A}$-origins of table ρ, goes over all subsets of these origins and looks up stored counts (s-ipasc) in $\mathbb{PROJ}$-tables of children t_i of t.

Example 8. Consider again program Π and TD $\mathcal{T}$ from Example 1 and Fig. 2. First, we compute the projected count $\text{pasc}(t_4, \{\mathbf{u_{4.1}}\}, \langle \pi(t_3) \rangle)$ for row $\mathbf{u_{4.1}}$ of table $\nu(t_4)$, where $\pi(t_3) := \{ \langle \{\mathbf{u_{3.1}}\}, 1 \rangle, \langle \{\mathbf{u_{3.2}}\}, 1 \rangle, \langle \{\mathbf{u_{3.1}}, \mathbf{u_{3.2}}\}, 1 \rangle \}$ with $\mathbf{u_{3.1}} = \langle \emptyset, \emptyset, \langle \rangle \rangle$ and $\mathbf{u_{3.2}} = \langle \{a\}, \emptyset, \langle a \rangle \rangle$. Note that t_5 has only the child t_4 and therefore the product in s-ipasc consists of only one factor. Since $\mathbb{PHC}\text{-origins}(t_4, \mathbf{u_{4.1}}) = \{\langle \mathbf{u_{3.1}} \rangle\}$, only the value of s-ipasc for set $\{\langle \mathbf{u_{3.1}} \rangle\}$ is non-zero. Hence, we obtain $\text{pasc}(t_4, \{\mathbf{u_{4.1}}\}, \langle \pi(t_3) \rangle) = 1$. Next, we compute $\text{pasc}(t_4, \{\mathbf{u_{4.1}}, \mathbf{u_{4.2}}\}, \langle \pi(t_3) \rangle)$. Observe that $\mathbb{PHC}\text{-origins}(t_4, \{\mathbf{u_{4.1}}, \mathbf{u_{4.2}}\}) = \{\langle \mathbf{u_{3.1}} \rangle, \langle \mathbf{u_{3.2}} \rangle\}$. We sum up the values of s-ipasc for sets $\{\mathbf{u_{4.1}}\}$ and $\{\mathbf{u_{4.2}}\}$ and subtract the one for set $\{\mathbf{u_{4.1}}, \mathbf{u_{4.2}}\}$. Hence, we obtain $\text{pasc}(t_4, \{\mathbf{u_{4.1}}, \mathbf{u_{4.2}}\}, \langle \pi(t_3) \rangle) = 1+1-1 = 1$. ■

Next, we provide a definition to compute ipasc at a node t for given table $\rho \subseteq \nu(t)$ by computing pasc for children t_i of t using stored ipasc values from tables $\pi(t_i)$, and subtracting and adding ipasc values for subsets $\emptyset \subsetneq \varphi \subsetneq \rho$ accordingly. Formally, $\text{ipasc}(t, \rho, s) := 1$ if $\text{type}(t) = \textit{leaf}$ and otherwise $\text{ipasc}(t, \rho, s) := \big| \text{pasc}(t, \rho, s) + \Sigma_{\emptyset \subsetneq \varphi \subsetneq \rho} (-1)^{|\varphi|} \cdot \text{ipasc}(t, \varphi, s) \big|$ where $s = \langle \pi(t_1), \ldots \rangle$. In other words, if a node is of type $\textit{leaf}$ the ipasc is one, since bags of leaf nodes are empty. Otherwise, we compute the "non-overlapping" count of given table $\rho \subseteq \nu(t)$ with respect to P, by exploiting inclusion-exclusion principle on $\mathbb{A}$-origins of ρ such that we count every projected answer set only once. Then we have to subtract and add ipasc values ("all-overlapping" counts) for strict subsets φ of ρ, accordingly. Finally, Listing 3 presents table algorithm $\mathbb{PROJ}$, which stores $\pi(t)$ consisting of every sub-bucket of given table $\nu(t)$ together with its ipasc.

Example 9. Recall instance (Π, P), TD $\mathcal{T}$, and tables $\tau_1, \ldots, \tau_{14}$ from Examples 2, 5, and Fig. 2. Figure 3 depicts selected tables of $\pi_1, \ldots, \pi_{14}$ obtained after running $\text{DP}_{\mathbb{PROJ}}$ for counting projected answer sets. We assume that row i in table π_t corresponds to $\mathbf{v_{t.i}} = \langle \rho_{t.i}, c_{t.i} \rangle$ where $\rho_{t.i} \subseteq \nu(t)$. Recall that there are rows among different $\mathbb{PHC}$-tables that are removed (highlighted gray in Fig. 2) during purging. By purging we avoid to correct stored counters (backtracking) whenever a row has no "succeeding" row in the parent table. Next, we discuss selected rows obtained by $\text{DP}_{\mathbb{PROJ}}((\Pi, P), (T, \chi, \nu))$. Tables $\pi_1, \ldots, \pi_{14}$ are shown in Fig. 3. Since $\text{type}(t_1) = \textit{leaf}$, we have $\pi_1 = \langle \{\langle \emptyset, \emptyset, \langle \rangle \rangle\}, 1 \rangle$. Intuitively, at t_1 the row $\langle \emptyset, \emptyset, \langle \rangle \rangle$ belongs to 1 bucket. Node t_2 introduces atom a, which results in table $\pi_2 := \{ \langle \{\mathbf{u_{2.1}}\}, 1 \rangle, \langle \{\mathbf{u_{2.2}}\}, 1 \rangle, \langle \{\mathbf{u_{2.1}}, \mathbf{u_{2.2}}\}, 1 \rangle \}$, where $\mathbf{u_{2.1}} = \langle \emptyset, \emptyset, \langle \rangle \rangle$ and $\mathbf{u_{2.2}} = \langle \{a\}, \emptyset, \langle a \rangle \rangle$ (derived similarly to table π_4 as in Example 8). Node t_{10} introduces projection atom e, and node t_{11} removes e. For row $\mathbf{v_{11.1}}$ we compute the count $\text{ipasc}(t_{11}, \{\mathbf{u_{11.1}}\}, \langle \pi_{10} \rangle)$ by means of pasc. Therefore, take for φ the singleton set $\{\mathbf{u_{11.1}}\}$. We simply have $\text{ipasc}(t_{11}, \{\mathbf{u_{11.1}}\}, \langle \pi_{10} \rangle) = $

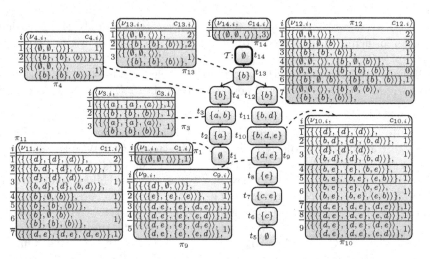

Fig. 3. Selected tables of π obtained by $\mathrm{DP_{PROJ}}$ on TD $\mathcal{T}$ and purged table mapping ν (obtained by purging on τ, c.f, Fig. 2).

$\mathrm{pasc}(t_{11}, \{\mathbf{u_{11.1}}\}, \langle \pi_{10} \rangle)$. To compute $\mathrm{pasc}(t_{11}, \{\mathbf{u_{11.1}}\}, \langle \pi_{10} \rangle)$, we take for O the sets $\{\mathbf{u_{10.1}}\}$, $\{\mathbf{u_{10.6}}\}$, $\{\mathbf{u_{10.7}}\}$, and $\{\mathbf{u_{10.6}}, \mathbf{u_{10.7}}\}$ into account, since all other non-empty subsets of origins of $\mathbf{u_{11.1}}$ in ν_{10} do not occur in π_{10}. Then, we take the sum over the values $\mathrm{s\text{-}ipasc}(\langle \pi_{10} \rangle, \{\mathbf{u_{10.1}}\}) = 1$, $\mathrm{s\text{-}ipasc}(\langle \pi_{10} \rangle, \{\mathbf{u_{10.6}}\}) = 1$, $\mathrm{s\text{-}ipasc}(\langle \pi_{10} \rangle, \{\mathbf{u_{10.7}}\}) = 1$ and subtract $\mathrm{s\text{-}ipasc}(\langle \pi_{10} \rangle, \{\mathbf{u_{10.6}}, \mathbf{u_{10.7}}\}) = 1$. This results in $\mathrm{pasc}(t_{11}, \{\mathbf{u_{11.1}}\}, \langle \pi_{10} \rangle) = c_{10.1} + c_{10.7} + c_{10.8} - c_{10.9} = 2$. We proceed similarly for row $v_{11.2}$, resulting in $c_{11.2} = 1$. Then for row $v_{11.3}$, $\mathrm{ipasc}(t_{11}, \{\mathbf{u_{11.1}}, \mathbf{u_{11.6}}\}, \langle \pi_{10} \rangle) = |\mathrm{pasc}(t_{11}, \{\mathbf{u_{11.1}}, \mathbf{u_{11.6}}\}, \langle \pi_{10} \rangle) - \mathrm{ipasc}(t_{11}, \{\mathbf{u_{11.1}}\}, \langle \pi_{10} \rangle) - \mathrm{ipasc}(t_{11}, \{\mathbf{u_{11.6}}\}, \langle \pi_{10} \rangle)| = |2 - c_{11.1} - c_{11.2}| = |2 - 2 - 1| = |-1| = 1 = c_{11.3}$. Hence, $c_{11.3} = 1$ represents the number of projected answer sets, both rows $\mathbf{u_{11.1}}$ and $\mathbf{u_{11.6}}$ have in common. We then use it for table t_{12}. Node t_{12} removes projection atom d. For node t_{13} where $\mathrm{type}(t_{13}) = join$ one multiplies stored $\mathrm{s\text{-}ipasc}$ values for A-rows in the two children of t_{13} accordingly. In the end, the projected answer sets count of Π is $\mathrm{s\text{-}ipasc}(\langle \pi_{14} \rangle, \mathbf{u_{14.1}}) = 3$. ∎

Next, we present upper bounds on the runtime of $\mathrm{DP_{PROJ}}$. Therefore, let $\gamma(n) \in \mathcal{O}(n \cdot \log n \cdot \log \log n)$ [16] be the runtime for multiplying two n-bit integers.

Theorem 4 ($\star$). $\mathrm{DP_{PROJ}}$ *runs in time* $\mathcal{O}(2^{4m} \cdot g \cdot \gamma(\|\Pi\|))$ *for instance* (Π, P) *and TTD* $\mathcal{T}_{purged} = (T, \chi, \nu)$ *of* G_Π *of width* k *with* g *nodes, where* $m := \max_{t \, in \, T}(|\nu(t)|)$.

Corollary 1 ($\star$). *Given an instance* (Π, P) *of #PAs where* Π *is head-cycle-free and* $k = tw(G_\Pi)$. *Then,* $\mathrm{PCNT_{PHC}}$ *runs in time* $\mathcal{O}(2^{3^{k+1.27} \cdot k!} \cdot \|\Pi\| \cdot \gamma(\|\Pi\|))$.

Theorem 5 (Lower Bound, $\star$). *Under ETH, #PAs cannot be solved in time* $2^{2^{o(k)}} \cdot \|\Pi\|^{o(k)}$ *for* (Π, P) *s.t.* Π *is head-cycle-free, normal or tight,* $k = tw(G_\Pi)$.

Solving #PAs for Disjunctive Programs. We extend our algorithm to projected answer set counting for disjunctive programs. Therefore, we simply use a table algorithm $\mathbb{A} = \mathbb{PRIM}$ for disjunctive ASP as in previous literature [12]. Recall algorithm $\mathrm{PCNT_A}$. First, we heuristically compute a TD of the primal graph. Then, we run $\mathrm{DP_{PRIM}}$ as first traversal resulting in TTD (T, χ, τ). Next, we purge rows of τ, which cannot be extended to an answer set resulting in TTD (T, χ, ν). Finally, we use (T, χ, ν) to compute the projected answer sets count by $\mathrm{DP_{PROJ}}$.

Table 1. Overview of upper and lower bounds using treewidth k of the primal graph of instance Π; bold entries were established in the course of this paper.

Problem	Restriction	Upper Bound	Lower Bound (under ETH)
SAT, #SAT	-	$2^{\mathcal{O}(k)} \cdot poly(\|\Pi\|)$ [21]	$2^{\Omega(k)} \cdot poly(\|\Pi\|)$ [17]
As, #As	tight	$\mathbf{2^{\mathcal{O}(k)} \cdot poly(\|\Pi\|)}$	$2^{\Omega(k)} \cdot poly(\|\Pi\|)$ [17]
As, #As	normal, HCF	$\mathbf{2^{\mathcal{O}(k \cdot \log(k))} \cdot poly(\|\Pi\|)}$	$2^{\Omega(k)} \cdot poly(\|\Pi\|)$ [17]
As, #As	disjunctive	$2^{2^{\mathcal{O}(k)}} \cdot poly(\|\Pi\|)$ [18]	$2^{2^{\Omega(k)}} \cdot poly(\|\Pi\|)$ [12]
Proj. #SAT	-	$2^{2^{\mathcal{O}(k)}} \cdot poly(\|\Pi\|)$ [13]	$2^{2^{\Omega(k)}} \cdot poly(\|\Pi\|)$ [13]
#PAs	tight	$\mathbf{2^{2^{\mathcal{O}(k)}} \cdot poly(\|\Pi\|)}$	$\mathbf{2^{2^{\Omega(k)}} \cdot poly(\|\Pi\|)}$
#PAs	normal, HCF	$\mathbf{2^{2^{\mathcal{O}(k \cdot \log(k))}} \cdot poly(\|\Pi\|)}$	$\mathbf{2^{2^{\Omega(k)}} \cdot poly(\|\Pi\|)}$
#PAs	disjunctive	$\mathbf{2^{2^{2^{\mathcal{O}(k)}}} \cdot poly(\|\Pi\|)}$	$\mathbf{2^{2^{\Omega(k)}} \cdot poly(\|\Pi\|)}$

Lemma 1 ($\star$). $\mathrm{PCNT_{PRIM}}$ *runs in time* $\mathcal{O}(2^{2^{2^{k+3}}} \cdot \|\Pi\| \cdot \gamma(\|\Pi\|))$ *for given instance* (Π, P) *of* #PAs *where* Π *is a disjunctive program, and* $k = tw(G_\Pi)$.

Theorem 6 (Lower Bound, $\star$). #PAs *cannot be solved in time* $2^{2^{2^{o(k)}}} \cdot \|\Pi\|^{o(k)}$ *for given instance* (Π, P), *where* $k = tw(G_\Pi)$, *unless ETH fails.*

In total, we obtain results presented in Table 1. Indeed, there is an increase of complexity when going from As and #As to #PAs (c.f., Theorem 4). For solving As (#As) on tight programs one can again reuse Algorithm $\mathbb{PHC}$ (Listing 2) without the orderings σ, or encode [10] to SAT and use established DP algorithms [21] for SAT (#SAT). Then, #PAs on tight programs can be solved after purging, followed by computing projected answer sets by means of $\mathrm{DP_{PROJ}}$.

5   Conclusions

We introduced novel algorithms to count the projected answer sets (#PAs) of tight, normal, head-cycle-free, and arbitrary disjunctive programs. Our algorithms employ dynamic programming and exploit small treewidth of the primal graph of the input program. More precisely, for disjunctive programs, the runtime is triple exponential in the treewidth and polynomial in the size of the instance, which can not be significantly improved under the exponential time hypothesis. When we restrict the input to tight, normal, and head-cycle-free programs, the runtime drops to double exponential, c.f., Table 1. Our results extend previous work to answer set programming and we believe it is applicable to further hard combinatorial problems, such as quantified Boolean formulas and circumscription [8].

References

1. Aziz, R.A.: Answer set programming: founded bounds and model counting. Ph.D. thesis, The University of Melbourne, September 2015
2. Ben-Eliyahu, R., Dechter, R.: Propositional semantics for disjunctive logic programs. Ann. Math. Artif. Intell. **12**(1), 53–87 (1994)
3. Bidoít, N., Froidevaux, C.: Negation by default and unstratifiable logic programs. TCS **78**(1), 85–112 (1991)
4. Bodlaender, H.L.: A linear-time algorithm for finding tree-decompositions of small treewidth. SIAM J. Comput. **25**(6), 1305–1317 (1996)
5. Bodlaender, H.L., Kloks, T.: Efficient and constructive algorithms for the pathwidth and treewidth of graphs. J. Algorithms **21**(2), 358–402 (1996)
6. Brewka, G., Eiter, T., Truszczyński, M.: Answer set programming at a glance. Commun. ACM **54**(12), 92–103 (2011)
7. Cygan, M., et al.: Parameterized Algorithms. Springer, Heidelberg (2015). https://doi.org/10.1007/978-3-319-21275-3
8. Durand, A., Hermann, M., Kolaitis, P.G.: Subtractive reductions and complete problems for counting complexity classes. TCS **340**(3), 496–513 (2005)
9. Eiter, T., Gottlob, G.: On the computational cost of disjunctive logic programming: propositional case. Ann. Math. Artif. Intell. **15**(3–4), 289–323 (1995)
10. Fages, F.: Consistency of Clark's completion and existence of stable models. Meth. Logic CS **1**(1), 51–60 (1994)
11. Fichte, J.K., Hecher, M.: Exploiting treewidth for counting projected answer sets. In: KR 2018, pp. 639–640. AAAI Press (2018)
12. Fichte, J.K., Hecher, M., Morak, M., Woltran, S.: Answer set solving with bounded treewidth revisited. In: Balduccini, M., Janhunen, T. (eds.) LPNMR 2017. LNCS (LNAI), vol. 10377, pp. 132–145. Springer, Cham (2017). https://doi.org/10.1007/978-3-319-61660-5_13
13. Fichte, J.K., Hecher, M., Morak, M., Woltran, S.: Exploiting treewidth for projected model counting and its limits. In: Beyersdorff, O., Wintersteiger, C.M. (eds.) SAT 2018. LNCS, vol. 10929, pp. 165–184. Springer, Cham (2018). https://doi.org/10.1007/978-3-319-94144-8_11
14. Gebser, M., Kaufmann, B., Schaub, T.: Solution enumeration for projected boolean search problems. In: van Hoeve, W.-J., Hooker, J.N. (eds.) CPAIOR 2009. LNCS, vol. 5547, pp. 71–86. Springer, Heidelberg (2009). https://doi.org/10.1007/978-3-642-01929-6_7
15. Gelfond, M., Lifschitz, V.: Classical negation in logic programs and disjunctive databases. New Gener. Comput. **9**(3/4), 365–386 (1991)
16. Harvey, D., van der Hoeven, J., Lecerf, G.: Even faster integer multiplication. J. Complex. **36**, 1–30 (2016)
17. Impagliazzo, R., Paturi, R., Zane, F.: Which problems have strongly exponential complexity? J. Comput. Syst. Sci. **63**(4), 512–530 (2001)
18. Jakl, M., Pichler, R., Woltran, S.: Answer-set programming with bounded treewidth. In: IJCAI 2009, vol. 2, pp. 816–822 (2009)

19. Lin, F., Zhao, J.: On tight logic programs and yet another translation from normal logic programs to propositional logic. In: IJCAI 2003, pp. 853–858. Morgan Kaufmann (2003)

20. Lokshtanov, D., Marx, D., Saurabh, S.: Slightly superexponential parameterized problems. In: SODA, pp. 760–776. SIAM (2011)

21. Samer, M., Szeider, S.: Algorithms for propositional model counting. J. Discrete Algorithms **8**(1), 50–64 (2010)

Splitting Epistemic Logic Programs

Pedro Cabalar[1(✉)], Jorge Fandinno[2], and Luis Fariñas del Cerro[2]

[1] University of Corunna, Corunna, Spain
cabalar@udc.es
[2] IRIT, University of Toulouse, CNRS, Toulouse, France
{jorge.fandinno,farinas}@irit.fr

Abstract. Epistemic logic programs constitute an extension of the stable models semantics to deal with new constructs called *subjective literals*. Informally speaking, a subjective literal allows checking whether some regular literal is true in all or some stable models. As it can be imagined, the associated semantics has proved to be non-trivial, as the truth of subjective literals may interfere with the set of stable models it is supposed to query. As a consequence, no clear agreement has been reached and different semantic proposals have been made in the literature. Unfortunately, comparison among these proposals has been limited to a study of their effect on individual examples, rather than identifying general properties to be checked. In this paper, we propose an extension of the well-known splitting property for logic programs to the epistemic case. We formally define when an arbitrary semantics satisfies the *epistemic splitting property* and examine some of the consequences that can be derived from that, including its relation to conformant planning and to epistemic constraints. Interestingly, we prove (through counterexamples) that most of the existing proposals fail to fulfill the epistemic splitting property, except the original semantics proposed by Gelfond in 1991.

1 Introduction

The language of *epistemic specifications*, proposed by Gelfond in 1991 [3], constituted an extension of disjunctive logic programming that introduced modal operators to quantify over the set of stable models [5] of a program. These new constructs were later incorporated as an extension of the Answer Set Programming (ASP) paradigm in different implemented solvers (see [8] for a recent survey). The new constructs, *subjective literals*, have the form $\mathbf{K}\,l$ and $\mathbf{M}\,l$ and allow respectively checking whether regular literal l is true in every stable model (cautious consequence) or in some stable model (brave consequence) or in some stable model (brave consequence). In many cases, these subjective literals can be seen as simple queries, but what makes

A preliminary version of this work was presented at [1]. Partially supported by MINECO, Spain, grant TIC2017-84453-P, Xunta de Galicia, Spain (GPC ED431B 2016/035 and 2016-2019 ED431G/01, CITIC). The second author is funded by the Centre International de Mathématiques et d'Informatique de Toulouse (CIMI) through contract ANR-11-LABEX-0040-CIMI within the program ANR-11-IDEX-0002-02.

© Springer Nature Switzerland AG 2019
M. Balduccini et al. (Eds.): LPNMR 2019, LNAI 11481, pp. 120–133, 2019.
https://doi.org/10.1007/978-3-030-20528-7_10

them really interesting is their use in rule bodies, which may obviously affect the set of stable models they are meant to quantify. This feature makes them suitable for modelling introspection but, at the same time, easily involves cyclic specifications whose intuitive behaviour is not always easy to define. For instance, the semantics of an epistemic logic program may yield alternative sets of stable models, each set being called a *world view*. Deciding the intuitive world views of a cyclic specification has motivated a wide debate in the literature. In fact, in Gelfond's original semantics (G91) [3] or in its extension [12], some cyclic examples manifested self-supportedness, so in [4] Gelfond himself and, later on, other authors [2,6,10,11] proposed different variants trying to avoid unintended results. Unfortunately, comparison among these variants was limited to studying their effect on a set of "test" examples, leading to a lack of confidence as any proposal is always subject to the appearance of new counterintuitive examples. A next methodological step would consist in defining formal properties to be established and that would cover complete families of examples and, hopefully, could help to reach an agreement on some language fragments. For instance, one would expect that, at least, the existing approaches agreed on their interpretation of acyclic specifications. Regretfully, as we will see, this is not the case.

In this paper we propose a candidate property, we call *epistemic splitting*, that not only defines an intuitive behaviour for stratified epistemic specifications but also goes further, extending the splitting theorem [9], well-known for standard logic programs, to the epistemic case. Informally speaking, we say that an epistemic logic program can be split if a part of the program (the *top*) only refers to the atoms of the other part (the *bottom*) through subjective literals. A given semantics satisfies epistemic splitting if, given any split program, it is possible to get its world views by first obtaining the world views of the bottom and then using the subjective literals in the top as "queries" on the bottom part previously obtained. If epistemic splitting holds, the semantics immediately satisfies other properties. For instance, if the use of epistemic operators is stratified, the program has a unique world view at most. Similarly, epistemic constraints (those only consisting of subjective literals) can be guaranteed to only rule out candidate world views. As we will see, however, only the G91 semantics satisfies epistemic splitting among the previously cited approaches. So, somehow, the recent attempts to fix the behaviour of cycles has neglected the attention on the effects produced on acyclic specifications. In fact, a different property of epistemic splitting was already proved in [13] as a method to compute world views for this semantics. However, this definition is based on a "safety" condition that needs to be checked for all possible world views and is specific for G91 semantics, so it is harder to justify as a general property required for other approaches.

The rest of the paper is organised as follows. First, we motivate the main idea through a well-known example. After that, we recall basic definitions of (non-epistemic) ASP and splitting, introduce the language of epistemic specifications and define the G91 semantics. In the next section, we proceed to define the property of epistemic splitting and study some of its consequences. Then, we formally prove that G91 satisfies this property while we provide counterexamples for the other approaches, concluding the paper after that.

2   Motivation

To illustrate the intuition behind our proposal, let us consider the well-known standard example introduced in [3].

Example 1. A given college uses the following set of rules to decide whether a student X is eligible for a scholarship:

$$eligible(X) \leftarrow high(X) \tag{1}$$

$$eligible(X) \leftarrow minority(X), fair(X) \tag{2}$$

$$\sim eligible(X) \leftarrow \sim fair(X), \sim high(X) \tag{3}$$

Here, '$\sim$' stands for strong negation and $high(X)$ and $fair(X)$ refer to the grades of student X. We want to encode the additional college criterion "*The students whose eligibility is not determined by the college rules should be interviewed by the scholarship committee*" as another rule in the program. ☐

The problem here is that, for deciding whether $eligible(X)$ "*can be determined*," we need to check if it holds in all the answer sets of the program, that is, if it is one of the cautious consequences of the latter. For instance, if the only available information for some student *mike* is the disjunction

$$fair(mike) \vee high(mike) \tag{4}$$

we get that program $\{(1)–(4)\}$ has two stable models, $\{high(mike),$ $eligible(mike)\}$ and $\{fair(mike)\}$ so $eligible(mike)$ cannot be determined and an interview should follow. Of course, if we just want to query cautious and brave consequences of the program, we can do it inside ASP. For instance, the addition of constraint:

$$\bot \leftarrow eligible(mike)$$

allows us to decide if $eligible(mike)$ is a cautious consequence by just checking that the resulting program has no answer sets. The difficulty comes from the need to *derive* new information from a cautious consequence. This is where subjective literals come into play. Rule

$$interview(X) \leftarrow \mathbf{not}\,\mathbf{K}\,eligible(X), \mathbf{not}\,\mathbf{K}\,\sim eligible(X) \tag{5}$$

allows us to prove that $interview(X)$ holds whenever neither $eligible(X)$ nor $\sim eligible(X)$ are cautious consequences of $\{(1)–(4)\}$. Recall that $\mathbf{K}l$ holds when the literal l is true in all stable models of the program. The novel feature here is that (5) is also part of the program, and so, it affects the answer sets queried by $\mathbf{K}$ too, which would actually be:

$$\{fair(mike), interview(mike)\} \tag{6}$$

$$\{high(mike), eligible(mike), interview(mike)\} \tag{7}$$

So, there is a kind of cyclic reasoning: operators $\mathbf{K}$ and $\mathbf{M}$ are used to query a set of stable models that, in their turn, may depend on the application of that query. In the general case, this kind of cyclic reasoning is solved by resorting to multiple world views, but in our particular example, however, this does not seem to be needed. One would expect that separating the queried part {(1)–(4)} and the rule that makes the query (5) should be correct, since the first four rules do not depend on (5) and the latter exclusively consults them without interacting with their results. This same reasoning could be applied if we added one more level such as, for instance, by including the rule:

$$appointment(X) \leftarrow \mathbf{K}\, interview(X) \tag{8}$$

The two answer sets of program {(1)–(5)} contain $interview(mike)$ and so $appointment(mike)$ can be added to both answer sets incrementally. This method of analysing a program by division into independent parts shows a strong resemblance to the *splitting theorem* [9], well-known in standard ASP. Splitting is applicable when the program can be divided into two parts, the *bottom* and the *top*, in such a way that the bottom never refers to head atoms in the top. When this happens, we can first compute the stable models of the bottom and then, for each one, simplify the top accordingly, getting new stable models that complete the information. We could think about different ways of extending this method for the case of epistemic logic programs, depending on how restrictive we want to be on the programs where it will be applicable. However, we will choose a very conservative case, looking for a wider agreement on the proposed behaviour. The condition we will impose is that our top program can only refer to atoms in the bottom through epistemic operators. In this way, the top is seen as a set of rules that derive facts from epistemic queries on the bottom. Thus, each world view W of the bottom will be used to replace the subjective literals in the top by their truth value with respect to W. For the sake of completeness, we recall next the basic definitions of ASP and splitting, to proceed with a formalization of epistemic splitting afterwards.

3 Background of ASP and Epistemic Specifications

Given a set of atoms At, a *regular literal* is either an atom or a truth constant[1], that is $a \in At \cup \{\top, \bot\}$, or its default negation, $\mathbf{not}\, a$. A *rule* r is an implication of the form:

$$a_1 \vee \cdots \vee a_n \leftarrow L_1, \ldots, L_m \tag{9}$$

with $n \geq 0$ and $m \geq 0$, where each $a_i \in At$ is an atom and each L_j a regular literal. The left hand disjunction of (9) is called the rule *head* and abbreviated as $Head(r)$. When $n = 0$, it corresponds to $\bot$ and r is called a *constraint*. The right hand side of (9) is called the rule *body* and abbreviated as $Body(r)$. When

---

[1] For a simpler description of program transformations, we allow truth constants with their usual meaning.

$m = 0$, the body corresponds to $\top$ and r is called a *fact* (in this case, the body and the arrow symbol are usually omitted). A *(regular) program* Π is a (possibly infinite) set of rules. We write $Atoms(F)$ to represent the set of atoms occurring in any syntactic construct F (a literal, head, body, rule or program). A propositional interpretation I is a set of atoms. We assume that strong negation '$\sim a$' is just another atom in At and that the constraint $\bot \leftarrow a, \sim a$ is implicitly included in the program. We allow the use of variables, but understood as abbreviations of their possible ground instances. Given any syntactic construct F, we write $I \models F$ to stand for "I satisfies F" in classical propositional logic, where the commas correspond to conjunctions, 'not' corresponds (under this interpretation) to classical negation and '$\leftarrow$' is just a reversed material implication. An interpretation I is a *(classical) model* of a program Π if it satisfies all its rules. The *reduct* of a program Π with respect to some propositional interpretation I, in symbols Π^I, is obtained by replacing in Π every negative literal not a by $\top$ if $I \models$ not a or by $\bot$ otherwise. A propositional interpretation I is a *stable model* of a program Π iff it is a $\subseteq$-minimal model of Π^I. By SM$[\Pi]$, we denote the set of all stable models of Π. The following is a well-known property in ASP.

Property 1 (Supraclassicality). Any stable model of a (regular) program Π is also a classical model of Π.

We extend now the syntax of ASP to the language of epistemic specifications. Given a set of atoms At, we call *subjective literal* to any expression of the form $\mathbf{K} l$, $\mathbf{M} l$, not $\mathbf{K} l$ or not $\mathbf{M} l$, for any regular literal l. We keep the same syntax for rules as in (9) excepting that body literals L_j can also be subjective literals now. Given rule r we define the sets $Body^{reg}(r)$ and $Body^{sub}(r)$ respectively containing the regular and the subjective literals in $Body(r)$. Rules or programs are *regular* if they do not contain subjective literals. We say that a rule is a *subjective constraint* if it is a constraint, $Head(r) = \bot$, and its body exclusively consists of subjective literals, that is $Body(r) = Body^{sub}(r)$.

We can define the concept of *model* of a program, in a similar way as we did for classical models in regular ASP. A *modal interpretation* $\mathcal{M} = \langle W, I \rangle$ is pair where I is a propositional interpretation and $W \subseteq 2^{At}$ is a non-empty set of propositional interpretations. A modal interpretation $\mathcal{M} = \langle W, I \rangle$ *satisfies* a literal L, written $\langle W, I \rangle \models L$, if

1. $\langle W, I \rangle \models \top$,
2. $\langle W, I \rangle \not\models \bot$,
3. $\langle W, I \rangle \models a$ if $a \in I$, for any atom $a \in At$,
4. $\langle W, I \rangle \models \mathbf{K} l$ if $\langle W, I' \rangle \models l$ for all $I' \in W$,
5. $\langle W, I \rangle \models \mathbf{M} l$ if $\langle W, I' \rangle \models l$ for some $I' \in W$, and
6. $\langle W, I \rangle \models$ not L if $\langle W, I \rangle \not\models L$.

Since for a subjective literal L, $\langle W, I \rangle \models L$ does not depend on I, we sometimes write $W \models L$. For a rule r of the form (9), we write $\langle W, I \rangle \models r$ iff either $\langle W, I \rangle \models a_i$ for some $1 \le i \le n$ or $\langle W, I \rangle \not\models L_j$ for some $1 \le j \le m$. We say that $\langle W, I \rangle$ is a *model* of a program Π, written $\langle W, I \rangle \models \Pi$, if it satisfies all its rules. Among the possible models of an epistemic logic program, all semantic approaches agree on selecting some preferred models called *world views*, each one being characterized by the W component. These world views satisfy a similar property to that of supraclassicality (Property 1) in non-epistemic ASP. In this case, however, rather than talking about classical models, we resort to modal logic S5, so all world views of a program are also S5 models of the program. This property can be formally stated as follows:

Property 2 (Supra-S5). A semantics satisfies *supra-S5* when for every world view W of an epistemic program Π and for every $I \in W$, $\langle W, I \rangle \models \Pi$.   □

To the best of our knowledge, all existing semantics satisfy supra-S5. Another property that is shared by all semantics is that, when Π is a regular ASP program (it has no modal epistemic operators) then it has a unique world view containing all the stable models of Π. We will formalize this property in the following way.

Property 3 (Supra-ASP). A semantics satisfies *supra-ASP* if for any regular program Π either Π has a unique world view $W = \mathrm{SM}[\Pi] \neq \emptyset$ or $\mathrm{SM}[\Pi] = \emptyset$ and Π has no world view at all.   □

Originally, some semantics like [3] or [12], allowed empty world views $W = \emptyset$ when the program has no stable models, rather than leaving the program without world views. Since this feature is not really essential, we exclusively refer to non-empty world views in this paper.

We define next a useful transformation extending the idea of the reduct to epistemic specifications, and generalized for a given signature.

Definition 1 (Subjective reduct). *The* subjective reduct *of a program Π with respect to a set of propositional interpretations W and a signature $U \subseteq$ At, also written Π_U^W, is obtained by replacing each subjective literal L with $Atoms(L) \subseteq U$ by; $\top$ if $W \models L$ or by $\bot$ otherwise. When $U = \mathrm{At}$ we just write Π^W.*   □

We use the same notation Π^W as for the standard reduct, but ambiguity is removed by the type of W (a set of interpretations now). This subjective reduct can be used to define [3] (G91) semantics in the following way.

Definition 2 (G91-world view). *A* non-empty set of interpretations W is a G91-world view *of an epistemic program Π if $W = \mathrm{SM}[\Pi^W]$.*   □

We will not provide the formal definitions of the rest of semantics compared in this paper, since none of them satisfies our goal property of epistemic splitting. In those cases, it will suffice with providing counterexamples and the reader can check their behaviour by resorting to the corresponding original definition.

4   Epistemic Splitting

We proceed now to introduce our definition of the epistemic splitting property. To do so, we begin extending the idea of splitting set from [9]. For space reasons, we refer the reader to [9] for the formal definition of splitting set.

Definition 3 (Epistemic splitting set). *A set of atoms $U \subseteq At$ is said to be an* epistemic splitting set *of a program Π if for any rule r in Π one of the following conditions hold*

(i) $Atoms(r) \subseteq U$,
(ii) $(Atoms(Body^{reg}(r) \cup Head(r))) \cap U = \emptyset$

We define an splitting *of Π as a pair $\langle B_U(\Pi), T_U(\Pi) \rangle$ satisfying $B_U(\Pi) \cap T_U(\Pi) = \emptyset$, $B_U(\Pi) \cup T_U(\Pi) = \Pi$, all rules in $B_U(\Pi)$ satisfy (i) and all rules in $T_U(\Pi)$ satisfy (ii).* □

With respect to the original definition of splitting set, we have replaced the condition for the top program, $Atoms(Head(r)) \cap U = \emptyset$, by the new condition (ii), which in other words means that the top program may only refer to atoms U in the bottom through epistemic operators. Note that this introduces a new kind of "dependence," so that, as happens with head atoms, regular literals in the body also depend on atoms in subjective literals. For instance, if $U = \{p, q\}$, the program $\Pi_1 = \{p \vee q, \; s \leftarrow p, \mathbf{K}\, q\}$ would not be splittable due to the second rule, since $s \notin U$ and we would also need the regular literal $p \notin U$. The reason for this restriction is to avoid imposing (to a potential semantics) a fixed way of evaluating p with respect to the world view $[\{p\}, \{q\}]$ for the bottom.

Another observation is that we have kept the definition of $B_U(\Pi)$ and $T_U(\Pi)$ non-deterministic, in the sense that some rules can be arbitrarily included in one set or the other. These rules correspond to subjective constraints on atoms in U, since these are the only cases that may satisfy conditions (i) and (ii) simultaneously.

If we retake our example program $\Pi_2 = \{(1)-(5)\}$, we can see that the set U consisting of atoms $high(mike), fair(mike), eligible(mike), minority(mike)$ and their corresponding strong negations is an epistemic splitting set that divides the program into the bottom $B_U(\Pi_2) = \{(1)-(4)\}$ and the top $T_U(\Pi_2) = \{(5)\}$. As in regular splitting, the idea is computing first the world views of the bottom program $B_U(\Pi)$ and for each one, W, simplifying the corresponding subjective literals in the top program. Given an epistemic splitting set U for a program Π and set of interpretations W, we define $E_U(\Pi, W) \stackrel{\text{def}}{=} T_U(\Pi)_U^W$, that is, we make the subjective reduct of the top with respect to W and signature U. A pair $\langle W_b, W_t \rangle$ is said to be a *solution* of Π with respect to an epistemic splitting set U if W_b is a world view of $B_U(\Pi)$ and W_t is a world view of $E_U(\Pi, W_b)$. Notice that this definition is semantics-dependent in the sense that each alternative semantics for epistemic specifications will define its own solutions for a given U and Π, since it defines the selected world views for a program in a different way. Back to our example, notice that $B_U(\Pi_2)$ is a regular program without epistemic operators. Thus, any semantics satisfying supra-ASP will provide $W_b = [\{fair(mike)\}, \{high(mike), eligible(mike)\}]$ as the unique world view for the bottom. The corresponding simplification of the top would be $E_U(\Pi_2, W_b)$ containing (after grounding) the single rule $interview(mike) \leftarrow \mathbf{not}\, \bot, \mathbf{not}\, \bot$ Again, this program is regular and its unique world view would be $W_t = [\{interview(mike)\}]$. Now, in the general case, to reconstruct the world views for the global program we define the operation:

$$W_b \sqcup W_t \;\; = \;\; \{\, I_b \cup I_t \mid I_b \in W_b \text{ and } I_t \in W_t \,\} \cdot$$

(remember that both the bottom and the top may produce multiple world views, depending on the program and the semantics we choose). In our example, $W_b \sqcup W_t$ would exactly contain the two stable models (6) and (7) we saw in the introduction.

Property 4 (Epistemic splitting). A semantics satisfies *epistemic splitting* if for any epistemic splitting set U of any program Π: W is a world view of Π iff there is a solution $\langle W_b, W_t \rangle$ of Π with respect to U such that $W = W_b \sqcup W_t$. □

In the example, this means that the world view we obtained in two steps is indeed the unique world view of the whole program, under any semantics satisfying epistemic splitting. Uniqueness of world view was obtained in this case because both the bottom program $B_U(\Pi_2)$ and the top, after simplification, $E_U(\Pi_2, W_b)$ were regular programs and we assumed supra-ASP. In fact, as we see next, we can still get a unique world view (at most) when there are no cyclic dependences among subjective literals. This mimics the well-known result for *stratified negation* in logic programming. Let us define a modal dependence relation among atoms in a program Π so that $dep(a, b)$ is true iff there is a rule $r \in \Pi$ such that $a \in Atoms(Head(r) \cup Body^{reg}(r))$ and $b \in Atoms(Body^{sub}(r))$.

Definition 4. *We say that an epistemic program Π is* epistemically stratified *if we can assign an integer mapping* $\lambda : At \to \mathbb{N}$ *to each atom such that* $\lambda(a) > \lambda(b)$ *for any pair of atoms* a, b *satisfying* $dep(a, b)$. □

Take, for instance, the extended program $\Pi_3 = \{(1)–(5), (8)\}$. We can assign atoms $high(mike)$, $fair(mike)$, $minority(mike)$ and $eligible(mike)$ layer 0. Then $interview(mike)$ could be assigned layer 1 and, finally, $appointment(mike)$ can be located at layer 2. So, Π_3 is epistemically stratified.

Theorem 1. *Let Π be a finite, epistemically stratified program. Then, any semantics satisfying supra-ASP and epistemic splitting assigns, at most, a unique world view to Π.* □

The proof of the theorem just relies on multiple applications of splitting to each layer backwards and the fact that each simplification $E_U(\Pi, W_b)$ will be a regular program. This is very easy to see in the extended example Π_3. We can split the program using as U all atoms but $appointment(mike)$ to get a bottom Π_2 and a top $\{(8)\}$. Program Π_2 can be split in its turn as we saw before, producing the unique world view $[(6), (7)]$. Then $E_U(\Pi_3, \{(6), (7)\})$ contains the single rule $appointment(mike) \leftarrow \top$ that is a regular program whose unique world view is $[\{appointment(mike)\}]$ and, finally, the combination of these two world views yields again a unique world view $[(6) \cup \{appointment(mike)\}, (7) \cup \{appointment(mike)\}]$.

Another consequence of epistemic splitting is that subjective constraints will have a monotonic behaviour. Note first that, for a subjective constraint r, we can abbreviate $\langle W, I \rangle \models r$ as $W \models r$ since the I component is irrelevant. Additionally, $W \models r$ means that $Body(r) = Body^{sub}(r)$ is falsified, since $Head(r) = \bot$.

Property 5 (subjective constraint monotonicity). A semantics satisfies *subjective constraint monotonicity* if, for any epistemic program Π and any subjective constraint r, W is a world view of $\Pi \cup \{r\}$ iff both W is a world view of Π and $W \models r$.   □

Theorem 2. *Epistemic splitting implies subjective constraint monotonicity.*   □

To conclude the exploration of consequences of epistemic splitting, let us consider a possible application to conformant planning. To this aim, consider the following simple example.

Example 2. To turn on the light in a room, we can toggle one of two lamps l_1 or l_2. In the initial state, lamp l_1 is plugged but we ignore the state of l_2. Our goal is finding a plan that guarantees we get light in the room in one step.

A logic program that encodes this scenario for a single transition[2] could be Π_4:

$$plugged(l_1) \qquad\qquad light \leftarrow toggle(L), plugged(L)$$
$$plugged(l_2) \vee \sim plugged(l_2) \qquad \bot \leftarrow toggle(l_1), toggle(l_2)$$

for $L \in \{l_1, l_2\}$. As we can see, $toggle(l_1)$ would constitute a conformant plan, since we obtain *light* regardless of the initial state, while this does not happen with plan $toggle(l_2)$. In order to check whether a given sequence of actions $A_0, \ldots, A_n$ is a valid conformant plan one would expect that, if we added those facts to the program, a subjective constraint should be sufficient to check that the goal holds in all the possible outcomes. In our example, we would just use:

$$\bot \leftarrow \textbf{not } \textbf{K} \, light \qquad\qquad\qquad (10)$$

and check that the program $\Pi_4 \cup \{toggle(L)\} \cup \{(10)\}$ has some world view, varying $L \in \{l_1, l_2\}$. Subjective constraint monotonicity guarantees that the addition of this "straighforward" formalisation has the expected meaning.

This method would only allow testing if the sequence of actions constitutes a conformant plan, but does not allow generating those actions. A desirable feature would be the possibility of applying the well-known ASP methodology of separating the program into three sections: generate, define and test. In our case, the "define" and the "test" sections would respectively be Π_4 and (10), but we still miss a "generate" part, capable of considering different alternative conformant plans. The problem in this case is that we cannot use a simple choice:

$$toggle(L) \vee \sim toggle(L)$$

because this would allow a same action to be executed in some of the stable models and not executed in others, all inside a *same* world view. Let us assume that our epistemic semantics has some way to non-deterministically generate

---

[2] For simplicity, we omit time arguments or inertia, as they are not essential for the discussion.

a world view in which either $\mathbf{K}\,a$ or $\mathbf{K}\,\mathrm{not}\;a$ holds using a given set of rules[3] $Choice(a)$. Then, take the program Π_5 consisting of rules

$$Choice(toggle(L)) \tag{11}$$

with $L \in \{l_1, l_2\}$ plus Π_4 and (10). If our semantics satisfies epistemic splitting, it is safe to obtain the world views in three steps: generate first the alternative world views for $toggle(l_1)$ and $toggle(l_2)$ using (11), apply Π_4 and rule out those world views not satisfying the goal *light* in all situations using (10). To fulfill the preconditions for applying splitting, we would actually need to replace regular literal $toggle(L)$ by $\mathbf{K}\,toggle(L)$ in all the bodies of Π_4, but this is safe in the current context. Now, we take the bottom program to obtain 4 possible world views $W_0 = [\{toggle(l_1)\}]$, $W_1 = [\{toggle(l_2)\}]$, $W_2 = [\{toggle(l_1), toggle(l_2)\}]$ and $W_3 = [\emptyset]$. When we combine them with the top Π_4 we obtain W_0' consisting of two stable models:

$$\{toggle(l_1), plugged(l_2'), light, \dots\} \qquad \{toggle(l_1), \sim plugged(l_2), light, \dots\}$$

and W_1' consisting of other two stable models:

$$\{toggle(l_2), plugged(l_2), light, \dots\} \qquad \{toggle(l_2), \sim plugged(l_2), \dots\}$$

where the latter does not contain *light*. Finally, constraint (10) would rule out W_1'.

To sum up, epistemic splitting provides a natural way of formulating conformant planning problems by a separation into three sections: a generation part, the usual encoding of the actions scenario and a test part consisting of a subjective constraint to guarantee that the goal is always reached.

5   Splitting in Some Existing Semantics

In this section we study the property of epistemic splitting for the approaches mentioned in the introduction. We will begin by stating that G91 actually satisfies this property. The proof of the following theorem can be found in the appendix.

Main Theorem. *Semantics G91 satisfies epistemic splitting.*   □

A similar proof can be developed to show that [12], that generalises[4] [3] from subjective literals to subjective formulas, also satisfies epistemic splitting.

To illustrate the behaviour of other semantics with respect to splitting, we will use several examples. Let us take the program Π_6 consisting of rules:

$$a \vee b \tag{12}$$

$$c \vee d \leftarrow \mathrm{not}\;\mathbf{K}\,a \tag{13}$$

---

[3] For instance, in the G91-semantics, this could be just the rule $a \leftarrow \mathrm{not}\;\mathbf{K}\,\mathrm{not}\;a$. Other semantics may have alternative ways of expressing this intended behaviour.

[4] In fact, [12] defines several semantics but, among them, we refer here to the epistemic stable model semantics.

The set $U = \{a, b\}$ splits the program into the bottom (12) and the top (13). The bottom has a unique world view $W_b = [\{a\}, \{b\}]$ so $\mathbf{K}\,a$ does not hold and the top is simplified as $E_U(\Pi_6, W_b)$ containing the unique rule

$$c \vee d \leftarrow \mathbf{not}\ \bot \tag{14}$$

This program has a unique world view $W_t = [\{c\}, \{d\}]$ that, combined with W_b yields $[\{a, c\}, \{b, c\}, \{a, d\}, \{b, d\}]$ as the unique solution for Π_6, for any semantics satisfying epistemic splitting (and so, also for G91). Let us elaborate the example a little bit further. Suppose we add now the constraint:

$$\bot \leftarrow c \tag{15}$$

The top must also include this rule and has now a unique stable model, yielding the world view $W_t = [\{d\}]$, so the world view for the complete program would be $[\{a, d\}, \{b, d\}]$. Finally, let us forbid the inclusion of atom d too:

$$\bot \leftarrow d \tag{16}$$

so we consider $\Pi_7 = \{(12), (13), (15), (16)\}$. This last constraint leaves the simplified top program $E_U(\Pi_6, W_b) = \{(14), (15), (16)\}$ without stable models, so epistemic splitting would yield that program Π_7 has no world view at all. This is the result we obtain, indeed, in [3,4][5] and in [12]. Surprisingly, recent approaches like [2,6,10,11] yield world view $[\{a\}]$, violating the epistemic splitting property. For instance, in the case of [6], the reduct of Π_7 with respect to $[\{a\}]$ is the program

$$a \leftarrow \mathbf{not}\ b \qquad c \vee d \leftarrow \mathbf{not}\ a \qquad \bot \leftarrow c$$
$$b \leftarrow \mathbf{not}\ a \qquad\qquad\qquad\qquad\qquad \bot \leftarrow d$$

which has a unique stable model $\{a\}$. As a second example, take the program Π_8 consisting of the same bottom program (12) and the rule:

$$c \leftarrow \mathbf{K}\,a \tag{17}$$

As expected, all approaches agree that Π_8 has a unique world view $W_b = [\{a\}, \{b\}]$ because $\mathbf{K}\,a$ is not satisfied and rule (17) is not applicable. Under epistemic splitting, we get that $E_U(\Pi_8, W_b)$ is the rule:

$$c \leftarrow \bot \tag{18}$$

whose unique world view is $[\emptyset]$, so that $W_b \sqcup [\emptyset] = W_b$. But let us further elaborate the example taking Π_8' containing Π_8 plus:

$$\bot \leftarrow \mathbf{not}\ c \tag{19}$$

---

[5] These two semantics actually produce empty world views, but as we said before, we disregard them, as they just point out that the program has no solution.

Under epistemic splitting, the new top $E_U(\Pi'_8, W_b)$ contains now (19) and (18) which have no stable models. As a result, no world view can be combined with W_b and we obtain that Π'_8 has no world views at all. This is the result we obtain under [3,12], which agree that the program is inconsistent. However, [4] joins [2,6,10,11] in the group of approaches that provide the world view $[\{a,c\}]$. That is, in all these approaches, adding a constraint intended to remove all belief sets that do not satisfy c, may surprisingly lead to justify c. Note that, according to [3,12], the reduct of Π'_8 with respect to $[\{a,c\}]$ is $\{a \leftarrow \text{not } b, \ b \leftarrow \text{not } a, \}$ $c \leftarrow \top, \bot \leftarrow \text{not } c$ which has two stable models, $\{a,c\}$ and $\{b,c\}$, so $[\{a,c\}]$ is not a world view. In contrast, the reduct with respect to [4] and [6] is $\{a \leftarrow \text{not } b, \}$ $b \leftarrow \text{not } a, \ c \leftarrow a, \ \bot \leftarrow \text{not } c$ which has a unique stable model $\{a,c\}$, so $[\{a,c\}]$ is a world view.

6 Conclusions

We have introduced a formal property for semantics of epistemic specifications. This property that we call *epistemic splitting* has a strong resemblance to the splitting theorem well-known for regular ASP programs. Epistemic splitting can be applied when we can divide an epistemic logic program into a bottom part for a subset U of atoms and a top part, that only refers to atoms in U through subjective literals (those using modal epistemic operators). When this happens, the property of splitting states that we should be able to compute the world views of the program in two steps: first, computing the world views of the bottom and, second, using each bottom world view W to replace subjective literals for atoms in U in the top by their truth value with respect to W.

We have studied several consequences of epistemic splitting: for instance, if the program is stratified with respect to subjective literals then it will have a unique world view, at most. Another consequence is that constraints only consisting of subjective literals will have a monotonic behaviour, ruling out world views that satisfy the constraint body.[6] We have also explored how epistemic splitting may facilitate the simple application of the generate-define-test methodology, well-known in ASP, to the formalisation of conformant planning. The application of epistemic specifications to conformat planning was first discussed in [6], though with a more complex formulation due to the lack of epistemic splitting.

Our study of the main semantics in the literature has shown that only the original semantics [3] (G91), and its generalisation [12], satisfy epistemic splitting while the rest of approaches we considered do not, as we showed with counterexamples. As said in the introduction, a different kind of epistemic splitting had also been proved for G91 in [13], reinforcing the idea that this semantics can be interpreted in a modular way. Notice that the sets of programs that can be split under these two definitions is incomparable. We do not mean with this, however, that G91 is always intuitive. As it is well-known, G91 suffers from self-supportedness: for instance, the program consisting of the single rule $p \leftarrow \mathbf{K}\,p$

---

[6] The lack of monotonicity suffered by epistemic constraints in some semantics has been recently discussed by [7].

yields two world views $[\emptyset]$ and $[\{p\}]$ but the latter justifies p by the mere assumption of $\mathbf{K}p$ without further evidence, something that seems counterintuitive. What we claim instead is that G91 has a reasonable behaviour when subjective literals are stratified. Unfortunately, later attempts to solve self-supportedness on cyclic epistemic specifications have somehow spoiled that feature.

Acknowledgements. We are thankful to Michael Gelfond, Richard Watson and Patrick T. Kahl for their helpful comments on early versions of this work. We are also thankful to the anonymous reviewers for their valuable feedback, which helped to improve the paper.

References

1. Cabalar, P., Fandinno, J., Fariñas del Cerro, L.: Splitting epistemic logic programs. In: Proceedings of the 17th International Workshop on Non-monotonic Reasoning (NMR 2018), pp. 81–89 (2018)
2. Fariñas del Cerro, L., Herzig, A., Su, E.I.: Epistemic equilibrium logic. In: Proceedings of the International Joint Conference on Artificial Intelligence (IJCAI 2015), pp. 2964–2970. AAAI Press (2015)
3. Gelfond, M.: Strong introspection. In: Dean, T.L., McKeown, K. (eds.) Proceedings of the AAAI Conference, vol. 1, pp. 386–391. AAAI Press/The MIT Press (1991)
4. Gelfond, M.: New semantics for epistemic specifications. In: Delgrande, J.P., Faber, W. (eds.) LPNMR 2011. LNCS (LNAI), vol. 6645, pp. 260–265. Springer, Heidelberg (2011). https://doi.org/10.1007/978-3-642-20895-9_29
5. Gelfond, M., Lifschitz, V.: The stable model semantics for logic programming. In: Proceedings of the 5th International Conference on Logic Programming (ICLP 1988), pp. 1070–1080 (1988)
6. Kahl, P., Watson, R., Balai, E., Gelfond, M., Zhang, Y.: The language of epistemic specifications (refined) including a prototype solver. J. Log. Comput. (2015). (Special issue article)
7. Leclerc, A.P., Kahl, P.T.: Epistemic logic programs with world view constraints. In: Technical communication of the 34th International Conference on Logic Programming (ICLP 2018) (2018)
8. Leclerc, A.P., Kahl, P.T.: A survey of advances in epistemic logic program solvers. In: Proceedings of the 11th International Workshop on Answer Set Programming and Other Computer Paradigms (ASPOCP 2018) (2018)
9. Lifschitz, V., Turner, H.: Splitting a logic program. In: Proceedings of the International Conference on Logic Programming (ICLP 1994), pp. 23–37. MIT Press (1994)
10. Shen, Y., Eiter, T.: Evaluating epistemic negation in answer set programming (extended abstract). In: Proceedings of the International Joint Conference on Artificial Intelligence (IJCAI 2017), pp. 5060–5064 (2017)
11. Son, T.C., Le, T., Kahl, P.T., Leclerc, A.P.: On computing world views of epistemic logic programs. In: Proceedings of the International Joint Conference on Artificial Intelligence (IJCAI 2017), pp. 1269–1275 (2017). https://www.ijcai.org

12. Truszczyński, M.: Revisiting epistemic specifications. In: Balduccini, M., Son, T.C. (eds.) Logic Programming, Knowledge Representation, and Nonmonotonic Reasoning. LNCS (LNAI), vol. 6565, pp. 315–333. Springer, Heidelberg (2011). https://doi.org/10.1007/978-3-642-20832-4_20
13. Watson, R.: A splitting set theorem for epistemic specifications. CoRR: Proceedings of the 8th International Workshop on Non-monotonic Reasoning, NMR 2000 cs.AI/0003038 (2000). http://arxiv.org/abs/cs.AI/0003038

Founded World Views with Autoepistemic Equilibrium Logic

Pedro Cabalar[1]([⊠]), Jorge Fandinno[2], and Fariñas del Cerro Luis[2]

[1] University of A Coruña, A Coruña, Spain
cabalar@udc.es
[2] IRIT University of Toulouse, CNRS, Toulouse, France
{jorge.fandinno,farinas}@irit.fr

Abstract. Defined by Gelfond in 1991 (G91), epistemic specifications (or programs) are an extension of logic programming under stable models semantics that introduces *subjective literals*. A subjective literal allows checking whether some regular literal is true in all (or in some of) the stable models of the program, being those models collected in a set called *world view*. One epistemic program may yield several world views but, under the original G91 semantics, some of them resulted from self-supported derivations. During the last eight years, several alternative approaches have been proposed to get rid of these self-supported world views. Unfortunately, their success could only be measured by studying their behaviour on a set of common examples in the literature, since no formal property of "self-supportedness" had been defined. To fill this gap, we extend in this paper the idea of unfounded set from standard logic programming to the epistemic case. We define when a world view is *founded* with respect to some program and propose the *foundedness* property for any semantics whose world views are always founded. Using counterexamples, we explain that the previous approaches violate foundedness, and proceed to propose a new semantics based on a combination of Moore's Autoepistemic Logic and Pearce's Equilibrium Logic. The main result proves that this new semantics precisely captures the set of founded G91 world views.

1 Introduction

The language of *epistemic specifications*, proposed by Gelfond in 1991 [4], extends disjunctive logic programs (under the *stable model* [6] semantics) with modal constructs called *subjective literals*. Using these constructs, it is possible to check

This work was partially supported by MINECO, Spain, grant TIC2017-84453-P, Xunta de Galicia, Spain (GPC ED431B 2016/035 and 2016–2019 ED431G/01, CITIC). The second author is funded by the Centre International de Mathématiques et d'Informatique de Toulouse (CIMI) through contract ANR-11-LABEX-0040-CIMI within the program ANR-11-IDEX-0002-02.

M. Balduccini et al. (Eds.): LPNMR 2019, LNAI 11481, pp. 134–147, 2019.
https://doi.org/10.1007/978-3-030-20528-7_11

whether a regular literal l is true in *every* stable model (written $\mathbf{K}\,l$) or in *some* stable model (written $\mathbf{M}\,l$) of the program. For instance, the rule:

$$a \leftarrow \neg\mathbf{K}\,b \tag{1}$$

means that a must hold if we cannot prove that all the stable models contain b. The definition of a "satisfactory" semantics for epistemic specifications has proved to be a non-trivial enterprise, as shown by the list of different attempts proposed so far [2,4,5,9,20–22]. The main difficulty arises because subjective literals query the set of stable models but, at the same time, occur in rules that determine those stable models. As an example, the program consisting of:

$$b \leftarrow \neg\mathbf{K}\,a \tag{2}$$

and (1) has now two rules defining atoms a and b in terms of the presence of those same atoms in all the stable models. To solve this kind of cyclic interdependence, the original semantics by Gelfond [4] (G91) considered different alternative *world views* or sets of stable models. In the case of program (1)–(2), G91 yields two alternative world views[1], $[\{a\}]$ and $[\{b\}]$, each one containing a single stable model, and this is also the behaviour obtained in the remaining approaches developed later on. The feature that made G91 unconvincing, though, was the generation of self-supported world views. A prototypical example for this effect is the epistemic program consisting of the single rule:

$$a \leftarrow \mathbf{K}\,a \tag{3}$$

whose world views under G91 are $[\emptyset]$ and $[\{a\}]$. The latter is considered as counter-intuitive by all authors[2] because it relies on a self-supported derivation: a is derived from $\mathbf{K}\,a$ by rule (3), but the only way to obtain $\mathbf{K}\,a$ is rule (3) itself. Although the rejection of world views of this kind seems natural, the truth is that all approaches in the literature have concentrated on studying the effects on individual examples, rather than capturing the absence of self-supportedness as a formal property. To achieve such a goal, we would need to establish some kind of *derivability* condition in a very similar fashion as done with *unfounded sets* [3] for standard logic programs. To understand the similarity, think about the (tautological) rule $a \leftarrow a$. The classical models of this rule are $\emptyset$ and $\{a\}$, but the latter cannot be a stable model because a is not derivable applying the rule. Intuitively, an unfounded set is a collection of atoms that is not derivable from a given program and a fixed set of assumptions, as happens to $\{a\}$ in the last example. As proved by [12], the stable models of any disjunctive logic program are precisely its classical models that are *founded*, that is, that do not admit any unfounded set. As we can see, the situation in (3) is pretty similar to $a \leftarrow a$ but, this time, involves derivability through subjective literals. An immediate option

---

[1] For the sake of readability, sets of propositional interpretations are embraced with [ ] rather than { }.

[2] This includes Gelfond himself, who proposed a new variant in [5] motivated by this same example and further modified this variant later on in [9].

is, therefore, extending the definition of unfounded sets for the case of epistemic programs – this constitutes, indeed, the first contribution of this paper.

Once the property of *founded* world views is explicitly stated, the paper proposes a new semantics for epistemic specifications, called *Founded Autoepistemic Equilibrium Logic* (FAEEL), that fulfills that requirement. In the spirit of [2,22], our proposal actually constitutes a full modal non-monotonic logic where **K** becomes the usual necessity operator applicable to arbitrary formulas. Formally, FAEEL is a combination of Pearce's *Equilibrium Logic* [17], a well-known logical characterisation of stable models, with Moore's *Autoepistemic Logic* (AEL) [15], one of the most representative approaches among modal non-monotonic logics. The reason for choosing Equilibrium Logic is quite obvious, as it has proved its utility for characterising other extensions of ASP, including the already mentioned epistemic approaches in [2,22]. As for the choice of AEL, it shares with epistemic specifications the common idea of *agent's introspection* where **K** φ means that φ is one of the agent's beliefs. The only difference is that those beliefs are just classical models in the case of AEL whereas epistemic specifications deal with stable models instead. Interestingly, the problem of self-supported models has also been extensively studied in AEL [11,13,16,18], where the formula **K** $a \rightarrow a$, analogous to (3), also yields an unfounded world view[3] $[\{a\}]$. Our solution consists in combining the monotonic bases of AEL and Equilibrium Logic (the modal logic KD45 and the intermediate logic of Here-and-There (HT) [8], respectively), but defining a two-step models selection criterion that simultaneously keeps the agent's beliefs as stable models and avoids unfounded world views from the use of the modal operator **K**. As expected, we prove that FAEEL guarantees the property of founded world views, among other features. Our main result, however, goes further and asserts that the FAEEL world views of an epistemic program are precisely the set of founded G91 world views. We reach, in this way, an analogous situation to the case of standard logic programming, where stable models are the set of founded classical models of the program.

The rest of the paper is organised as follows. Section 2 and 3 respectively revisit the background knowledge about equilibrium logic and epistemic specifications necessary for the rest of the paper. Section 4 introduces the foundedness property for epistemic logic programs. In Sect. 5, we introduce FAEEL and show that its world views precisely coincide with the set of founded G91 world views. Finally, Sect. 6 concludes the paper.

2   Background

We begin recalling the basic definitions of equilibrium logic and its relation to stable models. We start from the syntax of propositional logic, with formulas built from combinations of atoms in a set $\mathcal{AT}$ with operators $\wedge, \vee, \bot$ and $\rightarrow$ in the usual way. We define the derived operators $\varphi \leftrightarrow \psi \overset{\text{def}}{=} (\varphi \rightarrow \psi) \wedge (\psi \rightarrow \varphi)$, $(\varphi \leftarrow \psi) \overset{\text{def}}{=} (\psi \rightarrow \varphi)$, $\neg\varphi \overset{\text{def}}{=} (\varphi \rightarrow \bot)$ and $\top \overset{\text{def}}{=} \neg\bot$.

---

[3] Technically, AEL is defined in terms of *theory expansions* but each one can be characterised by a canonical S5-model with the same form of a world view [14,19].

A *propositional interpretation* T is a set of atoms $T \subseteq \mathcal{AT}$. We write $T \models \varphi$ to represent that T classically satisfies formula φ. An *HT-interpretation* is a pair $\langle H, T \rangle$ (respectively called "here" and "there") of propositional interpretations such that $H \subseteq T \subseteq \mathcal{AT}$; it is said to be *total* when $H = T$. We write $\langle H, T \rangle \models \varphi$ to represent that $\langle H, T \rangle$ *satisfies* a formula φ under the recursive conditions:

- $\langle H, T \rangle \not\models \bot$
- $\langle H, T \rangle \models p$ iff $p \in H$
- $\langle H, T \rangle \models \varphi \land \psi$ iff $\langle H, T \rangle \models \varphi$ and $\langle H, T \rangle \models \psi$
- $\langle H, T \rangle \models \varphi \lor \psi$ iff $\langle H, T \rangle \models \varphi$ or $\langle H, T \rangle \models \psi$
- $\langle H, T \rangle \models \varphi \to \psi$ iff both (i) $T \models \varphi \to \psi$ and (ii) $\langle H, T \rangle \not\models \varphi$ or $\langle H, T \rangle \models \psi$

As usual, we say that $\langle H, T \rangle$ is a *model* of a theory Γ, in symbols $\langle H, T \rangle \models \Gamma$, iff $\langle H, T \rangle \models \varphi$ for all $\varphi \in \Gamma$. It is easy to see that $\langle T, T \rangle \models \Gamma$ iff $T \models \Gamma$ classically. For this reason, we will identify $\langle T, T \rangle$ simply as T and will use '$\models$' indistinctly. By $\mathrm{CL}[\Gamma]$ we denote the set of all classical models of Γ. Interpretation $\langle T, T \rangle = T$ is a *stable (or equilibrium) model* of a theory Γ iff $T \models \Gamma$ and there is no $H \subset T$ such that $\langle H, T \rangle \models \Gamma$. We write $\mathrm{SM}[\Gamma]$ to stand for the set of all stable models of Γ. Note that $\mathrm{SM}[\Gamma] \subseteq \mathrm{CL}[\Gamma]$ by definition.

3   G91 Semantics for Epistemic Theories

In this section we provide a straightforward generalisation of G91 allowing its application to arbitrary modal theories. Formulas are extended with the necessity operator $\mathbf{K}$ according to the following grammar:

$$\varphi ::= \bot \mid a \mid \varphi_1 \land \varphi_2 \mid \varphi_1 \lor \varphi_2 \mid \varphi_1 \to \varphi_2 \mid \mathbf{K}\varphi \qquad \text{for any atom } a \in \mathcal{AT}.$$

An *(epistemic) theory* is a set of formulas. In our context, the epistemic reading of $\mathbf{K}\psi$ is that "ψ is one of the agent's beliefs." Thus, a formula φ is said to be *subjective* if all its atom occurrences (having at least one) are in the scope of $\mathbf{K}$. Analogously, φ is said to be *objective* if $\mathbf{K}$ does not occur in φ. For instance, $\neg\mathbf{K} a \lor \mathbf{K} b$ is subjective, $\neg a \lor b$ is objective and $\neg a \lor \mathbf{K} b$ none of the two.

To represent the agent's beliefs we will use a set $\mathbb{W}$ of propositional interpretations. We call *belief set* to each element $I \in \mathbb{W}$ and *belief view* to the whole set $\mathbb{W}$. The difference between belief and knowledge is that the former may not hold in the real world. Thus, satisfaction of formulas will be defined with respect to an interpretation $I \subseteq \mathcal{AT}$, possibly $I \notin \mathbb{W}$, that accounts for the real world: the pair $(\mathbb{W}, I)$ is called *belief interpretation* (or interpretation in modal logic KD45). Modal satisfaction is also written $(\mathbb{W}, I) \models \varphi$ (ambiguity is removed by the interpretation on the left) and follows the conditions:

- $(\mathbb{W}, I) \not\models \bot$,
- $(\mathbb{W}, I) \models a$ iff $a \in I$, for any atom $a \in \mathcal{AT}$,
- $(\mathbb{W}, I) \models \psi_1 \land \psi_2$ iff $(\mathbb{W}, I) \models \psi_1$ and $(\mathbb{W}, I) \models \psi_2$,
- $(\mathbb{W}, I) \models \psi_1 \lor \psi_2$ iff $(\mathbb{W}, I) \models \psi_1$ or $(\mathbb{W}, I) \models \psi_2$,
- $(\mathbb{W}, I) \models \psi_1 \to \psi_2$ iff $(\mathbb{W}, I) \not\models \psi_1$ or $(\mathbb{W}, I) \models \psi_2$, and

– $(\mathbb{W}, I) \models \mathbf{K}\,\psi$ iff $(\mathbb{W}, J) \models \psi$ for all $J \in \mathbb{W}$.

Notice that implication here is classical, that is, $\varphi \rightarrow \psi$ is equivalent to $\neg\varphi \vee \psi$ in this context. A belief interpretation $(\mathbb{W}, I)$ is a *belief model* of Γ iff $(\mathbb{W}, J) \models \varphi$ for all $\varphi \in \Gamma$ and all $J \in \mathbb{W} \cup \{I\}$. We say that $\mathbb{W}$ is an *epistemic model* of Γ, and abbreviate this as $\mathbb{W} \models \Gamma$, iff $(\mathbb{W}, J) \models \varphi$ for all $\varphi \in \Gamma$ and all $J \in \mathbb{W}$. Belief models defined in this way correspond to modal logic KD45 whereas epistemic models correspond to S5.

Example 1. Take the theory $\Gamma_1 = \{\neg\mathbf{K}\,b \rightarrow a\}$ corresponding to rule (1). An epistemic model $\mathbb{W} \models \Gamma_1$ must satisfy: $\langle \mathbb{W}, J \rangle \models \mathbf{K}\,b$ or $\langle \mathbb{W}, J \rangle \models a$, for all $J \in \mathbb{W}$. We get three epistemic models from $\mathbf{K}\,b$, $[\{b\}]$, $[\{a, b\}]$, and $[\{b\}, \{a, b\}]$ and the rest of cases must force a true, so we also get $[\{a\}]$ and $[\{a\}, \{a, b\}]$. In other words, Γ_1 has the same epistemic models as $\mathbf{K}\,b \vee \mathbf{K}\,a$. □

Note that rule (1) alone did not seem to provide any reason for believing b, but we got three epistemic models above satisfying $\mathbf{K}\,b$. Thus, we will be interested only in some epistemic models (we will call *world views*) that minimize the agent's beliefs in some sense. To define such a minimisation we rely on the following syntactic transformation provided by [21].

Definition 1 (Subjective reduct). *The* subjective reduct *of a theory Γ with respect to a belief view $\mathbb{W}$, also written $\Gamma^{\mathbb{W}}$, is obtained by replacing each maximal subformula of the form $\mathbf{K}\,\varphi$ by: $\top$, if $\mathbb{W} \models \mathbf{K}\,\varphi$; by $\bot$, otherwise. Notice that $\Gamma^{\mathbb{W}}$ is a classical, non-modal theory.* □

Finally, we impose a fixpoint condition where, depending on whether each belief set $I \in \mathbb{W}$ is required to be a stable model of the reduct or just a classical model, we get G91 or AEL semantics, respectively.

Definition 2 (AEL and G91 world views). *A belief view $\mathbb{W}$ is called an* AEL-world view *of a theory Γ iff $\mathbb{W} = \mathrm{CL}[\Gamma^{\mathbb{W}}]$, and is called a* G91-world view *of Γ iff $\mathbb{W} = \mathrm{SM}[\Gamma^{\mathbb{W}}]$.* □

Example 2 (Example 1 revisited). Take any $\mathbb{W}$ such that $\mathbb{W} \models \mathbf{K}\,b$. Then, $\Gamma_1^{\mathbb{W}} = \{\bot \rightarrow a\}$ with $\mathrm{CL}[\Gamma_1^{\mathbb{W}}] = [\emptyset, \{a\}, \{b\}, \{a, b\}]$ and $\mathrm{SM}[\Gamma_1^{\mathbb{W}}] = [\emptyset]$. None of the two satisfy $\mathbf{K}\,b$ so $\mathbb{W}$ cannot be fixpoint for G91 or AEL. If $\mathbb{W} \not\models \mathbf{K}\,b$ instead, we get $\Gamma_1^{\mathbb{W}} = \{\top \rightarrow a\}$, whose classical models are $\{a\}$ and $\{a, b\}$, but only the former is stable. As a result, $\mathbb{W} = [\{a\}, \{a, b\}]$ is the unique AEL world view and $\mathbb{W} = [\{a\}]$ the unique G91 world view. □

Example 3. Take now the theory $\Gamma_3 = \{\mathbf{K}\,a \rightarrow a\}$ corresponding to rule (3). If $\mathbb{W} \models \mathbf{K}\,a$ we get $\Gamma_3^{\mathbb{W}} = \{\top \rightarrow a\}$ and $\mathrm{CL}[\Gamma_3^{\mathbb{W}}] = \mathrm{SM}[\Gamma_3^{\mathbb{W}}] = \{a\}$ so $\mathbb{W} = [\{a\}]$ is an AEL and G91 world view. If $\mathbb{W} \not\models \mathbf{K}\,a$, the reduct becomes $\Gamma_3^{\mathbb{W}} = \{\bot \rightarrow a\}$, a classical tautology with unique stable model $\emptyset$. As a result, $\mathbb{W} = [\emptyset, \{a\}]$ is the other AEL world view, while $\mathbb{W} = [\emptyset]$ is the a second G91 world view. □

As we can see, the difference between AEL and G91 is that we use classical $CL[\Gamma^{\mathbb{W}}]$ instead of stable $SM[\Gamma^{\mathbb{W}}]$ models, respectively. It is well known that adding the excluded middle axiom $a \vee \neg a$ for all atoms makes equilibrium logic collapse into classical logic. This leads us to the following result.

Theorem 1. $\mathbb{W}$ *is an AEL world view of some theory* Γ *iff* $\mathbb{W}$ *is a G91-world view of* $\Gamma \cup \{a \vee \neg a \mid a \in \mathcal{AT}\}$. $\qquad\qquad\square$

4   Founded World Views of Epistemic Specifications

As we explained in the introduction, world view $[\{a\}]$ of $\{\mathbf{K}\,a \to a\}$ is considered to be "self-supported" in the literature but, unfortunately, there is no formal definition for such a concept, to the best of our knowledge. To cover this lack, we proceed to extend here the idea of unfounded sets from disjunctive logic programs to the epistemic case. For this purpose, we focus next on the original language of *epistemic specifications* [4] (a fragment of epistemic theories closer to logic programs) on which most approaches have been actually defined.

Let us start by introducing some terminology. An *objective literal* is either an atom $a \in \mathcal{AT}$, its negation $\neg a$ or its double negation $\neg\neg a$. A *subjective literal* is any of the formulas[4] $\mathbf{K}\,l$, $\neg\mathbf{K}\,l$ or $\neg\neg\mathbf{K}\,l$ where l an objective literal. A *literal* is either an objective or a subjective literal, and is called *negative* if it contains negation and *positive* otherwise. A *rule* is a formula of the form

$$a_1 \vee \ldots \vee a_n \leftarrow B_1 \wedge \ldots \wedge B_m \qquad (4)$$

with $n \geq 0$, $m \geq 0$ and $m + n > 0$, where each a_i is an atom and each B_j is a literal. For any rule r like (4), we define its body as $Body(r) \stackrel{\text{def}}{=} B_1 \wedge \ldots \wedge B_m$ and its head $Head(r) \stackrel{\text{def}}{=} a_1 \vee \ldots \vee a_n$, which we sometimes use as the set of atoms $\{a_1, \ldots, a_n\}$. When $n = 0$, $Head(r) = \bot$ and the rule is a *constraint*, whereas if $m = 0$ then $Body(r) = \top$ and the rule is a *fact*. The set $Body_{ob}^+(r)$ collects all atoms occurring in positive objective literals in the body while $Body_{sub}^+(r)$ collects all atoms occurring in positive subjective literals. An *epistemic specification* or *program* is a set of rules. As with formulas, a program without occurrences of $\mathbf{K}$ is said to be objective (it corresponds to a standard disjunctive logic program with double negation).

Definition 3 (Unfounded set). *Let* Π *be a program and* $\mathbb{W}$ *a belief view. An unfounded set* $\mathbb{S}$ *with respect to* Π *and* $\mathbb{W}$ *is a non-empty set of pairs where, for each* $\langle X, I \rangle \in \mathbb{S}$, *we have that* X *and* I *are sets of atoms and there is no rule* $r \in \Pi$ *with* $Head(r) \cap X \neq \emptyset$ *satisfying:*

1. $(\mathbb{W}, I) \models Body(r)$
2. $Body_{ob}^+(r) \cap X = \emptyset$

---

[4] We focus here on the study of the operator $\mathbf{K}$, but epistemic specifications also allow a second operator $\mathbf{M}\,l$ whose relation to $\mathbf{K}$ is also under debate and, for this reason, we leave it future work.

3. $(Head(r) \setminus X) \cap I = \emptyset$
4. $Body_{sub}^{+}(r) \cap Y = \emptyset$ with $Y = \bigcup\{ X' \mid \langle X', I' \rangle \in \mathbb{S} \}$.   □

The definition works in a similar way to standard unfounded sets [12, Definition 3.1]. In fact, the latter corresponds to the first three conditions above, except that we use $(\mathbb{W}, I)$ to check $Body(r)$, as it may contain now subjective literals. Intuitively, each I represents some potential belief set (or stable model) and X is some set of atoms without a "justifying" rule, that is, there is no $r \in \Pi$ allowing a positive derivation of atoms in X. A rule like that should have a true $Body(r)$ (condition 1) but not because of positive literals in X (condition 2) and is not used to derive other head atoms outside X (condition 3). The novelty in our definition is the addition of condition 4: to consider r a justifying rule, we additionally require not using any positive literal $\mathbf{K}\,a$ in the body such that atom a also belongs to any of the unfounded components X' in $\mathbb{S}$.

Definition 4 (Founded world view). *Let Π be a program and $\mathbb{W}$ be a belief view. We say that $\mathbb{W}$ is* unfounded *if there is some unfounded-set $\mathbb{S}$ s.t., for every $\langle X, I \rangle \in \mathbb{S}$, we have $I \in \mathbb{W}$ and $X \cap I \neq \emptyset$. $\mathbb{W}$ is called* founded *otherwise.*
□

When Π is an objective program, each pair $\langle X, I \rangle$ corresponds to a standard unfounded set X of some potential stable model I in the traditional sense of [12].

Example 4. Given the single disjunctive rule $a \lor b$ suppose we check the (expected) world view $\mathbb{W} = [\{a\}, \{b\}]$. For $I = \{a\}$ and $X = \{a\}$, rule $a \lor b$ satisfies the four conditions and justifies a. The same happens for $I = \{b\} = X$. So, $\mathbb{W}$ is founded. However, suppose we try with $\mathbb{W}' = [\{a, b\}]$ instead. For $I = \{a, b\}$ we can form $X = \{a\}$ and $X' = \{b\}$ and in both cases, the only rule in the program, $a \lor b$, violates condition 3. As a result, $\mathbb{W}'$ is unfounded due to the set $\mathbb{S}' = \{\langle\{b\}, \{a, b\}\rangle, \langle\{a\}, \{a, b\}\rangle\}$.   □

To illustrate how condition 4 works, let us continue with Example 3.

Example 5 (Example 3 continued). Theory $\Gamma_3 = \{\mathbf{K}\,a \to a\}$ is also a program. Given belief set $\mathbb{W} = [\{a\}]$ we can observe that $\mathbb{S} = [\langle\{a\}, \{a\}\rangle]$ makes $\mathbb{W}$ unfounded because the unique rule in Γ_3 does not fulfill condition 4: we cannot derive a from a rule that contains $a \in Body_{sub}^{+}(r)$. On the other hand, the other G91 world view, $\mathbb{W} = [\emptyset]$, is trivially founded.   □

Since Definition 4 only depends on some epistemic program and its selected world views, we can raise it to a general property for any epistemic semantics.

Property 1 (Foundedness). A semantics satisfies *foundedness* when all the world views it assigns to any program Π are founded.   □

Approaches proposed after G91 do remove unfounded world views in the examples studied in the literature, but unfortunately, this does not mean that they generally satisfy foundedness. Let us consider a common counterexample.

Example 6. Take the epistemic logic program:

$$a \vee b \qquad\qquad a \leftarrow \mathbf{K}\, b \qquad\qquad b \leftarrow \mathbf{K}\, a \qquad\qquad (\varPi_1)$$

whose G91-world views are $\mathbb{W} = [\{a\}, \{b\}]$ and $\mathbb{W}' = [\{a, b\}]$. These are, indeed, the two cases we analysed in Example 4. $\mathbb{W}$ is again founded because $a \vee b$ keeps justifying both possible $\langle X, I\rangle$ pairs, that is, $[\langle\{a\}, \{a\}\rangle]$ and $[\langle\{b\}, \{b\}\rangle]$. However, for $\mathbb{W}'$ we still have the unfounded set $\mathbb{S}' = [\langle\{a\}, \{a, b\}\rangle, \langle\{b\}, \{a, b\}\rangle]$ which violates condition 3 for the first rule as before, but also condition 4 for the other two rules. □

Note how $\mathbb{S}'$ allows us to spot the root of the derivability problem: to justify a in $\langle\{a\}, \{a, b\}\rangle$ we cannot use $a \leftarrow \mathbf{K}\, b$ because b is part of the unfounded structure X in the other pair $\langle\{b\}, \{a, b\}\rangle$, and vice versa. Since the variants by Gelfond in [5] (G11) and Kahl et al. [9] (K15) also assign the unfounded world view $\mathbb{W}'$ to $\varPi_1$ (in fact, they coincide with G91 for this program), we can conclude that G11 and K15 *do not satisfy foundedness* either.

A more elaborated strategy is adopted by the recent approaches by Fariñas et al. [2] (F15) and Shen and Eiter [20] (S17), that treat the previous world views as candidate solutions[5], but select the ones with *minimal knowledge* in a second step. This allows removing the unfounded world view $[\{a, b\}]$ in Example 6, because the other solution $[\{a\}, \{b\}]$ provides less knowledge. Unfortunately, this strategy does not suffice to guarantee foundedness, since other formulas (such as constraints) may remove the founded world view, as explained below.

Example 7 (Example 6 continued). Take the program $\varPi_2 = \varPi_1 \cup \{\bot \leftarrow \neg\mathbf{K}\, a\}$. The constraint rules out $\mathbb{W} = [\{a\}, \{b\}]$ because the latter satisfies $\neg\mathbf{K}\, a$. In G91, G11, F15 and S17, only world view $\mathbb{W}' = [\{a, b\}]$ is left, so knowledge minimisation has no effect. However, $\mathbb{W}'$ is still unfounded in $\varPi_2$ since constraints do not affect that feature (their empty head never justifies any atom). □

As a conclusion, semantics F15 and S17 *do not satisfy foundedness* either.

5 Founded Autoepistemic Equilibrium Logic

We present now the semantics proposed in this paper, introducing *Founded Autoepistemic Equilibrium Logic* (FAEEL). The basic idea is an elaboration of the belief (or KD45) interpretation $(\mathbb{W}, I)$ already seen but replacing belief sets by HT pairs. Thus, we extend now the idea of *belief view* $\mathbb{W}$ to a non-empty set of HT-interpretations $\mathbb{W} = \{\langle H_1, T_1\rangle, \ldots, \langle H_n, T_n\rangle\}$ and say that $\mathbb{W}$ is *total* when $H_i = T_i$ for all of them, coinciding with the form of belief views $\mathbb{W} = \{T_1, \ldots, T_n\}$ we had so far. Similarly, a *belief interpretation* is now redefined as $(\mathbb{W}, \langle H, T\rangle)$, or simply $(\mathbb{W}, H, T)$, where $\mathbb{W}$ is a belief view and $\langle H, T\rangle$ stands for the real world, possibly not in $\mathbb{W}$. Next, we redefine the satisfaction relation from a combination of modal logic KD45 and HT. A belief interpretation $\mathcal{I} = (\mathbb{W}, H, T)$ satisfies a formula φ, written $\mathcal{I} \models \varphi$, iff:

---

[5] In [2], these candidate world views are called *epistemic equilibrium models* while selected world views receive the name of *autoepistemic equilibrium models*.

- $\mathcal{I} \not\models \bot$,
- $\mathcal{I} \models a$ iff $a \in H$, for any atom $a \in \mathcal{AT}$,
- $\mathcal{I} \models \psi_1 \wedge \psi_2$ iff $\mathcal{I} \models \psi_1$ and $\mathcal{I} \models \psi_2$,
- $\mathcal{I} \models \psi_1 \vee \psi_2$ iff $\mathcal{I} \models \psi_1$ or $\mathcal{I} \models \psi_2$,
- $\mathcal{I} \models \psi_1 \rightarrow \psi_2$ iff both: (i) $\mathcal{I} \not\models \psi_1$ or $\mathcal{I} \models \psi_2$; and (ii) $(\mathbb{W}^t, T) \not\models \psi_1$ or $(\mathbb{W}^t, T) \models \psi_2$, where $\mathbb{W}^t = \{T_i \mid \langle H_i, T_i \rangle \in \mathbb{W}\}$.
- $\mathcal{I} \models \mathbf{K}\psi$ iff $(\mathbb{W}, H_i, T_i) \models \psi$ for all $\langle H_i, T_i \rangle \in \mathbb{W}$.

For total belief interpretations, this new satisfaction relation collapses to the one in Sect. 3 (that is, KD45). Interpretation $(\mathbb{W}, H, T)$ is a *belief model* of Γ iff $(\mathbb{W}, H_i, T_i) \models \varphi$ for all $\langle H_i, T_i \rangle \in \mathbb{W} \cup \{\langle H, T \rangle\}$ and all $\varphi \in \Gamma$ – additionally, when $\langle H, T \rangle \in \mathbb{W}$, we further say that $\mathbb{W}$ is an *epistemic model* of Γ, abbreviated as $\mathbb{W} \models \Gamma$.

Proposition 1 (Persistence). $(\mathbb{W}, H, T) \models \varphi$ implies $(\mathbb{W}^t, T) \models \varphi$. □

A belief model just captures collections of HT models which need not be in equilibrium. To make the agent's beliefs correspond to stable models we impose a particular minimisation criterion on belief models.

Definition 5. *We define the partial order $\mathcal{I}' \preceq \mathcal{I}$ for belief interpretations $\mathcal{I}' = (\mathbb{W}', H', T')$ and $\mathcal{I} = (\mathbb{W}, H, T)$ when the following three conditions hold:*

1. $T' = T$ and $H' \subseteq H$, and
2. *for every $\langle H_i, T_i \rangle \in \mathbb{W}$, there is some $\langle H_i', T_i \rangle \in \mathbb{W}'$, with $H_i' \subseteq H_i$.*
3. *for every $\langle H_i', T_i \rangle \in \mathbb{W}'$, there is some $\langle H_i, T_i \rangle \in \mathbb{W}$, with $H_i' \subseteq H_i$.* □

As usual, $\mathcal{I}' \prec \mathcal{I}$ means $\mathcal{I}' \preceq \mathcal{I}$ and $\mathcal{I}' \neq \mathcal{I}$. The intuition for $\mathcal{I}' \preceq \mathcal{I}$ is that $\mathcal{I}'$ contains less information than $\mathcal{I}$ for each fixed T_i component. As a result, $\mathcal{I}' \models \varphi$ implies $\mathcal{I} \models \varphi$ for any formula φ without implications other than $\neg \psi = \psi \rightarrow \bot$.

Definition 6. *A total belief interpretation $\mathcal{I} = (\mathbb{W}, T)$ is said to be an* equilibrium belief model *of some theory Γ iff $\mathcal{I}$ is a belief model of Γ and there is no other belief model $\mathcal{I}'$ of Γ such that $\mathcal{I}' \prec \mathcal{I}$.* □

By $\text{EQB}[\Gamma]$ we denote the set of equilibrium belief models of Γ. As a final step, we impose a fixpoint condition to minimise the agent's knowledge as follows.

Definition 7. *A belief view $\mathbb{W}$ is called an* equilibrium world view *of Γ iff:*

$$\mathbb{W} = \{\, T \mid (\mathbb{W}, T) \in \text{EQB}[\Gamma] \,\}$$ □

Example 8 (Example 5 continued). Back to $\Gamma_3 = \{\mathbf{K}a \rightarrow a\}$, remember its unique founded G91-world view was $[\emptyset]$. It is easy to see that $\mathcal{I} = ([\emptyset], \emptyset) \in \text{EQB}[\Gamma_3]$ because $([\emptyset], \emptyset) \models \Gamma_3$ and no smaller belief model can be obtained. Moreover, $[\emptyset]$ is an equilibrium world view of Γ_3 since no other $T \not\in [\emptyset]$ satisfies $([\emptyset], T) \in \text{EQB}[\Gamma_3]$. The only possibility is $([\emptyset], \{a\})$ but it fails because there is a smaller belief model $([\emptyset], \emptyset, \{a\})$ satisfying $\mathbf{K}a \rightarrow a$. As for the other potential world view $[\{a\}]$, it is not in equilibrium: we already have $\mathcal{I}' = ([\{a\}], \{a\}) \not\in \text{EQB}[\Gamma_3]$ because the smaller interpretation $\mathcal{I}'' = ([\langle \emptyset, \{a\} \rangle], \{a\}, \{a\})$ also satisfies Γ_3. In particular, note that $\mathcal{I}'' \not\models \mathbf{K}a$ and, thus, clearly satisfies $\mathbf{K}a \rightarrow a$. □

The logic induced by equilibrium world views is called *Founded Autoepistemic Equilibrium Logic* (FAEEL). A first important property is:

Theorem 2. *FAEEL satisfies foundedness.*   □

A second interesting feature is that equilibrium world views are also G91-world views though the converse may not be the case (as we just saw in Example 8). This holds, not only for programs, but in general for any theory:

Theorem 3. *For any theory Γ, its equilibrium world views are also G91-world views of Γ.*   □

In other words, FAEEL is strictly stronger than G91, something that, as we see next, is not the case in other approaches in the literature.

Example 9. The following program:

$$a \vee b \qquad\qquad c \leftarrow \mathbf{K}\, a \qquad\qquad \bot \leftarrow \neg c \qquad\qquad (\Pi_3)$$

has no G91-world views, but according to G11, K15, F15 and S17 has world view $[\{a, c\}]$. This example was also used in [1] to show that these semantics do not satisfy another property, called there *epistemic splitting*.   □

Example 10 (Example 6 continued). Take again program Π_1 whose G91-world views were $\mathbb{W} = [\{a\}, \{b\}]$ and $\mathbb{W}' = [\{a, b\}]$. Since $\mathbb{W}'$ is unfounded, it cannot be an equilibrium world view (Theorem 2), leaving $\mathbb{W}$ as the only candidate (Theorem 3). Let us check that this is in fact an equilibrium world view. First, note that $\mathcal{I} = ([\{a\}, \{b\}], \{a\}) \in \mathrm{EQB}[\Pi_1]$ because there is no model $\mathcal{I}'$ of Π_1 such that $\mathcal{I}' \preceq \mathcal{I}$. In fact, it is easy to see that $([\langle H_1, \{a\}\rangle, \langle H_2, \{b\}\rangle], H_3, \{a\})$ is not a model of the rule $a \vee b$ if $H_i = \emptyset$ for any $i \in \{1, 2, 3\}$. Symmetrically, we have that $\mathcal{I}' = ([\{a\}, \{b\}], \{b\}) \in \mathrm{EQB}[\Pi_1]$ too. Finally, we have to check that no other $T \not\subseteq [\{a\}, \{b\}]$ can form an equilibrium belief model. For the case $T = \emptyset$, it is easy to check that $([\{a\}, \{b\}], \emptyset)$ does not satisfy $a \vee b$. For $T = \{a, b\}$, we have that $\mathcal{I}'' = ([\{a\}, \{b\}], \{a, b\}) \notin \mathrm{EQB}[\Pi_1]$ because, for instance, the smaller $\mathcal{I}''' = ([\{a\}, \{b\}], \{a\}, \{a, b\})$ is a model of Π_1.   □

Theorems 2 and 3 assert that any equilibrium world view is a founded G91-world view. The natural question is whether the opposite also holds. In Examples 8, 9 and 10 we did not find any counterexample, and this is in fact a general property, as stated below.

Main Theorem. *Given any program Π, its equilibrium world views coincide with its founded G91-world views.*   □

An interesting observation is that in all the original examples of epistemic specifications [4, 7] used by Gelfond to introduce G91, modal operators occurred in the scope of negation. Negated beliefs never incur unfoundedness, so this feature could not be spotted using this family of examples. In fact, under this syntactic restriction, FAEEL and G91 coincide.

program	world views
$a \vee b$	$[\{a\}, \{b\}]$
$a \vee b$ $a \leftarrow \mathbf{K} b$	$[\{a\}, \{b\}]$
$a \vee b$ $a \leftarrow \neg \mathbf{K} b$	$[\{a\}]$
$a \vee b$ $c \leftarrow \neg \mathbf{K} b$	$[\{a, c\}, \{b, c\}]$
$a \leftarrow \neg \mathbf{K} b$ $b \leftarrow \neg \mathbf{K} a$	$[\{a\}]$, $[\{b\}]$
$a \leftarrow \neg \mathbf{K} \neg a$ $a \leftarrow \neg \mathbf{K} a$	$[\{a\}]$

program	G91/G11/FAEEL	K15/F15/S17
$a \leftarrow \neg \mathbf{K} \neg a$	$[\emptyset]$, $[\{a\}]$	$[\{a\}]$
$a \vee b$ $a \leftarrow \neg \mathbf{K} \neg b$	none	$[\{a\}]$
$a \vee b$ $a \leftarrow \mathbf{K} \neg b$	$[\{a\}]$, $[\{a\}, \{b\}]$	$[\{a\}, \{b\}]$
$a \leftarrow b$ $b \leftarrow \neg \mathbf{K} \neg a$	$[\emptyset]$, $[\{a, b\}]$	$[\{a, b\}]$
$a \leftarrow \neg \mathbf{K} \neg b$ $b \leftarrow \neg \mathbf{K} \neg a$	$[\emptyset]$, $[\{a\}, \{b\}]$	$[\{a\}, \{b\}]$

Fig. 1. On the left, examples where G91, G11, K15, F15, S17 and FAEEL agree. On the right, examples where FAEEL/G91/G11 differ from K15/F15/S17.

Proposition 2. *For any theory where all occurrences of* $\mathbf{K}$ *are in the scope of negation, we have that the equilibrium world views and the G91-world views coincide.* □

Proposition 2 also holds for semantics [21,22] that are conservative extensions of G91, as well as for G11. Apart from foundedness, [1] recently proposed other four properties for semantics of epistemic specifications. We analyse here three of them, omitting the so-called *epistemic splitting* due to lack of space.

1. *supra-ASP* holds when, for any objective theory Γ, either Γ has a unique world view $\mathbb{W} = \mathrm{SM}[\Gamma] \neq \emptyset$ or $\mathrm{SM}[\Gamma] = \emptyset$ and Γ has no world view.
2. *supra-S5* holds when every world view $\mathbb{W}$ of a theory Γ is also an S5-model of Γ (that is, $\mathbb{W} \models \Gamma$).
3. *subjective constraint monotonicity* holds when, for any theory Γ and any subjective constraint $\bot \leftarrow \varphi$, we have that $\mathbb{W}$ is a world view of $\Gamma \cup \{\bot \leftarrow \varphi\}$ iff both $\mathbb{W}$ is a world view of Γ and $\mathbb{W}$ is not an S5-model of φ.

Proposition 3. *FAEEL satisfies supra-ASP, supra-S5 and subjective constraint monotonicity.* □

All semantics discussed in this paper satisfy the above first two properties but most of them fail for subjective constraint monotonicity, as first discussed in [10]. In fact, a variation of Example 9 can be used to show that K15, F15 and S17 do not satisfy this property.

Example 11 (Example 9 continued). Suppose we remove the constraint (last rule) from Π_3 getting the program $\Pi_4 = \{a \vee b, c \leftarrow \mathbf{K} a\}$. All semantics, including G91 and FAEEL, agree that Π_4 has a unique world view $[\{a\}, \{b\}]$. Suppose we add now a subjective constraint $\Pi_5 = \Pi_4 \cup \{\bot \leftarrow \neg \mathbf{K} c\}$. This addition leaves G91 and FAEEL without world views (due to subjective constraint monotonicity) the same happens for G11, but not for K15, F15 and S17, which provide a *new* world view $[\{a, c\}]$ not obtained before adding the subjective constraint. □

Tables 1 and 2 show a list of examples taken from Table 4 in [2] and their world views according to different semantics.

program	G91	G11/FAEEL	K15	F15/S17
$a \leftarrow \neg\mathbf{K}\neg b \wedge \neg b$ $b \leftarrow \neg\mathbf{K}\neg a \wedge \neg a$		$[\emptyset] \, , [\{a\}, \{b\}]$		$[\{a\}, \{b\}]$
$a \leftarrow \mathbf{K}\, a$	$[\emptyset] \, , [\{a\}]$		$[\emptyset]$	
$a \leftarrow \mathbf{K}\, a$ $a \leftarrow \neg\mathbf{K}\, a$	$[\{a\}]$		none	

Fig. 2. Examples splitting different semantics. Examples 6 and 9 in the paper can be used to further split FAEEL and G11.

6   Conclusions

In order to characterise self-supported world-views, already present in Gelfond's 1991 semantics [4] (G91), we have extended the definition of unfounded sets from standard logic programs to epistemic specifications. As a result, we proposed the *foundedness* property for epistemic semantics, which is not satisfied by other approaches in the literature. Our main contribution has been the definition of a new semantics, based on the so-called *Founded Autoepistemic Equilibrium Logic* (FAEEL), that satisfies foundedness. This semantics actually covers the syntax of any arbitrary modal theory and is a combination of Equilibrium Logic and Autoepistemic Logic. As a main result, we were able to prove that, for the syntax of epistemic specifications, FAEEL world views coincide with the set of G91 world views that are founded. We showed how this semantics behaves on a set of common examples in the literature and proved that it satisfies other three basic properties: all world views are S5 models (*supra-S5*); standard programs have (at most) a unique world view containing all the stable models (*supra-ASP*); and subjective constraints just remove world views (monotonicity). FAEEL also satisfies the property of *epistemic splitting* as proposed in [1], but we leave the proof and discussion for future work, together with a formal comparison with other approaches.

Acknowledgements. We are thankful to Michael Gelfond and David Pearce for their helpful comments on early versions of this work and to the anonymous reviewers for their valuable feedback in improving the paper.

References

1. Cabalar, P., Fandinno, J., Fariñas del Cerro, L.: Splitting Epistemic Logic Programs. arXiv e-prints arXiv:1812.08763. December 2018
2. Fariñas del Cerro, L., Herzig, A., Su, E.I.: Epistemic equilibrium logic. In: Proceedings of the International Joint Conference on Artificial Intelligence, IJCAI 2015, pp. 2964–2970. AAAI Press (2015)
3. Gelder, A.V., Ross, K.A., Schlipf, J.S.: The well-founded semantics for general logic programs. J. ACM **38**(3), 620–650 (1991)
4. Gelfond, M.: Strong introspection. In: Dean, T.L., McKeown, K. (eds.) Proceedings of the AAAI Conference, vol. 1, pp. 386–391. AAAI Press/The MIT Press (1991)
5. Gelfond, M.: New semantics for epistemic specifications. In: Delgrande, J.P., Faber, W. (eds.) LPNMR 2011. LNCS (LNAI), vol. 6645, pp. 260–265. Springer, Heidelberg (2011). https://doi.org/10.1007/978-3-642-20895-9_29
6. Gelfond, M., Lifschitz, V.: The stable model semantics for logic programming. In: Proceedings of the 5th International Conference on Logic Programming, ICLP 1988, pp. 1070–1080 (1988)
7. Gelfond, M., Przymusinska, H.: Reasoning on open domains. In: Proceedings of the International Conference on Logic Programming and Non-Monotonic Reasoning, LPNMR 1993, pp. 397–413. MIT Press (1993)
8. Heyting, A.: Die formalen Regeln der intuitionistischen Logik. Sitzungsberichte der Preussischen Akademie der Wissenschaften, Physikalisch-mathematische Klasse, pp. 42–56 (1930)
9. Kahl, P., Watson, R., Balai, E., Gelfond, M., Zhang, Y.: The language of epistemic specifications (refined) including a prototype solver. J. Logic Comput. (2015). (Special issue article)
10. Kahl, P.T., Leclerc, A.P.: Epistemic logic programs with world view constraints. In: ICLP (Technical Communications), vol. 64, pp. 1:1–1:17. OASICS, Schloss Dagstuhl - Leibniz-Zentrum fuer Informatik (2018)
11. Konolige, K.: On the relation between default and autoepistemic logic. Artif. Intell. **35**(3), 343–382 (1988)
12. Leone, N., Rullo, P., Scarcello, F.: Disjunctive stable models: unfounded sets, fixpoint semantics, and computation. Inf. Comput. **135**(2), 69–112 (1997)
13. Marek, V.W., Truszczynski, M.: Relating autoepistemic and default logics. In: KR, pp. 276–288. Morgan Kaufmann (1989)
14. Moore, R.C.: Possible-world semantics for autoepistemic logic. In: Proceedings of the Non-Monotonic Reasoning Workshop, Mohonk Mountain House, New Paltz, NY 12561, USA, 17–19 October 1984. pp. 344–354. American Association for Artificial Intelligence (AAAI) (1984)
15. Moore, R.C.: Semantical considerations on nonmonotonic logic. Artif. Intell. **25**(1), 75–94 (1985). https://doi.org/10.1016/0004-3702(85)90042-6
16. Niemelä, I.: Constructive tightly grounded autoepistemic reasoning. In: IJCAI, pp. 399–405. Morgan Kaufmann (1991)
17. Pearce, D.: A new logical characterisation of stable models and answer sets. In: Dix, J., Pereira, L.M., Przymusinski, T.C. (eds.) NMELP 1996. LNCS, vol. 1216, pp. 57–70. Springer, Heidelberg (1997). https://doi.org/10.1007/BFb0023801
18. Schwarz, G.: Autoepistemic logic of knowledge. In: Nerode, A., Marek, V.W., Subrahmanian, V.S. (eds.) Logic Programming and Non-monotonic Reasoning, Proceedings of the First International Workshop, Washington, D.C., USA, July 1991, pp. 260–274. The MIT Press (1991)

19. Schwarz, G.: Minimal model semantics for nonmonotonic modal logics. In: Proceedings of the Seventh Annual IEEE Symposium on Logic in Computer Science 1992, LICS 1992, pp. 34–43. IEEE (1992)
20. Shen, Y., Eiter, T.: Evaluating epistemic negation in answer set programming (extended abstract). In: Proceedings of the International Joint Conference on Artificial Intelligence, IJCAI 2017, pp. 5060–5064 (2017)
21. Truszczyński, M.: Revisiting epistemic specifications. In: Balduccini, M., Son, T.C. (eds.) Logic Programming, Knowledge Representation, and Nonmonotonic Reasoning. LNCS (LNAI), vol. 6565, pp. 315–333. Springer, Heidelberg (2011). https://doi.org/10.1007/978-3-642-20832-4_20
22. Wang, K., Zhang, Y.: Nested epistemic logic programs. In: Baral, C., Greco, G., Leone, N., Terracina, G. (eds.) LPNMR 2005. LNCS (LNAI), vol. 3662, pp. 279–290. Springer, Heidelberg (2005). https://doi.org/10.1007/11546207_22

Towards Dynamic Answer Set Programming over Finite Traces

Pedro Cabalar[2] ⓘ, Martín Diéguez[1] ⓘ, and Torsten Schaub[3,4,5(✉)] ⓘ

[1] ENIB, Brest, France
martin.dieguez@enib.fr
[2] University of Corunna, A Coruña, Spain
pedro.cabalar@udc.es
[3] University of Potsdam, Potsdam, Germany
torsten@cs.uni-potsdam.de
[4] Simon Fraser University, Burnaby, Canada
[5] Griffith University, Brisbane, Australia

Abstract. Our ultimate goal is to conceive an extension of Answer Set Programming with language constructs from dynamic (and temporal) logic to provide an expressive computational framework for modeling dynamic applications. To address this in a semantically well founded way, we generalize the definition of Dynamic Equilibrium Logic to accommodate finite linear time and extend it with a converse operator in order to capture past temporal operators. This results in a general logical framework integrating existing dynamic and temporal logics of Here-and-There over both finite and infinite time. In the context of finite time, we then develop a translation of dynamic formulas into propositional ones that can in turn be translated into logic programs.

1 Introduction

Answer Set Programming (ASP [13]) has become a popular approach to solving knowledge-intense combinatorial search problems due to its performant solving engines and expressive modeling language.However, both are mainly geared towards static domains and lack native support for handling dynamic applications. We have addressed this shortcoming over the last decade by creating a temporal extension of ASP [1] based on Linear Temporal Logic (LTL [15]) that has recently led to the temporal ASP system *telingo* [5]. The approach of LTL has however its limitations when it comes to expressing control over temporal trajectories. Such control can be better addressed with Dynamic Logic (DL [16]), offering a more fine-grained approach to temporal reasoning thanks to the possibility to form complex actions from primitive ones. [1] To this end, DL relies on modal propositions, like $[\rho]\,\varphi$, to express that all executions of (complex) action ρ terminate in a state satisfying φ. As an example, consider a "Russian roulette" variation of the Yale-shooting-scenario, so the turkey is dead after we pull the

---

[1] The same consideration led to GOLOG [12] in the context of the situation calculus.

© Springer Nature Switzerland AG 2019
M. Balduccini et al. (Eds.): LPNMR 2019, LNAI 11481, pp. 148–162, 2019.
https://doi.org/10.1007/978-3-030-20528-7_12

trigger as many times as needed until we reach the loaded chamber. This can be expressed in DL via the proposition: [**while** ¬*loaded* **do** *trigger*; *trigger*] *dead*. The term within brackets delineates trajectories matching the regular expression '(¬*loaded*?; *trigger*)*; *loaded*?; *trigger*', where φ? tests whether φ holds at the state at hand, and ';' and '*' are the sequential composition and iteration operators, respectively. With this, the above proposition is satisfied whenever the state following a matching trajectory entails *dead*.

This expressive power motivated us to introduce the basic foundations of an extension of ASP with dynamic operators from DL in [4]. In what follows, we build upon these foundations (i) to introduce a general logical framework comprising previous dynamic and temporal extensions and (ii) to elaborate upon a translation to propositional theories that can in turn be compiled into logic programs. To this end, we follow the good practice of first introducing an extension to ASP's base logic, the *Logic of Here-and-There* (HT [11]), and then to devise an appropriate reduction. An HT interpretation $\langle H, T \rangle$ is a pair of interpretations that can be seen as being three-valued, where atoms in H are "*certainly true*," atoms not in T are "*false*" and atoms in T are "*potentially true*." This explains the usual condition $H \subseteq T$, meaning that anything certainly true is also potentially true. An HT interpretation $\langle H, T \rangle$ is said to be *total* if $H = T$, that is, the mapping becomes two-valued. Total interpretations satisfying a certain minimality condition are known to correspond to stable models; they are also referred to as equilibrium models, and the resulting logic is called *Equilibrium Logic* (EL). For capturing (linear) time, sequences of such HT interpretations are considered, similar to LTL. In accord with [7], we argue that such linear traces provide an appropriate semantic account of time in our context, and thus base also our dynamic extension of ASP on the same kind of semantic structures.

Our ultimate goal is to conceive an extension of ASP with language constructs from dynamic (and temporal) logic in order to provide an expressive computational framework for modeling dynamic applications. To address this in a semantically well founded way, we generalize the definition of *Dynamic* HT *and* EL (DHT/DEL [4]) to accommodate finite traces and augment it with a converse operator (in order to capture past temporal operators). This not only allows us to embed temporal extensions of ASP, such as *Temporal Equilibrium Logic* over finite traces (TEL$_f$ [5]) along with its past and future operators, and more standard ones like LTL$_f$ [7], but moreover provides us with blueprints for implementation on top of existing (temporal) ASP solvers like *telingo*. Indeed, DEL$_f$ can be regarded as a non-monotonic counterpart of LTL$_f$ [7], being in an analogous relationship as classical and equilibrium logic, or SAT and ASP, respectively.

More precisely, we start in Sect. 2 by defining a general logical framework integrating existing dynamic and temporal logics of Here-and-There and their associated Equilibrium logics over both finite and infinite traces. Section 3 is dedicated to the computational development of our approach in the context of finite traces. We introduce a translation from dynamic formulas to propositional ones by relying on a normal form for complex actions. Finally, Sect. 4 concludes the paper.

2   Linear Dynamic Equilibrium Logic

Given a set $\mathcal{A}$ of propositional variables (called *alphabet*), *dynamic formulas* φ and *path expressions* ρ are mutually defined as in [7] by the pair of grammar rules:

$$\varphi ::= a \mid \bot \mid \top \mid [\rho]\,\varphi \mid \langle \rho \rangle\,\varphi \,, \qquad \rho ::= \top \mid \varphi? \mid \rho + \rho \mid \rho\,;\rho \mid \rho^* \mid \rho^- \,.$$

Each ρ is a regular expression formed with the truth constant $\top$ plus the test construct φ? typical of Dynamic Logic (DL [9]). An important feature that departs from DL is that, in the latter, atomic path expressions are formed with a sort of so-called *atomic actions* that is separated from propositional atoms in $\mathcal{A}$, used for formulas. We adopt the approach of [7] and considering that the only atomic path expression is $\top$, keeping the test construct φ? that may refer to propositional atoms in the (single) alphabet $\mathcal{A}$.

As we show further below, the above language allows us to capture several derived operators, like the Boolean and temporal ones:

$$\varphi \wedge \psi \overset{def}{=} \langle \varphi? \rangle\,\psi \qquad\qquad \varphi \vee \psi \overset{def}{=} \langle \varphi? + \psi? \rangle\,\top$$

$$\varphi \to \psi \overset{def}{=} [\varphi?]\,\psi \qquad\qquad \neg\varphi \overset{def}{=} \varphi \to \bot$$

$$\mathbb{F} \overset{def}{=} [\top]\bot \qquad\qquad \mathsf{I} \overset{def}{=} [\top^-]\bot$$

$$\circ\varphi \overset{def}{=} \langle\top\rangle\,\varphi \qquad\qquad \bullet\varphi \overset{def}{=} \langle\top^-\rangle\,\varphi$$

$$\widehat{\circ}\varphi \overset{def}{=} [\top]\,\varphi \qquad\qquad \widehat{\bullet}\varphi \overset{def}{=} [\top^-]\,\varphi$$

$$\Diamond\varphi \overset{def}{=} \langle\top^*\rangle\,\varphi \qquad\qquad \blacklozenge\varphi \overset{def}{=} \langle\top^{*-}\rangle\,\varphi$$

$$\Box\varphi \overset{def}{=} [\top^*]\,\varphi \qquad\qquad \blacksquare\varphi \overset{def}{=} [\top^{*-}]\,\varphi$$

$$\varphi \,\mathsf{U}\, \psi \overset{def}{=} \langle(\varphi?;\top)^*\rangle\,\psi \qquad\qquad \varphi \,\mathsf{S}\, \psi \overset{def}{=} \langle(\varphi?;\top)^{*-}\rangle\,\psi$$

$$\varphi \,\mathbb{R}\, \psi \overset{def}{=} (\psi \,\mathsf{U}\, (\varphi \wedge \psi)) \vee \Box\psi \qquad\qquad \varphi \,\mathsf{T}\, \psi \overset{def}{=} (\psi \,\mathsf{S}\, (\varphi \wedge \psi)) \vee \blacksquare\psi$$

While negation $\neg$ is expressed as usual in HT via implication, all other connectives are defined in terms of the dynamic operators $\langle\cdot\rangle$ and $[\cdot]$. This involves the Booleans' $\wedge$, $\vee$, and $\to$, among which the definition of $\to$ is most noteworthy since it hints at the implicative nature of $[\cdot]$, as well as the future temporal operators $\mathbb{F}, \circ, \widehat{\circ}, \Diamond, \Box, \mathsf{U}, \mathbb{R}$, standing for *final, next, weak next, eventually, always, until,* and *release,* and their past-oriented counterparts: $\mathsf{I}, \bullet, \widehat{\bullet}, \blacklozenge, \blacksquare, \mathsf{S}, \mathsf{T}$. The weak one-step operators, $\widehat{\circ}$ and $\widehat{\bullet}$, are of particular interest when dealing with finite traces, since their behavior differs from their genuine counterparts only at the ends of a trace. In fact, $\widehat{\circ}\varphi$ can also be expressed as $\circ\varphi \vee \mathbb{F}$ (and $\widehat{\bullet}$ as $\bullet\varphi \vee \mathsf{I}$). Finally, note that the converse operator ρ^- is essential for expressing all temporal past operators, whose addition in temporal logic is exponentially more succinct than using only future operators [2]. A formula is *propositional*, if all its connectives are Boolean, and *temporal*, if it includes only Boolean and temporal ones. A dynamic formula is said to be *conditional* if it contains some occurrence of an atom $p \in \mathcal{A}$ inside a $[\cdot]$ operator; it is called *unconditional* otherwise. Note that formulas with atoms in implication antecedents or negated formulas are also conditional, since they are derived from $[\cdot]$. For instance, $[p?]\bot$ is conditional, and is actually the same as $p \to \bot$ and $\neg p$. As usual, a *(dynamic) theory* is a set of (dynamic) formulas.

Following the definition of *linear* DL (LDL) in [7], we sometimes use a propositional formula ϕ as a path expression actually standing for $(\phi?; \top)$. Another abbreviation is the sequence of n repetitions of some expression ρ defined as $\rho^0 \stackrel{def}{=} \top?$ and $\rho^{n+1} \stackrel{def}{=} \rho; \rho^n$. For instance, $\rho^3 = \rho; \rho; \rho; \top?$ which amounts to $\rho; \rho; \rho$, as we see below.

Given $a \in \mathbb{N}$ and $b \in \mathbb{N} \cup \{\omega\}$, we let $[a..b]$ stand for the set $\{i \in \mathbb{N} \mid a \leq i \leq b\}$ and $[a..b)$ for $\{i \in \mathbb{N} \mid a \leq i < b\}$. For the semantics, we start by defining a *trace* of length λ over alphabet $\mathcal{A}$ as a sequence $\langle H_i \rangle_{i \in [0..\lambda)}$ of sets $H_i \subseteq \mathcal{A}$. A trace is *infinite* if $\lambda = \omega$ and *finite* otherwise, that is, $\lambda = n$ for some natural number $n \in \mathbb{N}$. Given traces $\mathbf{H} = \langle H_i \rangle_{i \in [0..\lambda)}$ and $\mathbf{H}' = \langle H'_i \rangle_{i \in [0..\lambda)}$ both of length λ, we write $\mathbf{H} \leq \mathbf{H}'$ if $H_i \subseteq H'_i$ for each $i \in [0..\lambda)$; accordingly, $\mathbf{H} < \mathbf{H}'$ iff both $\mathbf{H} \leq \mathbf{H}'$ and $\mathbf{H} \neq \mathbf{H}'$.

A *Here-and-There trace* (for short HT-*trace*) of length λ over alphabet $\mathcal{A}$ is a sequence of pairs $\langle H_i, T_i \rangle_{i \in [0..\lambda)}$ such that $H_i \subseteq T_i \subseteq \mathcal{A}$ for any $i \in [0..\lambda)$. As before, an HT-trace is infinite if $\lambda = \omega$ and finite otherwise. We often represent an HT-trace as a pair of traces $\langle \mathbf{H}, \mathbf{T} \rangle$ of length λ where $\mathbf{H} = \langle H_i \rangle_{i \in [0..\lambda)}$ and $\mathbf{T} = \langle T_i \rangle_{i \in [0..\lambda)}$ and $\mathbf{H} \leq \mathbf{T}$. A particular type of HT-traces satisfy $\mathbf{H} = \mathbf{T}$ and are called *total*.

We proceed by generalizing the extension of HT with dynamic operators, called DHT in [4], to HT-traces of fixed length in order to integrate finite as well as infinite traces, and by adding the converse operator. The overall definition of DHT satisfaction relies on a double induction. Given any HT-trace $\mathbf{M} = \langle \mathbf{H}, \mathbf{T} \rangle$, we define DHT satisfaction of formulas, $\mathbf{M}, k \models \varphi$, in terms of an accessibility relation for path expressions $\|\rho\|^{\mathbf{M}} \subseteq \mathbb{N}^2$ whose extent depends again on $\models$.

Definition 1 (DHT satisfaction). *An* HT-*trace* $\mathbf{M} = \langle \mathbf{H}, \mathbf{T} \rangle$ *of length* λ *over alphabet* $\mathcal{A}$ *satisfies a dynamic formula* φ *at time point* $k \in [0..\lambda)$, *written* $\mathbf{M}, k \models \varphi$, *if the following conditions hold:*

1. $\mathbf{M}, k \models \top$ *and* $\mathbf{M}, k \not\models \bot$
2. $\mathbf{M}, k \models a$ *if* $a \in H_k$ *for any atom* $a \in \mathcal{A}$
3. $\mathbf{M}, k \models \langle \rho \rangle \varphi$ *if* $\mathbf{M}, i \models \varphi$ *for some* i *with* $(k, i) \in \|\rho\|^{\mathbf{M}}$
4. $\mathbf{M}, k \models [\rho] \varphi$ *if* $\mathbf{M}', i \models \varphi$ *for all* i *with* $(k, i) \in \|\rho\|^{\mathbf{M}'}$
   for both $\mathbf{M}' = \mathbf{M}$ *and* $\mathbf{M}' = \langle \mathbf{T}, \mathbf{T} \rangle$

where, for any HT-*trace* $\mathbf{M}$, $\|\rho\|^{\mathbf{M}} \subseteq \mathbb{N}^2$ *is a relation on pairs of time points inductively defined as follows.*

5. $\|\top\|^{\mathbf{M}} \stackrel{def}{=} \{(i, i+1) \mid i, i+1 \in [0..\lambda)\}$
6. $\|\varphi?\|^{\mathbf{M}} \stackrel{def}{=} \{(i, i) \mid \mathbf{M}, i \models \varphi\}$
7. $\|\rho_1 + \rho_2\|^{\mathbf{M}} \stackrel{def}{=} \|\rho_2\|^{\mathbf{M}} \cup \|\rho_2\|^{\mathbf{M}}$
8. $\|\rho_1 ; \rho_2\|^{\mathbf{M}} \stackrel{def}{=} \{(i, j) \mid (i, k) \in \|\rho_1\|^{\mathbf{M}} \text{ and } (k, j) \in \|\rho_2\|^{\mathbf{M}} \text{for some } k\}$
9. $\|\rho^*\|^{\mathbf{M}} \stackrel{def}{=} \bigcup_{n \geq 0} \|\rho^n\|^{\mathbf{M}}$
10. $\|\rho^-\|^{\mathbf{M}} \stackrel{def}{=} \{(i, j) \mid (j, i) \in \|\rho\|^{\mathbf{M}}\}$ □

The following properties can be easily observed by inspection of the semantics.

Proposition 1. *Relation* $\|\rho\|^{\mathbf{M}}$ *defined above satisfies* $\|\rho\|^{\mathbf{M}} \subseteq [0..\lambda) \times [0..\lambda)$. $\square$

Proposition 2. *If* ρ *is converse-free and* $(i, j) \in \|\rho\|^{\mathbf{M}}$ *then* $i \leq j$. $\square$

As we can see, $\langle \rho \rangle \, \varphi$ and $[\rho] \, \varphi$ quantify over time points i that are reachable under path expression ρ at the current point k, that is, $(k, i) \in \|\rho\|^{\mathbf{M}}$. The main difference with respect to [4] is that $\|\rho\|^{\mathbf{M}} \subseteq [0..\lambda) \times [0..\lambda)$ so that all pairs in that relation are now confined to the set of defined time points $[0..\lambda)$. This additional restriction is due to two reasons. First, it is now possible to access time points in the past $i < k$ using the converse operator ρ^-, something impossible with the converse-free path expressions in [4]. As a result, we must restrict $i \geq 0$ to avoid going backwards, further than the initial situation. Second, for a similar reason, when we have a finite length $\lambda = n$, we must also impose $i < n$, something not needed for infinite traces $\lambda = \omega$ since any natural number obviously satisfies $i < \omega$.

An HT-trace $\mathbf{M}$ is a *model* of a dynamic theory Γ if $\mathbf{M}, 0 \models \varphi$ for all $\varphi \in \Gamma$. We write $\mathrm{DHT}(\Gamma, \lambda)$ to stand for the set of DHT models of length λ of a theory Γ, and define $\mathrm{DHT}(\Gamma) \overset{def}{=} \bigcup_{\lambda=0}^{\omega} \mathrm{DHT}(\Gamma, \lambda)$, that is, the whole set of models of Γ of any length. When $\Gamma = \{\varphi\}$ we just write $\mathrm{DHT}(\varphi, \lambda)$ and $\mathrm{DHT}(\varphi)$.

A formula φ is a *tautology* (or is *valid*), written $\models \varphi$, iff $\mathbf{M}, k \models \varphi$ for any HT-trace and any $k \in [0..\lambda)$. We call the logic induced by the set of all tautologies *(Linear) Dynamic logic of Here-and-There* (DHT for short). Two formulas φ, ψ are said to be *equivalent*, written $\varphi \equiv \psi$, whenever $\mathbf{M}, k \models \varphi$ iff $\mathbf{M}, k \models \psi$ for any HT-trace $\mathbf{M}$ and any $k \in [0..\lambda)$. This allows us to replace φ by ψ and vice versa in any context, and is the same as requiring that $\varphi \leftrightarrow \psi$ is a tautology. Note that this relation, $\varphi \equiv \psi$, is stronger than coincidence of models $\mathrm{DHT}(\varphi) = \mathrm{DHT}(\psi)$. For instance, $\mathrm{DHT}(\bullet\top) = \mathrm{DHT}(\langle\top^-\rangle \top) = \emptyset$ because models are checked at the initial situation $k = 0$ and there is no previous situation at that point, so $\mathrm{DHT}(\bullet\top) = \mathrm{DHT}(\bot)$. However, in general, $\bullet\top \not\equiv \bot$ since $\bullet\top$ is satisfied for any $k > 0$ (for instance $\circ\bullet\top \not\equiv \circ\bot$ but $\circ\bullet\top \equiv \top$ instead).

As with formulas, we say that path expressions ρ_1, ρ_2 are *equivalent*, written $\rho_1 = \rho_2$, when $\|\rho_1\|^{\mathbf{M}} = \|\rho_2\|^{\mathbf{M}}$ for any HT-trace $\mathbf{M}$. For instance, it is easy to see that:

$$(\rho_1; \rho_2); \rho_3 = \rho_1; (\rho_2; \rho_3) \qquad \rho^* = \top? + (\rho; \rho^*)$$
$$\top?; \rho = \rho; \top? = \rho \qquad \rho; \rho^* = \rho^*; \rho$$

The following equivalences of path expressions allow us to push the converse operator inside, until it is only applied to $\top$.

Proposition 3. *For all path expressions* ρ_1, ρ_2 *and* ρ *and for all formulas* φ, *the following equivalences hold:*

$$(\rho^-)^- = \rho \qquad\qquad (\varphi?)^- = \varphi? \qquad\qquad (\rho^*)^- = (\rho^-)^*$$
$$(\rho_1 + \rho_2)^- = \rho_1^- + \rho_2^- \qquad (\rho_1; \rho_2)^- = \rho_2^-; \rho_1^-$$

We prove next that a pair of basic properties from HT already satisfied in [4] are maintained in the current extension of DHT.

Proposition 4 (Persistence). *For any HT-trace* $\langle \mathbf{H}, \mathbf{T} \rangle$ *of length* λ, *any dynamic formula* φ *and any path expression* ρ, *we have:*

1. $\langle \mathbf{H}, \mathbf{T} \rangle, k \models \varphi$ *implies* $\langle \mathbf{T}, \mathbf{T} \rangle, k \models \varphi$, *for all* $k \in [0..\lambda)$
2. $\|\rho\|^{\langle \mathbf{H}, \mathbf{T} \rangle} \subseteq \|\rho\|^{\langle \mathbf{T}, \mathbf{T} \rangle}$.   □

Persistence is a property known from intuitionistic logic; it expresses that accessible worlds satisfy the same or more formulas than the current world, where $\mathbf{T}$ is "accessible" from $\mathbf{H}$ in HT. This also explains the semantics of $[\rho]\,\varphi$, which behaves as a kind of intuitionistic implication (used to define '$\rightarrow$' as a derived operator) and so, it must hold for all accessible worlds, viz. $\langle \mathbf{H}, \mathbf{T} \rangle$ and $\langle \mathbf{T}, \mathbf{T} \rangle$.

For simplicity, we refrain from introducing the semantics of LDL [7], since it just corresponds to DHT on total traces $\langle \mathbf{T}, \mathbf{T} \rangle$, as stated below. Let us simply use $\mathbf{T}, k \models \varphi$ to denote the satisfaction of φ by a trace $\mathbf{T}$ at point k in LDL and $\|\rho\|^{\mathbf{T}}$ the LDL accessibility relation for ρ and $\mathbf{T}$.

Proposition 5. *For any total* HT-trace $\langle \mathbf{T}, \mathbf{T} \rangle$ *of length* λ, *any dynamic formula* φ *and any path expression* ρ, *we have: (1)* $\langle \mathbf{T}, \mathbf{T} \rangle, k \models \varphi$ *iff* $\mathbf{T}, k \models \varphi$, *for all* $k \in [0..\lambda)$; *and (2)* $\|\rho\|^{\langle \mathbf{T}, \mathbf{T} \rangle} = \|\rho\|^{\mathbf{T}}$.   □

Accordingly, any total HT-trace $\langle \mathbf{T}, \mathbf{T} \rangle$ can be seen as the LDL-trace $\mathbf{T}$. In fact, under total models, the satisfaction of dynamic operators $\langle \rho \rangle$ and $[\rho]$ in DHT collapses to that in LDL. Moreover, the first item implies that any DHT tautology is also an LDL tautology, so the former constitutes a weaker logic. To show that, in fact, DHT is *strictly* weaker, note that it does not satisfy some classical tautologies like the *excluded middle* $\varphi \vee \neg\varphi$, while LDL is a proper extension of classical logic. In fact, the addition of the axiom schema

$$\square(a \vee \neg a) \quad \text{for each atom } a \in \mathcal{A} \text{ in the alphabet} \qquad \text{(EM)}$$

forces total models and so, makes DHT collapse to LDL. Propositions 4 and 5 imply that φ is DHT$_f$ satisfiable iff it is LDL$_f$ satisfiable. Since the latter is a PSPACE-complete problem [7], the same applies to DHT$_f$ satisfiability.

The next theorem shows that derived operators follow the expected definitions from HT and THT (and LTL).

Theorem 1. *Let* $\mathbf{M} = \langle \mathbf{H}, \mathbf{T} \rangle$ *be an* HT-trace *of length* λ *over alphabet* $\mathcal{A}$. *Given the respective definitions of derived operators, we get the following satisfaction conditions:*

1. $\mathbf{M}, k \models \varphi \wedge \psi$ *iff* $\mathbf{M}, k \models \varphi$ *and* $\mathbf{M}, k \models \psi$
2. $\mathbf{M}, k \models \varphi \vee \psi$ *iff* $\mathbf{M}, k \models \varphi$ *or* $\mathbf{M}, k \models \psi$
3. $\mathbf{M}, k \models \varphi \rightarrow \psi$ *iff* $\mathbf{M}', k \not\models \varphi$ *or* $\mathbf{M}', k \models \psi$, *for both* $\mathbf{M}' = \mathbf{M}$ *and* $\mathbf{M}' = \langle \mathbf{T}, \mathbf{T} \rangle$

4. $\mathbf{M}, k \models \neg\varphi$ iff $\langle \mathbf{T}, \mathbf{T} \rangle, k \not\models \varphi$

5. $\mathbf{M}, k \models \mathbb{F}$ iff $k + 1 = \lambda$
6. $\mathbf{M}, k \models \circ\varphi$ iff $k + 1 < \lambda$ and $\mathbf{M}, k{+}1 \models \varphi$
7. $\mathbf{M}, k \models \hat{\circ}\varphi$ iff $k + 1 = \lambda$ or $\mathbf{M}, k{+}1 \models \varphi$
8. $\mathbf{M}, k \models \Diamond\varphi$ iff $\mathbf{M}, i \models \varphi$ for some $i \in [k..\lambda)$
9. $\mathbf{M}, k \models \Box\varphi$ iff $\mathbf{M}, i \models \varphi$ for all $i \in [k..\lambda)$
10. $\mathbf{M}, k \models \varphi \, \mathbb{U} \, \psi$ iff for some $j \in [k..\lambda)$, we have $\mathbf{M}, j \models \psi$ and $\mathbf{M}, i \models \varphi$ for all $i \in [k..j)$
11. $\mathbf{M}, k \models \varphi \, \mathbb{R} \, \psi$ iff for all $j \in [k..\lambda)$, we have $\mathbf{M}, j \models \psi$ or $\mathbf{M}, i \models \varphi$ for some $i \in [k..j)$

12. $\mathbf{M}, k \models \mathsf{I}$ iff $k = 0$
13. $\mathbf{M}, k \models \bullet\varphi$ iff $k > 0$ and $\mathbf{M}, k{-}1 \models \varphi$
14. $\mathbf{M}, k \models \hat{\bullet}\varphi$ iff $k = 0$ or $\mathbf{M}, k{-}1 \models \varphi$
15. $\mathbf{M}, k \models \blacksquare\varphi$ iff $\mathbf{M}, i \models \varphi$ for all $i \in [0..k]$
16. $\mathbf{M}, k \models \blacklozenge\varphi$ iff $\mathbf{M}, i \models \varphi$ for some $i \in [0..k]$
17. $\mathbf{M}, k \models \varphi \, \mathsf{S} \, \psi$ iff for some $j \in [0..k]$, we have $\mathbf{M}, j \models \psi$ and $\mathbf{M}, i \models \varphi$ for all $i \in [j+1..k]$
18. $\mathbf{M}, k \models \varphi \, \mathsf{T} \, \psi$ iff for all $j \in [0..k]$, we have $\mathbf{M}, j \models \psi$ or $\mathbf{M}, i \models \varphi$ for some $i \in [j+1..k]$

as well as the relation:

19. $\|\phi\|^{\mathbf{M}} = \{(i, i+1) \mid \mathbf{M}, i \models \phi\}$ for any propositional formula ϕ.   □

An important observation above is that the satisfaction conditions for the Boolean operators amounts to standard HT while the interpretation of LTL operators (temporal formulas) subsume all the different previous versions of the *Temporal logic of Here and There* (THT), including the original definition for infinite traces [1], its extension to past operators [2], and its variant on finite traces [5].

Corollary 1. *Let φ be a temporal formula, $\mathbf{M}$ an HT-trace and $k \geq 0$. Then, $\mathbf{M}, k \models \varphi$ under THT satisfaction iff $\mathbf{M}, k \models \varphi$ under DHT satisfaction.*   □

Since our new definition also subsumes DHT for infinite traces [4] (when $\lambda = \omega$), we may classify all these previous approaches as follows. In analogy to [5], we consider several logics that are stronger than DHT and that can be obtained by the addition of axioms (or the corresponding restriction on sets of traces). For instance, we denote [4] as DHT_ω and define it as $\mathrm{DHT} + \{\neg\Diamond\mathbb{F}\}$, that is, DHT where we exclusively consider infinite HT-traces. The finite-trace version, we call DHT_f, corresponds to $\mathrm{DHT} + \{\Diamond\mathbb{F}\}$ instead. Linear Dynamic Logic for possibly infinite traces, LDL, can be obtained as $\mathrm{DHT} + \{(\mathrm{EM})\}$, that is, DHT with total HT-traces. Accordingly, we can define LDL_ω as $\mathrm{DHT}_\omega + \{(\mathrm{EM})\}$, i.e. infinite and total HT-traces, and obtain LDL_f as $\mathrm{DHT}_f + \{(\mathrm{EM})\}$, that is, LDL on finite traces [7]. Then, the variants THT_ω, THT_f, LTL_ω, LTL_f respectively refer to DHT_ω, DHT_f, LDL_ω, LDL_f on the restricted syntax of temporal formulas.

We now introduce non-monotonicity by selecting a particular set of traces that we call *temporal equilibrium models*. First, given an arbitrary set $\mathfrak{S}$ of HT-traces, we define the ones in equilibrium as follows.

Definition 2 (Temporal Equilibrium/Stable models). *Let $\mathfrak{S}$ be some set of HT-traces. A total HT-trace $\langle \mathbf{T}, \mathbf{T} \rangle \in \mathfrak{S}$ is an equilibrium trace of $\mathfrak{S}$ iff there is no other $\langle \mathbf{H}, \mathbf{T} \rangle \in \mathfrak{S}$ such that $\mathbf{H} < \mathbf{T}$. If this is the case, we also say that trace $\mathbf{T}$ is a stable trace of $\mathfrak{S}$. We further talk about temporal equilibrium or temporal stable models of a theory Γ when $\mathfrak{S} = \mathrm{DHT}(\Gamma)$, respectively.* □

We write $\mathrm{DEL}(\Gamma, \lambda)$ and $\mathrm{DEL}(\Gamma)$ to stand for the temporal equilibrium models of $\mathrm{DHT}(\Gamma, \lambda)$ and $\mathrm{DHT}(\Gamma)$ respectively. Note that, due to Proposition 5, stable traces in $\mathrm{DEL}(\Gamma)$ are also LDL-models of Γ and, thus, DEL is stronger than LDL. Besides, as the ordering relation among traces is only defined for a fixed λ, it is easy to see:

Proposition 6. *The set of temporal equilibrium models of Γ can be partitioned by the trace length λ, that is, $\bigcup_{\lambda=0}^{\omega} \mathrm{DEL}(\Gamma, \lambda) = \mathrm{DEL}(\Gamma)$.* □

(Linear) *Dynamic Equilibrium Logic* (DEL) is the non-monotonic logic induced by temporal equilibrium models of dynamic theories. We obtain the variants DEL_ω and DEL_f by applying the corresponding restriction to infinite or finite traces, respectively.

To illustrate non-monotonicity, take the formula:

$$[(\neg h)^*](\neg h \rightarrow s) \tag{1}$$

whose reading is "keep sending an sos (s) while no help (h) is perceived." Intuitively, $[(\neg h)^*]$ behaves as a conditional referring to any future state after $n \geq 0$ repetitions of $(\neg h?; \top)$. Then, $\neg h \rightarrow s$ checks whether h fails one more time at $k = n$: if so, it makes s true again. Without additional information, this formula has a unique temporal stable model per each length λ satisfying $\square(\neg h \wedge s)$, that is, h is never concluded, and so, we repeat s all over the trace. Suppose we add now the formula $\langle \top^5 \rangle h$, that is, h becomes true after five transitions. Then, there is a unique temporal stable model for each $\lambda > 5$ satisfying:

$$\langle (\neg h \wedge s)^5; h \wedge \neg s; (\neg h \wedge \neg s)^* \rangle \top$$

Clearly, $\square(\neg h \wedge s)$ is not entailed any more (under temporal equilibrium models) showing that DEL is non-monotonic.

One important logical feature that emerges when dealing with a non-monotonic logic is the concept of *strong equivalence* [14]. Under a non-monotonic inference relation, the fact that two theories Γ_1 and Γ_2 yield the same consequences is too weak to consider that one can be "safely" replaced by the other, since the addition of new information Γ may make them behave in a different way. Instead, we normally define a stronger notion of equivalence, requiring that $\Gamma_1 \cup \Gamma$ and $\Gamma_2 \cup \Gamma$ have the same behavior, for any additional theory Γ (providing a context). An important property proved in [14] is that strong equivalence of propositional logic programs (and in fact, of arbitrary propositional theories) corresponds to regular equivalence in the monotonic logic of HT. This result reinforces the adequacy of the logic of HT as a monotonic basis for equilibrium logic and Answer Set Programming. Now, considering our setting, we can still prove that DHT plays a similar role with respect to DEL. Formally, we say that two dynamic theories Γ_1, Γ_2 are *strongly equivalent* if $\Gamma_1 \cup \Gamma$ and $\Gamma_2 \cup \Gamma$ have the same temporal equilibrium models, for any additional LDL theory Γ. Then, we get the following result, by a direct application of the proof obtained for (converse-free) DHT_ω (Theorem 2 in [4]) to the general case with converse operator and arbitrary length $\lambda \in \mathbb{N} \cup \{\omega\}$:

Theorem 2. *Dynamic theories Γ_1 and Γ_2 are strongly equivalent iff $\Gamma_1 \equiv \Gamma_2$ in* DHT.

This result shows that DHT-equivalence precisely captures the property of strong equivalence of dynamic theories. Thus, it is worth commenting some possible ways of deriving DHT equivalences. We already know that any DHT equivalence must also hold in LDL while, in general, the opposite does not hold, as with $[\rho] q \equiv \neg \langle \rho \rangle \neg q$. Still, some LDL equivalences are preserved in DHT, like the following unfolding properties.

Proposition 7. *The following equivalences hold in* DHT.

$$\langle \rho + \rho' \rangle \, \varphi \equiv \langle \rho \rangle \, \varphi \vee \langle \rho' \rangle \, \varphi \qquad\qquad [\rho + \rho'] \, \varphi \equiv [\rho] \, \varphi \wedge [\rho'] \, \varphi$$
$$\langle \rho \,;\, \rho' \rangle \, \varphi \equiv \langle \rho \rangle \, \langle \rho' \rangle \, \varphi \qquad\qquad [\rho \,;\, \rho'] \, \varphi \equiv [\rho] \, [\rho'] \, \varphi$$
$$\langle \rho^* \rangle \, \varphi \equiv \varphi \vee \langle \rho \rangle \, \langle \rho^* \rangle \, \varphi \qquad\qquad [\rho^*] \, \varphi \equiv \varphi \wedge [\rho] \, [\rho^*] \, \varphi$$

In Proposition 2 in [4], we proved that (converse-free) LDL_ω equivalences for unconditional formulas can also be guaranteed in DHT_ω. We extend below the same result for DHT and LDL with converse operator and traces of arbitrary length.

Proposition 8. *For unconditional formulas φ and ψ, $\varphi \equiv \psi$ in* LDL *iff $\varphi \equiv \psi$ in* DHT.

This result suffices to prove the three leftmost equivalences above by resorting to LDL, but cannot be applied for proving the right ones, as they are conditional—they contain arbitrary path expressions inside $[\cdot]$. An interesting fragment are temporal formulas without $\rightarrow$ or $\neg$. They are unconditional, since the definition of temporal operators only use $[\cdot]$ for $\Box \varphi = [\top^*] \, \varphi$ and its dual $\blacksquare \varphi = [\top^{*-}] \, \varphi$, and these formulas do not use atoms in the path expressions. As a consequence of Proposition 8, the DHT equivalence for temporal formulas without implications or negations can be directly checked in LTL.

Given any dynamic formula φ, we define φ^- as the result of replacing in φ each (maximal) path expression ρ by ρ^-. For instance, given $\varphi = [p; q] \, \langle r^- \rangle \, s$ we get $\varphi = [(p; q)^-] \, \langle r^{--} \rangle \, s$. Notice that the effect of this transformation on temporal operators is just switching their future/past versions. As an example:

$$(\lozenge \widehat{\bullet} p)^- = (\langle \top^* \rangle \, [\top^-] \, p)^- = \langle \top^{*-} \rangle \, [\top^{--}] \, p = \blacklozenge \widehat{\circ} p$$

Lemma 1. *There exists a mapping ϱ on finite HT-traces of a fixed length $\lambda = n \in \mathbb{N}$ such that, $\mathbf{M}, k \models \varphi$ iff $\varrho(\mathbf{M}), n - k \models \varphi^-$, for any $k \in [0..\lambda)$, any dynamic formula φ and any HT-trace $\mathbf{M}$ of length $\lambda = n$.*

Theorem 3 (Temporal duality theorem). *A dynamic formula φ is a DHT_f tautology iff φ^- is a DHT_f tautology.*

This property does not hold for infinite traces, where $\neg \Diamond \mathbb{F}$ is valid but its dual, $\neg \blacklozenge \mathbb{I}$, is false in all traces (we can always reach the initial situation at some point in the past).

3   Reducing Converse-Free DEL_f to Propositional ASP

In this section, we show that converse-free DEL_f can be reduced to propositional theories (under stable models semantics) by using indexed atoms. Given a set $\mathcal{A}$ of atoms and $\lambda \in \mathbb{N}$, we define $\mathcal{A}^\lambda \stackrel{def}{=} \{a_i \mid i \in [0..\lambda) \text{ and } a \in \mathcal{A}\}$. We define the translation of a converse-free dynamic formula φ at $i \in [0..\lambda)$, in symbols $(\varphi)_i$, as follows:

$$(\bot)_i \stackrel{def}{=} \bot \qquad (\top)_i \stackrel{def}{=} \top \qquad (p)_i \stackrel{def}{=} p_i \quad \text{for each } p \in \mathcal{A}$$

$$(\langle \varphi? \rangle \psi)_i \stackrel{def}{=} (\varphi)_i \wedge (\psi)_i \qquad\qquad ([\varphi?] \psi)_i \stackrel{def}{=} (\varphi)_i \to (\psi)_i$$

$$(\langle \top \rangle \varphi)_i \stackrel{def}{=} \begin{cases} (\varphi)_{i+1} & \text{if } i+1 < \lambda \\ \bot & \text{if } i+1 = \lambda \end{cases} \qquad ([\top] \varphi)_i \stackrel{def}{=} \begin{cases} (\varphi)_{i+1} & \text{if } i+1 < \lambda \\ \top & \text{if } i+1 = \lambda \end{cases}$$

and, for any other formula α starting with $\langle \cdot \rangle$ or $[\cdot]$, we apply the equivalences $\alpha \equiv \beta$ in Proposition 7 to unfold $(\alpha)_i$ into $(\beta)_i$, further assuming $(\varphi \otimes \psi)_i = (\varphi)_i \otimes (\psi)_i$ for $\otimes \in \{\wedge, \vee\}$. As an example, consider the formula $[p^*] q$ and assume that $\lambda = 3$:

$$
\begin{aligned}
([p^*] q)_0 &= (q)_0 \wedge ([p] [p^*] q)_0 \\
&= q_0 \wedge ([p?] [\top] [p^*] q)_0 \\
&= q_0 \wedge (p_0 \to ([p^*] q)_1) &&\text{then, repeating the pattern} \\
&= q_0 \wedge (p_0 \to (q_1 \wedge (p_1 \to ([p^*] q)_2))) &&\text{that is HT-equivalent to} \\
&= q_0 \wedge (p_0 \to q_1) \wedge (p_0 \wedge p_1 \to ([p^*] q)_2) \\
&= q_0 \wedge (p_0 \to q_1) \wedge (p_0 \wedge p_1 \to (p_2 \wedge \underbrace{([p] [p^*] q)_2}_{\top})) \\
&= q_0 \wedge (p_0 \to q_1) \wedge (p_0 \wedge p_1 \to p_2)
\end{aligned}
$$

It is easy to see that, applying the same pattern for $((1))_0$ and $\lambda = 3$, we get:

$$
\begin{aligned}
&(\neg h_0 \to s_0) \wedge (\neg h_0 \to (\neg h_1 \to s_1)) \wedge (\neg h_0 \wedge \neg h_1 \to (\neg h_2 \to s_2)) \\
&= (\neg h_0 \to s_0) \wedge (\neg h_0 \wedge \neg h_1 \to s_1) \wedge (\neg h_0 \wedge \neg h_1 \wedge \neg h_2 \to s_2)
\end{aligned}
$$

Theorem 4 (Partial correctness). *Let $(\alpha)_i$ terminate for formula α and $i \in [0..\lambda)$ with $\lambda \in \mathbb{N}$. For any finite HT-trace $\mathbf{M} = \langle \mathbf{H}, \mathbf{T} \rangle$ of length λ, and its (one-to-one) corresponding HT-interpretation $M = \langle \{a_i \mid a \in H_i\}, \{a_i \mid a \in T_i\} \rangle$ on $\mathcal{A}^\lambda$, we have $\mathbf{M}, i \models \alpha$ in DHT iff $M \models (\alpha)_i$ in HT.*

As stated above, the previous result only guarantees a *partial correctness* for the recursive translation $(\varphi)_i$—to get *total correctness* we further need to guarantee termination, and this does not hold in the general case. To see why, just consider the formula $[\top?^*]\, q$ (being equivalent to q) whose translation at i yields

$$\left([\top?^*]\, q\right)_i = q_i \wedge \left([\top?]\,[\top?^*]\, q\right)_i = q_i \wedge \left(\top \rightarrow \left([\top?^*]\, q\right)_i\right) = q_i \wedge \left([\top?^*]\, q\right)_i$$

and generates an infinite sequence of calls to $\left([\top?^*]\, q\right)_i$. This problem arises because the starred expression, $\top?$, leaves situation i unaltered, something that does not happen with $p^* = (p?; \top)^*$ used before, as it generated incremental jumps $i + 1 > i$ and a sequence of calls $\left([p^*]\, q\right)_0$, $\left([p^*]\, q\right)_1$, $\left([p^*]\, q\right)_2$ progressing towards $i = \lambda - 1$. We show next that any converse-free path expression ρ^* can be equivalently reformulated in such a way that its translation proceeds in a strictly incremental way, guaranteeing termination. We begin by defining the following types of path expressions: a *(sequential) component* θ, a *sequence* σ and a *normalized disjunction* δ are defined by the grammar rules:

$$\theta ::= \top \mid \varphi? \mid \delta^* \qquad \sigma ::= \theta \mid \sigma_1; \sigma_2 \qquad \delta ::= \theta \mid \delta_1 + \delta_2$$

Given that addition satisfies distributivity with respect to sequence, viz.

$$(\rho_1 + \rho_2); \rho_3 \equiv (\rho_1; \rho_2) + (\rho_2; \rho_3) \qquad \rho_1; (\rho_2 + \rho_3) \equiv (\rho_1; \rho_2) + (\rho_1; \rho_3),$$

it is easy to obtain the following result.

Proposition 9 (Disjunctive Normal Form). *Any arbitrary path expression ρ can be equivalently reformulated as a normalized disjunction δ.*

As an example, to normalize the expression $(a^* + b); (c?; d + e?)^*$ we can proceed, for instance, by reducing the inner expression $(c?; d + e?)$ to $(c?; d) + (c?; e?)$ and then go on applying distributivity outside:

$$(a^* + b); (c?; d + e?)^* = (a^* + b); ((c?; d) + (c?; e?))^*$$
$$= (a^*; ((c?; d) + (c?; e?))^*) + (b; ((c?; d) + (c?; e?))^*)$$

The last expression is already in normal form. We say that a sequence $\sigma = \theta_1; \ldots; \theta_n$ is *incremental* if $\theta_i = \top$ for some $i = 1, \ldots, n$. A normalized disjunction $\delta = \sigma_1 + \cdots + \sigma_m$ is *incremental* if σ_i is incremental for every $i = 1, \ldots, m$.

Proposition 10. *Let δ be an incremental, normalized disjunction and $\mathbf{M}$ an HT-trace. Then, $(i, j) \in \|\delta\|^{\mathbf{M}}$ implies $j > i$.*

In other words, incremental disjunctions always shift the time point strictly forward. Obviously, not any normalized disjunction δ is incremental, but this is not a problem as long as it is not combined with the star operator. We say that a normalized disjunction δ is *star-incremental* if all the sub-expressions $(\delta')^*$ of δ satisfy that δ' is incremental. The key point for guaranteeing termination is that we can transform any arbitrary path expression into a star-incremental, normalized disjunction.

Proposition 11. *For any expression ρ and formulas $\varphi_1, \ldots, \varphi_n$, we have that $(\rho + (\varphi_1?; \ldots; \varphi_n?))^* = (\rho)^*$ and $(\varphi_1?; \ldots; \varphi_n?)^* = \top?$.*

In other words, we can remove test-only sequences from any iterated disjunction. As an example $((c?; d) + (c?; e?))^*$ amounts to $(c?; d)^*$. Similarly, if we only have tests $(a?; b?)^*$ the whole expression can be just replaced by $\top?$.

Now, to transform any normalized disjunction to become star-incremental, we can proceed in a bottom-up manner, as described in the proof of the following proposition, included below to illustrate the process.

Proposition 12. *Any converse-free path expression can be transformed into an equivalent star-incremental, normalized disjunction.*

Proof. By Proposition 9, we can assume that we start from a normalized disjunction. Then, we begin with all the sub-expressions δ^* where δ is star-free, and so, trivially star-incremental. To make δ^* star-incremental too, it suffices with removing its test-only sequences, applying Proposition 11. Then, we proceed with δ^* where δ is not star-free, but is already star-incremental by application of previous steps. Any non-incremental sequence in δ is a combination of tests and starred expressions. Suppose we take some non-incremental sequence of δ of the form $\sigma; \rho^*; \sigma'$. Note that, if σ_1 or σ_2 are not present, we can assume they correspond to $\top?$. Then, we can apply the unfolding:

$$\sigma; \rho^*; \sigma' = \sigma; (\top? + \rho; \rho^*); \sigma'$$
$$= (\sigma; \top?; \sigma') + (\sigma; \rho; \rho^*; \sigma')$$
$$= (\sigma; \sigma') + (\sigma; \rho; \rho^*; \sigma')$$

where ρ^* does not occur in the first sequence, whereas in the second, we can apply distributivity on all sequences from the first occurrence of ρ. Since δ is star-incremental, ρ is incremental and so, all the sequences obtained in that way are incremental too. We would then proceed in the same way with the next starred-expression in $(\sigma; \sigma')$. The final result, δ', is equivalent to δ but contains incremental sequences or test-only expressions. But in $(\delta')^*$ we can further remove the test-only expressions (Property 11) and we eventually get a star-incremental expression. $\qquad\square$

As an example, given $(a?; (b + c)^*; d?; e^*)^*$, we can unfold $(b + c)^*$ into

$$(a?; \underline{(b + c)^*}; d?; e^*)^* = ((a?; d?; e^*) + (a?; (b + c); (b + c)^*; d?; e^*))^*$$

and unfold again the first sequence into:

$$= (\, (a?; d?) + (a?; d?; e; e^*) + (a?; (b+c); (b+c)^*; d?; e^*))^*$$

By Proposition 11, the test-only sequence $(a?; d?)$ can be removed

$$= (\, (a?; d?; e; e^*) + (a?; (b+c); (b+c)^*; d?; e^*))^*$$

and, now, applying distributivity on $(b+c)$, we get

$$= (\, (a?; d?; e; e^*) + (a?; b; (b+c)^*; d?; e^*) + (a?; c; (b+c)^*; d?; e^*))^*$$
$$= (\, (a?; d?; e?; \top; e^*) + (a?; b?; \top; (b+c)^*; d?; e^*) + (a?; c?; \top; (b+c)^*; d?; e^*))^*$$

and all remaining sequences are incremental.

Theorem 5. *Let φ be a formula where all its path expressions are star-incremental, normalized disjunctions, and let $i \in [0..\lambda)$ with $\lambda \in \mathbb{N}$, $\lambda > 0$. Then, $(\varphi)_i$ terminates.*

Corollary 2. *Given a fixed length $\lambda \in \mathbb{N}$, any converse-free dynamic theory can be reduced to a propositional theory with a one-to-one correspondence among the respective HT-traces (of length λ) and HT-models.*

Given that any propositional theory can be translated into an HT-equivalent disjunctive logic program (cf. [6]), we get the following result.

Corollary 3. *Given a fixed length $\lambda \in \mathbb{N}$, any converse-free dynamic theory can be reduced to a disjunctive logic program with a one-to-one correspondence among the respective HT-traces (of length λ) and HT-models.*

4   Discussion and Conclusions

As we have seen, our current definition of Dynamic Equilibrium Logic (DEL), covers the previous modal variants of Equilibrium Logic for dealing with time, including the original Temporal Equilibrium Logic (TEL) [1], its extension to past operators [2] and its variant on finite traces [5], but also generalizes the first definition of DEL in [4] by possibly allowing for finite traces and a converse operator. The recent introduction of Dynamic Logic operators in modal Equilibrium Logic and the use of finite traces have been obviously motivated by [7], that previously presented LTL and LDL on finite traces. DEL can be seen as a non-monotonic extension that allows for capturing temporal stable models of LDL theories. As happens in the non-temporal case, when we add the excluded middle axiom, DEL and TEL respectively collapse to the monotonic versions LDL and LTL. A different approach for extending ASP with linear-time and dynamic operators was studied in [8], for a rule-based syntax, and later generalized in [3] for arbitrary dynamic logic theories. The main difference with respect to DEL is that [8] starts from the linear version of DL in [10] and keeps separate alphabets for atomic actions and propositions. Still, as shown in [4], both [8] and [3] can be encoded in DEL$_\omega$. The approaches in [17,18] give encodings of GOLOG-like control in ASP planning by enforcing that traces are compatible with a given path expression without any logical underpinnings.

Apart from the general definition of DEL and its relation to other formalisms, a second contribution of the paper is the translation of any converse-free arbitrary DEL$_f$ theory into a propositional logic program. This translation has proved to be non-trivial: it is based on unfolding path expressions, something potentially equivalent to the execution of a sequential program. Termination was guaranteed by a previous preprocessing of path expressions. Future work includes the implementation of this translation for the converse-free fragment of the language together with the extension to other fragments involving the converse operator.

Acknowledgments. This work was partially supported by MINECO, Spain, (grant TIC2017-84453-P), Xunta de Galicia, Spain, (grant 2016–2019 ED431G/01, CITIC), ANR, France, (grant ANR-16-ASMA-0002) and DFG, Germany, (grant SCHA 550/9).

References

1. Aguado, F., Cabalar, P., Diéguez, M., Pérez, G., Vidal, C.: Temporal equilibrium logic: a survey. J. Appl. Non-Class. Log. **23**(1–2), 2–24 (2013)
2. Aguado, F., Cabalar, P., Diéguez, M., Pérez, G., Vidal, C.: Temporal equilibrium logic with past operators. J. Appl. Non-Class. Log. **27**(3–4), 161–277 (2017)
3. Aguado, F., Pérez, G., Vidal, C.: Integrating temporal extensions of answer set programming. In: Cabalar, P., Son, T.C. (eds.) LPNMR 2013. LNCS (LNAI), vol. 8148, pp. 23–35. Springer, Heidelberg (2013). https://doi.org/10.1007/978-3-642-40564-8_3
4. Bosser, A., Cabalar, P., Diéguez, M., Schaub, T.: Introducing temporal stable models for linear dynamic logic. In: Proceedings of the International Conference on Principles of Knowledge Representation and Reasoning, pp. 12–21. AAAI Press (2018)
5. Cabalar, P., Kaminski, R., Schaub, T., Schuhmann, A.: Temporal answer set programming on finite traces. Theor. Pract. Log. Program. **18**(3–4), 406–420 (2018)
6. Cabalar, P., Pearce, D., Valverde, A.: Reducing propositional theories in equilibrium logic to logic programs. In: Bento, C., Cardoso, A., Dias, G. (eds.) EPIA 2005. LNCS (LNAI), vol. 3808, pp. 4–17. Springer, Heidelberg (2005). https://doi.org/10.1007/11595014_2
7. De Giacomo, G., Vardi, M.: Linear temporal logic and linear dynamic logic on finite traces. In: Proceedings of the International Joint Conference on AI, pp. 854–860. IJCAI/AAAI Press (2013)
8. Giordano, L., Martelli, A., Dupré, D.T.: Reasoning about actions with temporal answer sets. Theor. Pract. Log. Program. **13**(2), 201–225 (2013)
9. Harel, D., Tiuryn, J., Kozen, D.: Dynamic Logic. MIT Press, Cambridge (2000)
10. Henriksen, J., Thiagarajan, P.: Dynamic linear time temporal logic. Ann. Pure Appl. Log. **96**(1–3), 187–207 (1999)
11. Heyting, A.: Die formalen Regeln der intuitionistischen Logik. In: Sitzungsberichte der Preussischen Akademie der Wissenschaften, p. 42–56. (1930)
12. Levesque, H., Reiter, R., Lespérance, Y., Lin, F., Scherl, R.: GOLOG: a logic programming language for dynamic domains. J. Log. Program. **31**(1–3), 59–83 (1997)

13. Lifschitz, V.: Answer set planning. In: Proceedings of the International Conference on Logic Programming, pp. 23–37. MIT Press (1999)
14. Lifschitz, V., Pearce, D., Valverde, A.: Strongly equivalent logic programs. ACM Transact. Comput. Log. **2**(4), 526–541 (2001)
15. Pnueli, A.: The temporal logic of programs. In: Proceedings of the Symposium on Foundations of Computer Science, pp. 46–57. IEEE Computer Society Press (1977)
16. Pratt, V.: Semantical consideration on Floyd-Hoare logic. In: Proceedings of the Symposium on Foundations of Computer Science, pp. 109–121. IEEE Computer Society Press (1976)
17. Ryan, M.: Efficiently implementing GOLOG with answer set programming. In: Proceedings of the AAAI Conference on Artificial Intelligence, pp. 2352–2357. AAAI Press (2014)
18. Son, T., Baral, C., Nam, T., McIlraith, S.: Domain-dependent knowledge in answer set planning. ACM Transact. Comput. Log. **7**(4), 613–657 (2006)

A Sequent-Type Calculus
for Three-Valued Default Logic, Or:
Tweety Meets Quartum Non Datur

Sopo Pkhakadze$^{(\boxtimes)}$ ⓘ and Hans Tompits ⓘ

Institute of Logic and Computation, Knowledge-Based Systems Group E192-03,
Technische Universität Wien, Favoritenstraße 9-11, 1040 Vienna, Austria
{pkhakadze,tompits}@kr.tuwien.ac.at

Abstract. Sequent-type proof systems constitute an important and widely-used class of calculi well-suited for analysing proof search. In this paper, we introduce a sequent-type calculus for a variant of default logic employing Łukasiewicz's three-valued logic as the underlying base logic. This version of default logic has been introduced by Radzikowska addressing some representational shortcomings of standard default logic. More specifically, our calculus axiomatises brave reasoning for this version of default logic, following the sequent method first introduced in the context of nonmonotonic reasoning by Bonatti, which employs a *complementary calculus* for axiomatising invalid formulas, taking care of expressing the consistency condition of defaults.

1 Introduction

Sequent-type proof systems, first introduced in the 1930s by Gerhard Gentzen [15] for classical and intuitionistic logic, are among the basic calculi used in automated deduction for analysing proof search. In the area of non-monotonic reasoning, Bonatti [8] introduced in the early 1990s sequent-style systems for default logic [31] and autoepistemic logic [25], and a few years later together with Olivetti [9] also for circumscription [24]. A distinguishing feature of these calculi is the usage of a *complementary calculus* for axiomatising invalid formulas, i.e., of non-theorems, taking care of formalising consistency conditions, which makes these calculi arguably particularly elegant and suitable for proof-complexity elaborations as, e.g., recently undertaken by Beyersdorff et al. [5]. In a complementary calculus, the inference rules formalise the propagation of refutability instead of validity and establish invalidity by deduction and thus in a purely syntactic manner. Complementary calculi are also referred to as *refutation calculi* or *rejection calculi* and the first axiomatic treatment of rejection was done by Łukasiewicz in his formalisation of Aristotle's syllogistic [18].

The first author was supported by the European Master's Program in Computational Logic (EMCL).

M. Balduccini et al. (Eds.): LPNMR 2019, LNAI 11481, pp. 163–177, 2019.
https://doi.org/10.1007/978-3-030-20528-7_13

In this paper, we introduce a sequent-type calculus for brave reasoning in the style of Bonatti [8] for a variant of default logic due to Radzikowska [30]. This version of default logic uses Łukasiewicz's three-value logic [17] as underlying logical apparatus for addressing certain shortcomings of standard default logic [31]. In particular, three-valued default logic allows a more fine-grained distinction between formulas obtained by applying defaults and formulas which are known for certain, in order to avoid counter-intuitive conclusions by successive applications of defaults.

Our calculus, called B_3, consists of three parts, similar to Bonatti's calculus for standard default logic [31], viz. a sequent calculus for Łukasiewiz's three-valued logic, a complementary *anti-sequent* calculus for three-valued logic, and specific default inference rules. For many-valued logics, different kinds of sequent-style systems exist in the literature, like systems [4,6] based on (two-sided) sequents in the style of Gentzen [15] employing additional non-standard rules, or using *hypersequents* [2], which are tuples of Gentzen-style sequents. In our sequent and anti-sequent calculi for Łukasiewicz's three-valued logic, we adopt the approach of Rousseau [33], which is a natural generalisation for many-valued logics of the classical two-sided sequent formulation of Gentzen. The respective calculi are obtained from a systematic construction for many-valued logics as described by Zach [37] and Bogojeski [7].

2   Background

We first recapitulate the basic elements of the three-valued logic $Ł_3$ of Łukasiewicz for the propositional case and afterwards we discuss a propositional version of the three-valued default logic DL_3 of Radzikowska [30] which is based on $Ł_3$. Our exposition of both formalisms follows Radzikowska [30].

Łukasiewicz's Three-Valued Logic $Ł_3$. The alphabet of $Ł_3$ consists of (i) a denumerable set P of propositional constants, (ii) the primitive logical connectives $\neg$ ("negation") and $\supset$ ("implication"), (iii) the truth constants $\top$ ("truth"), $\bot$ ("falsehood"), and $\sqcup$ ("undetermined"), and (iv) the punctuation symbols "(" and ")". The class of *formulas* is built from the elements of the alphabet of $Ł_3$ in the usual inductive fashion, whereby the propositional constants and the truth constants constitute the *atomic formulas*.

The additional connectives $\vee$ ("disjunction"), $\wedge$ ("conjunction"), and $\equiv$ ("equivalence") are defined in the following way: $(A \vee B) := ((A \supset B) \supset B)$, $(A \wedge B) := \neg(\neg A \vee \neg B)$, and $(A \equiv B) := ((A \supset B) \wedge (B \supset A))$. Furthermore, we make use of the unary operators L ("certainty operator") and M ("possibility operator"), defined by $LA := \neg(A \supset \neg A)$ and $MA := (\neg A \supset A)$, which, according to Łukasiewicz [17], were first formalised in 1921 by Tarski. Intuitively, LA expresses that A is certain, whilst MA means that A is possible. These operators will be used below to distinguish between *certain knowledge* and *defeasible conclusions*. Given L and M, we also define $IA := (MA \wedge \neg LA)$, expressing that A is *contingent* or *modally indifferent*.

¬		⊃	t	u	f	∨	t	u	f	∧	t	u	f	≡	t	u	f	L		M		I	
t	f	t	t	u	f	t	t	t	t	t	t	u	f	t	t	u	f	t	t	t	t	t	f
u	u	u	t	t	u	u	t	u	u	u	u	u	f	u	u	t	u	u	f	u	t	u	t
f	t	f	t	t	t	f	t	u	f	f	f	f	f	f	f	u	t	f	f	f	f	f	f

Fig. 1. Truth tables for the connectives of $\mathbf{L_3}$.

A (*three-valued*) *interpretation* is a mapping m assigning to each propositional constant from $\mathcal{P}$ an element from $\{\mathbf{t}, \mathbf{f}, \mathbf{u}\}$. We refer to each of the symbols $\mathbf{t}$, $\mathbf{f}$, and $\mathbf{u}$ as a *truth value*, and of $m(p)$ as the *truth value of p under m*. We assume a total order $\leq$ over the truth values such that $\mathbf{f} \leq \mathbf{u} \leq \mathbf{t}$ holds.

The truth value, $V^m(A)$, of an arbitrary formula A under an interpretation m is given subject to the following conditions: (i) if $A = \top$, then $V^m(A) = \mathbf{t}$; (ii) if $A = \sqcup$, then $V^m(A) = \mathbf{u}$; (iii) if $A = \bot$, then $V^m(A) = \mathbf{f}$; (iv) if A is an atomic formula, then $V^m(A) = m(A)$; and (v) if $A = \neg B$, for some formula B, or $A = (C \supset D)$, for some formulas C and D, then $V^m(A)$ is determined according to the truth tables in Fig. 1 (there, the corresponding truth conditions for the defined connectives are also given).

If $V^m(A) = \mathbf{t}$, then A is *true under m*, if $V^m(A) = \mathbf{u}$, then A is *undetermined under m*, and if $V^m(A) = \mathbf{f}$, then A is *false under m*. If A is true under m, then m is a *model* of A. If A is true in every interpretation, then A is *valid* (in $\mathbf{L_3}$), written $\models_{\mathbf{L_3}} A$.

Clearly, the classically valid principle of *tertium non datur*, i.e., the law of excluded middle, $A \vee \neg A$, as well as the corresponding law of non-contradiction, $\neg(A \wedge \neg A)$, are not valid in $\mathbf{L_3}$. However, their three-valued pendants, viz., the principle of *quartum non datur*, i.e., the law of excluded fourth, $A \vee \mathrm{I}A \vee \neg A$, and the corresponding extended non-contradiction principle, $\neg(A \wedge \neg \mathrm{I}A \wedge \neg A)$, are valid in $\mathbf{L_3}$.

As usual, by a *theory* we understand a set of formulas. An interpretation is a model of a theory T iff it is a model of each element of T. A theory is *satisfiable* iff it has a model; otherwise, it is *unsatisfiable*. Theories T and T' are *equivalent* iff they have the same models. A theory T is said to *entail* a formula A, or A is a *consequence* of T, symbolically $T \models_{\mathbf{L_3}} A$, iff every model of T is also a model of A.

Sound and complete Hilbert-style axiomatisations of $\mathbf{L_3}$ can be readily found in the literature [22,32]; the first one was introduced by Wajsberg in 1931 [36]. We write $T \vdash_{\mathbf{L_3}} A$ if A has a derivation (in some fixed Hilbert-style calculus) from T in $\mathbf{L_3}$. As well, the *deductive closure operator* of $\mathbf{L_3}$ is given by $\mathrm{Th}_{\mathbf{L_3}}(T) := \{A \mid T \vdash_{\mathbf{L_3}} A\}$, where T is a theory. A theory T is *deductively closed* iff $T = \mathrm{Th}_{\mathbf{L_3}}(T)$. We say that a theory T is *consistent* iff there is a formula A such that $T \nvdash_{\mathbf{L_3}} A$. Clearly, T is consistent iff it is satisfiable. Moreover, a formula A is *consistent with* T iff $T \nvdash_{\mathbf{L_3}} \neg A$. Note that the consistency of a formula A with a theory T implies the consistency of the theory $T \cup \{\mathrm{M}A\}$, but not necessarily of the theory $T \cup \{A\}$. For instance, $\neg p$ is consistent with $\{\mathrm{M}p\}$, so $\{\mathrm{M}p, \mathrm{M}\neg p\}$ is consistent, but $\{\mathrm{M}p, \neg p\}$ is not.

Three-Valued Default Logic. Radzikowska's three-valued default logic $\mathbf{DL_3}$ [30] differs from Reiter's standard default logic [31] in two aspects: not only is in $\mathbf{DL_3}$ the deductive machinery of classical logic replaced with $\mathbf{L_3}$, but there is also a modified consistency check for default rules employed in which the consequent of a default is taken into account as well. The latter feature is somewhat reminiscent to the consistency checks used in *justified default logic* [19] and *constrained default logic* [12,34], where a default may only be applied if it does not lead to a contradiction *a posteriori*.

Formally, a *default rule*, or simply a *default*, d, is an expression of form

$$\frac{A : B_1, \ldots, B_n}{C} \,,$$

where A is the *prerequisite*, $B_1, \ldots, B_n$ are the *justifications*, and C is the *consequent* of d. The intuitive meaning of such a default is: if A is believed, and $B_1, \ldots, B_n$ and LC are consistent with what is believed, then MC is asserted. Note that under this reading, by applying a default of the above form, it is assumed that C cannot be false, but it is not assumed that C is true in all situations. It is only assumed that C must be true in at least one such situation. This reflects the intuition that accepting a default conclusion, we are prepared to rule out all situations where it is false, but we can imagine at least one such situation in which it is true. As a consequence, we cannot conclude both MC and $M\neg C$ simultaneously.

In what follows, formulas of the form MC obtained by applying defaults will be referred to as *default assumptions*. For simplicity, defaults will also be written in the form $(A : B_1, \ldots, B_n/C)$.

A *default theory*, T, is a pair $\langle W, D \rangle$, where W is a set of formulas (i.e., a theory in $\mathbf{L_3}$) and D is a set of defaults. An *extension* of a default theory $T = \langle W, D \rangle$ in the three-valued default logic $\mathbf{DL_3}$ is defined thus: For a set S of formulas, let $\Gamma_T(S)$ be the smallest set K of formulas obeying the following conditions:

(i) $K = \mathrm{Th}_{\mathbf{L_3}}(K)$;
(ii) $W \subseteq K$;
(iii) if $(A : B_1, \ldots, B_n/C) \in D$, $A \in K$, $\neg B_1 \notin S, \ldots, \neg B_n \notin S$, and $\neg LC \notin S$, then $MC \in K$.

Then, E is an extension of T iff $\Gamma_T(E) = E$.

Note that the criterion of the applicability of a default in $\mathbf{DL_3}$ makes the two defaults $d = (A : B_1, \ldots, B_n/C)$ and $d' = (A : MB_1, \ldots, MB_n/C)$ equivalent in the sense that the application of d implies the application of d' and vice versa. Thus, in a default theory $T = \langle W, D \rangle$, we can replace all $d \in D$ with their corresponding version d' without changing extensions.

There are two basic reasoning tasks in the context of default logic, viz., *brave reasoning* and *skeptical reasoning*. The former task is the problem of checking whether a closed formula A belongs to at least one extension of a given closed default theory T, whilst the latter task examines whether A belongs to all extensions of T. Our aim is to give a sequent-type axiomatisation of brave default reasoning, following the approach of Bonatti [8] for standard default logic.

To conclude our review of three-valued default logic, we give two examples, as discussed by Radzikowska [30], showing the representational advantages of **DL₃**.

Example 1 ([20]). Consider $T = \langle W, D \rangle$, where $W = \{Summer, \neg Sun\_Shining\}$ and $D = \{(Summer : \neg Rain/Sun\_Shining)\}$. The only default of this theory is inapplicable since $W \vdash_{\mathbf{L_3}} \neg L Sun\_Shining$. Hence, T has one extension, $E = \mathrm{Th}_{\mathbf{L_3}}(W)$. Note that T has no extension in Reiter's default logic due to the weaker consistency check which yields to a vicious circle where the application of the default violates its justification for applying it. □

Example 2 ([29]). Consider the default rules $d_1 = (P : Q/Q)$ and $d_2 = (Q : R/R)$, where P, Q, and R are atomic formulas respectively standing for "Joe recites passages from Shakespeare", "Joe can read and write", and "Joe is over seven years old". Obviously, common sense suggests that, given P, there are perfect reasons to apply both defaults to infer that Joe is over seven years old. Suppose now that we add the default rule $d_3 = (S : Q/Q)$, where S stands for "Joe is a child prodigy". Given S, it is reasonable to infer that Joe can read and write, but the inference that Joe is over seven years old seems to be unjustified. In standard default logic, a common way of suppressing R in the second case of this example would be to employ a default rule with exceptions of the form $d_2' = (Q : R \wedge \neg S)/R)$. However, this remedy is somewhat unsatisfactory as it requires every default with a possibly large number of conceivable exceptions which, each time a new default is added, the previous ones must be revised, which is arguably ad hoc. In **DL₃**, however, this can easily be accommodated by using the defaults $(P : LQ/LQ)$, $(Q : LR/LR)$, and $(MS : Q/Q)$ instead of d_1, d_2, and d_3, respectively. □

3   Preparatory Characterisations: Residues and Extensions

We now discuss some properties of extensions concerning adding defaults to default theories which lays the groundwork on which our subsequent calculus is built. In doing so, we first introduce an alternative formulation of **DL₃** extensions, adapting a proof-theoretical characterisation as described by Marek and Truszczyński [23] for standard default logic, and afterwards we provide results concerning so-called *residues*, which are inference rules resulting from defaults satisfying their consistency condition. The latter endeavour generalises the approach of Bonatti [8] to the three-valued case and follows the exposition given by Tompits [35] for standard default logic.

Definition 1. *Let E be a set of formulas. A default $(A : B_1, \ldots, B_n/C)$ is* active *in E iff $E \vdash_{\mathbf{L_3}} A$ and $\{\neg B_1, \ldots, \neg B_n, \neg LC\} \cap E = \emptyset$.*

Definition 2. *Let D be a set of defaults and E a set of formulas. The* reduct *of D with respect to E, denoted by D_E, is the set consisting of the following inference rules:*

$$D_E := \left\{ \frac{A}{MC} \;\middle|\; \frac{A : B_1, \ldots, B_n}{C} \in D \text{ and } \{\neg B_1, \ldots, \neg B_n, \neg LC\} \cap E = \emptyset \right\}.$$

An inference rule A/MC is called residue *of a default $(A : B_1, \ldots, B_n/C)$.*

For a set R of inference rules, let $\vdash^R_{\mathbf{L_3}}$ be the inference relation obtained from $\vdash_{\mathbf{L_3}}$ by augmenting the postulates of the Hilbert-type calculus underlying $\vdash_{\mathbf{L_3}}$ with the inference rules from R. The corresponding deductive closure operator for $\vdash^R_{\mathbf{L_3}}$ is given by $\mathrm{Th}^R_{\mathbf{L_3}}(W) := \{A \mid W \vdash^R_{\mathbf{L_3}} A\}$. Clearly, $\mathrm{Th}^\emptyset_{\mathbf{L_3}}(W) = \mathrm{Th}_{\mathbf{L_3}}(W)$.

We then obtain the following characterisation of the operator Γ_T, mirroring the analogous property for standard default logic as discussed by Marek and Truszczyński [23]:

Theorem 1. *Let $T = \langle W, D \rangle$ be a default theory, E a set of formulas, and D_E the reduct of D with respect to E. Then, $\Gamma_T(E) = \mathrm{Th}^{D_E}_{\mathbf{L_3}}(W)$.*

Corollary 1. *Let $T = \langle W, D \rangle$ be a default theory. A set E of formulas is an extension of T iff $\mathrm{Th}^{D_E}_{\mathbf{L_3}}(W) = E$.*

Now we show some properties of extensions with respect to active and non-active defaults which are relevant for our sequent calculus. We start with two obvious results whose proofs are straightforward.

Lemma 1. *Let R, R' be sets of inference rules, and W, W' sets of formulas. Then:*

(i) $W \subseteq \mathrm{Th}^R_{\mathbf{L_3}}(W)$;
(ii) $\mathrm{Th}^R_{\mathbf{L_3}}(W) = \mathrm{Th}^R_{\mathbf{L_3}}(\mathrm{Th}^R_{\mathbf{L_3}}(W))$;
(iii) if $R \subseteq R'$, then $\mathrm{Th}^R_{\mathbf{L_3}}(W) \subseteq \mathrm{Th}^{R'}_{\mathbf{L_3}}(W)$; and
(iv) if $W \subseteq W'$, then $\mathrm{Th}^R_{\mathbf{L_3}}(W) \subseteq \mathrm{Th}^R_{\mathbf{L_3}}(W')$.

Lemma 2. *Let A and B be formulas, W and E sets of formulas, and R a set of inference rules. Then:*

(i) if $A \notin \mathrm{Th}^R_{\mathbf{L_3}}(W)$, then $\mathrm{Th}^R_{\mathbf{L_3}}(W) = \mathrm{Th}^{R \cup \{A/B\}}_{\mathbf{L_3}}(W)$;
(ii) if $A \in \mathrm{Th}^{R \cup \{A/B\}}_{\mathbf{L_3}}(W)$, then $\mathrm{Th}^{R \cup \{A/B\}}_{\mathbf{L_3}}(W) = \mathrm{Th}^R_{\mathbf{L_3}}(W \cup \{B\})$.

For convenience, we employ the following notation in what follows: for a default $d = (A : B_1, \ldots, B_n/C)$, we write $\mathsf{p}(d) := A$, $\mathsf{j}(d) := \{B_1, \ldots, B_n, LC\}$, and $\mathsf{c}(d) := MC$. Furthermore, for a set S of formulas, $\neg S := \{\neg A \mid A \in S\}$.

Theorem 2. *Let $T = \langle W, D \rangle$ be a default theory, E a set of formulas, and d a default not active in E. Then, E is an extension of $\langle W, D \rangle$ iff E is an extension of $\langle W, D \cup \{d\} \rangle$.*

Proof. If $\neg j(d) \cap E \neq \emptyset$, then $(D \cup \{d\})_E = D_E$. So, $\mathrm{Th}_{\mathbf{L_3}}^{(D \cup \{d\})_E}(W) = \mathrm{Th}_{\mathbf{L_3}}^{D_E}(W)$ and the statement of the lemma holds quite trivially by Corollary 1.

For the rest of the proof, assume thus $\neg j(d) \cap E = \emptyset$. Since d is not active in E, $E \nvdash_{\mathbf{L_3}} p(d)$ must then hold. Furthermore, $(D \cup \{d\})_E = D_E \cup \{p(d)/c(d)\}$ holds.

Suppose E is an extension of $T = \langle W, D \rangle$, i.e., $E = \mathrm{Th}_{\mathbf{L_3}}^{D_E}(W)$. Since $E \nvdash_{\mathbf{L_3}} p(d)$ and E is deductively closed, we obtain $p(d) \notin E$, and so $p(d) \notin \mathrm{Th}_{\mathbf{L_3}}^{D_E}(W)$. By Lemma 2(i), $\mathrm{Th}_{\mathbf{L_3}}^{D_E}(W) = \mathrm{Th}_{\mathbf{L_3}}^{D_E \cup \{p(d)/c(d)\}}(W)$. But $D_E \cup \{p(d)/c(d)\} = (D \cup \{d\})_E$, hence $\mathrm{Th}_{\mathbf{L_3}}^{D_E}(W) = \mathrm{Th}_{\mathbf{L_3}}^{(D \cup \{d\})_E}(W)$. Since $E = \mathrm{Th}_{\mathbf{L_3}}^{D_E}(W)$, we obtain $E = \mathrm{Th}_{\mathbf{L_3}}^{(D \cup \{d\})_E}(W)$ and E is extension of $\langle W, D \cup \{d\} \rangle$.

This proves the "only if" direction; the "if" direction follows by essentially the same arguments, but employing additionally Lemma 1(iii). □

Theorem 3. *Let E be a set of formulas and d a default.*

(i) *If E is an extension of $\langle W, D \cup \{d\} \rangle$ and d is active in E, then E is an extension of $\langle W \cup \{c(d)\}, D \rangle$.*

(ii) *If E is an extension of the default theory $\langle W \cup \{c(d)\}, D \rangle$, $W \vdash_{\mathbf{L_3}} p(d)$, and $\neg j(d) \cap E = \emptyset$, then E is an extension of $\langle W, D \cup \{d\} \rangle$.*

Proof. We only show item (ii); the proof of (i) is similarly. Assume that the preconditions of (ii) hold. Since E is an extension of $\langle W \cup \{c(d)\}, D \rangle$, $E = \mathrm{Th}_{\mathbf{L_3}}^{D_E}(W \cup \{c(d)\})$. Furthermore, by the hypothesis $W \vdash_{\mathbf{L_3}} p(d)$, we have $p(d) \in \mathrm{Th}_{\mathbf{L_3}}^{D_E \cup \{p(d)/c(d)\}}(W)$. We thus get $\mathrm{Th}_{\mathbf{L_3}}^{D_E \cup \{p(d)/c(d)\}}(W) = \mathrm{Th}_{\mathbf{L_3}}^{D_E}(W \cup \{c(d)\})$ in view of Lemma 2(ii), and therefore $E = \mathrm{Th}_{\mathbf{L_3}}^{D_E \cup \{p(d)/c(d)\}}(W)$. By observing that the assumption $\neg j(d) \cap E = \emptyset$ implies $D_E \cup \{p(d)/c(d)\} = (D \cup \{d\})_E$, the result follows. □

4   A Sequent Calculus for DL₃

We now introduce our sequent calculus for brave reasoning in **DL₃**. Our calculus adapts the approach of Bonatti [8], defined for standard default logic, for the three-valued case.

Analogous to Bonatti's system, our calculus, which we denote by B₃, comprises three kinds of sequents: assertional sequents for axiomatising validity in **L₃**, *anti-sequents* for axiomatising *invalidity*, i.e., non-theorems of **L₃**, taking care of the consistency check of defaults, and proper default sequents. Although it would be possible to use just one kind of sequents, this would be at the expense of losing clarity of the sequents' structure. As well, the current separation of types of sequents also reflects the interactions between the underlying monotonic proof machinery the nonmonotonic inferences in a much clearer manner.

As far as sequent-type calculi for three-valued logics are concerned—or, more generally, many-valued logics—, different techniques have been discussed in the literature [2,3,6,11,16,37]. Here, we use an approach due to Rousseau [33],

$$\frac{\Gamma \mid \Delta \mid \Pi, A \qquad \Gamma, B \mid \Delta \mid \Pi}{\Gamma, A \supset B \mid \Delta \mid \Pi} \ (\supset : \mathbf{f})$$

$$\frac{\Gamma \mid \Delta, A, B \mid \Pi \qquad \Gamma, B \mid \Delta \mid \Pi, A}{\Gamma \mid \Delta, A \supset B \mid \Pi} \ (\supset : \mathbf{u})$$

$$\frac{\Gamma, A \mid \Delta, A \mid \Pi, B \qquad \Gamma, A \mid \Delta, B \mid \Pi, B}{\Gamma \mid \Delta \mid \Pi, A \supset B} \ (\supset : \mathbf{t})$$

$$\frac{\Gamma \mid \Delta \mid \Pi, A}{\Gamma, \neg A \mid \Delta \mid \Pi} \ (\neg : \mathbf{f}) \qquad \frac{\Gamma \mid \Delta, A \mid \Pi}{\Gamma \mid \Delta, \neg A \mid \Pi} \ (\neg : \mathbf{u}) \qquad \frac{\Gamma, A \mid \Delta \mid \Pi}{\Gamma \mid \Delta \mid \Pi, \neg A} \ (\neg : \mathbf{t})$$

$$\frac{\Gamma \mid \Delta \mid \Pi}{\Gamma, A \mid \Delta \mid \Pi} \ (w : \mathbf{f}) \qquad \frac{\Gamma \mid \Delta \mid \Pi}{\Gamma \mid \Delta, A \mid \Pi} \ (w : \mathbf{u}) \qquad \frac{\Gamma \mid \Delta \mid \Pi}{\Gamma \mid \Delta \mid \Pi, A} \ (w : \mathbf{t})$$

Fig. 2. Rules of the sequent calculus SL_3.

which is a natural generalisation for many-valued logics of the classical two-sided sequent formulation as pioneered by Gentzen [15]. In Rousseau's approach, a sequent for a three-valued logic is a triple of sets of formulas where each component of the sequent represents one of the three truth values.

Formally, we introduce sequents for $\mathbf{L_3}$ as follows:

Definition 3. *A (three-valued) sequent is a triple of form* $\Gamma_1 \mid \Gamma_2 \mid \Gamma_3$, *where each* Γ_i ($i \in \{1, 2, 3\}$) *is a finite set of formulas, called* component *of the sequent.*

For an interpretation m, *a sequent* $\Gamma_1 \mid \Gamma_2 \mid \Gamma_3$ *is* true under m *if, for at least one* $i \in \{1, 2, 3\}$, Γ_i *contains some formula* A *such that* $V^m(A) = v_i$, *where* $v_1 = \mathbf{f}$, $v_2 = \mathbf{u}$, *and* $v_3 = \mathbf{t}$. *Furthermore, a sequent is* valid *if it is true under each interpretation.*

Obviously, a standard classical sequent $\Gamma \vdash \Delta$ corresponds to a pair $\Gamma \mid \Delta$ with the usual two-valued semantics. As customary for sequents, we write sequent components comprised of a singleton set $\{A\}$ simply as "A" and similarly $\Gamma \cup \{A\}$ as "Γ, A".

For obtaining the postulates of a many-valued logic in Rousseau's approach, the conditions of the logical connectives of the given logic are encoded in two-valued logic by means of a so-called *partial normal form* [32] and expressed by suitable inference rules.

The calculus we introduce for $\mathbf{L_3}$, which we denote by SL_3, is obtained from a systematic construction of sequent-style calculi for many-valued logics due to Zach [37] and by applying some optimisations of the corresponding partial normal form [7].[1] The axioms of SL_3 consist of sequents of the form $A \mid A \mid A$, where A is a formula, and the inference rules depicted in Fig. 2. Note that from

---

[1] SL_3 has optimised rules for $\supset$ compared to those of the calculus for $\mathbf{L_3}$ given by Malinowski [22]; also note that SL_3 does not require a cut rule.

$$\frac{\Gamma \mid \Delta \mid \Pi, A}{\Gamma, A \supset B \mid \Delta \mid \Pi}\ (\supset : \mathbf{f}^1)^r \qquad \frac{\Gamma, B \mid \Delta \mid \Pi}{\Gamma, A \supset B \mid \Delta \mid \Pi}\ (\supset : \mathbf{f}^2)^r$$

$$\frac{\Gamma \mid \Delta, A, B \mid \Pi}{\Gamma \mid \Delta, A \supset B \mid \Pi}\ (\supset : \mathbf{u}^1)^r \qquad \frac{\Gamma, B \mid \Delta \mid \Pi, A}{\Gamma \mid \Delta, A \supset B \mid \Pi}\ (\supset : \mathbf{u}^2)^r$$

$$\frac{\Gamma, A \mid \Delta, A \mid \Pi, B}{\Gamma \mid \Delta \mid \Pi, A \supset B}\ (\supset : \mathbf{t}^1)^r \qquad \frac{\Gamma, A \mid \Delta, B \mid \Pi, B}{\Gamma \mid \Delta \mid \Pi, A \supset B}\ (\supset : \mathbf{t}^2)^r$$

$$\frac{\Gamma \mid \Delta \mid \Pi, A}{\Gamma, \neg A \mid \Delta \mid \Pi}\ (\neg : \mathbf{f})^r \qquad \frac{\Gamma \mid \Delta, A \mid \Pi}{\Gamma \mid \Delta, \neg A \mid \Pi}\ (\neg : \mathbf{u})^r \qquad \frac{\Gamma, A \mid \Delta \mid \Pi}{\Gamma \mid \Delta \mid \Pi, \neg A}\ (\neg : \mathbf{t})^r$$

$$\frac{\Gamma, A \mid \Delta \mid \Pi}{\Gamma \mid \Delta \mid \Pi}\ (w : \mathbf{f})^r \qquad \frac{\Gamma \mid \Delta, A \mid \Pi}{\Gamma \mid \Delta \mid \Pi}\ (w : \mathbf{u})^r \qquad \frac{\Gamma \mid \Delta \mid \Pi, A}{\Gamma \mid \Delta \mid \Pi}\ (w : \mathbf{t})^r$$

Fig. 3. Rules of the anti-sequent calculus RL_3.

the inference rules of SL_3 we can easily obtain derived rules for the defined connectives of $\mathbf{L_3}$. Furthermore, the last three rules in Fig. 2 are also referred to as *weakening rules*.

Soundness and completeness of SL_3 follows directly from the method described by Zach [37].

Theorem 4. *A sequent $\Gamma \mid \Delta \mid \Pi$ is valid iff it is provable in SL_3.*

Note that sequents in the style of Rousseau are *truth functional* rather than formalising entailment directly, but the latter can be expressed simply as follows:

Theorem 5. *For a theory T and a formula A, $T \vdash_{\mathbf{L_3}} A$ iff the sequent $T \mid T \mid A$ is provable in SL_3.*

As for axiomatising non-theorems of $\mathbf{L_3}$, Bogojeski [7] describes a systematic construction of refutation calculi for many-valued logics, which is obtained by adapting the approach of Zach [37]. The refutation calculus we introduce now for axiomatising invalid sequents in $\mathbf{L_3}$, denoted by RL_3, is obtained from the method of Bogojeski [7].

Definition 4. *A (three-valued) anti-sequent is a triple of form $\Gamma_1 \mid \Gamma_2 \mid \Gamma_3$, where each Γ_i ($i \in \{1,2,3\}$) is a finite set of formulas, called* component *of the anti-sequent.*

For an interpretation m, an anti-sequent $\Gamma_1 \mid \Gamma_2 \mid \Gamma_3$ is refuted by m, or m refutes $\Gamma_1 \mid \Gamma_2 \mid \Gamma_3$, if, for every $i \in \{1,2,3\}$ and every formula $A \in \Gamma_i$, $V^m(A) \neq \mathsf{v}_i$, where v_i is defined as in Definition 3.

If m refutes $\Gamma_1 \mid \Gamma_2 \mid \Gamma_3$, then m is also said to be a counter-model *of $\Gamma_1 \mid \Gamma_2 \mid \Gamma_3$. An anti-sequent $\Gamma_1 \mid \Gamma_2 \mid \Gamma_3$ is refutable, if there is at least one interpretation that refutes $\Gamma_1 \mid \Gamma_2 \mid \Gamma_3$.*

$$\frac{\Gamma \mid \Gamma \mid A}{\Gamma; \emptyset \Rightarrow A; \emptyset} \; l_1 \qquad \frac{\Gamma \nmid \Gamma \nmid A}{\Gamma; \emptyset \Rightarrow \emptyset; A} \; l_2 \qquad \frac{\Gamma; \emptyset \Rightarrow \Sigma_1; \Theta_1 \quad \Gamma; \emptyset \Rightarrow \Sigma_2; \Theta_2}{\Gamma; \emptyset \Rightarrow \Sigma_1, \Sigma_2; \Theta_1, \Theta_2} \; mu$$

$$\frac{\Gamma; \Delta \Rightarrow \Sigma; \Theta, A}{\Gamma; \Delta, (A : B_1, \ldots, B_n/C) \Rightarrow \Sigma; \Theta} \; d_1 \qquad \frac{\Gamma; \Delta \Rightarrow \Sigma, \neg B; \Theta}{\Gamma; \Delta, (A : \ldots, B, \ldots /C) \Rightarrow \Sigma; \Theta} \; d_2$$

$$\frac{\Gamma; \Delta \Rightarrow \Sigma, \neg LC; \Theta}{\Gamma; \Delta, (A : B_1, \ldots, B_n/C) \Rightarrow \Sigma; \Theta} \; d_3$$

$$\frac{\Gamma; \emptyset \Rightarrow A; \emptyset \qquad \Gamma, MC; \Delta \Rightarrow \Sigma; \Theta, \neg B_1, \ldots, \neg B_n, \neg LC}{\Gamma; \Delta, (A : B_1, \ldots, B_n/C) \Rightarrow \Sigma; \Theta} \; d_4$$

Fig. 4. Additional rules of the calculus B_3.

Clearly, an anti-sequent $\Gamma_1 \nmid \Gamma_2 \nmid \Gamma_3$ is refutable iff the corresponding sequent $\Gamma_1 \mid \Gamma_2 \mid \Gamma_3$ is not valid.

The postulates of RL_3 are as follows: the axioms of RL_3 are anti-sequents whose components are sets of propositional constants such that no constant appears in all components. Furthermore, the inference rules of RL_3 are given in Fig. 3.

Note that, in contrast to SL_3, the inference rules of RL_3 have only single premises. Indeed, this is a general pattern in sequent-style rejection calculi: if an inference rule for standard (assertional) sequents for a connective have n premises, then there are usually n corresponding unary inference rules in the associated rejection calculus. Intuitively, what is exhaustive search in a standard sequent calculus becomes nondeterminism in a rejection calculus.

Again, soundness and completeness of RL_3 follows from the systematic construction as described by Bogojeski [7]. Likewise, non-entailment in $\mathbf{L_3}$ is expressed similarly as for SL_3.

Theorem 6. *An anti-sequent $\Gamma \nmid \Delta \nmid \Pi$ is refutable iff it is provable in RL_3. Moreover, for a theory T and a formula A, $T \nvdash_{\mathbf{L_3}} A$ iff $T \nmid T \nmid A$ is provable in RL_3.*

We are now in a position to specify our calculus B_3 for brave reasoning in $\mathbf{DL_3}$.

Definition 5. *By a (brave) default sequent we understand an ordered quadruple of the form $\Gamma; \Delta \Rightarrow \Sigma; \Theta$, where Γ, Σ, and Θ are finite sets of formulas and Δ is a finite set of defaults.*

A default sequent $\Gamma; \Delta \Rightarrow \Sigma; \Theta$ is true iff there is an extension E of the default theory $\langle \Gamma, \Delta \rangle$ such that $\Sigma \subseteq E$ and $\Theta \cap E = \emptyset$; E is called a witness of $\Gamma; \Delta \Rightarrow \Sigma; \Theta$.

The default sequent calculus B_3 consists of three-valued sequents, anti-sequents, and default sequents. It incorporates the systems SL_3 for three-valued sequents and RL_3 for anti-sequents. Additionally, it has axioms of the form

$\Gamma; \emptyset \Rightarrow \emptyset; \emptyset$, where Γ is a finite set of formulas, and the inference rules as depicted in Fig. 4.

The informal meaning of the nonmonotonic inference rules is the following. First of all, rules l_1 and l_2 combine three-valued sequents and anti-sequents with default sequents, respectively. Rule mu is the rule of "monotonic union"; it allows the joining of information in case that no default is present. Rules d_1–d_4 are the default introduction rules: rules d_1, d_2, and d_3 take care of introducing non-active defaults, whilst rule d_4 allows to introduce an active default.

Theorem 7 (Soundness). *If $\Gamma; \Delta \Rightarrow \Sigma; \Theta$ is provable in B_3, then it is true.*

Proof. We show that all axioms are true, and that the conclusions of all inference rules are true whenever its premises are true (resp., valid or refutable in case of l_1 and l_2).

First of all, an axiom $\Gamma; \emptyset \Rightarrow \emptyset; \emptyset$ is trivially true, because $\mathrm{Th}_{\mathbf{L_3}}(\Gamma)$ is the unique extension of the default theory $\langle \Gamma, \emptyset \rangle$ and hence the unique witness of $\Gamma; \emptyset \Rightarrow \emptyset; \emptyset$.

Suppose $\Gamma \mid \Gamma \mid A$ is the premiss of the rule l_1 and assume it is valid. Hence, $\Gamma \vdash_{\mathbf{L_3}} A$ and therefore $A \in \mathrm{Th}_{\mathbf{L_3}}(\Gamma)$. But $\mathrm{Th}_{\mathbf{L_3}}(\Gamma)$ is the unique extension of $\langle \Gamma, \emptyset \rangle$, so $\mathrm{Th}_{\mathbf{L_3}}(\Gamma)$ is the unique witness of $\Gamma; \emptyset \Rightarrow A; \emptyset$. Likewise, if the premiss $\Gamma \nmid \Gamma \nmid A$ of the rule l_2 is refutable, then $A \notin \mathrm{Th}_{\mathbf{L_3}}(\Gamma)$, and therefore $\mathrm{Th}_{\mathbf{L_3}}(\Gamma)$ is the (unique) witness of $\Gamma; \emptyset \Rightarrow \emptyset; A$.

If the two premises $\Gamma; \emptyset \Rightarrow \Sigma_1; \Theta_1$ and $\Gamma; \emptyset \Rightarrow \Sigma_2; \Theta_2$ of the rule mu are true, then they must have the same witness $E = \mathrm{Th}_{\mathbf{L_3}}(\Gamma)$. Hence, E is also the (unique) witness of $\Gamma; \emptyset \Rightarrow \Sigma_1, \Sigma_2; \Theta_1, \Theta_2$.

As for the soundness of the rules d_1, d_2, and d_3, we only show the case for d_3; the other two are similar. Let E be a witness of $\Gamma; \Delta \Rightarrow \Sigma, \neg LC; \Theta$. Then, E is an extension of $\langle \Gamma, \Delta \rangle$, $\Sigma \cup \{\neg LC\} \subseteq E$, and $\Theta \cap E = \emptyset$. So, $\neg LC \in E$ and thus the default $(A : B_1, \ldots, B_n/C)$ is not active in E. By Theorem 2, it follows that E is an extension of $\langle \Gamma, \Delta \cup \{(A : B_1, \ldots, B_n/C)\} \rangle$. Moreover, since $\Sigma \subseteq E$ and $\Theta \cap E = \emptyset$, E is a witness of $\Gamma; \Delta, (A : B_1, \ldots, B_n/C) \Rightarrow \Sigma; \Theta$.

Finally, assume that the premises of rule d_4 are true. Let E_1 be a witness of $\Gamma; \emptyset \Rightarrow A; \emptyset$ and E_2 a witness of $\Gamma, MC; \Delta \Rightarrow \Sigma; \Theta, \neg B_1, \ldots, \neg B_n, \neg LC$. Thus, E_2 is an extension of $\langle \Gamma \cup \{MC\}, \Delta \rangle$ and $\{\neg B_1, \ldots, \neg B_n, \neg LC\} \cap E_2 = \emptyset$. So, E_1 is an extension of $\langle \Gamma, \emptyset \rangle$ with $A \in E_1$, and therefore $\Gamma \vdash_{\mathbf{L_3}} A$. Hence, by Theorem 3(ii), E_2 is an extension of $\langle \Gamma, \Delta \cup \{(A : B_1, \ldots, B_n/C)\} \rangle$. Clearly, $\Sigma \subseteq E_2$ and $\Theta \cap E_2 = \emptyset$, so E_2 is a witness of $\Gamma; \Delta, (A : B_1, \ldots, B_n/C) \Rightarrow \Sigma; \Theta$. □

Theorem 8 (Completeness). *If $\Gamma; \Delta \Rightarrow \Sigma; \Theta$ is true, then it is provable in B_3.*

Proof. Suppose $S = \Gamma; \Delta \Rightarrow \Sigma; \Theta$ is true, with E as its witness. The proof proceeds by induction on the cardinality $|\Delta|$ of Δ.

INDUCTION BASE. Assume $|\Delta| = 0$. If $\Sigma = \Theta = \emptyset$, then S is an axiom and hence provable in B_3. So suppose that either $\Sigma \neq \emptyset$ or $\Theta \neq \emptyset$. Since $\mathrm{Th}_{\mathbf{L_3}}(\Gamma)$ is the unique extension of $\langle \Gamma, \emptyset \rangle$, we have $E = \text{Th}_{\mathbf{L_3}}(\Gamma)$. Furthermore, $\Sigma \subseteq E$ and $\Theta \cap E = \emptyset$. It follows that for any $A \in \Sigma$, $\Gamma \mid \Gamma \mid A$ is provable in SL_3, and for any $B \in \Theta$, $\Gamma \nmid \Gamma \nmid B$ is provable in RL_3. Repeated applications of rules l_1, l_2, and mu yield a proof of S in B_3.

INDUCTION STEP. Assume $|\Delta| > 0$, and let the statement hold for all default sequents $\Gamma'; \Delta' \Rightarrow \Sigma'; \Theta'$ such that $|\Delta'| < |\Delta|$. We distinguish two cases: (i) there is some default in Δ which is active in E, or (ii) none of the defaults in Δ is active in E.

If (i) holds, then there must be some default $d = (A : B_1, \ldots, B_n/C)$ in Δ such that d is active in E and $\Gamma \vdash_{\mathbf{L_3}} A$. Consider $\Delta_0 := \Delta \setminus \{d\}$. Then, $|\Delta_0| = |\Delta| - 1$ and $\Delta_0 \cup \{d\} = \Delta$. By Theorem 3(i), E is an extension of $\langle \Gamma \cup \{MC\}, \Delta_0 \rangle$. Since d is active in E, $\{\neg B_1, \ldots, \neg B_n, \neg LC\} \cap E = \emptyset$; and since E is a witness of $S = \Gamma; \Delta \Rightarrow \Sigma; \Theta$, $\Sigma \subseteq E$ and $\Theta \cap E = \emptyset$. So, E is a witness of $S' = \Gamma, MC; \Delta_0 \Rightarrow \Sigma; \Theta, \neg B_1, \ldots, \neg B_n, \neg LC$. Since $|\Delta_0| < |\Delta|$, by induction hypothesis there is some proof α in B_3 of S'. Furthermore, $\Gamma \vdash_{\mathbf{L_3}} A$, so there is some proof β of $\Gamma \mid \Gamma \mid A$ in SL_3. The following figure is a proof of S in B_3:

$$\dfrac{\dfrac{\beta}{\Gamma \mid \Gamma \mid A}}{\Gamma; \emptyset \Rightarrow A; \emptyset} l_1 \qquad \dfrac{\dfrac{\alpha}{\Gamma, MC; \Delta_0 \Rightarrow \Sigma; \Theta, \neg B_1, \ldots, \neg B_n, \neg LC}}{\Gamma; \Delta \Rightarrow \Sigma; \Theta} d_4$$

Now assume that (ii) holds, i.e., no default in Δ is active in E. Since $|\Delta| > 0$, there is some default $d = (A : B_1, \ldots, B_n/C)$ in Δ such that $\Delta = \Delta_0 \cup \{d\}$ with $\Delta_0 := \Delta \setminus \{d\}$. Since d is not active in E, according to Theorem 2, E is an extension of $\langle \Gamma, \Delta_0 \rangle$. Furthermore, either (i) $E \nvdash_{\mathbf{L_3}} A$, (ii) there is some $B_{i_0} \in \{B_1, \ldots, B_n\}$ such that $\neg B_{i_0} \in E$, or (iii) $\neg LC \in E$. Consequently, E is either a witness of (i) $\Gamma; \Delta_0 \Rightarrow \Sigma; \Theta, A$, (ii) $\Gamma; \Delta_0 \Rightarrow \Sigma, \neg B_{i_0}; \Theta$, or (iii) $\Gamma; \Delta_0 \Rightarrow \Sigma, \neg LC; \Theta$. Since $|\Delta_0| < |\Delta|$, by induction hypothesis there is either (i) a proof α in B_3 of $\Gamma; \Delta_0 \Rightarrow \Sigma; \Theta, A$, (ii) a proof β in B_3 of $\Gamma; \Delta_0 \Rightarrow \Sigma, \neg B_{i_0}; \Theta$, or (iii) a proof γ in B_3 of $\Gamma; \Delta_0 \Rightarrow \Sigma, \neg LC; \Theta$. Therefore, one of the three figures below constitutes a proof of S :

$$\dfrac{\dfrac{\alpha}{\Gamma; \Delta_0 \Rightarrow \Sigma; \Theta, A}}{\Gamma; \Delta \Rightarrow \Sigma; \Theta} d_1 \qquad \dfrac{\dfrac{\beta}{\Gamma; \Delta_0 \Rightarrow \Sigma, \neg B_{i_0}; \Theta}}{\Gamma; \Delta \Rightarrow \Sigma; \Theta} d_2 \qquad \dfrac{\dfrac{\gamma}{\Gamma; \Delta_0 \Rightarrow \Sigma, \neg LC; \Theta}}{\Gamma; \Delta \Rightarrow \Sigma; \Theta} d_3$$

$\square$

5   Conclusion

In this paper, we introduced a sequent-type calculus for brave reasoning for a three-valued version of default logic [30] following the method of Bonatti [8]. This form of axiomatisation yields a particular elegant formulation mainly due to their usage of anti-sequents. Also, the approach is flexible and can be applied to formalise different versions of nonmonotonic reasoning. Indeed, other variants of default logic besides the three-valued version studied in our paper, including justified default logic [19] and constrained default logic [12,34], have also been axiomatised by this sequent method [13,21].

Related to the sequent approach discussed here are also works employing tableau methods. In particular, Niemelä [26] introduces a tableau calculus for inference under circumscription. Other tableau approaches, however, do not encode inference directly, rather they characterise models (resp., extensions) associated with a particular nonmonotonic reasoning formalism [1,10,14,28].

A variation of our calculus can be obtained by using different calculi for the underlying three-valued logic. We opted here for the style of calculi as discussed by Rousseau [33] and Zach [37] because they naturally model the underlying semantic conditions of the considered logic. Alternatively, we could also use two-sided sequent and anti-sequent calculi like the ones described by Avron [2] and Oetsch and Tompits [27], respectively. By employing such two-sided sequents, however, one then deals with calculi having also "non-standard" inference rules introducing two connectives simultaneously. Another prominent proof method for many-valued logics are *hypersequent calculi* [3] which are basically disjunctions of two-sided sequents. However, no rejection calculus based on hypersequents exist as far as we know; establishing such a system in particular for $\mathbf{L_3}$ would be worthwhile.

Another topic for future work is to develop a calculus for skeptical reasoning in $\mathbf{DL_3}$ and other variants of default logic, similar to the system for skeptical reasoning in standard default logic as introduced by Bonatti and Olivetti [9]. In that work, they introduced also a different version of a calculus for brave default reasoning—extending this calculus to $\mathbf{DL_3}$ would provide an alternative to B_3.

References

1. Amati, G., Aiello, L.C., Gabbay, D., Pirri, F.: A proof theoretical approach to default reasoning I: Tableaux for default logic. J. Log. Comput. **6**(2), 205–231 (1996)
2. Avron, A.: Natural 3-valued logics - Characterization and proof theory. J. Symb. Log. **56**(1), 276–294 (1991)
3. Avron, A.: The method of hypersequents in the proof theory of propositional non-classical logics. In: Logic: From Foundations to Applications, pp. 1–32. Clarendon Press (1996)
4. Avron, A.: Classical Gentzen-type methods in propositional many-valued logics. In: Fitting, M., Orlowska, E. (eds.) Theory and Applications in Multiple-Valued Logics, pp. 113–151. Springer, Heidelberg (2002). https://doi.org/10.1007/978-3-7908-1769-0_5
5. Beyersdorff, O., Meier, A., Thomas, M., Vollmer, H.: The complexity of reasoning for fragments of default logic. J. Log. Comput. **22**(3), 587–604 (2012)
6. Béziau, J.Y.: A sequent calculus for Lukasiewicz's three-valued logic based on Suszko's bivalent semantics. Bull. Sect. Log. **28**(2), 89–97 (1999)
7. Bogojeski, M.: Gentzen-type Refutation Systems for Finite-valued Logics. Bachelor's thesis, Technische Universität Wien, Institut für Informationssysteme (2014)
8. Bonatti, P.A.: Sequent calculi for default and autoepistemic logics. In: Miglioli, P., Moscato, U., Mundici, D., Ornaghi, M. (eds.) TABLEAUX 1996. LNCS, vol. 1071, pp. 127–142. Springer, Heidelberg (1996). https://doi.org/10.1007/3-540-61208-4_9

9. Bonatti, P.A., Olivetti, N.: Sequent calculi for propositional nonmonotonic logics. ACM Transact. Comput. Log. **3**(2), 226–278 (2002)

10. Cabalar, P., Odintsov, S.P., Pearce, D., Valverde, A.: Partial equilibrium logic. Ann. Math. Artif. Intell. **50**(3–4), 305–331 (2007)

11. Carnielli, W.A.: On sequents and tableaux for many-valued logics. J. Non-Class. Log. **8**(1), 59–76 (1991)

12. Delgrande, J., Schaub, T., Jackson, W.: Alternative approaches to default logic. Artif. Intell. **70**(1–2), 167–237 (1994)

13. Egly, U., Tompits, H.: A sequent calculus for intuitionistic default logic. In: Proceedings of WLP 1997, pp. 69–79. Forschungsbericht PMS-FB-1997-10, Institut für Informatik, Ludwig-Maximilians-Universität München (1997)

14. Gebser, M., Schaub, T.: Tableau calculi for logic programs under answer set semantics. ACM Transact. Comput. Log. **14**(2), 15:1–15:40 (2013)

15. Gentzen, G.: Untersuchungen über das logische Schließen I. Math. Z. **39**(1), 176–210 (1935)

16. Hähnle, R.: Tableaux for many-valued logics. In: Handbook of Tableaux Methods, pp. 529–580. Kluwer (1999)

17. Łukasiewicz, J.: Philosophische Bemerkungen zu mehrwertigen Systemen des Aussagenkalküls. Comptes rendus des séances de la Société des Sciences et des Lettres de Varsovie Cl. **3**(23), 51–77 (1930)

18. Łukasiewicz, J.: O sylogistyce Arystotelesa. Sprawozdania z Czynności i Posiedzeń Polskiej Akademii Umiejętności **44**, 220–227 (1939)

19. Łukaszewicz, W.: Considerations on default logic - An alternative approach. Comput. Intell. **4**, 1–16 (1988)

20. Łukaszewicz, W.: Non-Monotonic Reasoning: Formalization of Commonsense Reasoning. Ellis Horwood Series in Artificial Intelligence. Ellis Horwood, Chichester (1990)

21. Lupea, M.: Axiomatization of credulous reasoning in default logics using sequent calculus. In: Proceedings of SYNASC 2008. IEEE Xplore (2008)

22. Malinowski, G.: Many-valued logic and its philosophy. In: Handbook of the History of Logic, vol. 8, pp. 13–94. North-Holland (2007)

23. Marek, W., Truszczyński, M.: Nonmonotonic Logic: Context-Dependent Reasoning. Springer, Berlin (1993). https://doi.org/10.1007/978-3-662-02906-0

24. McCarthy, J.: Circumscription - A form of non-monotonic reasoning. Artif. Intell. **13**, 27–39 (1980)

25. Moore, R.C.: Semantical considerations on nonmonotonic logic. Artif. Intell. **25**, 75–94 (1985)

26. Niemelä, I.: Implementing circumscription using a tableau method. In: Proceedings of ECAI 1996, pp. 80–84. Wiley (1996)

27. Oetsch, J., Tompits, H.: Gentzen-type refutation systems for three-valued logics with an application to disproving strong equivalence. In: Delgrande, J.P., Faber, W. (eds.) LPNMR 2011. LNCS (LNAI), vol. 6645, pp. 254–259. Springer, Heidelberg (2011). https://doi.org/10.1007/978-3-642-20895-9_28

28. Pearce, D., de Guzmán, I.P., Valverde, A.: A tableau calculus for equilibrium entailment. In: Dyckhoff, R. (ed.) TABLEAUX 2000. LNCS (LNAI), vol. 1847, pp. 352–367. Springer, Heidelberg (2000). https://doi.org/10.1007/10722086_28

29. Pearl, J.: Probabilistic Reasoning in Intelligent Systems: Networks of Plausible Inference. Morgan Kaufmann Publishers, San Mateo (1988)

30. Radzikowska, A.: A three-valued approach to default logic. J. Appl. Non-Class. Log. **6**(2), 149–190 (1996)

31. Reiter, R.: A logic for default reasoning. Artif. Intell. **13**, 81–132 (1980)
32. Rosser, J.B., Turquette, A.R.: Many-valued Logics. North-Holland, Amsterdam (1952)
33. Rousseau, G.: Sequents in many valued logic I. Fundamenta Math. **60**, 23–33 (1967)
34. Schaub, T.: On constrained default theories. Technical report AIDA-92-2, FG Intellektik, FB Informatik, TH Darmstadt (1992)
35. Tompits, H.: On Proof Complexities of First-Order Nonmonotonic Logics. Ph.D. thesis, Technische Universität Wien, Institut für Informationssysteme (1998)
36. Wajsberg, M.: Aksjomatyzacja trójwartościowego rachunku zdań. Comptes rendus des séances de la Société des Sciences et des Lettres de Varsovie Cl. **3**(24), 136–148 (1931)
37. Zach, R.: Proof Theory of Finite-valued Logics. Master's thesis, Technische Universität Wien, Institut für Computersprachen (1993)

Knowledge Representation and Reasoning

Diagnosing Data Pipeline Failures Using Action Languages

Jori Bomanson[1] and Alex Brik[2]($\boxtimes$)

[1] Department of Computer Science, Aalto University, Espoo, Finland
[2] Google Inc., Mountain View, USA
abrik@google.com

Abstract. This paper discusses diagnosis of industrial data processing pipelines using action languages. Solving the problem requires reasoning about actions, effects of the actions and mechanisms for accessing outside data sources. To satisfy these requirements, we introduce an action language, Hybrid $\mathcal{ALE}$ that combines elements of the action language Hybrid $\mathcal{AL}$ [6] and the action language C_{TAID} [8]. We discuss some of the practical aspects of implementing Hybrid $\mathcal{ALE}$ and describe an example of its use.

Answer Set Programming (ASP) is a knowledge representation formalism with the stable model semantics [11] that allows for a concise representation of defaults and uncertainty. Action languages [12] allow to formalize reasoning about effects of actions in dynamic domains. Descriptions in an action language are usually compiled into ASP. ASP solvers can then be used to find answer sets of the compiled descriptions, which specify possible trajectories of the modeled dynamic domain. Action languages have been used in various applications, such as planning [13], biological modeling [2], and diagnostic reasoning [1]. In this paper we discuss our work towards automating diagnosis of certain data processing pipelines at Google Inc. using action languages.

Industrial data processing pipelines can consists of hundreds of jobs, with outputs of some jobs consumed as inputs by others within the pipeline. In addition, pipelines themselves can have input dependencies on other pipelines. When working well, this architecture allows efficient and effective processing of large amounts of data. When a malfunction occurs, it can bring related data processing tasks to a halt, causing a set of cascading failures. The failures can cause an alert being dispatched to on-call engineers.

For the engineers, an alert presents a diagnostic challenge, as it can point to one of the later among the cascading failures, rather than an earlier one. The earlier causes have to be found before the underlying problem can be resolved thoroughly, and this can be tedious and time consuming. Moreover, multiple possible causes of failure may have to be investigated. Automating the diagnosing process can decrease the time required to fix failures. This can improve the fault tolerance of the system as well as decrease the workload for the engineers.

Earlier action languages, such as $\mathcal{AL}$ [3] focus on formalizing possible state-action-state transitions as well as applicability of actions. In diagnosing data

© Springer Nature Switzerland AG 2019
M. Balduccini et al. (Eds.): LPNMR 2019, LNAI 11481, pp. 181–194, 2019.
https://doi.org/10.1007/978-3-030-20528-7_14

processing pipelines, we found that reasoning also about the necessity of actions is conducive for creative adequate diagnostic software. $\mathcal{C}_{TAID}$ [8] is the earliest action language we found that provides all the needed language constructs.

In the context of our application, there remains, however a problem that $\mathcal{C}_{TAID}$ does not solve. In order to limit the number of possible diagnoses, it may be necessary to query outside sources for information about the diagnosed system (*outside information*). Such outside information may be, for instance the completion status of a diagnosed job, or properties of temporary files created while the diagnosed pipeline was running. In some cases precomputing all of the outside information is impractical, because of the large amount of data required to address the needs of all plausible trajectories. A more practical approach is to query the outside environment during the inference, since as the inference progresses the set of the plausible trajectories decreases in size.

Standard ASP does not provide the ability to interact with the outside environment during inference. Since action languages such as $\mathcal{AL}$ or $\mathcal{C}_{TAID}$ are translated into ASP, their ability to interact with the outside environment is likewise limited. There are extensions of ASP, however that provide the needed functionality. These include DLV^{DB} [14], VI programs [7], GRINGO grounder [10], HEX [9] and Hybrid ASP (H-ASP) [4]. The only action language known to us that translates into one of these extensions is Hybrid $\mathcal{AL}$ [6], which translates into H-ASP. We introduce a new action language Hybrid $\mathcal{ALE}$, which extends Hybrid $\mathcal{AL}$ with the language constructs of $\mathcal{C}_{TAID}$. We then discuss the use of Hybrid $\mathcal{ALE}$ for diagnostic reasoning in our application.

In this paper we refer to an example data processing pipeline and focus on a single job *process_data1* that requires an input file *input.data* before it starts processing and is suspended until the input file is produced. Upon successful termination, the job produces a single output file, *output_<timestamp>.data*, which can then be used as an input into a next job in the data processing pipeline. The *timestamp* is the timestamp of the output file and is part of its name. Upon a malfunction, the output file is not created.

To provide a meaningful diagnosis, in our example it is necessary to determine whether the input file and the output files exist. This can be done outside of the system description. In general, however such precomputing may not be feasible because of the large number of the possible trajectories of the diagnosed system. During inference, however, the space of the possible trajectories decreases as some possible trajectories are found invalid. Thus, if the checks are performed as needed during the inference, the computations can become more feasible.

The rest of the paper is structured as follows. In Sect. 1 we review H-ASP. In Sect. 2 we define Hybrid $\mathcal{ALE}$. In Sect. 3 we discuss the compilation of Hybrid $\mathcal{ALE}$ descriptions into H-ASP programs. A theorem demonstrating the correctness of the translation is discussed in the same section. In Sect. 4 we discuss an example of the use of Hybrid $\mathcal{ALE}$ for diagnostic reasoning. A discussion of some of the practical aspects of implementing Hybrid $\mathcal{ALE}$ is in Sect. 5 followed by the conclusion.

1 Hybrid ASP

We now give a brief overview of H-ASP restricted to rules used in this work. A H-ASP program P has an underlying parameter space S and a set of atoms At. Elements of S, called *generalized positions*, are of the form $\mathbf{p} = (t, x_1, \ldots, x_m)$ where t is time and x_i are parameter values. We let $t(\mathbf{p})$ denote t and $\mathbf{p}_i$ denote x_i for $i = 1, \ldots, m$. For convenience we name certain parameters, and use their names instead of their indexes so that for instance if a parameter i is named n we may use $n(\mathbf{p})$ to mean $\mathbf{p}_i$.

A *literal* is an atom a or its negation $\neg a$. For a literal b we define $\bar{b} = \neg a$ if $b = a$ for some atom a, and $\bar{b} = a$ if $b = \neg a$ for some atom a.

The *universe* of P is $At \times S$. A pair $(Z, \mathbf{p})$ where $Z \subseteq At$ and $\mathbf{p} \in S$ is referred to as a *hybrid state*. For $M \subseteq At \times S$ we write $\mathbb{GP}(M) = \{\mathbf{p} \in S : (\exists a \in At)((a, \mathbf{p}) \in M)\}$, $W_M(\mathbf{p}) = \{a \in At : (a, \mathbf{p}) \in M\}$, and $(Z, \mathbf{p}) \in M$ if $\mathbf{p} \in \mathbb{GP}(M)$ and $W_M(\mathbf{p}) = Z$. A *block* B is an object of the form $B = a_1,$ $\ldots, a_n, not\ b_1, \ldots, not\ b_m$ where $a_1, \ldots, a_n, b_1, \ldots, b_m \in At$. We let $B^- = not$ $b_1, \ldots, not\ b_m$, and $B^+ = a_1, \ldots, a_n$. We write $M \models (B, \mathbf{p})$, if $(a_i, \mathbf{p}) \in M$ for $i = 1, \ldots, n$ and $(b_j, \mathbf{p}) \notin M$ for $j = 1, \ldots, m$.

Advancing rules are of the form: $a \leftarrow B : A, O$. Here B is a block, $O \subseteq S$, for all $\mathbf{p} \in O$ $A(\mathbf{p}) \subseteq S$, and for all $\mathbf{q} \in A(\mathbf{p})$, $t(\mathbf{q}) > t(\mathbf{p})$. The idea is that if $\mathbf{p} \in O$ and B is satisfied at $\mathbf{p}$, then A can be applied to $\mathbf{p}$ to produce a set of generalized positions O' such that if $\mathbf{q} \in O'$, then $t(\mathbf{q}) > t(\mathbf{p})$ and $(a, \mathbf{q})$ holds. A is called an *advancing algorithm*.

Stationary-i rules (for $i = 1$ or $i = 2$) are of the form: $a \leftarrow B_i; B_1 : H, O$ (where for $i = 1$ we mean $a \leftarrow B_1 : H, O$). Here B_i are blocks and H is a Boolean algorithm defined on O. The idea is that if $(\mathbf{p}_i, \mathbf{p}_1) \in O$ (where for $i = 1$ we mean $\mathbf{p}_1 \in O$), B_k is satisfied at $\mathbf{p}_k$ for $k = 1, i$, and $H(\mathbf{p}_i, \mathbf{p}_1)$ is true (where for $i = 1$ we mean $H(\mathbf{p}_1)$), then $(a, \mathbf{p}_i)$ holds. H is called a *predicate algorithm*.

The stable model semantics for H-ASP [4] defines a set of *answer sets* for an H-ASP program in terms of a reduct in a way similar to ASP, but it is omitted here due to space constraints.

We now introduce additional definitions which are used later in this paper. An advancing algorithm A lets a parameter y be *free* if the domain of y is Y and for all generalized positions $\mathbf{p}$ and $\mathbf{q}$ and all $y' \in Y$, whenever $\mathbf{q} \in A(\mathbf{p})$, then there exist $\mathbf{q}' \in A(\mathbf{p})$ such that $y(\mathbf{q}') = y'$ and that $\mathbf{q}$ and $\mathbf{q}'$ are identical in all parameter values except possibly y. An advancing algorithm A *fixes* a parameter y if A does not let y be free. Intuitively, A fixes y if A is intended to specify values for y, and A lets y be free otherwise.

We use T to indicate a predicate algorithm or a set constraint that always returns true. As a short hand notation, if we omit a predicate algorithm or a set constraint from a rule, then by that we mean that T is used.

A pair of generalized positions $(\mathbf{q}, \mathbf{p})$ is a *step* (with respect to a H-ASP program P) if there exists an advancing rule $a \leftarrow B : A, O$ in P such that $\mathbf{p} \in O$ and $\mathbf{q} \in A(\mathbf{p})$. Then we say that $\mathbf{p}$ is a *source* and $\mathbf{q}$ is a *destination*. We assume that the underlying parameter space of P contains a parameter $Prev$ defined so that, for a step $(\mathbf{q}, \mathbf{p})$, we have $Prev(\mathbf{q}) = (x_1(\mathbf{p}), ..., x_n(\mathbf{p}))$. We also define a Boolean algorithm $IsStep(\mathbf{p}, \mathbf{q})$ that is true iff $Prev(\mathbf{q}) = (x_1(\mathbf{p}), ..., x_n(\mathbf{p}))$ and $[t(\mathbf{q}) = t(\mathbf{p}) + stepSize]$.

Given one-place Boolean algorithms A, B, we write $A \vee B$, $A \wedge B$, and $\overline{A}$ for Boolean algorithms that map generalized positions $\mathbf{q}$ to $A(\mathbf{q}) \vee B(\mathbf{q})$, $A(\mathbf{q}) \wedge B(\mathbf{q})$, and *not* $A(\mathbf{q})$ respectively. The same holds for two-place Boolean algorithms.

For a set of literals M, we denote by $rules(M)$ and $defaults(M)$ the sets of stationary-1 rules $\{m \leftarrow : T \mid m \in M\}$ and $\{m \leftarrow not\ \overline{m} \mid m \in M\}$ respectively.

A notation of the form $\leftarrow a_1, ..., a_m : P$ stands for a *constraint*, i.e., a stationary-1 rule $\_fail \leftarrow a_1, ..., a_m$, $not\ \_fail : P$, where $\_fail$ is a new auxiliary atom. An analogous notation holds for a stationary-2 rule.

If we omit an advancing algorithm from an advancing rule, by that we mean an advancing rule where an algorithm A is used such that if $\mathbf{q} \in A(\mathbf{p})$ then $(\mathbf{q}, \mathbf{p})$ is a step, and A lets all the parameters except *time* and *Prev* be free.

An algorithm $Dest[P]$ is defined to hold for $\mathbf{p}, \mathbf{q}$ iff $P(\mathbf{p})$.

2   Action Language Hybrid $\mathcal{ALE}$

A key concept related to action languages is that of a *transition diagram*, which is a labeled directed graph, where vertices are states of a dynamic domain, and edge labels are subsets of actions. An edge indicates that simultaneous execution of the actions in the label of an edge can transform a source state into a destination state. The transformation is not necessarily deterministic, and for a given source state there can be multiple edges having different destination states, labeled with the same set of actions. In Hybrid $\mathcal{ALE}$, just as in Hybrid $\mathcal{AL}$, one considers *hybrid transition diagrams*, which are directed graphs with two types of vertices: action states and domain states. A *domain state* is a pair $(A, \mathbf{p})$ where A is a set of propositional atoms and $\mathbf{p}$ is a vector of sequences of 0s and 1s. We can think of A as a set of Boolean properties of a system, and $\mathbf{p}$ as a description of the parameters used by external computations. An *action state* is a tuple $(A, \mathbf{p}, a)$ where A and $\mathbf{p}$ are as in the domain state, and a is a set of actions. An out edge from a domain state must have an action state as its destination. An out edge from an action state must have a domain state as its destination. Moreover, if $(A, \mathbf{p})$ is a domain state that has an out-edge to an action state $(B, \mathbf{r}, a)$, then $A = B$ and $\mathbf{p} = \mathbf{r}$. We note that there is a simple bijection between the set of transition diagrams and the set of hybrid transition diagrams.

We now define Hybrid $\mathcal{ALE}$ **syntax**. In Hybrid $\mathcal{ALE}$, there are two types of atoms: *fluents* and *actions*. There are two types of parameters: *domain parameters* and *time*. The fluents are partitioned into *inertial* and *default*. A *domain literal* l is a fluent atom p or its negation $\neg p$. For a generalized position $\mathbf{q}$, we let $\mathbf{q}|_{domain}$ denote a vector of domain parameters. The domain parameters are partitioned into *inertial* and *default*.

A *domain algorithm* is a Boolean algorithm P such that for all generalized positions $\mathbf{q}$ and $\mathbf{r}$, if $\mathbf{q}|_{domain} = \mathbf{r}|_{domain}$, then $P(\mathbf{q}) = P(\mathbf{r})$. An *action algorithm* is an advancing algorithm A such that for all $\mathbf{q}$ and for all $\mathbf{r} \in A(\mathbf{q})$, $time(\mathbf{r}) =$

$time(\mathbf{q}) + 1$. For an action algorithm A, the signature of A, $sig(A)$, is the vector of parameter indices $i_1, ..., i_k$ of domain parameters fixed by A.

Hybrid $\mathcal{ALE}$ allows the following types of statements.

1. **Default declaration for fluents:** *default fluent l*
2. **Default declaration for parameters:** *default parameter i with value w*
3. **Causal laws:** *a causes* $\langle l, L \rangle$ *with A if* $p_0, ..., p_m : P$,
4. **State constraints:** $\langle l, L \rangle$ *if* $p_0, ..., p_m : P$,
5. **Noconcurrency condition:** *impossible* $a_0, ..., a_k$ *if* $p_0, ..., p_m : P$,
6. **Allow condition:** *allow a if* $p_0, ..., p_m : P$,
7. **Trigger condition:** *trigger a if* $p_0, ..., p_m : P$,
8. **Inhibition condition:** *inhibit a if* $p_0, ..., p_m : P$

where l is a domain literal, i is a parameter index, w is a parameter value, a is an action, A is an action algorithm, $i_0, ..., i_k$ are parameter indices, L and P are domain algorithms, $p_0, ..., p_m$ are domain literals, and $a_0, ..., a_k$ are actions $k \geq 0$ and $m \geq -1$. If L or P are omitted then the algorithm T is substituted.

A *default declaration for fluents* declares a default fluent and specifies its default value. If l is a positive literal, then the default value is *true*, and if l is a negative fluent then the default value is *false*. A *default declaration for parameters* declares that i is a default parameter and that w is its default value. A *causal law* specifies that if $p_0, ..., p_m$ hold and P is true when a occurs, then l holds and L is true after the occurrence of a. In addition, after a occurs, the values of the parameters $sig(A)$ are specified by the output of the action algorithm A. A *state constraint* specifies that whenever $p_0, ..., p_m$ hold and P is true, l also holds and L is true. A *noconcurrency condition* specifies that whenever $p_0, ..., p_m$ hold and P is true, $a_0, ..., a_k$ cannot occur concurrently pairwise. An *allow condition* specifies that whenever $p_0, ..., p_m$ hold and P is true, an action a can occur (although not necessarily so). A *trigger condition* specifies that whenever $p_0, ..., p_m$ hold and P is true, an action a necessarily occurs (unless inhibited). An *inhibition condition* specifies that whenever $p_0, ..., p_m$ hold and P is true, action a cannot occur. A *system description* SD is a set of Hybrid $\mathcal{ALE}$ statements.

There are several differences between Hybrid $\mathcal{AL}$ and Hybrid $\mathcal{ALE}$. First, Hybrid $\mathcal{ALE}$ allows specifying defaults for fluents and parameters. This is not allowed in Hybrid $\mathcal{AL}$. In Hybrid $\mathcal{ALE}$ the noconcurrency condition specifying pairwise noconcurrency replaces the executability condition specifying set noconcurrency of Hybrid $\mathcal{AL}$. The compatibility condition of Hybrid $\mathcal{AL}$ allowing concurrent evaluation of action algorithms with intersecting signatures is not in Hybrid $\mathcal{ALE}$. The allow condition, trigger condition and inhibition condition, which allow reasoning about actions, are new to Hybrid $\mathcal{ALE}$.

The H-ASP programs discussed below assume the parameter space consisting of parameters t (time), domain parameters and the parameter Prev. Such a parameter space is called *the parameter space of SD*.

Let $\Pi_c(SD)$ denote the logic program: for every state constraint of the form (4), $\Pi_c(SD)$ contains the rules $l \leftarrow p_0, ..., p_m : P$ and $\leftarrow p_0, ..., p_m : P \wedge \overline{L}$.

Definition 1. *Let $(\sigma, \mathbf{q})$ be a hybrid state, and let $\sigma' \subseteq \sigma$ and $\sigma'' \subseteq \sigma$. If σ is a complete and consistent set of domain literals, then $(\sigma, \mathbf{q})$ is a Hybrid $\mathcal{ALE}$ state relative to σ', σ'' if $(\sigma, \mathbf{q})$ is an answer set of the program $\Pi_c(SD) \cup rules(\sigma') \cup defaults(\sigma'')$ with the initial condition $\mathbf{q}$.*

Next, we introduce a number of definitions needed to specify a transition.

A causal law or a state constraint is *applicable* in $(\sigma, \mathbf{q})$ if $\{p_0, ..., p_m\} \subseteq \sigma$ and $P(\mathbf{q})$ holds. The *logical effects* of an action a in a state $(\sigma, \mathbf{q})$ are $LE((\sigma, \mathbf{q}), a) = \{l : (a \text{ causes } \langle l, L \rangle \text{ with } A \text{ if } p_0, ..., p_m : P) \text{ is applicable in } (\sigma, \mathbf{q})\}$. For a set of actions B we define $LE((\sigma, \mathbf{q}), B) = \bigcup_{a \in B} LE((\sigma, \mathbf{q}), a)$.

For a generalized position $\mathbf{q}$ and action algorithm A with signature $(i_1, ..., i_k)$ we define the *binary effects* of A in $\mathbf{q}$ as $BE(\mathbf{q}, A) = \{((i_1, r_1), ..., (i_k, r_k)) : (r_1, ..., r_k) \in A(\mathbf{q})\}$.

A tuple $u = ((i_1, r_1), ..., (i_k, r_k))$ where i_js are parameter indexes and r_js are the values of the corresponding parameters is called an *assignment tuple*. We define $sig(u) = (i_1, ..., i_k)$ and $values(u) = (r_1, ..., r_k)$.

The *binary effects* of a set of actions D, in a state $(\sigma, \mathbf{q})$ are $BE((\sigma, \mathbf{q}), D) = \{BE(\mathbf{q}, A) : (a \text{ causes } \langle l, L \rangle \text{ with } A \text{ if } p_0, ..., p_m : P) \text{ is applicable in } (\sigma, \mathbf{q}) \text{ and } a \in D\}$.

For the binary effects of the actions B let $\Delta_p(B) = ((j_1, r_1), ..., (j_n, r_n))$ where $(j_1, ..., j_n)$ are the parameters not present among those that are in B, and for a parameter j_m, $r_m = \mathbf{q}_{j_m}$ if j_m is an inertial parameter, and $r_m = w$ if j_m is a default parameter with the default w. A *binary effects completion* of B is $\overline{B} = B \cup \{\Delta_p(B)\}$. That is a binary effects completion of B contains B and the assignment tuple for the parameters not found in B.

If w is an assignment tuple $((j_1, q_1), ..., (j_k, q_k))$ and $sig(u) \cap sig(w) = \emptyset$ then the *product* of u and w is an assignment tuple $((l_1, p_1), ..., (l_{k+n}, p_{k+n}))$ where $l_1, ..., l_{k+n}$ is the arrangement of the indexes $i_1, ..., i_k, j_1, ..., j_n$ in increasing order and $p_1, ..., p_{k+n}$ is the corresponding arrangement of the values.

For a set S of assignment tuples let $sig(S) = \{sig(u) : u \in S\}$. We say that S is *valid* if whenever $s_1, s_2 \in sig(S)$ are such that $s_1 \cap s_2 = \emptyset$ where the intersection of the two tuples is a tuple of the elements in the intersection of s_1, s_2 with s_1 and s_2 treated as sets.

For a valid set S of assignment tuples and a signature $s \in sig(S)$ we define $AT(s, S) = \{x : x \in S \text{ and } sig(x) = s\}$. A *partition of S by signatures* is $Part(S) = \{AT(s, S) : s \in sig(S)\}$.

The *set of the candidate successor generalized positions* at $(\sigma, \mathbf{q})$ with respect to a set of actions D is

$CSGP((\sigma, \mathbf{q}), D) = \emptyset$ if $\overline{BE}((\sigma, \mathbf{q}), D)$ is not valid, and otherwise

$CSGP((\sigma, \mathbf{q}), D) = values(\prod Part(\overline{BE}((\sigma, \mathbf{q}), D) \cup \{(0, t(\mathbf{q}) + 2)\} \cup \{(\text{Prev}, \mathbf{q}|_{domain})\}))$.

This specifies that given the binary effects of the action algorithms of the applicable causal laws, the candidate successor generalized positions can be constructed by taking the "cross products" of the binary effects of the corresponding action algorithms and by substituting any missing parameters i with $\mathbf{q}_i$ if i is an inertial parameter, or the default value of i if it is a default parameter.

For a state $(\sigma_0, \mathbf{q})$ and a set of actions B we define *the set of consequent states* as:

$CS((\sigma_0, \mathbf{q}), \ B) = \{ \ (\sigma, \mathbf{r}) \ : \mathbf{r} \in CSGP((\sigma_0, \mathbf{q}), \ B)$ and $L(\mathbf{r})$ holds for all L s.t. $(a \ causes \ \langle l, L \rangle \ with \ A \ if \ p_0, ..., \ p_m : P)$ is applicable at $(\sigma_0, \mathbf{q})$ and $a \in B$ and $LE((\sigma_0, \mathbf{q}), \ B) \subseteq \sigma$ and $(\sigma, \mathbf{r})$ is a Hybrid $\mathcal{ALE}$ state relative to $LE((\sigma_0, \mathbf{q}), \ B), \{l : \ l \in \sigma_0 \text{ and } l \text{ is inertial}\} \cup \{l : l \text{ is a default fluent}\} \ \}$.

That is the set of consequent states are constructed by combining the set of the candidate successor generalized positions with the Hybrid $\mathcal{ALE}$ states relative to the set of the logical effects of the applicable actions.

Finally, we specify the sets of possible and necessary actions similarly to [8]. An inhibition condition, an allow condition, a trigger condition and a noncon-currency condition is *active in* $(\sigma, \mathbf{q})$ if $\{p_0, ..., p_m\} \subseteq \sigma$ and $P(\mathbf{q})$ holds. Let $A_I(\sigma, \mathbf{q}) = \{a : \text{there exists an active inhibition condition in } SD \text{ containing } a\}$. Let $A_T(\sigma, \mathbf{q}) = \{a : \text{there exists an active trigger condition in } SD \text{ containing } a \text{ and } a \notin A_I(\sigma, \mathbf{q})\}$. Let $A_A(\sigma, \mathbf{q}) = \{a : \text{there exists an active allow condition in } SD \text{ containing } a \text{ and } a \notin A_I(\sigma, \mathbf{q})\}$. Let $A_N(\sigma, \mathbf{q}) = \{(a_1, ..., a_n) : \text{there exists an active noconcurrency condition with } a_1, ..., a_n\}$.

Definition 2 *(Transition).* *Hybrid $\mathcal{ALE}$ states* $(\sigma_0, \mathbf{q})$, $(\sigma_1, \mathbf{r})$ *and a nonempty set of actions* B *form a transition of* SD *if* $(\sigma_1, \mathbf{r}) \in CS((\sigma_0, \mathbf{q}), B)$ *and* $A_T(\sigma_0, \mathbf{q}) \subseteq B \subseteq A_T(\sigma_0, \mathbf{q}) \cup A_A(\sigma_0, \mathbf{q})$ *and for all* $B' \in A_N(\sigma_0, \mathbf{q})$ *we have* $|B \cap B'| \leq 1$.

In a transition there is always a reason for an action occurring. The definition ensures that no inhibited action is included in B, that all the triggered actions that are not inhibited are in B, that the remaining actions in B are allowed and that actions prohibited from executing concurrently by a noconcurrency condition are not all in B.

3   Compilation

A system description SD in Hybrid $\mathcal{ALE}$ is compiled into H-ASP. In the definition below we assume that the Hybrid $\mathcal{ALE}$ statements are of the form (1)–(8) specified in the syntax definition. *The encoding $\Pi(SD)$ of the system description SD consists of the following:*

1. For every action algorithm A, we have an atom $alg(A)$. If A has a signature $(i_0, ..., i_k)$ then we add the following rules for $j \in \{0, ..., k\}$ that specify all the parameters fixed by A and execute the algorithm A when appropriate:
   a stationary-1 rule, $will\_fix(i_j) \leftarrow action\_state, \ exec(alg(A))$,
   a stationary-2 rule, $fix(i_j) \leftarrow; \ action\_state, \ exec(alg(A))$,
   an advancing rule, $domain\_state \leftarrow action\_state, \ exec(alg(A)) : A$.
   For every pair of algorithms A_1 and A_2 with a nonempty signature inter-section, we add the following stationary-1 rule,

$\leftarrow action\_state,\ exec\,(alg\,(A_1)),\ exec(alg\,(A_2))$, to prevent situations where two different algorithms are setting the values of the same parameter in the same state.

2. *Inertia axioms for parameters.* For every inertial domain parameter i, we have an advancing rule

$fix\,(i) \leftarrow action\_state,\ not\ will\_fix\,(i) : Default\,[i]$

where $Default\,[i]\,(\mathbf{p}) = \{\mathbf{q}:\ \mathbf{p}_i = \mathbf{q}_i\}$. The inertia axioms for parameters cause the values of the inertial parameters not fixed by one of the action algorithms to be copied to the successor states.

3. *Default axioms for parameters.* For every default parameter i with the value w, we have an advancing rule

$fix\,(i) \leftarrow action\_state,\ not\ will\_fix\,(i) : Default\,[i, w]$

where $Default[i, w]\,(\mathbf{p}) = \{\mathbf{q} : \mathbf{p}_i = w\}$. The default axioms for parameters cause the values of the default parameters not fixed by one of the action algorithms to be set to the default value.

4. *State restriction constraints for the parameters.* We restrict the possible domain states to only those where every parameter is marked as fixed. For every domain parameter i, we have a stationary-1 rule

$\leftarrow not\ fix\,(i),\ domain\_state$

5. For every causal law $c \in SD$ of the form (3):

   (a) a stationary-2 rule specifying that the law is applicable if the prerequisites are satisfied

   $causal\,(c) \leftarrow action\_state,\ occurs\,(a),\ h\,(p_0),...,h\,(p_m) : P$

   where $causal\,(c)$ is an atom uniquely identifying the causal law.

   (b) a stationary-1 rule specifying that the advancing algorithm A is to be evaluated if the prerequisites are satisfied,

   $exec\,(alg\,(A)) \leftarrow causal\,(c)$

   (c) a stationary-2 rule to derive $h\,(l)$ in the successor state,

   $h\,(l) \leftarrow ;\ causal\,(c) : IsStep$

   (d) a stationary-2 rule specifying that L must be true in the successor state,

   $\leftarrow ;\ causal\,(c) : IsStep \wedge Dest[\overline{L}].$

6. For every state constraint $s \in SD$ of the form (4):

   (a) a stationary-1 rule indicating that the state constraint is applicable

   $constraint\,(s) \leftarrow domain\_state,\ h\,(p_0),...,\ h\,(p_m) : P$

   where $constraint\,(s)$ is an atom identifying s.

   (b) a stationary-1 rule to derive $h\,(l)$,

   $h\,(l) \leftarrow constraint\,(s),\ domain\_state$

   (c) and a stationary-1 rule to verify that L holds if the rule is applicable

   $\leftarrow constraint\,(s),\ domain\_state : \overline{L}$

7. For every noconcurrency condition $n \in SD$ of the form (5):

   (a) a stationary-1 rule indicating that the condition is applicable

   $noconcurrency\,(n) \leftarrow action\_state,\ h\,(p_0),...,\ h\,(p_m) : P$

   (b) a stationary-1 rule for every pair $a_i, a_j \in \{a_0,...,a_k\}$ to make the concurrent occurrence of a_i and a_j impossible

   $\leftarrow occurs\,(a_i),\ occurs\,(a_j),\ noconcurrency\,(n)$

8. For every trigger condition of the form (7), a stationary-1 rule to trigger the occurrence of a

   $occurs\,(a) \leftarrow action\_state,\ not\ ab\,(occurs\,(a)),\ h\,(p_0),...,\ h\,(p_m) : P$

9. For every inhibition condition of the form (8), a stationary-1 rule to inhibit the occurrence of a

   $ab\,(occurs\,(a)) \leftarrow action\_state,\ h\,(p_0),...,\ h\,(p_m) : P$

10. For every allow condition of the form (6) to make the occurrence of the action a possible:

    $allow\,(a) \leftarrow action\_state,\ h\,(p_0),...,\ h\,(p_m),\ not\ ab\,(occurs\,(a)) : P$

    $occurs\,(a) \leftarrow allow\,(a),\ not\ \neg occurs\,(a)$

    $\neg occurs\,(a) \leftarrow allow\,(a),\ not\ occurs\,(a)$

11. Axioms for interleaving domain states and action states. A stationary-2 rule

    $domain\_state \leftarrow\ ;\ action\_state : IsStep$

    and an advancing rule

    $action\_state \leftarrow domain\_state : CreateActionState$

    where for a generalized position $\mathbf{p}$

    $CreateActionState\,(\mathbf{p}) = \{\mathbf{q}:\ where\ \mathbf{p}|_{domain} = \mathbf{q}|_{domain}\ and\ time\,(\mathbf{q}) = time\,(\mathbf{p}) + 1,\ Prev\,(\mathbf{q}) = \mathbf{p}|_{domain}\ \}$.

12. Stationary-1 rules for making an action state with no actions invalid:

    a constraint, $\leftarrow action\_state,\ not\ valid\_action\_state,$

    and for every action a the rule, $valid\_action\_state \leftarrow action\_state,\ occurs\,(a)$.

13. Rules for copying fluents from a domain state to an action state. For every fluent l, stationary-2 rules

    $h\,(l) \leftarrow\ ;\ domain\_state,\ h\,(l) : IsStep$

14. For every inertial literal l, a stationary-2 rule encoding *inertia axioms*

    $h\,(l) \leftarrow not\ \overline{h\,(l)};\ action\_state,\ h\,(l) : IsStep$

15. For every default literal l, a stationary-1 rule encoding the default

    $h\,(l) \leftarrow domain\_state,\ not\ \overline{h\,(l)}$

16. $\Pi\,(SD)$ contains closed world assumptions (CWA, for short) for actions. For every action a, a stationary-1 rule

    $\neg occurs\,(a) \leftarrow action\_state,\ not\ occurs\,(a)$

The encoding $H\,(\sigma_0)$ of the initial state is a set of stationary-1 rules:

$H\,(\sigma_0) = \{\ h\,(l) \leftarrow\ : IsTime\,[0]\ : l \in \sigma_0\} \cup \{\ domain\_state \leftarrow\ : IsTime\,[0]\}$,

where $IsTime\,[0]\,(\mathbf{p})$ holds iff $t\,(\mathbf{p}) = 0$.

Theorem 1 *(correctness of the translation). Hybrid $\mathcal{ALE}$ states $(\sigma_0, \mathbf{q})$, $(\sigma_1, \mathbf{r})$ where $t\,(\mathbf{q}) = 0$ and a set of actions B is a transition of SD iff there exists a stable model M of $\Pi\,(SD) \cup H\,(\sigma_0)$ with respect to $\mathbf{q}$ such that $\{q, \mathbf{r}\} \subseteq GP\,(M)$*

and $\{\ l : h\,(l) \in W_M\,(\mathbf{q})\} = \sigma_0$

and $\{\ l : h\,(l) \in W_M\,(\mathbf{r})\} = \sigma_1$

and there exists $\mathbf{s} \in GP\,(M)$ with $IsStep\,(\mathbf{s}, \mathbf{q})$ and $IsStep\,(\mathbf{r}, \mathbf{s})$ holding (i.e. $\mathbf{s}$ is a successor generalized position of $\mathbf{q}$ and $\mathbf{r}$ is a successor generalized position of $\mathbf{s}$) and $\{\ a : occurs\,(a) \in W_M\,(\mathbf{s})\} = B$.

The proof of the forward direction is by constructing M and then applying induction on the reduct of $\Pi(SD) \cup H(\sigma_0)$ with respect to M and $\mathbf{q}$ to show that M is a stable model of $\Pi(SD) \cup H(\sigma_0)$ with respect to $\mathbf{q}$. The proof of the reverse direction uses induction on the reducts to show that a stable model of $\Pi(SD) \cup H(\sigma_0)$ is a transition. The proof is omitted due to space constraints.

4   Example

In this section, we will discuss the example described in the beginning of the paper. Note that in the example the output file has a timestamp dependent name, which therefore cannot be hard coded. We use an advancing algorithm to find the name and to store it under a parameter. The parameter value can then be used in subsequent diagnosis stages to check the existence of the file.

We have two actions *do(1)* and *fail(1)*. The action *do(1)* indicates the attempted execution of a job. The action *fail(1)* indicates a malfunction. We use a default parameter *input_filename1* to contain the name of the input file, and we use a default parameter *output_filename1* to contain the name of the output file. We use the default fluent *ready(1)* with the default value *false*, to indicate that the input file exists and that the processing can start. All other fluents are inertial. *finished(1)* indicates a completed processing, whether successful or not. *failed(1)* indicates that the processing has failed, and *succeeded(1)* indicates that the processing has succeeded. Because *ready(1)* is a default fluent with the default value false, we know that the fluent holds only at a specific time in the trajectory. Thus, we do not need to check the negative conditions when checking the existence of the fluent. The predicate algorithm *Exists[file_name]* returns true if the value of the parameter *file_name* is not empty, which indicates the existence of the corresponding file. We use an advancing algorithm *GetOutputFileName1* to determine the output file name if it exists, and to associate the file name (or empty value, if the file does not exist) with the parameter *output_filename1*.

We then use a state constraint to determine whether the processing can start:
(1) *ready(1)* **if** *-finished(1)* : *Exists[input_filename1]*

ready(1) triggers the processing with an optional failure:
(2) **trigger** *do(1)* **if** *ready(1)*
(3) **allow** *fail(1)* **if** *ready(1)*

Indicate the completion of the processing and determine the output file name, if the file exists.
(4) *do(1)* **causes** *finished(1)* **with** *GetOutputFileName1*
(5) *fail(1)* **causes** *failed(1)*

Define success as an absence of failure.
(6) *succeeded(1)* **if** *finished(1)*, *-failed(1)*

Make it invalid to fail if an output file exists, and to succeed if it does not.

(7) $<$ *failed(1), -Exists[output_filename1]* $>$ **if** *failed(1)*

(8) $<$ *succeeded(1), Exists[output_filename1]* $>$ **if** *succeeded(1)*

We now consider the two trajectories described by the above system description. We assume that the input file exists, the parameter *input_filename1* at the generalized position **q** contains the input file name, and *-finished(1)* is derived at a generalized position **q**. We consider the case where the output file exists.

(1) derives (*ready(1)*, **q**). Consequently (2) and the absence of active inhibition conditions for the action *do(1)* cause an action *do(1)* to occur at state corresponding to **q**. (3) is active and creates two transitions: one containing action *fail(1)* and one not containing the action. In both transitions, (4) derives (*finished(1)*, **r**). Since the output file exists, (4) makes the parameter *output_filename1* at the generalized position **r** contain the name of the file. (5) is not active in the first transition, but in the second transition it derives (*failed(1)*, **r**). (6) derives (*succeeded(1)*, **r**) in the first transition, and (6) is not active in the second transition. (7) is not active in the first transition, but it invalidates the second transition, since *-Exists[output_filename1]* returns false. (8) is active in the first transition, but it simply rederives (*succeeded(1)*, **r**).

Then the following transition is derived (we omit negative atoms from the description for brevity):

({ *ready(1)* }, **q**), { *do(1)* }, ({*finished(1), succeeded(1)*}, **r**)

where *input_filename1(**q**)*, *output_filename1(**r**)* contain the name of the input file and the name of the output file respectively.

Since only one transition is valid, and it contains (*succeeded(1)*, **r**), the diagnosing engineer can conclude that *process_data1* has not failed.

If the output file did not exist, then the following transition would be derived:

({ *ready(1)* }, **q**), { *do(1), fail(1)* }, ({*finished(1), failed(1)*}, **v**)

where *input_filename1(**q**)* contains the name of the input file, and *output_filename1(**v**)* is empty.

Since only one transition is valid, and it contains (*failed(1)*, **r**), the diagnosing engineer can conclude that *process_data1* has failed.

In our example we consider a data processing job typical of those found in the data pipelines we have worked with. Such data pipelines may contain many jobs, with outputs of some being the inputs of others. Each such jobs requires its own Hybrid $\mathcal{ALE}$ description. To create a diagnostic description for the entire pipeline, individual job descriptions need to be assembled into a single pipeline description. In many cases doing so is simplified because the interactions of the jobs is limited to the following scenario: an output of a job X is an input to a job Y. We can thus "chain" the descriptions together by using *finished(X)* as a condition for *ready(Y)*. If Y starts only upon a successful termination of X then - *failed(X)* has to be added to the condition for *ready(Y)* as well.

5 Computation

While a detailed discussion of all the relevant computational aspects is outside of the scope of this paper, we would like to note a few here. To compute with the Hybrid ASP programs compiled from Hybrid $\mathcal{ALE}$ descriptions, supporting only advancing rules of arity 1, and stationary rules of arity 1 and arity 2 is required. Moreover, computations can be made more efficient by assuming that any stationary-2 rule are applicable only in the generalized positions that form a step. In [5] it was shown that with the above and some additional adaptations all of the maximal trajectories can be computed using the *Local Algorithm*. Informally, the algorithm does the following. For a given hybrid state $(A, \mathbf{p})$ it first computes a set $S = \{ (B, \mathbf{q}) \}$ of candidate successor states via the use of the advancing rules applicable at $(A, \mathbf{p})$. Then for each $(B, \mathbf{q}) \in S$ it uses stationary-2 rules applicable at $(B, \mathbf{q})$, $(A, \mathbf{p})$ and stationary-1 rules applicable at $(B, \mathbf{q})$ to compute a set of the successor states at the generalized position $\mathbf{q}$. This is an iterative process that produces a tree, with hybrid states $(A, \mathbf{p})$ as nodes having their successor states as children. The trajectories can then be recovered by following tree paths from leaf nodes to the root.

Another adaptation is a deferred evaluation of domain algorithms. Evaluation of the domain algorithms can be computationally expensive, and for stationary rules, it is thus desirable to evaluate domain algorithms only once the satisfaction of boolean atoms is verified. We illustrate the deferred domain algorithm evaluation using the example of a stationary-1 rule: $constraint\,(s) \leftarrow domain\_state,\ h\,(p_0)\,, ...,\ h\,(p_m) : P$. For stationary-2 rules the implementation is similar. We introduce two atoms $pos(domain(P))$ and $neg(domain(P))$ that encode the possible values of evaluating P. We also add an atom $exec(domain(P))$ to indicate domain algorithms P that need to be evaluated. We then substitute the above stationary-1 rule with the following rules.

$$constraint\,(s) \leftarrow domain\_state,\ h\,(p_0)\,, ...,\ h\,(p_m)\,,\ pos(domain(P))$$

to indicate that $constraint\,(s)$ can be derived only if all the predicate requirements are satisfied and P evaluates to true. We add a rule to indicate that P needs to be evaluated if all the propositional constraints of the original stationary-1 rule are satisfied:

$$exec(domain(P)) \leftarrow domain\_state,\ h\,(p_0)\,, ...,\ h\,(p_m)$$

We then add rules that guess the value of P:

$$pos(domain(P)) \leftarrow exec(domain(P)),\ not\ neg(domain(P)),\ \text{and}$$
$$neg(domain(P)) \leftarrow exec(domain(P)),\ not\ pos(domain(P)).$$

The guess is then verified by the Hybrid ASP solver in the following way. In every state where $exec(domain(P))$ atom is present, P is evaluated. If the state contains atom $pos(domain(P))$ and the value of P is false, or if the state contains atom $neg(domain(P))$ and the value of P is positive then the state is rejected.

6   Conclusion

In this paper we introduced an action language Hybrid $\mathcal{ALE}$ in order to facilitate the development of diagnostic programs for the industrial data processing pipelines. The nature of the application is such as to require the diagnostic program to access outside sources. As precomputing all of the facts derivable from the outside sources can be impractical, access to those sources has to be done during inference. This poses a challenge to action languages that compile to ASP, since ASP does not provide mechanisms for accessing outside sources. We have thus chosen as a starting point action language Hybrid $\mathcal{AL}$, which compiles into Hybrid ASP—one of the extensions of ASP that provides access to outside sources. While Hybrid $\mathcal{AL}$ provides the syntactic structure for reasoning about the consequences of actions, it lacks structure such as found in C_{TAID} for reasoning about the actions themselves. We thus extended Hybrid $\mathcal{AL}$ with the structure for reasoning about actions, as found in C_{TAID}. The resulting action language Hybrid $\mathcal{ALE}$ can be viewed as a more expressive version of C_{TAID} that compiles to Hybrid ASP instead of ASP. A system implementing Hybrid $\mathcal{ALE}$ was developed and is now being used at Google Inc. to help engineers with diagnosing malfunctions of certain data processing pipelines.

References

1. Balduccini, M., Gelfond, M.: Diagnostic reasoning with A-Prolog. TPLP **3**(4–5), 425–461 (2003)
2. Baral, C., Chancellor, K., Nam, T.H., Tran, N., Joy, A.M., Berens, M.E.: A knowledge based approach for representing and reasoning about signaling networks. In: Proceedings Twelfth International Conference on Intelligent Systems for Molecular Biology/Third European Conference on Computational Biology 2004, 31 July–4 August 2004, Glasgow, UK, pp. 15–22 (2004)
3. Baral, C., Gelfond, M.: Reasoning agents in dynamic domains. In: Minker, J. (ed.) Logic Based Artificial Intelligence, vol. 597, pp. 257–279. Springer, Boston (2000). https://doi.org/10.1007/978-1-4615-1567-8_12
4. Brik, A., Remmel, J.B.: Hybrid ASP. In: Gallagher, J.P., Gelfond, M. (eds.) ICLP (Technical Communications). LIPIcs, vol. 11, pp. 40–50. Schloss Dagstuhl - Leibniz-Zentrum fuer Informatik (2011)
5. Brik, A., Remmel, J.B.: Computing a finite horizon optimal strategy using hybrid ASP. In: NMR (2012)
6. Brik, A., Remmel, J.: Action language hybrid AL. In: Balduccini, M., Janhunen, T. (eds.) LPNMR 2017. LNCS (LNAI), vol. 10377, pp. 322–335. Springer, Cham (2017). https://doi.org/10.1007/978-3-319-61660-5_29
7. Calimeri, F., Cozza, S., Ianni, G.: External sources of knowledge and value invention in logic programming. Ann. Math. Artif. Intell. **50**(3–4), 333–361 (2007)
8. Dworschak, S., Grell, S., Nikiforova, V.J., Schaub, T., Selbig, J.: Modeling biological networks by action languages via answer set programming. Constraints **13**(1–2), 21–65 (2008)
9. Eiter, T., Ianni, G., Schindlauer, R., Tompits, H.: A uniform integration of higher-order reasoning and external evaluations in answer-set programming. In: Kaelbling, L.P., Saffiotti, A. (eds.) IJCAI 2005, Proceedings of the Nineteenth International Joint Conference on Artificial Intelligence, 30 July–5 August 2005, Edinburgh, Scotland, UK, pp. 90–96. Professional Book Center (2005)
10. Gebser, M., Kaufmann, B., Kaminski, R., Ostrowski, M., Schaub, T., Schneider, M.T.: Potassco: the potsdam answer set solving collection. AI Commun. **24**(2), 107–124 (2011)

11. Gelfond, M., Lifschitz, V.: The stable model semantics for logic programming. In: ICLP/SLP, pp. 1070–1080 (1988)
12. Gelfond, M., Lifschitz, V.: Action languages. Electron. Trans. Artif. Intell. **2**, 193–210 (1998)
13. Lifschitz, V.: Answer set programming and plan generation. Artif. Intell. **138**(1–2), 39–54 (2002)
14. Terracina, G., Leone, N., Lio, V., Panetta, C.: Experimenting with recursive queries in database and logic programming systems. TPLP **8**(2), 129–165 (2008)

Repair-Based Degrees of Database Inconsistency

Leopoldo Bertossi[1,2]([envelope]) [iD]

[1] RelationalAI Inc., Toronto, Canada
[2] Carleton University, Ottawa, Canada
bertossi@scs.carleton.ca

Abstract. We propose and investigate a concrete numerical measure of the inconsistency of a database with respect to a set of integrity constraints. It is based on a database repair semantics associated to cardinality-repairs. More specifically, it is shown that the computation of this measure can be intractable in data complexity, but answer-set programs are exhibited that can be used to compute it. Furthermore, its is established that there are polynomial-time deterministic and randomized approximations. The behavior of this measure under small updates is analyzed, obtaining fixed-parameter tractability results. We explore abstract extensions of this measure that appeal to generic classes of database repairs. Inconsistency measures and repairs at the attribute level are investigated as a particular, but relevant and natural case.

1 Introduction

Intuitively, a relational database may be more or less consistent than other databases with the same schema, and with respect to the same integrity constraints (ICs). This comparison can be accomplished by assigning a *measure of inconsistency* to databases, which represents a quantitative degree of satisfaction of the intended ICs by the database. In this work we propose such an inconsistency measure, we investigate its computational properties, and we propose a generalization and abstraction that gives rise to a whole family of inconsistency measures that depend on how consistency is restored.

The problem of measuring inconsistency has been investigated mostly by the knowledge representation (KR) community, but scarcely by the data management community. Furthermore, the approaches and results obtained in KR do not immediately apply to databases, or do not address problems that are natural and relevant in databases, such as the computational complexity in terms of the size of the database, i.e. in data complexity. Actually, several (in)consistency measures have been considered in KR [20,21,32], mostly for propositional knowledge bases, or have been applied with grounded first-order representations, obtaining in essence a propositional representation. It becomes interesting to

---

Member of the "Millenium Institute for Foundational Research on Data" (IMFD, Chile).

M. Balduccini et al. (Eds.): LPNMR 2019, LNAI 11481, pp. 195–209, 2019.
https://doi.org/10.1007/978-3-030-20528-7_15

consider inconsistency measures that are closer to database applications, and whose formulation and computation stay at the relational, first-order level.

In this work we make these ideas concrete by introducing and investigating a particular and natural inconsistency measure. We provide an approach to the computation of the inconsistency measure that is based on *answer-set programming* (ASP) [9], also known as *logic programming with stable model semantics* [19]. This is a natural choice since: (a) an inconsistency measure is non-monotonic in general; (b) the complexity results for its computation show that ASPs provide the exact expressive and computational power needed to compute this measure; (c) database repairs are the basis for the measure, and there are already ASPs that specify them [12] (more on this point below).

The investigation we carry out for the particular inconsistency measure is, independently from possible alternative measures, interesting *per se*: In addition to staying at the relational level, we stress computability and complexity issues in terms of the size of the database. This provides a pattern for the investigation of other possible consistency measures, along similar lines. We are not aware of research that emphasizes computational aspects of inconsistency measures; and here we start filling in this gap. It is likely that other possible consistency measures in the relational setting are also polynomially-reducible to the one we investigate here (or the other way around), and results for one of them can be leveraged for the others. This is a matter of future research.

The particular inconsistency measure we investigate in detail is motivated by one used before to measure the degree of satisfaction of *functional dependencies* (FDs) in a relational database [25]. We extend and reformulate it in terms of database repairs that are based on tuple deletions.[1] As such, it can be applied to the larger class of *denial constraints* [3], and even more, to any class of monotonic ICs (in the sense that, as the database grows, only more violations can be added). However, this measure can also be applied to non-monotonic classes of ICs, such as inclusion- and tuple-generating dependencies, as long as we repair, i.e. restore consistency, only through tuple deletions.[2] Actually, the connection between the inconsistency measure and database repairs motivates our use of ASPs for its computation: We can rely on ASPs that specify and compute the repairs of a database (cf. [3] for a survey and references).

The particular connection of the inconsistency measure and a particular class of database repairs is used here as a basis for proposing more general and abstract inconsistency measures, which have origin in different classes of repairs. From this point of view, we can capture the intuition that the inconsistency degree of a database D with respect to (wrt.) a set of ICs Σ depends on how complex it is to restore consistency (as represented by the admissible class of *repairs* of D wrt. Σ). More technically, our take is that a degree of inconsistency depends

---

[1] Intuitively, a repair of an inconsistent database D is an alternative instance for the same schema that satisfied the given ICs, and is "maximally close" to D.

[2] The measure can be easily redefined using the symmetric difference between the original database and the repairs when tuple insertions are also allowed as repair actions.

upon a repair semantics, and then, on the admissible repair actions, and on how close we want stay to the instance at hand.

Our main contributions are the following: (a) We introduce an inconsistency measure that is based on cardinality-repairs (Sect. 3). (b) We introduce answer-set programs to compute the inconsistency-measures (Sect. 4); and we show that they provide the required expressive power (Sect. 5). (c) We obtain data complexity results for the inconsistency measure, showing that its computation (as a decision problem) is NP-complete for denial constraints (DCs) and some classes of FDs (Sect. 5). (d) We obtain deterministic and randomized PTIME approximation results for the inconsistency measure, with approximation ratio d (Sect. 5). (e) We establish that the inconsistency measure behaves well under updates, in that small updates keep the inconsistency measure within narrow boundaries. Furthermore, we establish that the computation of the inconsistency measure is fixed-parameter tractable when one starts with a consistent instance, and the parameter is the number of updates (Sect. 6). (f) We introduce a general inconsistency-measure based on an abstract repair-semantics (Sect. 7), and we instantiate it using attribute-based repairs (Sect. 8). (g) We briefly introduce a causality-based notion of contribution of individual tuples to the inconsistency of the database (Sect. 9). All the proofs, additional examples, and an extended discussion can be found in the extended version of this work [1]. All the complexity statements refer to *data complexity*, i.e. in the size of the DB instance at hand.

2   Background on Relational Databases and Repairs

A relational schema $\mathcal{R}$ contains a domain of constants, $\mathcal{C}$, and a set of predicates of finite arities, $\mathcal{P}$. $\mathcal{R}$ gives rise to a language $\mathfrak{L}(\mathcal{R})$ of first-order (FO) predicate logic with built-in equality, $=$. Variables are usually denoted with $x, y, z, ...$, and finite sequences thereof with $\bar{x}, ...$; and constants with $a, b, c, ...$, etc. An *atom* is of the form $P(t_1, \ldots, t_n)$, with n-ary $P \in \mathcal{P}$ and $t_1, \ldots, t_n$ *terms*, i.e. constants, or variables. An atom is *ground* (a.k.a. a tuple) if it contains no variables. A DB instance, D, for $\mathcal{R}$ is a finite set of ground atoms; and it serves as an interpretation structure for $\mathfrak{L}(\mathcal{R})$.

A *conjunctive query* (CQ) is a FOformula, $\mathcal{Q}(\bar{x})$, of the form $\exists \bar{y} \, (P_1(\bar{x}_1 \wedge \cdots \wedge P_m(\bar{x}_m))$, with $P_i \in \mathcal{P}$, and (distinct) free variables $\bar{x} := (\bigcup \bar{x}_i) \smallsetminus \bar{y}$. If $\mathcal{Q}$ has n (free) variables, $\bar{c} \in \mathcal{C}^n$ is an *answer* to $\mathcal{Q}$ from D if $D \models \mathcal{Q}[\bar{c}]$, i.e. $\mathcal{Q}[\bar{c}]$ is true in D when the variables in $\bar{x}$ are componentwise replaced by the values in $\bar{c}$. $\mathcal{Q}(D)$ denotes the set of answers to $\mathcal{Q}$ from D. $\mathcal{Q}$ is a *boolean conjunctive query* (BCQ) when $\bar{x}$ is empty; and when *true* in D, $\mathcal{Q}(D) := \{true\}$. Otherwise, it is *false*, and $\mathcal{Q}(D) := \emptyset$. Sometimes CQs are written in Datalog notation as follows: $\mathcal{Q}(\bar{x}) \leftarrow P_1(\bar{x}_1), \ldots, P_m(\bar{x}_m)$.

We consider as integrity constraints, i.e. sentences of $\mathfrak{L}(\mathcal{R})$: (a) *denial constraints* (DCs), i.e. of the form $\kappa : \neg \exists \bar{x}(P_1(\bar{x}_1) \wedge \cdots \wedge P_m(\bar{x}_m))$, where $P_i \in \mathcal{P}$, and $\bar{x} = \bigcup \bar{x}_i$; and (b) *functional dependencies* (FDs), i.e. of the form

$\varphi \colon \neg \exists \bar{x}(P(\bar{v}, \bar{y}_1, z_1) \wedge P(\bar{v}, \bar{y}_2, z_2) \wedge z_1 \neq z_2).$[3] Here, $\bar{x} = \bar{y}_1 \cup \bar{y}_2 \cup \bar{v} \cup \{z_1, z_2\}$, and $z_1 \neq z_2$ is an abbreviation for $\neg z_1 = z_2$. A *key constraint* (KC) is a conjunction of FDs: $\bigwedge_{j=1}^{k} \neg \exists \bar{x}(P(\bar{v}, \bar{y}_1) \wedge P(\bar{v}, \bar{y}_2) \wedge y_1^j \neq y_2^j)$, with $k = |\bar{y}_1| = |\bar{y}_2|$, and generically y^j stands for the jth variable in $\bar{y}$. For example, $\forall x \forall y \forall z (Emp(x, y) \wedge Emp(x, z) \to y = z)$, is an FD (and also a KC) that could say that an employee (x) can have at most one salary. This FD is usually written as $EmpName \to EmpSalary$. In the following, we will include FDs and key constraints among the DCs. If an instance D does not satisfy the set Σ of DCs associated to the schema, we say that D is *inconsistent*, which is denoted with $D \not\models \Sigma$.

When a database instance D does not satisfy its intended ICs, it is *repaired*, by deleting or inserting tuples from/into the database. An instance obtained in this way is a *repair* of D if it satisfies the ICs and minimally departs from D [3]. In this work, mainly to fix ideas and simplify the presentation, we consider mostly sets Σ of ICs that are monotone, in the sense that $D \not\models \Sigma$ and $D \subseteq D'$ imply $D' \not\models \Sigma$. This is the case for DCs.[4] For monotone ICs, repairs are obtained by tuple deletions (later on we will also consider value-updates as repair actions). We introduce the most common repairs of databases wrt. DCs by means of an example.

Example 1. The DB $D = \{P(a), P(e), Q(a, b), R(a, c)\}$ is inconsistent wrt. Σ containing the DCs $\kappa_1 \colon \neg \exists x \exists y(P(x) \wedge Q(x, y))$, and $\kappa_2 \colon \neg \exists x \exists y(P(x) \wedge R(x, y))$. Here, $D \not\models \{\kappa_1, \kappa_2\}$.

A *subset-repair*, in short *S-repair*, of D wrt. Σ is a $\subseteq$-maximal subset of D that is consistent, i.e. no proper superset is consistent. The following are S-repairs: $D_1 = \{P(e), Q(a, b), R(a, c)\}$ and $D_2 = \{P(e), P(a)\}$. Under this repair semantics, both repairs are equally acceptable. A *cardinality-repair*, in short a *C-repair*, is a maximum-cardinality S-repair. D_1 is the only C-repair.   □

For an instance D and a set Σ of DCs, the sets of S-repairs and C-repairs are denoted with $Srep(D, \Sigma)$ and $Crep(D, \Sigma)$, resp. It holds: $Crep(D, \Sigma) \subseteq Srep(D, \Sigma)$. More generally, for a set Σ of ICs, not necessarily DCs, they can be defined by (cf. [3]):   (a) $Srep(D, \Sigma) = \{D' \colon D' \models \Sigma$, and $D \triangle D'$ is minimal under set inclusion$\}$; and (b) $Crep(D, \Sigma) = \{D' \colon D' \models \Sigma$, and $D \triangle D'$ is minimal in cardinality$\}$. Here, $D \triangle D'$ is the symmetric set-difference $(D \smallsetminus D') \cup (D' \smallsetminus D)$.

3   An Inconsistency Measure

In this section we consider a concrete inconsistency measure. It is natural, and has been consider already in knowledge representation [21], but its investigation

---

[3] The variables in $\bar{v}$ do not have to go first in the atomic formulas; what matters is keeping the correspondences between the variables in those formulas.

[4] Put in different terms, a DC is associated to (or is the negation of) a conjunctive queries Q, which is monotone in the usual sense: $D \models Q$ and $D \subseteq D' \Rightarrow D' \models Q$.

in a database context has not been undertaken yet. It has also appeared in [25], as measure g_3, among other possible measures and in a restricted form in relation to the satisfaction of FDs, but it was not analyzed much. Its analysis in terms of applicability and properties in the context of DBs, that we here undertake, should serve as a pattern to follow for the analysis of other possible inconsistency measures for DBs. To fix ideas, we consider only DCs. For them, the repair semantics $Srep(D, \Sigma)$ and $Crep(D, \Sigma)$ provide repairs D' that are is maximally contained in the initial instance D. On this basis, we define:

$$inc\text{-}deg^{s,g_3}(D, \Sigma) := \frac{|D| - max\{|D'| \; : \; D' \in Srep(D, \Sigma)\}}{|D|}, \tag{1}$$

$$inc\text{-}deg^{c,g_3}(D, \Sigma) := \frac{|D| - max\{|D'| \; : \; D' \in Crep(D, \Sigma)\}}{|D|}. \tag{2}$$

The first is relative to S-repairs and the second, to C-repairs.

Example 2. (Example 1 cont.) Here, $Srep(D, \Sigma) = \{D_1, D_2\}$, and $Crep(D, \Sigma) = \{D_1\}$. They provide the inconsistency degrees:

$$inc\text{-}deg^{s,g_3}(D, \Sigma) = \frac{4 - |D_1|}{4} = \frac{1}{4}, \text{ and } inc\text{-}deg^{c,g_3}(D, \Sigma) = \frac{4 - |D_1|}{4} = \frac{1}{4}. \quad \square$$

It holds $Crep(D, \Sigma) \subseteq Srep(D, \Sigma)$, but $max\{|D'| \; : \; D' \in Crep(D, \Sigma)\} = max\{|D'| \; : \; D' \in Srep(D, \Sigma)\}$, so it holds $inc\text{-}deg^{s,g_3}(D, \Sigma) = inc\text{-}deg^{c,g_3}(D, \Sigma)$. This measure always takes a value between 0 and 1. The former when D is consistent (so it itself is its only repair). This measure will be generalized in Sect. 7. Before that, in the next sections we investigate this measure of inconsistency.

4   ASP-Based Computation of the Inconsistency Measure

We concentrate here on the computation of the inconsistency measure $inc\text{-}deg^{c,g_3}(D, \Sigma)$ in (2), which appeals to repairs in $Crep(D, \Sigma)$. This can be done through a compact specification of repairs by means of ASPs.[5] More precisely, given a database instance D and a set of ICs Σ (not necessarily DCs), it is possible to write an ASP whose intended models, i.e. the *stable models* or *answer sets*, are in one-to-one correspondence with the S-repairs of D wrt. Σ (cf. [12] for a general formulation). Here we show only some cases of ICs and examples. In them we use, only to ease the formulation and presentation, global unique tuple identifiers (tids), i.e. every tuple $R(\bar{c})$ in D is represented as $R(t; \bar{c})$ for some integer (or constant) t that is not used by any other tuple in D.

If Σ is a set of DCs containing $\kappa : \neg \exists \bar{x}(P_1(\bar{x}_1) \wedge \cdots \wedge P_m(\bar{x}_m))$, we first introduce for a predicate P_i of the database schema, a nickname predicate P_i' that has, in addition to a first attribute for tids, an extra, final attribute to

---

[5] This approach was followed in [2] to compute maximum *responsibility degrees* of database tuples as causes for violations of DCs, appealing to a causality-repair connection [7].

hold an annotation from the set $\{\mathsf{d},\mathsf{s}\}$, for "delete" and "stays", resp. Nickname predicates are used to represent and compute repairs. Next, the *repair-ASP*, $\Pi(D,\Sigma)$, for D and Σ contains all the tuples in D as facts (with tids), plus the following rules for κ:

$$P_1'(t_1;\bar{x}_1,\mathsf{d}) \vee \cdots \vee P_m'(t_n;\bar{x}_m,\mathsf{d}) \leftarrow P_1(t_1;\bar{x}_1), \ldots, P_m(t_m;\bar{x}_m).$$
$$P_i'(t_i;\bar{x}_i,\mathsf{s}) \leftarrow P_i(t_i;\bar{x}_i),\ not\ P_i'(t_i;\bar{x}_i,\mathsf{d}). \quad i = 1,\cdots,m.$$

A stable model M of the program determines a repair D' of D: $D' := \{P(\bar{c}) \,|\, P'(t;\bar{c},\mathsf{s}) \in M\}$, and every repair can be obtained in this way [5,12].

For an FD in Σ, say φ: $\neg\exists xyz_1 z_2 vw(R(x,y,z_1,v) \wedge R(x,y,z_2,w) \wedge z_1 \neq z_2)$, which makes the third attribute functionally depend upon the first two, the repair program contains the rules:

$$R'(t_1;x,y,z_1,v,\mathsf{d}) \vee R'(t_2;x,y,z_2,w,\mathsf{d}) \leftarrow R(t_1;x,y,z_1,v), R(t_2;x,y,z_2,w),$$
$$z_1 \neq z_2.$$
$$R'(t;x,y,z,v,\mathsf{s}) \leftarrow R(t;x,y,z,v),\ not\ R'(t;x,y,z,v,\mathsf{d}).$$

For DCs and FDs, the repair programs can be made *normal*, i.e. non-disjunctive, by moving all the disjuncts but one, in turns, in negated form to the body of the rule [12]. For example, the rule $P(a) \vee R(b) \leftarrow Body$, can be written as the two rules $P(a) \leftarrow Body, not\ R(b)$ and $R(b) \leftarrow Body, not\ P(a)$.[6] Still the resulting program can be *non-stratified* if there is recursion via negation [18], e.g. for FDs and DCs with self-joins.

Example 3. (Example 1 cont.) The initial instance with tids is $D = \{P(1,e), P(2,a), Q(3,a,b), R(4,a,c),\}$. The repair program contains the following rules, with the first and second for κ_1 and κ_2, resp.:

$$P'(t_1;x,\mathsf{d}) \vee Q'(t_2;x,y,\mathsf{d}) \leftarrow P(t_1;x), Q(t_2;x,y).$$
$$P'(t_1;x,\mathsf{d}) \vee R'(t_2;x,y,\mathsf{d}) \leftarrow P(t_1;x), R(t_2;x,y).$$
$$P'(t;x,\mathsf{s}) \leftarrow P(t;x),\ not\ P'(t;x,\mathsf{d}). \quad \text{etc.}$$

The *repair program* $\Pi(D,\{\kappa_1,\kappa_2\})$ has the stable models: $\mathcal{M}_1 = \{P'(1,e,\mathsf{s}), Q'(3,a,b,\mathsf{s}), R'(4,a,c,\mathsf{s}), P'(2,a,\mathsf{d})\} \cup D$ and $\mathcal{M}_2 = \{P'(1,e,\mathsf{s}), P'(2,a,\mathsf{s}), Q'(3,a,b,\mathsf{d}), R'(4,a,c,\mathsf{d})\} \cup D$, which correspond to the S-repairs D_1, D_2, resp. $\square$

In order to compute $inc\text{-}deg^{c,g_3}(D,\Sigma)$ via C-repairs, we need to specify the latter, which can be achieved by adding to Π: (a) rules to collect the *tids* of deleted tuples; (b) a rule with aggregation to compute the number of deleted tuples; and (c) a *weak program-constraint* (WC) [26] that eliminates all the stable models (equivalently, S-repairs) that violate the body of the WC a non-minimum number of times:

(a) $Del(t) \leftarrow P_i'(t,\bar{x}_i,\mathsf{d}). \quad i = 1,\ldots,m$

(b) $NumDel(n) \leftarrow \#count\{t : Del(t)\} = n.$ \quad (c) $:\sim Del(t).$

---

[6] This transformation preserves the semantics, because these repair-ASPs turn out to be head-cycle-free [12].

With them, in each model of the program the tids of deleted tuples are collected and counted; only the models where the number of deletions is a minimum are kept.[7] With the WC we keep only cardinality repairs, but not the S-repairs that are maximal, but not maximum subinstances of D.

Example 4. (Example 3 cont.) If we add to Π the rule $Del(t) \leftarrow R'(t, x, y, \mathsf{d})$, similarly for Q' and P'; and the rule counting the deleted tuples, $NumDel(n) \leftarrow \#count\{t : Del(t)\} = n$, the stable model $\mathcal{M}_1$ of the original program would be extended with the atoms $Del(2), NumDel(1)$. Similarly for $\mathcal{M}_2$. If we also add the WC $:\sim Del(t)$, only (the extended) model $\mathcal{M}_1$ remains. It corresponds to the only C-repair. □

The value for $NumDel$ in any of the remaining models can be used to compute $inc\text{-}deg^{c,g_3}(D, \Sigma)$. So, there is no need to explicitly compute all stable models, their sizes, and compare them. This value can be obtained by means of the query ": $- NumDel(x)$?", answered by the extended program under the *brave semantics* (returning answers that hold in *some* stable model). An extended example with DLV-Complex [11, 26] is shown in the extended version [1].

Brave reasoning under ASPs with weak constraints is $\Delta_2^P(log(n))$-complete in data complexity, i.e. in the size of the database [10]. As we will see in Sect. 5 (cf. Theorem 1), this complexity matches the intrinsic complexity of the computation of the inconsistency measure.

5   Complexity of the Inconsistency Measure Computation

We recall that the *functional complexity class* $FP^{NP(log(n))}$ contains computation problems whose counterparts as decision problems are in the class $P^{NP(log(n))}$, i.e. they are solvable in polynomial time with a logarithmic number of calls to an *NP*-oracle [30].

Theorem 1. For DCs, computing $inc\text{-}deg^{c,g_3}(D, \Sigma)$ belongs to the functional class $FP^{NP(log(n))}$; and there is a relational schema and a set of DCs Σ for which computing $inc\text{-}deg^{c,g_3}(D, \Sigma)$ is $FP^{NP(log(n))}$-complete (in data complexity). □

This result still holds for a set $\mathcal{F}$ of two FDs of the form: $A \rightarrow B$, $B \rightarrow C$ [1], which deserves a comment: In [27] it is established that if a set of FDs is "simplifiable", then a C-repair can be computed in polynomial time. Clearly if we can build such a repair, we can immediately compute the inconsistency measure in polynomial time (one C-repair suffices). As expected, the set $\mathcal{F}$ is not simplifiable.

---

[7] If we had a (hard) program-constraint instead, written $\leftarrow Del(t)$, we would be prohibiting the satisfaction of the rule body (in this case, deletions would be prohibited), and we would be keeping only the models where there are no deletions. This would return no model or the original D depending on whether D is inconsistent or not.

Remark 1. In the following we make use several times of the fact that, for a set Σ of DCs and an instance D, one can build a *conflict-hypergraph*, $CG(D, \Sigma)$, whose vertices are the tuples in D and hyperedges are subset-minimal sets of tuples that simultaneously participate in the violation of one of the DCs in Σ [13,28]. More precisely, for a DC $\kappa\colon \neg \exists \bar{x}(P_1(\bar{x}_1) \wedge \ldots \wedge P_l(\bar{x}_l))$ in Σ, $S \subseteq D$ forms a hyperedge, if S satisfies the BCQ associated to κ, $\mathcal{Q}^\kappa \leftarrow P_1(\bar{x}_1), \ldots, P_l(\bar{x}_l)$, and S is subset-minimal for this property.[8] A C-repair turns out to be the complement of a minimum-size vertex cover for the conflict-hypergraph; equivalently, of a minimum-size hitting-set for the set of hyperedges; or, equivalently, a maximum-size independent set of $CG(D, \Sigma)$. □

The complexity results above show that the normal ASPs introduced in Sect. 4 have the right expressive power to deal with the computational problem at hand. Despite the high-complexity results above, there is a good polynomial-time algorithm, *appID*, that approximates *inc-deg^{c,g_3}*(D, Σ).

Theorem 2. There is a polynomial-time, deterministic algorithm that returns an approximation *appID(D, Σ)* to *inc-deg^{c,g_3}*(D, Σ), with the maximum number d of atoms in a DC in Σ as constant factor: *appID$(D, \Sigma) \leq d \times$ inc-deg^{c,g_3}*(D, Σ). □

Another approach to the approximate computation of the inconsistency measure is based on randomization applied to a relaxed, linear-programming version of the hitting-set (HS) problem for the set of d-bounded hyperedges (or, equivalently, as vertex-covers in hypergraphs with d-bounded hyperedges). In our case, this occurs when each of the DCs in Σ has a number of atoms bounded by d. In this case, we say Σ is d-bounded, and the hyperedges in the conflict-hypergraph have all size at most d. The algorithm in [15] returns a "small", possibly non-minimum HS, which in our case is a set of database tuples whose removal from D restores consistency. The size of this HS approximates the numerator of the inconsistency measure.

Proposition 1. There is a polynomial-time, randomized algorithm that approximates *inc-deg^{c,g_3}*(D, Σ) within a ratio d, and with probability $\frac{3}{5}$. □

In this result, d is determined by the fixed set of DCs, and does not depend on D. Actually, as shown in [15], the ratio of the algorithm can be improved to $(d - \frac{8}{\Delta})$, where $\Delta \leq \frac{1}{4}|D|^{\frac{1}{4}}$, and d is the maximum degree of a vertex, i.e. in our case the maximum number of tuples that co-violate a DC.[9] For FDs we have conflict-graphs, and $d = 2$.

---

[8] More technically, each DC $\kappa\colon \neg \exists \bar{x}(P_1(\bar{x}_1) \wedge \ldots \wedge P_l(\bar{x}_l) \wedge \ldots)$ gives rise to conjunctive queries $\mathcal{Q}^\kappa_{P_l}(\bar{x}_l) \leftarrow P_1(\bar{x}_1), \ldots, P_l(\bar{x}_l), \ldots$. A tuple $P(\bar{a})$ participates in the violation of κ if $\bar{a}$ is an answer to $\mathcal{Q}^\kappa_P(\bar{x})$.

[9] It is known that there is no polynomial-time approximation with ratio of the form $(d - \epsilon)$ for any constant ϵ [24].

6 Inconsistency Degree Under Updates

Let us assume we have a $inc\text{-}deg^{s,g_3}(D, \Sigma)$ for an instance D and a set of DCs Σ. If, possibly virtually or hypothetically for exploration purposes, we insert m new tuples into D, the resulting instance, D', may suffer from more IC violations than D. The question is how much can the inconsistency measure change. The next results tell us that the inconsistency degree does not experiments unexpected jumps under small updates. They can be seen as a *sensitivity analysis*, and the result as a *continuity property* of the inconsistency measure.

Proposition 2. Given an instance D and a set Σ of DCs, if $\epsilon \times |D|$ new tuples are added to D, with $0 < \epsilon < 1$, obtaining instance D', then $inc\text{-}deg^{c,g_3}(D', \Sigma) \leq inc\text{-}deg^{c,g_3}(D, \Sigma) + \frac{1}{1+\frac{1}{\epsilon}}$; and $inc\text{-}deg^{c,g_3}(D, \Sigma) \leq \frac{1}{1-\epsilon} \times inc\text{-}deg^{c,g_3}(D', \Sigma)$. □

When tuples are deleted, the number of DC violations can only decrease, but also the reference size of the database decreases. However, the inconsistency degree stays within a tight upper bound.

Proposition 3. Given an instance D and a set Σ of DCs, if $\epsilon \times |D|$ tuples are deleted from D, with $0 < \epsilon < 1$, obtaining instance D', then $inc\text{-}deg^{c,g_3}(D', \Sigma) \leq \frac{1}{1-\epsilon} \times inc\text{-}deg^{c,g_3}(D, \Sigma)$; and $inc\text{-}deg^{c,g_3}(D, \Sigma) \leq \frac{1}{1-\epsilon} \times inc\text{-}deg^{c,g_3}(D', \Sigma) + \epsilon$. The last term can be dropped if the tuples deleted form D did not participate in DC violations. □

A natural situation occurs when D is consistent wrt. a set Σ of DCs, and one adds a set U of m tuples (deletions will not affect consistency). It turns out that if Σ is d-bounded, then computing the inconsistency measure is fixed-parameter tractable [16], where the fixed parameter is m.

Theorem 3. For a fixed set of d-bounded DCs Σ, a database D that is consistent wrt. Σ, and U a set of extra tuples, computing $inc\text{-}deg^{c,g_3}(D \cup U, \Sigma)$ is *fixed-parameter tractable* with parameter $m = |U|$. More precisely, there is an algorithm that computes the inconsistency measure in time $O(log(m) \times (C^m + mN))$, where $N = |D|$, $m = |U|$, and C is a constant that depends on d. □

The complexity is exponential in the number of updates, but linear in the size of the initial database. In many situations, m would be relatively small in comparison to $|D|$.

7 Repair Semantics and Inconsistency Degrees

In general terms, a *repair semantics* S for a schema $\mathcal{R}$ that includes a set Σ of ICs assigns to each instance D for $\mathcal{R}$ (which may not satisfy Σ), a class $Rep^S(D, \Sigma)$ of S-*repairs* of D wrt. Σ. These are the instances for $\mathcal{R}$ that satisfy Σ and minimally depart from D according to some minimization criterion. Beside the repairs introduced in Example 1, several repair semantics have been investigated, e.g. *prioritized repairs* [31], *attribute-based repairs* that change attribute values by other data values [33], or by a null value, NULL, as in SQL databases [2]. The latter will be retaken in Sect. 8.

According to our take on how an inconsistency degree depends on database repairs, we define the *inconsistency degree* of an instance D wrt. a set of ICs Σ in relation to a given repair semantics S. Namely, as the distance from D to the class $Rep^S(D, \Sigma)$:

$$inc\text{-}deg^S(D, \Sigma) := dist(D, Rep^S(D, \Sigma)). \tag{3}$$

This is an abstract measure that depends on S and a numerical function that gives the distance, $dist(W, \mathcal{W})$, from a world W to a set $\mathcal{W}$ of possible worlds, which in this case are database instances. Under the assumption that any repair semantics should return D when D is consistent wrt. Σ and $dist(D, \{D\}) = 0$, a consistent instance D should have 0 as inconsistency degree.[10]

The class $Rep^S(D, \Sigma)$ might contain instances that are not sub-instances of D, for example, for different forms of *inclusion dependencies* (INDs) we may want to insert tuples;[11] or even under DCs, we may want to appeal to attribute-based repairs. *In the rest of this section, we consider only repairs that are sub-instances of the given instance.* Still this leaves much room open for different kinds of repairs. For example, we may prefer to delete some tuples over others [31]. Or, as in database causality [7,29], the database can be partitioned into *endogenous* and *exogenous* tuples, assuming we have more control on the former, or we trust more the latter; and we prefer *endogenous repairs* that delete only, or preferably, endogenous tuples [2]. The consistency measure we have investigated so far can be defined with an abstract class $Rep^S(D, \Sigma)$:

$$inc\text{-}deg^{S,93}(D, \Sigma) := dist^{93}(D, Rep^S(D, \Sigma)) := \frac{|D| - max\{|D'| : D' \in Rep^S(D, \Sigma)\}}{|D|}$$

$$= \frac{min\{|D \setminus D'| \; : \; D' \in Rep^S(D, \Sigma)\}}{|D|}. \tag{4}$$

This measure can be applied more generally as a "quality measure", not only in relation to inconsistency, but also whenever possibly several intended "quality versions" of a dirty database exist, e.g. as determined by additional contextual information [8]. Particularly prominent is the instantiation of (4) on S-repairs (cf. Sect. 3).

The measure in (4) takes the value 1 only when $Rep^S(D, \Sigma) = \emptyset$ (assuming that $max\{\, |D'| \; : \; D' \in \emptyset\} = 0$), i.e. the database is *irreparable*, which is never the case for DCs and S-repairs: there is always an S-repair. However, it could be irreparable with different, but related repair semantics. As mentioned before, in database causality [29] tuples can be endogenous or exogenous, being the former those we can play with, e.g. applying virtual updates on them, producing

---

[10] Abstract distances between two point-sets are investigated in [14], with their computational properties. Our setting is a particular case.

[11] For INDs repairs based only on tuple deletions can be considered [13].

counterfactual scenarios. One can define *endogenous repairs* as those obtained updating only endogenous tuples [7].

Example 5. (Example 2 cont.) Assume D is partitioned into endogenous and exogenous tuples, say resp. $D = D^n \,\dot\cup\, D^x$, with $D^n = \{Q(a,b), R(a,c)\}$ and $D^x = \{P(a), P(e)\}$. In this case, the *endogenous-repair semantics* that allows only a minimum number of deletions of endogenous tuples, defines the class of repairs: $Crep^n(D, \Sigma) = \{D_2\}$, with D_2 as above. In this case,[12] $inc\text{-}deg^{c,n,g_3}(D, \Sigma) = \frac{4-2}{4} = \frac{1}{2}$. Similarly, if now $D^n = \{P(a), Q(a,b)\}$ and $D^x = \{P(e), R(a,c)\}$, there are no endogenous repairs, and $inc\text{-}deg^{c,n,g_3}(D, \Sigma) = 1$.

□

8 Adapting $inc\text{-}deg^{s,g_3}$ to Attribute-Based Repairs

Database repairs that are based on changes of attribute values in tuples have been considered in [6,33], and implicitly in [4]. In this section we adapt the inconsistency measure we have considered so far, to make it depend upon attribute-repairs. We emphasize that these repairs may not be subinstances of the initial instance even in the presence of DCs. We rely here on repairs introduced in [2], which we show with an example.[13]

Example 6. For the database instance $D = \{S(a_2), S(a_3), R(a_3, a_1), R(a_3, a_4), R(a_3, a_5)\}$, and the DC $\kappa : \neg \exists x \exists y (S(x) \wedge R(x, y))$, it holds $D \not\models \kappa$. Notice that value a_3 matters here in that it enables the join, e.g. $D \models S(a_3) \wedge R(a_3, a_1)$, which could be avoided by replacing it by a null value as used in SQL databases.

More precisely, for the instance $D_1 = \{S(a_2), S(a_3), R(null, a_1), R(null, a_4), R(null, a_5)\}$, where *null* stands for the null value, which cannot be used to satisfy a join, it holds $D_1 \models \kappa$. Similarly with $D_2 = \{S(a_2), S(null), R(a_3, a_1), R(a_3, a_4), R(a_3, a_5)\}$, and $D_3 = \{S(a_2), S(null), R(null, a_1), R(null, a_4), R(null, a_5)\}$, among others obtained from D through replacement of attribute values by *null*.

□

In relation to the special constant *null* we assume that all atoms with built-in comparisons, say $null \,\theta\, null$, and $null \,\theta\, c$, with c a non-null constant, are all false for $\theta \in \{=, \neq, <, >, \ldots\}$. In particular, since a join, say $R(\ldots, x) \wedge S(x, \ldots)$, can be written as $R(\ldots, x) \wedge S(x', \ldots) \wedge x = x'$, it can never be satisfied through *null*. This assumption is compatible with the use of NULL in SQL databases (cf. [5, sect. 4] for a detailed discussion, also [4, sect. 2]). Changes of attribute values by *null* as repair actions offer a natural and deterministic solution. It appeals to *the* generic data value used in SQL databases to represent the uncertainty and

---

[12] For certain forms of *prioritized repairs*, such as endogenous repairs, the normalization coefficient $|D|$ might be unnecessarily large. In this particular case, it might be better to use $|D^n|$.

[13] We believe the developments in this section could be applied to inconsistency measures based on repairs that update attribute values using other constants from the domain [6,33].

incompleteness of the database that inconsistency produces. In order to keep track of changes, we introduce numbers as first arguments in tuples, as global, unique tuple identifiers (tids).

Example 7. (Example 6 cont.) With tids D becomes $D = \{S(1; a_2), S(2; a_3), R(3; a_3, a_1), R(4; a_3, a_4), R(5; a_3, a_5)\}$; and D_1 becomes $D_1 = \{S(1; a_2), S(2; a_3), R(3; null, a_1), R(4; null, a_4), R(5; null, a_5)\}$. The changes are collected in $\Delta^{null}(D, D_1) := \{R[3; 1], R[4; 1], R[5; 1]\}$, showing that (the original) tuple (with tid) 3 has its first-argument changed into *null*, etc. Similarly, $\Delta^{null}(D, D_2) := \{S[2; 1]\}$, and $\Delta^{null}(D, D_3) := \{S[2; 1], R[3; 1], R[4; 1], R[5; 1]\}$.

D_1 and D_2 are the only repairs based on attribute-value changes (into *null*) that are minimal under set inclusion of changes. More precisely, they are consistent, and there is not other consistent repaired version of this kind D' for which $\Delta^{null}(D, D') \subsetneqq \Delta^{null}(D, D_1)$. Similarly for D_2. We denote this class of repairs (and the associated repair semantics) by $Srep^{null}(D, \Sigma)$. Since $\Delta^{null}(D, D_1) \subsetneqq \Delta^{null}(D, D_3)$, $D_3 \notin Srep^{null}(D, \{\kappa\})$. So, $Srep^{null}(D, \{\kappa\}) = \{D_1, D_2\}$.

As with S-repairs, we can consider the subclass of repairs that minimize the number of changes, denoted $Crep^{null}(D, \Sigma)$. In this example, $Crep^{null}(D, \{\kappa\}) = \{D_2\}$ □

Inspired by (4), we define:

$$inc\text{-}deg^{c, null, g_3}(D, \Sigma) := \frac{min\{|\Delta^{null}(D, D')| : D' \in Crep^{null}(D, \Sigma)\}}{|atv(D)|},$$

where $atv(D)$ is the number of values in attributes of tuples in D.

Example 8. (Example 7 cont.) $inc\text{-}deg^{c, null, g_3}(D, \{\kappa\}) = \frac{1}{8}$, but $inc\text{-}deg^{c, g_3}(D, \{\kappa\}) = \frac{1}{5}$. Here, it is easy to restore consistency: only one attribute value has to be changed. □

The computation of this measure can be done on the basis of ASPs that specify null-based attribute repairs that were introduced in [2], to specify and compute causes for query answers at the attribute level.

9   Tuple-Level Inconsistency Degrees

The inconsistency measure is global in that it applies to the whole database. However, one could also investigate and measure the contribution by individual tuples to the degree of inconsistency of the database. Such local measures have been investigated before in a logical setting [22]. In our case, the global inconsistency measure can be expressed in terms of the *responsibility* of tuples as *causes* for the violation of the DCs.

Connections between database causality [29] and repairs were investigated in [7], where it was established that the *responsibility* of a tuple τ as a cause for $D \not\models \Sigma$ is:

$$\rho_{D, \Sigma}(\tau) = \frac{1}{|D| - max(|S|)},$$

where $S \subseteq D$ is an S-repair of D wrt. Σ and $\tau \notin S$ (but $\rho_{D,\Sigma}(\tau) := 0$ if there is not such an S). Combining this with (1) and (2), we can see that

$$inc\text{-}deg^{c,g_3}(D, \Sigma) = \frac{1}{\rho_{D,\Sigma}(\tau) \times |D|}, \tag{5}$$

where τ is one and any of the *maximum-responsibility* tuples τ as causes for $D \not\models \Sigma$. We can also consider the responsibility of tuple, $\rho_{D,\Sigma}(\tau)$, as its degree of contribution to the inconsistency of the database, and those with the highest responsibility as those with a largest degree of contribution. According to (5), the global inconsistency measure turns out to be an aggregation over local, tuple-level, degrees of inconsistency.

10   Conclusions

We have scratched the surface of some of the problems and research directions we considered in this work. Certainly all of them deserve further investigation, most prominently, the analysis of other possible distance-based inconsistency measures along the lines of our work; and also the relationships between those measures. Also a deeper analysis of the incremental case (cf. Sect. 6) would be interesting. It is also left for ongoing and future research establishing a connection to the problem of computing specific repairs, and using them [27]. The same applies to the use of the inconsistency measure to explore the *causes for inconsistency*, in particular, to analyze how the measure changes when tuples or combinations thereof are removed from the database. Such an application sounds natural given the established connection between database repairs, causality and causal responsibility [2,7].

It is natural to think of a principled, postulate-based approach to inconsistency measures, similar in spirit to postulates for belief-updates [23]. This has been done in logic-based knowledge representation [20], but as we argued before, a dedicated, specific approach for databases becomes desirable.

In relation to the abstract setting of Sect. 7, we could consider a class $Rep^{S^{\preceq}}(D, \Sigma)$ of *prioritized repairs* [31], and through them introduce *prioritized measures of inconsistency*. Repair programs for the kinds of priority relations $\preceq$ investigated in [31] could be constructed from the ASPs introduced and investigated in [17] for capturing different optimality criteria. The repair programs could be used to specify and compute the corresponding prioritized inconsistency measures.

Acknowledgments. Research supported by NSERC Discovery Grant #06148. The author is grateful to Jordan Li for his help with DLV; and to Benny Kimelfeld, Sudeepa Roy and Ester Livshits for stimulating general conversations. The author appreciates the support from RelationalAI, and its excellent human and research environment.

References

1. Bertossi, L.: Repair-based degrees of database inconsistency: computation and complexity. Corr arxiv Paper cs.DB/1809.10286 (2018). (extended version of this work)

2. Bertossi, L.: Characterizing and computing causes for query answers in databases from database repairs and repair programs. In: Ferrarotti, F., Woltran, S. (eds.) FoIKS 2018. LNCS, vol. 10833, pp. 55–76. Springer, Cham (2018). https://doi.org/10.1007/978-3-319-90050-6_4

3. Bertossi, L.: Database Repairing and Consistent Query Answering. Synthesis Lectures on Data Management. Morgan & Claypool, San Rafael (2011)

4. Bertossi, L., Li, L.: Achieving data privacy through secrecy views and null-based virtual updates. IEEE Trans. Knowl. Data Eng. **25**(5), 987–1000 (2013)

5. Bertossi, L., Bravo, L.: Consistency and trust in peer data exchange systems. Theory Pract. Log. Program. **17**(2), 148–204 (2017)

6. Bertossi, L., Bravo, L., Franconi, E., Lopatenko, A.: The complexity and approximation of fixing numerical attributes in databases under integrity constraints. Inf. Syst. **33**(4), 407–434 (2008)

7. Bertossi, L., Salimi, B.: From causes for database queries to repairs and model-based diagnosis and back. Theory Comput. Syst. **61**(1), 191–232 (2017)

8. Bertossi, L., Rizzolo, F., Jiang, L.: Data quality is context dependent. In: Castellanos, M., Dayal, U., Markl, V. (eds.) BIRTE 2010. LNBIP, vol. 84, pp. 52–67. Springer, Heidelberg (2011). https://doi.org/10.1007/978-3-642-22970-1_5

9. Brewka, G., Eiter, T., Truszczynski, M.: Answer set programming at a glance. Commun. ACM **54**(12), 93–103 (2011)

10. Buccafurri, F., Leone, N., Rullo, P.: Enhancing disjunctive datalog by constraints. IEEE Trans. Knowl. Data Eng. **12**(5), 845–860 (2000)

11. Calimeri, F., Cozza, S., Ianni, G., Leone, N.: An ASP system with functions, lists, and sets. In: Erdem, E., Lin, F., Schaub, T. (eds.) LPNMR 2009. LNCS (LNAI), vol. 5753, pp. 483–489. Springer, Heidelberg (2009). https://doi.org/10.1007/978-3-642-04238-6_46

12. Caniupan-Marileo, M., Bertossi, L.: The consistency extractor system: answer set programs for consistent query answering in databases. Data Knowl. Eng. **69**(6), 545–572 (2010)

13. Chomicki, J., Marcinkowski, J.: Minimal-change integrity maintenance using tuple deletions. Inf. Comput. **197**(1–2), 90–121 (2005)

14. Eiter, T., Mannila, H.: Distance measures for point sets and their computation. Acta Informatica **34**, 109–133 (1997)

15. El Oualia, M., Fohlin, H., Srivastav, A.: A randomised approximation algorithm for the hitting set problem. Theor. Comput. Sci. **555**, 23–34 (2014)

16. Flum, J., Grohe, M.: Parameterized Complexity Theory. Springer, Heidelberg (2006). https://doi.org/10.1007/3-540-29953-X

17. Gebser, M., Kaminski, R., Schaub, T.: Complex optimization in answer set programming. Theory Pract. Log. Program. **11**(4–5), 821–839 (2011)

18. Gelfond, M., Kahl, Y.: Knowledge Representation and Reasoning, and the Design of Intelligent Agents. Cambridge University Press, Cambridge (2014)

19. Gelfond, M., Lifschitz, V.: Classical negation in logic programs and disjunctive databases. New Gener. Comput. **9**(3/4), 365–386 (1991)

20. Grant, J., Martinez, M.V. (eds.): Measuring Inconsistency in Information. College Publications (2018)

21. Grant, J., Hunter, A.: Analysing inconsistent information using distance-based measures. Int. J. Approx. Reason. **89**, 3–26 (2017)
22. Hunter, A., Konieczny, S.: On the measure of conflicts: shapley inconsistency values. Artif. Intell. **174**(14), 1007–1026 (2010)
23. Katsuno, H., Mendelzon, A.O.: Propositional knowledge base revision and minimal change. Artif. Intell. **52**(3), 263–294 (1992)
24. Khot, S., Regev, O.: Vertex cover might be hard to approximate to within 2-epsilon. J. Comput. Syst. Sci. **74**(3), 335–349 (2008)
25. Kivinen, J., Mannila, H.: Approximate inference of functional dependencies from relations. Theor. Comput. Sci. **149**, 129–149 (1995)
26. Leone, N., et al.: The DLV system for knowledge representation and reasoning. ACM Trans. Comput. Logic. **7**(3), 499–562 (2006)
27. Livshits, E., Kimelfeld, B., Roy, S.: Computing optimal repairs for functional dependencies. In: Proceedings of PODS 2018, pp. 225–237 (2018)
28. Lopatenko, A., Bertossi, L.: Complexity of consistent query answering in databases under cardinality-based and incremental repair semantics. In: Schwentick, T., Suciu, D. (eds.) ICDT 2007. LNCS, vol. 4353, pp. 179–193. Springer, Heidelberg (2006). https://doi.org/10.1007/11965893_13
29. Meliou, A., Gatterbauer, W., Moore, K.F., Suciu, D.: The complexity of causality and responsibility for query answers and non-answers. In: Proceedings of VLDB 2010, pp. 34–41 (2010)
30. Papadimitriou, C.: Computational Complexity. Addison-Wesley, Boston (1994)
31. Staworko, S., Chomicki, J., Marcinkowski, J.: Prioritized repairing and consistent query answering in relational databases. Ann. Math. Artif. Intell. **64**(2–3), 209–246 (2012)
32. Thimm, M.: On the compliance of rationality postulates for inconsistency measures: a more or less complete picture. Künstliche Intelligenz **31**(1), 31–39 (2017)
33. Wijsen, J.: Database repairing using updates. ACM Trans. Database Syst. **30**(3), 722–768 (2005)

Elect: An Inconsistency Handling Approach for Partially Preordered Lightweight Ontologies

Sihem Belabbes[1(✉)] [iD], Salem Benferhat[1(✉)] [iD], and Jan Chomicki[2(✉)] [iD]

[1] CRIL, CNRS, Université d'Artois, Lens, France
{belabbes,benferhat}@cril.fr
[2] SUNY at Buffalo, Buffalo, NY, USA
chomicki@buffalo.edu

Abstract. We focus on the problem of handling inconsistency in light-weight ontologies. We assume terminological knowledge bases (TBoxes) are specified in DL-Lite and that assertional facts (ABoxes) are partially preordered and may be inconsistent with respect to TBoxes. One of the main contributions of this paper is the provision of an efficient and safe method, called Elect, to restore consistency of the ABox with respect to the TBox. In the case where the assertional bases are flat (no priorities are associated with the ABoxes) or totally preordered, our method collapses with the well-known IAR semantics and non-defeated semantics, respectively. The semantic justification of Elect is obtained by first viewing a partially preordered ABox as a family of totally preordered ABoxes, and then applying non-defeated inference to each of the totally preordered ABoxes. We introduce the concept of elected assertions which allows us to provide an equivalent characterization of Elect without explicitly generating all totally preordered ABoxes. Finally we show that the computation of Elect is done in polynomial time.

Keywords: Inconsistency · Lightweight ontologies ·
Partially preordered knowledge bases

1 Introduction

In this paper, we are interested in handling inconsistencies arising in ontologies that are specified in DL-Lite [13], a family of lightweight fragments of Description Logics (DLs) with good computational properties. In the context of Description Logics, a knowledge base (KB) consists of two components, namely the TBox which contains the terminological knowledge and the ABox which is an assertional base (set of ground facts). The content of the TBox is oftentimes considered as correct and free of conflicts. In this paper, we adopt such reasonable assumption and hence elements of the TBox are not questionable in the presence of conflicts. However, assertions in the ABox may be questionable when the whole KB is inconsistent. Several strategies have been designed to allow for

© Springer Nature Switzerland AG 2019
M. Balduccini et al. (Eds.): LPNMR 2019, LNAI 11481, pp. 210–223, 2019.
https://doi.org/10.1007/978-3-030-20528-7_16

meaningful reasoning with inconsistent KBs [10,12,23] (see also [2] for a survey). This often amounts to computing repairs for the ABox. A repair is a maximal subset of the ABox that is consistent with respect to the TBox.

The well-known ABox Repair (AR) semantics [17] amounts to repairing the ABox in a minimal way (in terms of set inclusion) without modifying the TBox. Query answering is based on the answers holding in every repair. The AR semantics is often viewed as a safe way to deal with conflicts. However, the computation of AR query answers is expensive, even for lightweight ontology logic such as DL-Lite. The Intersection ABox Repair (IAR) semantics [17] is more cautious. It queries one consistent sub-base of the ABox obtained from the intersection of all the repairs. The IAR-repair has the advantage of being computable in polynomial time. In [3], the notion of non-defeated repair of an inconsistent prioritized ABox was introduced. The approach assumes the ABox is partitioned into strata by way of a total preorder on the assertions. Intuitively, the non-defeated repair is based on the iterative application of IAR semantics to a cumulative sequence of strata. This is also achieved in polynomial time [21] for DL-Lite.

In this paper, we address the problem of seeking for a tractable computation of repairs of an inconsistent DL-Lite knowledge base where the priority relation over assertions is a partial preorder. Namely, certain statements are deemed as more reliable than others and there are some statements whose reliability is incomparable. We provide an efficient and safe method, called Elect, to restore consistency of the ABox with respect to the TBox. We show that Elect generalizes both IAR semantics and non-defeated semantics. This is achieved in the case where the assertional bases are flat (no priorities are associated with the ABoxes) for the former, and for totally preordered ABoxes for the latter.

The semantic justification of Elect is obtained by first viewing the partial preorder associated with the ABox as a family of total preorders, then applying non-defeated inference to each of the totally preordered ABoxes and lastly computing their intersection to produce a single repair. Elect is safe since there is no arbitrary choice between the total preorders and hence all total pre-orders are taken into account for defining Elect. We introduce the concept of elected assertions which intuitively are those assertions that are strictly preferred to all of their opponents. This allows us to provide an equivalent characterization of Elect, hence a repair is obtained without explicitly computing all total preorders. Finally we show that the computation of Elect is done in polynomial time. Hence Elect maintains the tractability of IAR semantics and non-defeated semantics for partially preordered ABoxes.

This paper is structured as follows. Section 2 contains preliminaries on DL-Lite. Section 3 presents the IAR semantics for non-prioritized ABoxes. Section 4 discusses the non-defeated repair for ABoxes prioritized with a total preorder. Section 5 deals with partially preordered ABoxes. We introduce our method called Elect and provide a characterization for it. Section 6 provides some discussions on how to go beyond Elect.

2   The Description Logic DL-Lite

Description Logics (DLs) [1] are a family of successful logic-based knowledge representation formalisms meeting many applications, notably in the formalisation of ontologies. The so-called lightweight fragments of DLs, of which DL-Lite [13] is an example, are particularly interesting since they provide a good trade-off between expressive power and computational complexity. Indeed, query answering from a DL-Lite knowledge base can be carried out efficiently. There are a few variants of DL-Lite, such as DL-Lite$_R$ and on which we shall focus.

The language of DL-Lite$_R$ is built upon a finite set of *concept names* C, a finite set of *role names* R and a finite set of *individual names* I, such that C, R and I are pairwise disjoint. DL-Lite$_R$ concepts are defined according to the following rules: $R \longrightarrow P \mid P^-$ $E \longrightarrow R \mid \neg R$ $B \longrightarrow A \mid \exists R$ $C \longrightarrow B \mid \neg B$.
Above, A denotes a concept name, P a role name, and P^- the *converse* of P. With R we denote a *basic role*, while E stands for a *complex role*. Moreover, B denotes a *basic concept* and C a *complex* one.

Example 1. For a concrete example, we can have:

- C = {*Dances, Mdances, Tdances, DancesWP, DancesWoP, Props*}, standing for: dances, modern dances, traditional dances, dances with props, dances without props as well as the props that are used in some dances, respectively.
- R = {*HasProps*}, representing the props used in some dances and which can be flowers (*fl* for short), a hat, or handkerchiefs (*hk* for short).
- I = {d_1, d_2, d_3, d_4, d_5} ∪ {*fl, hat, hk*} where each $d_i, i = 1, ..., 5$, represents dances and the rest represents props.

Some examples of complex concepts are: ¬*DancesWP* and ¬∃*HasProps*.   □

An *inclusion axiom* on concepts (resp. on roles) is a statement of the form $B \sqsubseteq C$ (resp. $R \sqsubseteq E$). Concept inclusions with ¬ in the right-hand side are called *negative inclusion axioms*, otherwise they are called *positive inclusion axioms*. Concrete examples of concept inclusion axioms are:
$DancesWoP \sqsubseteq \neg DancesWP$ and $\exists HasProps^- \sqsubseteq Props$.
A DL-Lite$_R$ *TBox* $\mathcal{T}$ is a finite set of inclusion axioms (including positive and negative ones). An *assertion* is a statement of the form $A(a)$ or $P(a, b)$, with $a, b \in$ I. Examples of assertions are $Mdances(d_1)$ and $HasProps(d_3, hat)$.

A DL-Lite$_R$ *ABox* $\mathcal{A}$ is a finite set of assertions. Given $\mathcal{T}$ and $\mathcal{A}$, we denote a DL-Lite$_R$ *knowledge base* (KB) with $\mathcal{K} =_{\text{def}} \langle \mathcal{T}, \mathcal{A} \rangle$.

We shall use the following running example throughout the paper.

Example 1. Assume that we have the following TBox:

$$\mathcal{T} = \begin{cases} 1.\ Mdances \sqsubseteq Dances, & 2.\ Tdances \sqsubseteq Dances, \\ 3.\ Tdances \sqsubseteq DancesWP, & 4.\ Mdances \sqsubseteq DancesWoP, \\ 5.\ DancesWoP \sqsubseteq \neg DancesWP, & 6.\ DancesWoP \sqsubseteq \neg\exists HasProps, \\ 7.\ \exists HasProps^- \sqsubseteq Props, & 8.\ \exists HasProps \sqsubseteq DancesWP \end{cases}$$

The first two axioms state that modern dances and traditional dances are dances. The third axiom means that traditional dances are dances that use props. Axiom 4 states that modern dances do not use props. Axiom 5 expresses the fact that the list of modern dances and the list of traditional dances are disjoint. Axiom 6 represents the fact that a modern dance does not have props. Axiom 7 expresses the fact that elements used by dances, given by role name *HasProps*, should belong to the list of elements specified by the concept name *Props*. Axiom 8 specifies that anything having props must be a dance with props.

Let us now describe the ABox given by the following assertions:

$$\mathcal{A} = \left\{ \begin{array}{l} Mdances(d_1), Mdances(d_2), \\ Tdances(d_2), Tdances(d_3), Tdances(d_4), \\ DancesWP(d_3), DancesWP(d_5), \\ DancesWoP(d_5), HasProps(d_2, fl), \\ HasProps(d_3, hat), HasProps(d_4, hk) \end{array} \right\}$$

□

A knowledge base $\mathcal{K}$ is said to be *consistent* if it admits at least one model, it is *inconsistent* otherwise. A TBox $\mathcal{T}$ is *incoherent* if there is $A \in C$ such that A is empty in every model of $\mathcal{T}$, it is *coherent* otherwise. For more details on the DL-Lite family of DLs, we refer the reader to the work of Calvanese et al. [13]. In the rest of this paper, we shall refer to DL-Lite$_R$ as DL-Lite for simplicity.

3   IAR Semantics for Flat Assertional Bases

In this section, we consider a KB $\mathcal{K} = \langle \mathcal{T}, \mathcal{A} \rangle$ that may be inconsistent. We assume that the TBox $\mathcal{T}$ is coherent and reliable, that is, its elements are not questionable in the presence of conflicts, unlike assertions in $\mathcal{A}$ which may be questionable. Besides, we assume that the ABox $\mathcal{A}$ is flat (or non-prioritized), that is, all assertions have the same level of priority. A standard way of dealing with inconsistency proceeds by first computing the set of maximal consistent subsets of $\mathcal{A}$, called repairs, then using them to perform inference (i.e. query answering). More formally a repair is defined as follows [17]:

Definition 1. *Let* $\mathcal{K} = \langle \mathcal{T}, \mathcal{A} \rangle$ *be a flat and inconsistent DL-Lite KB. A subbase* $\mathcal{R} \subseteq \mathcal{A}$ *is a repair if* $\langle \mathcal{T}, \mathcal{R} \rangle$ *is consistent, and* $\forall \mathcal{R}': \mathcal{R} \subsetneq \mathcal{R}', \langle \mathcal{T}, \mathcal{R}' \rangle$ *is inconsistent. Furthermore if* $\langle \mathcal{T}, \mathcal{A} \rangle$ *is consistent, then there exists only one repair* $\mathcal{R} = \mathcal{A}$.

Consequently, when $\mathcal{K}$ is inconsistent, adding any assertion f from $\mathcal{A} \setminus \mathcal{R}$ to $\mathcal{R}$ entails the inconsistency of $\langle \mathcal{T}, \mathcal{R} \cup \{f\} \rangle$. We denote by $MAR(\mathcal{A})$ the set of repairs of $\mathcal{A}$ with respect to $\mathcal{T}$. Using the notion of repairs, handling inconsistency from flat DL-Lite KB can be done by applying standard query answering, either using the whole set of repairs (universal entailment or AR entailment [17]) or using only one repair (namely, using the so-called brave entailment [9]). It is well known that brave semantics is very adventurous and may return unsafe conclusions, while AR semantics is safe but computationally expensive.

An alternative is the IAR semantics [17] which selects one consistent sub-base of $\mathcal{A}$, denoted by $IAR(\mathcal{A})$. Before introducing IAR semantics, let us first introduce the notion of an assertional conflict. Basically, it is a minimal inconsistent subset of assertions that contradicts the TBox.

Definition 2. *Let* $\mathcal{K} = \langle \mathcal{T}, \mathcal{A} \rangle$ *be a DL-Lite KB. A sub-base* $\mathcal{C} \subseteq \mathcal{A}$ *is an assertional conflict of* $\mathcal{K}$ *iff* $\langle \mathcal{T}, \mathcal{C} \rangle$ *is inconsistent and* $\forall f \in \mathcal{C}$, $\langle \mathcal{T}, \mathcal{C} \setminus \{f\} \rangle$ *is consistent.*

We denote by $\mathcal{C}(\mathcal{A})$ the set of conflicts in $\mathcal{A}$. From Definition 2, we see that removing any fact f from $\mathcal{C}$ restores the consistency of $\langle \mathcal{T}, \mathcal{C} \rangle$. A nice feature of DL-Lite is that computing the set of conflicts is done in polynomial time [12]. Besides, a conflict $\mathcal{C}$ involves exactly two assertions [12]. In this case, if f and g are two assertions that belong to a conflict, we simply denote the conflict as a pair (f, g) and we say that f and g are conflicting.

We now introduce the notion of non-conflicting or free elements.

Definition 3. *Let* $\mathcal{K} = \langle \mathcal{T}, \mathcal{A} \rangle$ *be a DL-Lite KB. An assertion* $f \in \mathcal{A}$ *is free iff* $\forall \mathcal{C} \in \mathcal{C}(\mathcal{A}) : f \notin \mathcal{C}$.

Intuitively, *free* assertions correspond to elements that are not involved in any conflict. The notion of *free* elements was originally proposed in [4] in the context of propositional logic.

Henceforth, we shall denote by $IAR(\mathcal{A})$ the set of free elements in $\mathcal{A}$. Namely:

Definition 4. $IAR(\mathcal{A}) = \{f : f \in \mathcal{A} \text{ and } f \text{ is free}\}$.

Definition 4 is an equivalent rewriting of the standard definition of $IAR(\mathcal{A})$ given by $IAR(\mathcal{A}) = \bigcap_{\mathcal{R} \in MAR(\mathcal{A})} \mathcal{R}$ [4,17]. Namely, $IAR(\mathcal{A})$ is the intersection of all repairs. Query answering in IAR semantics comes down to performing standard query answering from $\langle \mathcal{T}, IAR(\mathcal{A}) \rangle$ (since $\langle \mathcal{T}, IAR(\mathcal{A}) \rangle$ is consistent).

Example 2. Let us consider Example 1. The list of conflicts in $\langle \mathcal{T}, \mathcal{A} \rangle$ is:

$$\mathcal{C}(\mathcal{A}) = \left\{ \begin{array}{l} \{Mdances(d_2), Tdances(d_2)\}, \\ \{Mdances(d_2), HasProps(d_2, fl)\}, \\ \{DancesWP(d_5), DancesWoP(d_5)\} \end{array} \right\}$$

In order to define $IAR(\mathcal{A})$, it is enough to remove all assertions of $\mathcal{C}(\mathcal{A})$ from $\mathcal{A}$. This leads to:

$$IAR(\mathcal{A}) = \left\{ \begin{array}{l} Mdances(d_1), Tdances(d_3), Tdances(d_4), \\ DancesWP(d_3), HasProps(d_3, hat), HasProps(d_4, hk) \end{array} \right\}$$

4   Non-defeated Repair for Prioritized Assertional Bases

In this section, we shall consider prioritized DL-Lite KBs wherein a total preorder relation $\geq$ is applied only to the ABox component which we denote by $(\mathcal{A}, \geq)$. The relation $\geq$ is reflexive, transitive and $\forall f, g \in \mathcal{A}$, either $f \geq g$ or $g \geq f$. Let $>$ and $=$ stand for the strict and equality relations associated with $\geq$. Besides, for convenience, we represent $(\mathcal{A}, \geq)$ by a well-ordered partition of $\mathcal{A}$ induced by $\geq$. Namely, given $(\mathcal{A}, \geq)$, we view $\mathcal{A}$ as being partitioned into n layers (or strata) of the form $\mathcal{A} = (\mathcal{S}_1, \ldots, \mathcal{S}_n)$, such that:

- $\mathcal{S}_1 = \{f : \forall g \in \mathcal{A}, f \geq g\}$, and
- $\mathcal{S}_i = \{f : \forall g \in \mathcal{A} \setminus (\mathcal{S}_1 \cup \cdots \cup \mathcal{S}_{i-1}), f \geq g\}$, for $i = 2, \ldots, n$.

In other words, assertions in each layer $\mathcal{S}_i$ have the same level of priority i and they are considered as more reliable than the ones contained in a layer $\mathcal{S}_j$ for $j > i$. Thus $\mathcal{S}_1$ contains the most important assertions, while $\mathcal{S}_n$ contains the least important ones. Obviously, $\mathcal{A} = \mathcal{S}_1 \cup \cdots \cup \mathcal{S}_n$.

Several studies consider the notion of priority when querying inconsistent databases (e.g. [18,20]) or DL knowledge bases (e.g. [8,15]). Most of these frameworks extend the notions of repair and AR semantics, hence they are computationally expensive. In particular, the concepts of preferred repairs semantics were introduced in [8] (in the spirit of what has been done in prioritized propositional logic [11,19]). It revisits AR and IAR semantics by replacing the notion of repair by different types of preferred repairs based on: set cardinality, priority levels on the ABox and weights on the assertions. However, this formalism often induces an increase in computational complexity for the proposed semantics. Most notably, the tractability of IAR semantics in a flat context (i.e. polynomial time) is lost when a total preorder is applied to the ABox.

In [3], a particular attention was devoted to approaches that select a single preferred repair. One of such approaches is the so-called non-defeated repair which is tractable without being adventurous. Basically, non-defeated repair consists of iteratively collecting, layer per layer, the set of free assertions like so:

Definition 5. *Let $\mathcal{K}$ be a prioritized DL-Lite KB where the ABox $(\mathcal{A}, \geq)$ is totally preordered. Let $\mathcal{A} = (\mathcal{S}_1, \ldots, \mathcal{S}_n)$ be the well-ordered partition associated with $\geq$. The non-defeated repair, denoted by $nd(\mathcal{A}, \geq) = \mathcal{S}_1' \cup \ldots \cup \mathcal{S}_n'$, is:*

$$\forall i = 1, .., n : \mathcal{S}_i' = IAR(\mathcal{S}_1 \cup \ldots \cup \mathcal{S}_i)$$

where $\forall i : IAR(\mathcal{S}_1 \cup \ldots \cup \mathcal{S}_i)$ denotes the set of IAR base of $(\mathcal{S}_1 \cup \ldots \cup \mathcal{S}_i)$, given by Definition 4.

The definition of the non-defeated sub-base is an adaptation of the one proposed in [5] within a propositional logic framework. However, non-defeated repair is computed in polynomial time in DL-Lite while its computation is hard in propositional logic. Lastly, in [6] a rewriting (similar to that of $IAR(\mathcal{A})$) is given for $nd(\mathcal{A}, \geq)$. Basically, an assertion $f \in \mathcal{S}_i$ is said to be defeated if there exists an assertion $g \in \mathcal{S}_j$ such that $j \leq i$ and g is conflicting with f. It has been shown in [6] that $nd(\mathcal{A}, \geq)$ consists of all non-defeated assertions.

Example 3. Let us continue our running example and consider a total preorder $\geq$ over assertions of the ABox as per Fig. 1, where $f = g$ means that the two assertions have the same level of priority, and the arrow $f \to g$ means that f has a higher priority than g (i.e. $f > g$).

$$Tdances(d_2) = Mdances(d_1) = Tdances(d_3) = HasProps(d_3, hat)$$
$$\downarrow$$
$$HasProps(d_2, fl) = DancesWP(d_5) = DancesWoP(d_5) = DancesWP(d_3)$$
$$\downarrow$$
$$Mdances(d_2) = Tdances(d_4) = HasProps(d_4, hk)$$

Fig. 1. A total preorder over the ABox

From this totally preordered ABox, one can compute the non-defeated sub-class of $\mathcal{A}$. The well-ordered partition associated with this ordering is:

$\mathcal{S}_1 = \{Tdances(d_2), Mdances(d_1), Tdances(d_3), HasProps(d_3, hat)\}$.
$\mathcal{S}_2 = \{HasProps(d_2, fl), DancesWP(d_5), DancesWoP(d_5), DancesWP(d_3)\}$
$\mathcal{S}_3 = \{Mdances(d_2), Tdances(d_4), HasProps(d_4, hk)\}$.

We have $nd(\mathcal{A}, \geq) = IAR(\mathcal{S}_1) \cup IAR(\mathcal{S}_1 \cup \mathcal{S}_2) \cup IAR(\mathcal{S}_1 \cup \mathcal{S}_2 \cup \mathcal{S}_3)$, where:

- $IAR(\mathcal{S}_1) = \{Tdances(d_2), Mdances(d_1), Tdances(d_3), HasProps(d_3, hat)\}$
- $IAR(\mathcal{S}_1 \cup \mathcal{S}_2) = \{Tdances(d_2), Mdances(d_1), Tdances(d_3), HasProps(d_3, hat),$
  $\qquad\qquad HasProps(d_2, fl), DancesWP(d_3)\}$
- $IAR(\mathcal{S}_1 \cup \mathcal{S}_2 \cup \mathcal{S}_3) = IAR(\mathcal{A})$ (given in Example 2).

Therefore:
$nd(\mathcal{A}, \geq) = \{Tdances(d_2), Mdances(d_1), Tdances(d_3), HasProps(d_3, hat),$
$\qquad\qquad HasProps(d_2, fl), DancesWP(d_3), Tdances(d_4), HasProps(d_4, hk)\}$.

5　Partially Preordered Assertional Bases

A nice feature about IAR semantics (for a flat ABox) and non-defeated semantics (for a totally preordered ABox) is their efficiency in dealing with inconsistency since they produce a single sub-base of the ABox as a repair and they do so in polynomial time. In this section, we also aim at producing a single repair when only a partial preorder (denoted $\unrhd$) is applied to assertions of the ABox which we denote by $(\mathcal{A}, \unrhd)$. We denote by $\rhd$ the strict order (irreflexive and transitive) and by $\overset{\unrhd}{=}$ the equality order associated with $\unrhd$.

A minimal requirement is to maintain tractability. Namely, we seek for a tractable method that also returns one (preferred) repair for a partially pre-ordered ABox. We call our method 'Elect' and denote by $Elect(\mathcal{A}, \unrhd)$ the repair it returns. As we shall see later, Elect extends both IAR semantics and non-defeated semantics in the cases where $\unrhd$ is flat and totally preordered respectively. Henceforth, we do not make explicit the TBox $\mathcal{T}$.

5.1   From a Partial Preorder to a Family of Total Preorders

In order to achieve our aim, we first view a partial preorder $\unrhd$ as a family of total preorders, each of which should be a total extension of $\unrhd$ defined like so:

Definition 6. *A total preorder $\geq$ over $\mathcal{A}$ is a total extension of $\unrhd$ over $\mathcal{A}$ iff $\forall f, g \in \mathcal{A}$, if $f \unrhd g$ then $f \geq g$.*

Viewing a partially preordered KB as a family of totally preordered KBs is a natural representation that has been used in other frameworks such as partially ordered possibilistic logic [7, 22] and credal probabilistic networks [14].

Example 4. Let us assume a partial preorder $\unrhd$ over assertions of the ABox which are split up into the following four subsets:

$$A = \{Tdances(d_2) \stackrel{\unrhd}{=} Mdances(d_1) \stackrel{\unrhd}{=} Tdances(d_3) \stackrel{\unrhd}{=} HasProps(d_3, hat)\},$$
$$B = \{HasProps(d_2, fl) \stackrel{\unrhd}{=} DancesWP(d_3) \stackrel{\unrhd}{=} DancesWoP(d_5) \stackrel{\unrhd}{=} Dances$$
$$WP(d_5)\},$$
$$C = \{Mdances(d_2)\},$$
$$D = \{Tdances(d_4) \stackrel{\unrhd}{=} HasProps(d_4, hk)\},$$

where $f \stackrel{\unrhd}{=} g$ means that the two assertions have the same level of priority. The relation $\unrhd$ is depicted in Fig. 2, where the arrow $A \rightarrow B$ (for instance) means that $\forall f \in A, \forall g \in B$, f has a higher priority than g (i.e. $f \rhd g$).

Fig. 2. A partial preorder over the ABox

It follows that set A (resp. D) contains assertions having the highest (resp. lowest) priority. Assertions of sets B and C are not comparable. Hence the partial preorder $\unrhd$ can be viewed as a family of three total preorders: in $\geq_1$ set B is strictly preferred to set C, in $\geq_2$ sets B and C are equally preferred, and in $\geq_3$ set C is strictly preferred to set B. This is depicted in Fig. 3.   □

Now the question is how to handle this family of totally preordered ABoxes? We would like to avoid arbitrary choice consisting in the selection of one total preorder over others. Hence, all total preorders should be taken into account. A safe way to get a single consistent assertional sub-base is to consider the intersection of all non-defeated repairs associated with all total preorders. Formally:

Definition 7. *Let $\mathcal{K}$ be a DL-Lite KB with a partially preordered ABox $(\mathcal{A}, \unrhd)$.*

- *$Elect(\mathcal{A}, \unrhd) = \bigcap \{nd(\mathcal{A}, \geq)$ s.t. $\geq$ is a total extension of $\unrhd\}$, where $nd(\mathcal{A}, \geq)$ is given by Definition 5.*

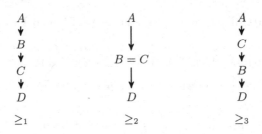

Fig. 3. Total extensions of the partial preorder

- *Let q be a query. Then q is an Elect-consequence of $\mathcal{K}$ if q follows from $Elect(\mathcal{A}, \trianglerighteq)$ (using standard DL-lite inference).*

We illustrate this idea on our running example.

Example 5. The non-defeated repairs associated with the totally preordered ABoxes $(\mathcal{A}, \geq_1)$, $(\mathcal{A}, \geq_2)$ and $(\mathcal{A}, \geq_3)$ are:

- $nd(\mathcal{A}, \geq_1) = A \cup \{HasProps(d_2, fl), DancesWP(d_3)\} \cup D$
- $nd(\mathcal{A}, \geq_2) = A \cup \{DancesWP(d_3)\} \cup D$
- $nd(\mathcal{A}, \geq_3) = A \cup \{DancesWP(d_3)\} \cup D$

$$Elect(\mathcal{A}, \trianglerighteq) = nd(\mathcal{A}, \geq_1) \cap nd(\mathcal{A}, \geq_2) \cap nd(\mathcal{A}, \geq_3)$$
$$= A \cup \{DancesWP(d_3)\} \cup D.$$

$\square$

An important result stated in Proposition 1 is that the computation of $Elect(\mathcal{A}, \trianglerighteq)$ can be achieved in polynomial time. This means that in order to compute $Elect(\mathcal{A}, \trianglerighteq)$, there is no need to exhibit all possible extensions of $\trianglerighteq$.

Proposition 1. *Computing $Elect(\mathcal{A}, \trianglerighteq)$ is done in polynomial time (w.r.t. the size of the ABox).*

The next proposition states that, as expected, the KB having $Elect(\mathcal{A}, \trianglerighteq)$ as ABox is consistent.

Proposition 2. $\langle \mathcal{T}, Elect(\mathcal{A}, \trianglerighteq) \rangle$ *is consistent.*

Another interesting feature of Elect is that it collapses with IAR semantics (resp. non-defeated semantics) when the ABox is flat (resp. totally preordered).

Proposition 3. *If the partial preorder $\trianglerighteq$ is flat, then $Elect(\mathcal{A}, \trianglerighteq) = IAR(\mathcal{A})$. If the partial preorder $\trianglerighteq$ is a total preorder, then $Elect(\mathcal{A}, \trianglerighteq) = nd(\mathcal{A}, \trianglerighteq)$.*

The proofs of Propositions 1–3 are established by providing a characterization of $Elect(\mathcal{A}, \trianglerighteq)$ presented in the next section.

5.2   Characterizing Elect($\mathcal{A}, \unrhd$)

In this section we provide a characterization of $Elect(\mathcal{A}, \unrhd)$ without having to compute all total extensions of $\unrhd$. This is done by introducing the concept of elected assertions. Intuitively, an assertion f is elected in $(\mathcal{A}, \unrhd)$ if f is strictly preferred to all of its conflicting assertions. Formally:

Definition 8. *An assertion $f \in \mathcal{A}$ is elected iff $\forall g \in \mathcal{A}$, if (f, g) are conflicting then $f \rhd g$ (i.e. f is strictly preferred to g).*

Definition 8 extends the concept of free assertions given in Definition 3. Indeed, if $\unrhd$ is flat (namely, $\forall f, g \in \mathcal{A}, f \unrhd g$ and $g \unrhd f$), then f is elected in $(\mathcal{A}, \unrhd)$ iff f is free. Obviously, the converse does not hold in general (when $\unrhd$ is no longer flat), since an elected assertion may not be a free assertion, however its reliability is strictly more important than that of its opponents. This definition also extends the notion of non-defeated assertions given for non-defeated repairs in totally preordered KBs [6]. Lastly, the concept of elected assertions is in the spirit of the one of accepted beliefs introduced in uncertainty theories [16].

As shown in Proposition 4, it turns out that the set of elected assertions matches exactly the set of assertions in $Elect(\mathcal{A}, \unrhd)$.

Proposition 4. *An assertion $f \in \mathcal{A}$ is elected in $(\mathcal{A}, \unrhd)$ iff $f \in Elect(\mathcal{A}, \unrhd)$.*

Proof. Let $(\mathcal{A}, \unrhd)$ be a partially preordered assertional base.

(i) Let $f \in \mathcal{A}$ be an elected assertion. Let us show that for each total extension $(\mathcal{A}, \geq)$ of $(\mathcal{A}, \unrhd)$, we have $f \in nd(\mathcal{A}, \geq)$. Let $(\mathcal{S}_1, \ldots, \mathcal{S}_n)$ be the well-ordered partition associated with $\geq$. Let i be the first stratum where $f \in \mathcal{S}_i$.
Recall that f is elected in $(\mathcal{A}, \unrhd)$ means that $\forall g \in \mathcal{A}$, if (f, g) are conflicting then $f \rhd g$ (*i.e.* f is strictly preferred to g with respect to $\unrhd$). And since $\geq$ is a total extension of $\unrhd$, then this also means that $f > g$. This also means that $\forall g$ such that (f, g) are conflicting, $g \in \mathcal{S}_j$ with $j > i$. Hence, $f \in IAR(\mathcal{S}_1 \cup \ldots \cup \mathcal{S}_i)$. Therefore $f \in nd(\mathcal{A}, \geq)$.

(ii) Let us now show the converse. Assume that $f \in \mathcal{A}$ is not elected and let us build a total extension $(\mathcal{A}, \geq)$ of $(\mathcal{A}, \unrhd)$ such that $f \notin nd(\mathcal{A}, \geq)$.
f is not elected means that $\exists g \in \mathcal{A}$ such that (f, g) are conflicting but $f \rhd g$ does not hold. This means that there exists a total extension $\geq$ of $\unrhd$ where $g \geq f$. If (f, g) are conflicting and $(\mathcal{S}_1, \ldots, \mathcal{S}_n)$ is the well-ordered partition associated with $\geq$, then if $f \in \mathcal{S}_i$ it follows that $g \in \mathcal{S}_j$ with $j \leq i$. Hence, $\forall k \in \{1, \ldots, n\}, f \notin IAR(\mathcal{S}_1 \cup \ldots \cup \mathcal{S}_k)$ which means that $f \notin nd(\mathcal{A}, \geq)$.

With this result at hand, we can now prove Propositions 1, 2 and 3.

1. Regarding the computational complexity, we recall that computing the set of conflicts $\mathcal{C}(\mathcal{A})$ is done in polynomial time with respect to the size of $\mathcal{A}$. Hence, computing $Elect(\mathcal{A}, \unrhd)$ is also done in polynomial time. Indeed, checking if some assertion $f \in \mathcal{A}$ is elected boils down to parsing all assertional conflicts in $\mathcal{C}(\mathcal{A})$. This is done in linear time with respect to the size of $\mathcal{C}(\mathcal{A})$ (the size is itself bounded by $\mathcal{O}(|\mathcal{A}|^2)$).

2. Let us show that $Elect(\mathcal{A}, \trianglerighteq)$ is consistent with respect to $\mathcal{T}$. Assume that this is not the case. This means that $\exists f \in Elect(\mathcal{A}, \trianglerighteq)$, $\exists g \neq f \in Elect(\mathcal{A}, \trianglerighteq)$ such that $\langle \mathcal{T}, \{f, g\} \rangle$ are conflicting. Since f and g are in $Elect(\mathcal{A}, \trianglerighteq)$, then this means that $f \triangleright g$ and $g \triangleright f$ which is impossible.

3. Lastly, by construction of $Elect(\mathcal{A}, \trianglerighteq)$, it is easy to check that when $\trianglerighteq$ is a total preorder, then $Elect(\mathcal{A}, \trianglerighteq)$ collapses with the non-defeated repair of $\trianglerighteq$. And if $\trianglerighteq$ is flat (namely $\forall f, g \in \mathcal{A}, f \trianglerighteq g$ and $g \trianglerighteq f$), then $Elect(\mathcal{A}, \trianglerighteq) = IAR(\mathcal{A}) = \{f \in \mathcal{A} : \nexists g \in \mathcal{A}, (f, g) \text{ are conflicting}\}$.   □

Example 6. We reproduce the result of $Elect(\mathcal{A}, \trianglerighteq)$ given in Example 5 using the notion of elected assertions of Definition 8. One can check that:

- $Mdances(d_2)$ is not elected, since it is conflicting with $Tdances(d_2)$ and $Mdances(d_2) \triangleright Tdances(d_2)$ does not hold.
- $DancesWoP(d_5)$ and $DancesWP(d_5)$ are conflicting and have the same priority levels. Hence, they cannot be elected assertions.
- $HasProps(d_2, fl)$ is in conflict with $Mdances(d_2)$ but $HasProps(d_2, fl) \triangleright Mdances(d_2)$ is not true. Hence $HasProps(d_2, fl)$ is not an elected assertion.
- The remaining assertions are all elected. Namely:
  $Elect(\mathcal{A}, \trianglerighteq) = \{Mdances(d_1), Tdances(d_2), Tdances(d_3), Tdances(d_4),$

  $DancesWP(d_3), HasProps(d_3, hat), HasProps(d_4, hk)\}.$

We thus obtain the same result as in Example 5 where we considered all total extensions of $\trianglerighteq$.

6   Discussions on How to Go Beyond $Elect(\mathcal{A}, \trianglerighteq)$

This section provides a brief discussion on how to go beyond $Elect(\mathcal{A}, \trianglerighteq)$ (an in-depth investigation of these issues is left for future work).

How to Tractably Go Beyond Elect? A legitimate question is how to obtain a base that is larger (more productive) than Elect but without increasing its computational complexity? A natural solution to achieve this aim is to use the concept of positive deductive closure (the closure of the ABox is defined w.r.t. positive axioms in $\mathcal{T}$). But this begs the question of when is it appropriate to apply the closure: on the initial ABox or on all non-defeated repairs of all total extensions that have been computed? The first option, which consists in applying the positive closure to the initial ABox, in the spirit of ICAR semantics for flat ABoxes [17], raises two issues. Firstly in semantic terms, ICAR may be debatable since it may entail consequences which are derived from questionable assertions. Secondly, there are different ways to define the reliability of the derived elements. For instance, assume that the TBox contains $\{A \sqsubseteq B, E \sqsubseteq B\}$ and that the ABox contains $\{A(x), E(x)\}$. Assume that $A(x)$ and $E(x)$ are incomparable. $B(x)$ is entailed from $A(x)$ but also from $E(x)$. The question is then where to place $B(x)$? The intuition is to consider $B(x)$ is *at least as plausible as* $A(x)$ and

$E(x)$, but this is not straightforward to define in a general way (especially for expressive DLs).

The second option is to define the closure on all non-defeated repairs. This would be our favourite choice. Namely, this leads to computing a repair as the intersection of the closed non-defeated repairs [3], a method we would call CElect. CElect would then be larger than Elect. Besides, we argue that for flat ABoxes, CElect would be equivalent to the closure of IAR (which is different from ICAR), and for totally preordered ABoxes, CElect would be equivalent to the closure of non-defeated repair. Lastly, we expect to single out specific cases for which the complexity of CElect would also be polynomial in DL-Lite.

Beyond Non-defeated Repair. The question addressed here is whether one can use a semantics other than non-defeated as a basis for defining $Elect(\mathcal{A}, \unrhd)$? From a semantic point of view, the answer is yes. For instance, one can use a preferred repair defined in [8] instead of non-defeated repair in our definition of $Elect(\mathcal{A}, \unrhd)$. Let us first recall the concept of preferred repairs defined for totally preordered ABoxes. Let $\mathcal{A} = (\mathcal{S}_1, \ldots, \mathcal{S}_n)$ be a prioritized ABox. Let $\mathcal{R}_1$ and $\mathcal{R}_2$ be two consistent sub-bases of $\mathcal{S}_1 \cup \cdots \cup \mathcal{S}_n$. Then $\mathcal{R}_1$ is said to be preferred to $\mathcal{R}_2$ iff $\mathcal{R}_1 \cap \mathcal{S}_i = \mathcal{R}_2 \cap \mathcal{S}_i$ for every $i, 1 \leq i \leq n$, or there is some $i, 1 \leq i \leq n$ such that $\mathcal{R}_2 \cap \mathcal{S}_i \subsetneq \mathcal{R}_1 \cap \mathcal{S}_i$ and for all $j, 1 \leq j < i$, $\mathcal{R}_1 \cap \mathcal{S}_j = \mathcal{R}_2 \cap \mathcal{S}_j$ (in this case, $\mathcal{R}_1$ is strictly preferred to $\mathcal{R}_2$). Then $\mathcal{R}$ is said to be a preferred repair if $\nexists \mathcal{R}'$ s.t. $\mathcal{R}'$ is strictly preferred to $\mathcal{R}$ (see [8] for more details). The notion of preferred repairs can then be used as an alternative for defining a repair associated with partial preorders $\unrhd$. We would call the new setting $Partial_{PR}(\mathcal{A}, \unrhd)$ (where PR stands for preferred repairs). Like $Elect(\mathcal{A}, \unrhd)$, $Partial_{PR}(\mathcal{A}, \unrhd)$ would consider all total extensions $\geq$ of $\unrhd$. However instead of computing $\bigcap \{nd(\mathcal{A}, \geq)$ s.t. $\geq$ is an extension of $\unrhd\}$ like in $Elect(\mathcal{A}, \unrhd)$, we would compute $\bigcap \{IAR(\mathcal{A}, \geq)$ s.t. $\geq$ is an extension of $\unrhd\}$, where $IAR(\mathcal{A}, \geq) = \bigcap_{\mathcal{R}} \{\mathcal{R}$ is a preferred repair of $\geq\}$ as defined in [8]. We argue that $Partial_{PR}(\mathcal{A}, \unrhd)$ produces a repair that is larger than a base computed by $Elect(\mathcal{A}, \unrhd)$. However $Partial_{PR}(\mathcal{A}, \unrhd)$ is intractable since the complexity of $IAR(\mathcal{A}, \unrhd)$ is coNP [8] if $\unrhd$ is simply a total preorder. Thus Proposition 1 no longer holds.

Beyond DL-Lite. Another question is whether one can generalize the Elect method to partially preordered ABoxes expressed in logics other than DL-Lite? From a semantic point of view, we see no limitations and the obtained results would also collapse with IAR (for flat ABoxes) and non-defeated repair (for totally preordered ABoxes). However from a computational point of view, it is mandatory to have an efficient way to handle conflicts in order for Proposition 1 to still hold. In particular, assertional conflicts $\mathcal{C} \in \mathcal{C}(\mathcal{A})$ need not be binary (i.e. involve two assertions) provided that they can be computed in polynomial time. In the presence of non-binary conflicts, we need to redefine the notion of an elected assertion as the one that is more preferred than all its conflicting assertions. This would allow for our characterization (without computing all total preorders) to still hold. Hence, $Elect(\mathcal{A}, \unrhd)$ could be generalized into languages that are more expressive than DL-Lite provided that the computation of conflicts is efficient.

7   Conclusion

We tackled the problem of restoring consistency of a partially preordered ABox that may be inconsistent w.r.t. the TBox in DL-Lite ontologies. We proposed a method called Elect which generalizes the IAR semantics (flat ABox) and the non-defeated semantics (totally preordered ABox). Basically, using Elect, a partial preorder is viewed as a family of total preorders to which non-defeated inference is applied, thus producing non-defeated repairs. We introduced the concept of elected assertions that help us to have an equivalent characterization of Elect. Most importantly, we showed that the complexity of Elect is polynomial. In future work, we plan to investigate the three issues raised in Sect. 6 on how to go beyond Elect.

Acknowledgements. This work was supported by the European project H2020-MSCA-RISE: AniAge (High Dimensional Heterogeneous Data based Animation Techniques for Southeast Asian Intangible Cultural Heritage).

References

1. Baader, F., Calvanese, D., Mcguinness, D., Nardi, D., Patel-Schneider, P.: The Description Logic Handbook: Theory, Implementation, and Applications (2007)
2. Baget, J., et al.: A general modifier-based framework for inconsistency-tolerant query answering. In: KR, Cape Town, South Africa, pp. 513–516 (2016)
3. Benferhat, S., Bouraoui, Z., Tabia, K.: How to select one preferred assertional-based repair from inconsistent and prioritized DL-Lite knowledge bases? In: IJCAI, Buenos Aires, Argentina, pp. 1450–1456 (2015)
4. Benferhat, S., Dubois, D., Prade, H.: Representing default rules in possibilistic logic. In: Knowledge Representation and Reasoning, pp. 673–684 (1992)
5. Benferhat, S., Dubois, D., Prade, H.: Some syntactic approaches to the handling of inconsistent knowledge bases: a comparative study: Part 2: the prioritized case. Studia Logica **24**, 473–511 (1998). Physica-Verlag, Heidelberg
6. Benferhat, S., Bouraoui, Z., Chadhry, H., Fc, M.S.B.M.R., Tabia, K., Telli, A.: Characterizing non-defeated repairs in inconsistent lightweight ontologies. In: SITIS, pp. 282–287 (2016)
7. Benferhat, S., Lagrue, S., Papini, O.: Reasoning with partially ordered information in a possibilistic logic framework. Fuzzy Sets Syst. **144**(1), 25–41 (2004)
8. Bienvenu, M., Bourgaux, C., Goasdoué, F.: Querying inconsistent description logic knowledge bases under preferred repair semantics. In: AAAI, pp. 996–1002 (2014)
9. Bienvenu, M., Rosati, R.: Tractable approximations of consistent query answering for robust ontology-based data access. In: IJCAI, pp. 775–781 (2013)
10. Bienvenu, M., Bourgaux, C.: Inconsistency-tolerant querying of description logic knowledge bases. In: Pan, J.Z., et al. (eds.) Reasoning Web 2016. LNCS, vol. 9885, pp. 156–202. Springer, Cham (2017). https://doi.org/10.1007/978-3-319-49493-7_5

11. Brewka, G.: Preferred subtheories: an extended logical framework for default reasoning. In: IJCAI, pp. 1043–1048 (1989)
12. Calvanese, D., Kharlamov, E., Nutt, W., Zheleznyakov, D.: Evolution of DL-lite knowledge bases. In: International Semantic Web Conference, vol. 1. pp. 112–128 (2010)
13. Calvanese, D., De Giacomo, G., Lembo, D., Lenzerini, M., Rosati, R.: Tractable reasoning and efficient query answering in description logics: the DL-Lite family. J. Autom. Reason. **39**(3), 385–429 (2007)
14. Cozman, F.G.: Credal networks. Artif. Intell. J. **120**, 199–233 (2000)
15. Du, J., Qi, G., Shen, Y.: Weight-based consistent query answering over inconsistent SHIQ knowledge bases. Knowl. Inf. Syst. **34**(2), 335–371 (2013)
16. Dubois, D., Fargier, H., Prade, H.: Ordinal and probabilistic representations of acceptance. J. AI Res. **22**, 23–56 (2004)
17. Lembo, D., Lenzerini, M., Rosati, R., Ruzzi, M., Savo, D.F.: Inconsistency-tolerant semantics for description logics. In: Hitzler, P., Lukasiewicz, T. (eds.) RR 2010. LNCS, vol. 6333, pp. 103–117. Springer, Heidelberg (2010). https://doi.org/10. 1007/978-3-642-15918-3_9
18. Martinez, M.V., Parisi, F., Pugliese, A., Simari, G.I., Subrahmanian, V.S.: Inconsistency management policies. In: KRR, pp. 367–377. AAAI Press (2008)
19. Rescher, N., Manor, R.: On inference from inconsistent premisses. Theory Decis. **1**(2), 179–217 (1970)
20. Staworko, S., Chomicki, J., Marcinkowski, J.: Prioritized repairing and consistent query answering in relational databases. AMAI **64**(2–3), 209–246 (2012)
21. Telli, A., Benferhat, S., Bourahla, M., Bouraoui, Z., Tabia, K.: Polynomial algorithms for computing a single preferred assertional-based repair. KI **31**(1), 15–30 (2017)
22. Touazi, F., Cayrol, C., Dubois, D.: Possibilistic reasoning with partially ordered beliefs. J. Appl. Log. **13**(4), 770–798 (2015)
23. Trivela, D., Stoilos, G., Vassalos, V.: Querying expressive DL ontologies under the ICAR semantics. In: Proceedings of the 31st DL Workshop, Tempe, USA (2018)

Elaboration Tolerant Representation of Markov Decision Process via Decision-Theoretic Extension of Probabilistic Action Language $p\mathcal{BC}+$

Yi Wang[(✉)] and Joohyung Lee

School of Computing, Informatics, and Decision Systems Engineering,
Arizona State University, Tempe, USA
{ywang485,joolee}@asu.edu

Abstract. We extend probabilistic action language $p\mathcal{BC}+$ with the notion of utility in decision theory. The semantics of the extended $p\mathcal{BC}+$ can be defined as a shorthand notation for a decision-theoretic extension of the probabilistic answer set programming language LP^{MLN}. Alternatively, the semantics of $p\mathcal{BC}+$ can also be defined in terms of Markov Decision Process (MDP), which in turn allows for representing MDP in a succinct and elaboration tolerant way as well as leveraging an MDP solver to compute a $p\mathcal{BC}+$ action description. The idea led to the design of the system PBCPLUS2MDP, which can find an optimal policy of a $p\mathcal{BC}+$ action description using an MDP solver.

Keywords: Answer set programming · Action language ·
Markov Decision Process

1 Introduction

Many problems in Artificial Intelligence are about what actions to choose to maximize the agent's utility. Since actions may also have stochastic effects, the main computational task is, rather than to find a sequence of actions that leads to a goal, to find an optimal policy, that states which actions to execute in each state to achieve the maximum expected utility.

While a few decades of research on action languages has produced several expressive languages, such as $\mathcal{A}$ [5], $\mathcal{B}$ [6], $\mathcal{C}+$ [7], $\mathcal{BC}$ [8], and $\mathcal{BC}+$ [1], that are able to describe actions and their effects in a succinct and elaboration tolerant way, these languages are not equipped with constructs to represent stochastic actions and the utility of a decision. In this paper, we present an action language that overcomes the limitation. Our method is to equip probabilistic action language $p\mathcal{BC}+$ [11] with the notion of utility and define policy optimization problems in that language.

Following the way that $p\mathcal{BC}+$ is defined as a shorthand notation of probabilistic answer set programming language LP^{MLN} for describing a probabilistic

ⓒ Springer Nature Switzerland AG 2019
M. Balduccini et al. (Eds.): LPNMR 2019, LNAI 11481, pp. 224–238, 2019.
https://doi.org/10.1007/978-3-030-20528-7_17

transition system, we first extend LP^{MLN} by associating a utility measure to each soft stable model in addition to its already defined probability. We call this extension DT-LP^{MLN}. Next, we define a decision-theoretic extension of $p\mathcal{BC}+$ as a shorthand notation for DT-LP^{MLN}. It turns out that the semantics of $p\mathcal{BC}+$ can also be directly defined in terms of Markov Decision Process (MDP), which in turn allows us to define MDP in a succinct and elaboration tolerant way. The result is theoretically interesting as it formally relates action languages to MDP despite their different origins, and furthermore justifies the semantics of the extended $p\mathcal{BC}+$ in terms of MDP. It is also computationally interesting because it allows for applying a number of algorithms developed for MDP to computing $p\mathcal{BC}+$. Based on this idea, we design the system PBCPLUS2MDP, which turns a $p\mathcal{BC}+$ action description into the input language of an MDP solver and leverages MDP solving to find an optimal policy for the $p\mathcal{BC}+$ action description.

The extended $p\mathcal{BC}+$ can thus be viewed as a high-level representation of MDP that allows for compact and elaboration tolerant encodings of sequential decision problems. Compared to other MDP-based planning description languages, such as PPDDL [18] and RDDL [13], it inherits the nonmonotonicity of the stable model semantics to be able to compactly represent recursive definitions and indirect effects of actions, which can save the state space significantly. Section 5 contains such an example.

This paper is organized as follows. After Sect. 2 reviews preliminaries, Sect. 3 extends LP^{MLN} with the notion of utility, through which we define the extension of $p\mathcal{BC}+$ with utility in Sect. 4. Section 5 defines $p\mathcal{BC}+$ as a high-level representation language for MDP and presents the prototype system PBCPLUS2MDP. We discuss the related work in Sect. 6.

2 Preliminaries

Due to the space limit, the reviews are brief. We refer the reader to the original papers [10,11], or the technical report of this paper [15] for the reviews of preliminaries. The technical report also contains all proofs and experiments with the system PBCPLUS2MDP.

2.1 Review: Action Language $p\mathcal{BC}+$

Like $\mathcal{BC}$ and $\mathcal{BC}+$, language $p\mathcal{BC}+$ assumes that a propositional signature σ is constructed from "constants" and their "values." A *constant* c is a symbol that is associated with a finite set $Dom(c)$, called the *domain*. The signature σ is constructed from a finite set of constants, consisting of atoms $c = v$ for every constant c and every element v in $Dom(c)$. If the domain of c is {FALSE, TRUE}, then we say that c is *Boolean*, and abbreviate $c=$TRUE as c and $c=$FALSE as $\sim c$.

There are four types of constants in $p\mathcal{BC}+$: *fluent constants*, *action constants*, *pf (probability fact) constants* and *initpf (initial probability fact) constants*. Fluent constants are further divided into *regular* and *statically determined*. The domain of every action constant is restricted to Boolean. An *action description*

Causal Laws	Syntax	Translation into LP^{MLN}
static law	**caused** F **if** G where F and G are fluent formulas	$i:F \leftarrow i:G$ $(i \in \{0,\ldots,m\})$
fluent dynamic law	**caused** F **if** G **after** H where F and G are fluent formulas, H is a formula, F does not contain statically determined constants and H does not contain initpf constants	$i{+}1:F \leftarrow (i{+}1:G) \wedge (i:H)$ $(i \in \{0,\ldots,m-1\})$
pf constant declaration	**caused** $c = \{v_1 : p_1, \ldots, v_n : p_n\}$ where c is a pf constant with domain $\{v_1,\ldots,v_n\}$, $0 < p_i < 1$ for each $i \in \{1,\ldots,n\}$ and $\sum\limits_{i \in \{1,\ldots,n\}} p_i = 1$	For each $j \in \{1,\ldots,n\}$: $ln(p_i) : (i{:}c) = v_j$ $(i \in \{0,\ldots,m-1\})$
initpf constant declaration	**caused** $c = \{v_1 : p_1, \ldots, v_n : p_n\}$ where c is a initpf constant with domain $\{v_1,\ldots,v_n\}$, $0 < p_i < 1$ for each $i \in \{1,\ldots,n\}$	For each $j \in \{1,\ldots,n\}$: $ln(p_i) : (0{:}c) = v_j$
initial static law	**initially** F **if** G where F is a fluent constant and G is a formula that contains neither action constants nor pf constants	$\bot \leftarrow \neg(0{:}F) \wedge 0{:}G$

Fig. 1. Causal laws in $p\mathcal{BC}+$ and their translations into LP^{MLN}

is a finite set of *causal laws*, which describes how fluents depend on each other statically and how their values change from one time step to another. Figure 1 lists causal laws in $p\mathcal{BC}+$ and their translations into LP^{MLN}. A *fluent formula* is a formula such that all constants occurring in it are fluent constants.

We use σ^{fl} (σ^{act}, σ^{pf}, and σ^{initpf}, respectively) to denote the set of all atoms $c = v$ where c is a fluent constant (action constant, pf constant, initpf constant, respectively) of σ and v is in $Dom(c)$. For any subset σ' of σ and any $i \in \{0,\ldots,m\}$, we use $i:\sigma'$ to denote the set $\{i:A \mid A \in \sigma'\}$. For any formula F of signature σ, by $i:F$ we denote the result of inserting $i:$ in front of every occurrence of every constant in F.

The semantics of a $p\mathcal{BC}+$ action description D is defined by a translation into an LP^{MLN} program $Tr(D,m) = D_{init} \cup D_m$. Below we describe the essential part of the translation that turns a $p\mathcal{BC}+$ description into an LP^{MLN} program.

The signature σ_m of D_m consists of atoms of the form $i:c = v$ such that

- for each fluent constant c of D, $i \in \{0,\ldots,m\}$ and $v \in Dom(c)$,
- for each action constant or pf constant c of D, $i \in \{0,\ldots,m-1\}$ and $v \in Dom(c)$.

D_m contains LP^{MLN} rules obtained from static laws, fluent dynamic laws, and pf constant declarations as described in the third column of Fig. 1, as well as $\{0:c = v\}^{\mathrm{ch}}$ for every regular fluent constant c and every $v \in Dom(c)$, and $\{i:c = \mathrm{TRUE}\}^{\mathrm{ch}}, \{i:c = \mathrm{FALSE}\}^{\mathrm{ch}}$ ($i \in \{0,\ldots,m-1\}$) for every action constant c to state that the fluents at time 0 and the actions at each time are exogenous.[1] D_{init} contains LP^{MLN} rules obtained from initial static laws and initpf constant declarations as described in the third column of Fig. 1. Both D_m and D_{init} also contain constraints asserting that each constant is mapped to exactly one value

---

[1] $\{A\}^{\mathrm{ch}}$ denotes the choice rule $A \leftarrow not\ not\ A$.

in its domain. In the presence of these constraints, we identify an interpretation of σ_m with the value assignment function that maps each constant to its value.

For any LP^{MLN} program Π of signature σ_1 and an interpretation I of a subset σ_2 of σ_1, we say I is a *residual (probabilistic) stable model* of Π if there exists an interpretation J of $\sigma_1 \setminus \sigma_2$ such that $I \cup J$ is a (probabilistic) stable model of Π.

For any interpretation I of σ, by $i:I$ we denote the interpretation of $i:\sigma$ such that $i:I \models (i:c) = v$ iff $I \models c = v$. For $x \in \{act, fl, pf\}$, we use σ_m^x to denote the subset of σ_m, which is $\{i:c = v \in \sigma_m \mid c = v \in \sigma^x\}$.

A *state* of D is an interpretation I^{fl} of σ^{fl} such that $0:I^{fl}$ is a residual (probabilistic) stable model of D_0. A *transition* of D is a triple $\langle s, e, s' \rangle$ where s and s' are interpretations of σ^{fl} and e is an interpretation of σ^{act} such that $0:s \cup 0:e \cup 1:s'$ is a residual stable model of D_1. A *pf-transition* of D is a pair $(\langle s, e, s' \rangle, pf)$, where pf is a value assignment to σ^{pf} such that $0:s \cup 0:e \cup 1:s' \cup 0:pf$ is a stable model of D_1.

The following simplifying assumptions are made on action descriptions in $p\mathcal{BC}+$.

1. **No Concurrency**: For all transitions $\langle s, e, s' \rangle$, we have $e \models a = \text{TRUE}$ for at most one action constant a;
2. **Nondeterministic Transitions are Determined by pf constants**: For any state s, any value assignment e of σ^{act}, and any value assignment pf of σ^{pf}, there exists exactly one state s' such that $(\langle s, e, s' \rangle, pf)$ is a pf-transition;
3. **Nondeterminism on Initial States are Determined by Initpf constants**: For any value assignment pf_{init} of σ^{initpf}, there exists exactly one value assignment fl of σ^{fl} such that $0:pf_{init} \cup 0:fl$ is a stable model of $D_{init} \cup D_0$.

With the above three assumptions, the probability of a history, i.e., a sequence of states and actions, can be computed as the product of the probabilities of all the transitions that the history is composed of, multiplied by the probability of the initial state (Corollary 1 in [11]).

2.2 Review: Markov Decision Process

A *Markov Decision Process (MDP)* M is a tuple $\langle S, A, T, R \rangle$ where (i) S is a set of states; (ii) A is a set of actions; (iii) $T : S \times A \times S \to [0, 1]$ defines transition probabilities; (iv) $R : S \times A \times S \to \mathbb{R}$ is the reward function.

Given a history $\langle s_0, a_0, s_1, \ldots, s_{m-1}, a_{m-1}, s_m \rangle$ such that each $s_i \in S$ ($i \in \{0, \ldots, m\}$) and each $a_i \in A$ ($i \in \{0, \ldots, m-1\}$), the *total reward* R_M of the history under MDP M is defined as

$$R_M(\langle s_0, a_0, s_1, \ldots, s_{m-1}, a_{m-1}, s_m \rangle) = \sum_{i=0}^{m-1} R(s_i, a_i, s_{i+1}).$$

The probability P_M of $\langle s_0, a_0, s_1, \ldots, s_{m-1}, a_{m-1}, s_m \rangle$ under MDP is defined as

$$P_M(\langle s_0, a_0, s_1, \ldots, s_{m-1}, a_{m-1}, s_m \rangle) = \prod_{i=0}^{m-1} T(s_i, a_i, s_{i+1}).$$

A *non-stationary policy* $\pi : S \times ST \mapsto A$ is a function from $S \times ST$ to A, where $ST = \{0, \ldots, m-1\}$. The *expected total reward* of a non-stationary policy π starting from the initial state s_0 under MDP M is

$$ER_M(\pi, s_0) = \underset{\substack{\langle s_1, \ldots, s_m \rangle: \\ s_i \in S \text{ for } i \in \{1, \ldots, m\}}}{E} [R_M(\langle s_0, \pi(s_0, 0), s_1, \ldots, s_{m-1}, \pi(s_{m-1}, m-1), s_m \rangle)]$$

$$= \sum_{\substack{\langle s_1, \ldots, s_m \rangle: \\ s_i \in S \text{ for } i \in \{1, \ldots, m\}}} \left(\sum_{i=0}^{m-1} R(s_i, \pi(s_i, i), s_{i+1}) \right) \times \left(\prod_{i=0}^{m-1} T(s_i, \pi(s_i, i), s_{i+1}) \right).$$

The *finite horizon policy optimization* problem starting from s_0 is to find a non-stationary policy π that maximizes its expected total reward starting from s_0, i.e., $\mathrm{argmax}_\pi \ ER_M(\pi, s_0)$.

Various algorithms for MDP policy optimization have been developed, such as value iteration [3] for exact solutions, and Q-learning [16] for approximate solutions.

3   DT-LP^{MLN}

We extend the syntax and the semantics of LP^{MLN} to DT-LP^{MLN} by introducing atoms of the form

$$\texttt{utility}(u, t) \tag{1}$$

where u is a real number, and t is an arbitrary list of terms. These atoms can only occur in the head of hard rules of the form

$$\alpha : \texttt{utility}(u, t) \leftarrow Body \tag{2}$$

where $Body$ is a list of literals. We call these rules *utility rules*.

The weight and the probability of an interpretation are defined the same as in LP^{MLN}. The *utility* of an interpretation I under Π is defined as

$$U_\Pi(I) = \sum_{\texttt{utility}(u,t) \in I} u.$$

The *expected utility* of a proposition A is defined as

$$E[U_\Pi(A)] = \sum_{I \models A} U_\Pi(I) \times P_\Pi(I \mid A). \tag{3}$$

A DT-LP^{MLN} program is a pair (Π, Dec) where Π is an LP^{MLN} program with a propositional signature σ (including $\texttt{utility}$ atoms) and Dec is a subset of σ consisting of *decision atoms*. We consider two reasoning tasks with DT-LP^{MLN}.

- **Evaluating a Decision.** Given a propositional formula e ("evidence") and a truth assignment dec of decision atoms Dec, represented as a conjunction of literals over atoms in Dec, compute the expected utility of decision dec in the presence of evidence e, i.e., compute

$$E[U_\Pi(dec \wedge e)] = \sum_{I \models dec \wedge e} U_\Pi(I) \times P_\Pi(I \mid dec \wedge e).$$

- **Finding a Decision with Maximum Expected Utility (MEU).** Given a propositional formula e ("evidence"), find the truth assignment dec on Dec such that the expected utility of dec in the presence of e is maximized, i.e., compute

$$\underset{dec \,:\, dec \text{ is a truth assignment on } Dec}{\operatorname{argmax}} E[U_\Pi(dec \wedge e)]. \tag{4}$$

Example 1. Consider a directed graph G representing a social network: (i) each vertex $v \in V(G)$ represents a person; each edge (v_1, v_2) represents that v_1 influences v_2; (ii) each edge $e = (v_1, v_2)$ is associated with a probability p_e representing the probability of the influence; (iii) each vertex v is associated with a cost c_v, representing the cost of marketing the product to v; (iv) each person who buys the product yields a reward of r.

The goal is to choose a subset U of vertices as marketing targets so as to maximize the expected profit. The problem can be represented as a DT-LP^{MLN} program Π^{market} as follows:

$$\alpha : buy(v) \leftarrow marketTo(v).$$
$$\alpha : buy(v_2) \leftarrow buy(v_1), influence(v_1, v_2).$$
$$\alpha : utility(r, v) \leftarrow buy(v).$$

with the graph instance represented as follows:

- for each edge $e = (v_1, v_2)$, we introduce a probabilistic fact $ln(\frac{p_e}{1-p_e}) :$ $influence(v_1, v_2)$;
- for each vertex $v \in V(G)$, we introduce the following rule:
$\alpha : \mathtt{utility}(-c_v, v) \leftarrow marketTo(v).$

For simplicity, we assume that marketing to a person guarantees that the person buys the product. This assumption can be removed easily by changing the first rule to a soft rule.

The MEU solution of DT-LP^{MLN} program ($\Pi^{\mathrm{market}}, \{marketTo(v) \mid v \in V(G)\}$) corresponds to the subset U of vertices that maximizes the expected profit.

For example, consider the directed graph on the right, where each edge e is labeled by p_e and each vertex v is labeled by c_v. Suppose the reward for each person buying the product is 10. There are $2^6 = 64$ different truth assignments on decision atoms, corresponding to 64 choices of marketing targets. The best decision is to market to `Alice` only, which yields the expected utility of 17.96.

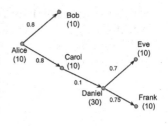

4 $p\mathcal{BC}+$ with Utility

We extend $p\mathcal{BC}+$ by introducing the following expression called *utility law* that assigns a reward to transitions:

$$\textbf{reward } v \textbf{ if } F \textbf{ after } G \tag{5}$$

where v is a real number representing the reward, F is a formula that contains fluent constants only, and G is a formula that contains fluent constants and action constants only (no pf, no initpf constants). We extend the signature of $Tr(D, m)$ with a set of atoms of the form (1). We turn a utility law of the form (5) into the LP^{MLN} rule

$$\alpha : \texttt{utility}(v, i+1, id) \ \leftarrow \ (i+1 : F) \wedge (i : G) \tag{6}$$

where id is a unique number assigned to the LP^{MLN} rule and $i \in \{0, \dots, m-1\}$.

Given a nonnegative integer m denoting the maximum timestamp, a $p\mathcal{BC}+$ action description D with utility over multi-valued propositional signature σ is defined as a high-level representation of the DT-LP^{MLN} program $(Tr(D, m), \sigma_m^{act})$.

We extend the definition of a probabilistic transition system as follows: A *probabilistic transition system $T(D)$* represented by a probabilistic action description D is a labeled directed graph such that the vertices are the states of D, and the edges are obtained from the transitions of D: for every transition $\langle s, e, s' \rangle$ of D, an edge labeled $e : p, u$ goes from s to s', where $p = Pr_{D_1}(1 : s' \mid 0 : s \wedge 0 : e)$ and $u = E[U_{D_1}(0 : s \wedge 0 : e \wedge 1 : s')]$. The number p is called the *transition probability* of $\langle s, e, s' \rangle$, denoted by $p(s, e, s')$, and the number u is called the *transition reward* of $\langle s, e, s' \rangle$, denoted by $u(s, e, s')$.

Example 2. The following action description D^{simple} describes a simple probabilistic action domain with two Boolean fluents P, Q, and two actions A and B. A causes P to be true with probability 0.8, and if P is true, then B causes Q to be true with probability 0.7. The agent receives the reward 10 if P and Q become true for the first time (after then, it remains in the state $\{P, Q\}$ as it is an absorbing state).

A causes P **if** Pf_1

B causes Q **if** $P \wedge Pf_2$

inertial P, Q

constraint $\neg(Q \wedge \sim P)$

caused $Pf_1 = \{\text{TRUE} : 0.8, \text{FALSE} : 0.2\}$

caused $Pf_2 = \{\text{TRUE} : 0.7, \text{FALSE} : 0.3\}$

reward 10 **if** $P \wedge Q$ **after** $\neg(P \wedge Q)$

caused $InitP = \{\text{TRUE} : 0.6, \text{FALSE} : 0.4\}$

initially $P = x$ **if** $InitP = x$

caused $InitQ = \{\text{TRUE} : 0.5, \text{FALSE} : 0.5\}$

initially Q **if** $InitQ \wedge P$

initially $\sim Q$ **if** $\sim P$.

The transition system $T(D^{simple})$ is as follows:

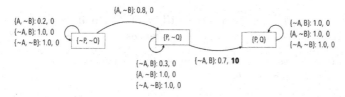

4.1 Policy Optimization

Given a $p\mathcal{BC}+$ action description D, we use $\mathbf{S}$ to denote the set of states, i.e, the set of interpretations I^{fl} of σ^{fl} such that $0 : I^{fl}$ is a residual (probabilistic) stable model of D_0. We use $\mathbf{A}$ to denote the set of interpretations I^{act} of σ^{act} such that $0 : I^{act}$ is a residual (probabilistic) stable model of D_1. Since we assume at most one action is executed each time step, each element in $\mathbf{A}$ makes either only one action or none to be true.

A *(non-stationary) policy* π (in $p\mathcal{BC}+$) is a function $\pi : \mathbf{S} \times \{0, \dots, m-1\} \mapsto \mathbf{A}$ that maps a state and a time step to an action (including doing nothing). By $\langle s_0, s_1 \dots, s_m \rangle^t$ (each $s_i \in \mathbf{S}$) we denote the formula $0 : s_0 \wedge 1 : s_1 \wedge \cdots \wedge m : s_m$, and by $\langle s_0, a_0, s_1 \dots, s_{m-1}, a_{m-1}, s_m \rangle^t$ (each $s_i \in \mathbf{S}$ and each $a_i \in \mathbf{A}$) the formula

$$0 : s_0 \wedge 0 : a_0 \wedge 1 : s_1 \wedge \cdots \wedge m-1 : a_{m-1} \wedge m : s_m.$$

We say a state s is *consistent* with D_{init} if there exists at least one probabilistic stable model I of D_{init} such that $I \models 0 : s$. The *Policy Optimization* problem from the initial state s_0 is to find a policy π that maximizes the expected utility starting from s_0, i.e., π with

$$\operatorname*{argmax}_{\pi \text{ is a policy}} E[U_{Tr(\Pi,m)}(C_{\pi,m} \cup \langle s_0 \rangle^t)]$$

where $C_{\pi,m}$ is the following formula representing policy π:

$$\bigwedge_{s \in \mathbf{S},\ \pi(s,i)=a,\ i \in \{0,\dots,m-1\}} i : s \rightarrow i : a.$$

We define the *total reward* of a history $\langle s_0, a_0, s_1, \dots, s_m \rangle$ *under the action description* D as

$$R_D(\langle s_0, a_0, s_1, \dots, s_m \rangle) = E[U_{Tr(D,m)}(\langle s_0, a_0, s_1, a_1, \dots, a_{m-1}, s_m \rangle^t)].$$

Although it is defined as an expectation, the following proposition tells us that any stable model X of $Tr(D,m)$ such that $X \models \langle s_0, a_0, s_1, \ldots, s_m \rangle$ has the same utility, and consequently, the expected utility of $\langle s_0, a_0, s_1, \ldots, s_m \rangle$ is the same as the utility of any single stable model that satisfies the history.

Proposition 1. *For any two stable models X_1, X_2 of $Tr(D,m)$ that satisfy a history $\langle s_0, a_0, s_1, a_1, \ldots, a_{m-1}, s_m \rangle$, we have*

$$U_{Tr(D,m)}(X_1) \;=\; U_{Tr(D,m)}(X_2) \;=\; E[U_{Tr(D,m)}(\langle s_0, a_0, s_1, a_1, \ldots, a_{m-1}, s_m \rangle^t)].$$

It can be seen that the expected utility of π can be computed from the expected utility from all possible state sequences.

Proposition 2. *Given any initial state s_0 that is consistent with D_{init}, for any non-stationary policy π, we have*

$$E[U_{Tr(D,m)}(C_{\pi,m} \wedge \langle s_0 \rangle^t)] =$$
$$\sum_{\langle s_1, \ldots, s_m \rangle : s_i \in \mathbf{S}} R_D(\langle s_0, \pi(s_0), s_1, \ldots, \pi(s_{m-1}), s_m \rangle) \times P_{Tr(D,m)}(\langle s_0, s_1, \ldots, s_m \rangle^t \mid \langle s_0 \rangle^t \wedge C_{\pi,m}).$$

Definition 1. *For a pBC+ action description D, let $M(D)$ be the MDP $\langle S, A, T, R \rangle$ where (i) the state set S is $\mathbf{S}$; (ii) the action set A is $\mathbf{A}$; (iii) transition probability T is defined as $T(s, a, s') = P_{D_1}(1 : s' \mid 0 : s \wedge 0 : a)$; (iv) reward function R is defined as $R(s, a, s') = E[U_{D_1}(0 : s \wedge 0 : a \wedge 1 : s')]$.*

We show that the policy optimization problem for a $pBC+$ action description D can be reduced to the policy optimization problem for $M(D)$ for the finite horizon. The following theorem tells us that for any history following a non-stationary policy, its total reward and probability under D defined under the $pBC+$ semantics coincide with those under the corresponding MDP $M(D)$.

Theorem 1. *Given an initial state $s_0 \in \mathbf{S}$ that is consistent with D_{init}, for any non-stationary policy π and any finite state sequence $\langle s_0, s_1, \ldots, s_{m-1}, s_m \rangle$ such that each s_i in $\mathbf{S}$ ($i \in \{0, \ldots, m\}$), we have*

- $R_D(\langle s_0, \pi(s_0), s_1, \ldots, \pi(s_{m-1}), s_m \rangle) = R_{M(D)}(\langle s_0, \pi(s_0,) \ldots, \pi(s_{m-1}), s_m \rangle)$
- $P_{Tr(D,m)}(\langle s_0, s_1, \ldots, s_m \rangle^t \mid \langle s_0 \rangle^t \wedge C_{\pi,m}) = P_{M(D)}(\langle s_0, \pi(s_0,) \ldots, \pi(s_{m-1}), s_m \rangle).$

It follows that the policy optimization problem for $pBC+$ action descriptions coincides with the policy optimization problem for MDP with finite horizon.

Theorem 2. *For any nonnegative integer m and an initial state $s_0 \in \mathbf{S}$ that is consistent with D_{init}, we have*

$$\underset{\pi \text{ is a non-stationary policy}}{argmax} E[U_{Tr(D,m)}(C_{\pi,m} \wedge \langle s_0 \rangle^t)] = \underset{\pi \text{ is a non-stationary policy}}{argmax} ER_{M(D)}(\pi, s_0).$$

Theorem 2 justifies using an implementation of DT-LP^{MLN} to compute optimal policies of MDP $M(D)$ as well as using an MDP solver to compute optimal policies of the $pBC+$ descriptions. Furthermore, the theorems above allow us to check the properties of MDP $M(D)$ by using formal properties of LP^{MLN}, such as whether a certain state is reachable in a given number of steps.

5 $p\mathcal{BC}+$ as a High-Level Representation Language of MDP

An action description consists of causal laws in a human-readable form describing the action domain in a compact and high-level way, whereas it is non-trivial to describe an MDP instance directly from the domain description in English. The result in the previous section shows how to construct an MDP instance $M(D)$ for a $p\mathcal{BC}+$ action description D so that the solution to the policy optimization problem of D coincide with that of MDP $M(D)$. In that sense, $p\mathcal{BC}+$ can be viewed as a high-level representation language for MDP.

As its semantics is defined in terms of $\mathrm{LP}^{\mathrm{MLN}}$, $p\mathcal{BC}+$ inherits the nonmonotonicity of the stable model semantics to be able to compactly represent recursive definitions or transitive closure. The static laws in $p\mathcal{BC}+$ prune out invalid states to ensure that only meaningful value combinations of fluents will be given to MDP as states, thus reducing the size of state space at the MDP level.

Example 3. **Robot and Blocks**   *There are two rooms* R1, R2, *and three blocks* B1, B2, B3 *that are originally located in* R1. *A robot can stack one block on top of another block if the two blocks are in the same room. The robot can also move a block to a different room, resulting in all blocks above it also moving if successful (with probability p). Each moving action has a cost of 1. What is the best way to move all blocks to* R2?

The example can be represented in $p\mathcal{BC}+$ as follows. x, x_1, x_2 *range over* B1, B2, B3; r, r_1, r_2 *ranges over* R1, R2. *TopClear(x), Above(x_1, x_2), and GoalNotAchieved are Boolean statically determined fluent constants; In(x) is a regular fluent constant with Domain* {R1, R2}, *and OnTopOf(x_1, x_2) is a Boolean regular fluent constant. MoveTo(x, r) and StackOn(x_1, x_2) are action constants and Pf_Move is a Boolean pf constant. In this example, we make the goal state absorbing, i.e., when all the blocks are already in* R2, *then all actions have no effect.*

Moving block x to room r causes x to be in r with probability p:

> *MoveTo(x, r)* **causes** *In(x) = r* **if** *Pf_Move ∧ GoalNotAchieved*
> **caused** *Pf_Move* = {TRUE : *p*, FALSE : 1 − *p*}.

Successfully Moving a block x_1 to a room r_2 causes x_1 to be no longer underneath the block x_2 that x_1 was underneath in the previous step, if r_2 is different from where x_2 is:

> *MoveTo(x_1, r_2)* **causes** ∼ *OnTopOf(x_1, x_2)*
> **if** *Pf_Move ∧ In(x_1) = r_1 ∧ OnTopOf(x_1, x_2) ∧ GoalNotAchieved*   ($r_1 \neq r_2$).

Stacking a block x_1 on another block x_2 causes x_1 to be on top of x_2, if the top of x_2 is clear, and x_1 and x_2 are at the same location:

> *StackOn(x_1, x_2)* **causes** *OnTopOf(x_1, x_2)*
> **if** *TopClear(x_2) ∧ At(x_1) = r ∧ At(x_2) = r ∧ GoalNotAchieved($x_1 \neq x_2$).*

Stacking a block x_1 on another block x_2 causes x_1 to be no longer on top of the block x where x_1 was originally on top of:

$$StackOn(x_1, x_2) \textbf{ causes } \sim OnTopOf(x_1, x) \textbf{ if } TopClear(x_2) \wedge At(x_1) = r \wedge At(x_2) = r \wedge$$
$$OnTopOf(x_1, x) \wedge GoalNotAchieved \qquad\qquad (x_2 \neq x, x_1 \neq x_2).$$

Two different blocks cannot be on top of the same block, and a block cannot be on top of two different blocks:

$$\textbf{constraint } \neg(OnTopOf(x_1, x) \wedge OnTopOf(x_2, x)) \qquad\qquad (x_1 \neq x_2)$$
$$\textbf{constraint } \neg(OnTopOf(x, x_1) \wedge OnTopOf(x, x_2)) \qquad\qquad (x_1 \neq x_2).$$

By default, the top of a block x is clear. It is not clear if there is another block x_1 that is on top of it:

$$\textbf{default } TopClear(x)$$
$$\textbf{caused } \sim TopClear(x) \textbf{ if } OnTopOf(x_1, x).$$

The relation Above between two blocks is the transitive closure of the relation OnTopOf: A block x_1 is above another block x_2 if x_1 is on top of x_2, or there is another block x such that x_1 is above x and x is above x_2:

$$\textbf{caused } Above(x_1, x_2) \textbf{ if } OnTopOf(x_1, x_2)$$
$$\textbf{caused } Above(x_1, x_2) \textbf{ if } Above(x_1, x) \wedge Above(x, x_2).$$

One block cannot be above itself; two blocks cannot be above each other:

$$\textbf{caused } \bot \textbf{ if } Above(x_1, x_2) \wedge Above(x_2, x_1).$$

If a block x_1 is above another block x_2, then x_1 has the same location as x_2:

$$\textbf{caused } At(x_1) = r \textbf{ if } Above(x_1, x_2) \wedge At(x_2) = r. \qquad\qquad (7)$$

Each moving action has a cost of 1:

$$\textbf{reward } -1 \textbf{ if } \top \textbf{ after } MoveTo(x, r).$$

Achieving the goal when the goal is not previously achieved yields a reward of 10:

$$\textbf{reward } 10 \textbf{ if } \sim GoalNotAchieved \textbf{ after } GoalNotAchieved.$$

The goal is not achieved if there exists a block x that is not at R2. It is achieved otherwise:

$$\textbf{caused } GoalNotAchieved \textbf{ if } At(x) = r \quad (r \neq R2)$$
$$\textbf{default } \sim GoalNotAchieved.$$

$At(x)$ and $OnTopOf(x_1, x_2)$ are inertial:

$$\textbf{inertial } At(x), OnTopOf(x_1, x_2).$$

Finally, we add $a_1 \wedge a_2$ causes $\bot$ for each distinct pair of ground action constants a_1 and a_2, to ensure that at most one action can occur each time step.

It can be seen that stacking all blocks together and moving them at once would be the best strategy to move them to R2.

In Example 3, many value combinations of fluents do not lead to a valid state, such as $\{\,OnTopOf(\texttt{B1},\texttt{B2}),\ OnTopOf(\texttt{B2},\texttt{B1}),\ldots\}$, where the two blocks $\texttt{B1}$ and $\texttt{B2}$ are on top of each other. Moreover, the fluents $TopClear(x)$ and $Above(x_1, x_2)$ are completely dependent on the value of the other fluents. There would be $2^{3+3\times3+3+3\times3} = 2^{24}$ states if we define a state as any value combination of fluents. On the other hand, the static laws in the above action description reduce the number of states to only $(13 + 9) \times 2 = 44.^2$

Furthermore, in this example, $Above(x, y)$ needs to be defined as a transitive closure of $OnTopOf(x, y)$, so that the effects of $StackOn(x_1, x_2)$ can be defined in terms of the (inferred) spatial relation of blocks. Also, the static law (7) defines an indirect effect of $MoveTo(x, r)$.

We implemented the prototype system PBCPLUS2MDP, which takes an action description D and time horizon m as input, and finds an optimal policy by constructing the corresponding MDP $M(D)$ and invoking an MDP solver MDP-TOOLBOX.^{3} The current system uses LP^{MLN} 1.0 [9] (http://reasoning.eas.asu. edu/lpmln) for exact inference to find states, actions, transition probabilities, and transition rewards. The system is publicly available at https://github.com/ ywang485/pbcplus2mdp, along with several examples. The current system is not quite scalable because generating exact transition probability and reward matrices requires enumerating all stable models of D_0 and D_1.

6   Related Work

There have been quite a few studies and attempts in defining factored representations of (PO)MDP, with feature-based state descriptions and more compact, human-readable action definitions. PPDDL [18] extends PDDL with constructs for describing probabilistic effects of actions and reward from state transitions. One limitation of PPDDL is the lack of static causal laws, which prohibits PPDDL from expressing recursive definitions or transitive closure. This may yield a large state space to explore as discussed in Sect. 5. RDDL (Relational Dynamic Influence Diagram Language) [13] improves the expressivity of PPDDL in modeling stochastic planning domains by allowing concurrent actions, continuous values of fluents, state constraints, etc. The semantics is defined in terms of lifted dynamic Bayes network extended with influence graph. A lifted planner can utilize the first-order representation and potentially achieve better performance. Still, indirect effects are hard to be represented in RDDL. Compared to PPDDL and RDDL, the advantages of $p\mathcal{BC}+$ are in its simplicity and expressivity originating from the stable model semantics, which allows for elegant representation of recursive definitions, defeasible behaviors, and indirect effects.

Zhang et al. [19] adopt ASP and P-Log [2] which respectively produces a refined set of states and a refined probability distribution over states that are then fed to POMDP solvers for low-level planning. The refined sets of states

---

^{2} This can be verified by counting all possible configurations of 3 blocks with 2 locations.

^{3} https://pymdptoolbox.readthedocs.io.

and probability distribution over states take into account commonsense knowledge about the domain, and thus improve the quality of a plan and reduce computation needed at the POMDP level. Yang *et al.* [17] adopts the (deterministic) action description language $\mathcal{BC}$ for high-level representations of the action domain, which defines high-level actions that can be treated as deterministic. Each action in the generated high-level plan is then mapped into more detailed low-level policies, which takes stochastic effects of low-level actions into account. Similarly, Sridharan *et al.* [14] introduce a framework with planning in a coarse-resolution transition model and a fine-resolution transition model. Action language $\mathcal{AL}_d$ is used for defining the two levels of transition models. The fine-resolution transition model is further turned into a POMDP for detailed planning with stochastic effects of actions and transition rewards. While a $p\mathcal{BC}+$ action description can fully capture all aspects of (PO)MDP including transition probabilities and rewards, the $\mathcal{AL}_d$ action description only provides states, actions and transitions with no quantitative information. Leonetti *et al.* [12], on the other hand, use symbolic reasoners such as ASP to reduce the search space for reinforcement learning based planning methods by generating partial policies from planning results generated by the symbolic reasoner. The exploration of the low-level RL module is constrained by actions that satisfy the partial policy.

Another related work is [4], which combines ASP and reinforcement learning by using action language $\mathcal{BC}+$ as a meta-level description of MDP. The $\mathcal{BC}+$ action descriptions define non-stationary MDPs in the sense that the states and actions can change with new situations occurring in the environment. The algorithm ASP(RL) proposed in this work iteratively calls an ASP solver to obtain states and actions for the RL methods to learn transition probabilities and rewards, and updates the $\mathcal{BC}+$ action description with changes in the environment found by the RL methods, in this way finding optimal policy for a non-stationary MDP with the search space reduced by ASP. The work is similar to ours in that ASP-based high-level logical description is used to generate states and actions for MDP, but the difference is that we use an extension of $\mathcal{BC}+$ that expresses transition probabilities and rewards.

7   Conclusion

Our main contributions are as follows.

- We presented a decision-theoretic extension of LP^{MLN}, through which we extended $p\mathcal{BC}+$ with the language constructs for representing rewards of transitions;
- We showed that the semantics of $p\mathcal{BC}+$ can be equivalently defined in terms of the decision-theoretic LP^{MLN} or MDP;
- We presented the system PBCPLUS2MDP, which solves $p\mathcal{BC}+$ policy optimization problems with an MDP solver.

Formally relating action languages and MDP opens up interesting research to explore. Dynamic programming methods in MDP can be utilized to compute action languages. In turn, action languages may serve as a formal verification tool for MDP as well as a high-level representation language for MDP that describes an MDP instance in a succinct and elaboration tolerant way. As many reinforcement learning tasks use MDP as a modeling language, the work may be related to incorporating symbolic knowledge to reinforcement learning as evidenced by [12,17,19].

DT-LP^{MLN} may deserve attention on its own for static domains. We are currently working on an implementation that extends LP^{MLN} system to handle utility. We expect that the system can be a useful tool for verifying properties for MDP.

The theoretical results in this paper limit attention to MDP in the finite horizon case. When the maximum step m is sufficiently large, we may view it as an approximation of the infinite horizon case, in which case, we allow discount factor γ by replacing v in (6) with $\gamma^{i+1}v$. While it appears intuitive to extend the theoretical results in this paper to the infinite case, it requires extending the definition of LP^{MLN} to allow infinitely many rules, which we leave for future work.

Acknowledgements. We are grateful to the anonymous referees for their useful comments and to Siddharth Srivastava, Zhun Yang, and Yu Zhang for helpful discussions. This work was partially supported by the National Science Foundation under Grant IIS-1815337.

References

1. Babb, J., Lee, J.: Action language $\mathcal{BC}+$. J. Log. Comput. exv062 (2015). https://doi.org/10.1093/logcom/exv062
2. Baral, C., Gelfond, M., Rushton, J.N.: Probabilistic reasoning with answer sets. Theory Pract. Log. Program. **9**(1), 57–144 (2009)
3. Bellman, R.: A markovian decision process. Indiana Univ. Math. J. **6**, 679–684 (1957)
4. Ferreira, L.A., Bianchi, R.A.C., Santos, P.E., de Mantaras, R.L.: Answer set programming for non-stationary Markov decision processes. Appl. Intell. **47**(4), 993–1007 (2017)
5. Gelfond, M., Lifschitz, V.: Representing action and change by logic programs. J. Log. Program. **17**, 301–322 (1993)
6. Gelfond, M., Lifschitz, V.: Action languages. Electron. Trans. Artif. Intell. **3**, 195–210 (1998). http://www.ep.liu.se/ea/cis/1998/016/
7. Giunchiglia, E., Lee, J., Lifschitz, V., McCain, N., Turner, H.: Nonmonotonic causal theories. Artif. Intell. **153**(1–2), 49–104 (2004)
8. Lee, J., Lifschitz, V., Yang, F.: Action language $\mathcal{BC}+$: preliminary report. In: Proceedings of International Joint Conference on Artificial Intelligence (IJCAI) (2013)
9. Lee, J., Talsania, S., Wang, Y.: Computing LPMLN using ASP and MLN solvers. Theory Pract. Log. Program. **17**(5–6), 942–960 (2017)
10. Lee, J., Wang, Y.: Weighted rules under the stable model semantics. In: Proceedings of International Conference on Principles of Knowledge Representation and Reasoning (KR), pp. 145–154 (2016)

11. Lee, J., Wang, Y.: A probabilistic extension of action language $\mathcal{BC}+$. Theory Pract. Log. Program. **18**(3–4), 607–622 (2018)
12. Leonetti, M., Iocchi, L., Stone, P.: A synthesis of automated planning and reinforcement learning for efficient, robust decision-making. Artif. Intell. **241**, 103–130 (2016)
13. Sanner, S.: Relational dynamic influence diagram language (RDDL): language description. Unpublished ms, p. 32. Australian National University (2010)
14. Sridharan, M., Gelfond, M.: Using knowledge representation and reasoning tools in the design of robots. In: Workshop on Knowledge-Based Techniques for Problem Solving and Reasoning (KnowProS) (2016)
15. Wang, Y., Lee, J.: Elaboration tolerant representation of Markov decision process via decision theoretic extension of pBC+. arXiv e-prints (2019). http://arxiv.org/abs/1904.00512
16. Watkins, C.J.C.H.: Learning from delayed rewards. Ph.D. thesis, King's College, Cambridge, UK, May 1989. http://www.cs.rhul.ac.uk/~chrisw/new_thesis.pdf
17. Yang, F., Lyu, D., Liu, B., Gustafson, S.: PEORL: integrating symbolic planning and hierarchical reinforcement learning for robust decision-making. In: Proceedings of International Joint Conference on Artificial Intelligence, pp. 4860–4866 (2018)
18. Younes, H.L., Littman, M.L.: PPDDL1.0: an extension to PDDL for expressing planning domains with probabilistic effects. Technical report, CMU-CS-04-162, April 2004
19. Zhang, S., Stone, P.: CORPP: commonsense reasoning and probabilistic planning, as applied to dialog with a mobile robot. In: Proceedings of the Twenty-Ninth AAAI Conference on Artificial Intelligence, pp. 1394–1400 (2015)

Systems

Evaluation of Disjunctive Programs
in WASP

Mario Alviano[1], Giovanni Amendola[1], Carmine Dodaro[2]([⊠]),
Nicola Leone[1], Marco Maratea[2], and Francesco Ricca[1]

[1] DEMACS, University of Calabria, Rende, Italy
{alviano,amendola,leone,ricca}@mat.unical.it
[2] DIBRIS, University of Genoa, Genoa, Italy
{dodaro,marco}@dibris.unige.it

Abstract. Answer Set Programming (ASP) is a well-established declarative programming language based on logic. The success of ASP is mainly due to the availability of efficient ASP solvers, therefore their development is still an important research topic. In this paper we report the recent improvements of the well-known ASP solver WASP. The new version of WASP includes several improvements of the main solving strategies and advanced reasoning techniques for computing paracoherent answer sets. Indeed, WASP is the first ASP solver handling paracoherent reasoning under two mainstream semantics, namely semi-stable and semi-equilibrium. However, semi-equilibrium semantics may require the introduction of several disjunctive rules, which are usually considered as a source of inefficiency for modern solvers. Such a drawback is addressed in WASP by implementing ad-hoc techniques to efficiently handle disjunctive logic programs. These techniques are presented and evaluated in this paper.

Keywords: Answer set programming · Answer set computation · Disjunctive logic programs

1 Introduction

Answer set programming (ASP) [17] is a declarative formalism for knowledge representation and reasoning based on the stable model semantics [27]. The success of ASP is witnessed by the increasing number of academic and industrial applications [1,11,14,20,28], and it is mainly due to the combination of its high knowledge-modeling power with robust solving technology [5,23]. For this reason, the development of new efficient solvers and solving techniques is still an important research topic.

In this paper we present the progress in the development of the ASP solver WASP [4,5]. Among the features recently included in WASP, advanced reasoning techniques for computing *paracoherent answer sets* [9] are of particular interest, as in fact WASP is the first solver that is able to compute paracoherent

© Springer Nature Switzerland AG 2019
M. Balduccini et al. (Eds.): LPNMR 2019, LNAI 11481, pp. 241–255, 2019.
https://doi.org/10.1007/978-3-030-20528-7_18

answer sets according to two mainstream semantics, namely *semi-stable* and *semi-equilibrium* [10,12,13]. In this context, it is important to emphasize that the evaluation of ASP programs under the semi-equilibrium semantics may lead to a deterioration of the performance of the solver due to a significant amount of disjunctive rules introduced by the implemented algorithm [8].

Disjunctive rules are a common source of inefficiency for many ASP solvers based on the Clark's completion [18], such as CMODELS [29], LP2SAT [30], and CLASP [23]. In particular, in the disjunctive case, such solvers apply a rewriting technique, called *shift* [16], that causes a quadratic blow-up of the input program. This drawback is addressed in WASP by applying a linear rewriting technique that extends Clark's completion to the disjunctive case [3] (see Sect. 3.1). Moreover, disjunctive rules might increase the computational complexity of several reasoning tasks because the evaluation of disjunctive logic programs may require to perform an additional co-NP-complete task, usually referred to as *answer set checking* (or *stability checking*).

Answer set checking is usually carried out by checking the unsatisfiability of a propositional formula, which can be constructed according to different strategies. The first of such strategies was implemented in the ASP solver DLV and is based on the reduct of the input program with respect to the answer set candidate to be checked [32]. Albeit the construction of such a formula can be done in polynomial time, in practice its creation is often more expensive than the unsatisfiability check. Moreover, the traditional reduct-based approach cannot reuse any information from previous checks and requires to build a new formula each time the stability check is required. An alternative strategy was implemented in the ASP solver CLASP, where a characterization of answer sets based on *unfounded sets* is used to obtain a formula that can be reused for all stability checks [24]. However, the formula built using this strategy is quadratic in the size of the program, while the reduct-based approach produces linear formulas.

The main contribution of this paper is to show how to improve the efficiency of the mainstream strategies for handling disjunctive logic programs under stable model semantics. In particular, we describe how the reduct-based approach can be modified in order to use the same formula in all answer set checks (Sect. 3.2), and we propose a slight, yet effective, modification of the unfounded-based approach so to make it linear (Sect. 3.3); the new algorithms are integrated in the solver WASP. After that, we empirically assess the impact of the new features on several benchmarks, showing that WASP can efficiently handle disjunctive ASP programs (Sect. 4).

2 Preliminaries

2.1 Propositional Logic

Syntax. Let $\mathcal{A}$ be a fixed, countable set of (propositional) *atoms*. A *literal* ℓ is either an atom p, or its negation $\neg p$. For a negative literal $\neg p$, $\neg\neg p := p$. A *clause* is a set of literals representing a disjunction, and a propositional formula φ is a set of clauses representing a conjunction, i.e., only formulas in *conjunctive normal form* (CNF) are considered here. For a formula φ, $size(\varphi) := \sum_{c \in \varphi} |c|$, and $At(\varphi)$ is the set of atoms appearing in φ. For $n \geq 0$, and $\ell_0, \ldots, \ell_n$ being literals, formula $\ell_0 \leftrightarrow \ell_1 \wedge \cdots \wedge \ell_n$ is a compact representation of the following clauses: $\{\ell_0\} \cup \{\neg \ell_i \mid i \in [1..n]\}$; $\{\neg \ell_0, \ell_i\}$, for all $i \in [1..n]$. Similarly, $\ell_0 \leftrightarrow \ell_1 \vee \cdots \vee \ell_n$ is a compact representation of the following clauses: $\{\ell_0, \neg \ell_i\}$, for all $i \in [1..n]$; $\{\neg \ell_0\} \cup \{\ell_i \mid i \in [1..n]\}$.

Semantics. An interpretation I is a set of atoms in $\mathcal{A}$. Intuitively, atoms in I are true, and those in $\mathcal{A} \setminus I$ are false. Relation $\models$ is defined as follows: for $p \in \mathcal{A}$, $I \models p$ if $p \in I$, and $I \models \neg p$ if $p \notin I$; for a clause c, $I \models c$ if $I \models \ell$ for some $\ell \in c$; for a formula φ, $I \models \varphi$ if $I \models c$ for all $c \in \varphi$. If $I \models \varphi$ then I is a *model* of φ, I *satisfies* φ, and φ is true w.r.t. I. If $I \not\models \varphi$ then I is not a model of φ, I *violates* φ, and φ is false w.r.t. I. Similarly for literals, and clauses. A formula φ is *satisfiable* if there is an interpretation I such that $I \models \varphi$; otherwise, φ is *unsatisfiable*.

2.2   Answer Set Programming

A *literal* ℓ is either an atom p, or its negation $\sim p$, where $\sim$ denotes *negation as failure*. $\sim p$ Let $\overline{\ell}$ denote the complement of ℓ, i.e., $\overline{p} := \sim p$, and $\overline{\sim p} := p$, for all $p \in \mathcal{A}$. This notation is extended to sets of literals, i.e., for a set S of literals, $\overline{S} := \{\overline{\ell} \mid \ell \in S\}$.

A disjunctive logic program Π is a finite set of rules of the following form:

$$a_1 \mid \cdots \mid a_n \leftarrow b_1, \cdots, b_k, \sim b_{k+1}, \cdots, \sim b_m \tag{1}$$

where $n \geq 1$, $m \geq k \geq 0$, and $a_1, \ldots, a_n, b_1, \ldots, b_m$ are atoms in $\mathcal{A}$. For a rule r of the form (1), set $\{a_1, \ldots, a_n\}$ is called *head* of r, and denoted $H(r)$; while $\{b_1, \ldots, b_k, \sim b_{k+1}, \ldots, \sim b_m\}$ is named *body* of r, and denoted $B(r)$; sets $\{b_1, \ldots, b_k\}$ and $\{b_{k+1}, \ldots, b_m\}$ of positive and negative literals in $B(r)$ are denoted $B^+(r)$ and $B^-(r)$, respectively. Given an atom p, $heads(\Pi, p) := \{r \mid r \in \Pi, p \in H(r)\}$. For a rule r of the form (1), $size(r) := n + m$. For a program Π, $size(\Pi) := \sum_{r \in \Pi} size(r)$ and $At(\Pi)$ denotes the set of atoms appearing in Π.

Semantics. An interpretation I is a set of atoms in $\mathcal{A}$. Relation $\models$ is extended as follows: for a negative literal $\sim a$, $I \models \sim a$ if $I \not\models a$; for a rule r, $I \models B(r)$ if $I \models \ell$ for all literals $\ell \in B(r)$, $I \not\models B(r)$ if $I \not\models \ell$ for a literal $\ell \in B(r)$, $I \models r$ if $H(r) \cap I \neq \emptyset$ whenever $I \models B(r)$; for a program Π, $I \models \Pi$ if $I \models r$ for all $r \in \Pi$. An interpretation I is a *model* of Π if $I \models \Pi$. An interpretation I is *supported* in Π if for all $p \in I$ there is a rule $r \in \Pi$ such that $I \models B(r)$ and $H(r) \cap I = \{p\}$. The definition of answer set is based on a notion of program reduct [27]: Let Π be a disjunctive logic program, and I an interpretation. The reduct of Π with respect to I, denoted Π^I, is obtained from Π by deleting each rule r such that $I \not\models B(r)$, and removing negative literals and false head atoms in the remaining rules. A supported model I of Π is an *answer set* if there is no $J \subset I$ such that $J \models \Pi^I$. Let $AS(\Pi)$ denote the set of answer sets of Π. Program Π is *coherent* if $AS(\Pi) \neq \emptyset$; otherwise, it is *incoherent*.

3   Answer Set Computation

In this section, we review the main techniques employed by WASP for the computation of an answer set. In particular, WASP first encodes the input program Π as a propositional formula by applying the (Clark's) completion (see Sect. 3.1), whose models are all supported models of Π [18,33]. After that, WASP searches for an answer set by implementing a variant of the CDCL backtracking algorithm on the completion of Π as described in [5].

The backtracking algorithm is based on the pattern *choose-propagate-learn*. In a nutshell, the algorithm builds an answer set step-by-step starting from an empty set of literals A. At each step, a literal, called *branching literal*, is added to A (*choice*), and the deterministic consequences of this choice are *propagated*, that is, other literals are added to A. Propagation is carried out by applying several inference rules, called *propagators*. In case the propagation leads to a *conflict*, i.e., an atom and its negation are both in A, the algorithm *learns* a new clause, undoes the choices leading to the conflict, and restores the consistency of A. This process is repeated until the incoherence of Π is proven or $I := A \cap atoms(\Pi)$ is a (supported) model of Π. In the latter case, a stability check on I is possibly performed (more specifically, if Π is *non head-cycle-free* [24]); if the stability check is successful, I is an answer set and the algorithm terminates, otherwise a conflict is raised and a new clause is learned. The stability check amounts to checking the satisfiability of a formula φ, built starting from Π and I. Actually, in WASP the formula φ can be created according to two strategies, referred to as reduct-based (Sect. 3.2) and unfounded-based (Sect. 3.3).

3.1   Completion

In the following, we briefly recall the *Clark's completion* [18] and we describe the completion implemented by WASP. First, consider programs without disjunction, i.e., where for each rule of the form (1), n is equal to 1. In particular, given a program Π without disjunction, the completion of Π, denoted $Comp(\Pi)$, is the set of clauses:

$$a_1^r \leftrightarrow b_1 \wedge \cdots \wedge b_k \wedge \neg b_{k+1} \wedge \cdots \wedge \neg b_m \tag{2}$$

for all $r \in \Pi$ of the form (1) with $n = 1$, where a_1^r is a fresh atom (true if and only if r is a support of a_1), together with

$$a \leftrightarrow \bigvee_{r \in heads(\Pi,a)} a^r \tag{3}$$

for all $a \in At(\Pi)$. Note that the construction of the completion is linear in size.

In order to apply completion to programs in general, a transformation known as *shift* [16] is first applied to the input program Π, so to obtain a program $Shift(\Pi)$ with the same supported models. Formally, for a program Π, $Shift(\Pi)$ is defined as follows. For all rules $r \in \Pi$ of the form (1) and for all $a_i \in H(r)$, $Shift(\Pi)$ contains a rule r', such that $H(r') := \{a_i\}$ and

$B(r') := B(r) \cup (\overline{H(r) \setminus \{a_i\}})$. The strength of the shift is to preserve supported models, however the construction is not linear, but quadratic in size. This weakness is circumvented in WASP by directly extending completion to the disjunctive case [3]. In particular, auxiliary atoms a_i^r will be used with the same meaning of the disjunction-free case, i.e., rule r of the form (1) supports atom a_i, for $i \in [1..n]$. However, since n may be greater than 1, other atoms occurring in the head of r have to be taken into account. Additional auxiliary atoms will be thus used, and in particular: s_i^r, true if and only if rule r may support a_i, for $i \in [1..n]$; d_i^r, true if and only if the disjunction $a_i \vee \cdots \vee a_n$ is true, for $i \in [2..n]$. The completion of a program Π, denoted $Comp^\vee(\Pi)$, is the set of clauses:

$$d_i^r \leftrightarrow a_i \vee d_{i+1}^r \quad \forall i \in [2..n-1] \tag{4}$$

$$d_n^r \leftrightarrow a_n \quad \text{if } n \geq 2 \tag{5}$$

$$s_1^r \leftrightarrow b_1 \wedge \cdots \wedge b_k \wedge \neg b_{k+1} \wedge \cdots \wedge \neg b_m \tag{6}$$

$$s_i^r \leftrightarrow s_{i-1}^r \wedge \neg a_{i-1} \quad \forall i \in [2..n] \tag{7}$$

$$a_i^r \leftrightarrow s_i^r \wedge \neg d_{i+1}^r \quad \forall i \in [1..n-1] \tag{8}$$

$$a_n^r \leftrightarrow s_n^r \tag{9}$$

for all $r \in \Pi$ of the form (1), together with (3) for all $a \in At(\Pi)$. Note that (5) defines d_n^r as an alias of a_n. Similarly, (9) defines s_n^r as an alias of a_n^r. It turns out that d_n^r and s_n^r could be simplified in the above construction, but they are left to ease the reading. Note that for $n = 1$ the above equations essentially give (2): only (6) and (9) are used in this case, and (6) is precisely (2) if s_1^r is replaced by its alias a_1^r.

Finally, we mention that WASP supports a *disjunctive propagator*, which is used to compactly represent clauses from (4) to (9), as detailed in [3]. The disjunctive propagator usually reduces the memory footprint and the solving time of WASP.

3.2 Reduct-Based Stability Check

Let Π be a program, and I be an interpretation. Let $\mathcal{C}(\Pi, I)$ be the propositional formula $\{\mathcal{C}(r, I) \mid r \in \Pi^I\}$, where for each rule r, $\mathcal{C}(r, I)$ is the following clause:

$$(H(r) \cap I) \cup \{\neg b \mid b \in B^+(r)\}.$$

Intuitively, the clauses $\mathcal{C}(\Pi, I)$ encode the program reduct Π^I. Let $c_\mathbb{C}(I)$ denote the clause $\{\neg a \mid a \in I\}$, enforcing at least one atom in I to be assigned false. Formula $red_{bas}(\Pi, I)$ is thus $\mathcal{C}(\Pi, I) \cup \{c_\mathbb{C}(I)\}$.

The following mapping between stability and satisfiability checks is established.

Proposition 1 (Theorem 4.2 of [32]). *Let Π be a program, and I be an interpretation. $I \in AS(\Pi)$ if and only if $red_{bas}(\Pi, I)$ is unsatisfiable.*

Note that both $\mathcal{C}(\Pi, I)$, and $c_{\mathsf{C}}(I)$ depend on I. Therefore, sensibly different propositional formulas have to be built for each stability check, and in general exponentially many checks may be performed while searching for an answer set of the input program. The following example should better clarify this aspect.

Example 1. Consider the following program Π_1:

$$a \mid b \leftarrow c \qquad a \leftarrow b, {\sim}e \qquad b \leftarrow a, {\sim}e \qquad c \mid d \leftarrow \qquad e \mid f \leftarrow \qquad a \leftarrow {\sim}b$$

and the answer set candidate to check is $I_1 := \{a, b, c, f\}$. Then, $\mathcal{C}(\Pi_1, I_1)$ is composed by $\{a, b, \neg c\}$, $\{a, \neg b\}$, $\{b, \neg a\}$, $\{c\}$, and $\{f\}$; while $c_{\mathsf{C}}(I_1) := \{\neg a, \neg b, \neg c, \neg f\}$. Formula $red_{bas}(\Pi_1, I_1)$ is unsatisfiable, thus I_1 is an answer set. Consider again the program Π_1 and suppose that the answer set candidate to check is $I_2 = \{a, b, d, f\}$. In this case, $\mathcal{C}(\Pi_1, I_2)$ is composed by $\{a, \neg b\}$, $\{b, \neg a\}$, $\{d\}$, and $\{f\}$; while $c_{\mathsf{C}}(I_2) = \{\neg a, \neg b, \neg d, \neg f\}$. Formula $red_{bas}(\Pi_1, I_2)$ is satisfiable, thus I_2 is not an answer set. Note that the two formulas $red_{bas}(\Pi_1, I_1)$, and $red_{bas}(\Pi_1, I_2)$ have in common several clauses, i.e., $\{a, \neg b\}, \{b, \neg a\}, \{f\}$. However, at each check the formula is rebuilt without taking into account this information. $\triangleleft$

In order to overcome the main weakness of the basic stability check, the propositional formula $red_{bas}(\Pi, I)$ is replaced by a refined formula $red_{adv}(\Pi, I)$ such that each of its clauses depends on either Π, or I, but not both. Actually, many clauses of the new formula will only depend on Π, which will allow to reuse them in subsequent stability checks. As will be clarified soon, these clauses compactly encode all possible reducts for the input program Π, so that the specific reduct Π^I for the interpretation I to be checked can be selected by properly adding to $red_{adv}(\Pi, I)$ a set of unit clauses, i.e., clauses consisting of a single literal.

Formally, for a rule r, let $\mathcal{C}(r)$ denote the following clause:

$$H(r) \cup \{\neg b \mid b \in B^+(r)\} \cup \{b' \mid b \in B^-(r)\}$$

where each b' is a fresh atom, i.e., an atom not occurring in Π. These fresh atoms are required because the interpretation of negative literals in program reducts is fixed by definition: their falsity implies the deletion of r, and their truth imply their own elimination. For a program Π, let $\mathcal{C}(\Pi)$ be the propositional formula $\{\mathcal{C}(r) \mid r \in \Pi\}$.

For an interpretation I, define $fix(I)$ to be the following set of clauses:

$$\{\{\neg a\} \mid a \in \mathcal{A} \setminus I\} \cup \{\{b'\} \mid b \in I\} \cup \{\{\neg b'\} \mid b \in \mathcal{A} \setminus I\}.$$

Intuitively, $fix(I)$ fixes the interpretation of false as well as fresh atoms. Finally, formula $red_{adv}(\Pi, I)$ is defined as $\mathcal{C}(\Pi) \cup fix(I) \cup \{c_{\mathsf{C}}(I)\}$.

It is important to observe that simplifying $\mathcal{C}(\Pi)$ by means of the unary clauses in $fix(I)$ would result in the formula $\mathcal{C}(\Pi, I)$. The analogous of Proposition 1 can thus be established for the advanced stability check.

Theorem 1. *Let Π be a program, and I be an interpretation. $I \in AS(\Pi)$ if and only if $red_{adv}(\Pi, I)$ is unsatisfiable.*

Example 2. Consider the program Π_1 of Example 1. Suppose that the answer set candidate to check is $I_1 := \{a, b, c, f\}$. Then, $\mathcal{C}(\Pi_1)$ comprises the clauses $\{a, b, \neg c\}$, $\{a, \neg b, e'\}$, $\{b, \neg a, e'\}$, $\{c, d\}$, $\{f, e\}$, and $\{a, b'\}$. The set of clauses $fix(I_1)$ comprises $\{\neg d\}$, $\{\neg e\}$, $\{\neg e'\}$ and $\{b'\}$; while $c_C(I_1) := \{\neg a, \neg b, \neg c, \neg f\}$. Note that $fix(I_1)$ should also contain the unit clauses $\{a'\}$, $\{c'\}$, $\{\neg d'\}$, $\{f'\}$ which however are not necessary since such atoms do not appear in any other clause. The formula $red_{adv}(\Pi_1, I_1)$ is then unsatisfiable, thus I_1 is an answer set. Consider again the program Π_1. Suppose that the answer set candidate to check is $I_2 = \{a, b, d, f\}$. Note that, $\mathcal{C}(\Pi_1)$ is not dependent on the interpretation thus it can be reused also in this check. Then, $fix(I_2)$ is composed by $\{\neg c\}$, $\{\neg e\}$, $\{\neg e'\}$, and $\{b'\}$; while $c_C(I_2) = \{\neg a, \neg b, \neg d, \neg f\}$. The formula $red_{adv}(\Pi_1, I_2)$ is satisfiable, thus I_2 is not an answer set.   ◁

3.3   Unfounded-Based Stability Check

Let Π be a program, and I be an interpretation. A set X of atoms is an unfounded set for Π with respect to I if for each $r \in \Pi$ with $H(r) \cap X \neq \emptyset$ then $I \not\models B(r)$, or $B^+(r) \cap X \neq \emptyset$, or $(H(r) \setminus X) \cap I \neq \emptyset$. Note that, I is an answer set of Π iff $I \models \Pi$ and no unfounded set X is such that $X \cap I \neq \emptyset$. In the following, for a rule r we define $\neg B(r) := \{\neg q \mid q \in B^+(r)\} \cup \{q \mid q \in B^-(r)\}$.

Given a program Π and an interpretation I, the stability of I can be checked by encoding the unfounded conditions. In more detail, for each atom $p \in \mathcal{A}$ two auxiliary atoms are used, namely u_p and h_p, where atom u_p is true iff p is unfounded and atom h_p is true iff p is true and founded. Then, $\mathcal{U}(r, p)$ denotes the following clause:

$$\{\neg u_p\} \cup \neg B(r) \cup \{u_q \mid q \in B^+(r)\} \cup \{h_q \mid q \in H(r) \setminus \{p\}\}$$

and $\mathcal{U}(\Pi)$ is the formula $\{\mathcal{U}(r, p) \mid r \in \Pi, p \in H(r)\}$. Moreover, let $\mathcal{H}(p)$ be the clauses $h_p \leftrightarrow p \wedge \neg u_p$, $\mathcal{H}(\Pi)$ be the formula $\{\mathcal{H}(p) \mid p \in At(\Pi)\}$ and $c(\Pi)$ be the clause $\{u_p \mid p \in At(\Pi)\}$. For an interpretation I, define $fix'(I)$ to be the formula:

$$\{\neg u_p \mid p \notin I\} \cup \{\neg p \mid p \notin I\} \cup \{p \mid p \in I\}$$

Finally, formula $unf_{qdt}(\Pi, I)$ is defined as $\mathcal{U}(\Pi) \cup \mathcal{H}(\Pi) \cup \{c(\Pi)\} \cup fix'(I)$.

Proposition 2 (Theorem 3 of [24]). *Let Π be a program, and I be an interpretation. $I \in AS(\Pi)$ if and only if $unf_{qdt}(\Pi, I)$ is unsatisfiable.*

Example 3. Consider the program Π_1 in Example 1. Suppose that the answer set candidate to check is $I_1 := \{a, b, c, f\}$. Then, $\mathcal{U}(\Pi_1)$ is $\{\neg u_a, \neg c, u_c, h_b\}$, $\{\neg u_b, \neg c, u_c, h_a\}$, $\{\neg u_a, \neg b, u_b, e\}$, $\{\neg u_b, \neg a, u_a, e\}$, $\{\neg u_c, h_d\}$, $\{\neg u_d, h_c\}$, $\{\neg u_e, h_f\}$, $\{\neg u_f, h_e\}$, and $\{\neg u_a, b\}$. Moreover, for $p \in \{a, b, c, d, e, f\}$, $\mathcal{H}(p)$ comprises $\{\neg h_p, p\}$, $\{\neg h_p, \neg u_p\}$, $\{h_p, \neg p, u_p\}$; while $c(\Pi_1)$ is the clause

$\{u_a, u_b, u_c, u_d, u_e, u_f\}$. The clauses in $fix'(I_1)$ are $\{\neg u_d\}$, $\{\neg u_e\}$, $\{\neg d\}$, $\{\neg e\}$, $\{a\}$, $\{b\}$, $\{c\}$, and $\{f\}$. The formula $unf_{qdt}(\Pi_1, I_1)$ is then unsatisfiable, thus I_1 is an answer set. Consider again the program Π_1. Suppose that the answer set candidate to check is $I_2 = \{a, b, d, f\}$. Interestingly, $\mathcal{U}(\Pi_1)$, $\mathcal{H}(\Pi_1)$, and $c(\Pi_1)$ are not dependent on the interpretation thus they can be reused also in this check. Then, $fix'(I_2)$ is composed by $\{\neg u_c\}$, $\{\neg u_e\}$, $\{\neg c\}$, $\{\neg e\}$, $\{a\}$, $\{b\}$, $\{d\}$, and $\{f\}$. The formula $unf_{qdt}(\Pi_1, I_2)$ is satisfiable, thus I_2 is not an answer set. ◁

A weakness of $unf_{qdt}(\Pi, I)$ is that its size is not always linear with respect to the size of Π, as formalized next.

Proposition 3. *In the worst case, for a rule r of a program Π, $size(\{\mathcal{U}(r, p) \mid p \in H(r)\})$ is quadratic with respect to $size(r)$.*

Proof. Let r be of the form (1). Hence, $|\{\mathcal{U}(r, p) \mid p \in H(r)\}| = n$, and each $\mathcal{U}(r, p)$ has size $n + m + k$. Hence, $size(\{\mathcal{U}(r, p) \mid p \in H(r)\}) = n \cdot (n + m + k)$. □

In order to circumvent this weakness, in the following we propose a modification of the formula $\mathcal{U}(\Pi)$. In particular, $\mathcal{U}'(r, p)$ denotes the clause $\{\neg u_p, aux_r\}$ and $\mathcal{U}'(r)$ denotes the clause $\{\neg aux_r\} \cup \neg B(r) \cup \{u_q \mid q \in B^+(r)\} \cup \{h_q \mid q \in H(r)\}$, where aux_r is a fresh atom not appearing elsewhere in the formula, and $\mathcal{U}'(\Pi)$ is the formula $\{\mathcal{U}'(r, p) \mid r \in \Pi, p \in H(r)\} \cup \{\mathcal{U}'(r) \mid r \in \Pi\}$. Finally, formula $unf_{lin}(\Pi, I)$ is defined as $\mathcal{U}'(\Pi) \cup \mathcal{H}(\Pi) \cup \{c(\Pi)\} \cup fix'(I)$.

Theorem 2. *Let Π be a program, and I be an interpretation. $I \in AS(\Pi)$ if and only if $unf_{lin}(\Pi, I)$ is unsatisfiable.*

Proof. We know that $I \in AS(\Pi)$ iff $unf_{qdt}(\Pi, I)$ is unsatisfiable (Theorem 3 of [24]). Hence, to prove our claim we can show that $unf_{lin}(\Pi, I)$ is satisfiable iff $unf_{qdt}(\Pi, I)$ is satisfiable. For an interpretation M, let $ext(M)$ be $(M \cap At(unf_{qdt}(\Pi, I))) \cup \{aux_r \mid r \in \Pi, M \models \mathcal{U}'(r) \setminus \{\neg aux_r\}\}$. We shall show the following properties:

(i) if $M \models unf_{qdt}(\Pi, I)$, then $ext(M) \models unf_{lin}(\Pi, I)$;
(ii) if $M \models unf_{lin}(\Pi, I)$, then $M \cap At(unf_{qdt}(\Pi, I)) \models unf_{qdt}(\Pi, I)$.

Proof of (i). Let $M \models unf_{qdt}(\Pi)$. We have to show that $ext(M) \models \mathcal{U}'(\Pi)$ (since the other clauses in $unf_{lin}(\Pi, I)$ also belong to $unf_{qdt}(\Pi, I)$). Recall that $\mathcal{U}'(\Pi)$ contains clause $\mathcal{U}'(r)$ for each $r \in \Pi$, and clause $\mathcal{U}'(r, p)$ for each atom $p \in H(r)$. Let us first consider a clause $\mathcal{U}'(r)$. If $ext(M) \models \neg aux_r$, then $ext(M) \models \mathcal{U}'(r)$ trivially. Otherwise, if $ext(M) \models aux_r$, then $M \models \mathcal{U}'(r) \setminus \{\neg aux_r\}$ by construction of $ext(M)$; hence, $ext(M) \models \mathcal{U}'(r)$. Let us now consider a clause $\mathcal{U}'(r, p)$. If $ext(M) \models aux_r$, then $ext(M) \models \mathcal{U}'(r, p)$ trivially. Otherwise, if $ext(M) \models \neg aux_r$ then $M \not\models \mathcal{U}'(r) \setminus \{\neg aux_r\}$ by construction of $ext(M)$; hence, $M \not\models \mathcal{U}(r, p) \setminus \{\neg u_p\}$ (because $\mathcal{U}(r, p) \setminus \{\neg u_p\} \subset \mathcal{U}'(r) \setminus \{\neg aux_r\}$), and therefore $M \models \neg u_p$ (because $M \models \mathcal{U}(r, p)$ by assumption). We can thus conclude that $ext(M) \models \mathcal{U}'(r, p)$.

Proof of (ii). Let $M \models unf_{lin}(\Pi)$ and M' be $M \cap At(unf_{qdt}(\Pi, I))$. We have to show that $M' \models \mathcal{U}(\Pi)$ (since the other clauses in $unf_{qdt}(\Pi, I)$ also belong to $unf_{lin}(\Pi, I)$). Recall that $\mathcal{U}(\Pi)$ contains clause $\mathcal{U}(r, p)$ for each rule $r \in \Pi$ and for each atom $p \in H(r)$. If $M \models \neg u_p$ then $M' \models \mathcal{U}(r, p)$ trivially. Otherwise, if $M \models u_p$, then $M \models aux_r$ (because $M \models \mathcal{U}'(r, p)$) and $M \models \neg h_p$ (because $M \models \mathcal{H}(p)$). Hence, $M' \models \mathcal{U}'(r) \setminus \{\neg aux_r, h_p\}$, and since $\mathcal{U}'(r) \setminus \{\neg aux_r, h_p\} = \mathcal{U}(r, p) \setminus \{\neg u_p\}$ we can conclude that $M' \models \mathcal{U}(r, p)$. $\qquad\square$

Example 4. Let r be the rule $a \mid b \leftarrow c$ of program Π_1 in Example 3. Then, $\mathcal{U}'(r)$ is $\{\neg aux_r, \neg c, u_c, h_a, h_b\}$, while $\mathcal{U}'(r, a)$ is $\{\neg u_a, aux_r\}$ and $\mathcal{U}'(r, b)$ is $\{\neg u_b, aux_r\}$. $\qquad\lhd$

Proposition 4. *In the worst case, for a rule r of a program Π, $size(\{\mathcal{U}'(r, p) \mid p \in H(r)\} \cup \{\mathcal{U}'(r)\})$ is linear with respect to $size(r)$.*

Proof. Let r be of the form (1). Then, $size(\{\mathcal{U}'(r, p) \mid p \in H(r)\}) = 2 \cdot n$, while $size(\{\mathcal{U}'(r) \mid r \in \Pi\}) = 1 + m + k + n$. Thus, $size(\{\mathcal{U}'(r, p) \mid p \in H(r)\} \cup \{\mathcal{U}'(r) \mid r \in \Pi\}) = 3 \cdot n + m + k + 1$. $\qquad\square$

4   Experiments

The impact of the techniques described in this paper on the performance of WASP was assessed empirically on three benchmarks: (i) instances from the latest ASP Competition [25] containing cyclic disjunctive rules; (ii) a synthetic benchmark containing disjunctive rules with increasing size of heads; and (iii) computation of paracoherent answer sets of programs from [8]. For (i) and (ii), WASP was executed with the reduct-based and unfounded-based strategies for answer set checking, referred to as WASP$_{RED}$ and WASP$_{UNF}$, respectively; and compared with CLASP [22,23] version 3.3.3. For (iii), WASP was also compared with CLASP version 3.3.3. Since the latter does not support paracoherent reasoning, we used the preprocessor of WASP for the computation of the *externally extended supported program* as described in [10]. Then, this program is extended by adding weak constraints as in the algorithm WEAK, described in [9], in such a way that each optimal answer set of the new program is guaranteed to be a paracoherent answer set. For both solvers, we used a similar algorithm based on *unsatisfiable cores* [6, 22] for computing an optimal answer set. In all cases, the completion was enabled using the strategy *auto* that applies the syntactic rewriting $Comp^\vee$ for rules whose head size is at most 4, and the propagator for rules with larger heads. The experiment was run on an Intel CPU 2.4 GHz with 16 GB of RAM. Time and memory were limited to 1200 seconds and 15 GB, respectively. All instances were grounded by GRINGO 4.5.4 [21], whose execution time and memory consumption are accounted in our analysis. Benchmarks can be found at https://doi.org/10.5281/zenodo.2605076.

Concerning benchmark (i), the tested encodings are *Complex Optimization Of Answer Sets*, *Minimal Diagnosis*, and *Random Disjunctive Programs* [15]. Results are provided in Table 1, where the number of solved instances is reported for each solver. WASP$_{\text{RED}}$ solves 47 instances, whereas the performance achieved by WASP$_{\text{UNF}}$ is slightly worse, with 43 solved instances. CLASP is the best performing solver on this benchmark: it solves 54 instances in the allotted time; its advantage is due to the good performance on *Random Disjunctive Programs*, where it solves 6 instances more than WASP.

Table 1. Results of benchmark (i) executed on the instances from the latest ASP competition.

Problem	#	CLASP	WASP$_{\text{RED}}$	WASP$_{\text{UNF}}$
Complex Optimization Of Answer Sets	20	20	19	16
Minimal Diagnosis	20	20	20	19
Random Disjunctive Programs	20	14	8	8

The advantage of the linear rewriting techniques for handling disjunctive rules does not emerge on the instances of benchmark (i), whose head sizes are at most 2. Hence, in order to assess the scalability of the proposed techniques, we considered the synthetic benchmark (ii). The idea is to have a prototypical family of programs that allows to link the efficiency of a solver with the size of disjunctive heads. Specifically, we generated programs of the following form varying the constant n: $\{a_1 \mid \cdots \mid a_n \leftarrow \} \cup \{a_{i+1} \leftarrow a_i \mid i \in [1..n-1]\} \cup \{a_1 \leftarrow a_n\}$. The results of our experiment are reported on Fig. 1. We observe that CLASP scales worse than both WASP$_{\text{RED}}$ and WASP$_{\text{UNF}}$, and cannot solve the instance with $n = 10000$ in the allotted time. On the contrary, we verified that WASP scales linearly also for larger values of n: WASP$_{\text{RED}}$ and WASP$_{\text{UNF}}$ solve the instance with $n = 100000$ in 60 and 90 s, respectively. We report that the advantage of the linear rewriting techniques is also visible in terms of memory usage. Indeed, the memory footprint of CLASP is 2450 MB for $n = 10000$, while WASP$_{\text{RED}}$ and WASP$_{\text{UNF}}$ use 40 and 49 MB, respectively. Actually, CLASP exceeds the allotted memory with $n \geq 30000$, while WASP$_{\text{RED}}$ and WASP$_{\text{UNF}}$ use 318 and 402 MB when $n = 100000$, respectively.

As for the benchmark (iii), we considered the *Stable Roommates Problem* as presented in [8], which is interesting since the semi-equilibrium transformation may produce long disjunctive rules. In our experiment, we considered different numbers of persons (from 500 to 1500), and for each of them we randomly generated 5 instances. Table 2 reports, for the different number of persons, the cumulative number, the minimum size, the maximum size, and the average size of disjunctions, respectively. Results show that WASP solves all 55 instances, while CLASP solves 30 instances, and in general WASP scales better than CLASP as shown in Fig. 2. Actually, WASP is faster than CLASP in all the tested instances as shown in the instance-wise comparison of the solving time reported in Fig. 3(a). Moreover, we observe that WASP uses less memory than CLASP as illustrated in Fig. 3(b). Indeed, the latter exceeds the allotted memory in all the instances

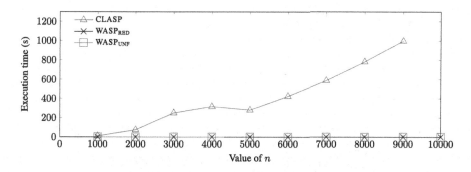

Fig. 1. Scalability analysis on the benchmark (ii).

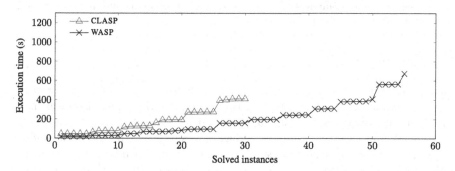

Fig. 2. Comparison of CLASP and WASP on benchmark (iii).

Table 2. Sizes of disjunctive rules after the semi-equilibrium transformation on benchmark (iii).

#Persons	#Disjunctive rules	Min size	Max size	Avg size
500	5246	2	499	238
600	6252	2	599	288
700	7240	2	699	338
800	8244	2	799	388
900	9282	2	899	436
1000	10304	2	999	485
1100	11260	2	1099	537
1200	12438	2	1199	579
1300	13246	2	1299	638
1400	14244	2	1399	688
1500	15304	2	1499	735

with a number of persons greater than or equal to 1100, whereas WASP uses on average 4205 MB on the instances with 1500 persons.

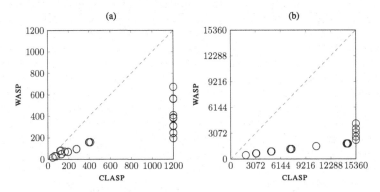

Fig. 3. Instance-wise comparison of solving time in seconds (a) and memory usage in MB (b) of CLASP and WASP on benchmark (iii).

5   Related Work

Answer set computation is performed by WASP applying the CDCL algorithm on the (Clark's) completion of the input program. Clark's completion was introduced in the solver ASSAT [33] and later on also adopted by CMODELS [29], LP2SAT [30] and CLASP [22,23], as well as by WASP 2 [5]. In case of disjunctive programs, such solvers apply a technique called *shift*, which is quadratic in size. The completion employed by the new version of WASP is instead linear and it can be applied as it is also by the aforementioned solvers. Interestingly, the quadratic blow-up of the shift does not affect DLV [7], GNT [31] and WASP 1 [4], which are not based on the Clark's completion but they employ custom data structures and algorithms to handle disjunction. However, the (Clark's) completion can lead to an exponential performance gain [26], and custom data structures are in general harder to maintain and require complex optimizations to achieve efficiency [5].

Concerning the stability checks, the reduct-based approach based on red_{bas} was introduced by DLV [32]. A major drawback of this approach consists of building a new propositional formula at each stability check. This limitation is overcome in WASP by using the formula red_{adv}, which is built once and then reused in all stability checks. The unfounded-based stability check based on the formula unf_{qdt} was instead introduced in [24] and implemented in CLASP. As observed in Sect. 3.3, the formula unf_{qdt} is in general quadratic in size. Such a drawback is addressed by WASP by applying the formula unf_{lin}, which is instead linear in size. Interestingly, the formula unf_{qdt} is more compact than unf_{lin} up to rules with disjunctive heads of size 3, since for a rule r with $|H(r)| \leq 3$, $size(\{\mathcal{U}(r,p) \mid p \in H(r)\}) < size(\mathcal{U}'(r) \cup \{\mathcal{U}'(r,p) \mid p \in H(r)\})$. Thus, one can also combine $\mathcal{U}$ and $\mathcal{U}'$ by selecting the best one according to the rule size.

6   Conclusion and Future Work

In this paper we presented the techniques employed by WASP for evaluating disjunctive logic programs. Results of our empirical analysis show that WASP can efficiently handle disjunctive programs, even with long disjunctive rules. As future work, we plan to revise strategy red_{adv} because in principle it may introduce exponentially many clauses of the form $c_\subset(I)$, even if we never observed such a drawback in our tests. Our idea is to replace $c_\subset(I)$ with alternative implementations, among them a compact representation via *pseudo-Boolean constraints*, introducing the notion of *or-assumptions literals*, or driving the heuristic choices as in the algorithm *opt* [19]. Finally, we mention that WASP is part of the system DLV2 [2] and is available at https://www.mat.unical.it/DLV2/wasp.

References

1. Adrian, W.T., Manna, M., Leone, N., Amendola, G., Adrian, M.: Entity set expansion from the web via ASP. In: Technical Communications of ICLP. OASICS, vol. 58, pp. 1:1–1:5. Schloss Dagstuhl - Leibniz-Zentrum fuer Informatik (2017). https://doi.org/10.4230/OASIcs.ICLP.2017.1
2. Alviano, M., et al.: The ASP system DLV2. In: Balduccini, M., Janhunen, T. (eds.) LPNMR 2017. LNCS (LNAI), vol. 10377, pp. 215–221. Springer, Cham (2017). https://doi.org/10.1007/978-3-319-61660-5_19
3. Alviano, M., Dodaro, C.: Completion of disjunctive logic programs. In: IJCAI, pp. 886–892. IJCAI/AAAI Press (2016)
4. Alviano, M., Dodaro, C., Faber, W., Leone, N., Ricca, F.: WASP: a native ASP solver based on constraint learning. In: Cabalar, P., Son, T.C. (eds.) LPNMR 2013. LNCS (LNAI), vol. 8148, pp. 54–66. Springer, Heidelberg (2013). https://doi.org/10.1007/978-3-642-40564-8_6
5. Alviano, M., Dodaro, C., Leone, N., Ricca, F.: Advances in WASP. In: Calimeri, F., Ianni, G., Truszczynski, M. (eds.) LPNMR 2015. LNCS (LNAI), vol. 9345, pp. 40–54. Springer, Cham (2015). https://doi.org/10.1007/978-3-319-23264-5_5
6. Alviano, M., Dodaro, C., Marques-Silva, J., Ricca, F.: Optimum stable model search: algorithms and implementation. J. Log. Comput. (2015, in press). https://doi.org/10.1093/logcom/exv061
7. Alviano, M., Faber, W., Leone, N., Perri, S., Pfeifer, G., Terracina, G.: The disjunctive datalog system DLV. In: de Moor, O., Gottlob, G., Furche, T., Sellers, A. (eds.) Datalog 2.0 2010. LNCS, vol. 6702, pp. 282–301. Springer, Heidelberg (2011). https://doi.org/10.1007/978-3-642-24206-9_17
8. Amendola, G.: Solving the stable roommates problem using incoherent answer set programs. In: RiCeRcA Workshop. CEUR Workshop Proceedings, vol. 2272. CEUR-WS.org (2018)
9. Amendola, G., Dodaro, C., Faber, W., Leone, N., Ricca, F.: On the computation of paracoherent answer sets. In: AAAI, pp. 1034–1040. AAAI Press (2017)
10. Amendola, G., Dodaro, C., Faber, W., Ricca, F.: Externally supported models for efficient computation of paracoherent answer sets. In: AAAI, pp. 1720–1727. AAAI Press (2018)
11. Amendola, G., Dodaro, C., Leone, N., Ricca, F.: On the application of answer set programming to the conference paper assignment problem. In: Adorni, G., Cagnoni, S., Gori, M., Maratea, M. (eds.) AI*IA 2016. LNCS (LNAI), vol. 10037, pp. 164–178. Springer, Cham (2016). https://doi.org/10.1007/978-3-319-49130-1_13

12. Amendola, G., Eiter, T., Fink, M., Leone, N., Moura, J.: Semi-equilibrium models for paracoherent answer set programs. Artif. Intell. **234**, 219–271 (2016). https://doi.org/10.1016/j.artint.2016.01.011
13. Amendola, G., Eiter, T., Leone, N.: Modular paracoherent answer sets. In: Fermé, E., Leite, J. (eds.) JELIA 2014. LNCS (LNAI), vol. 8761, pp. 457–471. Springer, Cham (2014). https://doi.org/10.1007/978-3-319-11558-0_32
14. Amendola, G., Greco, G., Leone, N., Veltri, P.: Modeling and reasoning about NTU games via answer set programming. In: IJCAI, pp. 38–45. IJCAI/AAAI Press (2016)
15. Amendola, G., Ricca, F., Truszczynski, M.: Generating hard random Boolean formulas and disjunctive logic programs. In: IJCAI, pp. 532–538 (2017). https://doi.org/10.24963/ijcai.2017/75. ijcai.org
16. Ben-Eliyahu, R., Dechter, R.: Propositional semantics for disjunctive logic programs. Ann. Math. Artif. Intell. **12**(1–2), 53–87 (1994). https://doi.org/10.1007/BF01530761
17. Brewka, G., Eiter, T., Truszczynski, M.: Answer set programming at a glance. Commun. ACM **54**(12), 92–103 (2011). https://doi.org/10.1145/2043174.2043195
18. Clark, K.L.: Negation as failure. In: Symposium on Logic and Data Bases, pp. 293–322. Advances in Data Base Theory. Plemum Press (1977)
19. Di Rosa, E., Giunchiglia, E., Maratea, M.: Solving satisfiability problems with preferences. Constraints **15**(4), 485–515 (2010). https://doi.org/10.1007/s10601-010-9095-y
20. Erdem, E., Gelfond, M., Leone, N.: Applications of answer set programming. AI Mag. **37**(3), 53–68 (2016)
21. Gebser, M., Harrison, A., Kaminski, R., Lifschitz, V., Schaub, T.: Abstract gringo. TPLP **15**(4–5), 449–463 (2015). https://doi.org/10.1017/S1471068415000150
22. Gebser, M., Kaminski, R., Kaufmann, B., Romero, J., Schaub, T.: Progress in *clasp* series 3. In: Calimeri, F., Ianni, G., Truszczynski, M. (eds.) LPNMR 2015. LNCS (LNAI), vol. 9345, pp. 368–383. Springer, Cham (2015). https://doi.org/10.1007/978-3-319-23264-5_31
23. Gebser, M., Kaufmann, B., Schaub, T.: Conflict-driven answer set solving: from theory to practice. Artif. Intell. **187**, 52–89 (2012). https://doi.org/10.1016/j.artint.2012.04.001
24. Gebser, M., Kaufmann, B., Schaub, T.: Advanced conflict-driven disjunctive answer set solving. In: IJCAI, pp. 912–918. IJCAI/AAAI (2013)
25. Gebser, M., Maratea, M., Ricca, F.: The design of the seventh answer set programming competition. In: Balduccini, M., Janhunen, T. (eds.) LPNMR 2017. LNCS (LNAI), vol. 10377, pp. 3–9. Springer, Cham (2017). https://doi.org/10.1007/978-3-319-61660-5_1
26. Gebser, M., Schaub, T.: Tableau calculi for logic programs under answer set semantics. ACM Trans. Comput. Log. **14**(2), 15:1–15:140 (2013). https://doi.org/10.1145/2480759.2480767
27. Gelfond, M., Lifschitz, V.: Classical negation in logic programs and disjunctive databases. New Gener. Comput. **9**(3/4), 365–386 (1991). https://doi.org/10.1007/BF03037169
28. Gençay, E., Schüller, P., Erdem, E.: Applications of non-monotonic reasoning to automotive product configuration using answer set programming. J. Intell. Manuf. **30**(3), 1407–1422 (2019). https://doi.org/10.1007/s10845-017-1333-3
29. Giunchiglia, E., Lierler, Y., Maratea, M.: Sat-based answer set programming. In: AAAI, pp. 61–66. AAAI Press/The MIT Press (2004)

30. Janhunen, T.: Cross-translating answer set programs using the ASPTOOLS collection. In: KI **32**(2-3), 183–184 (2018). https://doi.org/10.1007/s13218-018-0529-9
31. Janhunen, T., Niemelä, I.: GNT—a solver for disjunctive logic programs. In: Lifschitz, V., Niemelä, I. (eds.) LPNMR 2004. LNCS (LNAI), vol. 2923, pp. 331–335. Springer, Heidelberg (2003). https://doi.org/10.1007/978-3-540-24609-1_29
32. Koch, C., Leone, N., Pfeifer, G.: Enhancing disjunctive logic programming systems by SAT checkers. Artif. Intell. **151**(1–2), 177–212 (2003). https://doi.org/10.1016/S0004-3702(03)00078-X
33. Lin, F., Zhao, Y.: ASSAT: computing answer sets of a logic program by SAT solvers. Artif. Intell. **157**(1–2), 115–137 (2004). https://doi.org/10.1016/j.artint.2004.04.004

$telingo = \mathrm{ASP} + \mathrm{Time}$

Pedro Cabalar[1] , Roland Kaminski[2] , Philip Morkisch[2] ,
and Torsten Schaub[2,3,4(✉)]

[1] University of Corunna, A Coruña, Spain
pedro.cabalar@udc.es
[2] University of Potsdam, Potsdam, Germany
{kaminski,torsten}@cs.uni-potsdam.de, morkisch@uni-potsdam.de
[3] Simon Fraser University, Burnaby, Canada
[4] Griffith University, Brisbane, Australia

Abstract. We describe *telingo*, an extension of the ASP system *clingo* with temporal operators over finite linear time and provide insights into its implementation. *telingo* takes temporal logic programs as input whose rules contain only future and present operators in their heads and past and present operators in their bodies. Moreover, *telingo* extends the grammar of *clingo*'s input language with a variety of temporal operators that can even be used to represent nested temporal formulas. By using *clingo*'s interface for manipulating the abstract syntax tree of non-ground programs, temporal logic programs are transformed into regular ones before grounding. The resulting regular logic program is then solved incrementally by using *clingo*'s multi-shot interface. Notably, this involves the consecutive unfolding of future temporal operators that is accomplished via external atoms. Finally, we provide an empirical evaluation contrasting standard incremental ASP programs with their temporal counterparts in *telingo*'s input language.

1 Introduction

Answer Set Programming (ASP [15]) has become a popular approach to solving knowledge-intense combinatorial search problems due to its performant solving engines and expressive modeling language. However, both are mainly geared towards static domains and lack native support for handling dynamic applications. This shortcoming was addressed over the last decade by creating a temporal extension of ASP based on Linear Temporal Logic (LTL [17]) and referred to as Temporal Equilibrium Logic (TEL [1,5]). Recently, this was distilled into a computationally more feasible version based on finite linear time. The resulting logic, TEL_f [4] has meanwhile led to the temporal ASP system *telingo* [4], which we describe in this system description. *telingo* extends the full-fledged modeling language of the ASP system *clingo* by future and past temporal operators and solves the corresponding temporal logic programs incrementally by means of *clingo*'s multi-shot solving interface. Hence, we also provide insights into how *clingo*'s infrastructure can be used to implement more complex ASP languages.

© Springer Nature Switzerland AG 2019
M. Balduccini et al. (Eds.): LPNMR 2019, LNAI 11481, pp. 256–269, 2019.
https://doi.org/10.1007/978-3-030-20528-7_19

2   Temporal Equilibrium Logic over Finite Traces

The semantics of TEL$_f$ rests upon finite traces (or sequences) of equilibrium models (cf. [4]), just as LTL$_f$ rests upon finite traces of regular models [6]. In fact, LTL$_f$ is obtained by adding the law of the excluded middle for each propositional atom and each time point, or in terms of ASP, by adding a corresponding choice rule (see below). Hence, *telingo* can be used just as well for computational tasks in LTL$_f$.

TEL$_f$ extends the language of propositional logic by the future and past temporal operators listed in the second and fifth row of Table 1. The first line gives the two nullary operators **I** and $\mathbb{F}$ that hold exclusively at the initial and final state of a trace, respectively. The common one-step operators • and ○ allow us to test whether a proposition holds in the previous or next state in a trace, respectively. Their weak versions are defined as $\widehat{\bullet}\varphi \stackrel{def}{=} \bullet\varphi \vee$ **I** and $\widehat{\circ}\varphi \stackrel{def}{=} \circ\varphi \vee \mathbb{F}$, respectively. The unary operators ◆ and ■ allow us to refer to one or all states in the past, respectively, while their counterparts ◊ and □ relate to the future. Common to all operators, a bold version indicates a past operator, while an outlined one refers to the future. As a simple example, the proposition •□p requires that p must be true in all states of a trace starting from the state preceding the one at hand. For another example, consider the formula

Table 1. Past and future temporal operators in *telingo* and TEL$_f$

`&initial`	**I**	*initial*	`&final`	$\mathbb{F}$	*final*
`'p`	•p	*previous*	`p'`	○p	*next*
`<`	•	*previous*	`>`	○	*next*
`<?`	**S**	*since*	`>?`	$\mathbb{U}$	*until*
`<*`	**T**	*trigger*	`>*`	$\mathbb{R}$	*release*
`<?`	◆	*eventually before*	`>?`	◊	*eventually afterward*
`<*`	■	*always before*	`>*`	□	*always afterward*
`<:`	$\widehat{\bullet}$	*weak previous*	`>:`	$\widehat{\circ}$	*weak next*

$$\square(shoot \wedge \bullet\!\blacklozenge\, shoot \wedge \blacksquare unloaded \rightarrow \lozenge fail) \tag{1}$$

expressing the sentence: *"If we shoot twice with a gun that was never loaded, it will eventually fail."* Finally, an atom p is put under the semantics of LTL$_f$ by adding $\square(p \vee \neg p)$.

For the binary operators **S, T,** $\mathbb{U}$, **and** $\mathbb{R}$ along with more details and illustration regarding the temporal language and its semantics the interested reader is referred to [1,4].

Any temporal formula can be translated into a (strongly equivalent) *temporal logic program*. Given an alphabet $\mathcal{A}$, such programs consist of three types of *temporal rules*

- *initial rules* of form $\qquad\qquad B \to A$
- *dynamic rules* of form $\qquad \hat{\circ}\Box(B \to A)$
- *final rules* of form $\qquad \Box(\mathbb{F} \to (B \to A))$

where $B = b_1 \wedge \cdots \wedge b_n$ with $n \geq 0$, $A = a_1 \vee \cdots \vee a_m$ with $m \geq 0$ and the b_i and a_j are *temporal literals* as in $\{a, \neg a, \bullet a, \neg \bullet a \mid a \in \mathcal{A}\}$ for dynamic rules, and regular literals $\{a, \neg a \mid a \in \mathcal{A}\}$ for initial and final rules.

As their names suggest, initial and final rules impose conditions on the first and last state of a trace, respectively. The former can also be expressed in analogy to the latter as $\Box(\mathbb{I} \to (B \to A))$. A temporal program consisting of initial rules only amounts to a regular logic program. Dynamic rules capture transitions among states. To this end, they comprise regular and temporal literals that may refer to a preceding state via the previous operator $\bullet$. To avoid referring to states beyond the initial and final state, dynamic rules are preceded with the weak next operator $\hat{\circ}$ operator.

A temporal logic program can be converted into a regular one by adorning literals with explicit timestamps (cf. [14]). For this, let $\mathcal{A}_k = \{a_k \mid a \in \mathcal{A}\}$ be a time stamped copy of alphabet $\mathcal{A}$ for each time point k. We outline below the module-based translation introduced in [4] since it accounts for *telingo*'s incremental approach to computing traces: A module $\mathbb{P}$ is a triple (P, I, O) consisting of a logic program P over alphabet $\mathcal{A}_P$ and sets I and O of input and output atoms such that (i) $I \cap O = \emptyset$, (ii) $\mathcal{A}_P \subseteq I \cup O$, and (iii) $H(P) \subseteq O$, where $H(P)$ gives all atoms occurring in rule heads in P (cf. [16]). Whenever clear from context, we associate $\mathbb{P}$ with (P, I, O). In our setting, a set X of atoms is a stable model of $\mathbb{P}$, if X is a stable model of logic program P.[1] Two modules $\mathbb{P}_1$ and $\mathbb{P}_2$ are *compositional*, if $O_1 \cap O_2 = \emptyset$ and $O_1 \cap C = \emptyset$ or $O_2 \cap C = \emptyset$ for every strongly connected component C of the positive dependency graph of the logic program $P_1 \cup P_2$. In other words, all rules defining an atom must belong to the same module, and no positive recursion is allowed among modules. Whenever $\mathbb{P}_1$ and $\mathbb{P}_2$ are compositional, their *join* is defined as the module $\mathbb{P}_1 \sqcup \mathbb{P}_2 = (P_1 \cup P_2, (I_1 \setminus O_2) \cup (I_2 \setminus O_1), O_1 \cup O_2)$. The module theorem [16] ensures that compatible stable models of $\mathbb{P}_1$ and $\mathbb{P}_2$ can be mapped to one of $\mathbb{P}_1 \sqcup \mathbb{P}_2$, and vice versa.

Given this, the translation τ at time point k is defined for temporal literals as

$$\tau_k(a) \stackrel{def}{=} a_k \qquad\qquad \tau_k(\neg a) \stackrel{def}{=} \neg a_k \qquad\qquad \text{for } a \in \mathcal{A}$$
$$\tau_k(\bullet a) \stackrel{def}{=} a_{k-1} \qquad\qquad \tau_k(\neg \bullet a) \stackrel{def}{=} \neg a_{k-1} \qquad\qquad \text{for } a \in \mathcal{A}$$

and for temporal rules r in a temporal logic program P partitioned into its initial, $I(P)$, dynamic, $D(P)$, and final rules, $F(P)$, as

$$\tau_k(r) \stackrel{def}{=} \tau_k(a_1) \vee \cdots \vee \tau_k(a_m) \leftarrow \tau_k(b_1) \wedge \cdots \wedge \tau_k(b_n) \qquad \text{if } r \in I(P) \cup D(P)$$
$$\tau_k(r) \stackrel{def}{=} \tau_k(a_1) \vee \cdots \vee \tau_k(a_m) \leftarrow \tau_k(b_1) \wedge \cdots \wedge \tau_k(b_n) \wedge \neg q_{k+1} \qquad \text{if } r \in F(P)$$

---

[1] Note that the default value assigned to input atoms is *false* in multi-shot solving [10]; this differs from the original definition [16] where a choice rule is used.

for a new atom $q \notin \mathcal{A}$. The modules $\mathbb{P}_k$ corresponding to a temporal logic program P over $\mathcal{A}$ at time point k are then defined as

$$\mathbb{P}_0 \stackrel{def}{=} (P_0, \{q_1\}, \mathcal{A}_0) \quad \mathbb{P}_k \stackrel{def}{=} (P_k, \mathcal{A}_{k-1} \cup \{q_{k+1}\}, \mathcal{A}_k \cup \{q_k\}) \quad \text{for } k > 0$$

where

$$P_0 \stackrel{def}{=} \{\tau_0(r) \mid r \in I(P)\} \cup \{\tau_0(r) \mid r \in F(P)\} \tag{2}$$
$$P_k \stackrel{def}{=} \{\tau_k(r) \mid r \in D(P)\} \cup \{\tau_k(r) \mid r \in F(P)\} \cup \{q_k \leftarrow\} \tag{3}$$

The idea is to associate the rules at each time point with a module and to successively add modules corresponding to increasing time points (while leaving all previous modules unchanged). A stable model obtained after k compositions then corresponds to a trace of length k.

To ensure the compositionality of modules, dynamic rules are restricted to heads of regular literals; such rules are called *present-centered* [4]. This restriction warrants that modules only incorporate atoms from previous time points, as reflected by $\mathcal{A}_{k-1}$ in the input of $\mathbb{P}_k$, and thus that no positive cycles can occur across modules.

The exception are auxiliary atoms like q_{k+1} that belong to the input of each $\mathbb{P}_k$ for $k > 0$ but only get defined in the next module $\mathbb{P}_{k+1}$. The goal of introducing atoms like q_{k+1} in the translation of final rules $r \in F(P)$ is to deactivate their image $\tau_k(r)$ whenever k is incremented. More precisely, the idea is to let atom q_{k+1} be false at each horizon k (by declaring it as a yet undefined input atom), while all previous atoms $q_1, \ldots, q_k$ are set to true via the facts added in $P_1, \ldots, P_k$, respectively. In this way, for $r \in F(P)$ only $\tau_k(r)$ is potentially applicable at time point k, while all rules $\tau_i(r)$ are inapplicable for earlier time points $i = 1..k-1$.

3   The *telingo* Language

telingo extends the full-fledged modeling language of *clingo* by the future and past temporal operators listed in the first and fourth row of Table 1.

Although *telingo*'s inner workings rely on present-centered temporal logic programs (to support incremental ASP solving), it offers a more general input language. This is because the fragment of *past-future rules* is reducible to present-centered programs [4]. A temporal formula is a past-future rule if it has form $A \leftarrow B$ where B and A are just temporal formulas with the following restrictions: B and A contain no implications (other than negations[2]), B contains no future operators, and A contains no past operators. An example of a past-future rule is (1). This fragment is not only quite expressive but also rather natural when using the causal reading of program rules by drawing upon the past in rule bodies and referring to the future in rule heads. Considering that, past-future rules also serve as the design guideline for *telingo*'s input language.

---

[2] Recall that $\neg\varphi \stackrel{def}{=} \varphi \to \bot$ in the logic of here-and-there and thus in TEL_f, too.

To this end, *telingo* allows for enclosing a nested temporal formula φ in an expression of the form &tel{φ}. Formulas like φ are formed via the temporal operators in Line 3 to 8 in Table 1 along with the Boolean operators &, |, ~ for conjunction, disjunction, and negation, respectively (thus avoiding nested implications). The underlying idea is to use the *smaller* symbol < as the basis of all past operators, and to combine it with a *question mark* ? or a *Kleene star* * depending on whether the semantics of the respective operator relies on an existential or universal quantification over states. This is nicely exemplified by the always and eventually operators, represented by <* and <?. In fact, the symbols <* and <? are overloaded due to their usage as binary and unary operators. For a simple example, consider the formula $\bullet p \vee \blacklozenge r$ represented as '&tel{< p | <? p}'. Similarly, future operators are built with the *greater* symbol '>' as their basis. More generally, temporal expressions of the form &tel{φ} are treated like atoms in *telingo*'s input language (and constitute theory atoms in *clingo* [9]); they are compiled away by *telingo*'s preprocessing that ultimately yields present-centered logic programs. In order to keep this translation simple, the current version of *telingo*, viz 1.0, restricts their occurrence in temporal rules $A \leftarrow B$ to being positive in A and preceded by one or two negations in their body B.[3] No restriction is imposed on their occurrences in integrity constraints.

For example, the integrity constraint '*shoot* $\wedge$ ■*unloaded* $\wedge$ $\bullet\blacklozenge$*shoot* $\to \bot$' is expressible in several alternative ways.

```
:- &tel { shoot & <* unloaded & < <? shoot }.
:- shoot,  &tel { <* unloaded & < <? shoot }.
:- shoot,  &tel { <* unloaded }, &tel { < <? shoot }.
```

Alternatively, present-centered logic programs can be written directly by using the alternative notation for the common one-step operators $\bullet$ and $\circ$. Here, a quote is used either at the beginning or the end of a predicate symbol to indicate that the literal at hand must be true in the previous or next state in the trace, respectively. For instance, $\bullet p(7)$ is represented by 'p(7), while $\circ q(X)$ is q'(X). For convenience, *telingo* 1.0 allows for using $\circ$ in singleton rule heads;[4] as above, this is compiled away during preprocessing.

The distinction between different types of temporal rules is done in *telingo* via *clingo*'s #program directives [10], which allow us to partition programs into subprograms. More precisely, each rule in *telingo*'s input language is associated with a temporal rule r of form $A \leftarrow B$ and interpreted as r, $\hat{\circ}\Box r$, or $\Box(\mathbb{F} \to r)$ depending on whether it occurs in the scope of a program declaration headed by initial, dynamic, or final, respectively. Additionally, *telingo* offers always for gathering rules preceded by $\Box$ (thus dropping $\hat{\circ}$ from dynamic rules). A rule outside any such declaration is regarded to be in the scope of initial.

---

[3] The extension to arbitrary occurrences is no hurdle and foreseen in future versions of *telingo*.

[4] As above, the extension to disjunctions is no principal hurdle and foreseen in future versions of *telingo*; currently they must be expressed by using &tel.

```
1  #program always.

3  item(fox;beans;goose).
4  route(river_bank,far_bank). route(far_bank,river_bank).
5  eats(fox,goose). eats(goose,beans).

7  #program initial.

9  at(farmer,river_bank).
10 at(X,river_bank) :- item(X).

12 #program dynamic.

14 move(farmer).
15 0 { move(X) : item(X) } 1.

17 at(X,B) :- 'at(X,A), move(X), route(A,B).
18 :- move(X), item(X), 'at(farmer,A), not 'at(X,A).

20 at(X,A) :- 'at(X,A), not move(X).

22 #program always.

24 :- at(X,A), at(X,B), A<B.
25 :- eats(X,Y), at(X,A), at(Y,A), not at(farmer,A).

27 #program final.

29 :- at(X,river_bank).

31 #show move/1.
32 #show at/2.
```

Listing 1. *telingo* encoding for the Fox, Goose and Beans Puzzle

For illustration, we give in Listing 1 an exemplary *telingo* encoding of the
Fox, Goose and Beans Puzzle available at https://github.com/potassco/telingo/
tree/master/examples/river-crossing.

> *Once upon a time a farmer went to a market and purchased a fox, a goose,
> and a bag of beans. On his way home, the farmer came to the bank of a
> river and rented a boat. But crossing the river by boat, the farmer could
> carry only himself and a single one of his purchases: the fox, the goose, or
> the bag of beans. If left unattended together, the fox would eat the goose, or
> the goose would eat the beans. The farmer's challenge was to carry himself
> and his purchases to the far bank of the river, leaving each purchase intact.
> How did he do it?*
> (https://en.wikipedia.org/wiki/Fox,_goose_and_bag_of_beans_puzzle)

In Listing 1, lines 3–5 and 9–10 provide facts holding in all and the initial states,
respectively; this is indicated by the program directives headed by always and

initial. The dynamic rules in lines 14–22 describe the transition function. The farmer moves at each time step (Line 14), and may take an item or not (Line 15). Line 17 describes the effect of action move/1, Line 18 its precondition, and Line 20 the law of inertia. The second part of the always rules give state constraints in Line 24 and 25. The final rule in Line 29 gives the goal condition.

All in all, we obtain two shortest plans consisting of eight states in about 20 ms. Restricted to the move predicate, *telingo* reports the following solutions:

Time	Solution 1		Solution 2	
1				
2	move(farmer)	move(goose)	move(farmer)	move(goose)
3	move(farmer)		move(farmer)	
4	move(beans)	move(farmer)	move(farmer)	move(fox)
5	move(farmer)	move(goose)	move(farmer)	move(goose)
6	move(farmer)	move(fox)	move(beans)	move(farmer)
7	move(farmer)		move(farmer)	
8	move(farmer)	move(goose)	move(farmer)	move(goose)

We have chosen this example since it was also used by [3] to illustrate the working of *stelp*, a tool for temporal answer set programming with TEL$_\omega$. We note that *stelp* and *telingo* differ syntactically in describing transitions by using next or previous operators, respectively. Since *telingo* extends *clingo*'s input language, it offers a richer input language, as witnessed by the cardinality constraints in Line 15 in Listing 1. Finally, *stelp* uses a model checker and outputs an automaton capturing all infinite traces while *telingo* returns finite traces corresponding to plans.

4 The *telingo* System

The implementation of *telingo* draws heavily on the functionality provided by *clingo*'s application programming interface (API[5]). This is also why *telingo* allows us to extend the full-fledged modeling and solving capabilities of *clingo*.

We outline *telingo*'s operation below by following its workflow.

4.1 Parsing Temporal Logic Programs

All of the temporal language additions are designed to use available syntax features, so that *clingo*'s (or better *gringo*'s [11]) parser can be used as is. Atoms like &initial, &final, and &tel, as well as the temporal operators in the first and fourth column of Table 1 rely on *clingo*'s theory language capacities that allow for defining customized syntactic expressions by supplementing a dedicated (theory) grammar (cf. [9]). Also, *clingo* tolerates quotes in predicate names. Finally, *telingo* uses *clingo*'s #program directive [10] for partitioning temporal logic programs into their four types of rules.

---

[5] https://potassco.org/clingo.

4.2 Translating Temporal Logic Programs into Regular Ones

The translation of temporal logic programs into regular ones relies on the processing of the temporal adornments described in Sect. 4.1. This information is used for generating an (incremental) logic program, as described in Sect. 2. In practice, the resulting program is equipped with program directives that allow *clingo* to use its multi-shot solving capabilities (cf. [10,13]) for solving the program incrementally. The actual translation is accomplished by means of the functionalities of *clingo*'s API for manipulating the abstract syntax tree of a logic program. That is, the list of rules is extracted, rewritten, and finally passed back to *clingo*.

The most intriguing part in this process is the (incremental) rewriting of future-oriented operators in heads of past-future rules. In fact, the restriction of having future operators occur in rule heads only and past operators occur in rule bodies results in a normal form where all future operators occur negatively in rule bodies and rule heads do not contain temporal operators anymore. In general, this normal form creates a temporal program with an infinite number of rules but only a finite number of them are required for a fixed horizon. The translation rests on the idea that for past-future rules there can be no positive cycles involving an atom from the current step and an atom from a future step. This allows us to shift rule heads and bring a program in the above normal form. The formal elaboration of this translation is detailed in a companion paper, and we focus below on an example-driven presentation.

Let us begin by illustrating the elimination of negative occurrence of future operators in rule bodies. As just mentioned, they appear during *telingo*'s translation in an intermediate step but can be turned back into present-centered temporal logic programs.[6] For example, consider an occurrence of $\neg \circ \Diamond a$ (viz. 'not &tel { > >? a }') in a rule body, since this pops up below again. Each such negative occurrence of $\circ \Diamond a$ is replaced by an auxiliary atom $\ell_{\circ \Diamond a}$:

$$\Box(A \leftarrow \neg \circ \Diamond a \wedge B) \quad \mapsto \quad \Box(A \leftarrow \neg \ell_{\circ \Diamond a} \wedge B)$$

Since the occurrence of $\circ \Diamond a$ is negative, TEL allows us to treat it as in classical (linear time) logic, namely by starting from $\Box(\ell_{\circ \Diamond a} \leftrightarrow \circ \Diamond a)$, we get $\Box(\ell_{\circ \Diamond a} \leftrightarrow \circ a \vee \circ \circ \Diamond a)$,[7] which we decompose into three integrity constraints in the standard way:

$$\Box(\ell_{\circ \Diamond a} \vee \neg \ell_{\circ \Diamond a})$$
$$\Box(\bot \leftarrow \ell_{\circ \Diamond a} \wedge \neg \circ a \wedge \neg \circ \circ \Diamond a) \tag{4}$$
$$\Box(\bot \leftarrow \neg \ell_{\circ \Diamond a} \wedge \circ a)$$
$$\Box(\bot \leftarrow \neg \ell_{\circ \Diamond a} \wedge \circ \circ \Diamond a) \tag{5}$$

While the first rule makes us choose the truth value of $\ell_{\circ \Diamond a}$, the last three rules result from rewriting the above equivalence (into two classical implications).

---

[6] This is also why this extension to the past-future format is tolerated in *telingo*'s input language.

[7] $\circ \Diamond a \leftrightarrow \circ a \vee \circ \circ \Diamond a$ is valid in TEL.

Finally, replacing in (4) and (5) the remaining occurrences of $\circ\Diamond a$ by $\ell_{\circ\Diamond a}$ and time shifting the inner part backwards by one and the outer one forward again by prepending $\hat{\circ}$ results in the following set of present-centered rules

$$\Box(\ell_{\circ\Diamond a} \vee \neg\ell_{\circ\Diamond a})$$
$$\hat{\circ}\Box(\bot \leftarrow \bullet\ell_{\circ\Diamond a} \wedge \neg a \wedge \neg\ell_{\circ\Diamond a})$$
$$\hat{\circ}\Box(\bot \leftarrow \neg\bullet\ell_{\circ\Diamond a} \wedge a)$$
$$\hat{\circ}\Box(\bot \leftarrow \neg\bullet\ell_{\circ\Diamond a} \wedge \ell_{\circ\Diamond a})$$
$$\Box((\bot \leftarrow \ell_{\circ\Diamond a}) \leftarrow \mathbb{F}) \tag{6}$$

all of which are now ready to be compiled into regular rules with the translation given in Sect. 2. The application of the (weak) next operator shifts the temporal context of the actual rules one step ahead; the usage of the weak version $\hat{\circ}$ makes sure that they are not falsified at the end of the trace. The final rule in (6) is added to ensure that $\ell_{\circ\Diamond a}$ is false in the final state. All in all, we get a translation linear in the size of the original literal.

Now, to illustrate the actual rewriting of future-oriented operators in rule heads, let us start with a simple past-future temporal rule

$$\Box(a \vee \circ b \leftarrow \ell) \tag{7}$$

where ℓ can be thought of as an auxiliary atom, representing the original body. $a \vee \circ b$ means that a is true now or b is true at the next point in time.

The translation consists of three parts. First, we time-shift a rule for all possible time points, in which an atom, viz. a or b, can be made true. For the above rule, there are only two relevant rules:

$$\Box(a \vee \circ b \leftarrow \ell)$$
$$\hat{\circ}\Box(\bullet a \vee b \leftarrow \bullet\ell)$$

Until this point, both rules together are strongly equivalent to the original one in (7). Note that $\bullet a \vee b$ means (outside of any temporal context) that a is true at the previous point in time or b is true now.

Then, in the resulting rules, we double negate each outermost next and previous operator in the rule head. For our example, this results in:

$$\Box(a \vee \neg\neg\circ b \leftarrow \ell)$$
$$\hat{\circ}\Box(\neg\neg\bullet a \vee b \leftarrow \bullet\ell)$$

Here, we loose strong equivalence but the past-future condition guarantees that the solutions of the obtained programs are the same.

Finally, we can unfold the formulas in the usual way. For our example, this is:

$$\Box(a \leftarrow \neg\circ b \wedge \ell)$$
$$\hat{\circ}\Box(b \leftarrow \neg\bullet a \wedge \bullet\ell)$$

This is strongly equivalent to the rules obtained in the previous step of the translation. Once the negative occurrence of $\circ b$ is eliminated from the first rule (as shown above), we get a set of present-centered dynamic rules being equivalent to the one in (7).

Finally, let us consider the treatment of an inductive operator, and have a look at the eventually operator in the head of the following rule:

$$\Box(\Diamond a \leftarrow \ell) \tag{8}$$

$\Diamond a$ means that a is true now or at some point in the future; its unfolding relies on the temporal law $\Diamond a \leftrightarrow a \vee \circ \Diamond a$.

By letting $\bullet^0 \varphi = \varphi$ and $\bullet^i \varphi = \bullet\bullet^{i-1}\varphi$ for $i > 0$, we obtain in step one:

$$\Box(a \vee \circ \Diamond a \leftarrow \bullet^0 \ell)$$
$$\Box(\bullet^1 a \vee a \vee \circ \Diamond a \leftarrow \bullet^1 \ell)$$
$$\vdots$$
$$\Box(\bullet^i a \vee \cdots \vee \bullet^1 a \vee a \vee \circ \Diamond a \leftarrow \bullet^i \ell)$$

Taken together, these rules are equivalent to the rule in (8) but differ in the number of applications of the law $\Diamond a \leftrightarrow a \vee \circ \Diamond a$.[8]

For each $i \geq 0$, we can then add the double negations as in the example above:

$$\Box(\neg\neg\bullet^i a \vee \cdots \vee \neg\neg\bullet^1 a \vee a \vee \neg\neg\circ\Diamond a \leftarrow \bullet^i \ell)$$

And finally, we can shift the double negated literals into the rule body:

$$\Box(a \leftarrow \neg\bullet^i a \wedge \cdots \wedge \neg\bullet^1 a \wedge \neg\circ\Diamond a \wedge \bullet^i \ell)$$

Once all negative occurrences of $\circ\Diamond a$ are eliminated (as shown above), we get once more a linear number of present-centered dynamic rules (of successively increasing size) being equivalent to the one in (8). In this case, we thus get a translation of quadratic size.

In general, the unfolding of future formulas may result in an exponential translation whereas the one for past formulas is linear in size. Currently, *telingo* unfolds without introducing shortcuts. We might be able to use a full Tseitin-style translation introducing auxiliary atoms to keep the translation compact, along with a good strategy guaranteeing compactness, which might be more difficult in the presence of inductive operators.

4.3 Solving Regular Logic Programs Incrementally

The above translation results in two (non-ground) regular logic programs corresponding to P_0 and P_k in (2) and (3), respectively. A control loop, similar to the

---

[8] Unlike in the example above, we do not obtain strongly equivalent rules because we do not introduce weak next operators. This is safe in this context because the literal $\bullet^i \ell$ does not apply for horizons smaller i.

one in [13], starts with P_0 and successively adds P_k for increasing k, grounds it, and solves the accumulated program until a stop criterion is met. In other words, *telingo* computes the stable models of $P_0 \cup \bigcup_{k \geq 0} P_k$ for $k \geq 0$. This process is controlled by three options: `--imin` and `--imax`, the minimum and maximum number of solving steps, respectively, and `--istop`, the stop criterion, which defaults to `sat` and offers alternatives `unsat` and `unknown`.

An interesting detail concerns the treatment of the final rule in Line 29 of Listing 1, viz. ':- at(X, river_bank).' standing for $\Box(\mathbb{F} \rightarrow \neg\textbf{at}(\textbf{X}, \textbf{river\_bank}))$. As described in Sect. 2, final rules are equipped with a special-purpose literal, $\neg q_{k+1}$, during their translation into regular rules in order to control their range of applicability in view of increasing k. In terms of module theory, q_{k+1} is an input atom, and they are accounted for by `#external` declarations in *clingo*. In our example, the recurrent test of ':- at(X, river_bank).' at the final time point gives rise to the program:

```
1  #external q(k+1). [false]
2  :- at(X,river_bank,k), not q(k+1).
```

The time parameter `k` is handled by the aforementioned control loop through *clingo*'s API. The declaration of `q(k+1)` as an external exempts it from simplification and allows for assigning truth values via the API. The trailing `[false]` gives the initial truth value.[9] For brevity, we refrain from duplicating the rule for all instantiations of `X`. For `k = 0`, we thus get ':- at(X,river_bank,0), not q(1).' along with `q(1)` being `false`. Hence, the integrity constraint amounts to requiring that `at(X,river_bank)` is false for all instantiations of `X` at time point 0.

For `k = 1`, we have two instances of Line 2:

```
:- at(X,river_bank,0), not q(1).
:- at(X,river_bank,1), not q(2).
```

However, while as before `q(2)` is set to `false` by its declaration as an external (cf. Line 1 above), the control loop changes the truth of `q(1)` to `true`. As a result, the first integrity constraint becomes vacuous and only the second one applies, now requiring that `at(X,river_bank)` is false at time point 1 (for all instantiations of `X`). This mechanism ensures that final rules always apply exclusively to the last point in time. Note that the change of the truth value of external atoms via the API accounts for the addition of facts in (3).

4.4 Extracting Traces from Regular Stable Models

telingo translates a temporal logic program into a regular one, whose stable models are incrementally computed by *clingo*. The obtained model is then translated back into a temporal trace by reversing translation τ on the atoms in the model. That is, each atom a_k is turned into a and associated with the state numbered k.

---

[9] This feature is introduced with *clingo* 5.4.

5 Experiments

To check whether our approach imposes a significant burden on grounding and solving, we set up the following experiment: We took the benchmark suite used in [8] for incrementally solving ASP planning benchmarks.[10] This benchmark suite was obtained in [8] by manually producing incremental ASP encodings from encodings using a fixed plan length. This includes the benchmark domains *hanoi-tower*, *labyrinth*, *no-mystery*, *ricochet-robots*, *sokoban*, and *visit-all*, all originating in recent ASP competitions. In turn, we manually translated the incremental encodings from [8] into the temporal input language of *telingo*.[11] This resulted in two benchmark suites, in each case consisting of 69 benchmark instances. We then contrasted the results obtained by solving the incremental instances with *clingo* 5.3 and the temporal ones with *telingo* 1.0 (also based on *clingo* 5.3). The experiments ran under Linux on Intel Xeon E5-2650 v4 processors and 64 GB memory; we selected instances solvable within 24 h by both *clingo* and *telingo*, and computed a single model.

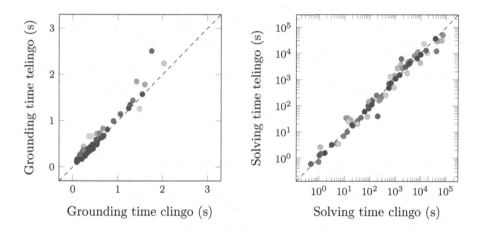

Fig. 1. Grounding and solving times of clingo and telingo

Figure 1 shows two scatter plots comparing the runtime of *clingo* and *telingo* for both grounding and solving. Each point in such a plot displays the runtimes for one instance; the runtime of *clingo* is displayed on the x-axis and the runtime of *telingo* on the y-axis. Thus, we find easier instances in the lower left part and harder instances in the upper right part of a plot. Furthermore, the farther a point is away from the diagonal, the more the runtimes of both systems diverge; for points in the lower right part of a plot, *telingo* is faster and for points in the upper left part, *clingo* is faster. To highlight runtime differences, we use the

---

[10] https://github.com/potassco/asp-planning-benchmarks.
[11] https://github.com/potassco/clingo-vs-telingo-planning/tree/v1.0.0.

colors from a heat map ranging from blue (both systems are equally fast) over yellow to red (highest runtime deviation of both systems).

First, let us look at the grounding times in the left plot in Fig. 1. We see that most points are close to the diagonal, showing that both systems perform quite similarly. All instances could be grounded in less than 3 seconds making grounding times negligible in the overall runtime. Furthermore, the resulting ground programs have nearly the same number of rules and atoms (each deviates by 0.01% on average). These results are not that surprising given that ASP planning benchmarks only deal with one-step transitions, and do not involve any complex temporal statements. Here, the translation in *telingo* boils down to adding time parameters to atoms. Hence, the translated program passed to the grounder is very similar to the incremental program used by *clingo*.

Next, we look at the solving times depicted in the right plot in Fig. 1. Note that both *clingo* and *telingo* find solutions for the smallest horizon where a problem is satisfiable. Since the difficulty of planning problems increases exponentially with the search horizon, we use logarithmic axes in the plot. We see that there are runtime fluctuations between both systems. This is due to different traversals of the search space of both systems induced by heuristic effects. Such fluctuations are to be expected with ASP solvers, which are sensitive to small changes in instances, where even changing the order in which rules are passed to a solver can make a big difference in runtime.

All in all, our experiments confirm that *telingo*'s machinery imposes no significant encumbrance compared to a direct treatment with *clingo*.[12]

6   Discussion

We have described the temporal ASP system *telingo*, starting from its input language, over its workflow on top of *clingo*, to an empirical demonstration of its lightweight machinery. Previous temporal extensions to ASP [3,12] relied on different semantics resulting in translations to automata and thus model checkers. What makes *telingo* interesting is that it constitutes a true extension of the ASP system *clingo*, and provides us with a full-fledged temporal modeling language. Moreover, it allows for an easy embedding of action languages (cf. [4]) and offers the specification of nested logic programs. For the future, we envisage the integration of constructs from dynamic logic, as proposed in [2], and the integration of more flexible reasoning modes, as used in [8].

Acknowledgments. This work was partially supported by MINECO, Spain, grant TIC2017-84453-P, Xunta de Galicia, Spain (GPC ED431B 2016/035 and 2016-2019 ED431G/01, CITIC), and DFG grant SCHA 550/9.

---

[12] Detailed results are obtainable at https://github.com/potassco/clingo-vs-telingo-planning/tree/v1.0.0/benchmark-results.

References

1. Aguado, F., Cabalar, P., Diéguez, M., Pérez, G., Vidal, C.: Temporal equilibrium logic: a survey. J. Appl. Non-Classical Log. **23**(1–2), 2–24 (2013)
2. Bosser, A., Cabalar, P., Diéguez, M., Schaub, T.: Introducing temporal stable models for linear dynamic logic. In: Proceedings of the International Conference on Principles of Knowledge Representation and Reasoning, pp. 12–21. AAAI Press (2018)
3. Cabalar, P., Diéguez, M.: STELP: a tool for temporal answer set programming. In: [7], pp. 370–375 (2011)
4. Cabalar, P., Kaminski, R., Schaub, T., Schuhmann, A.: Temporal answer set programming on finite traces. Theory Pract. Log. Program. **18**(3–4), 406–420 (2018)
5. Cabalar, P., Pérez Vega, G.: Temporal equilibrium logic: a first approach. In: Moreno Díaz, R., Pichler, F., Quesada Arencibia, A. (eds.) EUROCAST 2007. LNCS, vol. 4739, pp. 241–248. Springer, Heidelberg (2007). https://doi.org/10.1007/978-3-540-75867-9_31
6. De Giacomo, G., Vardi, M.: Linear temporal logic and linear dynamic logic on finite traces. In: Proceedings of the International Joint Conference on Artificial Intelligence, pp. 854–860. IJCAI/AAAI Press (2013)
7. Delgrande, J., Faber, W. (eds.): LPNMR 2011. LNCS, vol. 6645. Springer, Heidelberg (2011). https://doi.org/10.1007/978-3-642-20895-9
8. Dimopoulos, Y., Gebser, M., Lühne, P., Romero, J., Schaub, T.: plasp 3: Towards effective ASP planning. Theory Pract. Log. Program. (2018, to appear)
9. Gebser, M., Kaminski, R., Kaufmann, B., Ostrowski, M., Schaub, T., Wanko, P.: Theory solving made easy with clingo 5. In: Technical Communications of the International Conference on Logic Programming, vol. 52, pp. 2:1–2:15. OASIcs (2016)
10. Gebser, M., Kaminski, R., Kaufmann, B., Schaub, T.: Multi-shot ASP solving with clingo. Theory Pract. Log. Program. **19**(1), 27–82 (2019)
11. Gebser, M., Kaminski, R., König, A., Schaub, T.: Advances in gringo series 3. In: [7], pp. 345–351 (2011)
12. Giordano, L., Martelli, A., Theseider Dupré, D.: Reasoning about actions with temporal answer sets. Theory Pract. Log. Program. **13**(2), 201–225 (2013)
13. Kaminski, R., Schaub, T., Wanko, P.: A tutorial on hybrid answer set solving with *clingo*. In: Ianni, G., et al. (eds.) Reasoning Web 2017. LNCS, vol. 10370, pp. 167–203. Springer, Cham (2017). https://doi.org/10.1007/978-3-319-61033-7_6
14. Kamp, J.: Tense logic and the theory of linear order. Ph.D. thesis, UCLA (1968)
15. Lifschitz, V.: Answer set planning. In: Proceedings of the International Conference on Logic Programming, pp. 23–37. MIT Press (1999)
16. Oikarinen, E., Janhunen, T.: Modular equivalence for normal logic programs. In: Proceedings of the European Conference on Artificial Intelligence, pp. 412–416. IOS Press (2006)
17. Pnueli, A.: The temporal logic of programs. In: Proceedings of the Symposium on Foundations of Computer Science, pp. 46–57. IEEE Press (1977)

Verifying Strong Equivalence of Programs in the Input Language of GRINGO

Vladimir Lifschitz[1], Patrick Lühne[2], and Torsten Schaub[2,3,4]($\boxtimes$)

[1] University of Texas at Austin, Austin, USA
[2] University of Potsdam, Potsdam, Germany
torsten@cs.uni-potsdam.de
[3] Simon Fraser University, Burnaby, Canada
[4] Griffith University, Gold Coast, Australia

Abstract. The semantics of the input language of the ASP grounder GRINGO uses a translation that converts a logic program, which may contain variables and arithmetic operations, into a set of infinitary propositional formulas. In this note, we show that the result of that translation can be replaced in some cases by a finite set of first-order sentences. The translator ANTHEM constructs that set of sentences and converts it to a format that can be processed by automated reasoning tools. ANTHEM, in combination with the first-order theorem prover VAMPIRE, allows us to verify the strong equivalence of programs in the language of GRINGO.

1 Introduction

The semantics of the input language of the ASP grounder GRINGO [3] uses a translation τ that converts a logic program, which may contain variables and arithmetic operations, into a set of infinitary propositional formulas. In this note, we show that the set produced by τ can be replaced in some cases by a finite set of first-order sentences. The translator ANTHEM constructs that set of sentences and converts it to a format that can be processed by automated reasoning tools.

In combination with the first-order theorem prover VAMPIRE [7], ANTHEM allows us to verify strong equivalence of programs in the language of GRINGO with a computer-assisted proof. This relation between logic programs is important because it guarantees the possibility of replacing one program by the other in any context [9]. Earlier work on verifying strong equivalence [1,6] was restricted to programs that do not contain arithmetic operations.

The definition of a logic program in Sect. 2 largely follows [3,5], and it disregards some details of the syntax of GRINGO. For instance, about the set of symbolic constants we assume only that it is countably infinite and totally ordered; in GRINGO, symbolic constants are actually strings, and they are ordered lexicographically. Dropping the condition `abc < acb` from the body of a rule in a GRINGO program does not change the set of stable models, but this fact is not reflected in our more abstract theory of strong equivalence.

M. Balduccini et al. (Eds.): LPNMR 2019, LNAI 11481, pp. 270–283, 2019.
https://doi.org/10.1007/978-3-030-20528-7_20

The class of programs studied in this note is more restricted than that in the papers quoted above. In particular, local variables are not allowed. Accordingly, the version of τ defined in Sect. 3 does not use infinite conjunctions and disjunctions. It produces, generally, an infinite set of finite formulas. Some of the theorems in this paper refer, however, to infinitary propositional formulas and to the strong equivalence relation between them [4].

This paper is structured as follows. Sections 2 and 3 revisit background on logic programs and stable models. Section 4 extends strong equivalence from the propositional case to logic programs as defined in Sect. 2. Section 5 outlines the target language of τ^*, our new translation from logic programs to finite sets of first-order sentences. τ^* is then introduced in Sect. 6. Section 7 discusses the important special case of positive programs. The translator ANTHEM is presented in Sect. 8. Finally, Sect. 9 shows how to programmatically verify the strong equivalence of positive programs with ANTHEM and the theorem prover VAMPIRE, and Sect. 10 concludes this paper with ideas for future work.

2   Background: Logic Programs

We assume that three countably infinite sets of symbols are selected: *numerals*, *symbolic constants*, and *program variables*. (We talk about "program" variables to distinguish them from "integer" variables, introduced in Sect. 5 below. Integer variables are allowed in formulas but not in programs.) We assume that a 1-to-1 correspondence between numerals and integers is chosen; we denote the numeral corresponding to an integer n by $\overline{n}$.

Program terms are defined recursively as follows. (Program terms are to be distinguished from "formula terms," defined in Sect. 5.)

- Numerals, symbolic constants, program variables, and the symbols *inf* and *sup* are program terms;
- if t_1, t_2 are program terms and *op* is one of the *operation names*

$$+ \quad - \quad \times \quad / \quad \backslash \quad ..$$

then $(t_1 \ op \ t_2)$ is a program term.

If t is a term, then $-t$ is shorthand for $\overline{0} - t$. A program term, or another syntactic expression, is *ground* if it does not contain variables. A ground expression is *precomputed* if it does not contain operation names.

We assume that a total order on precomputed program terms is chosen, where

- *inf* is its least element and *sup* is its greatest element,
- for any integers m and n, $\overline{m} < \overline{n}$ iff $m < n$, and
- for any integer n and any symbolic constant c, $\overline{n} < c$.

An *atom* is an expression of the form $p(\mathbf{t})$, where p is a symbolic constant and $\mathbf{t}$ is a tuple of program terms. A *literal* is an atom possibly preceded by one or two occurrences of *not*. A *comparison* is an expression of the form $(t_1 \, rel \, t_2)$, where t_1, t_2 are program terms and *rel* is one of the *relation names*

$$= \; \neq \; < \; > \; \leq \; \geq \tag{1}$$

A *rule* is an expression of the form

$$Head \leftarrow Body, \tag{2}$$

where

- *Body* is a conjunction (possibly empty) of literals and comparisons, and
- *Head* is either an atom (then we say that (2) is a *basic rule*), or an atom in braces (then (2) is a *choice rule*), or empty (then (2) is a *constraint*).

A *program* is a finite set of rules.

3   Background: Stable Models

An *interpretation* is a set of precomputed atoms. We define which interpretations are stable models of a program Π by first transforming Π into a set $\tau\Pi$ of propositional formulas formed from precomputed atoms and then referring to the definition of a stable model (answer set) [2] of a set of propositional formulas.

In propositional formulas, we consider the connectives

$$\bot \; (\text{"false"}), \; \wedge, \; \vee, \; \rightarrow \tag{3}$$

primitives; $\top$ is shorthand for $\bot \rightarrow \bot$, $\neg F$ is shorthand for $F \rightarrow \bot$, and $F \leftrightarrow G$ is shorthand for $(F \rightarrow G) \wedge (G \rightarrow F)$.

Before defining τ, we define, for every ground program term t, the set $[t]$ of its *values*:

- if t is a numeral, a symbolic constant, *inf*, or *sup*, then $[t]$ is $\{t\}$;
- if t is $(t_1 + t_2)$, then $[t]$ is the set of numerals $\overline{n_1 + n_2}$ for all integers n_1, n_2 such that $\overline{n_1} \in [t_1]$ and $\overline{n_2} \in [t_2]$; similarly when t is $(t_1 - t_2)$ or $(t_1 \times t_2)$;
- if t is (t_1/t_2), then $[t]$ is the set of numerals $\lfloor n_1/n_2 \rfloor$ for all integers n_1, n_2 such that $\overline{n_1} \in [t_1]$, $\overline{n_2} \in [t_2]$, and $n_2 \neq 0$;
- if t is $(t_1 \backslash t_2)$, then $[t]$ is the set of numerals $\overline{n_1 - n_2 \cdot \lfloor n_1/n_2 \rfloor}$ for all integers n_1, n_2 such that $\overline{n_1} \in [t_1]$, $\overline{n_2} \in [t_2]$, and $n_2 \neq 0$;
- if t is $(t_1 .. t_2)$, then $[t]$ is the set of numerals $\overline{m}$ for all integers m such that some integers n_1, n_2 satisfy $\overline{n_1} \in [t_1]$, $\overline{n_2} \in [t_2]$, and $n_1 \leq m \leq n_2$.

It is clear that values of a ground program term are precomputed program terms. For example,

- the only value of $\overline{2} \times \overline{2}$ is $\overline{4}$;
- the values of $\overline{1} .. \overline{3}$ are $\overline{1}, \overline{2}, \overline{3}$;
- $\overline{1}/\overline{0}$ has no values;

– $a + \bar{1}$, where a is a symbolic constant, has no values.

For any ground terms $t_1, \ldots, t_n$, by $[t_1, \ldots, t_n]$ we denote the set of tuples $r_1, \ldots, r_n$ for all $r_1 \in [t_1], \ldots, r_n \in [t_n]$.

Now, we can turn to the definition of τ. For any ground atom $p(\mathbf{t})$,

– $\tau p(\mathbf{t})$ stands for $\bigvee_{\mathbf{r} \in [\mathbf{t}]} p(\mathbf{r})$,
– $\tau(not\, p(\mathbf{t}))$ stands for $\bigvee_{\mathbf{r} \in [\mathbf{t}]} \neg p(\mathbf{r})$, and
– $\tau(not\, not\, p(\mathbf{t}))$ stands for $\bigvee_{\mathbf{r} \in [\mathbf{t}]} \neg\neg p(\mathbf{r})$.

For example,

– $\tau p(\bar{1}\,..\,\bar{3})$ is $p(\bar{1}) \vee p(\bar{2}) \vee p(\bar{3})$,
– $\tau(not\, p(\bar{1}\,..\,\bar{3}))$ is $\neg p(\bar{1}) \vee \neg p(\bar{2}) \vee \neg p(\bar{3})$.

For any ground comparison $t_1 \, rel \, t_2$, we define $\tau(t_1 \, rel \, t_2)$ as

– $\top$ if the relation rel holds between some r_1 from $[t_1]$ and some r_2 from $[t_2]$;
– $\bot$ otherwise.

For example, $\tau(\bar{1} = \bar{1}\,..\,\bar{3})$ is $\top$.

If each of $C_1, \ldots, C_k$ is a ground literal or a ground comparison, then $\tau(C_1 \wedge \cdots \wedge C_k)$ stands for $\tau C_1 \wedge \cdots \wedge \tau C_k$.

If R is a ground basic rule $p(\mathbf{t}) \leftarrow Body$, then τR is the propositional formula

$$\tau(Body) \rightarrow \bigwedge_{\mathbf{r} \in [\mathbf{t}]} p(\mathbf{r}).$$

If R is a ground choice rule $\{p(\mathbf{t})\} \leftarrow Body$, then τR is the propositional formula

$$\tau(Body) \rightarrow \bigwedge_{\mathbf{r} \in [\mathbf{t}]} (p(\mathbf{r}) \vee \neg p(\mathbf{r})).$$

If R is a ground constraint $\leftarrow Body$, then τR is $\neg\tau(Body)$.

An *instance* of a rule is a ground rule obtained from it by substituting precomputed program terms for program variables. For any program Π, $\tau\Pi$ is the set of the propositional formulas τR for all instances R of the rules of Π.

For example, the instances of the rule

$$q(X + \bar{1}) \leftarrow p(X) \tag{4}$$

are the ground rules

$$q(r + \bar{1}) \leftarrow p(r)$$

for all precomputed program terms r. If r is a numeral $\bar{n}$, then the result of applying τ to this instance is

$$p(\bar{n}) \rightarrow q(\overline{n+1}). \tag{5}$$

If r is not a numeral, then the result is

$$p(r) \rightarrow \top \tag{6}$$

(because the empty conjunction is understood as $\top$). Consequently, the result of applying τ to rule (4) consists of propositional formulas (5) for all integers n and propositional formulas (6) for all precomputed program terms r except numerals.

Similarly, the result of applying τ to the rule

$$q(X) \leftarrow p(X - \overline{1}) \tag{7}$$

consists of the propositional formulas

$$p(\overline{n-1}) \rightarrow q(\overline{n}) \tag{8}$$

for all integers n and the propositional formulas

$$\bot \rightarrow q(r) \tag{9}$$

for all precomputed program terms r other than numerals.

An interpretation is a *stable model* of a program Π if it is a stable model of $\tau\Pi$.

4   Strong Equivalence

Recall that sets Γ_1 and Γ_2 of propositional formulas are said to be *strongly equivalent* to each other if for every set Γ of propositional formulas, $\Gamma_1 \cup \Gamma$ has the same stable models as $\Gamma_2 \cup \Gamma$. Two sets of propositional formulas are strongly equivalent iff each of them can be derived from the other in the propositional logic of here-and-there, which is intermediate between classical and intuitionistic [9].

We extend the definition of strong equivalence to programs in the sense of Sect. 2 as follows: Programs Π_1 and Π_2 are *strongly equivalent* to each other if $\tau\Pi_1$ is strongly equivalent to $\tau\Pi_2$.

For example, one-rule program (4) is strongly equivalent to (7). To justify this claim, note that the sets of formulas obtained from these two rules by applying the transformation τ are intuitionistically equivalent. Indeed, the set of formulas (5) for all integers n is identical to the set of formulas (8) for all integers n; on the other hand, all formulas (6) and (9) are provable intuitionistically.

This argument is quite simple, but it involves reasoning about infinite sets of propositional formulas. It is not immediately clear how to automate generating proofs of this kind. This is the challenge that we are interested in. Our approach is to replace τ by a transformation τ^*, defined in Sect. 6 below, which produces a finite set of first-order sentences. Sets of that kind can be processed by automated reasoning tools. The transformation τ^* is somewhat similar to the transformations defined in [5] and implemented in an earlier version of ANTHEM [8].

To take another example, consider the rules

$$q(X) \leftarrow p(X), \tag{10}$$

$$q(X + \overline{1}) \leftarrow p(X + \overline{1}). \tag{11}$$

They are not strongly equivalent to each other. Indeed, adding the rule $p(a)$, where a is a symbolic constant, to the former gives a program with the stable model $\{p(a), q(a)\}$; adding that rule to the latter gives a program with the stable model $\{p(a)\}$.

We call a rule *trivial* if it is strongly equivalent to the empty program. It is clear that a rule R is trivial iff τR is provable in the logic of here-and-there. Removing a trivial rule from a program does not affect its stable models. For example, the rule

$$p(\overline{4}) \leftarrow p(\overline{2} \times \overline{2}) \tag{12}$$

is trivial because the result

$$p(\overline{4}) \rightarrow p(\overline{4})$$

of applying τ to it is intuitionistically provable. The rule

$$p(\overline{1} .. \overline{3}) \leftarrow p(\overline{1} .. \overline{3}) \tag{13}$$

is not trivial because the program obtained by adding it to the fact $p(\overline{1})$ has $p(\overline{2})$ and $p(\overline{3})$ in its stable model.

Other examples of strong equivalence are given in Sect. 9.

5   Formulas

In this section, we define the target language of the new translation τ^*. This is a first-order language with variables of two sorts. First, we include program variables, introduced in Sect. 2; they range over precomputed program terms. Second, *integer variables* range over numerals (or, equivalently, integers).

Arithmetic terms are formed from numerals and integer variables using the operation symbols $+$, $-$, and $\times$. Note that $/$ and $\backslash$ are not allowed in arithmetic terms. This is because division by 0 is undefined, and in first-order logic, a function symbol is expected to denote a total function. Intervals are not allowed either because an interval expression, generally, does not have a single value.

We collectively refer to arithmetic terms, symbolic constants, program variables, and the symbols *inf* and *sup* as *formula terms*. Thus, the set of program terms (defined in Sect. 2) and the set of formula terms partially overlap. In a program term, integer variables are not allowed; on the other hand, in a formula term, arithmetic operations cannot be applied to symbolic constants and program variables. It is clear that the only precomputed arithmetic terms are numerals. Precomputed formula terms are identical to precomputed program terms so that we can talk simply about "precomputed terms."

Atomic formulas are expressions of the forms

- $p(\mathbf{t})$, where p is a symbolic constant and $\mathbf{t}$ is a tuple of formula terms (separated by commas, possibly empty), and
- $(t_1 \, rel \, t_2)$, where t_1, t_2 are formula terms and rel is one of relation names (1).

Formulas are formed from atomic formulas using propositional connectives (3) and the quantifiers $\forall$ and $\exists$ as usual in first-order logic. It is clear that every propositional formula in the sense of Sect. 3—a propositional combination of precomputed atoms—is a closed formula in the sense of this definition.

The satisfaction relation between interpretations and propositional formulas is extended to arbitrary closed formulas as usual in classical logic; program variables range over precomputed program terms, and integer variables range over numerals. Two closed formulas are *classically equivalent* to each other if they are satisfied by the same interpretations.

For describing the relationship between the translations τ and τ^*, we need a translation that converts closed formulas in this language into infinitary propositional formulas formed from precomputed atoms. The infinitary propositional formula F^{prop} corresponding to a closed formula F is defined as follows:

- if F is $p(\mathbf{t})$, then F^{prop} is obtained from F by replacing each member of $\mathbf{t}$ by its value;
- if F is $(t_1 \; rel \; t_2)$, then F^{prop} is $\top$ if the values of t_1 and t_2 are in the relation rel, and $\bot$ otherwise;
- $\bot^{\mathrm{prop}}$ is $\bot$;
- $(F \odot G)^{\mathrm{prop}}$ is $(F^{\mathrm{prop}} \odot G^{\mathrm{prop}})$ for every binary connective $\odot$;
- $(\forall X F(X))^{\mathrm{prop}}$ is the conjunction of the formulas $F(r)^{\mathrm{prop}}$ over all precomputed terms r if X is a program variable, and over all numerals r if X is an integer variable;
- $(\exists X F(X))^{\mathrm{prop}}$ is the disjunction of the formulas $F(r)^{\mathrm{prop}}$ over all precomputed terms r if X is a program variable, and over all numerals r if X is an integer variable.

It is clear that a closed formula F is satisfied by the same interpretations as the corresponding infinitary propositional formula F^{prop}. Closed formulas F and G are classically equivalent iff the infinitary propositional formulas F^{prop} and F^{prop} are classically equivalent. If F^{prop} and G^{prop} are strongly equivalent, then F and G are classically equivalent.

For example, if F is

$$\forall X \exists N (N \geq 0 \wedge p(X, N)),$$

where X is a program variable and N is an integer variable, then F^{prop} is

$$\bigwedge_r \left(\bigvee_{n \geq 0} (\top \wedge p(r, \overline{n})) \vee \bigvee_{n < 0} (\bot \wedge p(r, \overline{n})) \right),$$

where r ranges over precomputed terms and n ranges over integers. This formula is strongly equivalent to

$$\bigwedge_r \bigvee_{n \geq 0} p(r, \overline{n}).$$

6   Transforming Programs into Formulas

Prior to defining τ^*, we define, for every program term t, a formula $val_t(Z)$, where Z is a program variable that does not occur in t. That formula expresses, informally speaking, that Z is one of the values of t. This property is made precise in Proposition 1 below.

The definition is recursive:

- if t is a numeral, a symbolic constant, a program variable, inf, or sup, then $val_t(Z)$ is $Z = t$;
- if t is $(t_1 \, op \, t_2)$, where op is $+$, $-$, or $\times$, then $val_t(Z)$ is

$$\exists IJ(Z = I \, op \, J \wedge val_{t_1}(I) \wedge val_{t_2}(J)),$$

  where I, J are fresh integer variables;
- if t is (t_1/t_2), then $val_t(Z)$ is

$$\exists IJQR(I = J \times Q + R \wedge val_{t_1}(I) \wedge val_{t_2}(J)$$
$$\wedge \, J \neq 0 \wedge R \geq 0 \wedge R < Q \wedge Z = Q),$$

  where I, J, Q, R are fresh integer variables;
- if t is $(t_1 \backslash t_2)$, then $val_t(Z)$ is

$$\exists IJQR(I = J \times Q + R \wedge val_{t_1}(I) \wedge val_{t_2}(J)$$
$$\wedge \, J \neq 0 \wedge R \geq 0 \wedge R < Q \wedge Z = R),$$

  where I, J, Q, R are fresh integer variables;
- if t is $(t_1 .. t_2)$, then $val_t(Z)$ is

$$\exists IJK(val_{t_1}(I) \wedge val_{t_2}(J) \wedge I \leq K \wedge K \leq J \wedge Z = K),$$

  where I, J, K are fresh integer variables.

For example, $val_{X + \overline{1}}(Z)$ is

$$\exists IJ(Z = I + J \wedge I = X \wedge J = \overline{1}),$$

where I, J are integer variables.

Proposition 1. *For any ground program term t and any precomputed term r, the formula $val_t(r)^{\mathrm{prop}}$ is strongly equivalent to $\top$ if $r \in [t]$ and to $\bot$ otherwise.*

This assertion can be proved by induction on t.

The last thing to do in preparation for defining τ^* is to define the translation τ^B that is applied to expressions in the body of the rule:

- $\tau^B(p(t_1, \ldots, t_k))$ is

$$\exists Z_1 \ldots Z_k(val_{t_1}(Z_1) \wedge \cdots \wedge val_{t_k}(Z_k) \wedge p(Z_1, \ldots, Z_k));$$

- $\tau^B(not \, p(t_1, \ldots, t_k))$ is

$$\exists Z_1 \ldots Z_k(val_{t_1}(Z_1) \wedge \cdots \wedge val_{t_k}(Z_k) \wedge \neg p(Z_1, \ldots, Z_k));$$

$- \tau^B(not\ not\ p(t_1, \ldots, t_k))$ is

$$\exists Z_1 \ldots Z_k(val_{t_1}(Z_1) \wedge \cdots \wedge val_{t_k}(Z_k) \wedge \neg\neg p(Z_1, \ldots, Z_k));$$

$- \tau^B(t_1\ rel\ t_2)$ is

$$\exists Z_1 Z_2(val_{t_1}(Z_1) \wedge val_{t_2}(Z_2) \wedge Z_1\ rel\ Z_2);$$

where each Z_i is a fresh program variable.

From Proposition 1, we conclude:

Proposition 2. *If L is a ground literal or ground comparison, then $(\tau^B L)^{\mathrm{prop}}$ is strongly equivalent to τL.*

Now, we define

$$\tau^*(Head \leftarrow B_1 \wedge \cdots \wedge B_n)$$

as the universal closure of the formula

$$\tau^B(B_1) \wedge \cdots \wedge \tau^B(B_n) \rightarrow H,$$

where H is

- $\forall Z_1 \ldots Z_k(val_{t_1}(Z_1) \wedge \cdots \wedge val_{t_k}(Z_k) \rightarrow p(Z_1, \ldots, Z_k))$
  if $Head$ is $p(t_1, \ldots, t_k)$;
- $\forall Z_1 \ldots Z_k(val_{t_1}(Z_1) \wedge \cdots \wedge val_{t_k}(Z_k) \rightarrow p(Z_1, \ldots, Z_k) \vee \neg p(Z_1, \ldots, Z_k))$
  if $Head$ is $\{p(t_1, \ldots, t_k)\}$;
- $\bot$ if $Head$ is empty;

where each Z_i is a fresh program variable.

For example, the result of applying τ^* to rule (4) is

$$\forall X(\exists Z(Z = X \wedge p(Z)) \rightarrow \forall Z_1(\exists IJ(Z_1 = I+J \wedge I = X \wedge J = \bar{1}) \rightarrow q(Z_1))). \quad (14)$$

The result of applying τ^* to rule (7) is

$$\forall X(\exists Z(\exists IJ(Z = I-J \wedge I = X \wedge J = \bar{1}) \wedge p(Z)) \rightarrow \forall Z_1(Z_1 = X \rightarrow q(X))). \quad (15)$$

From Proposition 2, we conclude:

Proposition 3. *For any rule R, $(\tau^* R)^{\mathrm{prop}}$ is strongly equivalent to τR.*

For any program Π, $\tau^*\Pi$ stands for the set of formulas τR for all rules R of Π. From Proposition 3, we conclude:

Proposition 4. *A program Π_1 is strongly equivalent to a program Π_2 iff $(\tau^* \Pi_1)^{\mathrm{prop}}$ is strongly equivalent to $(\tau^* \Pi_2)^{\mathrm{prop}}$.*

For example, the question about the strong equivalence of rule (4) to rule (7), resolved in Sect. 4, can be reformulated as the question about the strong equivalence of the propositional counterparts of formulas (14) and (15).

With Proposition 4 available, our goal of verifying strong equivalence of programs using automated reasoning tools for classical logic is not yet within reach; what we need in addition is a way to use these tools to verify the condition

$$(\tau^* \Pi_1)^{\mathrm{prop}} \text{ is strongly equivalent to } (\tau^* \Pi_2)^{\mathrm{prop}}. \tag{16}$$

This can be achieved using an additional transformation that replaces each predicate symbol by two, corresponding to the two worlds of the logic of here-and-there, and thus reduces that logic to classical. A transformation of this kind is part of the design of SELP [1]. Implementing this idea in the context of ANTHEM is a topic for future work. In the next section, we show, however, that for "positive" rules, such as (4), (7), and (10)–(13), condition (16) can be replaced by

$$\tau^* \Pi_1 \text{ is classically equivalent to } \tau^* \Pi_2,$$

which can be verified by VAMPIRE and similar systems directly.

7   Positive Programs

A *positive rule* is a basic rule or constraint such that its body is a conjunction of atoms and comparisons.

Proposition 5. *A positive program Π_1 is strongly equivalent to a positive program Π_2 iff $\tau \Pi_1$ is classically equivalent to $\tau \Pi_2$.*

This is immediate from the following lemma:

For any positive program Π and any positive ground rule R, if τR is derivable from $\tau \Pi$ classically, then τR is derivable from $\tau \Pi$ intuitionistically.

This lemma can be proved using [10, Theorem 3].

Proposition 3 shows that for any program Π, $\tau \Pi$ is classically equivalent to $\tau^* \Pi$. In view of this fact, from Proposition 5, we can conclude:

Proposition 6. *A positive program Π_1 is strongly equivalent to a positive program Π_2 iff $\tau^* \Pi_1$ is classically equivalent to $\tau^* \Pi_2$.*

This theorem justifies the use of ANTHEM for verifying strong equivalence of positive programs described below.

8   ANTHEM

ANTHEM 0.2 implements τ^* as specified in Sect. 6. ANTHEM supports input programs in the input language of GRINGO of the form described in Sect. 2, including nonpositive programs (Sect. 7), and generates output formulas in human-readable form by default. For example, ANTHEM translates the simple positive program consisting of rule (7),

```
q(X) :- p(X - 1).
```
into the formula
```
forall X
  (exists X1
    (exists N1, N2 (X1 = N1 - N2 and N1 = X and N2 = 1)
     and p(X1))
  -> forall X2 (X2 = X -> q(X2)))
```

In the output language of ANTHEM, integer variables are denoted by N1, N2, etc., while all other variables are program variables. For this program, ANTHEM additionally prints a note that the input program was detected to be positive:

info: positive program

When instead passing a nonpositive program to ANTHEM, such as

q :- **not** p.

ANTHEM still performs the translation to

not p -> q

but issues the following note:

info: nonpositive program

ANTHEM's implementation takes advantage of GRINGO's library functionality for accessing the abstract syntax tree (AST) of a nonground program. The AST obtained from GRINGO is taken by ANTHEM and turned into the AST of the collection of formulas representing the rules of the program according to τ^*. Since both the input and output of ANTHEM are small, its runtime is negligible.

ANTHEM's source code and usage instructions are available at GitHub.[1]

9   Proving Strong Equivalence of Programs with VAMPIRE

When given two input programs, ANTHEM generates an output formula expressing that the collections of formulas obtained by applying τ^* to both programs are equivalent. For positive programs, it is sufficient to prove equivalence classically to conclude that both programs are strongly equivalent (because of Proposition 6).

In order to verify the strong equivalence of two positive programs programatically, ANTHEM is able to communicate with automated first-order theorem provers supporting integer arithmetic such as VAMPIRE. To that end, ANTHEM can be instructed to generate output in the syntax of TPTP [11], a standard input language for theorem provers. More precisely, ANTHEM leverages the *typed first-order form* (TFF) of TPTP with interpreted integer arithmetic.

In the output of ANTHEM, there are variables of two sorts—integer and program variables (see Sects. 5 and 8), where the domain of integer variables is a

---

[1] https://github.com/potassco/anthem.

subset of the domain of program variables. In TPTP, there may be variables of multiple sorts, but it is not clear how to express that one sort is a subsort of another. ANTHEM works around this limitation by applying an additional transformation to the output formulas when TPTP output is requested. For this purpose, a custom sort *object* is introduced; all integer and symbolic constants are then mapped to distinct values of type *object* through auxiliary functions *integer* and *symbolic*. Then, all variables in the output formulas are changed to the *object* domain; if a quantifier binds an integer variable, ANTHEM restricts it to the condition that the value of the variable is in the range of the function *integer*. For example, the TPTP counterpart of

forall N1 (p(N1))

is

![N1: object]: ((?[X1: $int]: N1 = integer(X1)) => p(N1))

With this transformation, ANTHEM can be used in combination with a first-order theorem prover to verify the strong equivalence of positive programs. The remainder of this section presents experimental results obtained with VAMPIRE. The experiments were conducted on a Linux system with an Intel Core i7-7700K (4 physical cores, 4.5 GHz) and 16 GB of RAM. VAMPIRE was invoked with the options **--mode casc --cores 4**.

Example 1: Predecessor/Successor

Program 1	Program 2
q(X + 1) :- p(X).	q(X) :- p(X - 1).

These two programs represent rules (4) and (7) from Sect. 3. VAMPIRE proves the strong equivalence of these programs in about 2.4 s.

Example 2: Multiplication by 2

Program 1	Program 2	Program 3
q(X + X) :- p(X).	q(X + Y) :- p(X), X = Y.	q(2 * X) :- p(X).

VAMPIRE proves the strong equivalence of Programs 1 and 2 in about 5 ms. The strong equivalence of the other combinations is proved in about 3.0 s.

Example 3: Integer Between 3 and 5

Program 1	Program 2
p(X) :- X > 3, X < 5.	p(4).

VAMPIRE proves the strong equivalence of these two programs in about 3.5 s. This result is particularly interesting because Program 1 contains an unsafe rule. While the program would be rejected by GRINGO, ANTHEM is able to prove the strong equivalence to Program 2.

Example 4: Trivial Rule

Program 1	Program 2
p(X) :- X < 3, X > 5.	q :- q.

VAMPIRE verifies that the rule in Program 1 is trivial by checking that Program 1 is strongly equivalent to Program 2. The trivial rule q :- q. is used here because ANTHEM does not support the empty program yet. VAMPIRE proves the strong equivalence in about 14 ms.

Example 5: Incorrect Refactoring

Program 1	Program 2
q(X) :- p(X).	q(X + 1) :- p(X + 1).

These programs contain rules (10) and (11) from Sect. 4, respectively. As explained earlier, these two programs aren't strongly equivalent, which might come as a surprise to a programmer rewriting Program 2 as Program 1. VAMPIRE refuses to prove the strong equivalence within 300 s.

Example 6: Infinite Stable Models

Program 1	Program 2	Program 3
p(X + 0).	p(X + 1).	p(X).

VAMPIRE proves the strong equivalence of Programs 1 and 2 in about 87 ms. The stable model of Program 3 is the infinite set of atoms p(r) for all precomputed terms r. In contrast, the stable models of Programs 1 and 2 include p(r) only if r is an integer. Consequently, VAMPIRE does not prove the strong equivalence of Program 3 to Programs 1 or 2.

10   Future Work

We plan to extend this research effort in several directions. First, investigate using theorem provers other than VAMPIRE to verify strong equivalence. Second, enable ANTHEM to use theorem provers for verifying strong equivalence of nonpositive programs. Third, enable ANTHEM to use theorem provers for verifying the correctness of tight programs in the language of GRINGO by proving the equivalence of the given specification to the program's completion. Fourth, extend ANTHEM to cover a larger subset of the language of GRINGO, including symbolic functions.

Acknowledgements. We would like to thank Pedro Cabalar for his suggestion to use ANTHEM for verifying the strong equivalence of logic programs.

References

1. Chen, Y., Lin, F., Li, L.: SELP—a system for studying strong equivalence between logic programs. In: Proceedings of LPNMR, pp. 442–446 (2005)
2. Ferraris, P.: Answer sets for propositional theories. In: Proceedings of LPNMR, pp. 119–131 (2005)
3. Gebser, M., Harrison, A., Kaminski, R., Lifschitz, V., Schaub, T.: Abstract Gringo. TPLP **15**(4–5), 449–463 (2015)
4. Harrison, A., Lifschitz, V., Pearce, D., Valverde, A.: Infinitary equilibrium logic and strongly equivalent logic programs. Artif. Intell. **246**, 22–33 (2017)
5. Harrison, A., Lifschitz, V., Raju, D.: Program completion in the input language of GRINGO. TPLP **17**(5–6), 855–871 (2017)
6. Janhunen, T., Oikarinen, E.: LPEQ and DLPEQ—translators for automated equivalence testing of logic programs. In: Proceedings of LPNMR, pp. 336–340 (2004)
7. Kovács, L., Voronkov, A.: First-order theorem proving and VAMPIRE. In: Sharygina, N., Veith, H. (eds.) CAV 2013. LNCS, vol. 8044, pp. 1–35. Springer, Heidelberg (2013). https://doi.org/10.1007/978-3-642-39799-8_1
8. Lifschitz, V., Lühne, P., Schaub, T.: anthem: Transforming gringo programs into first-order theories (preliminary report). In: Proceedings of ASPOCP (2018)
9. Lifschitz, V., Pearce, D., Valverde, A.: Strongly equivalent logic programs. TOCL **2**(4), 526–541 (2001)
10. Orevkov, V.: Three ways of recognizing inessential formulas in sequents. J. Math. Sci. **20**, 2351–2357 (1982)
11. Sutcliffe, G.: The TPTP problem library and associated infrastructure. J. Autom. Reason. **59**(4), 483–502 (2017)

The Return of *xorro*

Flavio Everardo[3] [iD], Tomi Janhunen[1,2] [iD], Roland Kaminski[3] [iD],
and Torsten Schaub[3,4,5(✉)] [iD]

[1] Aalto University, Espoo, Finland
[2] Tampere University, Tampere, Finland
[3] University of Potsdam, Potsdam, Germany
`torsten@cs.uni-potsdam.de`
[4] Simon Fraser University, Burnaby, Canada
[5] Griffith University, Brisbane, Australia

Abstract. Although parity constraints are at the heart of many relevant reasoning modes like sampling or model counting, little attention has so far been paid to their integration into ASP systems. We address this shortcoming and investigate a variety of alternative approaches to implementing parity constraints, ranging from rather basic ASP encodings to more sophisticated theory propagators (featuring Gauss-Jordan elimination). All of them are implemented in the *xorro* system by building on the theory reasoning capabilities of the ASP system *clingo*. Our comparative empirical study investigates the impact of the number and size of parity constraints on performance and indicates the merits of the respective implementation techniques. Finally, we benefit from parity constraints to equip *xorro* with means to sample answer sets, paving the way for new applications of ASP.

1   Introduction

Parity constraints constitute the basic building blocks of many relevant reasoning modes like sampling or (approximate) model counting [19], not to mention their pertinence to circuit verification and cryptography [18]. Although their application and computational treatment are very active research topics (cf. [3,4,11,12,23]) in the neighboring area of Satisfiability Testing (SAT [2]), almost no attention has so far been paid to their integration into ASP solving [17]. Modest approaches include the (discontinued) support of `#even` and `#odd` aggregates in *gringo* series 3[1] and their usage for sampling in the initial prototype of *xorro*[2] from 2009. In this earlier prototype, parity constraints were simply implemented via `#count` aggregates and a modulo-two operation (see Listing 1.1). An alternative idea was later used in *harvey* [13] (see Listing 1.2). Unlike these approaches, several SAT solvers feature rather sophisticated treatments of parity constraints, most popularly the award-winning solver *cryptominisat* [24]. The difficulty lies in the inadequacy of CDCL-based solvers [9]

---

[1] This is achieved by uncompiling them during grounding using meta-encodings.
[2] https://sourceforge.net/p/potassco/code/HEAD/tree/branches/xorro.

© Springer Nature Switzerland AG 2019
M. Balduccini et al. (Eds.): LPNMR 2019, LNAI 11481, pp. 284–297, 2019.
https://doi.org/10.1007/978-3-030-20528-7_21

(and more precisely their underlying resolution-based learning scheme) to effectively handle parity constraints. In fact, the translation of parity constraints into conjunctive normal form degrades search [14], although they could be directly solved with Gauss-Jordan elimination (GJE) in polynomial time [21]. Consequently, solvers like *crypto-minisat* pursue a hybrid approach, addressing parity constraints separately with GJE.

In what follows, we present the next generation of *xorro*, a full re-implementation, providing a wide spectrum of alternative ways for integrating parity constraints into ASP solving. On the one hand, this re-implementation draws upon the advanced interfaces of *clingo* for integrating foreign constraints and corresponding forms of inference. On the other hand, *xorro* takes advantage of the sophisticated solving techniques developed in SAT for handling parity constraints, such as GJE. More precisely, we propose two types of approaches in Sect. 2,[3] namely eager ones that rely on ASP encodings of parity constraints, and lazy ones using theory propagators within *clingo*'s Python interface. We then empirically evaluate the different approaches in view of their impact on solving performance, while varying the number and size of parity constraints.

2   Incorporating Parity Constraints into ASP

We expect the reader to be familiar with the basic syntax and semantics of logic programs as implemented by *clingo* (see [6,7] for details). In this section, we focus on the introduction of non-standard concepts needed in this paper.

Towards the definition of parity constraints, let $\top$ and $\bot$ stand for the Boolean constants *true* and *false*, respectively. Given atoms a_1 and a_2, the *exclusive or* (XOR for short) of a_1 and a_2 is denoted by $a_1 \oplus a_2$ and it is satisfied if *either* a_1 *or* a_2 is true (but not both). Generalizing the idea for n distinct atoms $a_1, \ldots, a_n$, we obtain an n-ary XOR constraint $(((a_1 \oplus a_2) \ldots) \oplus a_n)$ by multiple applications of $\oplus$. Since it is satisfied iff an odd number of atoms among $a_1, \ldots, a_n$ are true, it is called an *odd* XOR *constraint* and it can be written simply as $a_1 \oplus \ldots \oplus a_n$ due to associativity. Analogously, an *even* XOR *constraint* is defined by $a_1 \oplus \ldots \oplus a_n \oplus \top$ as it is satisfied iff an even number of atoms among $a_1, \ldots, a_n$ hold. Then, e.g., $a_1 \oplus a_2 \oplus \top$ is satisfied iff none or both of a_1 and a_2 hold. In the sequel, we also refer to even and odd XOR constraints as *parity constraints*. As shown in [18], any XOR constraint $a_1 \oplus \ldots \oplus a_n$ can be decomposed into two XOR constraints $a_1 \oplus a_2 \oplus aux$ and $aux \oplus a_3 \oplus \ldots \oplus a_n \oplus \top$ where aux is a new atom not used elsewhere. Finally, XOR constraints of forms $a \oplus \bot$ and $a \oplus \top$ are called *unary*.

To accommodate parity constraints in the input language, we rely on *clingo*'s theory language extension [8] that pertains to the common syntax of *aggregates*:

```
1    &odd{ 1 : p(1) }.
2    &even{ X : p(X), X>1 }.
```

---

[3] The distinction of eager and lazy approaches follows the methodology in Satisfiability modulo theories [1].

More precisely, *xorro* extends the input language of *clingo* by aggregate names
&even and &odd that are followed by a set, whose elements are *terms* conditioned
by conjunctions of literals separated by commas.[4] The semantics of aggregates
formed with keywords &even and &odd is defined by even and odd parity constraints, respectively. In the current implementation, they are interpreted as
directives that select answer sets satisfying the parity constraint in question.[5]
For now, parity constraints may not occur in the bodies nor the heads of rules
and the full integration of parity constraints into rules is left as future work. The
parity constraints shown above yield two answer sets, viz. {p(1)} and {p(1),
p(2), p(3)} in the context of a choice rule {p(1..3)}. Hence, the first constraint filters out answer sets not containing the atom p(1), while the second
requires that either none or both of the atoms p(2) and p(3) are included.

2.1 Eager Encodings of Parity Constraints

In the following, we present three different ways to encode parity constraints using
primitives available in standard ASP. We refer to these encodings by nicknames
Counting, *List*, and *Tree*, respectively. Each encoding leads to an *eager* evaluation of the corresponding parity constraint in terms of *nogoods*, which are used to
invalidate answer sets as well as to explain reasons behind conflicts encountered by
solvers. In the eager approach, nogoods resulting from parity constraints are generated in advance. As a consequence, the underlying answer-set solver may freely
propagate truth values over (parts of) parity constraints during search.

   Counting. Our first encoding is essentially the same as used in the previous
generation of *xorro*. As shown in Listing 1.1, the idea is to introduce an analogous
counting aggregate for the number of terms in the set and, in addition, to check
that this number matches with the given parity. Recalling the preceding example
in this section, the given parity constraints translate into integrity constraints
embedding #*count* aggregates coupled with appropriate modulo 2 conditions.
The net effect is that the first constraint enforces odd parity within {p(1)},
while the latter concerns even parity for the atoms in {p(2),p(3)}.

```
1    :- #count{ 1 : p(1)      } = N, N\2!=1.
2    :- #count{ X : p(X),X>1 } = N, N\2!=0.
```

Listing 1.1: Aggregate-based encoding parity constraints (count.lp).

   List. The encoding presented in Listing 1.2 is based on an ordered list of terms
expressed using predicates term/1, first/1, last/1, and next/2. The idea is
to perform a sequence of tests for odd parity based on this list.[6] Line 1 sets the
base case using the first term of the list. Then, Lines 2 and 3 recursively check
for odd parity following the structure of the list. Note that term(T) holds iff the
conditions related with the term T are satisfied. Line 4 determines if the parity

---

[4] In turn, multiple conditional terms within an aggregate are separated by semicolons.
[5] Our implementation of parity constraints fits perfectly with the parity constraints
   used in sampling and model counting.
[6] This is analogous to parity evaluation using *binary decision diagrams* (BDDs).

of the entire term sequence is odd based on the status of last term in the list. Finally, the encoding should be combined with exactly one of the constraints in Lines 5 and 6. The first eliminates answer sets with odd parity, while the one commented away in the listing removes the even cases with respect to the parity constraint in question. The given encoding has been deployed, e.g., in the previous *gringo* versions (2 and 3) [10] as well as randomized testing [13].

```
1  odd(T)  :- first(T), term(T).
2  odd(Y)  :- next(X,Y),       term(Y), not odd(X).
3  odd(Y)  :- next(X,Y), not term(Y),       odd(X).
4  odd      :- odd(T), last(T).
5  :- odd.
6  % :- not odd.
```

Listing 1.2: List-based encoding of parity constraints (`list.lp`).

Tree. Our last eager representation resembles the previous encoding but the underlying topology for parity checks is different. A *balanced* binary tree is created for each parity constraint and the recursive evaluation proceeds in a bottom-up fashion. The terms are associated with the leaves of the tree while the root corresponds to the final outcome of the parity check. The structure of the tree is expressed using predicates `leaf/1`, `root/1`, and `edge/2`. Line 1 in Listing 1.3 sets the base case using the leaves of the tree. Lines 2 and 3 accumulate the result of the parity check towards the root of the tree, the value for each parent P is set based on the values of children C1 and C2 that need not be ordered by symmetry. The value observed for the root R (see Line 4) sets the result. In addition to the given rules, we have to include constraints for selecting the intended parity value as done in Lines 5–6 in Listing 1.2.

```
1  odd(T)  :- leaf(T), term(T).
2  odd(P)  :- odd(C1), not odd(C2), edge(P,C1), edge(P,C2)
3  odd(P)  :- not odd(C1), odd(C2), edge(P,C1), edge(P,C2).
4  odd      :- odd(R), root(R).
```

Listing 1.3: Tree-based encoding of parity constraints (`tree.lp`).

2.2 Lazy Evaluation of Parity Constraints

Next, we switch our attention to the *lazy* evaluation techniques that generate nogoods related to parity constraints on demand only. This is in contrast with the eager approaches where such nogoods can be produced a priori. In practice, we have implemented parity reasoning modules in Python acting as *theory propagators* [8] for the *clingo* system. In what follows, we briefly explain how parity checking can be achieved in a more lazy fashion.

Lazy Counting. In this approach, the idea is to perform counting (modulo 2) in order to check parity constraints. However, such checks are performed only when a candidate answer set for the rest of the program has been found. Therefore, the evaluation of parity constraints does not interfere with the propagation of truth values while searching for answer sets. If a particular parity constraint is violated, then a corresponding nogood is generated.

Watched Literals. The propagation of truth values can be performed on demand by *watching* certain literals occurring in a constraint (such as 2 literals per clause [20]). The rough idea is to check the status of the constraint only if the truth values of the watched literals are changed. As a result, the constraint might be used for propagation or the literal(s) being watched is/are changed to some other literal(s). In case of parity constraints, however, all but one atom involved in a particular constraint must be assigned before the truth value of the final one is determined [18,24]. E.g., if $a_1, \ldots, a_{k-1}$ and $a_{k+1}, \ldots, a_n$ have been assigned false or, more generally, have an even parity in $a_1 \oplus \ldots \oplus a_n$, then a_k must be true. Therefore, we have to keep track of both parity values (even and odd) by watching 2×2 literals (two literals both phases) for each parity constraint. Is important to mention, that all atoms (or terms) contributing to parity constraints originate from the underlying logic program. Otherwise, they are removed by the *gringo* grounder due to closed world assumption (all occurrences of $\bot$ can be removed from parity constraints).

Figure 1 illustrates unit propagation over parity constraints $a \oplus b \oplus c$ and $c \oplus d \oplus \top$. Given the truth assignments a and $\neg b$ indicated in gray, the first constraint simplifies to $b \oplus c \oplus \top$. Furthermore, we get $\neg c$ and $\neg d$ through unit propagation. Had the assumptions originated from a candidate answer set $\{a\}$, no other answer sets would be feasible. The inferences made here can be recorded as learned

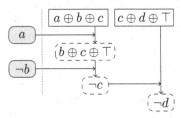

Fig. 1. Unit propagation involving parity constraints

nogoods $\{a, \neg b, c\}$ and $\{\neg c, d\}$ in order to perform similar (ordinary) unit propagation later on without consulting the parity propagator again.

Gauss-Jordan Elimination. Sets of parity constraints can also be cast as linear equation systems whose solutions can be determined using Gauss-Jordan elimination (GJE) [15,18,24]. The GJE method is complete for parity reasoning because it can be used to decide whether a conjunction of parity constraints is satisfiable as well as to find implied literals and equivalences. Plain Gaussian elimination can efficiently detect satisfiability, but not implied literals nor equivalences. This can be understood from the difference between the *row-echelon* and the *reduced row-echelon* forms for the matrix representations of parity equation systems.

For the sake of illustrating GJE, let us use the constraints from Fig. 1 along with $b \oplus c \oplus \top$. Figure 2(a) represents the respective equations as a matrix where the column "p" indicates parities for the equations. Figure 2(b) shows a column reduction when b is assigned true and reflected to the parity

$a\ b\ c\ d$	p
1 1 1 0	1
0 0 1 1	0
0 1 1 0	0
(a)	

$a\ c\ d$	p
1 1 0	0
0 1 1	0
0 1 0	1
(b)	

$a\ c\ d$	p
1 1 0	0
0 1 1	0
0 0 1	1
(c)	

$a\ c\ d$	p
1 0 0	1
0 1 0	1
0 0 1	1
(d)	

Fig. 2. Deducing a, c, and d by GJE after b given

values. Figure 2(c) shows a row-echelon form for the matrix, already indicating satisfiability and the truth of d. By further simplification into reduced row-echelon form in Fig. 2(d), we can clearly see how the values for other atoms are determined: a, c, and d must all be true. After the matrix is reduced, we need to find either a conflict or implications. If conflict, the nogood is the partial assignment. If implications, the nogood is the partial assignment coupled with each of the implication literals in negated form.

3   The *xorro* System

This re-implementation of *xorro* allows the user to solve parity constraints on top of an ASP program using a specific approach.[7] *xorro* is built on top of *clingo* 5.3, and the system architecture is shown in Fig. 3. *xorro* follows the standard grounding-solving workflow of ASP, plus three additional blocks shown in solid lines which are preprocessing, transformation, and translation. The preprocessing module has two optional flags --split and --pre-gje. The split flag takes an integer to cut larger constraints into smaller ones using auxiliary variables, and the pre-gje flag enables XOR simplification for more than one constraint. If both flags are used together, GJE is performed first followed by splitting. The transformation block is performed before grounding to parse each parity constraint into facts and normal ASP rules. The translation block is called before solving and it is responsible for building additional features for each approach. Additionally, this implementation of *xorro* preserves the same functionality as its predecessor for near-uniform sampling.

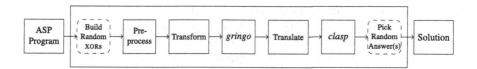

Fig. 3. Architecture of *xorro*

The workflow starts with an ASP program with parity constraints. Before grounding, we preprocess and transform each parity constraint using *clingo*'s Abstract Syntax Tree (AST) into auxiliary atoms of the form __parity/2 and __parity/3. The atom __parity/2 is added as a fact and it contains a numeric identifier and the parity as *odd* or *even*. The atom __parity/3 is added in the head of a new rule where the body corresponds to its conditional literal. This atom contains the same information as the fact __parity/2 plus the tuples of terms involved in the constraint.[8] For example, the transformation of the parity constraints from Fig. 2a is shown in Listing 1.4.

---

[7] https://github.com/potassco/xorro.

[8] The transformation process mimicks the use of a theory grammar for *clingo* [8].

```
1  __parity(0,odd). __parity(1,even). __parity(2,even).
2  __parity(0,odd,(a,)):-a.  __parity(0,odd,(b,)):-b.
3  __parity(0,odd,(c,)):-c.
4  __parity(1,even,(c,)):-c. __parity(1,even,(d,)):-d.
5  __parity(2,even,(b,)):-b. __parity(2,even,(c,)):-c.
```

Listing 1.4: Transformation of parity constraints to ASP.

The translation block depends on the given approach which is given by the flag `--approach` followed by a keyword indicating one of the approaches from Sects. 2.1 and 2.2. In the case of an eager approach, we add additional structures to the program. For the eager count approach, we add the count aggregates with respect to the atom `__parity/3` for every parity constraint `__parity/2`. For the list and tree approaches, we benefit from *clingo*'s Python API by using *clingo*'s backend class to extend a logic program by adding statements directly in the intermediate format of ASP (*aspif* [16]).

For the lazy approaches, we benefit from the theory propagator interface of *clingo* which consists of four functions, namely *init*, *propagate*, *undo*, and *check*. We rely on them, so each lazy approach performs at a specific part of the search, being during propagation or fixpoints (partial or total assignments). All propagators keep the state of each parity constraint by its (solver) literals. From the three lazy approaches, the lazy count works on total assignment whereas the UP and GJE during propagation. The lazy count approach does not propagate and do not interfere with clasp propagation. On total assignment under the *check* method, we count the number of true literals. In case of conflict, add the nogood (whole assignment per constraint) and let *clasp* to propagate again. The Unit-Propagation (UP) propagator performs plain propagation over parity constraints. As its name suggests, it is performed in the *propagate* function. The *check* method is not implemented, and the state keeps 2×2-watched literals. For implementing Gauss-Jordan Elimination, two alternatives are proposed, called "gje-fp" and "gje-prop". Their main difference is at which point of the search GJE is called. Both extend the UP approach. For "gje-fp" two propagators are registered, the UP followed by the "gje-fp" propagator, performing GJE on fixpoints. The "gje-prop" alternative registers only one propagator performing GJE when a unit clause is detected.

As mentioned, this implementation of *xorro* preserves the functionality of sampling following the concepts from the XORSample' algorithm [12], by solving a program with `--s` random parity constraints with a density `--q`. The sampling components are enabled with `--sampling` and shown in Fig. 3 in dotted rounded-corner squares. Unlike the algorithm from [12] which calls a model counter, *xorro* enumerates all remaining answer sets, and the last module randomly picks n (user-defined) answer sets. The sampling mode for *xorro* corresponds to the non-iterative algorithm from [12] recalling the possibility to get no answer set due to unsatisfiable parity constraints. Finally, the flag `--display` prints the random XOR constraints used in sampling.

4   Experiments

Different tests are proposed to measure the impact of solving a single or several parity constraints with *xorro*. We considered 301 satisfiable instances from 19 (9 tight, 10 non–tight) classes using all aforementioned approaches. However, we kept only 126 instances from eight classes (5 tight, 3 non-tight) for which *clingo*'s solving time surpasses one second. These benchmarks problems were taken from the second ASP competition [5], using encodings of the Potassco team.[9] No encoding or instance has been modified, just parity constraints are appended. The main objectives of our experiments are built around the following questions:

1. What is the impact of solving a single random parity constraint of different sizes ranging from 1, 10, 20, 30, 40, and 50% of unassigned variables?
2. Due to SAT solvers' good performance on small size parity constraints, is there any benefit of splitting a single parity into small ones? On average from the literature, the size of a small XOR constraint is 4.
3. Due to sampling using high-density constraints (50% of unassigned variables), what is the impact of solving more than one high-density parity constraint with and without GJE preprocessing?
4. Do the eager approaches count and list used in the previous *xorro* version, *gringo* up to version 3, and in *harvey*, respectively, scale when solving high-density parity constraints?
5. Is there any approach outstanding from the rest?

To address these questions, we designed five experiments, each with different tests. Each test uses the set of instances from the benchmark classes in Table 1 coupled with a single or several XORs. We use *clingo*, and Python to randomly build each constraint excluding facts with the only condition that at least one answer set remains. Table 1 shows the range of atoms per class and the number of instances under column "#".

For the first experiment, we solved all the instances each with a single parity constraint of different sizes ranging from one, 10, 20, 30, 40, to 50% of unassigned variables. In the second experiment, we used the same parity constraints but we split them into smaller ones of size four. The auxiliary atoms were added into each instance as choice rules. For the third, fourth, and fifth

Table 1. Range of atoms per class

Class	#	MIN	AVG	MAX
Tight				
15Puzzle	16	9841	10514	11332
BlockedNQueens	15	7996	8008	8012
GraphColouring	9	2707	2837	3087
SchurNumbers	13	1291	1291	1291
Solitaire	22	7687	8702	9920
Non-tight				
ConnectedDomSet	10	804	1463	2519
Labyrinth	29	56482	91733	120192
WireRouting	12	6085	15546	25330

---

[9] http://flavioeverardo.com/research/benchmarks/xorro/.

experiments, we increased the number of high-density XORs to two, three, four, and five. We first solved the instances without preprocessing. Then, we reduced the length of the XORs by applying GJE, and lastly, GJE plus a split of size four. It is important to remark that the difference between small XORs and shorter ones due to split, is their shared variables. If independently drawn small XORs contain variables in common, they mean the same as a longer XOR with equivalence reasoning.

Our tests follow the notation "cNxMperc" where N represents the number of parity constraints times M percentage or density per parity. For example the test "c03 × 50perc" solves an instance containing three XORs of 50% each. Our comparison considers solving each instance without parity constraints using *clingo* 5.3 in its default setting as benchmark reference. We ran *clingo* two times, once for the first two experiments and once more for the last three.

The experiments were run in parallel under Linux on an Intel Xeon E5-2650v4 high performance cluster equipped with 2.20 GHz processors. Each benchmark instance (in smodels output format, generated offline with *gringo* plus the parity constraints) was run three times per solver (*clingo* and *xorro*). Each run is restricted to 600 s time with 4 GB RAM. A run finished when the solver found an answer set or was aborted due to time or memory exhaustion.

4.1   Results

Our experiments' results are summarized in Tables 2a–3c giving average runtimes in seconds (using PAR–1 score) and the number of aborted runs is shown in parentheses.[10] All the tables show the experiments and *clingo*'s runtimes without parity constraints on the left side followed by the corresponding lazy and eager approaches. The last row of each table shows the average runtimes followed by the total number of time or memory exhaustion. All tables show the best score from each test in bold. Tables 2a and b correspond to the results from the first two experiments addressing questions 1 and 2, respectively. Both experiments divide the search space into two parts. However, the results are completely contrasting. The counting approach with aggregates does not scale from the 10 size when solving the parity constraint as it is. However, this approach scales when the XORs are split. The grounding becomes the bottleneck on longer XORs causing timeouts or memory exhaustion on most of the instances and runs, whereas roles switch with shorter XORs. Despite the best performance of the lazy count approach on four out of six tests, the best PAR–1 score belongs to the tree approach. Both approaches perform better than *clingo* in five out of six tests in the first experiment. Contrary, both approaches perform worst when splitting XORs. A similar case occurs with the two worst approaches when solving non-split XORs (the count with aggregates and the UP). Both outperform the rest if the XORs are split. The best PAR–1 score from the second experiment belongs

---

[10] For more detailed benchmarks results, including individual times per classes please go to http://flavioeverardo.com/research/benchmarks/xorro/.

to the UP approach. We can see from both experiments the feasibility to reach an answer set faster than *clingo* when solving with a single XOR.

To resume, the length of the parity constraint matters depending on the approach to use. To solve a single parity constraint without a split, better use the tree or the lazy counting approach. On shorter XORs or a longer split XOR, better use UP or the eager counting.

Table 2. Experiments solving a single parity constraint from different sizes.

test	clingo	lazy count	up	eager list	count	tree
1x01perc	883.19 (11)	1220.65 (15)	**644.72 (8)**	1035.84 (13)	1038.58 (13)	806.43 (10)
1x10perc	909.21 (11)	**802.27 (10)**	1026.35 (13)	951.96 (12)	2998.6 (39)	876.34 (11)
1x20perc	908.98 (11)	**802.52 (10)**	952.37 (12)	837 (10)	5025.73 (66)	882.33 (11)
1x30perc	884.17 (11)	827.38 (10)	1180.09 (15)	875.56 (11)	6885.11 (90)	**782.72 (10)**
1x40perc	884.07 (11)	**878.19 (11)**	1178.58 (15)	1103.47 (14)	7933.01 (104)	904.66 (11)
1x50perc	959.49 (12)	**877.13 (11)**	1178.37 (15)	959.15 (12)	8638.37 (113)	878.6 (11)
AVG (SUM)	904.85 (67)	901.36 (67)	1026.74 (78)	960.5 (72)	5419.9 (425)	**855.18 (64)**

(a) Average solving runtimes on a single XOR constraint ranging from 1 to 50 percent.

test	clingo	lazy count	up	eager list	count	tree
1x01perc	883.19 (11)	1196.01 (15)	**647.96 (8)**	804.07 (10)	1035.91 (13)	808.8 (10)
1x10perc	909.21 (11)	658.57 (8)	653.47 (8)	**644.19 (8)**	648.15 (8)	955.17 (12)
1x20perc	908.98 (11)	962.7 (12)	722.71 (9)	732.31 (9)	**568.47 (7)**	871.84 (11)
1x30perc	884.17 (11)	965.12 (12)	**571.27 (7)**	802.18 (10)	800.14 (10)	1029.28 (13)
1x40perc	884.07 (11)	1451.29 (18)	1032.9 (13)	1023.5 (13)	963.23 (12)	**880.07 (11)**
1x50perc	959.49 (12)	1512.16 (19)	725.18 (9)	1026.21 (13)	**508.78 (6)**	945.73 (12)
AVG (SUM)	904.85 (67)	1124.31 (84)	**725.58 (54)**	838.74 (63)	754.11 (56)	915.15 (69)

(b) Average solving runtimes on split XORs of size 4, ranging from 1 to 50 percent.

For the last three experiments, the search space is divided into four, eight, 16 and 32 parts showing the solving performance over more than one parity constraint. From here on, we include the GJE elimination approaches and we exclude for now the eager counting approach which only performs on shorter (or split) XORs. Table 3a shows the results from experiment number three. The hardness of solving dense XORs starts to arise. Lazy countinging outperforms the rest when solving with two XORs, opposed to *clingo* which performs the best in the remaining tests. Both eager approaches (tree and list) perform badly as the number of XORs increases. Lastly, there is a big difference between both GJE approaches. One (gje-prop) performing in between the eager and the other lazy approaches, whereas the other (gje-fp) does not scale at all. Both use the same routines to operate over columns, rows, detect conflicts, propagation and so on. Also, both perform exactly the same concerning the number of choices, restarts, conflicts, backjumps, etc. To recall, GJE outputs one of three results: variable(s) to propagate, conflict(s) or neither of both. The runtime difference occurs when performing GJE on fixpoints results in finding neither of both in most of the time. For example, "gje-prop" solves instances of the 15Puzzle class with an average of 10 calls to GJE without propagating or conflict. The same instances with "gje-fp" called on average over 5,000 times more GJE without finding a conflict or a literal to propagate.

Table 3. Experiments on multiple high-density parity constraints.

test	clingo	lazy				eager	
		count	up	gje-fp	gje-prop	list	tree
2x50perc	1113.02 (14)	**902.33 (11)**	952.39 (12)	3806.57 (48)	1025.23 (13)	960.53 (12)	1144.23 (14)
3x50perc	**934.33 (12)**	976.59 (12)	1028.65 (13)	4038.56 (51)	1097.16 (14)	1567.05 (20)	1570.77 (20)
4x50perc	**1034.74 (13)**	1105.75 (14)	1182.47 (15)	4347.56 (55)	1421.77 (18)	1546 (20)	1622.86 (21)
5x50perc	**1009.25 (13)**	1189.58 (15)	1032.25 (13)	4655.35 (59)	1468.04 (19)	1770.75 (23)	1928.74 (25)
AVG (SUM)	**1022.83 (63)**	1043.56 (64)	1048.94 (68)	4212.01 (228)	1253.05 (79)	1461.08 (87)	1566.65 (91)

(a) Average solving runtimes from two to five high-density constraints.

test	clingo	lazy			eager	
		count	up	gje-prop	list	tree
2x50perc	1113.02 (14)	877.85 (11)	956.17 (12)	1026.36 (13)	1261.7 (16)	**736.64 (9)**
3x50perc	**934.33 (12)**	1027.76 (13)	1028.87 (13)	1095.95 (14)	981.04 (12)	1343.69 (17)
4x50perc	**1034.74 (13)**	**1006.4 (13)**	1112.8 (14)	1374.6 (18)	1729.47 (22)	1711.62 (22)
5x50perc	**1009.25 (13)**	1112.83 (14)	1187.97 (15)	1470.44 (19)	1852.3 (24)	2151.83 (28)
AVG (SUM)	1022.83 (63)	**1006.21 (62)**	1071.45 (69)	1241.84 (79)	1456.13 (90)	1485.94 (91)

(b) Average solving runtimes from two to five high-density with GJE preprocess.

test	clingo	lazy			eager		
		count	up	gje-prop	list	count	tree
2x50perc	1113.02 (14)	2333.18 (30)	**729.96 (9)**	8613.63 (111)	941.51 (12)	1060.47 (13)	1042.54 (13)
3x50perc	**934.33 (12)**	2413.15 (31)	947.77 (12)	9177.39 (118)	1917.18 (25)	1215.5 (15)	1798.67 (23)
4x50perc	**1034.74 (13)**	2321.53 (30)	1776.73 (23)	9579.91 (123)	2130.86 (28)	1668.8 (21)	2284.37 (30)
5x50perc	**1009.25 (13)**	2417.51 (31)	1927.46 (25)	9438.35 (122)	2367.49 (31)	1552 (19)	2278.92 (30)
AVG (SUM)	**1022.83 (51)**	2371.34 (122)	1345.48 (69)	9202.32 (474)	1839.26 (96)	1374.19 (68)	1851.13 (97)

(c) Average solving runtimes from two to five high-density with GJE and split preprocess.

The fourth experiment solves the same parity constraints but with a GJE preprocessing step to reduce their length. The results are shown in Table 3b. From the five approaches, all except UP benefit from preprocessing. The tree and the lazy counting approaches got a speedup of 5.2 and 3.6% respectively. However, the tree approach remains worst, and the lazy counting now performs better than *clingo*.

The last experiment takes another notch by splitting the preprocessed XORs after GJE. We include the eager counting approach due to its performance on split constraints. The results from Table 3c show *clingo* outperforming the rest in three out of four tests, and also, in the overall score. The UP has the best score in only one test. Similarly to experiment number two, the lazy counting and the tree approaches perform poorly with shorter XORs. UP and the eager counting approach have the best scores but still quite far from *clingo*'s performance. None of the five approaches from the fourth experiment benefit from splitting in the fifth. It is the opposite. The tree, list, and UP downgrade their performance by 24–26%. The lazy counting by 135% and GJE by 600%. We confirm that splitting high-density parity constraints does not scale without further preprocessing. When split, we add more XORs and more variables (rows and columns respectively for GJE). We passed from five dense to 670 smaller constraints in the best case (Connected Dom Set class) against 100,160 shorter parity constraints in the worst (Labyrinth class). From a GJE perspective, we increased the size of the matrix from five rows and 402 columns in the best case, to 670 rows and 536 columns. The worst case passes from five rows and 64,596 columns to 100,160 rows and 86,128 columns. This makes our GJE implementation fail to scale without additional preprocessing. As stated in [18], so far, for larger matrices, the computational overhead of Gaussian elimination is significant. Also, [22,24] state that for efficient solving, the number of parity constraints and their density should be low. The tests show most of the approaches performed better with longer XORs. Additional preprocessing like equivalence reasoning reduces the number of constraints by creating longer XORs.

After running all experiments, we can see that the eager counting and list approaches stay behind when solving high-density constraints without any preprocessing (as in the previous *xorro* and *harvey* implementations). In contrary, they improved their performance especially when a split occurs. Also, it is difficult to identify an approach outstanding from the rest. From 24 tests, the lazy counting has the best score on six, followed by the UP and the tree approaches with four and three respectively. Plain *clingo* performs best on eight tests. On the other hand, depending on the number and the density of the parity constraints, some approaches perform best. From experiment number two, some *xorro* approaches perform better on XORs of lower densities than $n/2$ variables. This is sufficient for approximate model counting, but not for sampling [11].

5 Discussion

We presented different means of implementing parity constraints, ranging from ASP encodings to theory propagators. The fully re-implemented system *xorro* takes advantage of the hybrid reasoning capacities of the ASP system *clingo* for solving parity constraints on top of logic programs, providing an opening to develop new applications in ASP including sampling, (approximate) model counting, cryptography, and probabilistic reasoning.

Our experiments show that *xorro* scales depending on the combination of the number, density, and preprocessing of the parity constraints. For instance, cutting the search space by half helps *xorro* to reach an answer set faster than *clingo* even when using a high-density constraint. Some approaches scaled when splitting a single XOR as opposed to others who perform without preprocessing. On the other hand, solving high-density parity constraints hinders *xorro* performance compared to *clingo*'s, but there is evidence that preprocessing can lead to a significant speedup.

For future work, we plan to extend *clingo*'s input language with parity aggregates and investigate the performance of *clingo*'s multi-shot capabilities by incrementally solving parity constraints as an application for sampling. Finally, to improve our GJE approach, and inspired by [18,24], we want to explore an incremental GJE and strategies like ordered columns and turning GJE on/off automatically as well as cutoff values, rows and columns elimination with equivalence reasoning.

References

1. Barrett, C., Sebastiani, R., Seshia, S., Tinelli, C.: Satisfiability modulo theories. In: Biere et al. [2], chap. 26, pp. 825–885
2. Biere, A., Heule, M., van Maaren, H., Walsh, T. (eds.): Handbook of Satisfiability. Frontiers in Artificial Intelligence and Applications, vol. 185. IOS Press, Amsterdam (2009)
3. Chakraborty, S., Meel, K.S., Vardi, M.Y.: A scalable and nearly uniform generator of SAT witnesses. In: Sharygina, N., Veith, H. (eds.) CAV 2013. LNCS, vol. 8044, pp. 608–623. Springer, Heidelberg (2013). https://doi.org/10.1007/978-3-642-39799-8_40
4. Chakraborty, S., Meel, K.S., Vardi, M.Y.: A scalable approximate model counter. In: Schulte, C. (ed.) CP 2013. LNCS, vol. 8124, pp. 200–216. Springer, Heidelberg (2013). https://doi.org/10.1007/978-3-642-40627-0_18
5. Denecker, M., Vennekens, J., Bond, S., Gebser, M., Truszczyński, M.: The second answer set programming competition. In: Erdem, E., Lin, F., Schaub, T. (eds.) LPNMR 2009. LNCS (LNAI), vol. 5753, pp. 637–654. Springer, Heidelberg (2009). https://doi.org/10.1007/978-3-642-04238-6_75
6. Gebser, M., Harrison, A., Kaminski, R., Lifschitz, V., Schaub, T.: Abstract Gringo. Theory Pract. Logic Program. **15**(4–5), 449–463 (2015)
7. Gebser, M., et al.: Potassco User Guide, 2 edn. (2015). http://potassco.org
8. Gebser, M., Kaminski, R., Kaufmann, B., Ostrowski, M., Schaub, T., Wanko, P.: Theory solving made easy with clingo 5. In: Carro, M., King, A. (eds.) Technical Communications of the Thirty-second International Conference on Logic Programming (ICLP 2016), vol. 52, pp. 2:1–2:15. Open Access Series in Informatics (OASIcs) (2016)
9. Gebser, M., Kaminski, R., Kaufmann, B., Schaub, T.: Answer Set Solving in Practice. Synthesis Lectures on Artificial Intelligence and Machine Learning. Morgan and Claypool Publishers, San Rafael (2012)
10. Gebser, M., Kaminski, R., König, A., Schaub, T.: Advances in *gringo* series 3. In: Delgrande, J.P., Faber, W. (eds.) LPNMR 2011. LNCS (LNAI), vol. 6645, pp. 345–351. Springer, Heidelberg (2011). https://doi.org/10.1007/978-3-642-20895-9_39
11. Gomes, C.P., Hoffmann, J., Sabharwal, A., Selman, B.: Short XORs for model counting: from theory to practice. In: Marques-Silva, J., Sakallah, K.A. (eds.) SAT 2007. LNCS, vol. 4501, pp. 100–106. Springer, Heidelberg (2007). https://doi.org/10.1007/978-3-540-72788-0_13
12. Gomes, C., Sabharwal, A., Selman, B.: Near-uniform sampling of combinatorial spaces using XOR constraints. In: Schölkopf, B., Platt, J., Hofmann, T. (eds.) Proceedings of the Twentieth Annual Conference on Neural Information Processing Systems (NIPS 2006), pp. 481–488. MIT Press (2007)

13. Greßler, A., Oetsch, J., Tompits, H.: Harvey: a system for random testing in ASP. In: Balduccini, M., Janhunen, T. (eds.) LPNMR 2017. LNCS (LNAI), vol. 10377, pp. 229–235. Springer, Cham (2017). https://doi.org/10.1007/978-3-319-61660-5_21

14. Haanpää, H., Järvisalo, M., Kaski, P., Niemelä, I.: Hard satisfiable clause sets for benchmarking equivalence reasoning techniques. J. Satisfiability Boolean Model. Comput. **2**(1–4), 27–46 (2006)

15. Han, C.-S., Jiang, J.-H.R.: When boolean satisfiability meets gaussian elimination in a simplex way. In: Madhusudan, P., Seshia, S.A. (eds.) CAV 2012. LNCS, vol. 7358, pp. 410–426. Springer, Heidelberg (2012). https://doi.org/10.1007/978-3-642-31424-7_31

16. Kaminski, R., Schaub, T., Wanko, P.: A tutorial on hybrid answer set solving with *clingo*. In: Ianni, G., et al. (eds.) Reasoning Web 2017. LNCS, vol. 10370, pp. 167–203. Springer, Cham (2017). https://doi.org/10.1007/978-3-319-61033-7_6

17. Kaufmann, B., Leone, N., Perri, S., Schaub, T.: Grounding and solving in answer set programming. AI Mag. **37**(3), 25–32 (2016)

18. Laitinen, T.: Extending SAT solver with parity reasoning. Dissertation, Aalto University, November 2014

19. Meel, K.: Constrained counting and sampling: bridging the gap between theory and practice. Dissertation, Rice University, August 2018

20. Moskewicz, M., Madigan, C., Zhao, Y., Zhang, L., Malik, S.: Chaff: engineering an efficient SAT solver. In: Proceedings of the Thirty-Eighth Conference on Design Automation (DAC 2001), pp. 530–535. ACM Press (2001)

21. Schaefer, T.: The complexity of satisfiability problems. In: Lipton, R., Burkhard, W., Savitch, W., Friedman, E., Aho, A. (eds.) Proceedings of the Tenth Annual ACM Symposium on Theory of Computing (STOCS 1978), pp. 216–226. ACM Press (1978)

22. Soos, M.: Enhanced Gaussian elimination in DPLL-based SAT solvers. In: Le Berre, D. (ed.) Proceedings of the First Workshop on Pragmatics of SAT (PoS 2010). EPiC Series in Computing, vol. 8, pp. 2–14. EasyChair (2012)

23. Soos, M., Meel, K.: Bird: Engineering an efficient CNF-XOR sat solver and its applications to approximate model counting. In: Van Hentenryck, P., Zhou, Z. (eds.) Proceedings of the Thirty-Third National Conference on Artificial Intelligence (AAAI 2019). AAAI Press (2019, to appear)

24. Soos, M., Nohl, K., Castelluccia, C.: Extending SAT solvers to cryptographic problems. In: Kullmann, O. (ed.) SAT 2009. LNCS, vol. 5584, pp. 244–257. Springer, Heidelberg (2009). https://doi.org/10.1007/978-3-642-02777-2_24

Degrees of Laziness in Grounding

Effects of Lazy-Grounding Strategies on ASP Solving

Richard Taupe[1,2]([✉]) [iD], Antonius Weinzierl[3] [iD], and Gerhard Friedrich[2] [iD]

[1] Siemens AG Österreich, Vienna, Austria
richard.taupe@siemens.com
[2] Alpen-Adria-Universität Klagenfurt, Klagenfurt, Austria
gerhard.friedrich@aau.at
[3] Institute of Logic and Computation, Vienna University of Technology,
Vienna, Austria
weinzierl@kr.tuwien.ac.at

Abstract. The traditional ground-and-solve approach to Answer Set
Programming (ASP) suffers from the grounding bottleneck, which makes
large-scale problem instances unsolvable. Lazy grounding is an alternative approach that interleaves grounding with solving and thus uses space
more efficiently. The limited view on the search space in lazy grounding
poses unique challenges, however, and can have adverse effects on solving performance. In this paper we present a novel characterization of
degrees of laziness in grounding for ASP, i.e. of compromises between
lazily grounding as little as possible and the traditional full grounding
upfront. We investigate how these degrees of laziness compare to each
other formally as well as, by means of an experimental analysis using a
number of benchmarks, in terms of their effects on solving performance.
Our contributions are the introduction of a range of novel lazy grounding
strategies, a formal account on their relationships and their correctness,
and an investigation of their effects on solving performance. Experiments
show that our approach performs significantly better than state-of-the-
art lazy grounding in many cases.

Keywords: Answer Set Programming · Lazy grounding · Heuristics

1 Introduction

Answer Set Programming (ASP) [2,11,14,15] is a declarative knowledge representation formalism that has been applied in a variety of industrial and scientific
applications. The success of ASP is rooted in efficient solvers such as CLINGO [10]
or DLV [17], which apply the *ground-and-solve* approach, i.e. they first instantiate the given non-ground program and then apply a number of efficient solving
techniques to find the answer sets of the variable-free (i.e., ground) program.

This approach suffers from the *grounding bottleneck* since in many practical
and industrial applications the ground program is too large to fit in memory.

© Springer Nature Switzerland AG 2019
M. Balduccini et al. (Eds.): LPNMR 2019, LNAI 11481, pp. 298–311, 2019.
https://doi.org/10.1007/978-3-030-20528-7_22

One example for such applications is scheduling, where instances used in ASP competitions already yield very large ground programs and real-life instances are significantly larger [9]. Such problem instances cannot be grounded by modern grounders such as GRINGO [12] or I-DLV [3] in acceptable time and/or space [6].

Lazy-grounding ASP systems such as GASP [20], ASPeRiX [16], OMiGA [5], and most recently ALPHA [26] successfully avoid the grounding bottleneck by interleaving grounding and solving, but suffer from substandard search performance. For practical applications one can now decide between running out of memory with a ground-and-solve system, or running out of time with a lazy-grounding system. Since the grounding bottleneck is an inherent issue of the ground-and-solve approach, improvements of lazy-grounding ASP solving are an important contribution for dealing with large, real-world problem instances.

Therefore, we equipped ALPHA with state-of-the-art heuristics successfully employed by other ASP solvers, namely MOMs [21] for initialization of heuristic scores and VSIDS [19] for their dynamic modification. Both have been implemented in a similar fashion as in CLASP [13]. Somewhat surprisingly, however, those heuristics improved performance of lazy-grounding solving by a much smaller degree than expected. A subsequent investigation revealed that lazy grounding does not provide sufficient information on the search space for such heuristics to perform adequately, because by grounding lazily the solver has only a limited view on the search space. This is a novel challenge for ASP solving, which traditional ground-and-solve ASP solvers did not have to face.

In order to improve solving performance this work investigates ways to offset the limited view of the search space in lazy-grounding ASP solving. We explore various lazy-grounding strategies to find compromises between full upfront grounding and largely blind search heuristics. In summary, our contributions are:

- the inception of a field of novel lazy-grounding strategies for ASP evaluation,
- a formal investigation of how these grounding strategies compare to each other and to previously known ones, as well as
- an experimental analysis in terms of their effects on solving performance, showing that our approach is able to perform significantly better than state-of-the-art lazy grounding in many cases.

Outline: After preliminaries in Sect. 2, novel lazy-grounding strategies are introduced in Sect. 3 and their relationships are formally investigated. Section 4 presents experimental results, and Sect. 5 concludes.

2   Preliminaries

Let $\mathcal{C}$ be a finite set of constants, $\mathcal{V}$ be a set of variables and $\mathcal{P}$ be a finite set of predicates. An atom is an expression $p(t_1, \ldots, t_n)$ where p is an n-ary predicate and $t_1, \ldots, t_n \in \mathcal{C} \cup \mathcal{V}$ are terms, and a literal is either an atom a or its default negation not a. An ASP program P is a finite set of (normal) rules of the form

$$h \leftarrow b_1, \ \ldots \ , b_m, \ \text{not } b_{m+1}, \ \ldots, \ \text{not } b_n.$$

where h and $b_1, \ldots, b_m$ are positive literals (i.e. atoms) and not $b_{m+1}, \ldots,$ not b_n are negative literals. Given a rule r, we denote by $\mathrm{H}(r) = \{h\}$, $\mathrm{B}(r) = \{b_1, \ldots, b_m, \text{not } b_{m+1}, \ldots, \text{not } b_n\}$, $\mathrm{B}^+(r) = \{b_1, \ldots, b_m\}$, and $\mathrm{B}^-(r) = \{b_{m+1}, \ldots, b_n\}$ the head, body, positive body, and negative body of r, respectively. If $\mathrm{H}(r) = \emptyset$, r is a called a constraint, and a fact if $\mathrm{B}(r) = \emptyset$. Given a literal l, set of literals L, or rule r, we denote by $\mathrm{vars}(l)$, $\mathrm{vars}(L)$, or $\mathrm{vars}(r)$ the set of variables occurring in l, L, or r, respectively. A literal l or rule r is ground if $\mathrm{vars}(l) = \emptyset$ or $\mathrm{vars}(r) = \emptyset$, respectively. The set of all ground atoms is denoted by At_{grd}. A program P is ground if all its rules $r \in P$ are. As usual, in the remainder of this work we only consider safe programs P, where each rule $r \in P$ is safe, i.e., each variable occurring in r also occurs in its positive body, formally, $\mathrm{vars}(r) \subseteq \mathrm{vars}(\mathrm{B}^+(r))$. The function pred: $2^A \to 2^P$ maps a set of atoms to their predicates, e.g. $\mathrm{pred}(\{a(1,2), a(X,Y)\}) = \{a/2\}$. The set $\mathrm{heads}(P) = \{\mathrm{H}(r) \mid r \in P\}$ contains the heads of all rules in P, and the set $\mathrm{facts}(P) = \{r \mid r \in P \wedge \mathrm{B}(r) = \emptyset\}$ contains all facts.

An (Herbrand) interpretation I is a subset of the Herbrand base w.r.t. P, i.e., $I \subseteq At_{\mathrm{grd}}$. I satisfies a ground rule r, denoted $I \models r$, if $\mathrm{B}^+(r) \subseteq I \wedge \mathrm{B}^-(r) \cap I = \emptyset$ implies $\mathrm{H}(r) \subseteq I$ and $\mathrm{H}(r) \neq \emptyset$. Given an interpretation I and a ground program P, the FLP reduct P^I of P w.r.t. I is the set of rules $r \in P$ whose body is satisfied by I, i.e., $P^I = \{r \in P \mid \mathrm{B}^+(r) \subseteq I \wedge \mathrm{B}^-(r) \cap I = \emptyset\}$ [8]. I is an *answer set* of a ground program P if I is the subset-minimal model of P^I. A substitution $\sigma : \mathcal{V} \to \mathcal{C}$ is a mapping of variables to constants. Given an atom at the result of applying a substitution σ to at is denoted $at\sigma$; this is extended in the usual way to rules r, i.e., $r\sigma$ for a rule of the above form is $h\sigma \leftarrow b_1\sigma, \ldots, b_m\sigma, \text{not } b_{m+1}\sigma, \text{not } b_n\sigma$. The grounding of a rule is given by $\mathrm{grd}(r) = \{r\sigma \mid \sigma \text{ is a substitution for all } v \in \mathrm{vars}(r)\}$ and the grounding $\mathrm{grd}(P)$ of a program P is given by $\mathrm{grd}(P) = \bigcup_{r \in P} \mathrm{grd}(r)$. The answer sets of a nonground program P are given by the answer sets of $\mathrm{grd}(P)$.

Computing all answer sets such that $\mathrm{grd}(P)$ is constructed lazily is typically done by a loop composed of two phases: given a partial assignment (that is initially empty), first ground those rules that potentially fire under the current assignment, second expand the current assignment (using propagation and guessing). If the loop reaches a fixpoint, i.e., no more rules potentially fire and nothing is left to propagate or guess on, and no constraints are violated, then the current assignment is an answer set (cf. [18,26] for a detailed account of the ALPHA ASP system). A (partial) *assignment* A is a set of signed atoms where A^+ denotes the atoms assigned a positive value and A^- those assigned a negative value in A. Note that for this work it is sufficient to consider A to be Boolean (while the solving component of ALPHA also considers a third and positive truth value must-be-true). Also, we consider assignments to be *consistent*, i.e. $A^+ \cap A^- = \emptyset$. Given two assignments A, A' we define the combination $A \uplus A' = B$ to be an assignment such that $B^+ = A^+ \cup A'^+$ and $B^- = A^- \cup A'^-$.

3 Lazy-Grounding Strategies

Currently, a ground rule is only returned to the solver if it is of interest, i.e., if its positive body is fully satisfied. This is a very restrictive grounding strategy in order to save space and avoid the grounding bottleneck. As experience shows, this *maximally strict* grounding strategy employed by ALPHA results in non-optimal search performance, because state-of-the-art search procedures are propositional and only operate on grounded parts of the problem. With maximally strict lazy-grounding these search procedures (e.g. branching heuristics) are left mostly blind when large parts of the given problem instance are not yet grounded.

In the following we thus investigate more permissive lazy-grounding strategies that lie between the maximally strict one and the full upfront grounding (the *maximally permissive* grounding strategy). The more permissive a grounding strategy, the less restrictions it poses on ground rules returned by the grounder. Thus, ground rules are produced earlier and in higher quantity.

Definition 1. *Let P be an answer-set program, $\mathcal{A}$ be the set of assignments, $G_{\mathrm{m}} = 2^{At_{\mathrm{grd}}}$ be the set of possible grounder memories, and $R \subseteq P$ the set of rules of P that are not ground. Then, a lazy-grounding strategy is a function $s : \mathcal{A} \times G_{\mathrm{m}} \times R \to G_{\mathrm{m}} \times 2^{\mathrm{grd}(P)}$ mapping a triple of assignment, grounder memory, and a rule with variables to a new grounder memory and a set of ground instances of the rule, i.e., $(A, G, r) \mapsto (G', R')$ with $R' \subseteq \mathrm{grd}(r)$.*

A grounder memory $G \subseteq 2^{At_{\mathrm{grd}}}$ is a subset of the Herbrand base $\mathcal{HB}_P = At_{\mathrm{grd}}$ and thus can be seen as one half of an assignment, i.e., either A^+ or A^-. Since rules in ASP must be safe, a grounding substitution for all variables of the positive body of a rule is also a grounding substitution for the whole rule. Therefore, it is sufficient to consider only the positive body for lazy grounding.

Considering both negative and positive body atoms could allow a more restrictive grounding than currently employed in ALPHA, because a grounding instantiation could be rejected if one of the negative body literals is currently true. This approach, however, would require the solver to ground additional rules also when backtracking in the search, because backtracking removes assignments and those could then lead to negative body atoms no longer being true. Thus in ALPHA grounding only considers the positive body of a rule and we follow this choice here. In the remainder of this work we therefore identify a grounder memory G with an assignment A such that $A^+ = G$ and $A^- = \emptyset$, i.e., a grounder memory identifies a fully positive assignment.

In order to avoid ground instantiations of rules that can never be applicable we introduce a notion of deterministically inactive rules. Intuitively, a rule is inactive if it contains a positive literal over a predicate that does not occur in any rule head (or fact) and hence cannot be derived, or if it contains a negative literal that also occurs as a fact in the program hence its negation never holds. Formally, given a ground rule $r \in \mathrm{grd}(P)$, r is *inactive* if there exists $a \in \mathrm{B}^+(r)$ with $\mathrm{pred}(a) \notin \mathrm{pred}(\mathrm{heads}(P))$ or $a \in \mathrm{B}^-(r)$ with $a \in \mathcal{A}(\mathrm{facts}(P))$.[1]

---

[1] The notion of inactive rule could be generalized to cover more rules, but we decidedly chose a syntactic condition that is easy to check algorithmically.

Given an assignment A, a ground rule $r\sigma$ stemming from a non-ground rule $r \in P$ and a substitution σ, $r\sigma$ is *of interest* w.r.t. A if $B^+(r\sigma) \subseteq A^+$ holds and must be grounded, because $r\sigma$ potentially fires under A.

The formalization of ALPHA's default grounding strategy is as follows.

Definition 2. *The default grounding strategy for a program P is a lazy-grounding strategy* $\mathrm{gs}_{\mathrm{def}}(A, G, r) = (G', R)$ *such that* $G' = A^+$ *and* $R = \{r' \in \mathrm{grd}(r) \mid r'$ *is not inactive and of interest w.r.t.A*$\}$.

The following notion helps to characterize a class of grounding strategies that are at least as permissive as the maximally strict strategy and strictly less permissive than the maximally permissive strategy.

Definition 3. *A ground rule $r \in \mathrm{grd}(P)$ is* weakly applicable *w.r.t. an assignment A if* $B^+(r) \cap A^- = \emptyset$ *and r is not inactive.*

Intuitively, a ground rule r is weakly applicable if is not inactive and no positive body atom is assigned false. Given an assignment A, a (non-ground) rule r, and a substitution σ such that $r\sigma$ is ground, we call the set $L_A(r, \sigma)$ of positive literals of r whose grounding is in A, i.e., $L_A(r, \sigma) = \{l \in B^+(r) \mid l\sigma \in A^+\}$, the *assigned literals* of $r\sigma$ w.r.t. A; furthermore, if $\mathrm{vars}(L_A(r, \sigma)) = \mathrm{vars}(r)$ we say $r\sigma$ is *all-variable-assigning* w.r.t. A.

Definition 4. *A ground instance $r\sigma$ of a non-ground rule $r \in P$ is* k-unassigned *w.r.t. an assignment A if it is weakly applicable, its set $L_A(r, \sigma)$ of assigned literals is all-variable-assigning, and* $|B^+(r) \setminus L_A(r, \sigma)| \leq k$, *i.e. at most k literals in the positive body of $r\sigma$ are still unassigned.*

For grounding strategies based on k-unassignedness, we further distinguish between constraints and normal rules, because these two types affect the search procedure in different ways (as Sect. 4 shows). A modified grounder then returns all ground rules that can be produced w.r.t. the current partial assignment and that are k_{co}-unassigned in the case of constraints or k_{ru}-unassigned in the case of other rules, where k_{co} and k_{ru} are parameterizable. Values $k_{\mathrm{co}} = k_{\mathrm{ru}} = 0$ yield the maximally strict grounding strategy, i.e., a rule is 0-unassigned if and only if it is of interest. The field of novel grounding strategies then is as follows.

Definition 5. *The k-unassigned grounding strategy for a program P is a lazy-grounding strategy* $\mathrm{gs}_{k_{\mathrm{co}}, k_{\mathrm{ru}}}(A, G, r) = (G', R)$ *such that $G' = A^+$ and $R = \{r' \in \mathrm{grd}(r) \mid H(r') = \emptyset, r'$ is k_{co}-unassigned w.r.t. $A\} \cup \{r' \in \mathrm{grd}(r) \mid H(r') \neq \emptyset, r'$ is k_{ru}-unassigned w.r.t. $A\}$.*

Strategies with $k_{\mathrm{co}} > k_{\mathrm{ru}}$ ground more constraints than rules, allowing better-informed search heuristics and at the same time fewer superfluous ground rules. Intuitively, these grounding strategies yield a larger grounding in each step of a lazy-grounding solver, but they are still limited to only yield ground instances of rules that are very close to the current search path, since k-unassignedness requires all variables to be bound by instances in the current assignment.

To give the grounder more freedom such that ground instances can be obtained that are further away from the current search path, we introduce accumulator grounding strategies. The core idea is to use the grounder memory to store ground atoms that were encountered earlier in another branch of the search for answer sets but are not necessarily true in the current branch of the search.

Definition 6. *The* default accumulator grounding strategy *for a program P is a lazy-grounding strategy* $\mathrm{gs}_{\mathrm{def}}^{\mathrm{accu}}(A, G, r) = (G', R)$ *such that* $G' = G \cup A^+$ *and* $R = \{r' \in \mathrm{grd}(r) \mid r'$ *is not inactive and of interest w.r.t.* $G' \uplus A\}$.

Using such an accumulator the grounder is able to obtain ground instances resulting from a combination of different search paths. The accumulator can also be added to the k-unassigned grounding strategy as follows.

Definition 7. *The k-unassigned accumulator grounding strategy for a program P is a lazy-grounding strategy* $\mathrm{gs}_{k_{\mathrm{co}}, k_{\mathrm{ru}}}^{\mathrm{accu}}(A, G, r) = (G', R)$ *such that* $G' = G \cup A^+$ *and* $R = \{r \in \mathrm{grd}(r) \mid \mathrm{H}(r) = \emptyset, r$ *is* k_{co}*-unassigned w.r.t.* $G' \uplus A\} \cup \{r' \in \mathrm{grd}(r) \mid \mathrm{H}(r') \neq \emptyset, r'$ *is* k_{ru}*-unassigned w.r.t.* $G' \uplus A\}$.

Relationships Between Lazy-Grounding Strategies. Some of the lazy-grounding strategies introduced above are subsumed by others, i.e., the sets of ground rules produced by some grounding strategies are subsets of those produced by others. First, each k-unassigned grounding strategy is subsumed by a $k + 1$-unassigned grounding strategy, intuitively because a k-unassigned rule also is a $k + 1$-unassigned rule. Formally, and more detailed:

Proposition 1. *Given an assignment A, a grounding memory G, and a rule r. Let* $\mathrm{gs}_{k_{\mathrm{co}}, k_{\mathrm{ru}}}(A, G, r) = (G', R)$ *and* $\mathrm{gs}_{k'_{\mathrm{co}}, k'_{\mathrm{ru}}}(A, G, r) = (G'', R')$, *then* $R \subseteq R'$ *for any* $k'_{\mathrm{co}} \geq k_{\mathrm{co}}$ *and* $k'_{\mathrm{ru}} \geq k_{\mathrm{ru}}$.

Proof. Let $\mathrm{gs}_{k_{\mathrm{co}}, k_{\mathrm{ru}}}(A, G, r) = (G', R)$ and $r' \in R$. Then r' is either a k_{co}-unassigned constraint or a k_{ru}-unassigned rule and because $k'_{\mathrm{co}} \geq k_{\mathrm{co}}$ and $k'_{\mathrm{ru}} \geq k_{\mathrm{ru}}$ it follows that r' is either a k'_{co}-unassigned constraint or a k'_{ru}-unassigned rule, respectively. In either case it holds that $r' \in R'$ for $\mathrm{gs}_{k'_{\mathrm{co}}, k'_{\mathrm{ru}}}(A, G, r) = (G'', R')$.

Second, each k-unassigned strategy subsumes the default grounding strategy.

Proposition 2. *Given an assignment A, a grounding memory G, and a rule r. Let* $\mathrm{gs}_{\mathrm{def}}(A, G, r) = (G', R)$ *and* $\mathrm{gs}_{k_{\mathrm{co}}, k_{\mathrm{ru}}}(A, G, r) = (G'', R')$, *then* $R \subseteq R'$ *for any* $k_{\mathrm{co}}, k_{\mathrm{ru}} \geq 0$.

Proof. Let $\mathrm{gs}_{\mathrm{def}}(A, G, r) = (G', R)$ and $r \in R$, then r is not inactive and of interest w.r.t. A, i.e., $\mathrm{B}^+(r) \subseteq A^+$. By the latter, it holds that r is 0-unassigned and consequently $r \in R'$ for $\mathrm{gs}_{0,0}(A, G, r) = (G'', R')$. From Proposition 1 it then follows that $r \in R'$ for any $\mathrm{gs}_{k_{\mathrm{co}}, k_{\mathrm{ru}}}(A, G, r) = (G'', R')$ with $k_{\mathrm{co}}, k_{\mathrm{ru}} \geq 0$.

Third, the accumulator variant of a grounding strategy subsumes the grounding strategy without accumulator.

Proposition 3. *For an assignment A, a grounding memory G, and a rule r:*

1. *if* $\mathrm{gs}_{\mathrm{def}}(A, G, r) = (G', R)$ *and* $\mathrm{gs}_{\mathrm{def}}^{\mathrm{accu}}(A, G, r) = (G'', R')$ *then* $R \subseteq R'$.
2. *if* $\mathrm{gs}_{k_{\mathrm{co}}, k_{\mathrm{ru}}}(A, G, r) = (G', R)$ *and* $\mathrm{gs}_{k_{\mathrm{co}}, k_{\mathrm{ru}}}^{\mathrm{accu}}(A, G, r) = (G'', R')$ *then* $R \subseteq R'$
   for any $k_{\mathrm{co}}, k_{\mathrm{ru}} \geq 0$.
3. *if* $\mathrm{gs}_{k_{\mathrm{co}}, k_{\mathrm{ru}}}^{\mathrm{accu}}(A, G, r) = (G', R)$ *and* $\mathrm{gs}_{k_{\mathrm{co}}', k_{\mathrm{ru}}'}^{\mathrm{accu}}(A, G, r) = (G'', R')$ *then* $R \subseteq R'$
   for any $k_{\mathrm{co}}' \geq k_{\mathrm{co}}$ *and* $k_{\mathrm{ru}}' \geq k_{\mathrm{ru}}$.

Proof. 1. Let $\mathrm{gs}_{\mathrm{def}}(A, G, r) = (G', R)$ and $r \in R$, thus by definition it holds that r is not inactive and of interest w.r.t. $G' = A^+$. For the accumulator variant it holds that $G'' = G \cup A^+$ and $R' = \{r \in \mathrm{grd}(r) \mid r$ is not inactive and of interest w.r.t. $G''\}$. Since $G' \subseteq G''$ and the assignment corresponding to a grounder memory is an assignment A such that $A^+ = G'$ and $A^- = \emptyset$, it holds that r is of interest w.r.t. G'', i.e., $r \in R'$. 2. and 3. are analogous.

Soundness and Completeness. We show in the following that all grounding strategies are sound and complete, i.e., in a lazy-grounding ASP solver one may freely exchange one grounding strategy for another.

Proposition 4. *Given a lazy-grounding ASP solver S which is sound and complete for the default grounding strategy $\mathrm{gs}_{\mathrm{def}}$, then S is sound and complete for the k-unassigned grounding strategies $\mathrm{gs}_{k_{\mathrm{co}}, k_{\mathrm{ru}}}$, and their respective accumulator variants $\mathrm{gs}_{\mathrm{def}}^{\mathrm{accu}}$ and $\mathrm{gs}_{k_{\mathrm{co}}, k_{\mathrm{ru}}}^{\mathrm{accu}}$.*

Proof. Soundness immediately follows from the respective definition, because every ground rule returned by any of the above grounding strategies is a ground rule of the original program. Formally, let (G', R) be the returned pair of any of these strategies then for all $r \in R$ it holds that $r \in \mathrm{grd}(r)$ and thus $r \in \mathrm{grd}(P)$ where P is the input program.

Completeness: S is complete for $\mathrm{gs}_{\mathrm{def}}$ intuitively since if a ground rule r fires under some assignment A then r is of interest w.r.t. A and hence returned by $\mathrm{gs}_{\mathrm{def}}$. Observe that a rule that is inactive can never be applicable in any answer set, hence the additional requirement to only consider rules that are not inactive has no effect on completeness. Completeness for all other grounding strategies then follows from Propositions 1 to 3, showing that every other grounding strategy produces at least the same ground rules as $\mathrm{gs}_{\mathrm{def}}$.

The lazy-grounding strategies $\mathrm{gs}_{\mathrm{def}}, \mathrm{gs}_{k_{\mathrm{co}}, k_{\mathrm{ru}}}$, $\mathrm{gs}_{\mathrm{def}}^{\mathrm{accu}}$, and $\mathrm{gs}_{k_{\mathrm{co}}, k_{\mathrm{ru}}}^{\mathrm{accu}}$ are sound and complete for ALPHA, since ALPHA is sound and complete for $\mathrm{gs}_{\mathrm{def}}$ (cf. [26]).

The Effect of Domain Predicates. It is well-known for practical ASP solving that the choice of encoding employed for a task can have a major influence on solving performance, even though the semantics is still declarative. Such an effect can also be observed in conjunction with grounding strategies based on k-unassignedness. Assume that dom is a domain predicate in the sense of [25], i.e. a predicate defining the domain over which p and q are defined, and consider the constraint c as follows: $\leftarrow \mathrm{p}(X), \mathrm{q}(Y)$. If $\mathrm{p}(1) \in A^+$ and

$q(t) \notin A^+$ holds for all terms t then c is not 1-unassigned, because Y is not yet bound and thus c is not all-variable-assigning. Extending c with domain predicates to obtain c' gives $\leftarrow \mathrm{dom}(X), \mathrm{dom}(Y), \mathrm{p}(X), \mathrm{q}(Y)$. Assuming that $\mathrm{dom}(1)$ holds together with $\mathrm{p}(1) \in A^+$ and $\mathrm{q}(1) \notin A^+$ then yields the ground rule $\leftarrow \mathrm{dom}(1), \mathrm{dom}(1), \mathrm{p}(1), \mathrm{q}(1)$ which is 1-unassigned w.r.t. A^+. In such a case, the 1-unassigned lazy-grounding strategy yields no ground instances for c but some for c'. Hence an earlier grounding of constraints (and rules) can be initiated by adding (superfluous) domain predicates.

Adding domain predicates allows finding a solution with fewer backtracks, because the additional ground constraints support early propagation and inform the search heuristics better. This is not a guaranteed improvement, however, since more ground constraints also need more space. A grounder can add domain predicates automatically or use the heads of previously grounded rules to generate bindings even if those heads are not true yet. But this is future work.

4   Experimental Results

To asses their impact, we evaluate the novel grounding strategies on three benchmark problems: Graph Colouring, House Reconfiguration, and Stable Marriage.

Experimental Setup. Experiments were run on a cluster of machines each with two Intel® Xeon® CPU E5-2650 v4 @ 2.20 GHz with 12 cores each, 252 GB of memory, and Ubuntu 16.04.1 LTS Linux. Benchmarks were scheduled with the ABC Benchmarking System [22] together with HTCondor™.[2] Time and memory consumption were measured by PYRUNLIM,[3] which was also used to limit time consumption to 15 min per instance and swapping to 0.

Encodings and Instances. The encodings for Stable Marriage and Graph Colouring were taken from the Fourth Answer Set Programming Competition [1], the former without modifications, the latter with a choice rule replacing the equivalent disjunctive rule of the original. The encoding for the House Reconfiguration Problem was taken from [24] and changed to a decision problem. Instances from the ASP Competitions [1, 4] decidedly were not used, as these are hand-picked to exercise search techniques of ground-and-solve systems, which are not all available in lazy-grounding ASP solving, like restarts and equivalence preprocessing.[4]

Instead, instances for all three problems were generated randomly. For Graph Colouring, Erdős–Rényi graphs [7] were generated.[5] Let (V, E, C) denote a class of Graph Colouring instances, where V denotes the number of vertices, E the number of edges, and C the number of colours. A total of 1430 instances were generated for $V \in \{10, 20, \ldots, 190, 200, 250, \ldots, 450, 500\}$ and diverse choices for

---

[2] https://github.com/credl/abcbenchmarking, http://research.cs.wisc.edu/htcondor.

[3] https://alviano.com/software/pyrunlim/.

[4] Graph Colouring benchmark instances, for example, are prohibitive even for CLASP with those techniques disabled by `--sat-prepro=no --eq=0 -r no -d no`.

[5] Using the Python function `networkx.generators.random_graphs.gnm_random_graph`.

E and C based on values used for the ASP competitions. A total of 99 instances were generated for the House Reconfiguration Problem, where the number of things T ranged from 5 to 45. For each instance, the number of persons P was drawn from a uniform distribution $\mathcal{U}\{2, \lfloor \frac{T}{2} \rfloor + 1\}$ and the owner of every thing was drawn from $\mathcal{U}\{1, P\}$. Every thing had a 50% chance to be in a cabinet and a random subset of given things was considered as long things. For Stable Marriage, 341 instances with a number of people $P \in \{10, \ldots, 70\}$ were generated. The scores given by each person were drawn from $\{1, \ldots, \max(5, \lfloor \frac{P}{8} \rfloor)\}$, where every score had the same probability of being drawn except for the lowest and the highest score, whose probability of being drawn was reduced by 50% each.

Results and Discussion. For each instance, ALPHA was instructed to find 10 answer sets. To reduce the numbers of data points in the following scatter plots only the median performance data for each size and class of problem instances is shown.[6] For example, all 11 Graph Colouring instances of each class (V, E, C) are condensed into one data point for each pair of grounding strategies.

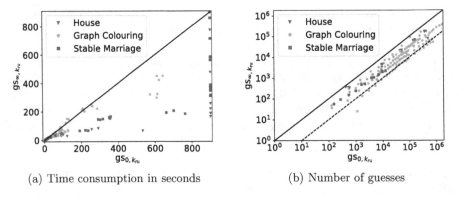

(a) Time consumption in seconds   (b) Number of guesses

Fig. 1. Time and guesses comparing $gs_{0,k_{ru}}$ to $gs_{\infty,k_{ru}}$ for $k_{ru} \in \{0, 1, \infty\}$

Figure 1 shows the resource usage needed to find the first 10 answer sets of each benchmark instance, comparing strict ($k_{co} = 0$) to permissive ($k_{co} = \infty$) grounding of constraints. Each data point in the scatter plots corresponds to one class of problem instances of the same size solved by two different grounder configurations for $k_{co} \in \{0, \infty\}$ and varying $k_{ru} \in \{0, 1, \infty\}$. The location of each data point on the x axis corresponds to resource usage with $k_{co} = 0$, its y location to resource usage with $k_{co} = \infty$.

Hence, a data point on the diagonal corresponds to a problem instance where strict ($k_{co} = 0$) and permissive ($k_{co} = \infty$) perform equally. Data points that are located below the diagonal indicate that an instance could be solved faster when

---

[6] Computing the median of an odd number of performance data allows to obtain a measure of central tendency that is unaffected by timeouts.

using $k_{co} = \infty$, while those above the diagonal represent an instance that could
be solved faster when using $k_{co} = 0$. Instances that exceeded the given time-out
of 900 s line up at the end of each axis. Time usage is shown in Fig. 1a, number
of guesses in Fig. 1b.[7] Guesses are scaled logarithmically, with a dashed second
reference diagonal to indicate an improvement of factor 10.

Permissive grounding of constraints is faster in most cases, as most data
points in Fig. 1 are below the diagonal. Figure 1b shows an even greater advantage of permissive grounding when the number of guesses is considered. Comparing strict and permissive settings for k_{ru} instead of k_{co}, no clear conclusion
can be drawn. Due to space constraints, the corresponding plots are not shown.

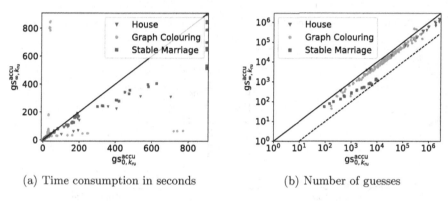

(a) Time consumption in seconds   (b) Number of guesses

Fig. 2. Time and guesses comparing $gs^{accu}_{0,k_{ru}}$ to $gs^{accu}_{\infty,k_{ru}}$ for $k_{ru} \in \{0, 1, \infty\}$

Figure 2 shows the same instances for the accumulator variants of the
same grounding strategies. Again, the general pattern indicates that permissive
grounding of constraints ($k_{co} = \infty$) improves performance. Comparing those
plots to Fig. 1 shows a noticeable change of the performance in Graph Colouring
instances. Most of the data points gather along the diagonal near the origin and
a small (but more visible) number of outliers is distributed near both axes, which
means that some Graph Colouring instances were hard to solve for $k_{co} = 0$ and
some were hard to solve for $k_{co} = \infty$. Deeper analysis of the solver revealed that
in these cases the branching heuristic completely leads the search astray, resulting in more guesses to solve the problem and to invest more time in propagation.

In Fig. 3, we compare results for accumulator grounding strategies to their
variants without accumulator. We observe a similar pattern as in Fig. 2: while
House and Stable Marriage are clearly able to benefit from the accumulator,
effects are mixed for Graph Colouring. Visually, outliers dominate the plot but
most data points are near the origin and below the diagonal.

Figure 4 offers a different perspective on time consumption data for two
classes of Graph Colouring instances. For each instance size (number of nodes),

---

[7] Numbers of guesses omit instances that could not be solved within the time limit.

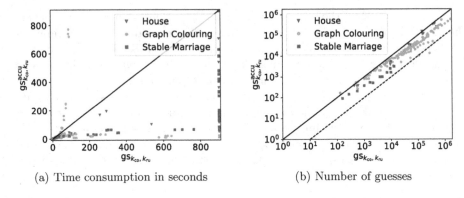

(a) Time consumption in seconds   (b) Number of guesses

Fig. 3. Time and guesses comparing $gs_{k_{co},k_{ru}}$ to $gs^{accu}_{k_{co},k_{ru}}$ for $k_{co}, k_{ru} \in \{0, 1, \infty\}$

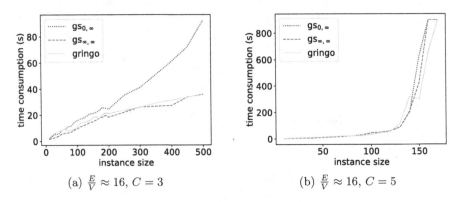

(a) $\frac{E}{V} \approx 16$, $C = 3$ (b) $\frac{E}{V} \approx 16$, $C = 5$

Fig. 4. Time for two classes of Graph Colouring instances (without accumulator).

the median time consumption of selected grounding strategies on all 11 instances is plotted. From the range of lazy grounding strategies, two representatives are shown, comparing strict to permissive grounding of constraints.[8] These are contrasted with ALPHA's performance when working on a fully ground input produced by GRINGO version 5.2.2. It appears that instances with $\frac{E}{V} \approx 16$ and three colours were able to benefit greatly from permissive grounding of constraints, while performance was rather unaffected by change of grounding strategies when five colours were used instead. For both classes we observe that having the full upfront grounding provides good performance compared to lazy grounding, which is in line with heuristics being fully informed. The k-unassigned grounding strategy with permissive grounding of constraints, however, performs similarly well. We observed that permissive grounding of constraints also reduces

---

[8] In Graph Colouring, changing the value of k_{ru} does not show an effect on the number of guesses needed to find an answer set. This is likely due to the encoding containing only one non-constraint rule whose body is not fully determined by facts.

memory usage. We assume this to be caused by the current lack of learned nogood forgetting, i.e. the longer ALPHA runs the more learned nogoods are kept in memory.

Overall, we observe that lazy grounding enables a whole range of new lazy-grounding strategies that face other challenges than previous approaches at grounding. Most importantly, in lazy grounding rules and constraints grounded earlier than necessary have a great effect on solving performance, because they inform the heuristics about the search space. While we cannot give a definite answer on which grounding strategy is the best, we uncovered a whole new field of possible strategies and identified some that improve efficiency significantly.

5   Conclusions and Future Work

In this work we introduced a field of novel grounding strategies for lazy-grounding ASP evaluation. Grounding lazily as little as possible adversely affects heuristics and search performance, because of the limited view of the search space. Our investigation aimed at new ways to offset this restriction while keeping the benefits of lazy grounding to avoid the grounding bottleneck. The main contribution of this paper is the introduction and formal characterization of various classes of grounding strategies ("degrees of laziness"), like k-unassigned grounding strategies and accumulator-based ones, which allow compromises between lazily grounding as little as possible and the traditional grounding upfront. Experimental results show a clear improvement over existing lazy-grounding strategies and that permissive grounding of constraints usually improves solving performance, while the performance improvements from other grounding strategies depend on the problem to be solved. Permissive lazy grounding of constraints could become the new default for ALPHA and may be applied in other lazy-grounding solvers.

Our work considers grounding from a very different (lazy) perspective than previous works on (upfront) grounding. As such, it cannot provide the conclusion but rather the beginning of a larger investigation on the effects of lazy-grounding strategies on solving performance. Future work may explore syntactic features of answer-set programs to automatically select an efficient grounding strategy and connect lazy grounding more closely with search heuristics. Investigating the relationship between our approach and instantiation heuristics for quantified formulas in SMT [23] as well as generalizing our approach beyond ASP, e.g. based on lattices, also seem promising.

Acknowledgments. This work was conducted in the scope of the research project *DynaCon (FFG-PNr.: 861263)*, which is funded by the Austrian Federal Ministry of Transport, Innovation and Technology (BMVIT) under the program "ICT of the Future" between 2017 and 2020 (see https://iktderzukunft.at/en/ for more information).

References

1. Alviano, M., et al.: The fourth answer set programming competition: preliminary report. In: Cabalar, P., Son, T.C. (eds.) LPNMR 2013. LNCS (LNAI), vol. 8148, pp. 42–53. Springer, Heidelberg (2013). https://doi.org/10.1007/978-3-642-40564-8_5

2. Baral, C.: Knowledge Representation, Reasoning and Declarative Problem Solving. Cambridge University Press, Cambridge (2003)

3. Calimeri, F., Fuscà, D., Perri, S., Zangari, J.: I-DLV: the new intelligent grounder of DLV. Intell. Artif. **11**(1), 5–20 (2017)

4. Calimeri, F., Gebser, M., Maratea, M., Ricca, F.: Design and results of the fifth answer set programming competition. Artif. Intell. **231**, 151–181 (2016)

5. Dao-Tran, M., Eiter, T., Fink, M., Weidinger, G., Weinzierl, A.: OMiGA : an open minded grounding on-the-fly answer set solver. In: del Cerro, L.F., Herzig, A., Mengin, J. (eds.) JELIA 2012. LNCS (LNAI), vol. 7519, pp. 480–483. Springer, Heidelberg (2012). https://doi.org/10.1007/978-3-642-33353-8_38

6. Eiter, T., Faber, W., Fink, M., Woltran, S.: Complexity results for answer set programming with bounded predicate arities and implications. Ann. Math. Artif. Intell. **51**(2–4), 123–165 (2007)

7. Erdős, P., Rényi, A.: On Random Graphs. I. Publicationes Mathematicae **6**, 290–297 (1959). https://users.renyi.hu/~p_erdos/1959-11.pdf

8. Faber, W., Pfeifer, G., Leone, N.: Semantics and complexity of recursive aggregates in answer set programming. Artif. Intell. **175**(1), 278–298 (2011)

9. Falkner, A.A., Friedrich, G., Schekotihin, K., Taupe, R., Teppan, E.C.: Industrial applications of answer set programming. KI **32**(2–3), 165–176 (2018)

10. Gebser, M., Kaminski, R., Kaufmann, B., Romero, J., Schaub, T.: Progress in *clasp* series 3. In: Calimeri, F., Ianni, G., Truszczynski, M. (eds.) LPNMR 2015. LNCS (LNAI), vol. 9345, pp. 368–383. Springer, Cham (2015). https://doi.org/10.1007/978-3-319-23264-5_31

11. Gebser, M., Kaminski, R., Kaufmann, B., Schaub, T.: Answer Set Solving in Practice. Morgan and Claypool Publishers, San Rafael (2012)

12. Gebser, M., Kaminski, R., König, A., Schaub, T.: Advances in *gringo* series 3. In: Delgrande, J.P., Faber, W. (eds.) LPNMR 2011. LNCS (LNAI), vol. 6645, pp. 345–351. Springer, Heidelberg (2011). https://doi.org/10.1007/978-3-642-20895-9_39

13. Gebser, M., Kaufmann, B., Schaub, T.: Conflict-driven answer set solving: from theory to practice. Artif. Intell. **187**, 52–89 (2012)

14. Gelfond, M., Kahl, Y.: Knowledge Representation, Reasoning, and the Design of Intelligent Agents: The Answer-Set Programming Approach. Cambridge University Press, New York (2014)

15. Gelfond, M., Lifschitz, V.: The stable model semantics for logic programming. In: ICLP/SLP, pp. 1070–1080. MIT Press (1988)

16. Lefèvre, C., Béatrix, C., Stéphan, I., Garcia, L.: ASPeRiX, a first-order forward chaining approach for answer set computing. TPLP **17**(3), 266–310 (2017)

17. Leone, N., et al.: The DLV system for knowledge representation and reasoning. ACM Trans. Comput. Log. **7**(3), 499–562 (2006)

18. Leutgeb, L., Weinzierl, A.: Techniques for efficient lazy-grounding ASP solving. In: Seipel, D., Hanus, M., Abreu, S. (eds.) WFLP/WLP/INAP -2017. LNCS (LNAI), vol. 10997, pp. 132–148. Springer, Cham (2018). https://doi.org/10.1007/978-3-030-00801-7_9

19. Moskewicz, M.W., Madigan, C.F., Zhao, Y., Zhang, L., Malik, S.: Chaff: engineering an efficient SAT solver. In: DAC, pp. 530–535. ACM (2001)
20. Palù, A.D., Dovier, A., Pontelli, E., Rossi, G.: GASP: answer set programming with lazy grounding. Fundam. Inf. **96**(3), 297–322 (2009)
21. Pretolani, D.: Efficiency, and stability of hypergraph SAT algorithms. In: Cliques, Coloring, and Satisfiability, vol. 26, pp. 479–498. DIMACS/AMS (1993)
22. Redl, C.: Automated benchmarking of KR-systems. In: RCRA@AI*IA, CEUR Workshop Proceedings, vol. 1745, pp. 45–56. CEUR-WS.org (2016)
23. Reynolds, A., Deters, M., Kuncak, V., Tinelli, C., Barrett, C.: Counterexample-guided quantifier instantiation for synthesis in SMT. In: Kroening, D., Păsăreanu, C.S. (eds.) CAV 2015. LNCS, vol. 9207, pp. 198–216. Springer, Cham (2015). https://doi.org/10.1007/978-3-319-21668-3_12
24. Ryabokon, A.: Knowledge-based (re)configuration of complex products and services. Dissertation, Alpen-Adria-Universität Klagenfurt, Klagenfurt (2015). https://permalink.obvsg.at/UKL/AC10777791
25. Syrjänen, T.: Omega-restricted logic programs. In: Eiter, T., Faber, W., Truszczyński, M. (eds.) LPNMR 2001. LNCS (LNAI), vol. 2173, pp. 267–280. Springer, Heidelberg (2001). https://doi.org/10.1007/3-540-45402-0_20
26. Weinzierl, A.: Blending lazy-grounding and CDNL search for answer-set solving. In: Balduccini, M., Janhunen, T. (eds.) LPNMR 2017. LNCS (LNAI), vol. 10377, pp. 191–204. Springer, Cham (2017). https://doi.org/10.1007/978-3-319-61660-5_17

Enhancing DLV
for Large-Scale Reasoning

Nicola Leone[1], Carlo Allocca[3], Mario Alviano[1], Francesco Calimeri[1,2],
Cristina Civili[3], Roberta Costabile[1], Alessio Fiorentino[1],
Davide Fuscà[1], Stefano Germano[1,2], Giovanni Laboccetta[2],
Bernardo Cuteri[2], Marco Manna[1], Simona Perri[1], Kristian Reale[2],
Francesco Ricca[1], Pierfrancesco Veltri[2], and Jessica Zangari[1,2(✉)]

[1] Department of Mathematics and Computer Science,
University of Calabria, Rende, Italy
{leone,alviano,calimeri,r.costabile,fiorentino,fusca,
manna,perri,ricca,zangari}@mat.unical.it
[2] DLVSystem L.T.D., Polo Tecnologico Unical, Rende, Italy
{calimeri,germano,laboccetta,reale,veltri}@dlvsystem.com,
cuteri@mat.unical.it
[3] Samsung R&D Institute, Staines, UK
{c.allocca,c.civili}@samsung.com

Abstract. Several real-world applications of DLV made evident the
need for efficiently handling multiple queries and reasoning tasks over
large-sized knowledge bases. In this paper we present some recent
enhancements in the ASP system DLV2 for enabling reasoning over
large-scale domains. In particular, we developed both an optimized
implementation, sensibly reducing memory consumption, and a server-
like behaviour to support efficiently multiple-query scenarios. The high
potential of DLV2 for large-scale reasoning is outlined by the results of an
experiment on data-intensive benchmarks. The applicability of the system in real-world scenarios is demonstrated employing DLV2 as reasoning
service to query, in natural language, the large DBpedia knowledge base.
The relevance and the high potential industrial value of this research is
also confirmed by the direct interest of a major international industrial
player, which has stimulated and partially supported this work.

Keywords: Large-scale reasoning · Data-intensive applications · ASP

1 Introduction

DLV [30] has been one of the first solid and reliable Answer Set Programming
(ASP) systems; its project started a few years after the definition of stable
models/answer set semantics [26], and has been continuously enhanced over the
years, becoming well suited also for real-world applications [23]. Recently, it
underwent a major set of updates, that count modern evaluation techniques and

© Springer Nature Switzerland AG 2019
M. Balduccini et al. (Eds.): LPNMR 2019, LNAI 11481, pp. 312–325, 2019.
https://doi.org/10.1007/978-3-030-20528-7_23

development platforms, fully complying with the ASP-Core-2 language standard. The new version is referred to as DLV2 [2], and it results as a proper integration of two sub-systems addressing the two main computational phases: $\mathcal{I}$-DLV [18] for the *grounding* phase and WASP [3] for the *solving* phase. A strong point of DLV2 is its grounding layer $\mathcal{I}$-DLV, which – thanks to advanced optimization techniques (like, e.g., Magic Sets [4]) – enables for efficient query answering; this makes DLV2 a powerful deductive database engine [18,19], employable for querying knowledge bases of various natures. One of the distinctive points of the project is the wide usage in real-world applications, some of which are extremely challenging. This is the case of reasoning tasks over large-scale domains, such as those emerging in industrial-level applications fostered by the advances in Industry 4.0, the Internet of Things, and Big Data [16]. When dealing with high volumes of data, however, performing heavy operations (such as loading or indexing) multiple times should be definitely avoided; thus, traditional ASP systems based on one-shot executions are rather unsuited.

In this work, we present an optimized version of DLV2 where key aspects of the computational process have been properly re-engineered with the aim of reducing memory consumption and performing efficient tasks over large knowledge bases. Moreover, we present the new DLV2-SERVER system, extending DLV2 with a server-like modality, which is able to keep the main process alive and to receive and process user's requests on demand. Furthermore, we designed dedicated optimizations and facilities oriented towards effective reasoning over different practical scenarios. We started to implement enhancements at the grounding stage, which is internally handled by $\mathcal{I}$-DLV [18], and we are currently integrating also the solving stage. We conducted an experimental evaluation on data-intensive benchmarks in order to assess the effectiveness of our approaches; the results confirm the high potential of the new system for large-scale reasoning. Both memory consumption and query-answering times are significantly reduced, even on the one-shot version of DLV2, and the new DLV2-SERVER system turns out to be well-suited for reasoning over large scale data. The challenge of the industrial partner was related to LUBM [28] – a standard benchmark for ontology reasoning collecting data of universities (in particular, LUBM-8000 collects about 1 billion factual assertions upon 8,000 universities). The challenge was: *making the system able to answer in "near time" the benchmark queries of LUBM-8000 over a machine with 256 GB RAM;* while the old DLV2 version was very far from the target, taking about 350 GB and 15,000 s. Eventually, not only the system was able to win the general challenge; amazingly, *the average time taken by DLV2-SERVER on the ten bound queries (out of fourteen) of LUBM-8000 (1 billion of assertions) eventually was less than one second.* Such a result is due to the new architecture, novel indexing and body ordering techniques, and improvements to the magic-set technique that, by simulating backward chaining, focuses the computation on the atoms which are relevant to derive the query result and drastically prunes the search space.

To practically test this potential, we also report on a use case where DLV2-SERVER is employed as a reasoning service in a system for querying, in natural language, DBpedia [12]. The latter models the knowledge present in Wikimedia projects, in a large RDF(S) [40] ontology containing more than 3 billions triples. In the use-case, we developed a fresh instantiation of the ASP-based question answering framework presented in [21], that is able to exploit the information in DBpedia. In particular, DLV2-SERVER is exploited to handle the ontology and process queries under a more expressive entailment regime w.r.t. the one of [21]. Answers to typical queries are returned to the user in hundredths of a second, thus confirming the suitability of our system in real-world scenarios.

2   Enhancing the DLV2 Core Engine

In the following we describe the main enhancements implemented in DLV2 for enabling reasoning on large knowledge bases where main issues come from huge memory requirements; we focussed both on the design of refined optimizations and on technical aspects having significant impact both on time and memory performance. A thorough description of the computational stages of the system is out of the scope of the this paper; we refer the reader to [18] for more details.

We have singled out and optimized the main sources of inefficiency in the core of the DLV2 grounder, starting from memory consumption, which appeared the main obstacle to win the challenge. For instance, we carefully re-designed internal data structures in order to minimize raw memory allocation, and tuned the overall computation by optimizing points that, being frequently executed, might significantly affect performance. Moreover, we designed a memory-releasing policy that, according to the computational machinery and the structure of the program at hand, drops data structures as soon as they are no longer needed (as an example, the extension of a predicate p, along with its associated metadata such as indices, are removed once all rules depending on p have been grounded).

A further set of optimizations is related to query answering, a largely common task especially in practical cases. An improvement has been obtained by identifying and handling *relevant predicates* w.r.t. the query at hand: a predicate is relevant if it either appears in the input query or in a rule featuring a relevant predicate in the head. Intuitively, the relevant predicates are the only ones needed in order to answer the query; hence, when processing the input facts, we can both speed-up loading times and reduce memory consumption by skipping all non-relevant ones. Moreover, we speeded up query answering, by improving our magic-sets query rewriting technique [4]. In particular, we introduced an ad-hoc postprocessing that identifies redundant rules and predicates. Specifically, a subsumption check is performed that allows to remove redundant rules, i.e., rules whose ground instances are included or turn out to be less general than those associated with others. Furthermore, the technique has been enhanced to properly handle the loss of binding propagation, and extended to efficiently deal with a *set* of queries to be evaluated at once.

3   DLV2-Server

We describe here how DLV2 has been enhanced with the capability of running in a server-like fashion reusing the loaded program and data for multiple query sessions. Currently, enhancements concern the grounding phase; a comprehensive version, including also the solving stage, is under development.

DLV2-SERVER keeps the main process alive while receiving commands expressed in XML that permit to handle a set of functionalities, such as loading logic programs and data, removing data, executing reasoning and query answering tasks, and resetting loaded programs and data. Moreover, it can behave as a local or a remote service: in the first case, it runs in a console mode via standard input, and provides results via standard output; in the latter case, the system listens to a specific port and manages connection requests incoming via network.

In addition, the system has been endowed with advanced facilities oriented towards the effective query-answering in large-scale contexts: we consider a scenario in which the system is required to repeatedly query a Knowledge Base (KB) on demand. Such scenario can be further specialized into three different settings, depending on what is known before the system is actually started to be queried: (i) KB is known (both data and program), and also the "structure" of the queries to be executed is known (i.e., as in many database applications, we know the query patterns, that is, we have the conjunction of the query atoms and know which arguments will be free or bound to constants at query time); (ii) KB is known, while no information is available about the incoming queries; (iii) only data are available. In more detail, our scenario includes a logic program (without queries) $\mathcal{P}$, a dataset $\mathcal{D}$ and a set of logic programs (containing queries) $\{Q_1, \ldots, Q_n\}$; what is going to be requested is to evaluate each logic program $P \cup Q_i$ for $i \in \{1, \ldots, n\}$ over $\mathcal{D}$. The three scenarios can be described as (i): $\mathcal{P}$, $\mathcal{D}$ and (modulo constant renaming) $\{Q_1, \ldots, Q_n\}$ are known; (ii): $\mathcal{P}$ and $\mathcal{D}$ are known; (iii): only $\mathcal{D}$ is known. Such scenario is of practical relevance: for instance, it fits many real-world applications over ontological domains, where $\mathcal{P}$ and $\mathcal{D}$ consist of a TBox and an ABox, respectively.

DLV2-SERVER can be advantageously applied in this context since, differently from standard DLV2, it allows to avoid to repeatedly perform heavy parts of the computation such as, for instance, loading and indexing input data. In addition, DLV2-SERVER features different execution modalities specifically designed for optimizing query answering times in the depicted settings by properly taking advantage from what is known in each of them. In the following, we briefly describe the modalities; all of them act on steps of the grounding process having a high impact on overall performance, especially in large-scale contexts. In particular, they change DLV2 default policies for body orderings and indexing by anticipating, to a pre-computation phase, the identification of an effective indexing schema, along with an appropriate body ordering for rules complying with such indexing schema and the actual index creation. This way the cost of such optimizations is paid only once before actual query answering. Setting (i) is the most friendly: indeed, given that also the structure of the incoming queries is known, the system performs a preliminary run for each query Q_i evaluating

WordNet-3.1

Query	Old DLV2		DLV2 no filter		DLV2		DLV2-server	
	time	mem	time	mem	time	mem	time	mem
Adj. Clusters	8.85	0.47	5.21	0.16	4.16	0.14	2.29	0.57
Antonyms	4.59	0.23	3.11	0.13	2.05	0.10	0.05	0.64
Dir. Adj. Clusters	4.94	0.25	3.10	0.11	2.06	0.09	0.21	0.64
Dir. Holonyms	5.20	0.26	3.00	0.11	2.05	0.09	0.22	0.64
Dir. Hypernyms	4.37	0.23	2.68	0.09	3.10	0.11	1.14	0.68
Dir. Hyponyms	6.67	0.36	3.96	0.13	3.10	0.10	1.09	0.71
Dir. Meronyms	4.94	0.25	3.11	0.11	2.04	0.09	0.21	0.71
Dir. Troponyms	4.73	0.23	2.78	0.11	1.83	0.09	0.01	0.71
Glosses	6.52	0.36	3.85	0.15	3.11	0.13	0.76	0.74
Holonyms	7.82	0.40	4.63	0.14	3.31	0.12	1.70	0.78
Hypernyms	21.54	1.08	12.68	0.32	11.90	0.28	9.25	0.82
Hyponyms	21.26	1.05	12.42	0.29	11.40	0.27	9.15	0.82
Meronyms	7.60	0.39	4.52	0.14	3.31	0.11	1.58	0.82
Same Synset	7.30	0.42	4.16	0.15	3.10	0.12	1.39	0.82
Troponyms	4.47	0.23	2.79	0.11	1.83	0.09	0.02	0.82
Loading	-		-		-		3.71	
Setting Configuration	-		-		-		2.48	
Total Time	120.78		72.00		58.35		35.24	
Max Memory	1.08		0.32		0.28		0.82	

LUBM-8000

Query	Old DLV2		DLV2 no filter		DLV2		DLV2-server	
	time	mem	time	mem	time	mem	time	mem
query1	9,863.77	228.69	3,908.19	71.92	943.07	36.76	0.00	238.12
query2	12,840.03	266.43	4,769.60	81.38	997.31	49.54	172.20	238.12
query3	10,888.88	220.27	3,922.89	74.89	803.00	42.96	0.00	238.12
query4	14,711.55	286.86	6,025.35	178.61	4,523.44	178.62	0.01	238.12
query5	10,162.18	235.92	4,936.03	118.16	2,969.36	105.28	0.03	238.12
query6	Out of Memory		5,562.51	92.68	3,325.02	77.30	852.57	247.33
query7	11,813.49	234.35	5,273.65	136.08	3,033.78	120.70	0.01	247.33
query8	12,259.71	249.34	5,496.10	139.65	3,900.14	138.48	0.33	247.33
query9	Out of Memory		5,979.65	93.25	3,439.40	77.30	1,009.05	250.37
query10	10,667.09	262.05	5,308.87	134.73	3,007.82	119.35	0.01	250.37
query11	9,241.15	211.59	3,693.48	71.91	17.73	1.24	0.00	250.37
query12	11,816.31	235.67	5,080.11	114.91	2,904.69	99.52	0.03	250.26
query13	12,246.33	245.66	5,132.99	103.92	2,926.40	88.94	6.64	250.26
query14	11,865.39	234.77	3,694.86	71.91	244.74	12.84	14.40	250.26
Loading	-		-		-		2,961.27	
Setting Configuration	-		-		-		3,657.47	
Total Time	167,798.97		68,784.27		33,035.89		8,674.02	
Max Memory	349.12		178.61		178.62		250.37	

Fig. 1. Comparison of different DLV2 versions; times are in seconds and memory is in GB. Bound queries are reported in bold.

$\mathcal{P} \cup Q_i \cup \mathcal{D}$ in order to pre-compute indices and body orderings that will be of use when the system will be actually queried; roughly, it saves the choices that DLV2 would make in case of a "one-shot" execution. When $\mathcal{D}$ is significantly large and a given subset of data is available, that is fairly representative of the whole set, the preliminary run can be performed over it in order to further save time and computational resources. In setting (ii), which is less informed, a more general strategy is adopted: the system performs a single preliminary run over $\mathcal{P} \cup \mathcal{D}$ (without any query) and similarly to the previous case, it stores information about body ordering and indexing for all rules in $\mathcal{P}$ that DLV2 would choose in a one-shot execution. Then, it analyses $\mathcal{P}$ trying to predict how, in case of an incoming query, rules could be rewritten if magic-sets are applied and enriches the set of created indices accordingly. Setting (iii), where body orderings can't be pre-computed, is dealt via an aggressive indexing policy: all possible indices are computed over input data right after loading; this will save the expensive creation of indices at execution time, at the price of high memory consumption due to the creation of possibly useless indices. The approach of setting (iii) is also used as default strategy whenever the system is executed using a setting which is not suitable for the scenario at hand.

4   Experiments and Benchmarks

We now describe an experiment devised to check the improvements of the new systems DLV2 and DLV2-SERVER over Old DLV2, and to assess their potential in two data-intensive contexts such as WordNet and LUBM [28] as they require to handle meaningful data and to perform non-trivial query answering tasks.

Benchmark Problems and Data. We next provide a description of considered benchmarks, specifying the used dataset and encodings. Tests on WordNet were performed on a machine having two 2.8 GHz AMD Opteron 6320 processors and 128 GB of RAM; for LUBM we relied on a machine with an Intel Xeon Gold 6140 CPU clocked at 2.30 GHz with 297 GB of RAM. The WordNet benchmarks have been extracted from the well-known OpenRuleBench suite [31]; they consist of real-life tests dealing with common tasks from natural language processing with the WordNet semantic lexicon. As input data we used the latest released dataset at the time of writing (v. 3.1); as queries we used the ones in OpenRuleBench. The LUBM benchmarks consist of an OWL 2 ontology over a university domain with synthetic data and 14 queries. The whole LUBM ontology falls in Horn-$\mathcal{SHIQ}$ [29], thus, the ontology and the queries have been properly rewritten into ASP via techniques generalizing those presented in [22], still ensuring both soundness and completeness of query answering. Data generation has been carried out via the LUBM data generator. The used dataset is LUBM-8000 with "8000" universities and features about 1 *billion* of facts.

Results and Discussion. The experimental analysis has been designed in order to test both the effects of the enhancements introduced in DLV2 (cf. Sect. 2) and the general applicability of the newborn DLV2-SERVER (cf. Sect. 3).

In Fig. 1 we compare on WordNet and LUBM, respectively, four different versions of DLV2: (*i*) [*Old* DLV2], (*ii*) [dlvdue *no filter*], (*iii*) [dlvdue] and (*iv*) [DLV2-SERVER]. [*Old* DLV2] is the latest stable release ($\mathcal{I}$-DLV *v*.1.1.2); [dlvdue *no filter*] and [dlvdue] are new versions of DLV2 both empowered with all enhancements described in Sect. 2, except for the filtering mechanism on input data based on "relevant" predicates, which is disabled in version (*ii*) and enabled in version (*iii*); [dlvdueserver] is the server version of DLV2 executed by using setting (*ii*), as described in Sect. 3. Given that DLV2-SERVER remains alive until all queries are answered, we were able to exactly determine the maximum used memory, while memory consumption for each query has been internally detected via facilities provided by the operating system. Moreover, since loading and setting configuration times are relevant only for the server version, corresponding fields for the other versions are marked with a dash (-). It is easy to see that significant improvements are obtained by the new versions of the system, both in terms of time and memory; indeed, [DLV2 *no filter*] behaves systematically better than [*Old* DLV2], showing, on the overall, a gain of about 40% in terms of time, and a reduction of about 60% in terms of memory consumption. Moreover, the filter mechanism allows to optimize the loading phase, thus further contributing at improving overall performance; notably, in cases of highly selective queries, as in *query11* of LUBM, times and memory improvements of [DLV2] are close to 100%. Concerning DLV2-SERVER, as expected for a server modality, there is an initial cost due to loading and set-up times; however, query answering is quite fast in all domains: even for LUBM-8000 almost all bound queries are answered in less than 0.1 s, with an average time of about 0.7 s.

In order to provide the reader with an overall picture of the improvements of DLV2, we report a summary of the experimental results in Fig. 2. We considered all configurations of the enhanced system, both in server and standard modalities, and compared them over WordNet and LUBM-8000 against the

	WordNet					LUBM-8000-unbound-queries					LUBM-8000-bound-queries				
	Old DLV2	DLV2		DLV2-server		Old DLV2	DLV2		DLV2-server		Old DLV2	DLV2		DLV2-server	
	Value	Value	Gain %	Value	Gain %	Value	Value	Gain %	Value	Gain %	Value	Value	Gain %	Value	Gain %
Avg. Query Time	8.1	3.9	52%	1.9	76%	13,532.1	2,001.6	85%	512.1	96%	11,367.0	2,502.9	78%	0.7	100%
Total Time	120.8	58.4	52%	35.2	71%	54,128.5	1,242.0	98%	8,667.0	84%	113,670.5	24,705.4	78%	6,625.8	94%
Max. Used Memory	1.1	0.3	74%	0.8	24%	349.1	77.3	78%	126.9	64%	286.9	178.6	38%	227.0	21%

Fig. 2. Summary of the results.

version [*Old* DLV2]. Moreover, for LUBM-8000 we distinguished between bound and unbound queries, given that they lead to different computation approaches (the former enjoy magic sets); for WordNet, no distinction is made, as all queries are unbound. The figure reports average times for query answering, total time, including also loading and setting configuration times, and the maximum used memory; all are computed over all queries. Moreover, for DLV2 and DLV2-SERVER we report the percentage gain obtained w.r.t. [*Old* DLV2]. In order to compute all aggregations, the performance of [*Old* DLV2] on *query6* and *query9* (where it runs out memory) have been suitably estimated in a cautious way, exploiting the regular behaviour we observed on LUBM. Both DLV2 and DLV2-SERVER show to be superior than [*Old* DLV2]; significant improvements are observable on the overall, especially on the LUBM-8000, where the old version was unable to answer all queries: there, the new versions solved all the tasks consuming at most 227 GB of RAM and enjoying improvements of up to 100% in terms of times.

5   Querying DBpedia in Natural Language: A Use Case

Motivated by the interest of a relevant industrial player, we designed a prototype system for Question Answering (QA) on the well-known DBpedia knowledge base. The idea is to devise an intelligent service that is able to exploit a large existing ontology to answer a variety of user questions. In this respect DBpedia [12], which models the knowledge present in Wikimedia projects (using more than 3 billion of RDF [40] triples), was a natural pick. The use case provides a useful assessment of the suitability of our system for the efficient implementation of ontological reasoning tasks on a large real-world knowledge base.

QA System Overview. The architecture of the QA system follows a standard three-layer pattern. The first layer implements a Web-based user interface that appears as a simple chat service. The user can ask questions either by speaking on his/her device microphone or by typing in the chat. The implementation of the interface uses libraries and speech recognition services that are nowadays standard in HTML 5. Questions posed by the user are then transformed in a request for the QA Layer, which has the role of understanding the question and transforming it in a SPARQL query to be posed on the underlying ontology. The query answering process is carried out by the Query Layer, which implements a web service compliant with the SPARQL endpoint specification [41]. The result of the query is then passed back to the QA Layer that transforms it in the answer in natural language that is sent to (and displayed by) the user interface.

Question Answering Layer. In order to implement the QA Layer we instantiated the ASP-based QA strategy presented in [21] with respect to the use-case of DBpedia. In the following we illustrate that strategy using an example, the reader can refer to [21] for a complete description of the technique. Essentially, the QA process consists of a series of subsequent phases. First, the question is processed by means of natural language processing (NLP) techniques, namely named-entity recognition, tokenization, parts-of-speech tagging and dependency parsing. The result of the NLP phase is transformed into ASP facts that are fed to DLV2 together with the question templates that are encoded in terms of ASP rules. The result of the ASP computation contains the best matching template and a set of terms extracted from the question. Then, by exploiting word semantic relations on question terms, a matching template is mapped into an intent (belonging to a fixed set of available ones) corresponding to a SPARQL query with empty slots filled by question terms. Next, the query is executed over the knowledge base (in the Query Layer) and the results are transformed into natural language. An example of a template rule is the following, which matches questions of the form *who are the **X** from **Y** ?*

```
template(template1,terms(X,Y),15) :-
word (1,"who"), word(3,"the"), word(4,X), word(5,"from"),
word(6,Y), word(7,"?"), pos(1,wp), pos(3,dt), pos(5,in), gr(1,2,cop),
gr(4,3,det),gr(1,4,nsubj), gr(6,5,case), gr(4,6,nmod), gr(1,7,punct).
```

In the example, `template1` is a constant that identifies the template, while `terms(X, Y)` is a function symbol that allows extracting the two terms from the input question. The predicates `word`, `pos` and `gr` specify, respectively, words, parts-of-speech and grammatical relations of the template question pattern. The integer values in the body identify positions of words, while strings like **wp** or **nsubj** are tags taken from a fixed vocabulary of tags for parts-of-speech and grammatical relations. In the rule head, the number 15 specifies the weight of the template. Weights are used to specify the importance of template rules so as to favor more specific templates over more general templates. The best matching template (i.e. the matching template with the highest weight), if exists, is the result of the template matching phase of the question answering. Once the best template is computed, the QA system determines a question intent and, possibly, the intent is identified by considering question terms.

As an example of intent, we can consider `ARTISTS_FROM_CITY` (i.e. find the artists born in a certain city). Once the template above matches, we can check that the intent is indeed `ARTISTS_FROM_CITY` by checking that term X is *artists* (or a synonym of *artists*) by using the Babelnet vocabulary [36]. The intent `ARTISTS_FROM_CITY` corresponds to the following SPARQL query:

```
SELECT DISTINCT ?p
WHERE { ?p dbo:birthPlace ?city. ?p rdf:type dbo:Artist }
```

In the query above, `?city` is the intent empty slot and, at runtime, is filled by a question term. For example, if the question is *who are the artists from Florence?*, the variable `?city` would be replaced by the constant `dbr:Florence` (`dbr` is the DBpedia namespace for resources). Reasoning capabilities are necessary in this context. Indeed, if we ignore types inference, the result set of the query in the example on DBPedia would not contain some artists that belong to a subclass of `dbo:Artist`. Note that, approaches that do not implement inference would be inadequate to answer such types of questions, which are possible in our use-case. In our prototype QA system we implemented a number of templates (about 50) and intents (about 20) determined from an initial requirement analysis.

Query Layer. The Query Layer implements a *SPARQL Protocol Service* [41] using DLV2-SERVER as reasoning engine. A SPARQL Protocol Service is an HTTP server that services HTTP requests and sends back responses for SPARQL Protocol operations. The SPARQL Protocol consists of two operations: query and update. Currently, the Query Layer supports conjunctive query operations. A query operation is used to send a SPARQL query to our service and receive the results of the query, and can be invoked with the HTTP GET method, where the SPARQL code is *URL percent* (see https://www.ietf.org/rfc/rfc3986.txt) encoded and passed as a string parameter within the URI.

The implementation of the service relies on the *DLVService* project [20], a RESTful Web Service implemented in Java which provides service-oriented features for managing and executing ASP programs with DLV, that has been suitably extended for dealing with DLV2-SERVER and to be compliant with the official SPARQL Protocol Service requirements. In particular, behind the "Entry Point" that is in charge of handling the REST invocations received by the client, we developed a "Query Dispatcher" module to decode the received SPARQL query q, rewrite q into a Datalog conjunctive query q' and deliver q' to DLV2-SERVER. This rewriting works on the subset of SPARQL that corresponds to conjunctive queries, and it is based on the results presented in [22] to take into account the ontological schema and correctly implement the reasoning in case it requires the more expressive entailments of OWL2-QL [39]. The interaction between the "Query Dispatcher" and DLV2-SERVER is granted by a Java API that we implemented to wrap and integrate DLV2-SERVER (that is written in C++) in any Java application. In the QA prototype, DLV2-SERVER has been instructed to load DBpedia in main-memory at the deployment of the application on the web server. Thanks to the server-like behaviour of DLV2-SERVER, the main process is kept alive and the data loaded at the beginning are then re-used for every incoming request received by the client. Results produced by DLV2-SERVER are caught by the "Result Listener" module that is in charge of producing the JSON object to be sent back to the client who made the request.

Query Layer Performance. To assess the performance of our query layer we report next the results of an experiment devised for validating the system on real-world data. As data source, we employed the DBpedia ontology (Turtle version) available at the DBPedia website. Tests were run on a machine with an Intel Xeon Gold 6140 CPU clocked at 2.30 GHz with 297 GB of RAM. For the experiment we considered 10 different queries of varying difficulty that form a representative sampling of the intents supported by our QA system.

The considered queries range from simple selections to more involved queries that require to reason on the ontology, and are used to compute the answers to the following questions: (Q1) *who is X?* (Q2) *who is the author of X?* (Q3) *who are the artists from X?* (Q4) *who are the people that were born in X?* (Q5) *what is the list of materials that X is composed of?* (Q6) *what are the works by X?* (Q7) *what are the paintings by X?* (Q8) *what are the parts of X?* (Q9) *what is the subject of X?* (Q10) *what are the islands of X?* In the questions X can be any instance of a named entity. Note that to answer correctly queries Q8–Q10 the system computes the inferences due by some subclass of axiom present in the schema of the ontology. This requirement makes the computation of the answer more costly; for this reason, these axioms are just ignored by default by commercial systems for query answering on ontologies (unless the user "enables ontological reasoning"), thus providing incomplete results. For each query, we replaced X with three different constants (URI of some individual) from the ontology, and measured the average time needed to retrieve the result. Since the system performs static optimization (as, e.g., data indexing) when a query is run for the first time, we discarded this warm up time (on average 10s per query). This is acceptable in our use case since all the intents are known in advance and all queries can be run once the system is deployed for the first time, and the user never experiences the times measured in the first execution. The average times for each query amount to few milliseconds (from 0.07 to 0.09 ms): a performance surely acceptable in practice, also considering that our system computes complete answers (i.e., it has "reasoning enabled" by default). The neat result of this experiment confirms the effectiveness of DLV2-SERVER in handling the considered use case.

6   Related Work

Traditional ASP systems [32] implement a "one-shot" processing model where an input program is processed and the one or more answer sets are produced in output. This is the case of the first versions state of the art systems such as DLV [30] and clingo [25]. Although this mode is adequate for solving a number of practical applications [1,5–8,24,34], one-shot processing showed its limits in various application scenarios [25]. Among the system that try to go beyond the traditional computational scheme, we mention the latest incarnation of clingo [25], where the idea is to consider evolving grounding and solving processes. This approach is oriented to making more efficient task specifications of high complexity (e.g., robot planning, complex optimization), but does not provide explicitly a server-like feature for efficient query answering on large knowledge bases as the DLV2-SERVER. By focusing on ontological reasoning we also recall RDFox [37] and Vadalog [14], which however have a limited expressiveness. Systems and techniques for Ontology Based Query Answering (OBQA) [43] are also related and can be implemented using our system [9–11]. As for the development of service-oriented architecture, preliminary efforts in the field of logic programming lead to client-server infrastructures for tuProlog and SWI-Prolog [17,42].

Focusing on ASP, a framework for developing service-oriented applications was presented in [20]; the SPARQL end point developed in our use-case is actually a proper extension of this framework. Concerning the Question Answering module, we mention that this is a new instantiation of the ASP-based framework for QA presented in [21], which also features a more powerful reasoning engine capable of answering queries in the more expressive OWL2-QL entailment regime. Basically, the pipeline of NLP tools is the same as in [21], but the syntactic question templates as well as the intents and queries have been designed from scratch to suit the needs of a different domain. In the literature there is a number of question answering systems that are able to translate natural language questions to queries posed on a knowledge base in SPARQL [15,33,38], as well as systems elaborating questions by transforming them into logic forms so as to be able to perform reasoning tasks [13,27,35]. As discussed in more details in [21] our approach requires human intervention to be ported to other domains, but it offers more control for creating precise NL-to-ontology mappings.

7   Conclusion

Recent real-world applications of DLV2 evidenced the need for efficiently handling multiple queries and reasoning tasks over large-sized knowledge bases. In this paper we presented some recent enhancements in DLV2 for enabling reasoning in these contexts. Key aspects of the computational process have been properly re-engineered and optimized, with the aim of reducing memory consumption and performing efficient tasks on high volumes of data. A new version of the system has been devised, featuring a server-like behaviour that keeps the main process alive and is capable to be queried on demand; this allows to avoid repeatedly performing heavy parts of the computation, such as loading/indexing data, when the same KB has to be queried many times, as often happens in real-world applications. An experimental evaluation on data-intensive benchmarks confirms the high potential for large-scale reasoning. On the benchmark ontology LUBM-8000, the total time for executing the 14 queries falls down from 46 h taken by the old DLV2 version to 2.4 h taken by the new DLV2-SERVER. Remarkably, most of the time (nearly 2 h) is spent *off line* for loading and configuration, once and for all, since the server does handle updates efficiently, and after updates remains *ready for querying*, without the need of any expensive re-configuration. Thus, *at run time, the user experiences very fast answers, taking less than one second for most queries, even on one billion data in this test.* Moreover, a use case where DLV2 is employed as reasoning service in a system for querying DBpedia confirms its applicability in real-world scenarios, indeed it is able to answer typical queries in hundredths of a second, and opens the door to supporting more questions requiring expressive ontology reasoning.

The relevance and the high-potential industrial value of the present research are also confirmed by the direct interest of a major international industrial player, which has stimulated and partially supported this work.

Acknowledgments. This work has been partially supported by Samsung under project "Enhancing the DLV system for large-scale ontology reasoning", by MISE under project "S2BDW" (F/050389/01-03/X32) – "Horizon2020" PON I&C2014-20 and by Regione Calabria under project "DLV LargeScale" (CUP J28C17000220006) – POR Calabria 2014-20.

References

1. Adrian, W.T., Manna, M., Leone, N., Amendola, G., Adrian, M.: Entity set expansion from the web via ASP. In: ICLP (TC), OASICS, vol. 58, pp. 1:1–1:5. Schloss Dagstuhl - Leibniz-Zentrum fuer Informatik (2017)
2. Alviano, M., et al.: The ASP system DLV2. In: Balduccini, M., Janhunen, T. (eds.) LPNMR 2017. LNCS (LNAI), vol. 10377, pp. 215–221. Springer, Cham (2017). https://doi.org/10.1007/978-3-319-61660-5_19
3. Alviano, M., Dodaro, C., Leone, N., Ricca, F.: Advances in WASP. In: Calimeri, F., Ianni, G., Truszczynski, M. (eds.) LPNMR 2015. LNCS (LNAI), vol. 9345, pp. 40–54. Springer, Cham (2015). https://doi.org/10.1007/978-3-319-23264-5_5
4. Alviano, M., Faber, W., Greco, G., Leone, N.: Magic sets for disjunctive datalog programs. Artif. Intell. **187**, 156–192 (2012)
5. Amendola, G.: Preliminary results on modeling interdependent scheduling games via answer set programming. In: RiCeRcA@AI*IA, CEUR WS, vol. 2272 (2018)
6. Amendola, G.: Solving the stable roommates problem using incoherent answer set programs. In: RiCeRcA@AI*IA, CEUR WS, vol. 2272 (2018)
7. Amendola, G., Dodaro, C., Leone, N., Ricca, F.: On the application of answer set programming to the conference paper assignment problem. In: Adorni, G., Cagnoni, S., Gori, M., Maratea, M. (eds.) AI*IA 2016. LNCS (LNAI), vol. 10037, pp. 164–178. Springer, Cham (2016). https://doi.org/10.1007/978-3-319-49130-1_13
8. Amendola, G., Greco, G., Leone, N., Veltri, P.: Modeling and reasoning about NTU games via answer set programming. In: IJCAI 2016, pp. 38–45 (2016)
9. Amendola, G., Leone, N., Manna, M.: Finite model reasoning over existential rules. TPLP **17**(5–6), 726–743 (2017)
10. Amendola, G., Leone, N., Manna, M.: Finite controllability of conjunctive query answering with existential rules: two steps forward. In: IJCAI, pp. 5189–5193. ijcai.org (2018)
11. Amendola, G., Leone, N., Manna, M., Veltri, P.: Enhancing existential rules by closed-world variables. In: IJCAI, pp. 1676–1682. ijcai.org (2018)
12. Auer, S., Bizer, C., Kobilarov, G., Lehmann, J., Cyganiak, R., Ives, Z.: DBpedia: a nucleus for a web of open data. In: Aberer, K., et al. (eds.) ASWC/ISWC 2007. LNCS, vol. 4825, pp. 722–735. Springer, Heidelberg (2007). https://doi.org/10.1007/978-3-540-76298-0_52
13. Balduccini, M., Baral, C., Lierler, Y.: Knowledge representation and question answering. In: Handbook of Knowledge Representation. Foundations of Artificial Intelligence, vol. 3, pp. 779–819. Elsevier (2008)
14. Bellomarini, L., Sallinger, E., Gottlob, G.: The vadalog system: datalog-based reasoning for knowledge graphs. PVLDB **11**(9), 975–987 (2018)
15. Benamara, F., Saint-Dizier, P.: WEBCOOP: a cooperative question answering system on the web. In: Proceedings of EACL, pp. 63–66 (2003)
16. Bernstein, A., Hendler, J.A., Noy, N.F.: A new look at the semantic web. Commun. ACM **59**(9), 35–37 (2016)

17. Calegari, R., Denti, E., Mariani, S., Omicini, A.: Towards logic programming as a service: experiments in tuProlog. In: Proceedings of EASSS, CEUR Workshop Proceedings, vol. 1664, pp. 79–84 (2016)
18. Calimeri, F., Fuscà, D., Perri, S., Zangari, J.: I-DLV: the new intelligent grounder of DLV. Intell. Artif. **11**(1), 5–20 (2017)
19. Calimeri, F., Fuscà, D., Perri, S., Zangari, J.: Optimizing answer set computation via heuristic-based decomposition. In: Calimeri, F., Hamlen, K., Leone, N. (eds.) PADL 2018. LNCS, vol. 10702, pp. 135–151. Springer, Cham (2018). https://doi.org/10.1007/978-3-319-73305-0_9
20. Catalano, G., Laboccetta, G., Reale, K., Ricca, F., Veltri, P.: A REST-based development framework for ASP: tools and application. In: Calimeri, F., Hamlen, K., Leone, N. (eds.) PADL 2018. LNCS, vol. 10702, pp. 161–169. Springer, Cham (2018). https://doi.org/10.1007/978-3-319-73305-0_11
21. Cuteri, B., Reale, K., Ricca, F.: A logic-based question answering system for cultural heritage. In: Proceedings of JELIA (2019, to appear)
22. Eiter, T., Ortiz, M., Simkus, M., Tran, T.-K., Xiao, G.: Query rewriting for Horn-SHIQ plus rules. In: Proceedings of AAAI (2012)
23. Erdem, E., Gelfond, M., Leone, N.: Applications of answer set programming. AI Mag. **37**(3), 53–68 (2016)
24. Garro, A., Palopoli, L., Ricca, F.: Exploiting agents in e-learning and skills management context. AI Commun. **19**(2), 137–154 (2006)
25. Gebser, M., Kaminski, R., Kaufmann, B., Schaub, T.: Multi-shot ASP solving with clingo. TPLP **19**(1), 27–82 (2019)
26. Gelfond, M., Lifschitz, V.: Classical negation in logic programs and disjunctive databases. New Gener. Comput. **9**(3/4), 365–386 (1991)
27. Green, C.: Theorem proving by resolution as a basis for question-answering systems. Mach. Intell. **4**, 183–205 (1969)
28. Guo, Y., Pan, Z., Heflin, J.: LUBM: a benchmark for OWL knowledge base systems. J. Web Semant. **3**(2–3), 158–182 (2005)
29. Hustadt, U., Motik, B., Sattler, U.: Data complexity of reasoning in very expressive description logics. In: Proceedings of IJCAI, pp. 466–471 (2005)
30. Leone, N., et al.: The DLV system for knowledge representation and reasoning. ACM Trans. Comput. Log. **7**(3), 499–562 (2006)
31. Liang, S., Fodor, P., Wan, H., Kifer, M.: OpenRuleBench: an analysis of the performance of rule engines. In: Proceedings of WWW, pp. 601–610 (2009)
32. Lierler, Y., Maratea, M., Ricca, F.: Systems, engineering environments, and competitions. AI Mag. **37**(3), 45–52 (2016)
33. Lopez, V., Pasin, M., Motta, E.: AquaLog: an ontology-portable question answering system for the semantic web. In: Gómez-Pérez, A., Euzenat, J. (eds.) ESWC 2005. LNCS, vol. 3532, pp. 546–562. Springer, Heidelberg (2005). https://doi.org/10.1007/11431053_37
34. Manna, M., Ricca, F., Terracina, G.: Taming primary key violations to query large inconsistent data via ASP. TPLP **15**(4–5), 696–710 (2015)
35. Moldovan, D.I., Clark, C., Harabagiu, S.M., Maiorano, S.J.: COGEX: a logic prover for question answering. In: Proceedings of HLT-NAACL (2003)
36. Navigli, R., Ponzetto, S.P.: BabelNet: the automatic construction, evaluation and application of a wide-coverage multilingual semantic network. Artif. Intell. **193**, 217–250 (2012)
37. Nenov, Y., Piro, R., Motik, B., Horrocks, I., Wu, Z., Banerjee, J.: RDFox: a highly-scalable RDF store. In: Arenas, M., et al. (eds.) ISWC 2015. LNCS, vol. 9367, pp. 3–20. Springer, Cham (2015). https://doi.org/10.1007/978-3-319-25010-6_1

38. Unger, C., Bühmann, L., Lehmann, J., Ngonga Ngomo, A.-C., Gerber, D., Cimiano, P.: Template-based question answering over RDF data. In: Proceedings of WWW, pp. 639–648 (2012)
39. W3C: The OWL standard page. https://www.w3.org/standards/techs/owl
40. W3C: The RDF standard page. https://www.w3.org/standards/techs/rds
41. W3C: The SPARQL standard page. https://www.w3.org/standards/techs/sparql
42. Wielemaker, J., Lager, T., Riguzzi, F.: SWISH: SWI-Prolog for sharing. CoRR, abs/1511.00915 (2015)
43. Xiao, G., et al.: Ontology-based data access: a survey. In: IJCAI, pp. 5511–5519. ijcai.org (2018)

Pruning External Minimality Checking for ASP Using Semantic Dependencies

Thomas Eiter and Tobias Kaminski(✉)

Institute of Logic and Computation, TU Wien, Vienna, Austria
{eiter,kaminski}@kr.tuwien.ac.at

Abstract. HEX-programs integrate external computations in ASP. For HEX-evaluation, an external (e)-minimality check is required to prevent cyclic justifications via external sources. As the check is a bottleneck in practice, syntactic information about atom dependencies has been used previously to detect when the check can be avoided. However, the approach largely overapproximates the real dependencies due to the black-box nature of external sources. We show how the dependencies can be approximated more closely by exploiting semantic information, which significantly increases pruning of e-minimality checking. Moreover, we analyze checking and optimization of semantic dependency information. An empirical evaluation exhibits a clear benefit of this approach.

1 Introduction

Answer Set Programming (ASP) [10] is a popular approach for declarative problem solving. The HEX-*formalism* [5] extends ASP to address the increasing need for integrating external computation sources. It enables a bidirectional exchange with arbitrary sources via so-called *external atoms*, and has been employed in many areas ranging from *Semantic Web* applications to robot planning [5]. For instance, an external atom $\&concat[X,Y](Z)$ can be used to concatenate strings in a rule $fullname(X) \leftarrow \&concat[X,Y](Z), firstname(X), lastname(Y)$. External atoms may also have predicate input, e.g. in the rule $closeCity(X) \leftarrow \&closeTo[city](X), location(X)$, where the external atom outputs all cities located close to cities in the extension of the predicate $city$.

For HEX-evaluation, advanced reasoning algorithms are required since external atoms must be considered in all solving phases. A notable difference to ordinary ASP is that an *external (e-)minimality check* is needed to avoid unfounded support by external atoms. For example, if the locations for the above rule are *osaka*, *kobe*, *bratislava* and *vienna*, and the rule $city(X) \leftarrow closeCity(X)$ as well as the fact $city(osaka)$ are added, only the atom $city(kobe)$ should be contained in an answer set in addition. Even though Bratislava and Vienna are located close to each other, the atoms $city(bratislava)$ and $city(vienna)$ can only cyclically support each other via the two rules and the external atom. The e-minimality check of HEX eliminates spurious answer sets containing the latter two atoms.

This research has been supported by the FWF-projects P27730 and W1255-N23.

M. Balduccini et al. (Eds.): LPNMR 2019, LNAI 11481, pp. 326–339, 2019.
https://doi.org/10.1007/978-3-030-20528-7_24

On the one hand, performing the e-minimality check efficiently is highly non-trivial as it is co-NP-complete already for ground *Horn* programs with polynomial external atoms [4]. On the other hand, if the rule $city(X) \leftarrow closeCity(X)$ is not added above, cyclic support via the external atom can be ruled out independent from the external semantics. Based on this observation, a syntactic criterion was presented in [4] for deciding whether the e-minimality check can be skipped for a program, which often results in significant speedups.

Alternatively, if the external atom $\&closeWest[city](X)$ in the example (only retrieving cities close *to the west* of input cities), cyclic support can also be excluded. This cannot be detected by a syntactic criterion, such that the e-minimality check needs to be performed in any case by the previous approach. Moreover, applying a semantic criterion is challenging, as before, external atoms have largely been considered as black-boxes that conceal semantic dependencies.

Skipping e-minimality checks in more cases is of special interest as it can often result in drastic speedups. For this reason, we develop a new approach for pruning e-minimality checking that also exploits semantic dependencies. It relies on additional information about *input-output (io-)dependencies* of external atoms, which may be provided by a user, or even generated automatically. Hidden io-dependencies are common in applications involving recursive processing, e.g. over external graphs or *Semantic Web* data. At this, supplied dependency information can be incomplete and added flexibly. The overall goal is to increase the efficiency of ASP programs with external atoms to promote their practical applicability.

After preliminaries in Sect. 2, we present our contributions as follows:

- In Sect. 3.1, we provide a novel formalization of io-dependencies that encode semantic dependency information, and we show under which condition they can safely be used for pruning the e-minimality check.
- In Sect. 3.2, we state theoretical properties crucial for checking and optimizing io-dependencies, and show when the associated costs can be reduced.
- In Sect. 4, we present an experimental evaluation using illustrative benchmark problems that confirms the advantage of exploiting io-dependencies.

Our new approach not only applies to HEX, but may also be employed analogously for other approaches that integrate external sources into ASP, such as CLINGO [8], if external cyclic support is not desired. Proofs and benchmark data can be found at www.kr.tuwien.ac.at/research/projects/inthex/dep-pruning.

2   Preliminaries

We assume disjoint sets $\mathcal{P}$, $\mathcal{C}$, $\mathcal{X}$ and $\mathcal{V}$ of predicates, constants, external predicates (prefixed with '&') and variables, respectively. Each $p \in \mathcal{P}$ has fixed arity $ar(p)$, and each $\&g \in \mathcal{X}$ has fixed input and output arity $ar_I(\&g)$ and $ar_O(\&g)$, respectively. An atom is of the form $p(\boldsymbol{t})$, where $p \in \mathcal{P}$, $\boldsymbol{t} = t_1, \ldots, t_\ell \in \mathcal{C} \cup \mathcal{V}$. A (signed) literal is a positive or a negative ground atom $\mathbf{T}p(\boldsymbol{c})$ or $\mathbf{F}p(\boldsymbol{c})$. An *assignment* $\mathbf{A}$ over a set $\mathcal{A}$ of ground atoms is a set of literals s.t. for each $a \in \mathcal{A}$, either $\mathbf{T}a \in \mathbf{A}$ or $\mathbf{F}a \in \mathbf{A}$, where $\mathbf{A}(a) = \mathbf{T}$ if $\mathbf{T}a \in \mathbf{A}$, and $\mathbf{A}(a) = \mathbf{F}$ otherwise.

HEX-Programs. HEX-*programs* extend answer set programs with *external atoms* in rule bodies (cf. [5] for more details).

Syntax. An *external atom* is of form $\&g[\mathbf{X}](\mathbf{Y})$, where $\&g \in \mathcal{X}$, $\mathbf{X} = X_1, \ldots, X_k$, with $k = ar_I(\&g)$, are input parameters (variables or predicates w.l.o.g.) and $\mathbf{Y} = Y_1, \ldots, Y_l$, with $l = ar_O(\&g)$, are output terms. An external atom is *ground* if $\mathbf{X} = X_1, \ldots, X_k$ are predicates and $\mathbf{Y} = Y_1, \ldots, Y_l$ are constants. Given a ground external atom $\&g[\mathbf{X}](\mathbf{Y})$, we call $\&g[\mathbf{X}]$ a *ground external (ge-)predicate*.

Definition 1 (HEX-Program). *A* HEX-*program Π is a set of rules of the form* $a_1 \vee \cdots \vee a_k \leftarrow b_1, \ldots, b_m, \text{not } b_{m+1}, \ldots, \text{not } b_n$, *where each a_i, $1 \le i \le k$, is an atom and each b_j, $1 \le j \le n$, is either an ordinary atom or an external atom.*

Given a rule r, $H(r) = \{a_1, \ldots, a_k\}$ is its *head*, $B(r) = \{b_1, \ldots, b_m, \text{not } b_{m+1}, \ldots, \text{not } b_n\}$ its *body*, and $B^+(r) = \{b_1, \ldots, b_m\}$ resp. $B^-(r) = \{b_{m+1}, \ldots, b_n\}$.

Semantics. As safety conditions allow to compute equivalent finite groundings of HEX-programs, in the following we assume assignments are over the set $A(\Pi)$ of atoms that occur in a ground program Π at hand. Moreover, definitions are implicitly parameterized with the according finite vocabulary. Following [6], the semantics of a ground external atom $\&g[\mathbf{p}](\mathbf{c})$, wrt. an assignment $\mathbf{A}$, is given by a $1+ar_I(\&g)+ar_O(\&g)$-ary *two-valued (Boolean) oracle function* $f_{\&g}$ defined for all possible values of $\mathbf{A}$, $\mathbf{p}$ and $\mathbf{c}$ s.t. $\&g[\mathbf{p}](\mathbf{c})$ is true (informally, $\mathbf{c}$ is an output of $\&g$ for input $\mathbf{p}$) relative to $\mathbf{A}$ iff $f_{\&g}(\mathbf{A}, \mathbf{p}, \mathbf{c}) = \mathbf{T}$. As usual, we assume that $f_{\&g}(\mathbf{A}, \mathbf{p}, \mathbf{c})$ depends only on the restriction of $\mathbf{A}$ to $\mathbf{p}$. Satisfaction of ASP rules and programs [10] is extended to HEX-rules and programs in the obvious way.

The answer sets of a HEX-program Π are defined as follows. Let the *FLP-reduct* [7] of Π wrt. an assignment $\mathbf{A}$ be the set $f\Pi^{\mathbf{A}} = \{r \in \Pi \mid \mathbf{A} \models b, \text{ for all } b \in B(r)\}$ of all rules whose body is satisfied by $\mathbf{A}$, and let for assignments $\mathbf{A}_1$, $\mathbf{A}_2$ denote $\mathbf{A}_1 \le \mathbf{A}_2$ that $\{\mathbf{T}a \in \mathbf{A}_1\} \subseteq \{\mathbf{T}a \in \mathbf{A}_2\}$. Then:

Definition 2 (Answer Set). *An assignment $\mathbf{A}$ is an answer set of a* HEX-*program Π, if $\mathbf{A}$ is a $\le$-minimal model of $f\Pi^{\mathbf{A}}$.*

Example 1. Consider $\Pi = \{p \leftarrow \&id[p]()\}$, where $\&id[p]()$ is true iff p is true. Then, Π has the answer set $\mathbf{A}_1 = \emptyset$; indeed it is a $\le$-minimal model of $f\Pi^{\mathbf{A}_1} = \emptyset$.

Evaluation. A HEX-program Π can be transformed to an ordinary program by replacing each external atom $\&g[\mathbf{p}](\mathbf{c})$ in Π by an ordinary *replacement atom* $e_{\&g[\mathbf{p}]}(\mathbf{c})$, and by adding a rule $e_{\&g[\mathbf{p}]}(\mathbf{c}) \vee ne_{\&g[\mathbf{p}]}(\mathbf{c}) \leftarrow$ that guesses its evaluation. An ordinary ASP solver can then be employed to compute the answer sets of the resulting *guessing program* $\hat{\Pi}$, where each answer set $\hat{\mathbf{A}}$ is a *candidate model*. If all truth values for atoms $e_{\&g[\mathbf{p}]}(\mathbf{c})$ correspond to $f_{\&g}(\hat{\mathbf{A}}, \mathbf{p}, \mathbf{c})$, $\hat{\mathbf{A}}$ is a *compatible set*. Still, the projection $\mathbf{A}$ of a compatible set $\hat{\mathbf{A}}$ to $A(\Pi)$ is not always an answer set due to the possibility of cyclic support via external atoms.

Example 2 (cont'd). The guessing program $\hat{\Pi} = \{p \leftarrow e_{\&id[p]}(); \; e_{\&id[p]} \vee ne_{\&id[p]} \leftarrow \}$ has the answer sets $\hat{\mathbf{A}}_1 = \emptyset$ and $\hat{\mathbf{A}}_2 = \{\mathbf{T}p, \mathbf{T}e_{\&id[p]}\}$. Here, $\mathbf{A}_1$ is a $\leq$-minimal model of $f\Pi^{\mathbf{A}_1} = \emptyset$, but $\mathbf{A}_2$ not of $f\Pi^{\mathbf{A}_2} = \Pi$ since $\emptyset \leq \mathbf{A}_2$ is a smaller model.

Consequently, an e-minimality check wrt. $f\Pi^{\mathbf{A}}$ is needed for finding answer sets of HEX-programs. A direct way to ensure minimality of the projection $\mathbf{A}$ of a compatible set $\hat{\mathbf{A}}$ for a HEX-program Π wrt. $f\Pi^{\mathbf{A}}$ consists in explicitly constructing $f\Pi^{\mathbf{A}}$ and checking that it has no model $\mathbf{A}'$ s.t. $\mathbf{A}' \leq \mathbf{A}$.

3   Pruning the External Minimality Check

Since an answer set $\hat{\mathbf{A}}$ of a guessing program $\hat{\Pi}$ must be a minimal model of the FLP-reduct $f\hat{\Pi}^{\hat{\mathbf{A}}}$, an e-minimality check is under certain conditions redundant. The criterion in [4] for deciding its necessity relies on an atom dependency graph induced by the HEX-program. Informally, an e-minimality check is only needed for programs that allow cyclic support via external atoms, which can be checked efficiently. For instance, the program $\Pi_1 = \{p \leftarrow \&id[p]()\}$ allows cyclic support for the atom p via $\&id[p]()$, while this is not the case for $\Pi_2 = \{p \leftarrow \&id[q](); \; q \leftarrow r; \; r \leftarrow q\}$, where the truth value of $\&id[q]()$ is independent of the value of p. If cyclic support via external atoms can be ruled out as for Π_2, the e-minimality check can be skipped for a program, potentially avoiding to invest many resources into a redundant check. Note, however, that a minimality check is still needed for computing the answer sets of $\hat{\Pi}$.

In this section, we introduce a new technique for skipping the e-minimality check wrt. a wider class of programs than previous approaches. More precisely, given Π, we present a new sufficient[1] criterion for deciding if every projection $\mathbf{A}$ of a compatible set $\hat{\mathbf{A}}$ for $\hat{\Pi}$ is an answer set of Π. The criterion exploits that output values of external atoms often do not depend on the complete extensions of their input predicates, which can be determined given additional information concerning dependencies between the inputs and outputs of external atoms.

3.1   Dependency Graph Pruning

We start by defining so-called *io-dependencies*, which specify that certain outputs of external atoms only depend on specific argument values of their inputs. For instance, whether a city c is in the output of $\&closeWest[city](X)$ from Sect. 1 only depends on cities c' that are located close to the east of c. Hence, the truth value of $\&closeWest[city](kobe)$ clearly only depends on the atom $city(osaka)$, and we want to encode that *kobe* as first output of $\&closeWest[city](X)$ only depends on the element *osaka* as first argument of the first input predicate *city*.

---

[1] Deciding the sufficient *and necessary* criterion is Π_2^p-complete for polynomial-time decidable external atoms and thus ill-suited for our aim to improve performance.

Definition 3 (Io-Dependency). *An io-dependency for a ge-predicate $\&g[p]$ is a tuple $\delta = \langle i, j : J, k : e \rangle$ where $1 \leq i \leq ar_I(\&g)$, $1 \leq j \leq ar(p_i)$, $1 \leq k \leq ar_O(\&g)$, $J \subseteq C$ and $e \in C$. The set of all δ for $\&g[p]$ is denoted by $(\&g[p])$.*

In the sequel, io-dependencies will be used to constrain the possible dependencies between inputs and outputs of external atoms $\&g[p](c)$. Intuitively, an io-dependency $\langle i, j : J, k : e \rangle$ states that if constant e occurs as the kth output of $\&g[p](c)$, then only those input predicates at position i are relevant for its evaluation where the jth argument matches some $e' \in J$. Thus, the io-dependency $\delta = \langle 1, 1 : \{osaka\}, 1 : kobe \rangle$ could be specified for the example above. Io-dependencies induce atom sets relevant for evaluating respective external atoms:

Definition 4 (Compliant Atoms). *A ground ordinary atom $p_i(d)$, with $d = d_1, ..., d_l$, is compliant with a set $D \subseteq dep(\&g[p])$ of io-dependencies for a ground external atom $\&g[p](c)$ if $d_j \in J$ for all $\langle i, j : J, k : e \rangle \in D$ with $e = c_k$. The set of all atoms compliant with D for $\&g[p](c)$ is denoted by $(D, \&g[p](c))$.*

For our example, we have $comp(\{\delta\}, \&closeWest[city](kobe)) = \{city(osaka)\}$. The semantics of external atoms is related to io-dependencies as follows.

Definition 5 (Faithfulness). *A set $D \subseteq dep(\&g[p])$ is faithful if for any assignments $\mathbf{A}, \mathbf{A}'$ and ground external atom $\&g[p](c)$, either $\mathbf{A}(p_i(d)) \neq \mathbf{A}'(p_i(d))$ for some $p_i(d) \in comp(D, \&g[p](c))$ or $f_{\&g}(\mathbf{A}, p, c) = f_{\&g}(\mathbf{A}', p, c)$.*

Thus, io-dependencies $D \subseteq dep(\&g[p])$ constrain the set of atoms that potentially impact the evaluation of $\&g[p](c)$, i.e. if D is faithful, changing only truth values of atoms $p_i(d) \notin comp(D, \&g[p](c))$ has no effect on the value of $\&g[p](c)$.

In the following, we denote by $D(\&g[p]) \subseteq dep(\&g[p])$ a set of io-dependencies specified for $\&g[p]$. By default, we assume that $D(\&g[p])$ is empty, but it can be utilized to supply additional dependency information. To ensure correctness of an algorithm that skips e-minimality checks based on $D(\&g[p])$, it is important that $D(\&g[p])$ is faithful; and we assume in the following that this is the case. Simultaneously, the goal is to approximate the real dependencies between atoms as close as possible for maximal performance gains. Note that while an extensional specification of $D(\&g[p])$ might be very verbose, they can often also be specified more concisely in an intensional manner, as in the following example.

Example 3. Consider $\&setDiff[dom, set](c)$, which is true for $c \in C$ and assignment $\mathbf{A}$ iff $\{\mathbf{T}dom(c), \mathbf{F}set(c)\} \subseteq \mathbf{A}$. Thus, the presence of an output value c only depends on atoms with predicate dom or set that have c as first argument. Hence, $D(\&setDiff[dom, set]) = \{\langle 1, 1{:}\{c\}, 1{:}c \rangle, \langle 2, 1{:}\{c\}, 1{:}c \rangle \mid c \in C\}$ is faithful.

We now introduce a notion of atom dependency in HEX-programs that accounts for io-dependencies and generalizes the corresponding notion from [4].

Definition 6 (Atom Dependency). *Given a ground HEX-program Π, a set $D(\&g[p])$ for each $\&g[p]$ in Π, and ordinary ground atoms $p(d)$ and $q(e)$, we say*

- $q(e)$ depends on $p(d)$, denoted $q(e) \to_d p(d)$ if for some rule $r \in \Pi$ it holds that $q(e) \in H(r)$ and $p(d) \in B^+(r)$; and
- $q(e)$ depends externally on $p(d)$, denoted $q(e) \to_e p(d)$ if some rule $r \in \Pi$ and some external atom $\&g[p](c) \in B^+(r) \cup B^-(r)$ with $p \in p$ exist such that $q(e) \in H(r)$ and $q(e) \in H(r)$ and $p(d) \in comp(D(\&g[p]), \&g[p](c))$.

Note that Definition 6 generalizes the corresponding one from [4] in that an external dependency is only added if the specified io-dependencies are satisfied. The definitions coincide if $D(\&g[p]) = \emptyset$ for all ge-predicates $\&g[p]$.

Example 4. Consider $\&suc[node](n)$, which evaluates to true wrt. an assignment **A** and an external directed graph $\mathcal{G} = (V, E)$ iff $n' \to n \in E$ for some node n' s.t. $\mathbf{T}node(n) \in \mathbf{A}$. It is utilized in the following HEX-program Π:

$$node(a). \quad node(X) \leftarrow \&suc[node](X)$$

Intuitively, the program computes all nodes reachable from node a via the edges in $\mathcal{G}$. If the external graph has nodes $V = \{a, b, c, d\}$ and directed edges $E = \{a \to b, a \to c, c \to d, e \to d\}$, the grounding of Π produced by the grounding algorithm of the HEX-program solver DLVHEX contains the following rules (omitting facts):

$$node(b) \leftarrow \&suc[node](b). \quad node(c) \leftarrow \&suc[node](c). \quad node(d) \leftarrow \&suc[node](d)$$

Without specifying io-dependencies for $\&suc[node]$, it holds, e.g., that $node(a) \to_e node(b)$ and $node(b) \to_e node(a)$. However, we can specify $D(\&suc[node]) = \{\langle 1, 1 : \{c_1 \mid c_1 \to c_2 \in E\}, 1 : c_2\rangle \mid c_2 \in \mathcal{C}\}$, exploiting that the presence of output nodes only depends on input nodes to which they are successors. In this case, $node(a) \to_e node(b)$ does not hold according to Definition 6 as $b \to a \notin E$.

We are now ready to introduce the atom dependency graph for a given program Π. From this graph, a property of Π can be derived which is subsequently employed to decide the necessity of the e-minimality check wrt. Π.

Definition 7 (Dependency Graph). *Given a ground HEX-program Π, the dependency graph $\mathcal{G}_\Pi^{dep} = (V, E)$ has the vertices $V = A(\Pi)$ and directed edges $E = \to_d \cup \to_e$; Π has an e-cycle, if $\mathcal{G}_\Pi^{dep}$ has a cycle with an edge $\to_e$.*

While the inverse of $\to_d$ was additionally included in $\mathcal{G}_\Pi^{dep}$ by Eiter et al. [4], we improve their results by showing that our more general definition suffices. Moreover, the following result differs from the previous result for e-minimality check skipping [4] in that it is based on our generalized definition of external dependencies. Consequently, it can be applied to a larger class of HEX-programs.

Theorem 1. *If a ground HEX-program Π contains no e-cycle, then every projection **A** of a compatible set $\hat{\mathbf{A}}$ for $\hat{\Pi}$ is an answer set of Π.*

Fig. 1. Full and pruned dependency graph for Π from Example 4 (all arrows are "$\to_e$").

Example 5 (cont'd). Figure 1 shows the dependency graphs for Π from Example 4, with and without specified io-dependencies. The full dependency graph has an e-cycle, but the pruned graph does not. Hence, Π does not require e-minimality checks (cf. Theorem 1), but this can only be detected using the pruned graph.

As a result, we obtain a flexible means for increasing the efficiency of evaluating a class of HEX-programs where the e-minimality check is performed due to an overapproximation of the real dependencies between atoms.

3.2 Properties of Faithful IO-Dependencies

We now consider checking, generating and optimizing io-dependencies.

Informally, given $D_1, D_2 \subseteq dep(\&g[\boldsymbol{p}])$, D_1 is better than D_2 if it induces less compliant atoms. We thus say that D_1 *tightens* D_2, denoted $D_1 \leq D_2$, if $comp(D_1, \&g[\boldsymbol{p}](\boldsymbol{c})) \subseteq comp(D_2, \&g[\boldsymbol{p}](\boldsymbol{c}))$ holds for all tuples $\boldsymbol{c}$. We call D_1 *tight* if no D_2 strictly tightens D_1, i.e., $D_2 \leq D_1$ but $D_1 \not\leq D_2$; furthermore D_1 and D_2 are *equally tight*, denoted $D_1 \equiv D_2$, if $D_1 \leq D_2$ and $D_2 \leq D_1$. We then have:

Proposition 1. *Suppose* $D_1, D_2 \subseteq dep(\&g[\boldsymbol{p}])$ *are such that* $D_1 \leq D_2$. *If* D_1 *is faithful, then* D_2 *is also faithful.*

As a consequence, faithfulness is anti-monotonic wrt. set-inclusion, and it is monotonic wrt. adding subsumed io-dependencies, where $\delta = \langle i, j : J, k : e \rangle$ *subsumes* $\delta' = \langle i, j : J', k : e \rangle$, if $J \subseteq J'$ holds.

Corollary 1. *If* $D \subseteq dep(\&g[\boldsymbol{p}])$ *is faithful, then (i) each* $D' \subseteq D$ *is faithful and (ii) each* $D' = D \cup D''$ *where each* $\delta'' \in D''$ *is subsumed by some* $\delta \in D$ *is faithful.*

Consequently, we can tighten a faithful set D by sequentially dropping constants c from io-dependencies $\delta = \langle i, j : J, k : e \rangle$ in D, i.e., check whether $D \cup \delta'$ for $\delta' = \langle i, j : J \setminus \{c\}, k : e \rangle$ is faithful and if so, replace D with $(D \setminus \{\delta\}) \cup \{\delta'\}$.

We can simplify D by exploiting the following equivalences; let $\delta^*(i, j, k{:}e) = \langle i, j : \mathcal{C}, k : e \rangle$ for any possible i, j, and $k : e$.

Proposition 2. *For* $D \subseteq dep(\&g[\boldsymbol{p}])$ *and* $\langle i, j : J, k : e \rangle \in dep(\&g[\boldsymbol{p}])$, *we have (i)* $D \equiv D \cup \{\delta^*(i, j, k{:}e)\} \equiv D \setminus \{\delta^*(i, j, k{:}e)\}$, *and (ii) for any* $\delta = \langle i, j : J, k : e \rangle$, $\delta' = \langle i, j : J', k : e \rangle \in D$ *that* $D \equiv D \cup \{\langle i, j : J \cap J', k : e \rangle\}$.

That is, $\delta^*(i,j,k{:}e)$ is like a tautology, and we can replace all dependencies for i,j and $k:e$ in D by one which contains the intersection of all their J-sets. We thus can *normalize* D into $nf(D)$ such that for each i,j, and $k:e$ exactly one io-dependency occurs, and then start tightening. We then obtain:

Proposition 3. *Given a faithful $D \subseteq dep(\&g[\boldsymbol{p}])$, exhaustive tightening of $nf(D)$ results in a tight faithful D'.*

The set $D = \emptyset$ is trivially faithful, and $nf(\emptyset)$ consists of all $\delta^*(i,j,k{:}c)$; thus even without user input, a tight faithful set D' for $\&g[\boldsymbol{p}]$ is constructible. Moreover, semantically faithful sets of compliant atoms have the intersection property.

Proposition 4. *If $D_1, D_2 \subseteq dep(\&g[\boldsymbol{p}])$ are faithful, then $D_1 \cup D_2$ is faithful, and for every c, $comp(D_1 \cup D_2, \&g[\boldsymbol{p}](c)) = comp(D_1, \&g[\boldsymbol{p}](c)) \cap comp(D_2, \&g[\boldsymbol{p}](c))$.*

Consequently, every ge-predicate has a semantically unique tight set of faithful io-dependencies. However, syntactically, different tight faithful sets may exist.

Example 6. Consider a ge-predicate $\&g[p]$ which is true for output (a,b) wrt. an assignment $\mathbf{A}$ iff $\mathbf{T}p(c) \in \mathbf{A}$, and false for all other output tuples. Then $\{\langle 1,1:\{c\},1:a\rangle\}$ and $\{\langle 1,1:\{c\},2:b\rangle\}$ are faithful, and both are tight.

To check faithfulness of a set $D \subseteq dep(\&g[\boldsymbol{p}])$, formally the oracle function $f_{\&g}(\mathbf{A}, \boldsymbol{p}, \boldsymbol{c})$ must be evaluated for all evaluations of predicates $p \in \boldsymbol{p}$ and output tuples $\boldsymbol{c}$, which naively is often not feasible in practice.

Example 7. Reconsider $\&suc[node](X)$ from Example 3. To check faithfulness of the specified io-dependencies wrt. output a, the oracle function needs to be evaluated under all possible assignments to atoms with predicate *node*.

In the worst case, this cannot be avoided by the following result, where we assume that $\&g[\boldsymbol{p}](c)$ is decidable in polynomial time.

Proposition 5. *Checking faithfulness of a given set $D \subseteq dep(\&g[\boldsymbol{p}])$ is co-NEXP-complete in general, and co-NP-complete for fixed predicate arities.*

When certain properties of external sources are known, less external calls are needed for faithfulness checking, e.g. for monotonic functions. An input $p_i \in \boldsymbol{p}$ of a ge-predicate $\&g[\boldsymbol{p}]$ is *monotonic*, if for any assignment $\mathbf{A}$ and output $\boldsymbol{c}$, $f_{\&g}(\mathbf{A}, \boldsymbol{p}, \boldsymbol{c}) = \mathbf{T}$ implies $f_{\&g}(\mathbf{A}', \boldsymbol{p}, \boldsymbol{c}) = \mathbf{T}$ for every $\mathbf{A}' \geq \mathbf{A}$ s.t. $\mathbf{A}(p_j(\boldsymbol{d})) = \mathbf{A}'(p_j(\boldsymbol{d}))$ for all predicates $p_j \in \boldsymbol{p}$ with $p_j \neq p_i$ (cf. [6]). Based on monotonicity, the number of assignments to consider in a faithfulness check can be decreased.

Proposition 6. *If $p_i \in \boldsymbol{p}$ for $\&g[\boldsymbol{p}]$ is monotonic, a set $D \subseteq dep(\&g[\boldsymbol{p}])$ is faithful for $\&g[\boldsymbol{p}]$ iff for any assignments $\mathbf{A}$, $\mathbf{A}'$ s.t. $\mathbf{T}p_i(\boldsymbol{d}) \in \mathbf{A}$ and $\mathbf{F}p_i(\boldsymbol{d}) \in \mathbf{A}'$ for every $p_i(\boldsymbol{d}) \notin comp(D, \&g[\boldsymbol{p}](c))$ and $\mathbf{A}(p_i(\boldsymbol{d})) = \mathbf{A}'(p_i(\boldsymbol{d}))$ for every $comp(D, \&g[\boldsymbol{p}](c))$, it holds that $f_{\&g}(\mathbf{A}, \boldsymbol{p}, \boldsymbol{c}) = f_{\&g}(\mathbf{A}', \boldsymbol{p}, \boldsymbol{c})$.*

Example 8 (cont'd). As *node* is a monotonic input parameter of $\&suc[node]$, for checking faithfulness wrt. a it suffices to evaluate $f_{\&suc}(\mathbf{A}, node, a)$ under two assignments $\mathbf{A}_t$ and $\mathbf{A}_f$, s.t. $\mathbf{A}_t \subseteq \{\mathbf{T}node(a), \mathbf{T}node(b), \mathbf{T}node(c), \mathbf{T}node(d)\}$ and $\mathbf{A}_f \subseteq \{\mathbf{F}node(a), \mathbf{F}node(b), \mathbf{F}node(c), \mathbf{F}node(d)\}$.

Under additional conditions, we obtain tractability:

Corollary 2. *If all $p_i \in \boldsymbol{p}$ for $\&g[\boldsymbol{p}]$ are monotonic and $|comp(D, \&g[\boldsymbol{p}](\boldsymbol{c}))|$ is bounded, then checking faithfulness is polynomial for fixed predicate arities.*

The same holds for computing a tight faithful set D for $\&g[\boldsymbol{p}]$. In practice, this applies to Example 3, if the external graph has bounded degree.

Relativized io-dependencies. So far, the context of a given HEX-program has not been exploited for specifying respective io-dependencies. However, without considering how dependencies in an external source may be affected by input parameters, all io-dependencies that may hold under any possible extension of input predicates must be respected. This is illustrated by the following example.

Example 9. Consider $\&suc[edge, node](X)$, where edges from *edge* are inserted into $\mathcal{G}$ before successor nodes are output. If it is unknown which edges can be added, io-dependencies must account for the complete graph (all edges), which is a maximal overapproximation. Now, consider the following HEX-program.

$$edge(b, c) \vee n\_edge(b, c). \quad node(a). \quad node(b) \leftarrow \&suc[edge, node](b)$$

As $edge(b, c)$ is the only atom with predicate *edge* that can potentially be true in the input of $\&suc[edge, node](b)$ in any answer set, it suffices to specify io-dependencies wrt. the graph $\mathcal{G}' = (V, E \cup \{b \rightarrow c\})$ to ensure e-minimality.

To account for the inputs to external sources that are possible in answer sets, we define faithfulness wrt. a HEX-program Π. Let $env(\Pi)$ denote the set of all atoms for Π that are true in some compatible set of Π.

Definition 8 (Relativized Faithfulness). *A set $D \subseteq dep(\&g[\boldsymbol{p}])$ is faithful wrt. a HEX-program Π, if for any assignments $\mathbf{A}, \mathbf{A}'$ s.t. $\{a \mid \mathbf{T}a \in \mathbf{A} \cup \mathbf{A}'\} \subseteq env(\Pi)$, and for any output tuple $\boldsymbol{c}$ for $\&g[\boldsymbol{p}]$, either $\mathbf{A}(p_i(\boldsymbol{d})) \neq \mathbf{A}'(p_i(\boldsymbol{d}))$ for some atom $p_i(\boldsymbol{d}) \in comp(D, \&g[\boldsymbol{p}](\boldsymbol{c}))$ or $f_{\&g}(\mathbf{A}, \boldsymbol{p}, \boldsymbol{c}) = f_{\&g}(\mathbf{A}', \boldsymbol{p}, \boldsymbol{c})$.*

We show that skipping e-minimality checks based on the relativized definition of faithful io-dependencies is still safe.

Proposition 7. *Theorem 1 still holds if the specified io-dependencies are faithful wrt. to the HEX-program Π at hand according to Definition 8.*

The properties of above can be adjusted to this setting.

4   Empirical Evaluation

To empirically evaluate our new technique, we integrated it into the HEX-solver DLVHEX 2.5.0, which uses GRINGO 4.4.0 and CLASP 3.1.1 as backends [9], and

Table 1. User access selection results (few cycles)

#	c-mod	c-mod + io-dep	part	part + io-dep	min-part	min-part + io-dep	#cyclic
10	0.46 (0)	**0.43** (0)	0.60 (0)	0.58 (0)	1.53 (0)	1.36 (0)	7/10
15	2.64 (0)	**2.18** (0)	4.58 (0)	3.91 (0)	7.41 (0)	4.43 (0)	3/10
20	16.43 (0)	**14.71** (0)	44.90 (0)	41.93 (0)	43.87 (0)	31.03 (0)	5/10
25	43.85 (0)	**38.25** (0)	102.39 (1)	93.65 (1)	81.51 (0)	67.59 (0)	5/10
30	110.24 (2)	**91.01** (2)	192.48 (4)	180.58 (4)	168.80 (2)	99.53 (2)	4/10
35	111.62 (1)	**79.69** (1)	217.58 (4)	178.62 (2)	161.86 (2)	83.18 (1)	3/10
40	189.64 (2)	**141.12** (2)	262.35 (6)	231.22 (5)	202.95 (3)	143.12 (2)	5/10
45	264.04 (5)	216.89 (4)	269.49 (6)	227.88 (5)	263.40 (5)	**202.55** (4)	5/10
50	300.00 (10)	227.15 (4)	300.00 (10)	249.55 (6)	300.00 (10)	**220.61** (3)	2/10

tested it on randomly generated instances. Io-depencendies for external atoms are specified by plugin-methods that compute whether a dependency between given input and output values exists. We used a Linux machine with two 12-core AMD Opteron 6238 SE CPUs and 512 GB RAM; the timeout was 300 s and the memout 8 GB per instance. The average runtime of 10 instances per problem size is reported (in secs) for computing all answer sets; timeouts are in parentheses.

Configurations. To gain insights into how dependency graph pruning and other techniques interact, we consider the frequency of external calls as further factor. While basic evaluation in Sect. 2 evaluates external atoms wrt. candidate models, we can evaluate them also wrt. partial assignments [6]. At this, investigating how e-minimality check skipping interacts with partial evaluation is of interest as early external evaluation can speed up model search as well as the e-minimality check and thus, potentially influence the impact of our new technique.

We compared three different configurations, each with and without dependency graph pruning based on specified io-dependencies (configuration **io-dep**):

- **c-mod**: external atoms are only evaluated wrt. *candidate models* (representing the standard configuration of DLVHEX);
- **part**: external atoms are evaluated wrt. *partial assignments* after every solver guess during the model search; and
- **min-part**: external atoms are evaluated wrt. *partial assignments* after every solver guess during the *e-minimality check*.

In the result tables, we show combinations of configurations where interactions are expected. We predicted **io-dep** to decrease the runtime if e-cycles can be removed from the dependency graph; and that the speedup is larger when **io-dep** is combined with **part** and smaller when combined with **min-part**, whenever partial evaluation is beneficial. If pruning does not skip e-minimality checks, we expected no significant overhead in terms of runtime with **io-dep**.

User Access Selection (UAS). Consider a set of computer nodes C and a set of directed connections A between nodes, where $n_1 \to n_2 \in A$, for $n_1, n_2 \in C$, iff node n_1 has access to node n_2. Hence, a node can be accessed directly, or indirectly via other nodes. Now, suppose a network admin has to assign access

$$y\_nd(X) \vee n\_nd(X) \leftarrow domain(X). \qquad \leftarrow nd(X), nd\_f(X).$$
$$nd(X) \leftarrow y\_nd(X). \qquad \leftarrow \text{not } nd(X), nd\_a(X).$$
$$nd(X) \leftarrow \&hasAccess[nd](X). \leftarrow \#count\{X:y\_nd(X)\} > 3.$$

Fig. 2. User access selection rules

Table 2. User access selection results (many cycles)

#	c-mod	c-mod + io-dep	part	part + io-dep	min-part	min-part + io-dep	#cyclic
10	0.41 (0)	0.41 (0)	**0.35** (0)	0.36 (0)	0.46 (0)	0.46 (0)	10/10
15	7.55 (0)	7.61 (0)	**6.17** (0)	6.38 (0)	7.95 (0)	8.15 (0)	10/10
20	44.03 (1)	43.92 (1)	**6.52** (0)	6.57 (0)	44.54 (1)	44.66 (1)	10/10
25	107.50 (2)	107.95 (2)	**51.60** (1)	51.62 (1)	87.53 (1)	87.51 (1)	10/10
30	84.97 (0)	84.64 (0)	**44.23** (0)	44.73 (0)	85.64 (0)	85.42 (0)	10/10
35	223.56 (5)	222.95 (5)	**111.29** (1)	110.98 (1)	223.26 (5)	224.26 (5)	10/10
40	268.27 (7)	268.73 (7)	**152.53** (1)	153.28 (1)	268.86 (7)	269.44 (7)	10/10
45	284.12 (8)	284.33 (8)	**251.08** (4)	252.54 (4)	286.90 (8)	286.56 (8)	10/10
50	300.00 (10)	300.00 (10)	300.00 (10)	**298.61** (9)	300.00 (10)	300.00 (10)	10/10

rights by selecting nodes $C' \subseteq C$ to which some user will be granted access, s.t. every node in a set $C_a \subseteq C$ (required access) is accessible from some $n \in C'$ and no node in a set $C_f \subseteq C$ (forbidden nodes) is accessible from any $n \in C'$.

We assume the network is not known initially, but each node can be queried for its connections. For this, we use an external atom $\&hasAccess[nodes](n)$, which interfaces external network information, and outputs all nodes that can be accessed by some node in the extension of *nodes*. Accordingly, it evaluates to true for an output node n_2 wrt. an assignment $\mathbf{A}$ iff $\mathbf{T}nodes(n_1) \in \mathbf{A}$ for some $(n_1, n_2) \in A$. Moreover, we specify $D(\&hasAccess[nodes]) = \{\langle 2, 1 : \{n_1 \mid n_1 \rightarrow n_2 \in A\}, 1 : n_2 \rangle \mid n_2 \in C\}$, i.e. there is a dependency of an output on an input node whenever the latter has access to the former. The HEX-program in Fig. 2 with facts $domain(n)$ for $n \in C$, facts $node\_a(n)$ for $n \in C_a$, and facts $node\_f(n)$ for $n \in C_f$ encodes UAS, where at most three nodes can be accessed directly.

First, we generated networks with $N \in [10, 50]$ nodes, where each node has access to another node with probability $\frac{1}{2 \times N}$ (cf. Table 1). This yields networks about half of which have no cycles and thus, dependency pruning can have an effect on the number of required e-minimality checks. Next, we increased the access probability to $\frac{2}{N}$ (cf. Table 2). This effects that nearly all networks contain cycles, which allowed us to investigate the effect of pruning when this does not impact the need for an e-minimality check. The rightmost column shows the fraction of instances where the computer network has a cycle.

Sequential Allocation of Indivisible Goods (SAIG). Next, we considered a problem from *Social Choice*, namely dividing a set G of m items among two agents a_1 and a_2 by allowing them to pick items in specific sequences $\sigma = o_1 o_2 \ldots o_m \in \{a_1, a_2\}^m$ [11]. Each agent a_i has a linear preference order $>_i$ over G; and the utility of $g \in G$ for a_i is $u_i(g) = |\{g' \mid g >_i g' \in G\}|$. We assume that

Table 3. Sequential Allocation Results

#	c-mod	c-mod + io-dep	part	part + io-dep	min-part	min-part + io-dep
3	**0.19** (0)	**0.19** (0)	0.25 (0)	0.24 (0)	0.38 (0)	**0.19** (0)
4	2.74 (0)	1.73 (0)	0.74 (0)	**0.64** (0)	2.54 (0)	1.72 (0)
5	300.00 (10)	78.28 (0)	152.33 (5)	**2.42** (0)	141.76 (1)	78.02 (0)
6	300.00 (10)	300.00 (10)	300.00 (10)	**8.22** (0)	300.00 (10)	300.00 (10)
7	300.00 (10)	300.00 (10)	300.00 (10)	**26.63** (0)	300.00 (10)	300.00 (10)
8	300.00 (10)	300.00 (10)	300.00 (10)	**89.97** (0)	300.00 (10)	300.00 (10)
9	300.00 (10)	300.00 (10)	300.00 (10)	**284.17** (4)	300.00 (10)	300.00 (10)
10	**300.00** (10)	**300.00** (10)	**300.00** (10)	**300.00** (10)	**300.00** (10)	**300.00** (10)

$$turn(a\_1, P) \vee turn(a\_2, P) \leftarrow position(P).$$
$$picked(A, P, G) \leftarrow \&pick[alreadyPicked](A, P, G), turn(A, P), item(G).$$
$$alreadyPicked(P, G) \leftarrow position(P), position(P1), P1 < P, picked(\_, P1, G).$$
$$\leftarrow not\ \&envyFree[picked]().$$

Fig. 3. Sequential allocation rules

an agent always picks the remaining item with maximal utility. The goal is to find a sequence σ resulting in an *envy-free* division of items, i.e. where no agent prefers the items of the other agent over its own items.

We use an external atom to obtain the choices of the agents, while their complete preferences are hidden, and a further one that checks whether an allocation is envy-free. The atom $\&pick[alreadyPicked](a_i, p, g)$ evaluates to true wrt. assignment **A** iff $p \in [1, m]$ and $g >_i g'$ for all g' s.t. $\mathbf{T}alreadyPicked(p-1, g) \notin$ **A**, where p represents the positions in a respective sequence. Furthermore, let $G(\mathbf{A}, i, j) = \sum_{g \in \{g | \mathbf{T}picked(a_i, p, g) \in \mathbf{A}\}} u_j(g)$. Then, the atom $\&envyFree[picked]()$ is true iff $G(\mathbf{A}, 1, 1) < G(\mathbf{A}, 2, 1)$ and $G(\mathbf{A}, 2, 2) < G(\mathbf{A}, 1, 2)$. The encoding is shown in Fig. 3. Together with facts $position(p)$ and $item(g)$ for all $p, g \in [1, m]$, its answer sets encode all sequences that induce an envy-free allocation.

We set $D(\&pick[alreadyPicked]) = \{\langle 1, 1:\{p_1\}, 2:p_2 \rangle \mid p_1, p_2 \in [1, m], p_2 = p_1 + 1\}$, i.e. items already picked at a sequence position only depend on previous positions. The io-dependencies eliminate all cyclic dependencies via external atoms in the instances; thus e-minimality checks can always be skipped. We tested instances with random preference orders and $N \in [3, 10]$ items (cf. Table 3).

Findings. When dependency graph pruning skips e-minimality checks, **io-dep** significantly improves the runtimes for all instance sizes and independent from the configuration it is combined with (cf. Tables 1 and 3). In many cases, we are able to solve significantly more instances than before. In Table 2, **io-dep** has only a negligible impact on the runtimes. As **io-dep** has no advantage for cyclic instances, this shows that dependency pruning yields not much overhead. Partial evaluation was only beneficial both in the model search and the e-minimality check for SAIG. As predicted, the speedup for **part + io-dep** is larger than for **min-part + io-dep** since **min-part** already reduces the runtimes required for e-minimality checks, while **part** needs to invest more time in the e-minimality check. The runtimes for **c-mod+io-dep** and **min-part+io-dep** are similar; this is expected as **min-part** only applies to the e-minimality check, which is skipped in both cases. In summary, there is no clear winner among the conditions, but adding **io-dep** is suggestive as a default when io-dependencies can be specified.

5   Discussion and Conclusion

We introduced io-dependencies to formalize semantic dependencies over external atoms that approximate the real dependencies more closely than previously possible. Based on this, more e-minimality checks can be skipped, which proved to be beneficial in practice. We also stated properties for checking and optimizing io-dependencies important for automatically constructing tight faithful dependency sets. While faithfulness checking is intractable in general, we identified cases where the costs can be reduced for certain oracles, or where checking is polynomial.

Our approach is related to *domain independence* techniques in [3], where external atoms are evaluated wrt. subsets of the domain while correct outputs are retained. This is similar to our notions of compliant atoms and faithfulness. Yet, io-dependencies are more general because in [3], only disjoint domain partitions for external inputs are considered, and dependencies are not used for argument positions. Another important difference is that their approach employs dependencies for *program splitting* as in [13], while we aim at detecting redundant e-minimality checks. They do not analyze the costs for generating dependencies.

Apart from HEX, there are several other approaches that integrate external theories into declarative problem solving, such as CLINGO [8], *SMT* [1] and *Constraint-ASP* [12]. However, to the best of our knowledge, external minimality has not been considered there. Nevertheless, our technique could also be employed directly by related rule-based formalisms if minimality involving external theories is required. Moreover, cyclic support may arise from *external propagators*, e.g. in the *WASP*-solver [2], where our approach could be applied as well.

While we only exploited semantic dependencies for e-minimality checking, additional dependency information is also useful for other parts of HEX-solving such as grounding and *External Behavior Learning* [6]. By limiting oracle calls to compliant input atoms, the number of external calls during HEX-evaluation could potentially be reduced significantly.

References

1. Barrett, C.W., Sebastiani, R., Seshia, S.A., Tinelli, C.: Satisfiability modulo theories. In: Biere, A., Heule, M., van Maaren, H., Walsh, T. (eds.) Handbook of Satisfiability. Frontiers in Artificial Intelligence and Applications, vol. 185, pp. 825–885. IOS Press, Amsterdam (2009)

2. Dodaro, C., Ricca, F., Schüller, P.: External propagators in WASP: preliminary report. In: Bistarelli, S., Formisano, A., Maratea, M. (eds.) RCRA@AI*IA 2016, CEUR-WS, vol. 1745, pp. 1–9. CEUR-WS.org (2016)

3. Eiter, T., Fink, M., Krennwallner, T.: Decomposition of declarative knowledge bases with external functions. In: Boutilier, C. (ed.) IJCAI 2009. pp. 752–758 (2009)

4. Eiter, T., Fink, M., Krennwallner, T., Redl, C., Schüller, P.: Efficient HEX-program evaluation based on unfounded sets. J. Artif. Intell. Res. **49**, 269–321 (2014)

5. Eiter, T., Kaminski, T., Redl, C., Schüller, P., Weinzierl, A.: Answer set programming with external source access. In: Ianni, G., et al. (eds.) Reasoning Web 2017. LNCS, vol. 10370, pp. 204–275. Springer, Cham (2017). https://doi.org/10.1007/978-3-319-61033-7_7

6. Eiter, T., Kaminski, T., Redl, C., Weinzierl, A.: Exploiting partial assignments for efficient evaluation of answer set programs with external source access. J. Artif. Intell. Res. **62**, 665–727 (2018)

7. Faber, W., Pfeifer, G., Leone, N.: Semantics and complexity of recursive aggregates in answer set programming. Artif. Intell. **175**(1), 278–298 (2011)

8. Gebser, M., Kaminski, R., Kaufmann, B., Ostrowski, M., Schaub, T., Wanko, P.: Theory solving made easy with clingo 5. In: Carro, M., King, A., Saeedloei, N., Vos, M.D. (eds.) ICLP-TC 2016. OASICS, vol. 52, pp. 2:1–2:15. Schloss Dagstuhl (2016)

9. Gebser, M., Kaufmann, B., Kaminski, R., Ostrowski, M., Schaub, T., Schneider, M.T.: Potassco: the potsdam answer set solving collection. AI Commun. **24**(2), 107–124 (2011)

10. Gelfond, M., Lifschitz, V.: Classical negation in logic programs and disjunctive databases. New Gener. Comput. **9**(3/4), 365–386 (1991)

11. Kalinowski, T., Narodytska, N., Walsh, T., Xia, L.: Strategic behavior when allocating indivisible goods sequentially. In: desJardins, M., Littman, M.L. (eds.) AAAI 2013. AAAI Press (2013)

12. Lierler, Y.: Relating constraint answer set programming languages and algorithms. Artif. Intell. **207**, 1–22 (2014)

13. Lifschitz, V., Turner, H.: Splitting a logic program. In: Hentenryck, P.V. (ed.) ICLP 1994, pp. 23–37. MIT Press (1994)

Declarative Local Search
for Predicate Logic

Tu-San Pham[1]([✉]), Jo Devriendt[2], and Patrick De Causmaecker[1]

[1] KU Leuven, Leuven, Belgium
san.pham@kuleuven.be
[2] KTH Royal Institute of Technology, Stockholm, Sweden

Abstract. In this paper we introduce a framework built on top of the Knowledge Base System IDP, which allows local search heuristics to be synthesized from their formal descriptions. It is introduced as a new inference to solve *optimization* problems in IDP. To model a local search heuristic, users need to specify its components, among which *neighbourhood moves* are the most important. Two types of neighbourhood moves, namely standard moves and Large Neighbourhood Search moves, are supported. A set of built-in local search heuristics are provided, allowing users to combine neighbourhoods in different ways. We demonstrate how the new local search inference can be used to complement the existing solving mechanisms for logic programming.

Keywords: Heuristics · Local search · Knowledge representation · Predicate logic

1 Introduction

IDP (*Imperative-Declarative Programming* [2]) is a Knowledge Base System (KBS) which consists of two main components: (i) a formal declarative language that allows describing domain knowledge (as a *knowledge base*); and (ii) a set of inference methods that allows solving a wide variety of tasks around a knowledge base. Its language FO(·) is based on classical first-order logic (FO), extended with inductive definitions, types, aggregates and arithmetics. In this paper, we focus on IDP's ability to solve combinatorial optimization problems, which is provided through the inference method *optimization* using MiniSAT(ID) [3] as the backend engine. As a CP-SAT-based solver, it shows limited performance on many optimization problems, such as the assignment problem [4], or real-world problems with large-sized instances. In the field of operational research, *local search heuristics* have shown their ability to solve such problems successfully.

In this work, we introduce *declarative local search*, a framework that allows specifying local search heuristics declaratively in IDP. Local search is provided as a new inference method, serving as an alternative to solve optimization problems. To use the inference, beside a problem's modelling, users need to specify

© Springer Nature Switzerland AG 2019
M. Balduccini et al. (Eds.): LPNMR 2019, LNAI 11481, pp. 340–346, 2019.
https://doi.org/10.1007/978-3-030-20528-7_25

necessary components of a local search heuristic, chief of which are the neighbourhood moves. The initial idea was reported in [12] where only the modelling of a single neighbourhood is supported. In this work, users can specify multiple neighbourhoods and combine them in different ways using a set of built-in heuristics and metaheuristics. Two types of moves are supported, namely standard moves and Large Neighbourhood Search moves. This work is similar in spirit to [1], where neighbourhoods are declaratively modelled in the constraint programming language MiniZinc [11]. The source code of the solver along with all the modellings in this paper and experimental results can be found at [10].

Section 2 shortly introduces IDP, while the modelling of local search heuristics is showcased in Sect. 3. In Sect. 4, we present how IDP is extended with a local search back-end to synthesize local search heuristics. Section 5 concludes the paper.

2   Modelling TSP in FO(·) with IDP

A thorough introduction to IDP and its language FO(·) can be found at dtai.cs.kuleuven.be/software/idp. An IDP specification (or modelling) consists of different components. The four most important components are: *vocabularies* specifying the symbols and types used; *theories* specifying problem constraints; *structures* representing both input data and feasible solutions; and *terms* for objective functions. These are combined and reused through imperative code written in the Lua scripting language [8]. As a running example we employ the Travelling Salesman Problem (TSP), which consists of finding the shortest Hamiltonian cycle of a given graph. A model for the TSP in IDP can be found at goo.gl/TTv85c.

Example 1 (TSP). The four components of the TSP modelling are as follows:

- The vocabulary V specifying the parameters (*Node, Distance, Depot*), whose values define a problem instance, and the decision variables (*Path, Reachable*), whose values define a solution of the problem.
- The theory T built over V, specifying the problem's constraints:

$$\forall x\colon \exists! y\colon Path(x,y).$$
$$\forall x\colon \exists! y\colon Path(y,x).$$
$$\{\; Reachable(Depot).$$
$$\quad Reachable(x) \leftarrow \exists y\colon Reachable(y) \wedge Path(y,x).\}$$
$$\forall x\colon Reachable(x).$$

The first two lines represent the flow constraints. Line three and four feature an *inductive definition* which defines the *Reachable* predicate, starting from the depot, and inductively adding neighbouring nodes according to the links present in *Path*. The last line then states that all nodes must belong to *Reachable*, forming a subtour elimination constraint.

- The term $\Sigma_{(x,y)\in Path} Distance(x, y)$ represents the total travelling distance and serves as objective function *obj*.
- A (partial) structure S describing parameter values.

3   Modelling Local Search Heuristics

Local search is a heuristic which iteratively applies local changes – known as *(neighbourhood) moves* – on solutions to improve solution quality. In a simple *descent* search, a solution becomes the starting point of a new iteration if it improves the current solution. Descent search ususally ends up in a *local optimum*, which can be quite far away from optimality. *Metaheuristics* are local search-based heuristics, which use some *diversification* techniques to escape from local optima. In this paper, "local search heuristics" indicate both heuristics and metaheuristics.

To model a local search algorithm in our framework, users first need to extend the knowledge base with a moves modelling. These are then passed to IDP as inputs to synthesize the desired local search algorithm – IDP is extended with some "off-the-shelf" (meta) heuristic techniques to combine moves in various ways. The following local search techniques are implemented: *first improvement search, best improvement search, Tabu search* [7], *Large Neighbourhood Search* [13] and *Iterated Local Search* [9]. Two types of moves are supported: standard moves and Large Neighbourhood Search moves.

3.1   Standard Neighbourhood Moves

To model a standard move, the following information is crucial: (i) how to get valid moves given a solution; (ii) how to compute a neighbour solution given a move and a current solution; (iii) how to evaluate a move. To represent these pieces of information, a user should add the following components to the specification: (1) a vocabulary $Vmove$ consisting of functions and predicates representing a move; (2) a query $getValidMoves$ built over V, describing how to get valid moves from a given solution; (3) a theory $Tnext$ built over $Vnext$ containing a definition for a neigbhour solution given a solution and a move, with $Vnext$ is the vocabulary representing the neighbour solution; and (4) a query $getDeltaObj$ calculating the difference between the objective values of the current solution and the neighbour solution resulting from a move.

Example 2. To illustrate the standard move modelling, we hereby model the *2-opt* move for the TSP, where two edges are removed from the solution and replaced by two new edges (see Fig. 1). To model the 2-opt move, an auxiliary predicate *Before* represents the order of nodes appearing along the solution path.

$$\{\forall x : Before(x, x).$$
$$\forall x, y : Before(x, y) \quad \leftarrow Path(x, y) \wedge y \neq Depot.$$
$$\forall x, y : Before(x, y) \quad \leftarrow \exists z : Path(x, z) \wedge Before(z, y) \wedge z \neq Depot.\}$$

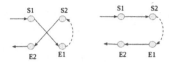

Fig. 1. 2-opt move of the TSP

Vmove consists of 4 constants $S1, E1, S2$ and $E2$ representing the four nodes involved in the 2-opt move. *Vnext* consists of the predicate *next_Path(Node, Node)*, whose values define a neighbour solution. The 2-opt move replaces two edges $(S1, E1)$, $(S2, E2)$ by $(S1, S2)$, $(E1, E2)$, and reverses the segment from $E1$ to $S2$. This mapping is defined in the theory *Tnext* as below:

$\{next\_Path(S1, S2).$

$\quad next\_Path(E1, E2).$

$\quad next\_Path(x, y) \qquad \leftarrow Path(x, y) \wedge Before(y, S1) \wedge y \neq Depot.$

$\quad next\_Path(x, y) \qquad \leftarrow Path(x, y) \wedge Before(E2, x) \wedge E2 \neq Depot.$

$\quad next\_Path(y, x) \qquad \leftarrow Path(x, y) \wedge Before(E1, x) \wedge Before(y, S2) \wedge y \neq Depot.\}$

To complete the modelling, two queries are specified. Query *getDeltaObj* evaluates a move by calculating the difference between the total travelling time of the current solution and its neighbour: $\Delta = d_{S1S2} + d_{E1E2} - (d_{S1E1} + d_{S2E2})$. Query *getValidMoves* defines valid moves of a given solution, which are the tuples of edges $(S1, E1)$ and $(S2, E2)$ appearing in this order on the solution path.

3.2 LNS Moves

Large Neighbourhood Search (LNS) [13] allows exploring a large neighbourhood of a solution by alternating a *destroy* and a *recreate* phase to gradually improve the objective value. In the destroy phase, a part of the solution is destroyed, resulting in a partial solution which is then repaired in the recreate phase. Destroying the "bad quality" parts of a solution is more likely to lead to a better solution in the recreate phase. Therefore, we support users to model the destroy phase in LNS moves, while the recreate phase is handled by the solver.

To get an intuition on how the destroy phase should be modelled, let us consider an example of the nurse scheduling problem (NSP) where shifts are assigned to nurses, subject to more complex constraints. An example of a meaningful LNS move for the NSP is to destroy the schedules of two, often randomly selected, nurses whose preferences are violated, and then reschedule them in the recreate phase. To model this move, users should be allowed to specify which parts of the solution can be destroyed (e.g. shift assignments to nurses whose preferences are violated).

With that intuition in mind, an LNS move can be modelled in our framework by specifying: (i) *random variables* – symbols which the framework can randomly interpret with (tuples of) values (domain elements); (ii) the set of valid interpretations to the random variables; and (iii) which parts of the solution should be destroyed given the selected values for the random variables. The first piece of information (i) is encoded in a vocabulary *Vmove* while (ii) is given through a query *getRandomVars*. By solving the query, possible options for the values to the random variables are obtained, from which the solver selects randomly. Given the chosen values to the random variables, users then can specify parts of the solution to be destroyed through (iii) the query *getMoves*. Besides a user-defined LNS move, the framework also supports automatic LNS moves, where parts of the solution to be destroyed are chosen randomly. An example of an LNS move modelling of the running example of the TSP is presented below.

Example 3. Each solution of the TSP is a Hamiltonian path that visits all vertices of the graph. Let say users want to destroy a part of this path, from node S to node E, given that S appears before E in the path starting from the depot. Vocabulary *Vmove* then consists of two constants S and E. S and E are random factors, which are chosen at each iteration of the algorithm. Query *getRandomVars* specifies valid values of S and E:

$$\{s, e \mid Before(s, e) \wedge s \neq e \wedge e \neq Depot\}$$

Given the chosen values of S and E, the part to be removed from the solution in the destroy phase of the LNS is the path from S to E, which is encoded in query *getMove*:

$$\{x, y \mid Before(S, x) \wedge Before(y, E)\}$$

4   Metaheuristics Framework

In this section, we explain how the descent first improvement search (FI) with a single standard move is synthesized in IDP. The synthesis of other local search algorithms with standard moves is straightforward given the description of FI while the synthesis of the LNS is straightforward from the description of LNS moves in Sect. 3.2.

Let us first recall the components of the modelling. A problem's modelling consists of a vocabulary V, a theory T, a query *getObjVal* and a term *obj*. Each neighbourhood move modelling consists of a vocabulary *Vmove*, a query *getValidMoves*, a theory *Tnext*, and finally a query *getDeltaObj*. Given an input instance, we let IDP execute its *model expansion* inference to obtain the first feasible solution, which will serve as the initial point of our FI search. At each iteration, a set of valid neighbourhood moves Ω from the current solution s is achieved by solving the query *getValidMoves*, using IDP's *query solving* inference. Each move $\omega \in \Omega$ is then evaluated by solving the query *getDeltaObj* on s_ω, where s_ω is a joined structure between the current solution s and the move ω. If the obtained delta objective improves the solution, the corresponding neighbour solution is created by applying *model expansion* on s_ω over theory *Tnext*, which contains a definition applying the move to the current solution. This neighbouring solution is the starting point of the next iteration, until a stopping criterion is met and the best solution found is returned.

Given this declarative local search framework, a user can easily mix-and-match several modelled neighborhoods and (meta) heuristics. For example, we modelled a set of neighbourhood moves, including three standard moves and 2 LNS moves, for the running example TSP, from which we synthesized no less than 15 local search heuristics [10]: 9 local search configurations based on *first improvement*, *best improvement* and *tabu search* for each standard move; 2 LNS configurations corresponding to two *LNS* moves; and 4 ILS configurations with different combination of simple local search configurations. We also ran a preliminary experiment comparing our framework to two black box approaches: IDP's *minimization* inference and optimization with clingo [6], both in their default settings. These early results demonstrate the fast prototyping potential of the framework: most of our local search heuristics outperformed IDP and clingo, especially two among the four ILS configurations result in a less than 10% average deviation from optimality, which is 7 or 8 times better than the two logic solvers. These results indicate that declarative local search could be a good complement to existing logic solvers.

5 Conclusion

In this paper, we propose a local search framework that synthesizes local search heuristics from their formal, declarative descriptions in predicate logic. Local search is introduced as an alternative back-end for IDP to solve optimization problems. The framework is illustrated by the modelling of local search heuristics for the TSP and some preliminary experiments are conducted.

A thorough experimental analysis of our declarative approach is to be performed in the future. Further work also includes extending the framework to allow more flexibility in metaheuristics modelling. The combination between user-defined neighbourhoods and automatically generated neighbourhoods [5] is also interesting.

Acknowledgements. This research was supported by Swedish Research Council grant 2016-00782, FWO research grant G.0922.13, and KU Leuven project C24/17/012.

References

1. Björdal, G., Flener, P., Pearson, J., Stuckey, P.J., Tack, G.: Declarative local-search neighbourhoods in MiniZinc. In: Tsoukalas, L.H., Grégoire, É., Alamaniotis, M. (eds.) IEEE 30th International Conference on Tools with Artificial Intelligence, ICTAI 2018, 5–7 November 2018, Volos, Greece, pp. 98–105. IEEE (2018). https://doi.org/10.1109/ICTAI.2018.00025

2. De Cat, B., Bogaerts, B., Bruynooghe, M., Janssens, G., Denecker, M.: Predicate logic as a modeling language: the IDP system. In: Declarative Logic Programming, pp. 279–323. Association for Computing Machinery and Morgan & Claypool (2018)

3. De Cat, B., Bogaerts, B., Devriendt, J., Denecker, M.: Model expansion in the presence of function symbols using constraint programming. In: 25th International Conference on Tools with Artificial Intelligence, 4–6 November 2013, USA, pp. 1068–1075 (2013)

4. Devriendt, J.: Exploiting symmetry in model expansion for predicate and propositional logic. Ph.D. thesis, Informatics Section, Department of Computer Science, Faculty of Engineering Science, February 2017

5. Devriendt, J., De Causmaecker, P., Denecker, M.: Transforming constraint programs to input for local search. In: The Fourteenth International Workshop on Constraint Modelling and Reformulation, pp. 1–16 (2015)

6. Gebser, M., Kaminski, R., Kaufmann, B., Schaub, T.: Clingo = ASP+ control: preliminary report. arXiv preprint arXiv:1405.3694 (2014)

7. Glover, F., Laguna, M.: Tabu search. In: Du, D.Z., Pardalos, P.M. (eds.) Handbook of Combinatorial Optimization, pp. 2093–2229. Springer, Boston (1998). https://doi.org/10.1007/978-1-4613-0303-9_33

8. Ierusalimschy, R., de Figueiredo, L.H., Celes, W.: Lua - an extensible extension language. Soft.: Pract. Exp. **26**(6), 635–652 (1996)

9. Lourenço, H.R., Martin, O.C., Stützle, T.: Iterated local search. In: Glover, F., Kochenberger, G.A. (eds.) Handbook of Metaheuristics, pp. 320–353. Springer, Boston (2003). https://doi.org/10.1007/0-306-48056-5_11

10. Modelling   and   instances   (2019).   https://github.com/tusanpham/DeclarativeLocalSearch

11. Nethercote, N., Stuckey, P.J., Becket, R., Brand, S., Duck, G.J., Tack, G.: MiniZinc: towards a standard CP modelling language. In: Bessière, C. (ed.) CP 2007. LNCS, vol. 4741, pp. 529–543. Springer, Heidelberg (2007). https://doi.org/10.1007/978-3-540-74970-7_38

12. Pham, T.-S., Devriendt, J., De Causmaecker, P.: Modelling local search in a knowledge base system. In: Daniele, P., Scrimali, L. (eds.) New Trends in Emerging Complex Real Life Problems. ASS, vol. 1, pp. 415–423. Springer, Cham (2018). https://doi.org/10.1007/978-3-030-00473-6_44

13. Shaw, P.: Using constraint programming and local search methods to solve vehicle routing problems. In: Maher, M., Puget, J.-F. (eds.) CP 1998. LNCS, vol. 1520, pp. 417–431. Springer, Heidelberg (1998). https://doi.org/10.1007/3-540-49481-2_30

Author Index

Printed in the United States
By Bookmasters